THE PAPERS OF

WOODROW WILSON

VOLUME 11
1898-1900

SPONSORED BY THE WOODROW WILSON
FOUNDATION
AND PRINCETON UNIVERSITY

THE PAPERS OF
WOODROW WILSON

ARTHUR S. LINK, *EDITOR*

JOHN WELLS DAVIDSON, DAVID W. HIRST, AND

JOHN E. LITTLE, *ASSOCIATE EDITORS*

JEAN MACLACHLAN, *CONTRIBUTING EDITOR*

M. HALSEY THOMAS, *CONSULTING EDITOR*

Volume 11 · 1898-1900

PRINCETON, NEW JERSEY
PRINCETON UNIVERSITY PRESS
1971

INTRODUCTION

THIS volume, covering the period from September 1898 to September 1900, reveals a man coming to maturity in political thought and religious understanding even while caught up in the midst of momentous changes in his life.

The degree to which Wilson's political thought had matured is compactly disclosed in the notes for his new course at Princeton, "Constitutional Government," printed herein for the first time. Suggestive also of his intellectual development are the random notes and memoranda for his projected *magnum opus*, "The Philosophy of Politics"; an outline for a newly conceived volume on statesmanship; notes for a series of lectures on "The Government of Cities"; and newspaper reports of five lectures in Richmond on "Constitutional Government."

Equally significant, perhaps, are the materials in this volume that illuminate Wilson's growth as an historian of the United States and his rise to the first rank among writers in the field at this time. "State Rights (1850-1860)" and "The Reconstruction of the Southern States"—surely two of his most brilliant pieces of historical work—display his powers of generalization and interpretation and his command of clear and unaffected, yet evocative, historical prose. During the period covered by this volume, moreover, Wilson works on and then abandons, because of the bankruptcy of his publisher, Harper and Brothers, his textbook in American history for high schools. Within a short time, but only after much careful negotiation, he signs a contract with the same publisher for, and begins work on, the series in *Harper's Magazine*, "Colonies and Nation," which he would later expand into *A History of the American People*.

As is disclosed by Wilson's essay, "When a Man Comes to Himself," the report of his address to the Philadelphian Society of Princeton on November 2, 1899, and other documents in this volume, a significant mutation in Wilson's religious thought was now taking place. Shedding his earlier moralism and pietism, he came for the first time fully to the understanding that, for the Christian, the law of love, as perfectly embodied in Jesus Christ, is the only force that can energize life and enable one to live in community both with fellow-men and God.

The years 1898-1900 saw the emergence of the United States to active world power, and in newspaper reports of speeches in this volume we can follow very clearly Wilson's reactions to events unfolding on the national and international scenes. At first reluctant to see his country embark upon the road of imperialism, he concludes that it is the duty of the United States to acquire the Philippine Islands and Puerto Rico and train their inhabitants in the arduous tasks of self-government. At the same time, he ardently defends the right to dissent of anti-imperialists then being widely accused of lack of patriotism, if not outright disloyalty.

All the while, Wilson was also maturing as a leader among the faculty at Princeton University. We find him helping to prepare the first statement of standards for graduate work; representing the university on the alumni circuit; and conducting a successful search for a new Professor of Politics, which, incidentally, led him into interesting correspondence with Theodore Roosevelt.

The letters between Wilson and his wife in this volume are unusually numerous because of two long separations—when Wilson made a two months' tour of the British Isles in the summer of 1899, and when Mrs. Wilson spent two months in early 1900 in New Orleans and elsewhere in the South. Wilson's travel letters from Great Britain are among the most revealing of his personality and esthetic perceptions that he ever wrote. Mrs. Wilson's letters yield delightful and graphic descriptions of New Orleans society and way of life at the turn of the century. They also afford interesting sidelights on a Creole culture in process of becoming Americanized.

Readers are again reminded that *The Papers of Woodrow Wilson* is a continuing series; that persons, institutions, and events that figure prominently in earlier volumes are not re-identified in subsequent ones; and that the Index to each volume gives cross references to fullest earlier identifications. We reiterate what we have said many times before—that it is our practice to print texts *verbatim et literatim*, repairing words and phrases only when necessary for clarity or ease of reading, and that we make silent corrections only of obvious typographical errors in typed copies.

We are grateful to Mrs. Bryant Putney of Princeton University Press for continued help in copyediting, and to Miss Marjorie Sirlouis and Colonel James B. Rothnie, U.S.A., Ret., for deciphering Wilson's shorthand.

The Editors wish here to record their deep gratitude to and affection for P. J. Conkwright upon his retirement as Typographer of Princeton University Press on January 1, 1971. At the very outset, he conceived the design, format, typography, and binding of the entire series, and we like to think that the volumes of *The Papers of Woodrow Wilson* are among the most handsome of his many works of art. Working with him over the years has been a joy, and we have learned much from him. So long as volumes in this series continue to come from the press, they will be monuments to his genius and craftsmanship.

Our colleague, John Wells Davidson, Ph.D., Senior Research Historian at Princeton University and Associate Editor of *The Papers of Woodrow Wilson* since the inauguration of work on the project on September 1, 1958, retired on June 30, 1971. In large measure responsible for the gathering and organization of our materials, he made a notable contribution to the planning and editing of the first large segment of this series. In addition, he mastered the mysteries of Graham shorthand and supervised the transcription of the bulk of Wilson's shorthand manuscripts. We here gratefully record our respect for his scholarly integrity, our admiration for his complete dedication to the cause of Wilsonian historiography, and our deep affection for him as a valued friend. We wish for him a happy retirement and many years of continued productive scholarship.

THE EDITORS

Princeton, New Jersey
July 15, 1971

CONTENTS

ILLUSTRATIONS

Following page 292

ABBREVIATIONS

ALI	autograph letter initialed
ALS	autograph letter(s) signed
att(s).	attached, attachment(s)
EAW	Ellen Axson Wilson
enc(s).	enclosed, enclosure(s)
env.	envelope
hw	handwriting, handwritten
L	letter
S	signed
sh	shorthand
T	typed
TCL	typed copy of letter
tel.	telegram
TLS	typed letter signed
WW	Woodrow Wilson
WWhw	Woodrow Wilson handwriting, handwritten
WWsh	Woodrow Wilson shorthand
WWT	Woodrow Wilson typed
WWTLS	Woodrow Wilson typed letter signed

ABBREVIATIONS FOR COLLECTIONS AND LIBRARIES

Following the National Union Catalog of the Library of Congress

A-Ar	Alabama Department of Archives and History, Montgomery
CSmH	Henry E. Huntington Library, San Marino
DLC	Library of Congress
ICU	University of Chicago Library
InI	Indianapolis Public Library
KyBB	Berea College Library
LNHT	Howard-Tilton Memorial Library of Tulane University
MH	Harvard University Library
NjP	Princeton University Library
NjR	Rutgers University Library
NN	New York Public Library
NNPM	Pierpont Morgan Library, New York
RSB Coll., DCL	Ray Stannard Baker Collection of Wilsoniana, Library of Congress
ViU	University of Virginia Library
WC, NjP	Woodrow Wilson Collection, Princeton University
WP, DLC	Woodrow Wilson Papers, Library of Congress

SYMBOLS

[Sept. 19, 1898]   publication date of a published writing; also
                    date of document when date is not part of
                    text
⟨Sept. 20, 1898⟩   matter deleted from manuscript by Wilson
                    and restored by editors
[[Jan. 29, 1899]]   delivery date of a speech if publication date
                    differs
[*Nov. 1, 1899*]   latest composition date of a published writing

THE PAPERS OF

WOODROW WILSON

VOLUME 11
1898-1900

THE PAPERS OF
WOODROW WILSON

To John Earle Brown[1]

My dear Sir,   Princeton, New Jersey, 16 September, 1898.

I cannot say that I think your article on the Philippines shows style. It shows a young hand by running to superlatives and being without moderation of statement, and also by a certain crudity which appears both in the fact that *some* of the arguments are taken for *all* and in the inadequate perception of the true force and meaning of individual words. No man can have a style or give distinction to anything he writes without the most careful discrimination and the most delicate imaginative appreciation in the use of words. For example, to take one or two instances from your article, the word *resourceful* ought to be used of persons and not of a land, and the same is true of the word *hostage* in the next sentence. It is entirely grotesque to speak of an *impetus* as having been *infused*, and more extraordinary still to speak of an impetus as having *laid open* or *recreated* anything.

My advice to you would be, to study diction with a view to hitting your meaning exactly, alike in the abstract statement and in the imagery of individual words; and to remember that good writing is based always and only upon a thorough, sober, and thoughtful study of the subject-matter, with a view not to writing well but to putting forth light into the world.

Very truly Yours,   Woodrow Wilson

WWTLS (WC, NjP).

[1] A sophomore at Brown University from Woonsocket, R.I., who afterward practiced law in his home town.

To John Lloyd Thomas[1]

Princeton, New Jersey,

My dear Mr. Thomas,   16 September, 1898.

I am keenly sensible of the honour the Nineteenth Century Club does me in urging again that I address it on the subject of colonial expansion, and when I first read your letter my first thought and impulse was to accept its invitation. But an examination of my list of engagements has shown me that I cannot.

II.

A. *The Origination and adaptation of Law*:

The movement of affairs which brought "constitutional" government into existence was *set afoot by a consciousness* (more or less clear and definite—generally clear upon items but not upon the scale of any systematic purpose) *that, in order to keep a right balance* between governmental power and individual right, *more than a statement (a Bill) of Rights* was necessary,—and more than a merely supervising and criticising representative body:—that it was necessary that there should be (a) *a veritably representative body*; (b) that that body should become a part, *a determining part, of the Government* itself; and (c) that permanent arrangements should be made to make and keep the gov't. of such *a structure and balance of parts* that it should at all points be reasonably regardful of the deliberately formed and definitely expressed wishes of the nation.

It is evident, ∴, in what sense *"constitutional" gov't.* practically means gov't. by the representation of either (1) the Community in some organic sense, or (2) the People collectively.

In order to understand representation, the fundamental arrangement of "constitutional" gov't., it is necessary, therefore, to define both "A Community" and "A People." This, then, the first topic.

I. [B] *A Community; A People.*

The conception of a Community is based, at heart, on *organization and social feeling*. (Older Eng. form, *"Commonty."* Lat., *communitas*=fellowship, a sense of fellowship,—or, in *ML.* a society, a division of people). We shall use the word rather in its older, essential significance than in its later, vague, collective sense.

((Comp. Notes on Politics.).)[2] The ideas [of] Community, People have this in common

    (1) A consciousness of common ties and interests.

    (2) A common way and standard of life or conduct.

    (3) A habit of union and common action.

But a Community adds to these

    (4) A *particular* social habit, giving it distinctive individual characteristics which mark it as a whole and are valid as generalizations.

2 The notes for Wilson's course, the Elements of Politics, are printed at March 5, 1898, Vol. 10.

(5) A solidarity or homogeneity of interests in great matters as well as in small, based upon some common social or economic peculiarities or features of development.

(6) A union in movement or action which is not only political and legal but also radical, social, habitual, and outside gov't. as well. Leading persons or families, e.g., and matter-of-course means of initiative, leading and following.

Such homogeneity and relationships as if of neighbours implies a simple social make-up, traditions of long standing, and either slow or stationary life.

Several of our States (like early Mass. and early Va.) have been at one stage of their development veritable Communities; but the United States has never been a Community within the meaning of this analysis

There is a sense in wh. it may be said that the object of "Constitutional" gov't. is to create a Community,—where it does not exist,—and that a People is not quite sufficiently coördinated and vitally united to form a perfect soil for "constitutional" principles and practices.

21 Sept., 1898

III.

The Government and the Community: the Government as Master, —the Community inorganic.

There can be *no Community without a government,*—if the word Community be used in a political sense. For a political Community a government,—i.e. an organ for the origination, interpretation, and enforcement of Law,—is *a neccessary means of coördination and action.*

A study of *the relation of the government to the Community* must give us a view, *not only of forms of gov't.,* but also of *essential principles of political action,* and of *the chief phases of political development.*

That Relation necessarily one or other of the following four:

(1) *The government master* of the Community, determining its law, conduct, and development.

(2) *The government checked* by the *beginnings of independent action on the part of the Community,* irregular and imperfectly organized, but definite enough and influential enough to demand the consideration and often to modify the course of the gov't., *lest it should fail of*

being obeyed and jeopard civil order if not its own authority and security.

(3) *The government itself as leader* of the Community,— as some modern gov'ts. have been, by reason of an *expert skill* in affairs, a *wide knowledge of conditions*, and a *sincere and systematic effort at* social and economic *development.*

(4) *The freely chosen leaders of the Community themselves the personnel of the government*, the authoritative masters of legislation and policy. ⟨(The *story of the French rustic* who was taken to the Chamber of Deputies and wished to be shown "The Government").⟩

Let us consider the first of these Relations,—

The Government as Master of the Community.

There is *practically no real absolutism for any man. Habit, environment, custom,* such *opinion* as he is sensitive to and can know, *temperament, time, space*, the necessity to act through *other men*, draw about every king a narrow circle of choice

What is really meant is, that *government* may, in certain circumstances be *practically free to choose for a Community (or* at any rate, if not for so sensitive and fully organized a thing as a Community, *at least for a People) its law and policy,*—if only the choosing be not too rapidly or violently changeful; and that *the dominating man at the centre* of a gov't. thus placed and empowered (if such a man there be) *is to all intents and purposes master of the State.*

It is not necessary to the analysis that the government should *have a king* at its centre. It may be the organ of a diffused group, *an aristocracy*, whose preëminence and power are too variously rooted to be easily explained.

Such a masterful Government can exist only—

(1) *At the sacred summit of a caste nation.*

(2) *As the* directing and controlling *organ of a nation* which is *practically an army encamped*, like the Teutonic peoples immediately after their taking possession of Roman Europe.

(3) As the *representative and* administrative *embodiment of a small* (generally *military) class* ruling a subjugated nation. *E.g. Russia* and China.

(4) *As "owner"* of the realm and the embodiment of all supreme legal powers, in such a nation as (at any rate

in France) emerged *by logical process from the Feudal System.*

Such gov'ts., in short, *represent always a stage of social development,*—that stage at which the Community as a whole is not conscious of any interest or purpose opposed to the authority and choices of the Government;—or, if conscious, is unable to utter or enforce its separate and differing wish. *Not necessarily an abnormal or unwholesome stage.*

A *nation may or may not linger at this stage.* The nation which is most apt to linger till it stagnate is *the caste nation. The encamped military nation* is quite sure to change rapidly, if we are to judge by the cases we know most about. *The population ruled by a limited class* who are its conquerors is apt to stand till the polity rots. *The modern monarch* of the developed feudal state is most apt to attempt progress and development.

It is *generally fatal for any nation to keep at this stage till* its forms and conceptions have a rootage many generations deep.

The characteristic limitations upon Gov'ts. wh. are *Masters* are *limitations of capacity, perception,* and *administrative integrity.* The conditions under wh. it acts are always demoralizing after it realizes and thinks that it has made sure of its power.

8 October, 1898

IV.

The Government as Leader.

When the Government acts as Leader it will usually be found to be because

(1) *The nation has to be prepared, organized, equipped* as an instrument in international rivalries and struggles, before its standing and security are such as to make it free or able to exercise a self-originated initiative *(Frederick the Great* and *Prussia); or because*

(2) *The nation is coming to self-consciousness* and a will and individuality of its own, but has not yet had such an organic growth as would fit or dispose it for self-government, and therefore *needs to be acted for,* being willing to submit to that initiative of the Gov't. so long as it leads and does not force or thwart or shock it. *(England and Elizabeth)*

In these cases the rulers are *really leaders; but* they are *self-constituted,* not set up by the deliberate choice of the Community. *The Community, nevertheless,* in the second case, *often offers advice,* and often *objects* to particular counsellors of the sovereign.

Successful leadership in this kind is possible only in circumstances like the the following,

(1) *When the objects of national policy are external* rather than internal and so *the government* is practically *forced to act upon national motives,* and not upon the motives of a class directing domestic development for its own selfish advantage.

(2) *When the nation is homogeneous and comparatively simple in its make-up* both of opinion and of economic conditions, so that its interests in matters of policy will in most large things be single and its advantage lie in vigorous and consistent action such as an alert government is apt to originate and pursue.

(3) *When the nation a-making,* finding its rôle and standing in the world.

(4) *When the nation has sufficiently found its tongue to make its leaders aware of its impulses, its possibilities, its character and temper. This can be* done *without the Press* (α) by a rural *gentry or* a trading or seafaring or colonizing *class;*

(β) by certain forms of *educational and administrative training,* creating a body of informed officials; as well as

(γ) by a *representative system,* consenting action, or suggestive resolutions.

This, too, is a period of transition, from which affairs *will pass,* stage by stage, into those arrangements whereby the freely chosen *leaders of the people conduct the government only if* while the autocratic rulers thus lead *a proper machinery* of constitutional action *exist or be formed* by means of wh. the transition may be effected.

This was the case in England, but not in Prussia. In England there were both Parliament and the self-governing country gentry, habituated to affairs. *In Prussia* there was nothing but a dependent bureaucracy, neither derived from the people nor capable of independent initiative in their interest.

As the last form of life (where the Government is Master) *repre-*

sents a stage of social development, this form represents a stage of *political development,* and will result in consequences good or bad according as *an adequate means* is or is not found *of accommodating* the needs and desires and principles of the nation and the will and motive force of the Government.

16 October, 1898

V.

The People and their Leaders vs. the Government

This is the next stage of progressive alteration in the relationship between the nation and its Government. *Things cannot stand still* where a whole arrangement depends upon the temper and insight of the rulers and the international, social, or economic situation of the Community.

National conditions are not often for long so simple or so comprehensible that the Government can retain *the sympathetic comprehension necessary to leadership.* Affairs alter, conditions grow complex.

Rulers seldom (if it depend on the personal equation) for any length of time *retain the* liberal and enlightened *temper of leadership.* Rulers grow too secure in the allegiance of their people and too selfish in the exercise of their power.

Then Nation and Rulers fall out of sympathy, draw apart into distinctly formed *parties,* and become antagonists in a contest for power, *if*

(1) *Deep common convictions* get abroad as the active principle in large, coherent, and *effective groups of men. E.g.,* In some states, the protestant *principle of the Reformation;* the *puritan party in England;* the revolutionary party in France. *1848* revolutionary excitement and example.

(2) *Circumstances produce leaders* capable of action and wise as well as bold and persistent in devising means of agitation. At this stage *leaders* are *self-constituted.* See Politics notes on Leadership.

(3) *Means of effective combination and continuous coöperation* be found. *May often be prevented* by a vigilant, prompt, and powerful government, acting with well trained force.

If, *in short opinion* become an *organized force* with *spokesmen* whom it is dangerous to silence.

This is "Agitation."

12 CONSTITUTIONAL GOVERNMENT NOTES

Agitation will produce "constitutional" understandings wh. will last and be observed only

> *If it* at the same time *bring about* the orderly establishment of such *arrangements* as will henceforth *transmute agitation* itself *into a regular originative agency.*

> This the Agitation which first came to a head at *Runnymede did not* at once do. This the *French revolutionists did not* do. This *America did* in the Continental Congresses.

So much for the People and their Leaders

The object of Agitation is *Law or Institutions*: for only in Law or in Institutions can constitutional understandings get *stable embodiment.*

A Government face to face with Agitation can either

> (1) *Fight*, trying to break parties and silence the utterance of opinion; or

> (2) *Compromise*, by yielding what is asked under such forms as will leave the new law or practice to its own moulding or interpretation; or

> (3) *Surrender*, yielding both the principle and the mode of its application.

It is *all a study in* {

the *formation of Opinion*

the *conscious genesis of Institutions*

the *repressive or guiding power of organized authority*

}

The question, who will side with the agitators, who with the Gov't. as *vs.* the agitators, is decided by

> *Habit or Affection* as *vs.*
> *Conviction or Interest.*

21 Oct., 1898

VI.

The People's Leaders as the Government.

There *may* very well *be several stages between* the state of affairs in which the people and their leaders are actively arrayed against the government and that in which the people's leaders actually constitute the government,—a considerable period, too, between the time when the government consents to mould its policy in the interest of the people, rather than of a class, and the time when the favour of the people regularly operates to put their leaders into office and into control of the government.

(1) *The Gov't. may obtain the consent of the people's representatives for each step* in the modification of the law; and

(2) *May even allow itself to be guided by the criticisms* of the people's representatives in the application of the law; without passing into the hands of the people's leaders.

It may be able to adjust itself to the general opinion and accommodate its action to the general desire, without impairing its separate choice and power,

(1) *When,* for example, *the leading classes of the community are in the interest of the Gov't.* without being out of sympathy with the general body of the people.

(2) *When the international situation of the country* and its government *is* so *difficult* and so constantly *liable to become critical* that continuity of organization and a trained and steady skill in affairs are necessary for the safety of the community.

(3) *When the Gov't. is enlightened and skilful enough* to constitute itself leader even of a developed nation, aroused to self-consciousness and the exercise of a quick and imperative critical faculty.

Organized opinion, however, *will always have a tendency to to make itself felt in the actual make-up of the Government,* as well as in the acceptance of governmental action. Such conditions as the above are seldom constant, while the pressure of opinion tends to grow; and it is always likely that the people's leaders will press nearer and nearer the seat of authority.

This aspiration and pressure may result in *one* or *other* of *two* now distinct and well recognized *forms of government*:

In order to understand these two forms we must observe that the function of government is two-fold,

(1) *The choice of policy,* i.e., courses of action under existing law (Executive); and

(2) *The modification of law* to suit actual changes of social condition or desired changes of policy. (Legislative)

Constitutional agitation may lead to one or other of two forms of popular government:

I. That under which *the people's leaders are both* heads of the Executive and guides of the Legislature,—generally called "Parliamentary Government."

II. That under which *the people's leaders* become *guides of legislation, but not necessarily chiefs of administration,* the Executive being constituted by some special process like that of popular election, which may or may not put real leaders in. Either of these is "constitutional," but the latter precariously so.

The Swiss federal government is of an intermediate kind produced by evolution from government by Assembly through executive committees. (See *The State*)

⟨7 November, 1898.⟩

VII.

Real and Formal Headship in the State.

Real, where *the vital processes* of politics *centre in the* person who is *legal head,*—where the monarch plans, or at least chooses the planners,—the ministers.

Formal, where those processes do not centre in the person who is legal head of the State. Of such States we may observe *two existing varieties*:

(1) *Where neither* the choice of policy nor the modification of law, nor even the administration of the law is left to the legal head of the State. As in England and France.

(2) *Where the administration* of the law, and to some extent a choice of policy rests with the legal head of the State,—*but not the initiative in law-making.* As in the United States.

We shall find from *an analysis of the two types* of formal headship *that the reality or mere formality* of headship in the State *does not turn upon the point of election. The French President* is elected as truly as our President is. He is elected by the chambers. *Our President* was meant to be elected by the electors, and is really elected by party convention.

In neither case is the process one which can be relied on to pick out real leaders. Real leaders must *pick themselves out:* and the process of self-selection cannot be carried on except *upon some public forum* where men may prove themselves with regard to the principal function they are called upon to perform.

Wherever we look, outside the field of international politics, *we find the Legislature the only real forum* of selection to leadership in the existing world of politics,—the only place where wisdom in affairs is publicly proved by service. (We are *not now considering "bosses"* as leaders. We are using the word leaders in a sense which does not apply to them. Bosses are managers, not leaders).

We find also that *only the "parliamentary" system,* whereby both functions of government are entrusted to the legislative leaders, *makes leadership distinct, effective, responsible.*

The President cannot get along without Congress.
Congress cannot act except through the President.

This largely because the Legislature is and must always be an administrative as well as a law-making body. The assent of the people's representatives to administrative choices as essential a part of modern popular government as their assent to law-making.

There can, therefore, be no leadership operating throughout the course of affairs, *without a single leadership* embracing both the Presidency and Congress.

So long as they are divorced and independent, we do not know *whom to trust* or *whom to blame.* Our real leaders are generally in Congress, where, amidst a very complex organization, they are very hard to distinguish. Sometimes leadership rests with the President,—who has been selected by processes not suited for the selection of real leaders.

Observe: The object of "constitutional" government is, *a cordial understanding between people and government.* The most developed form of constitutional government, therefore, is that under which the cordial understanding extends *beyond questions of fundamental law* to questions of administration and policy. This can be the case only when the people's real leaders constitute the government in both its parts, the planning *and* the executing,—between which in every well ordered government there must be unity, harmony, consistency.

Notice, too, *the entire self-selection of "bosses,"*—in a covert way which illustrates the truly singular manner in which we have *obscured the processes of leadership,* and *broken the direct course of "constitutional" government,* in this country, by a blind acceptance of the principle of a "division of powers."

13, 14 November, 1898

VIII.

[A.] *Petition* (proceeding from popular opinion)

"Congress shall make no law . . . *abridging* . . . *the right of the people peaceably to assemble, and to petition the government for a redress of grievances." Const. Amend.* I.

The right of Petition came slowly to complete recognition as one of the *undeniable rights* of *a people* constitutionally governed (i.e. *governed by consent*); and that *notwithstanding the fact* that Petition is necessarily an *inorganic* thing, originating privately and with limited and it may be *unrepresentative groups* of persons.

It was *at first resisted because inorganic,* under the idea that only the people's regularly elected representatives were the authentic spokesmen of the people and that petition was a process of *irregular and irresponsible agitation.*

It is noteworthy, too, that *in proportion as elective law-making bodies were made more truly representative,* more sensitively responsive to opinion (and *in proportion as opinion found such means of expression as* the *newspaper press*) *Petition has sunk* in influence and importance,—until it is *now hardly more than* an infrequent means of making representatives acquainted with new phases of opinion or new formulations of purpose amongst their constituents.

Petition, moreover, having become *familiar and frequent,* and the getting up of petitions an *easy* matter of soliciting signatures from indifferent persons, *its influence of course passes away with its dignity and significance.*

Imperative Petition is the most modern form, and is really but another name for an actual initiative in law-making. (See "The State," secs. 654, 655).

Upon this *it may be commented*

(1) That it permits *self-constituted spokesmen* to formulate measures to be submitted to the popular vote;

(2) That it may involve a use of *voting to* the extent of *inconvenience and disgust*;

(3) That it would have to be guarded carefully from the *danger of minority adoption,* through leth[ar]gy and inattention;

(4) That it is *apt to encourage* to an alert and *querulous uneasiness* which might make professional reformers a serious nuisance; above all,

(5) That *it discredits* and to a certain degree renders impossible *the most essential instrument of intelligent progress, viz., Responsible Leadership.*

(6) Does not secure face to face conference and discussion or the intimate comparison of views of legislative assemblies.

⟨21 Nov., 1898⟩

IX.

B. THE SANCTION OF LAW:

Representation

Representation is *the principal and characteristic instrumentality of "constitutional" government*: the means of maintaining *an understanding and a systematic union in opinion and purpose* between the people and the Government. It is the chief and only means so far devised for effecting the characteristic object of "constitutional" government, viz., *the organic association of the active parts of the nation in determining the choices of the Government in law and in policy.*

N.B. *"The active parts"* are those who regularly and intelligently busy and interest themselves in matters of political action. These may, if other men lie lethargic at most seasons, be only the *professional politicians*, who are managers and not leaders.

Historically, Representation was *a Germanic institution to begin with* (originally lying back of German and French history no less than of English); but it became *a peculiarly English institution in its development* into modern "constitutional" forms.

It was *never*, first or last, *intended as an instrumentality for the origination or formulation of law*; but

(1) For *the declaration of law* and for the making of coöperative plans of *action*, e.g., in the field of battle,—such as the choice of an acceptable leader.

(2) Finally, *for the development and maintenance of a constitutional understanding* between governors and the governed: a means of coöperative opinion and purpose.

It was *developed in order to obtain the* coöperation of the nation in the designs of the Crown,—to obtain *money* as a grant *based upon assent to the objects of expenditure. In organizing it for this purpose, representatives were chosen by classes*: the church, the baronage, the towns, the counties as organic units,—choosing at first in county court.

Only *an historical "accident"* (Freeman)[3] brought it about that there were *two instead of three or four "houses,"* or divisions, of Parliament,—as, for example, in France. And *this*

[3] Edward Augustus Freeman, *The Growth of the English Constitution from the Earliest Times* (London, 1872), p. 93.

circumstance (of the union of elements in each House) no doubt *gave England precedence* in the conception of the *principle that it was the nation* or community as a whole, and not classes or distinct sections of the people, *that should be represented in the assembly* that assented to law.

General Character: A Representative Body is *an instrument of criticism*, rejection, or assent: *a "grand inquest,"*—always intended to act *under the initiative of the Government*. It is a central and characteristic organ of a "constitutional" system, *not as itself a part of the Government*, but because that system cannot be maintained by constitutions merely, but must extend its understandings into the field of ordinary law,—must be *vitalized and sustained at every stage by the coöperation of representative assemblies*.

The Object of Representation.

To represent the Community?

To represent the People?

That must depend upon the actual historical *make-up and habitual organization* of the nation in question. Its object can be stated in only *one general proposition*: that *it must serve the objects of the national life*, or of the life of the community (e.g., one of our States) concerned,—whatever those may, historically, be.

28 Nov., 1898

The characteristic processes of constitutional government are the processes of *conference* and *discussion* between those who represent opinion and those who represent government, added to *conference and discussion amongst those who represent opinion*. The latter constitutes as essential a part of the method as the former. Opinion does not become national, single, and of a kind to be serviceable for guidance until it has ceased to be individual and peacemeal opinion and has become *agreement*. *Neither an average nor an aggregate* opinion is truly a national opinion. Government is organic, and the sort of opinion which should guide it cannot be got from a popular vote. It must be the result of *a careful comparison of views*,—of an agreement which takes into consideration, and so far as possible *combines, elements of thought and judgment as various as the interests and convictions of the communities which the representative body represents*.

And agreement between the people's representatives and the government must, likewise, be an agreement based upon both *general opinion* and *the actual exigencies* of affairs, which can be thoroughly known and intimately understood only by conference with those who are in the midst of the actual transactions which reveal them. Like opinion itself, this agreement must also be *compounded out of the circumstances of the case*. It can be wisely compounded in no other way. *An immediate and first-hand knowledge of the facts* is its indispensable foundation.

⟨20 Nov., 1900⟩

X.

The Referendum.

Introduction: Explanation of the Referendum as used in Switzerland and the United States ("*The State*," secs. 656-659, 699, 700, 1097, 1099, 1100; A. L. Lowell, "Gov'ts and Parties in Continental Europe," Chap. XII., vol II.)

Theory of the Referendum: That law-making should rest and may without practical inconvenience be made to rest upon *the explicit acceptance of a majority* of the enfranchised citizens of the State.

(1) *It rejects the whole idea of* the exercise of independent *individual judgment on the part of the elected representative* (and requires for its discussion, therefore, a re-examination of that idea). It, *in fact, rejects the idea of representation* altogether and substitutes that of *mere deputation* or agency.

(2) It *rejects guidance* and *substitutes persuasion.* The representative must first act and then, in order to make his act valid, convince a majority of the voters,—transmit to them his motives and reproduce in them his grounds of judgment. *Note the tendency* of the Swiss voter *to reject all complex measures* and all proposals for expenditures or new undertakings *not generally deemed necessary.*

(3) *Shuts law out from the exercise of all moulding or modifying power,* such as it may most wholesomely exert oftentimes when originated by men of experience or insight who are qualified to see (discern) special causes and understand special cases. (*This* influence and use of law to be *discussed next lecture*).

The Referendum is as *open* as Petition *to the objections* that it may entail *too much voting*; that it exposes a State to the *danger of minority control* in important matters; and that it *discredits responsible leadership.*

⟨5 December, 1898⟩

XI.

Adjustment: the Moulding and Modifying Power of Law.

This is an age, par excellence, *of Legislation,* of the conscious, deliberate, studious, almost ceaseless *adjustment of law to social conditions,* and, by intended consequence, of the alteration of those conditions

In this work of deliberate modification *there is to be seen,* e.g.,

(1) *The adjustment,* reconciliation, coördination *of social forces* which by their very nature produce *a minority to be protected* as well as *a majority to be satisfied.* E.g., capital and labour (factory acts, technical education, housing of the poor, &c. &c.).

(2) *The application of scientific laws,* which only experts can comprehend or apply: *e.g.,* sanitation and the prevention of disease, the punishment of crime, &c.

(3) *The application of social and political laws not of general observation: e.g.,* laws of commercial exchange, currency and banking, &c.

Such matters can be legislated upon successfully and with intelligence *only when* the Nation has *a real, organic selective organ,* i.e., *authoritative leadership,*—by which the knowledge of experts and the more subtle inferences of special observation and experience can be applied to subjects of *legislation without any actual acceptance on the part of the voter.*

Upon these matters *strong and general convictions are out of the question;* but for that very reason the general habit will the more readily yield itself to the guiding and modifying influences of the law. *E.g.,* the central regulation of *local government,* particularly, e.g., of local public works, local debts and loans, &c.

It is a field of experiment, moreover, in which statesmen sh. have leave to try the effects of first one and then another method of regulation. This is especially true in the field of *competitive interests,* like those of trade and manufacture, *wh. require a whole view and a long view.*

All that the principles of constitutional government demand in this sort of legislation is, not, of course, the assent of the nation to the opinions of experts and experienced judges of affairs, but only its *assent to leadership,*—a judgment, not of measures, but of the character and ability of its leaders: *an act of trust, not an act of legislative choice.*

⟨11 December, 1898⟩

XII

C. THE ADMINISTRATION OF LAW:

Popular Administration: Its Place and Limits.

We have seen that *the distinctive principle of "constitutional" government* demands that government should be conducted upon the basis of a cordial understanding between the Government and those who are governed,—and no doubt *this principle extends* beyond the making of laws and the inception of policies *to the administration of the laws* and the actual conduct of the government.

Unquestionably *the only sure and safe way* to bring this principle into action is, *to draw the administrative personnel of the government* by some free and open process *from out the general body of the nation*, without preferring in the selection one class or order or social station or blood or condition to another, if only fit and capable persons be found for each function.

But *fitness and capacity must vary with the function* to be performed, and so *we must distinguish*

(1) *Between those functions which require expert knowledge* and a special training for their proper performance *and those which do not*. This distinction will be *discussed in the next lecture*, wh. will treat especially of those matters of gov't. in wh. expert administration is necessary for the successful conduct of public affairs.

(2) *Between those functions wh. may be performed by any man of good intelligence* who is capable of understanding the simpler sorts of business, no matter what his antecedents may have been, *and those* functions *for which only special kinds of bringing up and special conditions of life and environment render men fit.*

Take the latter first.

In diplomacy, for example, quite aside from any special preliminary training that may be considered necessary, a man must have that *tact and address* in personal intercourse, that *self-possessed and self-respecting dignity*, that *knowledge of men and of social conventions*, and that *various knowledge of character* wh. come (except in extraordinary cases) only to men who have had *wide opportunities of culture and observation* and who have been *trained under the influence of leisured society*.

A consular service is thoroughly serviceable and efficient only when made up of men *experienced in commerce* and conversant with the *languages, tastes, resources,* and *economic conditions* of the countries in which they serve.

An unpaid civil service, though no doubt inadvisable, and indeed out of the question, in economically undeveloped countries, where very few enjoy an independent competence without the necessity for labour, in a country of widely diffused wealth *is likely to draw to the service of the country* (if the proper conditions of dignity and independence of tenure be established),—and that without limiting the selection to any special class,—*men very little exposed to the temptation* to peculate, apt to use their power with *independence*, not likely to make their places a means of *self-advancement, less petty, selfish,* and *servile* than those for whom place is a necessary means of livelihood and of social or political consideration.

Capacity is, of course, *a matter of developed*, and not merely of innate or latent, *intelligence. Fitness* has in it *moral as well as intellectual* elements, and may be acquired as well as native. *There can be no levels either of ability or of suitability. Suitability is a fact,* made up of *positive rather than* of *negative* elements; and no man can be said to be fit for public office simply because no special disability can be charged against him.

Moreover, a nation should be so constituted in respect of its government *as to be served ordinarily by its best minds*, upon a free and universal competitive principle; and *the administration is still "popular"* in the best sense of the term if *self-preparation* be free and unimpeded,—*individuals of every class admitted to the competition* without regard to social standing or derivation,—so that the whole wealth of capacity in the nation shall be drawn upon.

If wealth, and the opportunities wh. it brings give *some an advantage over others* in this self-preparation, that is *an economic, not a political, limitation* put upon the theoretical equality of competition; and the remedy for that inequality, if there be any remedy, must be sought for elsewhere than in constitutions and merely political arrangements.

The inequality is in part offset by the fact that the possession of *wealth as often enervates and relaxes effort as quickens it,* and the comparatively poor, if only by reason of the extra stimulus to exertion, outrun the rich in fitting themselves for achievement and the successful exercise of power.

The place, therefore, *of popular administration* is properly in the *untechnical matters of local self-gov't, and* in *all common counsel* about the scope and the plans of administrative action.

Wherever practicable, there should be associated with those by whom the daily tasks of administration are actually performed *a popular council* whose function it should be to sanction and direct.

The limits of popular administration lie where *the need for special training or technical skill* begins.

⟨18 and 20 Dec., 1898⟩

XIII.

Expert Administration: Its function and conditions:

Expert administration is that which is *founded* on knowledge or experience,—at best, *upon both knowledge and experience.*

It is *typified in the administration of justice:* the interpretation of the law, a function universally admitted to demand *professional training,*—if it is to be done at its best, *even profound scholarship.*

Its Object is: *to put the learning, experience, and skill of the country at the disposal of the government.*

The best equipped governments have even undertaken to *create the skill and the intellectual acquirements needed* in their service, where the ordinary educational and professional instrumentalities do not suffice to supply them,—as e.g., in familiarizing candidates for the civil service with the machinery of the government itself, with the relation of the several parts of its business to one another, and with the detail of the tasks it has to undertake.

A question of efficiency, not of "constitutionality."

It is absolutely necessary, e.g.,

    (1) *In things technical,*—like finance, the inspection of trades, of buildings, of ships, of boilers, of public works, and, of course, in the execution of public works.

    (2) *In things scientific,*—like education, sanitation, forest culture, coinage, agricultural experimentation, etc., etc.

    (3) *In matters which require various accomplishments* for their proper carrying out,—like diplomacy, which requires social training (which no school can give), a speaking knowledge of languages (which schools can give only imperfectly), and a knowledge of the customs and conventions of foreign countries (such as comes chiefly by travel and observation).

Requisite conditions for its success:

    (1) *Professional preparation*, by agencies public or private.

    (2) *Security of tenure.* (N.B. judicial removal).

    (3) *Impartial system of promotion.*

    (4) *A proper classification and division of functions*, of course.

Consistent with popular government, if it excludes monopoly

    I.e., limitation to a particular class, or to particular families by inheritance.

⟨7 January, 1899⟩

XIV.

D. THE GUARDIANSHIP AND INTERPRETATION OF LAW.

I. *Appointment or Election of Judges.*

    The interpretation of the law must have some place in the theory and practice of "constitutional" government. Experience has shown that law *can* be interpreted in the spirit and in the interest of a class or of personal power. *Its interpretation*, as well as its origination and formulation, ought to be imbued with the spirit of service, and *sh. have for its object the maintenance* in all frankness and good faith *of the understandings* as to personal freedom, governmental power, and equality before the law *upon which "constitutional" government rests.*

Considerations like these have led in some "constitutional" states *to the practice of electing judges*, as other officers of government are elected,—either directly by popular franchise, or else indirectly through the choice of representative bodies, like our state legislatures. *We have rejected*, in this country, it would appear, *the idea of appointment*—except in the case of the federal judiciary.

And yet Election is *by no means indisputably the best*, safest, fairest, most satisfactory method of choosing judges.

Its Advantages:

(1) *It imparts to the judge a sense of identification with the community* itself. *In practice, however*, this generally dwindles to a sense of identification with certain party managers.

(2) Theoretically, *it makes the bench attainable by men of ability who have had no advantages of birth or station* and who have, therefore, no adventitious means of advancing themselves,—and so enriches the public service. *In practice, however*, since nomination must precede election, it narrows the choice to men who have influence of another kind with local politicians.

(3) *It often draws the bar* of a locality or a country on *to exert a proper preference & show an active public spirit in influencing nominations and choices* for the bench.

Its Disadvantages:

(1) If connected with comparatively short terms of service, election is *apt to introduce* into the judge's mind that *subtle sort of corruption*, or, at any rate, bias, which comes *from thinking of the effect particular decisions* may have upon particular persons or groups of interests which are likely to be influential in securing or preventing his nomination for another term.

(2) *It makes each place on the bench subject to a particular set of influences*, personal or local,—and so, instead of intensifying, *disperses responsibility*, and makes it practically impossible to have a bench all of a kind in excellence or in any other quality. *Uniformity of quality is as important*, in this function, *as individual excellence.* (The superior impartiality, sometimes, of rural judges.)

(3) *It tempts obscure managing politicians* and the innumerable unwatched men who influence nominations *to make of the bench an instrument* for their own ends.

Appointment, on the other hand,

(1) *Centres and unifies responsibility.*

It is not to be overlooked that *the interpretation and application of law* is *an integral and essential part of administration as a whole*; and that the understandings of a "constitutional" government can be best maintained only when *the few persons who direct the government*, conspicuous in power and always closely observed and constantly criticised, *can be held responsible* for every part of their candid and careful maintenance. A responsible body of administrators *must choose judges as instruments of their own success in the just and acceptable conduct of affairs.*

(2) *The fitness of judges can be better assessed by persons themselves experienced in government* and acquainted with the practical temper and talents of the available persons from amongst whom they must choose than by the persons of smaller experience and responsibility who generally control the choice under a system of numerous nominations.

(3) While it is *probably true that appointment is apt to limit the range of choice* to the comparatively small number of men known and trusted by the few leaders of affairs, it is *also true that "constitutional" government* is, from its very nature, *best maintained when* its organization and structure are *simple and obvious.*

The object in constituting men judges is, *not to give* as large a number of persons as possible *a chance to get on the bench*, but simply *to make the interpretation of the law adjust itself* to the major purposes of government and of the development of legal relationships. *A responsible government* must be a government with a vital, guiding, organizing, controlling, mediating group of leaders who impart *to the whole conduct of affairs* their own spirit and integrity of serviceable purpose.

9 January, 1899

XV.

Judicial Term of Service.

In order that judges may be suitable instruments of "constitutional" government, it is necessary

(1) That *they should feel* a *constant* sense of *responsibility*, i.e., that they should all the time feel answerable to some definite power for their conduct in office.

(2) That *they should act* always *in a spirit of cordial sympathy with the rights of communities* or of individuals as against the government, as well as with the prerogatives of the government as *vs.* individuals or communities.

(3) That *they should not remain on the bench after their period of* physical and intellectual *efficiency* is passed and over.

Hence more or less frequent *re-election or re-appointment* under systems of popular government.

But the *power of removal*, coupled with the power of appointment, accomplishes all these objects, *if the appointing power* itself *be responsible* to the nation or community.

There are other objects to be sought in the constitution of courts of law quite as important as the three already mentioned

    (1) *The judges should* be so situated as to be encouraged to *exercise their powers independently and impartially*; and

    (2) *The bench should be* made to offer a secure and distinguished *career*. This it will not offer unless
    (a) *the tenure be secure,*—i.e. practically during good behaviour and physical and intellectual efficiency,— unless
    (b) *the service be* rendered such as to offer a place *of unusual dignity and elevation,*—and unless
    (c) *it be well-enough paid* to be worth the while of the best lawyers. This *includes retiring pensions.*

Emolument and Dignity of Judicial Service.

Few states can afford to pay their judges as much as the most successful practitioners earn (or, at any rate, receive); *but* it is not always the men with the most lucrative practice who have a taste or fitness for the bench; *and it is always possible to pay enough* to secure *a comfortable living at the highest dignified social levels* of the capital,—enough to secure to men of the highest culture and attainments their proper social standing, connections, and enjoyments.

Dignity comes, in such a calling, *with security of tenure and with the social position* obtained by an adequate income,—*no less than* by the exercise of *high and extensive powers* and by the enjoyment of *a conspicuous position of trust.* Security of tenure and adequate pay give dignity also to minor judgeships

For minor judgeships another principle may secure high consideration, viz., the principle that lower places are places of apprenticeship and preparation for the higher,—for the highest;—the principle which leads to systematic, impartial, well considered *Promotion.*

⟨16 January, 1899⟩

XVI.

E. THE CONCEPTION AND REALIZATION OF LAW.

The Field and Items of Individual Right.

There must in a constitutional government be a very clear and definite conception of Law,—*a very definite basis for the realization of Rights.* "Constitutional" government is by very definition based upon a limitation of the power of the government over the individual; and the principle of that limitation must be derived from *a conclusive analysis of individual rights, inherent or acquired.*

There are *two ways of determining* these rights:
(a) *by Theory*, that is, by speculative reason, and
(b) *by Experience*, the outcome, that is, of the inevitable and instinctive struggle of the individual for freedom of thought and action, on the one hand, and of the government for power and a directing control over the individual, on the other.

It is not our present business to follow either theory or experience in a *search for individual rights.* That inquiry belongs to the discussion of some particular system of government ⟨(such as we shall undertake next term)⟩: for *experience*, and *even theory, will differ with different cases of political development*, and each nation will follow its own ideals and work out its own experience, to the setting up of its own forms of government,—its own characteristic liberty.

A text from Burke: "If any ask me what *a free government* is, I answer, that, for any practical purpose, it is *what the people think so,*—and they, and not I, are the natural, lawful, and competent judges of the matter."[4]

"*Abstract liberty*, like other mere abstractions, is not to be found. *Liberty inheres in some sensible object*; and every nation has formed to itself some favourite point, which by way of eminence becomes the criterion of their happiness."[5]

"Nuns fret not at their convent's narrow room;
And hermits are contented with their cells;
And students with their pensive citadels;
Maids at the wheel, the weaver at his loom,

[4] "A Letter to the Sheriffs of the City of Bristol, on the Affairs of America, April 3, 1777," *Works of the Right Honorable Edmund Burke*, 5th edn. (12 vols., Boston, 1877), II, 227.
[5] "Speech on Moving His Resolutions for Conciliation with the Colonies, March 22, 1775," *ibid.*, p. 120.

Sit blithe and happy; bees that soar for bloom
High as the highest Peak of Furness-fells,
Will murmur by the hour in foxglove bells:
In truth the prison, unto which we doom
Ourselves, no prison is; and hence for me
In sundry moods, 'twas pastime to be bound
Within the Sonnet's scanty plot of ground;
Pleased if some Souls (for such there needs must be)
Who have felt the weight of too much liberty,
Should find brief solace there, as I have found."[6]

Wm. Penn:—"Any government is free to the people under it
(whatever be the frame) where the laws rule and the people
are a party to those laws."[7]

It is our business here *to inquire how Rights* against Government
actually come to light, and how they serve as a norm of constitutional order and freedom.

   In order to do this, we must *inquire*
   (1) *How they arise*
   (2) *How they find expression*
   (3) *How they persist*

I. *They arise,* as wants arise, *by the development both of the individual and of society*

II. *They find expression in Institutions,* i.e., in practices, privileges, exemptions, modes of dealing. So a nation will express its ideals, its genius for affairs, its social experience.

III. *They persist by habit,* and by a practical, stimulating and
helped by a speculative, unfolding, by passing through a
slowly found series of new or modified applications,—i.e.,
by being used and acted upon until they come to be accepted
as natural laws of life.

No Rights can mark the limits of government in any real or effectual fashion *which are not part and parcel of experience:* because *no nation can practice rights of which it is not conscious,* and consciousness of Right comes only with experience.

   Hence the inevitable experience of statesmen in periods
of constitutional experiment,—*that peoples cannot be given
Rights* for which they are not prepared by their circumstances, of which they are not consciously and definitely
desirous by reason of a practical realization of their own

6 By William Wordsworth.
7 Preface to *The Frame of the Government of the Province of Pennsylvania
in America* (1682).

interests and capacities. A *successful political change* must be *based, not upon a creation, but upon a recognition of Rights*. It is significant that among the English,—the most successful developers of "constitutional" government,— Rights have always been spoken of as *immemorial*, even at the moment of their *legal* inception.

WWhw and WWT notes (WP, DLC).

To William Oscar Rogers[1]

My dear Sir,   Princeton, New Jersey, 20 September, 1898

Allow me to acknowledge with great appreciation the receipt of the formal document conferring upon me the degree of Doctor of Laws at the hands of Tulane University.[2] It is a parchment which I shall greatly value, as evidence of an honour of the highest sort done me in quarters where I most desire to be thought highly of.   Most sincerely Yours,   Woodrow Wilson

ALS (LNHT).
  [1] Secretary of Tulane University.
  [2] See W. P. Johnston to WW, June 16, 1898, and WW to W. P. Johnston, June 27, 1898, both in Vol. 10.

From the Minutes of the Princeton University Faculty

3 P.M., Wednesday, September 21, '98

Princeton University was opened with the reading of Scripture, prayer and an address by the President of the University [Francis Landey Patton] in the Marquand Chapel, after which the Faculty assembled in the Faculty-room and the meeting was opened with prayer by the President.

The President then presented the following Remit from The Honorable, the Board of Trustees of Princeton University to the President of Princeton University announcing the adoption by the Board of the following Recommendation of the Committee on the Affairs of the University[1] on June 13th, 1898:

Division of the Faculty of the University into two Sub-Faculties.

"We recommend that in order to secure a more efficient administration of the affairs of the University, the Faculty of the University be divided into two Sub-Faculties, to be known respectively as the Academic Faculty and the School of Science Faculty; the former being composed of those Professors and Assistant Professors whose duties pertain mainly to the Academic Depart-

ment, and the latter being composed of those Professors and Assistant Professors whose duties pertain mainly to the School of
Science; that the President, or, in his absence, the Dean, shall
preside over each Sub-Faculty; that the Proceedings of the two
Sub-Faculties be reported regularly to the Faculty of the University at its Stated Meetings; that in all ordinary cases the Action
of the Sub-Faculties in reference to the Admission, Standing and
Discipline of Students be final and the University Faculty shall
deal mainly with questions pertaining to the general policy of the
University. . . ."

Attest. E. R. Craven, Clerk, &c.

The President then announced the names of the Professors
and Assistant Professors constituting the two Sub-Faculties as
follows. . . .

"Minutes of the Faculty, 1894-1902," bound minute book (University Archives,
NjP).
1 For the appointment of this committee, see the Minutes of the Trustees of
Princeton University, printed at Dec. 10, 1896, Vol. 10. For its reports, see the
Minutes of the Trustees, printed at June 14, 1897, March 10, 1898, and June
13, 1898, all in *ibid.*

From Gustav Eggena[1]

My dear Professor Wilson: New Brighton, N.Y. Sept 27/98.

Please let me thank you most sincerely for your great kindness
in writing those letters. The one to Columbia is so much more
than I deserve that I don't like to show it very much. They will
expect more than I can give. I shall ask to have it returned as a
memento of your classes in which I spent so many pleasant
hours. I shall always be more of a man for having been under
you.

Believe me,   Very sincerely yours,   Gustav Eggena

ALS (WP, DLC).
1 A special student at Princeton, 1895-98, who had just transferred to Columbia
University, from which he received the A.B. degree in 1899.

From the Minutes of the Princeton University Faculty

5 5′ P.M. Wednesday, September 28th, 1898.

. . . A Communication having been received from the Librarian
in reference to the arrangement and assignment of the Seminary
Rooms in the new Library Building Prof. West, the Dean and
Professors Ormond, Fine and Wilson were appointed a Commit-

tee to consider the matter and to report at the next meeting of the Faculty.[1]

The Committee in reference to the times of meeting of the respective Faculties of the University presented their report which was adopted and is as follows

The University Faculty shall meet on the Fifth Wednesday of any month in Term Time having five Wednesdays and also upon the Wednesdays preceding the meetings of the Board of Trustees.

The Academic Faculty shall meet upon the First and Third Wednesday of each month in Term time.

The Faculty of the School of Science shall meet upon the Second and Fourth Wednesday of each month in Term time.

The University Faculty is to have the precedence in the case of any conflict of dates of meeting

A Calendar of the Faculty Meetings was ordered to be prepared and published by the Clerk for the use of the Faculty. . . .

[1] For their report, see the Princeton University Faculty Minutes printed at October 19, 1898.

To Albert Shaw

My dear Shaw,   Princeton, 14 October, 1898

It seems fairly mean to say No to your request for an article on Wheeler;[1] but you know me well enough to believe that if I decline it is simply a case of must.

And it is! If you only knew!—what a slow mind I have, how hard to disengage from one subject and get going on another! It would take me a whole week of thinking about nothing else to write anything at all that I should be willing to sign my name to; and to take that much time from the imperative duty task I am now working at against time[2] would be nothing less than unconscientious. Don't be deceived by articles from me in the Atlantic.[3] They—with one to appear in the Century[4]—are the lectures I read at the Hopkins last February.[5]

I know that you will excuse me, and that you will believe me, despite all unserviceableness,

Faithfully Yours,   Woodrow Wilson

TCL (in possession of Virginia Shaw English).

[1] Joseph Wheeler, lieutenant general in the Confederate Army; congressman from Alabama, 1881-83 and 1885-1900; major general of volunteers in the Spanish-American War; and tireless advocate of reconciliation between the North and the South.

[2] The high school textbook in American history which Wilson had promised to deliver to Harper and Brothers by the end of 1898. See the Editorial Note, "Wilson's 'History of the United States for Schools,'" Vol. 10.

[3] "A Lawyer with a Style," Atlantic Monthly, LXXXII (Sept. 1898), 363-74.

printed in this series at Feb. 25, 1898, Vol. 10; and "A Wit and a Seer," *Atlantic Monthly*, LXXXII (Oct. 1898), 527-40, printed at Feb. 24, 1898, Vol. 10.

4 "Edmund Burke and the French Revolution," *Century Magazine*, LXII (Sept. 1901), 784-92, printed in this series at Feb. 23, 1898.

5 When he delivered the Donovan Lectures on February 23, 24, and 25, 1898.

A News Report

[Oct. 15, 1898]

In the Senior academic class the largest elective is History, with Prof. [Paul] van Dyke, who has 88 students. The next are English Literature, 63; Poetics, 50; Jurisprudence, 46, and History of Philosophy, 46. . . . The academic Junior electives stand thus: Jurisprudence, 76; English Literature, 71; Astronomy, 63; History of Philosophy, 63, and German, 42. . . . The electives generally indicate that the students as a rule select courses which tend to broad mental training and furnish a good foundation for future study.

Printed in the *Princeton Press*, Oct. 15, 1898.

From the Minutes of the Princeton University Faculty

5 5′ P.M. Wednesday, October 19th, 1898

. . . The Committee on Seminaries in the new Library made their report which after full discussion and slight amendment was adopted as follows:

Your Committee appointed September 28th to prepare for the consideration of the Faculty regulations for the organization and conduct of the proposed Seminaries in the new Library, respectfully reports as follows:

A Committee appointed by the Board of Trustees, consisting of the President, Mr. [Moses Taylor] Pyne, and the Librarian [Ernest Cushing Richardson], has advised the Faculty through a letter from the Librarian that there are thirteen rooms in the new Library now available for strictly Seminary purposes, and that these rooms are offered for the use of departments prepared to carry on Seminary work and not possessing special facilities in the form of laboratories, museums, observatories or other similar appliances. A provisional allocation of the rooms has accordingly been made, as follows: Of the five seminary rooms in the southeastern corner, one room on the first floor is set apart for Philosophy, and another for Jurisprudence and Political Science. The two rooms on the second floor are set apart for History, and the one room on the third floor for Economics and Sociology. Of the five rooms in the southwestern corner, one on the first floor is for the Germanic Languages and the other first floor room for the Romance Languages. The two rooms on the second floor are set apart, one for Latin and one for Greek, and the third floor room is for General Philology. In the northwestern corner three rooms are available; one on the first floor being allotted to English, one on the second floor to Mathematics, and one on the third floor to the mathematical side of Science. All these allotments are tentative, and are open to such modification as the Faculty may judge necessary. The fact that these rooms are now available makes it important for the Faculty to adopt some policy in regard to the reorganization and conduct of Seminaries, in order that that [sic] confusion may be avoided and the best obtainable results be realized. Two questions are therefore involved in this matter. The first is, On what plan should the Seminaries be organized and regulated? The second is, What resources are available for executing such a plan?

Your Committee assumes that the principal end to be aimed at is the development among our higher students of independent scholarly ability by extensive advanced study and training in the methods of original research, and unless this end can be realized, Seminaries are not fulfilling the object for which they are established. Of course, at this present time, we have few students in any department sufficiently qualified for such work, which is properly of a graduate character. Because of this limitation, it is not practicable, in the judgment of your Committee, to reserve the use of the seminary rooms solely for the seminary work. If successful Seminaries are to be developed in Princeton University we shall need to begin in a small way and develop them gradually, using all possible legitimate helps in the way of preparing our best students to enter the Seminaries. Accordingly we recommended that the rooms be used for the present for two purposes.

First, for the strictly seminary work, to which properly qualified individual graduate students and seniors may be admitted. Unless a Department has graduate students, it does not seem to your Committee that any Seminary should be established in that Department, because without graduate students it will be almost impossible to set or maintain proper seminary standards. But given some graduate students, a few seniors may be safely associated with them without disadvantage. These graduates and students who constitute the Seminary should be allowed individual private access, at all times when the Library is open, to the particular seminary room belonging to the Department of their studies.

Second, for small advanced elective classes of graduates or of seniors pursuing courses of study which are best prosecuted in the Library. Their exercises should not be considered or styled seminary work; but such classes would naturally be composed of the best material, and from them valuable members of the seminary might be selected.

To open the seminary rooms more freely than is here suggested seems to your Committee unwise. Probably no one would advocate the admission of underclassmen. Even the admission of classes of juniors and seniors, would probably impair the quality of the work that ought to be done and reduce the value of the privileges of the seminary rooms in the eyes of our higher students. If, however, after the experiment is tried on the basis here proposed it becomes clear to the Faculty that classes of Juniors should be admitted, it will be easy to make the change; but if juniors are admitted from the start and the experiment works unsatisfactorily, it will be difficult to deprive them of the privileges of the rooms.

Having considered the question as to what individual students should be eligible to membership in the Seminaries, and also what small advanced elective classes might be allowed for the present to hold their regular class exercises in seminary rooms, we pass to the question of the organization and conduct of the Seminaries. We recommend, first of all, that the Department be made the unit of organization, and suggest that the following be recognized for the present as single Departments so far as relates to the seminary work in the new Library:

1. Philosophy.
2. History.
3. Jurisprudence and Politics.
4. Economics and Sociology.
5. Mathematics.
6. Classics.
7. Romance Languages.
8. Germanic Languages.
9. English.

In view of this classification of Departments, we recommend that the allocation of rooms be so modified as not to include an assignment either to General Philology or to the mathematical side of Science, and that the two rooms assigned to these subjects be reserved for su[b]sequent assignment by the Faculty.

We further recommend that the entire seminary work of each Department be under the control of the Department, and immediately under the care of a Director chosen to represent the Department. Every Director should be a full Professor. He should serve for a term of one academic year, but should be eligible to reappointment. Each Department should nominate the Director of its seminary work. In order to do this, the Department should hold a conference, at which every professor and assistant professor in the Department should be entitled to vote on the nomination of the Director; but such nomination by the Department should not be sufficient of itself to constitute appointment. It should not amount to appointment unless confirmed by a vote of the University Faculty.

Of course, the Director ought not to have any exclusive control of the seminary work of his Department. The seminary work should be under the control of the Department, and all members of the Department prepared to conduct such work should have equal voice and opportunity with the Director, who should serve simply as the executive officer of the Department. Consequently all matters of policy should be settled by departmental conference and then carried out by the Director.

Subject always to these limitations, he should be the responsible head of the seminary work during his term of office, being individually accountable to the Library for the Seminary room and its contents, and to the University Faculty for the conduct of the seminary work. More particularly, it should be his indispensable duty to conduct personally some important portion of the seminary work; to see that arrangements are made for the participation of other qualified members of the Department; to suggest measures of coordinating work; to issue all orders for the purchase of books, journals and other supplies for the seminary library; to secure the use of the room to duly authorized classes at the hours of their exercises, and at the close of his term of office to present to the University Faculty a written report describing in detail the work done during the year.

The question of the proper library equipment for seminary work has also been considered by your Committee. If the possession of a well-furnished special library is made a condition prerequisite to the organization of any Seminary, no Seminary can be started at present, for no Department now possesses such equipment. But we do deem it indispensable that no seminary be organized and installed in the Library without enough books and journals to make a hopeful beginning in the strictly seminary work, and that they be established gradually as one Department after another is found to be prepared to this extent.

The student members attending any one seminary course will naturally need to be carefully limited to the maximum number that can receive full individual benefits in their work. The size of the rooms and the length of the academic year have also to be considered. In the opinion of your Committee, not more than eight or perhaps ten students can be accommodated with advantage in the seminary course of any one instructor; but in order to place as little restriction as possible, it is recommended that the maximum number of students allowed in the seminary course of any one instructor be twelve. In the admission of student members we recommend that approved graduates be given the preference and that the remaining places be filled, so far as filled at all, by admitting seniors selected from those entitled to study for Special Honors in the Department.

These suggestions comprise all that seem to us practicable. We are not yet in a position to organize Seminaries as thoroughly as it is hoped they may be organized in case of a great development of our graduate work in the proposed Graduate College. But in the meantime these suggestions may well be put in the form of a few simple rules to unify the policy of the Faculty for the present. We therefore conclude this report by submitting a list of rules for the organization and conduct of such Seminaries as may be installed in the Library.

◊

Regulations for the Organization and Conduct
of Seminaries held in the University Library.

I.   The Department is the unit of organization, and each Department shall have control of all its seminary work.

II.   The following are recognized for the present as single Departments, so far as concerns their seminary work in the Library.

1. Philosophy.
2. History.
3. Jurisprudence and Politics.
4. Economics and Sociology.
5. Mathematics.
6. Classics.
7. Romance Languages.
8. Germanic Languages.
9. English.

III. 1. A Department shall be admitted to the use of a seminary room in the Library only by vote of the University Faculty on written application of the Department.

2. In this written application any Department proposing to start seminary work in the Library shall satisfy the University Faculty that there are members of the Department prepared to give the necessary time for conducting seminary work, that the Department has graduate students, and that it possesses sufficient special library equipment to justify it in making a start. When the Faculty is satisfied that these three conditions have been complied with, and the Department has also presented a satisfactory nomination for its first Director, the University Faculty shall authorize the establishment of the proposed seminary course or courses, and shall certify to the Librarian that the Department is to be admitted to its appropriate room in the Library.

IV. Every Director shall be a full professor, and shall be nominated by a vote of the professors and assistant professors of the Department and elected by the University Faculty. The term of office of every Director shall be one academic year, but any Director may be reappointed.

V. Subject always to the control of the Department, every Director shall be the responsible head of the seminary work during his term of office, and shall be individually accountable to the Library for the seminary room and its contents, and to the University Faculty for the conduct of the seminary work. More particularly it shall be his indispensable duty to conduct personally some important portion of the seminary work; to see that arrangements are made for the participation of other instructors designated by the Department; to suggest means of coordinating work; to issue all orders for the purchase of books, journals and other supplies for the seminary library; to secure the use of the room to duly authorized classes at the hours of their exercises, and at the close of his term of office to present to the University Faculty a written report describing in detail the entire work done during the year.

VI. The total number of students admitted to the seminary course of any one instructor shall not exceed twelve. In admitting student members the preference shall be given to approved graduate students, and such places as may remain may be filled by admitting Seniors selected from the list of those eligible under regulations formulated by the several Departments and adopted by the University Faculty.

VII. Small elective classes of graduates and seniors pursuing advanced studies in the Department may be admitted to use the rooms, but only at the hours of their class exercises and provided these exercises do not interfere with the seminary work.

Whether the rooms should be opened to any Department before it is able to undertake strictly seminary work is an important question. In the judgment of your Committee, it is not best to do so. In planning the new library building these rooms were expressly intended for Seminaries and not as undergraduate class rooms. But if it should seem otherwise to the Faculty, we think it essential that the work done in seminary rooms by Departments not yet prepared to organize Seminaries should not be considered or styled seminary work, but should be given some other name.[1]

◊

Resolved, That it be recommended to the Board of Trustees that Seminary Work such as is described in the report adopted by the University Faculty, October 19th, 1898, be organized in the Seminary rooms of the new Library Building.[2]

[1] There is a printed copy of this report, dated Oct. 17, 1898, in WP, DLC.
[2] The report was approved by the Board of Trustees at their meeting on Dec. 8, 1898. "Minutes of the Trustees of Princeton University, Dec. 8, 1898-March 14, 1901," p. 30.

From Burton Alva Konkle[1]

My Dear Sir—   Philadelphia 20 Oct 98

It seems to me that if one has read a writer who, he hastily admits, has become his spokesman in certain fields of thought and expression and has become one of the two or three most stimulating of contemporary writers—that he might frankly say so to the man himself.

It has been my good fortune to live both in the North and South, although a Northern man, and to see that there was room for one of the younger men to express the contemporary political aspirations that thoughtful men of my generation feel vaguely. I have longed for such an one for years—say a decade—and as I have in the past couple of years read everything I could get of yours, it has been with a sense of the keen delight of the discoverer. I have read everything but "The State," which will be my next, and all of them have been so keen a pleasure that, after reading your recent *Atlantic* articles, I felt as if I wanted to say so. I doubt not that you would have done the same thing to Sir Henry Maine, so I will encourage myself in thinking that you will not feel this expression as an intrusion and a bore.

Sincerely Yours   Burton A. Konkle

ALS (WP, DLC) with WWhw notation on env.: "Ans. 23 Oct./98."
 [1] A former public school teacher and Presbyterian minister, Konkle had settled in Philadelphia in 1897 and devoted himself to writing American and Pennsylvania history.

To Burton Alva Konkle

My dear Sir,   Princeton, New Jersey, 23 October, 1898

It is certainly one of the rewards of authorship to get such a letter as yours of last Thursday. I am so far from regarding it as an intrusion that I wish to thank you for it most heartily.

A writer of course never sees his audience; he does not know how many he is reaching or in what way he is being regarded by his readers. He must keep heart amidst the embarrassing silence, and try to believe that what he writes is at any rate worth saying and deserving of an audience, for the sake of the truth or the cheer or the right moral impulse, or the mere human interest, that is in it. It's a lonely business at best. Your letter comes to me pitched in so genuine a key of friendliness and appreciation that I must accept it not only with pleasure but also with gratitude. It heartens me and touches me very near the quick.

With sincere appreciation,

Very cordially Yours,   Woodrow Wilson

ALS (photostat in RSB Coll., DLC).

To John Rogers Williams[1]

My dear Mr. Williams,   Princeton, New Jersey, 23 October, 1898

At last, despite innumerable interruptions, I have finished reading Mr. Fithian's Journal;[2] and I have passed it on to Professor Perry.

It seems to me most interesting, and I am really obliged to you for giving me the opportunity to read it. What are your plans (if you have formed any) about publishing it? I doubt if any of our big "popular" magazines would make room for it,—wishing nothing without rapid "go" and piquancy unless from the papers of some very famous personage; but I should think that the Virginia Historical Society, or the Southern History Association, or the American Historical Magazine[3] would be glad to publish most, if not all, of it. The last would be much the most noticeable place in which to have it appear. If you wish introductions in any of these quarters, I shall be very happy to give it to you, with a hearty recommendation of the manuscript.[4]

If published, it would need a little editing to explain incidents (e.g. in the Long Island fighting) and introduce persons referred to.

Do you wish the very charming photographs of Old Yeocomico Church returned? Pray do not think this is a hint. It is a frank question, introductory to an expression of very warm thanks for your thoughtful kindness in letting me see them.

With warm regard,

Very sincerely Yours,   Woodrow Wilson

ALS (in possession of George Fulton Brown).

[1] Born in Princeton about 1876, Williams had prepared for college but was prevented from entering by poor health, which also forced him to live in the South for several years. (Wilson's letter is addressed to Machodoc, Va.) Williams returned to Princeton in 1900 and later became associated with the University Library and the office of the Secretary of the University. He died in 1906 at the age of thirty.

[2] This was the manuscript diary of Philip Vickers Fithian (1747-76), A.B., College of New Jersey, 1772. After his graduation from college, Fithian spent the remainder of his short life as a tutor to the children of Robert Carter III of "Nomini Hall" in Virginia, 1773-74; as an itinerant Presbyterian missionary in New Jersey and in the frontier country of Pennsylvania and Virginia, 1774-76; and as a chaplain in the Continental army near New York City, where he died in camp from dysentery on October 8, 1776. The extant segments of his diary cover portions of the years 1766-67 and 1773-76 and are an important source for the social history both of the great plantations of tidewater Virginia and of the Pennsylvania and Virginia frontiers, as well as of the army in the early days of the American Revolution. In 1898, Fithian's diary and some of his other papers were in the hands of a descendant in Philadelphia. They were given to the Princeton University Library in 1908.

[3] Wilson meant the *American Historical Review*. Selections from Fithian's diary for 1773-74, edited by Williams, appeared in the "Documents" section of the *American Historical Review*, v (Jan. 1900), 290-319.

[4] In 1900, Williams edited and published, under the auspices of the short-lived Princeton Historical Association (of which he was the "General Editor"), *Philip Vickers Fithian: Journal and Letters, 1767-1774* (Princeton, N.J.: The University Library, 1900). The portion of the diary covering Fithian's tutorship at "Nomini Hall" has been re-edited and republished several times. The later portions of the diary did not appear in print until 1934, when Robert G. Albion and Leonidas Dodson edited *Philip Vickers Fithian: Journal, 1775-1776, Written on the Virginia-Pennsylvania Frontier and in the Army Around New York* (Princeton, N.J.: Princeton University Press, 1934).

From Ellen Axson Wilson

My own darling,   Princeton, Oct. 26 [1898].

It is eight o'clock, the children have just "gone up," and I have just come down from getting Jessie ready for the night,—and now I will keep my promise and write a few lines.

I hope Jessie is going to be *really* better now, for her fever has not risen tonight as usual; in fact it is lower than it was this morning. She still speaks with the same difficulty however, and the gargle sickens her so that she can not use it as thoroughly as I would like. Still I hope to be able to report decided progress tomorrow.

It has poured rain all day. I spent the morning reading to Jessie, the afternoon sewing for the mission box; so ends our brief history since you left. Father seems cheerful; he had a letter from Dr. Ralston Smith[1] just before dinner and was talking about him and his family very brightly during most of the meal.

But oh! how we *all* miss you, my darling![2] You are the very light of my eyes; the house certainly wears a changed aspect when you are out of it; the greatest comfort in your absence is the negative one that it is *not* Balt. and you won't be gone five weeks!

And now one day is past—that is another comfort. I love you, dear, profoundly and am as always,   Your own   Eileen

Your telegram[3] just received, much to my satisfaction.

ALS (WC, NjP).
  [1] Thomas Ralston Smith, first cousin of Joseph Ruggles Wilson. Born in Philadelphia, Feb. 13, 1830, the son of James Passmore Smith and Mary Adams Smith. A.B., University of Pennsylvania, 1847; D.D., Williams College, 1868. After private theological study he was ordained to the Presbyterian ministry in 1851 and served in pulpits in Delaware, New York City, and New York State, his longest pastorate being at the Westminster Presbyterian Church of Buffalo. He was at various times Corresponding Secretary of the American Bible Society, Moderator of the Synod of Western New York, Moderator of the Synod of New York, and a trustee of Hamilton College. Died Sept. 5, 1903. In 1898 he was retired and living in New York City.
  [2] Wilson had just gone to Richmond to give five lectures on constitutional government at Richmond College (now the University of Richmond).
  [3] It is missing.

To Ellen Axson Wilson

My own darling,   Richmond, Va., 27 Oct. 1898

I arrived last night *in statu quo*, and forgot more than my visiting cards. I forgot the notes of the talk I meant to make to the Ladies' Club![1] I begin my letter about that for fear I should forget it again. Wont my darling look in the bottom drawer of the right-hand tier of drawers in my desk (next the fire-place) and send me the little note-book[2] (the smallest of several of the same style and make standing on end) containing notes of a talk in Pittsburgh on *"The Fashion of the Age"*?[3] Please do it up in stout paper and send it by mail. Unfortunately, you will have to pay *letter postage* on it. So much for my absence of mind!

I have come into a most agreeable household.[4] The first thing

I noticed, almost, was the very gratifying fact, under the circumstances, that Mrs. P. is in "an interesting condition,"—the best cure, no doubt, for her distress of mind! I am likely to have to follow quite as lively a pace of entertainment as I care to follow and shall have no end of a good time. I am feeling very well indeed; the weather is delightful, cool and clear; and I am promised a full audience for to-night.

I love you more than I can say,—and carry about with me a deep sense of solicitude which disturbs me at the same time that it magnifies my love for you into a sort of passion that almost frightens me! You are so much the loveliest, most interesting, most loyal and devoted being I know that the sense of having possibly in some degree interfered with your future development or even enjoyment by foreign travel, or any other use of leisure or liberty, almost overwhelms me,—at the same time that, bringing with it, as it does, also a clearer view and realization than ever of what you are, it magnifies my love a thousand-fold. Ah, my darling, my darling! What shall,—what *can* I say.

I trust dear little Jessie is much better. Unbounded love to her and to all. Does Father sometimes break silence?

Your devoted lover   Woodrow

ALS (WC, NjP).
    [1] A news report of this talk is printed at Nov. 3, 1898.
    [2] It is described at Oct. 24, 1897, Vol. 10.
    [3] These notes are printed at Oct. 24, 1897, Vol. 10.
    [4] Wilson stayed in Richmond with the Archibald Williams Pattersons, 104 East Grace St. Patterson, a lawyer, was an old friend from the University of Virginia days.

From Ellen Axson Wilson

My own darling,   Princeton, Oct. 27/98

Jessie is, as I hoped, *much* better today; tonight her fever is entirely gone, her speech is improved, and it scarcely hurts her at all to swallow. The only symptom that disturbs me is a new one, viz. occasional twinges of pain in one ear with a slight deafness, also in the one ear.

The carpenters finished entirely this afternoon.[1] I meant to see the painter[2] today but couldn't leave Jessie in the morning,—it being Annie's day out,—and in the afternoon I couldn't leave Richard![3] We have been very busy getting things planted, and are by no means through yet, Mrs. Brown having sent me another dozen of fine roses! If all these things grow I shall be almost done with planting; shall have all I want, except perhaps a few hollyhocks and hyacinths.

I send your letters[4] with this; if I get out in the morning, as I expect to, I will give Mr. Wilder's message to Mr. DeVries.[5]

I suppose you are at this moment in the midst of your first lecture. How I wish I were there to hear! I am waiting impatiently for my first letter from my dear one. Oh, how I miss you—and how I love you, my *darling* Woodrow! Always & altogether,

Your own   Eileen.

ALS (WC, NjP).
  [1] The Wilsons were finishing a room on the third floor of their house.
  [2] James L. Briner of 9 John St.
  [3] A yard- and handyman.
  [4] They are missing.
  [5] William Royal Wilder, Secretary of the Class of 1879, and John Hendrik de Vries, pastor of the Second Presbyterian Church of Princeton.

A News Report of a Lecture on Constitutional Government

[Oct. 28, 1898]

CONSTITUTIONAL GOVERNMENT.

The audience that gathered in the chapel of Richmond College last night to hear the first of the twelfth course of lectures under the Thomas Museum Lecture Endowment[1] was a large and representative one. There were many of Richmond's most highly cultivated people present. Among these was a strikingly large number of professional men. The city bar was well represented, a number of the leading lawyers being noticed in the audience.

Quite a number of teachers, physicians and well known business men were present.

Dr. Woodrow Wilson, of Princeton University, the lecturer, who has been secured to deliver the series this year, was introduced by President [Frederick William] Boatwright, of the college.

The speaker has a pleasant voice, and an attractive delivery. He is forceful and pointed in style, and in his peculiar way of putting things. He was given the closest hearing throughout and evidently made a most favorable impression upon his hearers.

Dr. Wilson took as his subject: "What is Constitutional Government?"[2] He discussed this in a clear and instructive way, frequently illustrating his discourse in a striking and attractive manner.

Dr. Wilson said in part:

The subject seemed to be of new importance because we have since the war given too little thought to constitutional questions.

There is perhaps a little relaxation in an attitude towards constitutional restraints. But whether this be so or not, it is worth our while once and again to examine the essential nature of the sort of government we live under.

Every American who examines his own idea of the nature of a constitutional government will, I think, find that at the back of the notion somewhere [lies] a written constitution. He thinks of a constitutional government as one that has a definite character [charter] of powers, a charter which can be examined by any man and which must be interpreted by the courts. And yet inasmuch as England which gave us our notion and our practice of constitutional government has never had a written constitution, the existence of such a document cannot be an essential feature of the arrangement.

When we ask ourselves therefore, when it was histo[r]ically speaking that the idea of a constitutional government arose we will see that it cannot have been when governments began to have constitutions, for all governments have constitutions written or unwritten, that is all governments have regularly ordered ways of exercising authority[,] a carefully arranged inter-relationship of parts and a distribution of functions[;] and some of the most despotic have had from a business point of view the best constitutions.

It is evident that our idea therefore of a "constitutional" government has something to do with the liberty of those who have to submit to government, and that there is underneath it the idea of a difference between the community or the State and the government, and that the picture we form in our minds when we think of a constitutional government has in it some such scene as that at Runnymede when the Barons of England speaking in the name of the nation stood face to face with King John and made a covenant with him telling him very plainly what sort of liberty they should insist upon enjoying if they were to remain his subjects, and he their king. We think, in other words, of a power outside the government capable of independent organization, capable of restraining the government, knowing what sort of liberty free men are to enjoy, and steadfastly maintaining itself against the government. And by a constitutional government we mean one in which a definite understanding has been arrived at between those who govern and those who are governed as to how far the power of the government will be submitted to and at what point, if need be, it will be resisted.

An effort was made by the French Revolutionists, after breaking down the old monarchy, to establish a government upon the model set them in England. But the leaders of that Revolution did not understand the nature of the arrangement they were trying to bring about. They supposed that all they had to do was to make a government with a better structure, whereas what was really necessary was first to bring France to a real understanding of the nature of individual liberty and then devise means to erect a government of such a sort that it would be possible always to keep it mindful and regardful of the liberty of the individual.

The advantage of a written constitution is not that it makes the understanding which exists between the community and the government more stable than an unwritten constitution, but simply that it makes it more definite. It was necessary that we should have written constitutions at the period of our own revolution because we were making in many respects novel arrangements, and it was imperative that they should be made as clear and definite as possible. England has never been under the same necessity. Her political arrangements have grown slowly and insensibly and it has never been necessary for her to construct upon a large scale. Her arrangements, therefore, have been none the less definite because unwritten, inasmuch as they have been at every stage part of her though[t] and habit, and it is by habit that constitutions are made secure and by the allegiance of thought that they are made operative.

Such an analysis of our thought in these matters will show us why it is that we think of a constitutional government as necessarily including a representative assembly chosen by some sort of popular suffrage. It is by means of such an assembly that the wise adjustment of understanding and purpose which must subsist between the government and the community is kept up. We are sometimes wrong in supposing that a representative assembly is merely the law-making part of a government. Its other function is really more important—that is, its function of constantly subjecting the policy of the government to examination and discretion, and by its debates making it clear what sort of government including what sort of law-making a community desires. It is really this idea which has led us to include in our notion of a constitutional government not only a representative assembly, but also the principle that the executive branch of the government shall be in all things subject to the laws to which that assembly assents, which is simply another way of saying that they shall not have free choice as to the means which they shall use in governing, but shall always act in accordance with the common understandings embodied in precedent and statute. It is for this reason, too, that we have added to the stability of our laws by entrusting their interpretation to courts which are made as free as possible from the controlling influence of any other part of the government. It is for this reason that we have above all things else been careful to have in every one of our written constitutions a bill of rights—that is a careful statement of the items of individual liberty.

It was by the formulation of such a statement that the history of constitutional government began in Magna Carta from which our bills of rights get much of their phraseology. At every serious crisis in the history of English liberty some such statement has been drawn up—as, for example, in the petition of right and in the bill of rights which followed the revolution of 1688. Such statements really constitute the essence of the sort of government under which we live, for the object of that government is not so much to make perfect administrative arrangements or to devise the best means of making laws, but to secure such an arrangement as will draw the line between the sphere in which men may be free and the sphere in which they must submit to be governed and restrained.

A constitutional government then is one which is made to respect a great sentiment and a great habit on the part of free men, and it is necessary to its establishment that men should first have the thought and the purpose and the right conception of freedom. Constitutional governments do not make men free. It is only free men who can make constitutional governments. They are the consequences and the instruments, not the creators of freedom.

Dr. Wilson was warmly thanked for his discourse by a number of the most prominent people who heard it. He will deliver the second of the series to-night. His subject will be: "Political Liberty: Its Nature and Exercise."

Printed in the Richmond *Times*, Oct. 28, 1898; some editorial headings omitted.
  [1] An endowment of $10,000 donated by the family of James Thomas, Jr., to establish an annual lecture series at Richmond College. The Thomas Museum and Art Hall was also a memorial to James Thomas, Jr.
  [2] For this and his following lectures at Richmond College, Wilson used the notes printed at Nov. 15, 1893, Vol. 8.

To Ellen Axson Wilson

My own darling,   Richmond, Va., Friday 28 Oct. '98

I am kept on the go by these kind people here, and it is very hard to find time for a quiet word with you such as I need for my heart's comfort.

Not that I have "gone out" much: the formal entertaining does not begin till to-morrow; but I am taken out to see all the places and buildings worth seeing, and do not find myself often alone. This morning the things that interested me most were John Marshall's grave (very much neglected) and St. John's church, where Patrick Henry spoke, a *wooden* structure one hundred and fifty years old!

To-morrow I *breakfast* (at half past ten) with a Dr. Thomas near by;[1] in the evening I go to a small dinner at Patterson's club— just one or two intimate friends; on Sunday evening I take tea at the Lyons's, who—mother and daughter[2]—were at my lecture last night.

I did not think I did particularly well at my first effort, last night, but the audience, so far as I can tell, was quite delighted with what they heard, and so I have nothing to complain of. After the lecture this evening I am to hold an informal reception; but I shall probably not have to shake hands with many more people than spoke to me last night. The hall was crowded,—about 900 persons, I suppose.

Tell dear Father, with my love, that everybody I meet asks most cordially about him and regrets that he is not to be here again this winter.

I love you with every part and all of my whole nature, and am altogether   Your own   Woodrow

Love to all.

ALS (WC, NjP).
[1] The Rev. Dr. William D. Thomas, Professor of Philosophy at Richmond College and a son of James Thomas, Jr. William D. Thomas lived across the street from the Pattersons at 113 East Grace St.
[2] Lulie Lyons and her mother, who were not listed in the Richmond city directories of this period. Wilson had met Lulie Lyons in Hot Springs, Va., in August 1897. See Wilson's diary entry for Aug. 6, 1897, n. 1; EAW to WW, Feb. 9, 1898, n. 1; and WW to EAW, Feb. 12, 1898, all in Vol. 10.

From Ellen Axson Wilson

My own darling,   Princeton Oct 28/98

Your sweet note came duly to hand and made me very happy. I am delighted that everything is so pleasant and that you are

having, and are evidently *going* to have, such a "good time.["]
And if you are still disposed to disturb yourself about that little
matter I am truly glad that you are in the meantime away from
home and amid so many distractions that you can't think about
it much.

All goes very well here. Jessie's throat is "clear" at last, so
that now she has only to recover strength. The threat of trouble
with her ear has entirely passed. She is very weak still; can only
sit up a little while at a time. The rest of us are perfectly well.
Father is very bright and 'chatty.' He expects to preach on Sunday.[1] Mr Brenton Greene[2] came this afternoon to see about it,
and made a long call on Father, who was exceedingly pleased
with him. If at the last minute Father should not feel like preaching Mr. Greene will take his place.

Fraülein's sister[3] has actually landed and Fraülein has gone
to N. Y. That is the only news except alas! that Miss Getty[4] is
said to be slowly sinking. Be sure, darling, to write fully about the
lectures, how they are received &c. Father is anxious to know as
well as I.

Believe me, dear, that I love you beyond words—love you 'till
it *hurts*!   Your little wife   Eileen.

ALS (WC, NjP).
    [1] In Miller Chapel of Princeton Theological Seminary. The Seminary held
regular Sunday morning services in Miller Chapel at this time, at which Seminary professors usually preached.
    [2] William Brenton Greene, Jr., Stuart Professor of the Relation of Philosophy
and Science to the Christian Religion at Princeton Theological Seminary.
    [3] Marie Böhm, sister of Clara Böhm, former German governess of the Wilson
children. Clara Böhm was living with the Wilsons and teaching in a local girls'
school.
    [4] Margaret Getty, who lived with her sister, Eliza Getty (Mrs. Palmer Cham-
berlaine) Ricketts of 80 Stockton St. Miss Getty died on November 2, 1898.

A News Report of a Lecture on Constitutional Government

[Oct. 29, 1898]

ABLE DISCOURSE BY DR. WILSON.

Another large audience assembled in the chapel of Richmond
College last night to hear the second of the series of lectures
under the Thomas Museum Lecture Endownment. As on the
previous night there were many prominent people in the audience
including a number of well known lawyers and other professional
men.

Dr. Woodrow Wilson, the lecturer, took as his subject, "Political Liberty; Its Nature and Exercise."

His discourse was instructive and highly interesting, and was delivered, as was the one before it, in a clear, attractive style.

Dr. Wilson caught the attention of his hearers from the beginning, and he was listened to closely throughout.

Dr. Wilson said in part:

The difficulty in analyzing liberty is a difficulty of sentiment. It is a word of enthusiasm associated with adventure[,] with fortitude and with heroic endeavor. It is a word also of license and folly, stained with bloodshed and crime. It is difficult to dissociate it from the history that clings about struggles for liberty, and requires a distinct effort to regard it from a purely philosophical and dispassionate point of view. It is not even clear that liberty is best developed in those countries in which it has been speculatively analyzed. The countries which have enjoyed liberty have not usually been those which have speculated about it. It has been embodied where successfully established in institutions and laws rather than in theories.

The races, indeed, which have been strongest in the history of liberty have been those which have had an instinctive distrust of speculation and have showed a genius for affairs rather than for political philosophy. The French, for example, who regard liberty as a body of "natural rights[,]" have never managed to establish practical liberty, whereas the English who have never troubled themselves to inquire whether their rights were natural or artificial have for generations put liberty into practice.

Liberty, it would appear then, is a product of life and experience and not of mere rational speculation. It needs hard-headed sense to know what liberty is, and hard-headed sense is to be gotten out of experience and not out of books. An analysis of constitutional government such as we undertook in the last lecture sets us a great way forward in the comprehension of the nature of liberty. We saw that constitutional government had as its basis an understanding between the government and the community as to the limits beyond which the government should not venture to restrain the action of the individual, and manifestly such an understanding must itself be based upon a clear, experimental knowledge of the proper field of independent individual action. And this is the field of liberty. The nation that does not understand liberty cannot have constitutional government.

Liberty, it also becomes evident, is a product of society. It is the free action of the individual within the necessary social restraints. And it is the opposite, not of society—that is not of the reasonable association of individuals for mutual co-operation and helpfulness, but of rigid and arbitrary authority of an unchecked and wilful power on the part of the government unadjusted to and unmindful of the interest of individuals.

Despotism is a force checked only by friction which must sooner or later generate dangerous heat, whereas free government is a force balanced and held in equipois[e] by union and adjustment where the forces of action and restraint are like those of a perfectly adjusted machine where there is power without friction. The piston of a graeat [great] engine runs free not, of cause [course], becuase [because] it is not restrained, but because it is perfectly adjusted to the parts which restrains it. And so a free government is one in which there is a perfect adjustment between authority and liberty, between the power of the magistrate and the privilege of the citizen.

Liberty is so far from being a principle opposite to social organization as Rousseau and others have supposed it to be that it would be inconceivable without social organization. Man cannot do without society, and is free and strong in the exercise of his powers only by co-operation. Robinson Crusoe, obliged as he was to do everything for himself, was less free before he found his man Friday than after; less free to get the comforts of life; less free to understand his island and plan his future, tied to the drudgery which was slavery.

What we call the state—that, is the political community—is neither a mere necessity nor a mere convenience, but an abiding natural relationship without which man has never been strong or happy. It is the invariable and normal embodiment and expression of a higher form of life than the individual—namely, of that common life which makes a stage and an opportunity for the individual life, makes it full and complete, makes it spiritual. Leisure, that is some degree of freedom from drudgery, is necessary to the development of the spiritual part of man, the only part which makes him different from the beasts, and he could have no such chance of development if it were not for his social union with other men.

Liberty, then, is not the opposite of society, but simply of unreasonable restraint and experience. It must show what restraint is unreasonable. It is such an adjustment or systematic balance between private right and public power, between assistance and interference, as will give the individual spirit free play. And how far that can safely be accomplished is a question which can be determined, not by theoretical speculation, but by experiments tried by hard-headed men. Here is our explanation of why liberty has arisen out of experience, and not out of theory.

We ourselves get liberty from the English, and we can find in our own bills of rights which we copied out of the documents of English history a very clear and adequate notion of what practical Englishmen have found out about the native [nature] and use of liberty. It will be seen upon an examination of those documents that they all run in negatives, and not in affirmative statements. It is nowhere said in our law, for example, that there shall be freedom of speech and of the press, and we have laws of libel and of slander to show that we do not intend that there should be absolute freedom of speech and of the press. Our law says simply that freedom of speech and of the press shall not be restrained, except by uniform laws which place such restrictions as have been found reasonable and practical. Neither does our law say that no man's property shall be taken from him. It says only that it shall not be taken from him except by the judgment of his peers and the law of the land. And the law of the land may put any limitations we choose on the rights of property. All that we are after is to find those restraints which are for the convenience and best order of society. In other words, we are seeking the most reasonable adjustment between the rights of the individual and the powers of the community and the most reasonable adjustiment is the highest degree of liberty.

We do not pretend that men ought not to be restrained, but we are constantly seeking to find out the reasonable ways and degrees of restraint, and these every race must discover for itself, for every race has its own characteristic life and achievements.

Turn back now to the study of constitutions and it will be found that the very first step in the establishment of constitutional government was a definition of rights, and the object of constitutional government is to make a place for liberty. Only those peoples who have had constitutional government have had liberty. The two things are inseparable, and the constant effort of the constitutional statesman must be to perfect and adopt to changing circumstances that delicate adjustment between individual privilege and public power which constitutes liberty and is constitutional government.

Dr. Wilson will deliver the third of the series of lectures in the chapel of the college next Monday night at 8:15 o'clock. His subject will be "Written Constitutions."

Printed in the Richmond *Times*, Oct. 29, 1898; some editorial headings omitted.

From Ellen Axson Wilson

My own darling, Princeton, Oct. 29/98

Your satisfactory letter came safely to hand and gave great pleasure to Father as well as to me. We are delighted that you had such a splendid audience. Father wants to know in what hall you lectured.

I send with this three letters[.][1] That is an entertaining one from the Amherst man; is it not? But you will have to tell poor Mr. Heath to spare himself his time and pains? Will you not?[2]

I have just answered one of your letters myself. It is from the secretary of a home for self-supporting women in New York asking various questions about Miss Marie Bohm, who it seems has given you as her reference! My answer was discreet but plainly disclaimed *all* responsibility. A telegram came from her to *you* yesterday announcing her safe arrival![3] Such tender thought for your natural anxiety is truly touching.

Jessie is doing finely; made a great advance in strength today. I allowed the other children to be with her today and she and Nellie had a very happy time together. Nellie wouldn't leave her for a moment the whole day. The rest of us are quite well. I have been hard at work planting my daffodil bulbs, and am so tired from the unaccustomed labour that I can hardly keep my eyes open, so I will bid my darling goodnight.

With love unbounded, Your little wife, Eileen.

ALS (WC, NjP).

[1] They are missing.

[2] One of the missing letters was from the Boston publisher, Daniel Collamore Heath, probably enclosing copies of letters which he had recently written concerning the presidency of Amherst College. Following the resignation of Merrill Edward Gates from that post on June 9, 1898 (about which, see WW to E. R. Craven, July 1, 1897, n. 2, Vol. 10), the college was administered by a committee of three faculty members while the trustees looked for a new president. On September 22, 1898, Heath, an Amherst alumnus, wrote to Herbert Baxter Adams, a member of the Amherst Board of Trustees, suggesting Wilson as a desirable candidate for the position. Adams's reply of October 8 is missing, but it is clear from a second Heath letter of October 11 that Adams had indicated that the trustees were seeking a president who was both an Amherst alumnus and a clergyman. In his letter to Adams of October 11, Heath argued vigorously that it was unnecessary for the president to be an Amherst graduate and probably undesirable that he be a clergyman. There is no evidence known to the Editors that the Amherst trustees ever approached Wilson about the presidency. On June 27, 1899, the trustees unanimously elected the Rev. Dr. George Harris, Amherst '66 and Abbot Professor of Theology at Andover Theological Seminary, as the new President of Amherst. Heath's letters to Adams are printed in W. Stull Holt (ed.), *Historical Scholarship in the United States, 1876-1901: As Revealed in the Correspondence of Herbert B. Adams*, Johns Hopkins University Studies in Historical and Political Science, Series LVI (Baltimore, 1938), pp. 254-56. See also Claude Moore Fuess, *Amherst: The Story of a New England College* (Boston, 1935), pp. 257-58, 265.

[3] It is missing.

To Ellen Axson Wilson

My own darling,   Richmond, 30 Oct., 1898

It amuses me to think that I brought with me materials for work on my history![1] I have scarcely a moment alone, and have to plan carefully to get a chance to write even a few lines to my love. Yesterday I was *ten hours* in company! About three hours at the breakfast—eighteen people at the table, including almost all the most distinguished men in town, from the Governor[2] down, —and almost a course for each guest,—one of the most elaborate and elegant affairs I ever attended. As soon as breakfast was over (that is, at about one o'clock) we went to Mr. Valentine's studio,[3] and were with him until quite four o'clock. In the evening Patterson gave me a dinner (5 guests) at his Club, and there we spent three hours more. The whole day, practically, was spent in company, except the three hours from four to seven.

I keep well and chipper. On my lecture days I rigourously guard my afternoons, for rest and the study of my lectures,—and even yesterday I lay down for more than an hour and had a good snooze.

Oh, my sweet one, my heart fairly aches with loving you, and I am altogether   Your own   Woodrow

Love to all

ALS (WC, NjP).
  [1] That is, his high school textbook.
  [2] James Hoge Tyler.
  [3] Edward Virginius Valentine, Richmond sculptor, well known for his statues of Confederate military heroes.

From Ellen Axson Wilson

My own darling,   Princeton Oct 26 [30]/98

I know you will be glad to hear of Father's brilliant success this morning! His sermon was superb, really a model in *every* respect. And his manner was as good as his matter. His voice, somewhat husky in the first few sentences, seemed to become clearer and stronger with every word; and *so* expressive; it was beautiful to see the way in which he made every point tell. How I wish you could have been there! He had the most profound attention from everyone. After the service he was of course detained by different ones at the pulpit while I waited for him in the vestibule while the whole congregation passed by me, and I wish you could have heard the enthusiastic things they said to me, with the most evident note of sincerity in it all. Mr. [Joseph Heatly]

Dulles said it had been years since he had heard a sermon that he enjoyed so much. Mr. [John Howell] Westcott was there, quite running over with enthusiasm. Half a dozen of them said they were reminded constantly of *you*, and that it was so very interesting to see whence you had derived your eloquence, your style, &c. &c. I wonder if you remember the sermon; the text was, "And they all forsook him and fled." He was not at all the worse physically for it.

Since what I wrote last night will not start until tomorrow, I will leave this open and add a little tomorrow. I shall be very busy tomorrow getting some things made for the mission box; and I can't write tomorrow night because I must start quite early to the Prep. school, the Fines[1] having asked me to help them receive. The day after if nothing interferes I hope to go to Phila. The doctor made his final visit today, said Jessie could get out of doors in a day or two if the weather was good. She seems quite well except for a little weakness.

Fraülein [Clara Böhm] has just returned. She and her sister seem to have had quite a happy time together, meeting thus in a strange land. The sister leaves tonight for Hamilton, *Ontario*— a good safe distance I trust.

I have just had a pleasant call from Mrs. Scott; her admiration and affection for our children seems very strong and unfeigned.[2] She says she "thinks Nellie is *simply wonderful*" both for intelligence and sweetness;—so you will easily see that it *must* have been a "pleasant" call!

We are all well, and we all love you devotedly. *I* love you more than all the rest together,—tenderly, passionately absorbingly,— and am altogether   Your own   Eileen

Monday. Your note telling about the remarkable "breakfast" &c. has been received and enjoyed. I didn't know they were becoming so sophisticated in the South.

We are all well. Father goes to New York tomorrow to be gone over night. He has promised me to take a cab at 23 St. and keep it until he has finished his errands. He will be part of the time with his cousin Ralston,[3] and part of course with Sister Annie;[4] so I think he will be quite safe.

With a heart brimming over with love,

                    Your devoted little wife   Eileen.

ALS (WC, NjP).
    1 The John Burchard Fines. He was headmaster of the Princeton Preparatory School.
    2 Marian (Mrs. William Earl Dodge) Scott, proprietress and principal of a new girls' school in the building of the defunct Evelyn College (about which see

WW to EAW, April 8, 1892, n. 2, Vol. 7, and EAW to WW, Jan. 31, 1897, n. 3, Vol. 10). The Wilsons had sent their girls to Mrs. Scott's school when it opened in September 1898. Heretofore Mrs. Wilson had taught them at home. Mrs. Scott's husband was the ornithological curator in the Museum of Biology of Princeton University, 1897-1906.

[3] The Rev. Dr. Thomas Ralston Smith.

[4] Annie Wilson Howe.

To Ellen Axson Wilson, with Enclosure

My own darling,   Richmond, Va., 31 Oct., 1898

I am *so* relieved to hear that the threat of trouble in dear little Jessie's ear has passed away, and that the wretched trouble is really leaving her.

I am glad to report that the lectures are being well received,—*very* well,—as well as I could desire. The audience at the second lecture was considerably larger than at the first,—that is, a good many more were standing. They seemed really to enjoy my way of speaking and also greatly to appreciate the subject-matter. I knew that the second subject (Liberty) was not half so well handled as I had often handled it before; but they did not, and seemed altogether satisfied. I enclose a note, just received and answered, which will serve as a specimen of the kind of attentions and compliments I am receiving. I decline invitations for the afternoon, because I must rest then and fill up with my lecture.

Patterson and I took tea last evening with the Lyonss, and they gave us a dish of oysters so fearfully and wonderfully made, with wine and what not, that it quite sickened me, and I feel a little the worse for it; but I have gotten fairly over the effects of it now.

I am about to go to the Scott's ("Lady" Scott's)[1] for luncheon now. Good-bye, my sweet one, my matchless darling. I love you with all my heart and mind. Love to dear Father & the chicks.

Your own   Woodrow

ALS (WC, NjP).

[1] Lucy Blair Scott, wife of Judge R. Carter Scott, who lived at 406 East Franklin Street in Richmond.

ENCLOSURE

From Benjamin Franklin Johnson[1]

Dear Sir: Richmond, Va., October 31, 1898.

Should your engagements permit and you find that it will suit your convenience, I would be very glad to have you take a little drive with me Tuesday afternoon. Can call for you at 3:30, 4, or any hour that may suit you. I would like to show you some of the points of interest around the city.

Have had the pleasure of listening to both of your lectures, and have not only enjoyed them heartily but feel that I am greatly profited. I feel that I am learning how to be a better citizen.

Sincerely yours,   B. F. Johnson

TLS (WP, DLC).
[1] President of the B. F. Johnson Publishing Co. of Richmond.

To Ellen Axson Wilson

My own darling,   Richmond, Va.,   1 Nov., 1898

The third lecture is over, and after one more letter I will come myself to my darling. How glad I shall be! I am treated better here than I was ever treated anywhere else in my life, but in the midst of it all I am desperately homesick for you, my only delight.

I am feeling perfectly well again to-day, and am just about to go out driving with a most interesting man, Col. Archer Anderson.[1] I must rush this off before starting.

The hall I lecture in is at Richmond College.

My audiences keep up famously and seem really enthusiastic. With a heartful of love for all.   Your own   Woodrow

ALS (WC, NjP).
[1] Son of Joseph Reid Anderson, who succeeded his father as president of the Tregedar Iron Works. Prominent in the industrial and social life of Richmond, he lived at 103 West Franklin Street and was widely known for his scholarly interests in history and literature.

A News Report of a Lecture on Constitutional Government

[Nov. 1, 1898]

DOCTOR WILSON ON SECESSION
The Great Publicist Says Both Sections Were Right at the Time.

Another large and representative audience gathered in the chapel of Richmond College last night to hear the third of the series of lectures under the Thomas Museum Lecture Endowment by Dr. Woodrow Wilson. The speaker was given the closest attention throughout. He seems to grow more and more interesting in each lecture. He is clear and altogether instructive as a lecturer, and his delivery is attractive and impressive.

Dr. Wilson's subject last night was "Written Constitutions," and he handled his theme in a way which could not but be instructive and helpful to all who heard it.

Dr. Wilson spoke, in substance as follows:

We have in the United States a very specialized notion of a Constitution, which always has in it the notion of a document, a written fundamental law. We have considered ourselves the inventors of written constitutions, and have supposed that because written, they constituted a government of a new and unheard-of form. Foreign observers have been inclined to regard us as inventors of a new kind of government, whereas we have in reality been inventors only of a new way of formulating the Constitution of government.

There is a celebrated passage in one of Mr. Gladstone's essays, in which he speaks of the Constitution of the United States as having been "struck off at a given time by the brain and purpose" of the men of the convention of 1787. Mr. Gladstone probably did not suppose as his words would imply, that this was really an act of outright origination, but even he does not seem to have studied our institutions closely enough to see how really simple the part was which was played by origination.

Neither are those right who describe our government as mere corporations and speak of our constitutions as if they were the mere charters of business bodies. They are wrong in supposing that government is a business, though, of course, in its ministrative details it must be executed with business capacity, and they are wrong in comparing a government with a corporation. The conception of the government is much greater. It is nothing less than a frame for the whole life of society, and its functions shift and enlarge with the changes and growth which society undergoes. It is best to have no theory about the character of our constitutions, except that theory which is merely a general expression of facts of history.

As a matter of fact, the original thirteen States which formed the Union, had charters before they had constitutions, and when the Revolution came they merely transformed their charters into constitutions. In doing so they did not even make radical alteration of form, but the whole character of the new document was unlike the character of the old document, for the old document was derived from the will of another government. The Colonial charters were granted by the King in England, and were grants of as much of governmental power as he was willing to part with in the Colonies, or felt obliged under the circumstances to yield to the Colonies.

The State constitutions were a gift of power, not from a government, but from a community, and were more in their nature like constitutions of liberty, as we have before defined them, than like constitutions of government. Their object was not so much to make an efficient governing organization as to make such arrangements as would enable the people to guide and restrain, and control the organization of the government in the interests of their own liberty. The purpose was to set up such governments as would be most favorable to liberty, and the notion under which the whole process took place, was the notion which we put in the phrase, "popular sovereignty" or a sovereignty of the people. Under this arrangement, for example, the legislatures which were created were unlike the English Parliament, for they would be legislatures without absolute law-making power, checked and constrained in such a way as not to be real masters of the community.

The supreme law was to be the written constitution, which the legislature could not change. Lawyers were to recognize a sharp distinction between ordinary laws and fundamental laws and were to test legislation by the question whether it was in conformity with the written grant of powers, under which the legislatures were to act. Courts would be authorized to adopt an answer to this question, and with them was to rest the ultimate decision as to the powers of legislative action. All of this was but a way of making constitutional government an extension and safeguard of the constitution of liberty. It was this notion that was new and original, and which we ourselves at first only dimly conceived, though we were in fact acting upon it.

In constructing our governments during this process we used almost without exception old forms and principals [principles] which had been tested either by English or by colonial experience, generally by both; and so far as the actual institutions which we set up were concerned, the process of constitution making was a process altogether a selection and not at all an invention.

The same is true of the making of the Constitution of the United States as is true of the making of the Constitutions of the States. It also was conceived as if a part of the general constitution of liberty. It, too, was made to consist of tested bits of English and colonial practices, and had, though a rapid growth, as much a growth as the State Constitutions which had their origin in colonial charters.

It is worth noting that, though national action had begun with the Congress of 1774, it continued until 1781 without a formal Constitution of any sort, and the articles of confederation, afterward adopted in 1781, were hardly more than a formal expression of the practices and power of the Continental Congress. It is noteworthy, too, that during the eight years during which the country lived under the articles of confederation, it became evident not only that these articles were not sufficient or suitable for the national growth, but that it would be impossible to change them in the way in which they themselves had provided that changes should be made. They provided that their terms should be changed only when [the changes were first agreed upon] by the Congress of the Confederation and afterwards confirmed by the legislatures of every State. It would have been impossible to carry the legislatures of every State, and the proposition of the constitutional convention of 1787 that the new constitution which they had formed should go into effect if adopted by nine States was really, from a legal point of view, a revolutionary proposition. It was accordingly adopted, and its adoption marks a sharp break between the articles of confederation and the Constitution of the United States. That Constitution is not a mere body of amendments to the articles in whole, but cannot even be said to have any legal connection whatever with these articles. It is an entirely independent creation, and its adoption marks a peaceful but radical revolution. It shows the stage of growth and the capacity of the men of that day to recognize the growth of an adopted law without a too formal regard for the right of the existing law.

Our written constitutions have served not to originate notions or even forms of government, but to express and to record our political experience, and their stability exists not in the fact that they are written, but in the fact that they bear faithful record of the better part of what we have discovered by arduous experience.

Written constitutions are not mere legal documents; they are the skeleton frame of a living organism, and are subject to all the changes that living organisms undergo. This is proved in the case of our own Federal Constitution by the varying opinions as to the right of a State to withdraw from the Union. During the early days of our national experience this right, if not openly avowed, was tacitly assented to in every section of the country—

in the North as well as in the South. But in the North the course of events had nationalized the government that had once been deemed confederate. Before 1860 vast areas of new territory had been acquired by purchase and conquest, out of which twenty new States had been organized and added to the original thirteen, and almost all of these were actual creations of the Federal Government, first as Territories, then as States. Five of these new States had been carved out of that great Northwest Territory which Virginia with a princely liberality had given to the national government that the Union might be formed. Into this great domain and farther still into the ever expanding West the North had projected itself with its growing ideas of nationalization; and there had played upon the whole northern and northwestern regions those great forces of material development which made steadily for the unification of interests and purposes. During all these years the South had retained her social and industrial institutions unchanged, while the North and the Northwest had undergone a great social and industrial revolution. The South had stood still while the rest of the country had undergone profound changes, and standing still the South had retained the old principles and the old interpretation of the constitution that had once been universal.

The South in seceding from the Union was right from her point of view; the North in resisting secession was also right from her point of view. This national catastrophe resulted from the two different interpretations of the constitution. One of these methods may be called the lawyer's method, which looks at the constitution as a legal document without regard to subsequent events and accretions. The other is the statesman's or historian's method, which interprets constitutions not only in accordance with the intention of the framers but also in the light of subsequent events and the varying needs arising from new conditions of national life. One interprets constitutions ac[c]ording to the logic of words[,] the other according to the logic of events and the irresistable streams of national tendency. The historian's methods has mainly to do with interpreting written constitutions as a vehicle of life; and this method is now becoming accepted in the South as well as in the North. The conflict of ideas that resulted in the Civil War had to be fought out in the Court of Mars; and after the conflict was ended and the bitterness of sectional strife had subsided, the country emerged with a stronger national life permeating all sections and all parties.

Dr. Wilson was heard with profound attention and his philosophical utterances enthusiastically applauded. It is the general impression that Dr. Wilson's lecture last night was one of the most powerful and scholarly ever heard in this city.

Dr. Wilson will deliver the fourth of the series to-night in the college chapel. His subject will be "Theory and Practice of Organization."

Printed in the Richmond *Times*, Nov. 1, 1898; some editorial headings omitted.

From Ellen Axson Wilson

My own darling,   Princeton, Nov. 1, 1898

I am safely back from Phila., after a very successful day, tired of course but not worn out. It was a perfect day, mild and bright. Jessie was out, for the first time, in the middle of the day. She could go to school tomorrow were it not that that wretched hack has stopped running again, and the children have to walk both ways.

The painters began work yesterday and seem to be making good progress. Mr. Briner says the job will cost about $30.00. I am *so* delighted, darling, that the lectures are so well received and appreciated. It is a perfect ovation, is it not? Am very, very sorry for the little upset due to the oysters. I am awaiting your return anxiously as well as eagerly for I am a little afraid of all this feasting and excitement. Ah, how good it is to know that in three days from this very hour I will have my darling again! I think I will go to bed at once so as to hasten the time when I can say "it is the day after tomorrow." I cannot tell you, my love, with what infinite tenderness and passion my heart yearns toward you; oh I *do* love you, with all my soul I love you!

                                        Always all yours,   Eileen.

ALS (WC, NjP).

A News Report of a Lecture on Constitutional Government

                                                  [Nov. 2, 1898]

THE THEORY OF ORGANIZATION.

The fourth lecture of the series under the Thomas Museum Lecture Endowment in the chapel of Richmond College last night was marked by the largest attendance of the series and the audience were again charmed into appreciative listening by the forceful reasonings and the attractive delivery of Dr. Woodrow Wilson, who spoke upon "Theory and Practice in Organization."

The fifth and concluding lecture of the series will be given to-morrow night, when Dr. Wilson will discuss the "Organization and Powers of Congress."

Dr. Wilson spoke substantially as follows:

The theory I refer to is the theory of checks and balances, the theory under which we are very careful to separate the Legislative from the Judicial and both of these from the Executive Department of the government.

It is an interesting fact that we get this theory, not from English law books or English statesmen, but from a Frenchman's study of the English constitution as it appeared to him from across the English Channel. All of the generations which framed the Constitution of the United States, were fond of quoting Montesquieu, whose book on "The Spirit of the Laws" profoundly effected [affected] political speculation both on the Continent and in England. By borrowing this theory from a foreigner, which except a description of English institutions corresponded well enough with their appearance, but did not correspond with their reality, and yet our allegiance to this theory has been so constant, so consistent, that it might be said to have become almost a superstition amongst us. It exercises so great an influence over our imaginations that we are oftentimes incapable of perceiving what we very freely neglected in practice.

Our fancy for the theory has arisen purely out of our rulings upon the definitions which we have put into our fundamental law with regard to the functions and the organization of our government, and the operation of our constitutional law has been so successful that we have permitted ourselves to suppose that States existed because of law, whereas the fact has been that law existed because of States, and has had no vitality except in so far as it has expressed the appearance of life resident in them.

The result of our devotion to the exclusive study of constitutional law and the restraints which may be put by it upon the action of the government, has led us too much to neglect the study of the actual life of law which is to be seen not in statutes, but in administration under the action of the executive parts of the government, not only those executive parts which we describe as executive, but also under the application of the law to particular cases by the courts. No one who watches the interpretation and application of the law by the courts and administrative officers, can fail to observe how entirely the law takes its life and its adaptations to the necessities of society, from those who handle it day by day rather than from those who first formulated it in acts of legislation. The great body of our law which is customary and almost as old as English experience, is evidence of the fact that law has its springs in the fates of the world, rather than in the purpose of legislators[;] and the function of legislators is not one of origination so much as one of adaptation and formulation. By not studying administration as it has been studied in the other governments of the world we have missed some very useful lessons. We have supposed, for example, that the functions of our city councils were chiefly legislative functions, and we have organized these councils on the model of the State Legislatures, whereas everywhere else in the world, these bodies are recognized as business councils who formulate the rules of administration.

Everywhere else in the world all members of the town councils are thus given an active part in the carrying out of the general arrangement which they originate and put into the form of rules so that those who make the rules are constantly in a position to tell how well the rules operate and are constantly learning by contact with practical business. The new rules that ought to be made and the modifications of the old rules that ought to be adapted, we have so constantly thought the[m] restraining government, that we have not even enough thought of making it efficient. Administration is the experiencing part of government. The only part that stands in the midst of experience and fails in daily action is the expediency or inexpediency of existing law, and our deference to the theory of checks and balances has done us this disservice. It has led us so to separate those who make the laws and those who administer them that those who are entrusted with carrying the laws out are not free enough to suggest what the laws ought to be, and those who are appointed to determine what the laws shall be are not in position to determine their usefulness by the daily application of them. We have not as a matter of fact taken all the administrative functions away from our legislatures. The voting of moneys and their application to particular objects of expenditure, is an administrative and not a law making function. So are the yeld[1] subjects, the tax collections of the inferior organization, the discipline and development of the army and navy, the passage of bills of relief and the establishment of bureaus of the government, and only administrative experience can be a safe guidance in such matters.

We give our legislatures also such judicial functions as the determination of disputed election cases, the allowance of claims of individuals on the government for moneys or damages, the impeachment of delinquent officers, and in the case of Congress, the counting of the electoral votes. We give to our executives also the determination of claims of some classes, the conduct of prosecutions in which there is a wide range of discretion, and the granting of pardons. Our courts develop laws by decisions and precedent in a way which almost amounts to the making of law and in equity has a long history rule amended to the original, not only of processes but of principals [principles]. We entrust to our courts such purely administrative matters as carrying out of the provisions of wills, the record and registration of private documents, the incorporation of business bodies, the appointment of receivers, etc. In fact, we have had too much common sense to act always upon the theory that legislatures must have no administrative or judicial functions, that the executive must have no legislative nor judicial powers and that the courts shall have no right to administer the principles they adjudicate. But we have not gone the practical length the English have gone in recognizing the fact that any artificial cutting up of the government into parts is hurtful to it, and that whereas there should be a special person or body of persons for each of the three great functions, of making the laws, determining their meaning in individual cases, and carrying them out in action. These persons or bodies should be in close and sympathetic association and should be so joined as to form a single motive power like the organs of the same body and not like independent organizations.

It is at any rate profoundly true in experience with regard to the legislator and the executive, and the English so far from keeping their constitution true to the description given of it by Montesquieu, have not hesitated to entrust the executive action of the government to a body of ministers who are in reality representatives, not of the Crown, but of the House of Commons, and by doing so they have obtained a double benefit. Their laws have been formulated and proposed by those who were responsible for their execution and were in constant contact with actual affairs, and yet they have made the action of these officers dependent always upon the assent of the representatives of the people. They have yielded popular control but they have obtained experience[d] guidance and they have also obtained a better balance between the executive and the legislature by closely uniting them than they could possibly have done by divorcing them and treating them as if antagonistic in function.

Dr. Wilson indirectly referred to the now burning question of territorial expansion and in his very careful remarks upon the subject stated in effect that among the nations of the earth our greatest rivals are Germany and Russia. He intimated therefore, that if one of the three should acquire the mooted territory,[2] the United States should be that one, inasmuch as hers was the light of day, while theirs was the light of darkness.

While Dr. Wilson did not align himself with the expansionists of the extreme type, his remarks indicated a preference for a more liberal policy in this respect, in that he did not seem to possess any fears for the alleged perils of such policy.

Printed in the Richmond *Times*, Nov. 2, 1898; some editorial headings omitted.
[1] A variation of geld, in this context meaning payment of tax or tribute.
[2] That is, the Philippine Islands.

To Ellen Axson Wilson

My own darling,   Richmond, 2 Nov., 1898

This is my last letter,—next I come myself! Ah, how happy the thought makes me. I'd rather have a moment with you than all the entertainment and so-called pleasure in the world,—your love and sweetness and sympathy and intelligence are surely the most refreshing things in the world; and every time I am separated from you I realize that the chief part of my strength and the chief part of my delight in living are cut off. I come back to you to be renewed.

It was so delightful to hear of the appreciation with which dear Father's sermon was received last Sunday! Tell him that while he is reminding the people in Princeton of *me* a much more normal thing is happening here. I am reminding the Richmond people of *him*, in manner, style and vivid matter of reality. It makes me very happy and proud to have them tell me so!

I have just come back from another breakfast,—set this time for half-past eight, not half-past ten, at Judge Christian's,[1]—a much more interesting affair in its way than the other. The only guests, besides Patterson and myself, were Dr. Hoge and Dr. Kerr,[2] and we had an old-fashioned family meal, with family prayers to start off with.

I am well and too happy for words to think that I am coming to you. Love to all.   Your own   Woodrow

ALS (WC, NjP).
[1] George Llewellyn Christian, lawyer and businessman of Richmond, former Judge of the Hustings Court of the City of Richmond.
[2] The Rev. Dr. Moses Drury Hoge, pastor of the Second Presbyterian Church of Richmond, 1845-99, and the Rev. Dr. Robert Pollok Kerr, pastor of the First Presbyterian Church of Richmond, 1884-1903.

A News Report of a Lecture

[Nov. 3, 1898]

THE FASHION IN LITERATURE.

DR. WOODROW WILSON ADDRESSES THE WOMAN'S CLUB ON THIS SUBJECT.

Professor Woodrow Wilson, of Princeton, gave a charming talk yesterday before the Woman's Club, on the "Fashion of the Day in Literature." Professor Wilson's enunciation is so distinct and his English so perfect that not a word escaped his intensely interested audience. He said the whole world reads, but there are three distinctly separate circles of readers—one which reads only the best, another which seeks madly after sensation, and a third, which cares only for simple vulgarity. All these classes find their desire in the literature of the day. But there is still, as there always has been, a circle of readers who find delight in pure literature.

In speaking of the modern sensational novel, he said: "Anybody can turn on an electrical current who has no conscience for his connections." Further, he said, that once a young lady had asked him if he had ever read the "Heavenly Twins." He replied: "No; but may I ask if you have ever read 'Burton's Anatomy of Melancholia'?" In conclusion, he said pure literature would ever stand out above the baser sort, as the clear notes of a prima donna's soprano is heard far above the mixed voices of the chorus. . . .

Printed in the *Richmond Dispatch*, Nov. 3, 1898.

A News Report of a Lecture on Constitutional Government

[Nov. 4, 1898]

OUR CONGRESS AND ITS POWERS.

The last of the series of lectures at Richmond College under the Thomas Museum Lecture Endowment attracted a large and representative audience again last night. Dr. Woodrow Wilson, the lecturer, was given the closest attention throughout. He has won for himself a high place in the esteem of Richmond people as an attractive, instructive and interesting platform speaker, and many expressions of a most favorable character have been heard about the distinguished educator.

Dr. Wilson took as his subject last night, "The Organization and Powers of Congress."

He spoke in part as follows:

This subject is, in a certain sense, only a continuation of the last.

It is our object to see how Congress, separated as it is from the executive branch of the Government, conducts its business and fulfills the duties that fall to it. The way in which it does its work depends upon its rules, and it has not been often enough observed that parliamentary law is a very important part of the public law of the nation. The efficiency of Congress and its relation to the general business of the nation, must largely dep[e]nd upon its own rules and methods of action, and our Congress, though it started with the general parliamentary law of the English race, has in the course of a century, developed so many special rules and so distinct an organization of its own, that it is quite unlike the Parliament of Great Britain in almost every respect. Even in its original constitution it exhibited a marked feature of contrast from the English Parliament. Its two houses have been from the first rule, co-ordinate and equal in power, whereas in England the lower house, that is, the House of Commons, has for almost a century had a superiority of power which has steadily dwarfed that of the House of Lords.

Our Congress still enjoys the peculiar respect which has belonged to it from the outset, because it represented the equality of the States and stood for the Federal principals [principles] in our national Government. There is in it the same equality of votes that existed in the Congress of the old confederation, and the Senate may be said to be in a certain sense, a fragment of that old Congress. The senators retain in theory at least some of the dignity of the plenipotentiary representatives of the States.

There is still a doubt remaining among us whether the Senators represent the people of these several States, or the government which elects them. Unmistakably the tendency of the times is to make them representatives of the people. While we have not yet adopted the practice of electing senators by popular vote[,] for that would involve an amendment of the constitution, we have in several of the States invited the people to express their preference in the primaries and so have put in their hands, if not the actual choice, at any rate the authoritive [authoritative] nomination of the senators. This is a development which operates in some degree against federal principles, for the popular action which nominates Senators is no more confined by State boundaries than the popular election of members of the House of Representatives or the Congressional districts do not cross the State lines of each State, as it is not a distinct delegation in the House. Only equal representation of the States in the senate remains to remind us of the federal principles upon which it is made up.

When we come to examine the House of Representatives it is very difficult to determine what in fact it can be said to represent. No doubt it is the theory of this constitution that it represents not localities but the nation as a whole and in the early years of its existence when it was comparatively simple in its organization, this theory may have been possible to realize in action, but the later developments of its organization have made it more and more difficult to recognize it as a national instrument. There is no one on the floor who represents the country as a whole. Every member from the Speaker down represents a local district, and it has become more and more the habit of Congressmen to think of themselves as sent to Washington in order that their particular constituents may get such benefits as is possible from the legislation of Congress.

The one man who seems to stand above the rest as a recognized party leader, standing for the general policy which his party has put into power, is the Speaker or presiding officer of the House, but the Speaker himself in fact represents only the particular constituency from which he comes. The voters of the country at large have had no opportunity to express their confidence in him or their lack of confidence. He is too, afterward associated with men who have themselves no national vote behind them.

The rules of the House put extraordinary power in the hands of the Speaker. Its acts of legislation are practically without exception devised and formulated by its numerous committees. For each class of business there is a special standing committee which lead[s] the House with regard to that part of its action. Every committee is appointed by the Speaker of the House and he can of course give to any particular committee such a membership as will insure its acting in accordance with his purpose as a party leader. The rules of the House give to the committee the command of the floor and the control of debate practically at all times, and a private member can get the floor for the purpose of making a proposal of his own only if the Speaker knows what he has to say will not certainly interfere with the programme of the session, but with the plans of the group of leaders, whom the Speaker consults and represents. As a consequence of this system an amount of power falls to the Speaker which is hardly second to the power of the President of the United States himself, when it is remembered that the President himself cannot govern the course of the Legislature at all except as an unofficial private individual to govern it by persuasive conference with the leaders of the House, that he can only wait until the Houses act and then must interpose his veto. It will then be seen that there is in the whole arrangement no place of leadership whatever, but that leadership falls almost entirely to the Speaker and to those whom he cho[o]ses to consult.

In the Senate there is really no leadership. The committees of the Senate are elected by the votes of the Senators. The Vice-President is not a member of the Senate, and though he is chosen by the nation, as a whole, he really has no part in its deliverance [deliberations]. For each subject of business there is a special committee, as in the House, and each class of business gets the treatment to be expected from the members of the committee by which it is handled. There is no joint guidance except by the action of the party caucus. There is no central body to give unity [and] consistency to what is proposed or done. It is only in the House of Representatives, and the tendency in that House is unquestionably to always concentrate upon the Speaker the national responsibility as well as the power of leadership.

We come, then, to this singular conclusion that the President, who is elected by the whole people, is not a leader in the vital matters; consequently, in the consideration of the houses of Congress the policy, if formulated by one house without leaders, and passed to another house whose leader, though powerful, is not elected by the country at large, it would seem as if the great power of the Speaker would likely in the long run give him the power of dictation with respect to what the Senate shall do, which will make the Senate less independent than formerly in its action. If this should happen we would have a government in which the whole power of legislation would be practically concentrated in the hands of a local representative who is chosen by other local representatives to be Speaker of the House.

If that should come about it would be more noticeable and more inconvenient than either that this leader of policy should have nothing to do with its carrying out, or that he should be responsible only for plans and not for their execution, or that he should have no experience in execeutive [executive] business, no official intimacy or connection with those who actually put into effect the purpose of the government; that he should be able to dictate to the executive without being made responsible for the unfortunate results of what the executive might do under his dictation. It is hardly possible to believe that this is not merely a transitional condition of affars [affairs] illustrating more and more that in national leadership ·to hold those foremost immediately responsible for results, as we extend our power to the islands of the West Indies and the Far East, we shall certainly be unable to act with certainty unless we unite upon some plan of close legislation and may lay the responsibility on those who plan and those who execute the rule, makes the policy against the Senate and forces the latter to stand up as the responsible persons in the conduct of the government, and must at length be so arranged that they shall become the choice, not of the localities, but rather of the people's accepted leader and formal choice. We cannot govern an empire with disintegrated bodies; there must be unity of action in order that there may be efficiency and responsibility.

Printed in the Richmond *Times*, Nov. 4, 1898; some editorial headings omitted.

From Archibald Williams Patterson

My dear Wilson,   Richmond, Va., Nov. 10, 1898.

I received in due course your letter & photograph, both of which gave us much pleasure, and for them please accept our hearty thanks. It is indeed gratifying to be assured that you carried away from Richmond such pleasant memories, and especially that we contributed somewhat to those impressions. The assurance, however, will never be complete until it is confirmed by another visit—thus showing your faith by your works. I had intended to put the photo. in my office, but the ladies at home overruled the motion with a unanimity and emphasis which made me rather ashamed that I ever thought of anything but the parlor mantle as a suitable place.

It goes without saying that we have missed you very much, & that your name is a household word among us. Col. Archer Anderson stopped me the other day to enquire after you and to say that "he felt very flat now, with no more of those delightful lectures to stimulate him." Similar expressions have come from many others. The enclosed note from Mr. Newton explains why he did not call.[1] I am sure it was a real disappointment that he could not see & hear one whom he already knew so well through his writings.

Have you heard of Dr. Hoge's accident? A street car ran into his buggy, throwing the old gentleman violently to the ground & inflicting serious injuries. It is hardly probable that he will ever recover. The whole community is in deep distress over his misfortune, which amounts to a public calamity so great an *institution* is he in our midst.[2]

Of course, my people in the country understood why you could not see them again. They ask me to express their regret at this, and the very great pleasure you gave them by your visit & your lectures. My sister wants to take your class—the *subject* is so fascinating.

With kindest regards from each one of us to you all, I am, as ever,

Yours cordially & sincerely,   A. W. Patterson.

ALS (WP, DLC). Enc.: Virginius Newton to A. W. Patterson, Nov. 3, 1898, ALS (WP, DLC).
[1] In this letter, Virginius Newton, president of the First National Bank of Richmond, explained that he had been unable to come to Patterson's home to meet Wilson because he had been quite unwell.
[2] Dr. Hoge died from these injuries on January 6, 1899.

From Walter Hines Page

Dear Mr. Wilson,   [Cambridge, Mass.] November 12, 1898.

Except for the calendar and the little touch of frost I should not know that the summer had gone, for I have still been carrying in my mind the purpose to go up on the North Shore where you were spending the warm months and see you. The truth is, during the summer all the plans I had made beforehand were thrown into confusion by an illness and some unexpected absences; and my work has now only got to about the first of August. I am writing you, therefore, at this late date some of the things that I wished to ask you then.

And the main burden of my inquiry is what you, or what will you have, for the Atlantic this winter?

I have sent to you today a copy of the Fall Bulletin of Messrs. Houghton, Mifflin & Company showing the publications of the House during these two or three months, and I heartily wish there were a book on the list from you. May there not be some day in the future?   Very truly yours,   Walter H. Page

TLS (Houghton Mifflin Letterpress Books, MH).

A Report on Wilson's Richmond Lectures

[Nov. 17, 1898]

THE THOMAS LECTURES.

The following admirable synopsis of Professor Wilson's remarkable lectures is furnished us by Professor R. E. Gaines, of the chair of Mathematics in Richmond College:

The twelfth annual course of these lectures has just been given at Richmond College by Professor Woodrow Wilson, Ph.D., LL.D., of Princeton University, on the general theme, "Constitutional Government in the United States," and the people of Richmond have had another demonstration of the wisdom of those who founded this lectureship. For several years past the College has been exceedingly fortunate in the men who have been appointed to this position. Not only is each one a specialist, who by reason of the ability which he has brought to bear on some chosen field of labor has a message to give to the world, but each is endowed with unusual gifts as a speaker, so as to be able to rivet the attention of a large audience and present in an attractive and forceful way some of the results of years of patient investigation. All who heard Professor Wilson—and we have probably never seen at the College a larger number of people who were competent to judge—will concur in the opinion that he fully maintained the high reputation which has been made for this course of lectures by the distinguished scholars who have preceded him.

"Constitutional Government" sounds like a dry subject for a series of popular lectures; and in the hands of any but a master it would not be very inviting. But Professor Wilson possesses rare gifts as a speaker. With clear, strong voice and distinct, forceful utterance; with charming diction, which, without being especially ornate, is rich, varied, lucid, and vigorous; with remarkable discrimination in the use of words; choosing just the word to express his thought, and that without the slightest hesitation, so that one feels no sort of anxiety lest there might have been some miscalculation in the matter; with a vigorous mind, full of his subject, so that he feels at home in every phase of it and has at his command an almost endless variety of illustrations from which to choose precisely the one to suit his purpose, and with a fearlessness of utterance and a directness and earnestness of manner which bespeak not only firm conviction on the part of the speaker, but an ardent desire to unburden himself to others, he not only made it possible for each one of his thousand hearers to hear, but made it quite out of the question that any one should fail to hear, and, as if by magic, carried his audience with a thrill and momentum that were irresistible. . . .

Printed in the Richmond, Va., *Religious Herald*, LXXI (Nov. 17, 1898), 2.

To Henry Marcus Leipziger[1]

My dear Mr. Leipziger,   Princeton, 18 November, 1898

It is very kind of you to ask me to dine with you to-morrow,[2] and I appreciate it most warmly. But I am sorry (indeed I am almost ashamed) to say that I am one of those sensitive fellows who must be alone and keep quiet and ruminate before attempting to speak without manuscript; I know that you will excuse me, upon the confession.

Will you not stop at the Everett House for me on your way down to the Institute? That would give me great pleasure.

With regrets and regards,

In haste,   Sincerely Yours,   Woodrow Wilson

ALS (photostat in Presidential Series, NN).
  [1] Supervisor of Public Lectures, Board of Education, New York City.
  [2] Before Wilson was to give a lecture at Cooper Union, the notes for which are printed at Nov. 19, 1898. Undoubtedly Leipziger was to introduce Wilson.

Notes for Five Lectures on Municipal Government[1]

[Nov. 18-Dec. 15, 1898]

THE GOVERNMENT OF CITIES.

I.

Origins and Antecedents

We need, if we would be candid with ourselves, nothing less than *a reconception* of *the nature of city government,* and of *its place in a proper system* of local self-administration.

Let us clear the ground by acknowledging: that we have been misled

> (1) *By historical preconceptions.* Misleading to think of the modern city in terms originated in connection with *the mediaeval city,* whose life was one of privilege,—*the*

  [1] Given at the Brooklyn Institute of Arts and Sciences on Nov. 18 and 25 and Dec. 2, 9, and 16, 1898. The only news reports of these lectures found are the ones printed at Nov. 19 and Dec. 17, 1898. [Eds.' note]

privilege of a separate body politic. A mistake to think of our cities as first of all or chiefly political bodies. (Hence *Charters*)

The minute we make that mistake we begin to be misled

(2) *By theories of political organization,*—the whole literature of *Checks and Balances* begins to swim in our heads,—the confusing discussion of *functions* executive and legislative, of *veto and confirmation,*—of *nominations*, boards, and bureaux, estimates and appropriations,—none of which are to be rightly understood in the atmosphere of that region of theory.

All this confusion of ideas arises from

(3) *Our ignorance* (or, at any rate, neglect in thought) *of the real origins and elements* of modern city life,—its *actual genesis* and *motives,*—all so recent and so near to our view that we analyze it with difficulty.

The modern industrial city has arisen

(a) *By the superimposition* of the modern industrial features upon cities already politically made,—or made (at any rate located) by nature, at some point of natural advantage (Bost., N.Y., Phila., Balto., London, etc.)

(b) *By R.R. or canal creation*, a process most obvious in America, in the deliberate development of the country.

(c) *By* the *discovery* of extraordinary mineral or manufacturing resources at some single point of local concentration. (*Birmingham*, Ala.)

All of this growth has been not only

Rapid, and therefore without equable or adequate adjustment to its own necessities or to its environment, but also in a high degree

Artificial, i.e. brought about by forces neither physically nor politically natural. And so we have been sorely puzzled about political ways and means and even about political principles.

In order to obtain *a healthful political organization* a city must be also *a Community*, and the modern industrial city has greatly outstripped the hitherto possible speed of community-making and political integration.

(4) *By our quite exceptional* and in many ways extraor-

dinary *system of local government*, which is *statutory
and by means of the courts* rather than *administrative
and by means of vital processes* of integration and professional skill,—*by personnel and system.*

For Brooklyn Institute   18 November, 1898

II.

Bases and Objects of Organization and Action.

A. *The City Elements*: (I. Occupation   II. Origin)
   I. Analysis
   (1) *The Commercial Element*, composed generally of alert
       citizens, not necessarily brought under wide and com-
       plex organization, but both wholesale and retail, vari-
       ous, variously informed, wishing to see the city grow,
       jealous of hindrances and restrictions.
   (2) *The Manufacturing Element*, representing Capital wh.
       is for the most part immobile and liable in large part
       to loss from mistakes as to a market composed, not of
       the city, but of the country or the world.
           For this, *the City a mere local habitation.* No neces-
       sary identification with the city as a community, save
       that of convenience in commanding labour, transporta-
       tion, or etc.
       (a) *The Entrepreneur class*, controlling, with an almost
           absolute dominance the economic status and for-
           tunes of the labouring factory class.
       (b) *The labouring class* itself, living at city disadvan-
           tages,—under *conditions which threaten health and
           independence*, but over wh. they have no control be-
           cause of the collective, inevitable city pressure (The
           manufacturing cities said to be more closely peopled
           than others)
               The labouring class not permanent enough, in its
           individual units to get any strong identification of
           interest or community of sentiment.
   II. Analysis
   (1) *Natives in our cities*
       (a) *Natives of the cities* themselves
       (b) *Natives of the land* to wh. the cities belong.
           The interests and intelligence of both these will
       probably be harmonious with *a normal political de-*

velopment along lines of experience. They will know what they want and how to get it.

(2) *Foreigners,* (a) *by birth,* (b) *by descent.* These, if in the city without experience of the life of the country outside the city, tend to *make the city unlike the rest of the country,* socially and politically.

B. *The City Duties and Tasks:*

It *cannot* (1) *Regulate economic or political relations* between classes. This a State function.

(2) *Give legislative encouragement* to manufacturers or commerce, except within very narrow limits.

It *must* undertake

(1) *Discipline*—police.

(2) *Sanitation,*—including parks, housing of poor and labouring classes, etc.

(3) *Education,*—including Art, Music, Museums, etc. Technical education?

(4) *Facilitation of its characteristic life*: paving, lighting, locomotion, preparation of districts for occupation, etc.

(5) *Guardianship and relief of destitute and helpless* classes ruined by the city pressure.

Influence of the Classes on Performance of Functions:

Leading classes interested in Police; independent in *Sanitation* and *Education*; *selfish in paving,* lighting, locomotion, etc.; *apt to substitute philanthropy for civic duty* in relief of destitution and helplessness.

The *selfish interests* of the wealthy classes *cannot be relied on* to promote the delicate and difficult tasks wh. arise out of the presence of masses of men economically dependent

How Get and Hold the Attention and Interest of All?

(1) *Expensive way* of systematic *failure and corruption.*

(2) By *important action* and *simple organization*:

(a) Important, independent, wide-reaching, conspicuous functions wh. *must* succeed.

(b) By organization simple in principle, open, accessible, respected in action.

To be got by courage, agitation, experiment, communication of effort.

The modern industrial City, what?

An economic corporation, in which the chief stockholders ought to control expenditure? or

A political society (body politic), a delegate plenopotentiary of the State's in all local matters?

It is neither the one nor the other; *nor is it both.* It is, rather, *a humane economic society, whose object* is, *to facilitate, unite, and cleanse its life,—keep it quick, convenient, purged of disease, and morally wholesome.*

24 November, 1898

III.

The City "Executive."

Penalty of deliberate *constitutional formulation*: formal academic distinctions,—a scheme of thought,—*a philosophy of parts* and of their relations to one another.

Our philosophy of parts, derived from Montesquieu *really carried out in the Federal Government,*—carried out *only in form* in *State governments,*—carried out *in fact* again *in* our *city governments.*

We have applied the idea to no other area of local govt.,—not to township or county, e.g., but have given to the city a more separate and completely State-like organization than to our several commonwealths themselves.

Take the case of *Boston*

Charter of 1822 began the city *regime*, in respect of organization:

   (a) *Mayor and 8 aldermen* (at first called "selectmen"), with *powers of former selectmen.* Constituted "upper house."

   (b) *"Common Council"* of 48 (wh. it was at first proposed to call "Board of Assistants"), possessing *"all the powers* formerly exercised by *the inhabitants* in *town-meeting.*["]

Re-Analysis necessary,—wh. may at first sight appear more academic than the other, but wh. is in fact infinitely more practical and nearer to the lessons of experience.

LAW and ORDINANCE. The distinction
   (a) analyzes sovereignty
   (b) apportions function
   (c) fixes responsibility

General law sh. always rest upon *general consent*, and its determination is the natural field of Politics. *But in Administration* there sh. be the element of *professional expertness* and *technical knowledge. City government a field of Administration*, not of Law. Allow me to show this.

LAW is that expression of the will of the State which has for its object the *creation, modification, or clearer definition of some right or duty of the individual,* either as regards other individuals or as regards the State itself. *E.g.,* (a) property, contract, (b) franchise, objects of taxation. *Radical relationships, the field of legislation.*

ORDINANCE, alters no radical right or relationship, but *simply extends or alters governmental activity* within the sphere of powers or fields of action already recognized and established by law—creating, *not a new field* or a new kind of duty or privilege on the part of the individual, *but only new items* of duty or privilege. *E.g.,* police and sanitary measures; educational methods, means, subjects; paving, lighting, locomotion, "public improvements"; guardianship and relief.[2] For *every substantive extension* of these *fields* the *State* has to be applied to for *legislation.*

The City, then, is not a legislative, but *only an administrative body.* It makes administrative Ordinances and executes city tasks of Administration as thoroughly as possible. And, inasmuch as *its business throughout,* in every branch, is *administrative,* there sh. in its organization be *unity, intimate and systematic consultation, close integration, coördination, co-operation.*

Under every system but our own, accordingly, *the action is collegiate.* Nowhere else are mayors set apart as a separate, checking authority, except as agents of the central (i.e. the political, function-determining) Government, by whom they are used as an agency of restraint, or, etc. E.g., Germany (i.e. Prussia), France, England.

Method of executive (administrative) *action by Departments,* Boards, Commissions. E.g. Board of Police Commissioners, of Fire Commissioners, of Public Improvements, of Assessors, of Commissioners of Finance and Estimate, or Apportionment, &c. &c. For wh. we have latterly inclined to substitute *"single heads"* whom we have chosen to call "responsible," and concerning wh. we have debated only *methods of appointment, election, removal,* &c. However constituted, they remain

(1) *Separate in operation and in legal assignment of function* and ∴ legally independent;

(2) *Incapable of dealing with one another* by such consulta-

---

[2] Exhausts our list of city functions, p. 6. [WW's note. Wilson is here referring to Section B of the notes for his second lecture.]

tion as will *settle* and definitively arrange matters in which they *must* coöperate;

(3) *Unsuperintended,*—for the Mayor cannot in fact oversee them, and nothing but their own systematic coöperation can make them justly responsible.

Departments necessarily overlap. E.g. Police and Health; Health and street cleaning; Streets and Public Works; Fire and Police; Fire and building inspection, etc. *And yet these make no common plans,* and are coerced in action only by *the courts* and the Mayor's *power of removal. The power of removal can punish* but *it cannot cure,* integrate, guide.

Unless the work and plans of *all Departments meet in some truly "common" council,* acting as a veritable administrative body alike in method and responsibility, it is as if *hard and stiff horizontal lines* were drawn through the administrative frame of the city, *and fixed there,* unalterable, *by law* (charter provisions).

Take a final example.

    Police Duties: (1) *For the State,* enforcement of criminal law,—acting for the state's attorney.

    (2) *For the City,* (a) *Suppression of disorder*

        (b) Arrests for *breach of ordinances vs. vice,* (city atty. and city courts)

        (c) *Prevention of obstruction* or littering of the streets (Street-cleaning dep't.)

        (d) *Abatement of nuisances,* in aid of the Health Dep't.

        (e) *Enforcement of license laws,* in behalf of Excise Dep't.

The Police are thus manifestly *agents,* directly or indirectly, *of almost every branch of the city government.* No Dep't. is less suited, ∴, to be separately administered; none better *illustrates the need of administrative integration* at a common council-board.

Depends (1) *On other Dep'ts.* e.g., if Health Board will not prosecute for nuisances or Street Cleaning Dept. for obstructions.
(2) *On the Courts.*

                                    2 December, 1898

IV.

The City Council. (In effect a continuation of Lecture III.)

Let us take Prussian city government as a model *for discussion: The Mayor, a trained official,* chosen by the elective council, and *associated with other professional experts*, salaried and serving for long terms, for each class of work a professional director, *chosen by the Council* from the professional civil service. *These are*

The aldermen (to use our word), associated with the Mayor as *an administrative council*, to which is *added* an equal, often a larger, number of unpaid, *non-professional members*.

The work is done in Committees, over each of wh. the proper professional officer presides (e.g., the several experts in law, finance, education, engineering, sanitary science, charity, water supply, gas supply, electrical supply, etc.) over a *non-professional body* of fellow-aldermen and "select citizens."

The Council, with generally not more than 100 members, wholly *elective, unprofessional, unpaid*, which chooses the whole administrative force already indicated, controls the budget, makes the ordinances, and *performs every function of governing*.

Actual administration, a little more *in detail*, e.g.,

(1) *Elementary education*: a central Board or Committee with professional and non-professional aldermen & councillors, and select citizens associates; and in the several wards attendance committees (*Total, 1,258 persons*)

(2) *Poor relief*, overseen by commission composed of a professional alderman as chairman; 8 other aldermen, (*among them*, one legal expert, the Treasurer, and a school commissioner), 17 councillors, 10 select citizens,—a staff of clerks and servants.

   A poor commission in each ward (fr 4 to 12 citizens to a ward—*total of 1,594*) presided over by a citizen chairman, who must be in his office at certain hours, &c.

   N.B. Under this system *education expenses have increased* fr. 9¾% to 19¾% of the total municipal expenditure; while *poor relief expenses have decreased* fr. 18% to 14½%.

(3) *Income taxes*, both state and city, assessed by committees of citizens sitting under official presidency (total 3,396 citizens).

   At top of system, a citizen Court of Revision under the presidency of a state commissioner.

(4) *Citizens assist* in the *drawing up of jury lists*
            ”   ”   *trial of mercantile cases*
        ”   ”   ”   ”   *summary cases*
and serve *as permanent arbitrators* in the several wards.

Return to our original point:

A City Council is an Ordinance-making body.

What is an Ordinance? A formulation of administrative
rules, *a regulation of administrative action*, a prescription (often) of the ways in which citizens must coöperate with government toward certain ends.

It is the plan-making side of Administration: lies
close to daily *experience* and *experiment*. An ordinance
lies closer to fact, to practical conditions and detail,
than law does. *Its test* of excellence must be *feasibility*,
—administrative *practicability* and *efficiency*.

The bi-cameral idea of organization. There must, no doubt,
be *a difference*, in preparation and activity, if not of organization also, *between those* who, as representatives of
the general will, *guide and take counsel* as to what shall
shall be done *and those who execute* the plans made, as
day-to-day experts; *but can there be any good reason for
dividing the plan-making body into two parts?*

The system of Representation: *What* should be its *basis*?

Taxes?

Interests, separately or in groups?

Localities?

Individuals?

We *wish a system* which shall *make the city aware* in
all its action, and in each of its parts, *that it is not a
group* of wards, nor an aggregation of interests, nor a
mere corporation for public works.

Finance in the city *still further illustrates* its distinctively
administrative character.

"*The state taxes*, the interest on the city debt, the
amount to be raised for the payment of principal, the
salaries" of such departments as those of Fire, Police,
and Education, and to some extent of other dep'ts also,
are *often fixed by statute*; and many expenditures for public improvements are in the same way made mandatory
on the city,—and it sometimes happens that *very nearly,
if not quite one-half the annual appropriation* is for objects thus fixed and obligatory.

Limitations put *upon the taxing power* and *upon the debt-contracting power* of the city are common, almost universal.

In England all local-gov't. corporations have the right of *taxation by common law* (for local purposes); *but under our law* such powers must be granted and extend *only so far as the terms of the grant.*

Central control the question here involved, and the supplementary question whether that control should be by the *hard and fast* method of statute *or* by the *elastic* method of *administrative* oversight.

Money questions (*a*) so far as they concern *objects of expenditure* (outside the sphere in wh. the city is only an agent of the state gov't.), ought to be determined *by common counsel* (common council).

(*b*) So far as they are questions of *administrative efficiency*, they should be settled by the *coöperative action of Depts.* I.e.,

General policy of expenditure should be determined by the (representative) general voice, given full choice, and ∴ saddled with full responsibility.

Estimate and Appropriation (apportionment), on the other hand, should be accomplished by the coöperative action of Dep'ts., acting, not with final power, but as committees of Common Council.

8 and 9 Dec., 1898

V.

Reorganization.

I. *The Administration should be one Body,* and should be entrusted *with all counsel and origination,* and with the making of all plans of accommodation and coöperation between Dep'ts.

> *Finances, 2 functions*

If the actively *executive officials are separately organized* for action, *they ought not to be coördinated with the governing Council,* but sh. remain its advice-giving and advice-taking servants.

II. *Only the members of the* governing *Council should be elected,* —each voter voting for *a general borough list* of councilmen *or* for *a district group* of members. No ward *representation.* Such processes *simplify* and *clarify electoral choices.*

> *Basis of Representation*

Training?   III. *A minority of trained and experienced officials in the governing Council*—chosen by it, and themselves entrusted as the directing heads of Dep'ts. with the appointment of their administrative subordinates and agents.

IV. *Liberal salaries* for trained chiefs of service—as well well
[*sic*] as for all expert subordinates,—and, practically, a *tenure
during good behaviour.* "Civil service" rules of choice wherever practicable.

V. *A widening and concentration of city functions. Charities, e.g.,*
should be taken from the sphere of private, voluntary organization and endeavour and made the imperative legal duty
of the Whole. *Relief of the poor and a bettering of the conditions under which they live* is as much a governmental
function as Education (coming under the head, not only
of human duty, but also of social sanitation). *Private charities need not be prohibited.*

Street railways? Suburban preparation? Gas and *water*
and *electricity?*

But this widening and concentration would *not* be wise
without—

VI. *The enforcement of wide compulsory citizen duties,* e.g., in
*poor relief, tax assessment, mercantile and labour arbitra-
tion, orphan apprenticeship, education,* &c., &c., by *a system
of committees, both central and local,* under expert guidance
at the centre.

Will self-government ever become a matter of general interest and exertion if left to voluntary service and control
only at the polls? Should it not be made to rest (at any rate
first of all) upon *legal compulsion—like jury service?*

Limitation vs.   VII. *Central control, administrative integration* in *police, finance,*
Guidance   *health, education,* &c.,—*involving a reconstruction,* a vital-
ization, *of our State governments.* Here, again, no reform
can come till we desire and obtain *a professional service,*
controlled by elected councils.

VIII. *Separation of judicial from city organization* entirely,—except, perhaps, within the police jurisdiction of offences
against city ordinances.

15 Dec., 1898

WWhw notes (WP, DLC).

A Newspaper Report of a Lecture at the
Brooklyn Institute

[Nov. 19, 1898]

FAILURE TO GOVERN CITIES.

Prof. Woodrow Wilson of Princeton lectured last night on "Origins of City Government" before the members of the Brooklyn Institute, at the Art Building, on Montague Street. He ascribed the failure of our attempts to govern large cities to misconceptions as to their character and to the history of their development.

"One of the most wholesome signs about our city governments," he said, "is that we admit we have failed. The modern city is called a body politic, but is it in the same sense that the mediaeval city was a body politic? Your interests in living in the city are not political interests. They are economic interests. Why should we have a charter for a city, setting it off as a peculiar organization with a constitution of its own? We got the idea from mediaeval cities. They were chartered that they might have separate privileges as semi-independent bodies politic. You have not taken the pains to learn just how the modern city differs from the city that preceded it and how it came into existence.

"It began with the railway systems. The industrial revolution, most of it, has taken place since the year 1850. You can build a railroad or a canal and have a city. We have invented a process which we call 'developing the country.' If you arbitrarily create a city by running a railroad and enacting that there shall be a city, you have nothing whatever but a lot of factories, and men drawn there because the factories are there. You haven't got a community.

"Cities have been created by the beckoning of nature. If nature is going to lay your veins of iron right alongside your veins of coal and your business calls for iron and coal, of course you are going to plant your city there and have a great industrial centre.

"All this has taken place with such rapidity that we haven't stopped to think what we are doing. When I look at the endeavors of such societies as the City History Club[1] to make the people realize the unity of the place, I think with a certain hopelessness of the prospect of creating a sentiment about a modern city like this by talking about the pieces of it that existed at the beginning of the century, because the pieces are lost. If men will see what these places were when they were communities, then they will have some definite ground of hope for the time to come when they again shall be communities. But the way in which they shall realize that will be by studying the economic and social conditions of the modern city and realizing that so far it is artificial.

"We have grown not by attraction. We have grown by the running together of people to where they could be nearest to somebody who transacted a peculiar kind of business. Men did formerly come together that they might have a political organization. No city of modern times is formed for that purpose; but finding ourselves united for economic purposes, we have, as a second thought, and by the way, formed political organizations.

"Until we have dispossessed from our minds the misconceptions that have misled us it will be impossible to understand what has gone wrong."

Printed in the *New York Times*, Nov. 19, 1898; one editorial heading omitted.

[1] The City History Club of New York, founded in 1895, had "for its object the formation of popular classes for the study of the history of the City of New York, in the hope of awakening such an interest in its traditions, and in the possibilities of the future as shall tend to civic betterment." *New York Times*, Dec. 11, 1897. Wilson had spoken before the City History Club on December 10, 1897. About this speech, see the notes printed at Dec. 10, 1897, and the news report printed at Dec. 11, 1897, both in Vol. 10.

Outline of a Lecture[1]

New York (Free public lectures)   19 November, '98

Patriotism.

Words that move and stir us: *Liberty—Patriotism.*

Not a sentiment, but a principle—a thoughtful energy of character that looks abroad and operates beyond the narrow sphere of self-interest.

Simplicity of patriotism in the first days, when the country was a-making (*now* a matter of items of opinion and conduct.)
Service of a frontier—the Jingoe's justification.
    Rough and unthoughtful strength.

Now vision and insight,—and a careful service of the polity under which we live, with its need of an extraordinary "variety of information and excellence of discretion"
Study = Interest = Patience. The method: close local contacts.

Objects: Ideals:
Tennyson.[2]

Means: in an intellectual and debating polity—
Studious of the life about us

Studious of the conditions of practical success in politics
Fearless in criticism; fearful of radical change
Partisans of the right
Unclouded by books, unduped by men
Lovers and followers of good men.

WWhw MS. (WP, DLC).
   1 The Editors have been unable to find a report of this address in the New
York newspapers. Wilson's diary of 1898, described at Dec. 9, 1897, Vol. 10,
reveals that he spoke at Cooper Union in New York on "Education in Patriotism."
The outline printed here is a revision of the one printed at May 30, 1898, Vol. 10.
   2 Alfred Lord Tennyson, *The Princess*, "Conclusion," from which Wilson intended to quote.

From the Minutes of the Princeton University Faculty

5 5' P.M. Wednesday, Nov 30th, 1898.

. . . Upon report of the Committee on Discipline Mr. ——
(Acad. Special) was dismissed from the University for hazing
a member of the Freshman Class.

Upon recommendation of the same Committee Mr. ——'s case
. . . was reconsidered, and in view of mitigating circumstances he
was allowed to return to attend the Examinations of his Class in
February. . . .

Professors Young and Brackett were appointed a Committee
to call the attention of the Board of Trustees to the desirability
of lighting the Chapel by electricity. . . .

A News Item

[Dec. 3, 1898]

A '79 DINNER.—A jolly company of '79 men, numbering 45
in all, met at the residence of William B. Isham, Jr., Fifth Ave.
and 61st St., New York, on Thursday [Dec. 1] evening, to partake
of a dinner given in honor of C. C. Cuyler. An elegant repast was
served. Speeches were made by Woodrow Wilson and Robt.
Bridges.

Printed in the *Princeton Press*, Dec. 3, 1898.

To Lucy Marshall Smith

My dear Miss Lucy,   Princeton, 8 Dec., 1898

What you want is a "sentiment," is it not? that can be "proposed" as a toast.[1] How would this do:

To our Country: may her literary men do her honour by speaking the truth, of her and of all things; may they give her immortality by making the truth eloquent and beautiful.

It is a great pleasure to do *anything* for you! I could not tell you how often or with what deep affection Ellen and I think and speak of you both,[2]—or how eagerly we look forward to next summer's reunion. The summer of '97 was a lucky summer and made us rich with this new friendship, which now seems always to have been ours. The dear busy little woman has been meaning to write to one or both of you for some weeks, but seems always obliged to do something else, or to go at once to sleep when evening comes after the breathless day. You are generous, both of you, to write without reckoning exact exchanges of letters like exacting creditors, and we are *very much* in your debt because you write so much better letters than we do; but we do the best we can.

There is nothing to chronicle from this end. Nothing ever *happens* in this quiet house, except goings away to lecture or to speak at dinners (as, for example, tonight)[3] and returnings to lecture and to write. It is a busy and a happy routine, but it does not lend itself to narrative. How do studious men ever get together an autobiography? Besides, it's been years since I wrote a letter (except to Ellen). I conduct business, and send messages, give and get information, by correspondence,—just as one would communicate by telephone; but it has been many a year since I had "a correspondent," and I quit writing letters before I learned how! I feel it as a real privation and yet it seems impossible now to begin over. It would be that much more writing,—and I have enough writing to do in all conscience!

We are all well; father is still with us,—a fixture, we trust, for the winter,—and the children continue to regard their "up-to-date" school as a sort of elaborate entertainment which does not lose zest by repetition. Mrs. Daniels[4] is much liked (we have not met her yet), one of the young and enthusiastic men in the faculty, Jesse Carter,[5] describing her as "a sort of combination of Mrs. Hibben, Mrs. Westcott, and Mrs. Marquand." What that particular mixture would make I can't imagine!

Ellen and the children join me in a big message of love to you both, and I am, though writing as fast as I can,

Your devoted friend,   Woodrow Wilson

You must let me see that "pusillanimous" article, without fail.

ALS (photostat in RSB Coll., DLC).
  [1] The letter to which this was a reply is missing.
  [2] That is, she and her sister, Mary Randolph Smith, of New Orleans. They

had summered with the Wilsons in Markham, Va., in 1897 and visited them in Princeton during the summer of 1898.

3 For this affair, see the notes and news report printed following this letter.

4 Winthrop More Daniels had married Joan Robertson of Montville, Conn., on October 12, 1898.

5 Jesse Benedict Carter, Assistant Professor of Latin.

Notes for an After-Dinner Talk[1]

Trenton Alumni, 8 Dec., 1898.

The unawed scrutiny of graduates: "the missus."

The Univ. herself *makes* her constituency, the alumni,— and is, in turn, made by them.

Let us be careful to give no one cause to say of Princeton: "These lines were written fifty years ago by one who has, for a long time, slept in his grave merely for pastime."

Dare to be practical within the lines of scholarship: "Luckily Mr. Jorkin had deposited all his funds in the bank, and lost only his life."

The character of the College: a common school for citizens,— This at least "the common clash o' the kentry side."

But to realize this character, you *must be a candidate*.

Finally let us pray to be delivered "from witches, warlocks, lang-ribbed things, and things that go 'whoo.'"

WWhw MS. (WP, DLC).
1 See the following news report for a brief account of this affair.

A News Report

[Dec. 10, 1898]

PRINCETON CLUB OF TRENTON.

The Annual Banquet Held on Thursday Evening.

The Princeton Club of Trenton held its second annual dinner on Thursday night, in the banquet room of the Trenton House. Covers were laid for seventy, and the room was appropriately decorated in orange and black. The company was very enthusiastic, and "Old Nassau" and other college and national songs, alternated with repeated cheering during the course of the evening. . . .

John A. Campbell '77, president of the club, acted as toastmaster and introduced President Patton as the first speaker of the evening. . . .

Toasts were also responded to by Professor Andrew West,

Professor Woodrow Wilson, Adrian H. Joline '70, ex-president of the Princeton Club of New York, and Rev. Dr. James C. Mackenzie, head master of Lawrenceville School.

The committee which had the arrangements of the dinner, consisted of Henry Stafford Little '44, Bennett VanSyckle '46, and General William S. Stryker '58. . . .

Printed in the *Daily Princetonian*, Dec. 10, 1898.

A Newspaper Report of a Lecture at the Brooklyn Institute

[Dec. 17, 1898]

DISCUSSES CITY GOVERNMENT.

Prof. Woodrow Wilson of Princeton last night completed a series of lectures on "City Government" before the Brooklyn Institute. The lecture was delivered in the Art Building on Montague Street. Prof. Wilson presented his idea of the reforms necessary to improve city government, although he said that he had no hope of seeing them adopted for at least a generation.

First, he said, the city government should be ruled by a single elective body, which should be the only governing body of the community. The Board of Estimate and Apportionment should be composed of all the heads of departments. "City officials," he said, "do not consult each other; they hold each other at arm's length and regard themselves as in some sense rivals, whereas they ought to be cordial co-operators for the carrying out of a single set of plans to which they have all agreed."

Each voter should have only one person or one set of persons to vote for. Officials should be trained experts, for it is impossible for men without special training to properly discharge official duties. The City of New York had discovered that it was necessary to have an engineer at the head of the Street Cleaning Department. The old idea was that anybody could clean the streets, and anybody could if he had an engineer to tell him how.

"If we have bad government," said the Professor, "it isn't because we have bad men, but because we have ignorant men. And yet how are you going to get an expert? He must be trained somewhere, and there is no place in this country where he can be trained. We will have to find out, sooner or later, that our universities must train our public servants; not by teaching them sociology, which nobody can define, but by teaching them the science of administration, taught as technically as law itself, taught just exactly as we teach men to be civil engineers and doctors.

"We are not going to have expert officials by whistling for them, but we are going to have them by preparing them. Now we go to the expensive process of making the Government prepare them. There are some men whom politicians would love to turn out of the Department of State at Washington, but if they did there wouldn't be anybody in the department who remembered any precedents whatever. But this is simply the rough-and-ready Democratic way of getting experts by letting them learn.

"But after we have trained them we can't keep them unless we give them liberal salaries. We are the most niggardly people in the world in regard to paying salaries to public officials. We are asking men to do first-rate work at third and fourth rate salaries."

His last point was that judicial functions should be exercised by persons not elected as representatives of the city. Law should not be applied by tribunals which have local points of view. "But you say, 'There is appeal,'" he continued. "Yes, but how many cases are appealed? How many obscure persons suffer injustice because they cannot afford to appeal? The big cases are appealed, but I take it that a small case is just as important to the litigants in it as a big case is to the litigants in it. I believe there is more variety in our justice than you imagine."

Printed in the *New York Times*, Dec. 17, 1898; one editorial heading omitted.

From Cornelius Cuyler Cuyler

My dear Woodrow: New York. 23 Dec. 1898

To say that it gives me pleasure faintly expresses my feelings at this time in enclosing you my cheque as Treasurer for $2500. on behalf of your warm friends who last spring decided that Princeton could ill afford to lose you.[1]

I hope to have the pleasure of your company on the 23d when you speak before the YMCA.[2] This matter is closed as I understand it and your name is now being printed on the cards which are to be sent around next week. The other speaker as you know will be your classmate Tom Hall.[3]

Wishing you every joy and happiness in the coming year, I am with kindest regards to Mrs Wilson and yourself,

                    Sincerely yours   C C Cuyler

ALS (WP, DLC) with WWhw notation on env.: "Ans. 25 Dec. '98."
    [1] Cuyler refers to the arrangement which he and several other wealthy Princeton alumni made with Wilson in 1898. They agreed to augment Wilson's pro-

fessorial income by the sum of $2,500 a year for five years, and Wilson in return promised not to leave Princeton during this period. See the Agreement of April 30, 1898, printed as an enclosure with C. C. Cuyler to WW, May 16, 1898, Vol. 10.

² A news report of Wilson's speech is printed at Jan. 24, 1899.

³ The Rev. Dr. Thomas Cuming Hall, Princeton '79, who had just become Professor of Christian Ethics at Union Theological Seminary in New York.

To John Franklin Jameson

My dear Jameson,   Princeton, 27 Dec., 1898

I send you, under another cover, by registered mail, Mrs. Col. William Winthrop's¹ paper on *"The St. Clair Controversy."* You have examined it before, I know, for Mrs. Winthrop has told me the history of that; but she has let me read it, and I have grown anxious to see it published. It seems to me to have real importance, if for no other reason, because it is based upon papers to which others have not had access; and I for one should very much like to see it in permanent form, where it could be turned to and used.

I am, therefore, quite upon my own initiative, going to take a liberty in behalf of Mrs. Winthrop's paper which I certainly would not take for one of my own. I am going to beg, as a favour to myself, that you will submit it once more to the gentlemen of the Board of Editors and ask a reconsideration of their determination not to publish it in the American Historical Review. The St. Clair controversy is no doubt a foot-note to history, but it is a foot-note which, like some others I have seen, has more light in it for guidance than portions of the text.²

With warm regard, and the heartiest good wishes of the season to Mrs. Jameson and yourself from Mrs. Wilson and

Your sincere friend   Woodrow Wilson

ALS (J. F. Jameson Papers, DLC).

¹ Alice Worthington (Mrs. William Woolsey) Winthrop, whom Wilson had met in Washington in February 1898. For his description of her and Colonel Winthrop, see WW to EAW, Feb. 12, 1898, Vol. 10.

² Mrs. Winthrop's article was not published in the *American Historical Review* or, for that matter, anywhere else insofar as the Editors can determine.

A Financial Record

[c. Jan. 1, 1899-Dec. 31, 1901]

Inscribed on flyleaf (WWhw): "Woodrow Wilson"

A record of "extra earnings" for 1899-1901, showing dates and some subjects of public lectures, royalties from books, and fees for articles.

Bound notebook (WP, DLC).

A News Report of an Alumni Affair

[Jan. 14, 1899]

PRINCETON MEN DINE

Annual Banquet of Chicago Alumni a Jolly Affair.

TOASTS AND YELLS

Witty speeches and college yells were the features of the banquet of the Princeton club of Chicago, held at the University club last night. College songs also lent variety to the programme, and college spirit showed itself in the exuberance of the banqueters.

The serious side of life, however, was not lost sight of. The speeches, besides their witticisms and funny stories, dealt with the serious problems which confront the Nation, and the college men were exhorted by the speakers to come forth and prove themselves leaders of the people in solving the great problems before the Nation.

About fifty alumni of old Nassau gathered at the banquet tables, and the speakers represented Princeton, Yale, and Harvard, the three members of the triple alliance in athletics. . . .

Cyrus H. McCormick, president of the association, acted as toastmaster. The theme of his opening address was the old bulletin tree at Princeton, and his introductions of speakers were appropriate and witty.

Professor Woodrow Wilson of Princeton university, the well-known magazine writer, was the principal speaker of the evening, and his speech[1] was full of thoughts which may be profitably followed by the college graduate. For the alumni of colleges Professor Wilson outlined the sphere of leadership of the country in the new problems which confront it, for the college man has had opportunity to study past history, he has seen more than the average man has seen, and is better able to solve the new problems which are before the country.

Professor Wilson emphasized the change of international and domestic relations which had recently come to pass. The progress of civilization had obliterated the frontier and the result of the late war had extended our foreign relations. The Nation had broken its shell and bids fair to run a momentous career. Whether the Philippines are occupied or not conditions had changed and the university must change to meet changed conditions. The greatest province of the university is to serve the Nation; the university should be the highest school of citizenship for the men of the Nation.

The speaker, although, as he claimed, not an imperialist or expansionist, welcomed the new state of affairs, as it furnished the necessity of a foreign policy and gave to the executive of the Nation a national character.

"As long as we have only domestic subjects we have no real leaders," said he, "but we cannot have a foreign policy without the leadership of the executive. The President does not originate domestic policy, and the government has no national figure until we have a foreign policy, where the responsibility rests with the executive. Princeton must come to the aid of the country with a trained hand and a mind equal to the occasion." . . .[2]

Printed in the *Chicago Inter-Ocean*, Jan. 14, 1899; some editorial headings omitted.
  [1] There are brief WWhw notes for this talk, dated Jan. 13, 1899, in WP, DLC.
  [2] The *Chicago Daily Tribune*, Jan. 14, 1899, reported on Wilson's address in part as follows: "The orator of the occasion was Professor Woodrow Wilson of the university faculty. 'International Politics' was the subject of his remarks.
  " 'Each man present,' said the speaker, 'remembered a different college, but all held in affectionate memory "Old Nassau," and all are bound by the same common bonds of fraternity. The country has changed—is changing—and the university man should meet the changes. The country never in history underwent a greater change than it has in the last year. The nation is breaking its shell and is emerging from that shell. The ground of today is debatable. Shall we occupy the Philippines? That is the question we must meet. We cannot avoid it, and the university must take a national point of view.' "

To Edward Perkins Clark[1]

My dear Mr. Clark,   Princeton, 17 Jan'y, 1899

Evidently the passage from Bagehot to which Mr. Hyde alludes is this: "In youth the real plastic energy is not in tutors or lectures or in books 'got up,' but in Wordsworth and Shelley; in the books that all read because all like; in what all talk of because all are interested; in the argumentative walk or the disputatious lounge; in the impact of young thought upon young thought, of fresh thought on fresh thought, of hot thought on hot thought; in mirth and refutation, in ridicule and laughter: for these are the free play of the natural mind, and these cannot be got without a college."

It is a passage from an essay on "Oxford Reform" which I have never seen as a whole, but which I have seen referred to as having been published in *The Prospective Review* for August, 1852.

What you tell me of your sons interests me very much indeed,— what you say of George[2] most of all. He seems to have just the tastes I myself had as an undergraduate.

With much regard,

Sincerely Yours,   Woodrow Wilson

ALS (WC, NjP).
  [1] Editorial writer for the New York *Evening Post.*
  [2] George Maxwell Clark, a sophomore at Yale University.

From William Goodell Frost[1]

My dear Sir: Berea, Ky., January 23, 1899.

I have learned through friends in New York of your generous
—I may say chivalric—consent to present the cause of our belated
fellow-citizens in "Appalachian America" at the meeting in the
Brick Church on the 29th inst.[2]

It is one of the rewards of labors which are sometimes arduous
and exacting, to be brought by this cause into fellowship with
some of the best people in the land, and I am very grateful for
this kindness.

The general fact of our southern mountain region is coming to
consciousness with the public, but only a few scholars like yourself have measured the extent and significance of this region.
I have now had enough experiments and experience in the field
itself to verify the effectiveness of some simple measures for putting this population in step with the world, and with such enter-
prising friends as we are beginning to have in New York, and the
voice of one who can speak with authority—like Dr. Woodrow
Wilson—we shall secure adequate support.

You have of course the general facts of our cause before you,
and Mr. Cady[3] may have given you some of our literature. I venture to send herewith reprints of an article of my own in the
Outlook of last Sept.[4] and an article from the New England Magazine by Dr. Barton—one of our graduates;[5] and two copies of the
Berea Quarterly, each containing a marked article which may be
worthy of a glance.[6]

You may have noticed a paper by Dr. Geo. E. Vincent on "A
Retarded Frontier" in the September Number of the Journal of
Sociology. Another article of my own will probably appear in the
Atlantic Monthly for February, which will be out before the day
of our meeting.[7] I mention these different sources of information
in order that you may lay hold of those which are most convenient. Of course Shaler's History of Kentucky[8] is especially valuable from the fact that he is a native of the State and has tra-
versed the mountains as a geologist.

As I return from the East I am freshly impressed by the earnest
faces and character of our students. Some of the pictures I send
you tell the story—and photographs, like figures, cannot lie!

It is a thing to increase one's faith in human nature to find what noble friends can be rallied for a really important enterprise.

With grateful regard,

Faithfully yours,   Wm. Goodell Frost.

P. S. I had the pleasure of hearing your masterly address at Oberlin College some years ago,[9] where I was then Professor of Greek, but did not meet you personally.

TLS (WP, DLC).
[1] President of Berea College.
[2] The text of Wilson's speech is printed at Jan. 29, 1899, a news report at Jan. 30, 1899. See also WW to G. S. Webster, Jan. 17, 1899, printed as an addendum in this volume.
[3] Josiah Cleveland Cady, New York architect and trustee of Berea College.
[4] William Goodell Frost, "University Extension in Kentucky," New York Outlook, LX (Sept. 3, 1898), 73-79.
[5] William E. Barton, "The Cumberland Mountains and the Struggle for Freedom," New England Magazine, New Series, XVI (March 1897), 65-87.
[6] They are missing, as are the other enclosures.
[7] The article appeared in March as W. G. Frost, "Our Contemporary Ancestors in the Southern Mountains," Atlantic Monthly, LXXXIII (March 1899), 311-19.
[8] Nathaniel Southgate Shaler, Kentucky, A Pioneer Commonwealth (Boston, 1885).
[9] Frost's memory was hazy here. He left Oberlin to become President of Berea College in 1892. Wilson first spoke at Oberlin on June 19, 1895, when he delivered "Leaders of Men" as the commencement address. (See the news report of of Wilson's speech printed at June 20, 1895, Vol. 9.) Frost was perhaps present as a guest on that occasion.

A News Report

[Jan. 24, 1899]

Y.M.C.A. ANNIVERSARY CELEBRATED.

The forty-sixth anniversary of the Young Men's Christian Association of this city [New York] and the eleventh anniversary of the Twenty-third Street Branch was celebrated by a meeting at the association rooms last evening. A large audience was present. Highly satisfactory reports were read by the treasurer of the branch, and the treasurer of the association, and stereopticon views were displayed showing the work of the various city associations.

. . . Cleveland H. Dodge presided, and addresses were made by Professor Woodrow Wilson, of Princeton University, and by the Rev. Dr. Thomas C. Hall. Among those present were William E. Dodge, Morris K. Jesup, J. Edgar Leaycraft, Alfred E. Marling, Francis Schell, James Talcott, C. C. Cuyler, P. W. Henry, R. C. Morse, Edwin H. Weatherbee and William P. Howell.

Printed in the New York Tribune, Jan. 24, 1899.

A Final Examination

January 26, 1899.

EXAMINATION IN CONSTITUTIONAL GOVERNMENT

1. Is France a fully developed "constitutional" state? Give reasons for your answer.

2. What stage of "constitutional" government does the present political organization of Prussia illustrate?

3. Under what circumstances will the Government be most likely to be the leader of a progressive and developing nation? Give instances.

4. Is election the best process by which to pick out leaders under a "constitutional" government? Give reasons and illustrate.

5. In what country is the imperative petition used? In what forms is it used there? What criticisms may be made of it as an instrument of political action?

6. Show the necessary limitations of "popular" administration, and the proper field and most advantageous conditions of "expert" administration.

7. What are the advantages and what are the disadvantages of electing judges?

8. Why cannot a nation make rapid progress in freedom?

9. What are the various sources of English "constitutional" law and practice? (Boutmy).[1]

10. How does the conception of sovereignty differ in France, England, and the United States? (Boutmy).

"I pledge my honor as a gentleman that, during this examination, I have neither given nor received assistance."

Printed examination (WP, DLC).
[1] The textbook in the course, Émile Gaston Boutmy, *Studies in Constitutional Law: France—England—United States,* translated by E. M. Dicey (London and New York, 1891).

An Address on the Cause of Berea College[1]

[[Jan. 29, 1899]]

OUR LAST FRONTIER.

It is a cause of real personal gratification to me to have the privilege of standing upon this platform this evening with Dr. Frost and identifying myself with the interesting and noble cause which he represents.

It is a very significant fact that the people of the mountain regions of the South for whom Dr. Frost is working, and for whose benefit Berea College has made such important adaptations, are the inhabitants of what is really the only frontier we have left in this country. The Census of 1890 informs us that it is no longer possible to trace that waving line between us and the far coasts of the Pacific which once marked the front of our advance from sea to sea. We have reached the Pacific, and established our population with no considerable breaks that can be marked upon the map in the line of settlements that extends from ocean to ocean. And now we turn from this hurried work of advancing settlement, to observe the places we have skipped in the march and to do thoroughly what in our haste we had done but imperfectly or altogether overlooked; and it is in this turning about that we observe the frontier we have left within, at the heart of the older East, where the Appalachians spread their spurs from Pennsylvania to Georgia.

I have said that the gratification I feel this evening is a *personal* gratification, because in speaking for these people of the mountains I am speaking for the people of my own section of the country, I mean the South; and because there lies upon this subject for me the full light of many of the thoughts that spring out of my habitual studies. No one who observes the life of the nation now can fail to see the turning point which we have passed and the new character which our life has taken on. Hitherto in our breathless advance and conquest of the continent, our eager cry has always been, How far? We have pressed forward, forward, eager to complete upon its great scale that great work of settlement and of the establishment of states that has ever drawn us onward. We have sometimes been laughed at by foreigners for boasting of the size of our continent, as if we ourselves had made it; but the boast is not after all ridiculous, for by the size of the continent we are to measure our achievement in taking possession of it. It lay once pathless and with impenetrable forests massed thick upon it, the open plains far beyond, and unknown until we reached them,—themselves hard to till and difficult to subdue to the uses of men; and beyond them the great barrier of the Rockies with other forests to penetrate and another sea slope to make our own; and all this we have understood how to possess and how to use for the building of stable states and the expansion of a great common government, single and inseparable in spirit and in achievement. But now that this initial task is finished, we turn about and scrutinize more closely and critically the work we have done, see where it has been slipshod, imperfect, incomplete. The

cry is no longer, How far? but, How well? The task is no longer
one of achievement. It has become, rather, the sober study of
conduct, of the detail of life, of mutual responsibilities, of purification,—of readjustment. And it is with this duty in mind, and
with this new standard of effort, that we turn to look upon our
first forgotten frontier in the inner mountains that lie upon our
eastern seaboard, a place hitherto only touched and forgotten, and
holding still such people as those with whom the work began.

No one who has ridden, as I have, through the silent lengths
of that great region can fail to have his imagination touched by
what he has seen—the almost limitless forests lying there untouched upon the long slopes of the towering hills, as if they had
been there keeping their counsel and hold[ing] their secrets ever
since the creation; and here and there in the little clearings the
houses of a secluded people, as reticent as the hills about them,
slow to speak, their eyes watchful, holding back the secrets of
their quiet life. It moves one to know how like these people are, in
all but the absence of restless movement and of aggressive energy,
to the first settlers in these hills, who were our own precursors in
the establishment of civilization on the continent. And it is surely
not to be wondered at that those of us who have known the better
things that they have never had news of should feel the impulse
of duty to return to them. We should go to them as heralds of the
change, the invasion, the transformation that is to come upon
their hills,—the coming of the saw-mill and the road and the mine,
and then the railway and the last invasion of the forces of the
modern time. But we should go amongst them not to master them
and to take what they have so long possessed, but to teach them
self-mastery and the use of what they have, so that it shall be indeed their own, because they know its value and the uses they
may make of it.

In offering them the education which shall teach them these
things Berea surely does not differ from other colleges, nor even
from the great universities of the country in the essential features
of her task. Berea's unique features are simply adaptations to
unique conditions. No college nor even university amongst us is
yet a place whose chief and only function is research, the origination and discovery of truth. Every place of education amongst our
free people is still a place of schooling, where passion may be
cooled, prejudice enlightened, effort steadied, purpose given vision; where the chief product shall be, not men of the closet, but
chastened men of action, men schooled and fitted to carry forward the better tasks and make prevalent the established lessons

of the nation's life; men who can understand and lead and serve and interpret. And so, each in its rank, American colleges share with Berea this sacred function of enlightenment, and there ought to be universal comradeship with her. Every university man should call cheer to her and lend her aid as he can in the work which she has undertaken.[2]

Printed in the *Berea Quarterly*, IV (May 1899), 5-6.
  [1] For a note about the provenance of this address, see WW to W. G. Frost, Feb. 13, 1899, n. 2, printed as an addendum in this volume.
  [2] There is a WWhw outline of this address, dated Jan. 29, 1899, in WP, DLC.

A News Report

[Jan. 30, 1899]

AN APPEAL FOR BEREA COLLEGE.

"The Educational Development of the Native Americans in Our Southern Mountains" was the subject of considerable discussion at the Brick Presbyterian Church, Thirty-seventh-st. and Fifth-ave., last evening. The meeting was called more especially to present the claims of Berea College, situated at Berea, Madison County, Ky., which is making a hard struggle to obtain an endowment sufficient to carry on a work of education among the people of the isolated mountain region on the boarders [borders] of Kentucky and Tennessee.

Professor Woodrow Wilson, of Princeton University, was the first speaker, and spoke briefly of the need of the people of even the simplest education, and said that they were worthy as a race of the very best the government could give them. General O. O. Howard[1] also spoke, and President Frost of Berea made an earnest appeal for support for the college.

Printed in the *New York Tribune*, Jan. 30, 1899.
  [1] Oliver Otis Howard (1830-1909), Union general in the Civil War, head of the Freedman's Bureau, 1865-74, one of the founders and President, 1869-74, of Howard University, and founder of Lincoln Memorial University in Cumberland Gap, Tenn.

Ellen Axson Wilson to Anna Harris

My dear Anna,   Princeton   Jan. 31, 1899

I began a letter to you many weeks ago, was prevented from finishing that day and have positively never had an opportunity to resume until now,—thanks first to a house full of visitors and then to a six weeks struggle with the influenza. With the most fortunate exceptions of Woodrow and his father we have all had it,—including the servants—and had it two or three times over. All are pretty well again now however excepting myself who am still teased with a rather wearing cough.

It was a great pleasure, dear, to hear from you again after your long silence. I of course hear a little about you indirectly through the Hoyts, and so knew about your very successful school and how delighted all your patrons are with it. You don't know how much pleasure all this has given me, for I am sure you are one to prize and enjoy exceedingly the independence of a school of your own.

I on my part have just gone out of the business,—of teaching— to some extent. My children are all at school this year for the first time. Until last year I taught them altogether. Then we imported a governess from Germany who proved a great success. The children now speak German as fluently as English, and write it very correctly too. I still however had all the English branches. This year though a new school has been started at the beautiful place that was formerly Evelyn College. Our Fraülein teaches in it but still has her room with us, we giving her board for the sake of the German conversation. So we have the combined advantages of governess and school. We are delighted with the school,—are only afraid it is *too* good for the number of scholars and will break down.

The teachers are very enthusiastic about the children declaring that it is a "delight to teach them," that they are "the most intelligent, the best-trained, and the most thorough in their work of any they have ever seen." I knew they were very intelligent but I was honestly amazed to learn that they were "well-trained," for I have always taught them with so little regard for "method." By the way, they all say that Nellie especially is "*wonderful* in mind" as well as "angelic in character," and if you happen to think of it please repeat that to Mrs. *Goetchius*![1] We all enjoy having ourselves proved true prophets, and when Nell was a baby, Mrs. G. assured me that she would prove to have a remarkable intellect, judging simply from the *shape* of her *head*. She is now nine years old, and really so *lovely* that she almost frightens me. Jessie is the beauty of the family with her pale gold hair, her transparent complexion and her exquisitely delicate clear-cut profile. I wish you could see a bas-relief we had made of her last fall. It certainly looks like an angel. The artist said she had never hoped to find such an ideal head for a model. But I am bragging in the most shameful manner!

Woodrow keeps very well now,—with due care as to diet,—and

is working as usual very hard. In spite of the fact that he is as he says constantly "in a state of decline" he is *forced* to give by far too many lectures and addresses away from home. A little of it, of course, would be a wonderful relief from his writing &c. here. You speak of the vacancy at Athens.[2] He was approached on that subject,[3] but of course it is impossible on account of his literary work. The labours and interruptions of an executive office would almost certainly put an end to his career as a literary man so far as any *large* task was concerned, so he feels that he cannot consider such offers though they are very tempting to him, for he has a great taste for administration and is extremely successful in it. Of course he has a great deal of it here as chairman of important committees. He has declined the presidency of five universities, among them one of the most important in the country. . . .

I have a great sorrow lately in the death of Elizabeth Adams;[4] she literally gave her life to her children, of whom she has left eight. They were terribly poor and she has all these years done *everything* for them and taught school besides, kept so cheerful through it all too, and retained her vivid interest in books and affairs. It was a truly *heroic* life, but the end was inevitable. She has been slowly dying for months from nervous prostration. The end came last week. I cannot somehow shake off for a moment the weight it has laid upon my spirits, all the more so perhaps because for Woodrow's sake I must not show it. He is almost terribly dependent on me to keep up his spirits and to "rest" him as he says. So I dare not have the "blues." If I am just a little sky-blue he immediately becomes blue-black!

With sincere regards for all the family & love for yourself, believe me as ever   Your true friend   E. A. Wilson

ALS (WC, NjP); P.S. omitted.
   [1] Antoinette Wingfield Goetchius, wife of the Rev. Dr. George Thomas Goetchius, pastor of the Rome, Ga., Presbyterian Church.
   [2] That is, of the presidency of the University of Georgia.
   [3] There is no correspondence in the Wilson Papers relating to this matter.
   [4] Elizabeth Adams (Mrs. Hamilton) Erwin of Morganton, N.C., who had died on January 23, 1899.

To David Fentress[1]

Princeton, New Jersey,

My dear Mr. Fentress,   7 February, 1899.

I have not willingly let your interesting letter of December twenty-sixth remain all this time unanswered. It has simply been crowded to one side by innumerable matters of business, and countless claims of a very pressing sort on my time and attention.

You are undoubtedly right in thinking that there is something wrong in the debating business here. It is not a defect of organization or a lack of effort, however, it is a lack of resources, in the last analysis. In the Yale debate an almost incredible mistake of judgment was made in the choice of sides and our men were foredoomed to lose.[2] But the thing to remedy is deeper than that. We must give our men, not occasional, but constant and systematic practice in the study and discussion of questions of the day. And we shall do so. It requires for a proper debating drill that the Departments of History, Economics, and Politics should coöperate, and we were unable to arrange that coöperation for this college year, because the Department of History was not yet old enough in its reorganization.[3] But next year I sincerely hope to see the plan in operation.

What our men conspicuously lack is resources when caught at unawares in a debate. They know nothing more about the subject that [than] they have had time to get up in support of particular arguments since the subject was chosen. They move stiffly and a bit vaguely in any new region of discussion into which the other side may lead them. This is inevitable under the present system; but may the present system soon be a past one!

This is the fundamental matter. There are other minor ones; but too many and too particular for a letter.

With much regard,

Very sincerely Yours,   Woodrow Wilson

WWTLS (WC, NjP).

[1] A.B., Princeton, 1896; LL.B., Harvard, 1899.

[2] Yale had defeated Princeton in the debate held in New Haven on Dec. 6, 1898. Princeton argued the affirmative of the question, "Resolved, That the United States should annex Cuba."

[3] Wilson refers to the reorganization taking effect at the beginning of the academic year 1898-99 which separated political science and history and left history a separate section, or department, in the Department of Philosophy. It was at this time that Paul van Dyke took up his duties as Professor of History and Robert McNutt McElroy joined the department as Instructor in American History. Both men were to play significant roles in the development of the Department of History. Together with Assistant Professor John Haughton Coney, they offered a greatly expanded program of courses in history in 1898-99.

From William Goodell Frost

My Dear Friend: New York, Feb. 15th 1899.

I have been "swinging around the circle" and am again in New York by the fireside where we discussed so much of history, education, and philanthropy.

Mr. Cady shows me your recent letter containing the assurance that a report of your classic speech at the Brick Church is waiting for revision and will come to me soon. It will be *greatly* appreciated and highly useful. It was altogether too choice a thing to perish with perish with [*sic*] a single utterance, although even that was enough to give it a life as long as that of the most long-lived auditor.

I know you are "a man who can certainly divine," and will understand the gratitude for this great service which I can so inadequately express.

We are just sending to Mrs. Wilson, by express, a quilt or "bed kiver" of homespun which exhibits the skill of a woman who can neither read nor write! It is a genuine mountain product, and may serve its original purpose or be hung at a doorway as a kind of tapestry!

I expect to hover around New York for about a month.

With Grateful Regard,

Faithfully Yours,   Wm. Goodell Frost.[1]

ALS (WP, DLC).
[1] Wilson's reply, dated Feb. 17, 1899, is printed as an addendum in this volume.

Outline of an Address[1]

Address, Teachers College, N.Y.   16 Feb'y, 1899

The Teacher as Citizen.

Every profession has *its own ideal*: that of *the teacher*?
     Scholarship? An instrument. *Instruction*? With what aim?
The teacher's function *in the best sense a public function*.
     There is *a national spirit*, and *study* should be conducted *in that spirit*.
     What is our national spirit?
     So far as the teacher is concerned, it is *a spirit of liberal culture*. *'Liberal'* in the best sense means *'popular*,' i.e. open-minded, catholic, broadly human, without class prepossessions or narrownesses.
The idea of *culture under our polity* is, *Adjustable Capacity*, the condition precedent to *a free choice of occupation* and to the *specialization wh. must follow* that choice. It *involves*:
     (1) *Various preparation*
     (2) *Capacity for self-help*
     (3) *Appreciation of values* (i.e. the kind of thinking involved in each sort of Study)

Democracy = a polity of free success by effort,—*seeing chances and taking them.*

Are there studies without nationality,—the sciences, e.g.?
Even these have the same atmosphere, and must regard the pupil as an instrument of life in the nation.

How be such a teacher? Study
The variety of modern life
The processes of change
The distinctive principle of our polity (in *orators* and *poets*).

WWhw MS. (WP, DLC).
[1] The Editors have been unable to find a report of this address in the New York newspapers or in Columbia University student publications.

Notes for an Address on Statesmanship[1]

Congregational Club.   20 February, 1899. (N.Y.)

THE MAKING OF A STATESMAN.

Lincoln:
His *capacity for growth*, and his *actual growth*
(a) from *provincial to national* ways of thinking,
(b) from *seer to statesman*, after election to presidency.
"*A man of the people*"? No more than *Washington* was,—who, in a different way, showed the same qualities:—*vision* and *steady self-preparation*,—a man fit either for the frontier or for the council-room.

The heartening thing is, that, though exceptional in degree, the case is not exceptional in kind, but *in a sense typical* of what we may call *New-World capacity,—adjustable capacity.*

The "freedom" of a free polity = freedom of adjustment,—the admission of new elements, the free choice of men and means, the taking of a new situation as calmly as an old one, to meet it as steadily.

This freedom to adjust *has* so *eased critical,* and even *revolutionary junctures for us* that we have deemed them occasions, not of radical, but of conservative action

E.g. *the establishment of the Union* ⎱ the times of *Washing·*
    the re-establishment of the Union ⎰ *ton* and of *Lincoln.*

And now, shall we lose heart? *Avoid two things*
(1) A *sullen dismay*
(2) A *debonnair and irresponsible confidence*

A particular duty rests, as in the past, *upon men of education and of cultivated vision,*—upon the colleges.

A *burden, but* a burden to be carried with courage,—with the steadied confidence that is bred by sustained and watchful effort.   (19 Feby)[2]

WWhw MS. (WP, DLC).
   [1] The Editors have been unable to find a news report of this address.
   [2] Wilson's composition date.

From Thomas McAdory Owen[1]

My dear Sir: Carrollton, Alabama.   Feb. 20, 1899.

I have the honor to inform you of your nomination to corresponding membership in the Alabama Historical Society. No expense is attached. Your sympathy and cooperation in our work, however, is expected, with such contributions to our library of your own literary work as you may make. Please advise me of your acceptance at an early day.

The Society is now in excellent condition and has an encouraging future.   Very truly yours,   Thomas M. Owen.

TLS (WP, DLC).
   [1] Lawyer, historian, collector of southern Americana, and Secretary of the Alabama Historical Society. Owen was the prime mover in the establishment in 1901 of the Alabama State Department of Archives and History, the first such state agency in the United States. He served as its first director.

To Thomas McAdory Owen

My dear Sir,   Princeton, New Jersey, 23 February, 1899.

Allow me to acknowledge with very great appreciation your letter of the twentieth, notifying me of my election to corresponding membership in the Alabama Historical Society. I accept the election with real pleasure, and feel that the Society has done me a great honour.

I shall hope for the Society a long life and an increasing success in the too long neglected work of recording the detailed history of the South.

With much regard and appreciation,
                         Very truly Yours,   Woodrow Wilson

WWTLS (T. M. Owen Papers, A-Ar).

From Charles Scribner

Dear Mr. Wilson: [New York] February 24, 1899

You may remember some years ago we exchanged letters about your history.[1] You then thought that the work would occupy several years and that an arrangement for the work at that time would be premature. Are you prepared now to take up this question again? It would give us particular pleasure to act as your publishers and we should hope to arrange all questions in a way thoroughly satisfactory to you. I think that the interest in all questions connected with American history has greatly increased during the past few years and the market for the book is correspondingly greater.

Yours sincerely   Charles Scribner

TLS (Letterpress Books, Charles Scribner's Sons Archives, NjP).
  1 That is, Wilson's projected history of the United States, about which see the Editorial Note, "Wilson's 'Short History of the United States,'" Vol. 8. For the earlier exchange, see C. Scribner to WW, May 9, 1894, and WW to C. Scribner, May 11, 1894, both in Vol. 8.

A Newspaper Report of a Talk at the Hill School

[Feb. 25, 1899]

ADDRESS BY PROFESSOR WILSON
AT POTTSTOWN.

Professor Woodrow Wilson delivered an address last Wednesday morning [February 22] before the Hill School at Pottstown, Pa. His subject was "Patriotism," and he spoke in part as follows:

"There are some words which attract as if they were living things. The word Liberty is one of these, and the word Patriotism. There are times when words spring to a new significance, and this is such a time for the word Patriotism.

["]Conceived aright, Patriotism is not a sentiment, though it breeds and expresses itself in a sentiment. It is an energy of character, which manifests itself and seeks its object beyond the circle of self-interest; a sort of thoughtful energy which looks abroad for its satisfaction.

["]If a sentiment, it is a sentiment based on principle, a principle of service. It is a sentiment, not of taste, but of devotion. Its object is not self-pleasing. Devotion has always definite duties, based upon the nature of its object; and the country must be served in the same spirit as the friend.

["]The object of national life is character. The nation has only this world. In days of achievement, rough and unthoughtful strength suffices. In days of peace and dull routine, insight and vision are needed.

["]Ours is pre-eminently an intellectual and a debating policy [polity]. We should understand and be ready to demonstrate it.

We should be studious of the life of the nation, fearless in criticism, and partisans of the right."

Printed in the *Daily Princetonian*, Feb. 25, 1899.

To Charles Scribner

Princeton, New Jersey,

My dear Mr. Scribner,   28 February, 1899.

It is very kind of you to revert to the matter of my history; but, unhappily, only a small part of the work is yet written.[1] Soon after our last consideration of the matter I turned aside from it to write a Life of Washington. That done, tasks connected with the Sesquicentennial drew me off for a number of months. Since then I have been devoting my writing time, so far as I could, to the composition of a still briefer work on American History, for the Harpers, whose object is to win a place in southern schools which have become discontented with what they regard as "northern" views of the war and are much too apt to swing to the opposite extreme and use partisan "southern" accounts of the matters in controversy. So many men of influence in the South had urged the task upon me that it came to look like a sort of public duty. It remains to be seen whether the southern school committees will like it or not.[2]

The result of all which is, that my "Short History" has stood still, and must yet stand still for some months to come. I do not know, indeed just when I shall take it up again. My thought has filled to an almost uncomfortable degree with other matters of late, and I cannot wait much longer to do the work for which I have for some years been waiting to become mature enough.[3] The History must some time out, for I am full of matter on the subject; but the time when it shall out has now grown very uncertain.

I am none the less obliged to your [you] for your letter; and appreciate very much your wish to publish for me.

With much regard,   Sincerely Yours, Woodrow Wilson

WWTLS (Charles Scribner's Sons Archives, NjP).

[1] For an account of Wilson's progress on this work, see the Editorial Note, "Wilson's 'Short History of the United States,'" Vol. 8.

[2] See the Editorial Note, "Wilson's History of the United States for Schools," Vol. 10.

[3] That is, his projected "Philosophy of Politics," about which see the Editorial Note, "Wilson's First Treatise on Democratic Government," Vol. 5.

To Hunsdon Cary[1]

My dear Mr. Cary,   Princeton, New Jersey, 28 February, 1899.

It affords me pleasure to answer your letter of the twenty-fifth.[2] It is rather hard to pick out from almost a multitude of books on the subject just the one work on the development of English institutions which it is most interesting and instructive to use as a summary. Mr. Hannis Taylor's two volumes ("The Origin and Growth of the English Constitution," Houghton, Mifflin, & Co., Boston) is every way excellent; Mr. Freeman's little volume with almost the same title is stimulating and suggestive; Mr. Walter Bagehot's "English Constitution" is indispensable for the later phases of English constitutional growth and the real functions of the Cabinet under the parliamentary system. Perhaps, on the whole, you could not do better than begin with Professor Jesse Macy's "English Constitution," published in 1897 by the Macmillan Company, and read from that out.

I am by no means so well acquainted with the bibliography of English economic history; but I should say that you would not go astray in reading, at the outset J. E. Thorold Rogers' lectures on "The Industrial and Commercial History of England," published in 1892 by the Putnams, at New York. Professor Rogers is by no means infallible in details, but his general guidance is sage enough. No doubt the best book on the subject is Professor W. J. Ashley's "English Economic History"; but it is much more detailed and is not yet complete.

With much regard, and very pleasant recollections of our meeting,[3]   Sincerely Yours,   Woodrow Wilson

TCL (RSB Coll., DLC).
[1] A lawyer of Richmond, Va.
[2] It is missing.
[3] Cary probably met Wilson during the latter's visit to Richmond, October 26-November 4, 1898, to deliver the Thomas Museum Endowment Lectures at Richmond College.

A News Item

[March 1, 1899]

FINAL PRELIMINARY DEBATE.

The final preliminary Harvard debate will be held to-night in Murray Hall at 7.30 o'clock. Prof. Ormond will preside and Professors Wilson, Daniels, Perry, Fine, and Harper will act as judges.

There will be eleven contestants, five to represent each Hall, and one post-graduate. The opening speeches will be six minutes and the rebuttals five minutes in length.[1]

Six men will be chosen who will continue to debate against each other in practice until the final team is picked. . . .[2]

Printed in the *Daily Princetonian*, March 1, 1899; one editorial headiing omitted.
[1] The question was "Resolved, That a formal alliance between the United States and Great Britain, for the protection and advancement of their common interests, is advisable."
[2] See the news report printed at March 8, 1899.

From George Washington Miles[1]

My dear Doctor: Radford, Va., March 4, 1899.

Recalling our correspondence of a year ago,[2] I write to say to you that the situation at the University is even more favorable now than it was then for us to offer you the same position which we offered you then. While formal action has not been taken by the Board [of Visitors] as it was at that time, yet I am fully aware of their feelings and am quite sure of the ground upon which I stand when I say to you that, if you have received any new light regarding this and are now disentangled and in a position to accept, that we can offer you the election at our June meeting; and if you do not want to take any administrative work upon you, but will accept a simple professorship there at $3,000.00 a year and a house, with a light schedule of lectures, I am sure I could carry out your wishes in this matter. Everything is prospering with us at the University of Virginia. We have this year 589 students, about 125 of whom are in the law class. We confidently expect to have 700 students there next year, and are moving forward along all lines. It is the desire of the Board to make this law school one of the most powerful and influential and popular in the United States. I should like for you to associate your name and influence and your excellent work with us in reaching this goal. I do not write this to stir up a matter which has been adjudicated, or to further embarrass you; but I write it simply to recall a remark in one of your letters of a year ago wherein you said that "if this offer had come to you a year later you might be in a better position to accept it." I write now to say that here it is a year later; and you can either take the chairmanship of the faculty with the professorship in law at $4,000.00 a year and a house, or the professorship in law with a light schedule of lectures at $3,000.00 a year and a house.

I want to say that Mr. Minor[3] used to make as much as $5,000. ih [in] one summer out of his summer law school, and by joining in this work there you could no doubt largely add to this modest salary.

With cordial regards, I am

Very truly yours,   Geo. W. Miles

TLS (WP, DLC) with WWT notation on env.: "Answered 7 March, 1899."
    [1] Founder and Headmaster of St. Albans School, Radford, Va.; newspaper publisher and railroad promoter; and member of the Board of Visitors of the University of Virginia.
    [2] It is printed in Volume 10 and concerned an offer to Wilson of the chairmanship of the faculty of the University of Virginia and a professorship in the Law School of that institution.
    [3] John Barbee Minor, long-time law professor at the University of Virginia.

A News Item

[March 8, 1899]

PRELIMINARY DEBATE TO-DAY.

The first of the series of practice debates, preliminary to the contest with Harvard, will be held at 2.30 p.m. to-day, in Murray Hall. The six men who were chosen last week have been divided into two teams and will speak in the following order.

Affirmative—A. S. Weston '99, J. A. Jones '00, J. H. Northrup '99.

Negative—S. B. Scott '00, N. S. Reeves '99, J. H. Chidester '99.

Professors Fine, Wilson, and Daniels will act as judges. Both the first speeches and the rebuttals will be of the same length as in the Harvard Debate.[1]

Printed in the *Daily Princetonian*, March 8, 1899.
    [1] The Princeton-Harvard debate took place in Alexander Hall on April 5, 1899. Princeton defended the affirmative side of the question and lost the debate.

From Frank Louis Sevenoak[1]

My dear Wilson   New York, March 20, 1899

In the absence of Mr. Brett[2] your letter comes to me for attention.

The Dictionary of National Biography sells at $3.75 per volume list from which price professors receive a discount of 10%. I can secure a set for you at 20% off only asking that you will say nothing about the price—your cash offer and plan of paying the balance is satisfactory.

Some sets (so far as issued, 53 vols) are slightly damaged by rubbing &c but for a working library are just as good as any one would want and if such a set would be satisfactory I can probably get 25% off for you on those now in stock.

Let me know what you wish, and I will give the matter personal attention.   Sincerely yours   F. L. Sevenoak

ALS (WP, DLC).
    [1] Princeton '79, at this time employed by the Macmillan Company of New York.
    [2] George Platt Brett, president of the Macmillan Company of New York.

Francis Landey Patton to Grover Cleveland

My dear Mr. Cleveland: [Princeton, N.J.] March 23rd 1899

    Mr. H. S. Little of Trenton[1] as a mark of his admiration of you & his appreciation of your public services desires to give Ten Thousand dollars to Princeton University, with the understanding that the income of this fund is to be paid to you as an honorarium for such lectures or addresses as you may from year to year feel disposed to give the students of the University.

    Permit me to say that I very sincerely hope that you will be willing to render the University the great service which the acceptance of this lectureship would imply.

    We should not wish this undertaking to be at all burdensome to you; but I feel that if two or three times a year you would consent to talk to a picked body of men in the Senior Class on some phase of the administration of our government, and out of your large experience you would thereby confer a very unique benefit upon the University. Professor Woodrow Wilson concurs with me very fully in this judgment.

    We of course should wish to have the honour of announcing these lectures or addresses in our Catalogue but in publishing your name we should be careful to do it in a way that would comport entirely with the dignity that belongs to your position as an ex-President of the United States.

    I beg you not to give yourself the trouble of answering this letter. In a few days I hope to give myself the pleasure of calling upon you and we can then talk the matter over.[2]

    I am with great respect very faithfully yours
                                        Francis L. Patton

ALS (Patton Letterpress Books, University Archives, NjP).
    [1] Henry Stafford Little, Princeton, 1844, lawyer and businessman of Trenton, N.J. Trustee of Princeton University from 1901 until his death in 1904. He also gave the funds to build Stafford Little Hall, an undergraduate dormitory.
    [2] Cleveland did accept the lectureship. He delivered two lectures on "The Independence of the Executive" in 1900 and two on "The Venezuelan Boundary Controversy" in 1901. His next and last appearance as Stafford Little Lecturer did not occur until 1904, when he gave a single address on "The Government in the Chicago Strike of 1894." Since Cleveland's death in 1908, the Stafford Little Lecture Fund has been used to support an annual series of lectures by some distinguished visitor, usually in the areas of public affairs or the social sciences. For a brief characterization of Cleveland's lectures, see Allan Nevins, *Grover Cleveland: A Study in Courage* (New York, 1932), p. 736.

From Frank Louis Sevenoak

My dear Wilson   New York, March 24, 1899

Books will be shipped to-morrow by freight as it will only require about a day longer & there will be I am told a considerable saving in charges. Think you will find the set O.K. Will send contract in a day or two

Sincerely yours   F. L. Sevenoak

ALS (WP, DLC).

From the Minutes of the Princeton University Faculty

5 5' P.M. Tuesday, March 28th 1899

The Faculty met at the call of the President who announced that the meeting was called to take action in reference to the funeral of the Rev. James Ormsbee Murray, D.D., LL.D., Dean of the University, whose death occurred at 9 15' A.M., Monday, March 27th, 1899. . . .

Professors West, Woodrow Wilson, Westcott, Thompson and Libbey were appointed a Committee of arrangements in reference to the funeral which will take place tomorrow afternoon. . . .

Francis Landey Patton to Nancy Fowler McCormick[1]

My dear Mrs. McCormick   [Princeton, N.J.] 4 April 1899

. . . You will be glad to know that I have just been informed that a chair of politics is to be endowed in the sum of $100 000. If we can find a man as good as Professor Woodrow Wilson, we shall have a strong department of Jurisprudence & Politics.

The parties who give the money enjoin secrecy upon me: or rather they are anxious that their names should not be generally known in connection with this gift; but I dare say you know about it already; and if you do not there is no harm in my saying to you confidentially that the givers are John W. & Robert Garrett.[2]

It is a very handsome gift; is it not[?]

I am my dear Mrs McCormick

Very sincerely yours   Francis L. Patton

ALS (Patton Letterpress Books, University Archives, NjP).
  [1] Nancy, or Nettie, Fowler McCormick, widow of the elder Cyrus Hall McCormick and mother of Wilson's friend and classmate, the younger Cyrus Hall McCormick.
  [2] John Work Garrett, B.S., Princeton, 1895, and Robert Garrett, B.S., Princeton, 1897. At this time, John W. Garrett was a partner in the banking firm of Robert Garrett & Sons of Baltimore, founded in 1820, and Robert was a graduate student

in history at The Johns Hopkins University. John W. Garrett later had a distinguished career as a diplomat, while his brother Robert became a partner in the family banking firm. Both were to be frequent benefactors of Princeton, and Robert served as a trustee of the University from 1905 to 1946.

From the Minutes of the Princeton Academic Faculty

5 5′ P.M., Wednesday, April 5, '99.

. . . Professors Daniels, Wilson and Perry were appointed to confer with representatives of the Literary Societies in reference to the date of choosing sides for The Lynde Debate at Commencement.[1]

"Minutes of the Academic Faculty, Princeton University, 1898-1905," bound minute book (University Archives, NjP).
[1] About the Lynde Debate, see Wilson's diary for June 23, 1876, n. 1, Vol. 1; for the committee's report, see the Princeton Academic Faculty Minutes printed at April 19, 1899.

A News Report of an Address at the Hartford Theological Seminary

[April 6, 1899]

THIRD CAREW LECTURE.

Professor Woodrow Wilson Talks About "Democracy."

The third lecture in the Carew Course at Hosmer Hall was given last evening by Professor Woodrow Wilson of Princeton University, his subject being "Democracy." A large audience listened with interest and pleasure to the discourse. . . .[1]

Printed in the *Hartford Courant*, April 6, 1899.
[1] Here follows a summary of "Democracy," printed at Dec. 5, 1891, Vol. 7.

To Mark Antony DeWolfe Howe[1]

My dear Sir,   Princeton, 17 April, 1899

I am sincerely gratified that you should desire me to write one of the "Beacon Biographies." I have carefully considered the matter,—for the proposition is attractive,—but my first thought is inevitably my last: I am too busy. Tasks press which must be done at once and which I cannot in conscience leave within several years.

With sincere thanks and regrets,
Very truly Yours,   Woodrow Wilson

ALS (M. A. DeWolfe Howe Papers, MH).

1 At this time Associate Editor of *The Youth's Companion* and Editor of the "Beacon Biographies of Eminent Americans," a series of pocket-sized volumes published by Small, Maynard & Company of Boston. A total of thirty-one appeared under Howe's editorship from 1899 to 1910.

From the Minutes of the Princeton Academic Faculty

5 5′ P.M., Wednesday, April 19th, 1899.

. . . The Committee appointed to confer with representatives of the Literary Societies in regard to the Lynde Debate reported the following Recommendations which were adopted;

Regulations for the Lynde Debate;

I. That the subjects be posted two weeks before the Debate, (instead of ten days), and

II. That the time of the speeches be reduced to to [sic] ten (10) minutes for the first speech and to six (6) minutes for the second speech. . . .[1]

1 The Lynde Prize Debate was held in Alexander Hall on June 13, 1899. The question was "Resolved, That the United States should permanently retain and govern the Philippine Islands"; the winners were James Henry Northup of Augusta, N.J., Conover English of Elizabeth, N.J., and Alfred Sewall Weston of West Mount Vernon, Me.

From Horace Elisha Scudder

My dear Wilson   [Cambridge, Mass.] 26 April, 1899

Houghton, Mifflin & Co. have been making in conjunction with a London house a volume entitled "England and America after Independence."[1] It is a study and narrative of the diplomatic relations since 1783, and it may be available for use in college work. The author, an Englishman, frankly says in his Preface that his study has led him to a very favorable view of English diplomacy, and he emphasizes his position by more or less disparagement of the American share in diplomatic relations.

In the process of proofs, the author's attention has been called repeatedly to infelicities and partisan statements, and he has made a great many alterations. Nevertheless, on having the book all before us, we are haunted with the suspicion that it may be "offensively partisan," and thus a book which it is undesirable for this house to publish. Naturally, we wish to carry out the original design if possible, but it is better to call a halt at this stage if there is reason ultimately for chagrin at publication.

We want therefore a fresh and unbiassed mind to be exercised on it, and I write to ask if you will undertake an examination of it—we can send you the entire book in proof—to determine especially on the fairness of the book as well as its accuracy, and whether a self-respecting American house may properly publish it. Incidentally, also, we should be glad to know, if in your judgment the book is likely to have a college demand.[2]

Of course the house does not ask you to do this work for nothing. Perhaps you will put $25 worth of examination into it.

Sincerely yours   H. E. Scudder.

ALS (Houghton Mifflin Letterpress Books, MH).

[1] Edward Smith, *England and America after Independence: A Short Examination of Their International Intercourse,* 1783-1872 (London: A. Constable & Co., 1900).

[2] It is not known whether Wilson read the proofs. However, Houghton Mifflin did not publish the book; in fact, there does not seem to have been an American edition.

From William James Ashley[1]

My dear Wilson,   Edinburgh April 26. 99.

During the vacation you have a large choice of excellent rooms in Oxford—except when, in alternate years, there is a Summer School being held, as happens this year.[2] During the middle weeks of August this year (I think that is the time) most of the good lodgings will be preengaged; but even then you would have no serious difficulty in getting comfortable accommodation—though I imagine you would prefer to visit Oxford at some other time.

If you go up by an early train you can spend an hour or so in seeing half a dozen sets of rooms (with cards in their windows) & choose for yourself. The *Old Vicarage* next to St Giles' Church is delightfully quaint, and rooms are usually to be had there; or you might enjoy the sight of it more if you had rooms in one of the houses opposite—26 Banbury Rd., for instance, I have heard people speak well of. There are many good lodgings with charming outlooks in "St Giles"; and we were once very comfortable in one of the cottages in the quiet little court-yard numbered 10 St Giles. There are excellent rooms (dear for Oxford, but cheap for America!) in the Broad St., next to Kettel Hall (now part of Trinity) where Stubbs lived many years, & between it and Blackwell's well known bookshop. In the Parks' Road, almost opposite the Museum is "Museum Cottage" (so I think it is called), which has a charming & unsuspected garden. In Holywell, also, there are lots of good lodgings. It is an "embarras des richesses." In arranging, you must enquire about the subsidiary charges, besides rent—e.g. kitchen fire. Mrs. Wilson may either market herself, & then the landlady cooks &c.—this is the cheaper plan; or she may tell the landlady each morning what she would like, &

the landlady will get it. Some landladies are harpies; but most are excellent personages & considering their temptations, justify an optimistic view of human nature!

You doubtless know that all the college gardens are open without charge, & you will frequent those of New College, Magdalen, Ch. Ch., Worcester, Wadham & Trinity. The Cathedral services go on throughout the year. Get my friend Wells' admirable little guide book.[3]

We are now settled in Hampstead, London N.W. at Bentham House, Heath St. Let us know when you are in London, & you must come to us for a meal & meet Dr. Birkbeck Hill,[4] & let us put you up to everything worth knowing about Oxford![5]

Truly yours   W. J. Ashley

ALS (WP, DLC).
  [1] Professor of Economic History at Harvard University; a student, Fellow, and Lecturer at Oxford University, 1878-88.
  [2] Wilson's letter to which this is a reply is missing, but Wilson had obviously asked Ashley about accommodations in Oxford. Ashley's letter yields the first evidence that the Wilsons planned to go to Great Britain during the summer of 1899. However, by the time of sailing, the plans had been altered, with Stockton Axson accompanying Wilson on a bicycle trip around Britain while Mrs. Wilson remained at home. Wilson later indicated that it was his wife and Jenny Davidson Hibben who had persuaded him to go abroad for a much-needed rest. See WW to EAW, Aug. 9, 1899.
  [3] Joseph Wells, *Oxford and Its Colleges* (London, 1897).
  [4] George Birkbeck Norman Hill (1835-1903), specialist in the life and works of Samuel Johnson, many of which he brought out in critical editions.
  [5] Wilson did visit Ashley while he was in London. See WW to EAW, Aug. 4, 1899.

From John Emerich Edward Dalberg Acton, Lord Acton[1]

Sir,   Cambridge May 10 1899

Acting on behalf of the Syndics of the University Press, I venture to approach you with a request for your help in an important work they have undertaken.[2]

They are preparing a modern History on a large scale, from the end of the fifteenth century; and propose to dedicate an early volume to America. Several of your countrymen have been good enough to promise contributions; and there is one chapter which I know I could not do better than obtain from you.

It is the chapter I propose provisionally to call State Rights.

I imagine it beginning about 1850, and ending at the election of Lincoln, and the main object would be to explain the political substance of the dispute that then ripened. I daresay you would consider it necessary to recapitulate somewhat, and to describe, in this connection, the old debate between Webster and Calhoun, and the way in which the policy of Calhoun developed, among parties.

Quite apart from its consequences for America, it is a very important part of the history of political science.

We should be extremely gratified if we could induce you to discuss the matter, and to do it, so far as the ten years of national history allow, from this general point of view. We suppose a chapter to include somewhere about 17,000. words, and we should be glad to have the MS. early in the autumn. We give no footnotes, and we are anxious to be as plain as possible to the largest number of readers; but we seek in every instance to obtain the aid of an expert.[3]

I remain   Very Truly Yours   Acton

ALS (WP, DLC).
    [1] At this time Regius Professor of Modern History at Cambridge University.
    [2] *The Cambridge Modern History* (13 vols., New York and London, 1903-12).
    [3] Wilson did contribute this chapter, which is printed at Dec. 20, 1899. His copy of the contract for this chapter, dated Dec. 10, 1902, is in WP, DLC. It provided for payment at the rate of ten shillings per printed page of approximately 520 words per page.

To Robert Bridges

My dear Bobby,   Princeton, 13 May, 1899

Of course you understand that you and the rest of the usual gang are to stay with me at the Reunion.[1] We are counting on your coming, and a welcome awaits you as big, as cordial, and as inevitable as you can imagine. We couldn't enjoy the Reunion ourselves if we did not have you all here under our own roof.

As ever,   Affectionately Yours,   Woodrow Wilson[2]

ALS (Meyer Coll., DLC).
    [1] The twentieth reunion of the Class of 1879.
    [2] For virtually the same letters, see WW to C. A. Talcott, May 13, 1899, ALS (WC, NjP), and WW to R. R. Henderson, May 13, 1899, ALS (WC, NjP).

A News Item

[May 17, 1899]

Professor Woodrow Wilson has been elected one of the vice-presidents of the New York Alumni Association of the University of Virginia, where he took his law course after graduating at Princeton in the Class of 1879.

Printed in the *Daily Princetonian*, May 17, 1899.

A Newspaper Report of a Speech on Politics

[May 19, 1899]

PHILADELPHIAN SOCIETY.[1]

Professor Woodrow Wilson Addresses the Students in Murray Hall.

The regular meeting of the Philadelphian Society was addressed last night by Professor Woodrow Wilson, on "Politics." He spoke in part as follows:

There are two ways in which the subject of politics may be treated: first, as a life-work or career; and second, as the duty of every citizen of any country.

As a career, the political life is a very dangerous one for a man who has no independent means of support; first, because our politics are very complex, and there are no means of placing direct responsibility; secondly, for the reason that men will not keep in touch with politics at all times, no matter how much they may be interested in political questions. The necessary result of this is the party machine. If the man in public office should act contrary to the wishes of the machine, he is placed in a bad position unless he has independent means.

The man who has an income aside from that obtained in his political life is in a position to speak and act for those measures which he considers are for the best interests of his country. Even when not in office he can give time and attention to those questions which are of national import and thus keep before the public notice and influence, to a large extent, public opinion. If, then, a man should enter politics without means, he should be careful of his conduct when in office and be ready to sacrifice himself for principle, if need be.

However, most of us must act in the capacity of private citizens, and the question which comes before us is, "What does Citizenship require of a college-bred man?" First, his education should enable him to draw useful lessons from the history of the past and to apply them to the needs of the present. Second: The college man should be skilled in right criticism, and his criticism must be practical and based on experience. . . .[2]

Printed in the *Daily Princetonian*, May 19, 1899.
  [1] About this organization, see n. 1 to the news item printed at Nov. 1, 1890, Vol. 7.
  [2] There is a brief WWT outline of this talk, dated May 18, 1899, in WP, DLC.

Notes for an After-Dinner Address[1]

Princeton Inn, 19 May, 1899.

Dinner Society of Colonial Wars.

No more vitalizing thing than *to perpetuate the memory* of the colonial wars. They were parts of *a nationalizing process*, compelling separate and diverse colonies to think upon one another, with sympathy and with purpose.

> *The political capacity consists* in no small degree in this: in the power and the instinct to *generalize the wrongs and the rights of others and translate them* into the terms of a Cause, a duty laid upon ourselves, though they now touch our personal interests not at all
> *Virginia as forward as Massachusetts* in the Rev.

Significance of the names of the colonial wars: "King William's War," "Queen Anne's War," "King George's War,"—none of our making, a duty made for us; and then, as if at last a change had come and we were ourselves touched nearly, the "French and Indian War," as much ours as anybody's.

We condemn war now, but we grow no less jealous in the *celebration* of the *wars that are past*. And the instinct is a sound and honourable one. It is in this case a celebration not only of bravery, self-sacrifice, and success, but of *coöperation* also.

The moral is not hard to give a present-day significance to: *The colonies were diverse* and needed to be drawn together.

Are we not still diverse? Are there not wars to be waged against *prejudice*. Is not a cure of sympathy and common understanding to be found for *sectionalism? Can we enjoy peace while there is division?*

WWT MS. (WP, DLC).

[1] Delivered at the sixth annual meeting of the Society of Colonial Wars at the Princeton Inn on May 19, 1899. There is a brief report of this affair in the *Princeton Press*, May 20, 1899.

From Houghton, Mifflin and Company, with Enclosure

Dear Sir: Boston, May 26, 1899

We have your favor of yesterday,[1] enclosing a letter from M. Max Boucard, which we herewith return, and shall take pleasure in writing him by to-day's mail expressing our hearty approval of his making and publishing a French translation of your "Congressional Government."

Yours very truly,

Houghton, Mifflin & Co.   [per] F. J. T.

TL (WP, DLC).
¹ It is missing.

From Max Boucard¹

Sir,   Paris le 25th of January 1899

Wishing to popularize in France your remarkable work "Congressional Government a Study in American Politics" I come to ask your authorization to have it translated.

In a purely scientific point of view, I should like to make known to the French learned world the best works upon foreign public laws, and yours is one of those by which I should like to begin, it being very often refered to though so little read in our country.

Hoping for a favourable answer I beg you to accept my thanks and believe me, yours,²   M. Boucard

ALS (WP, DLC).
¹ Maître des Requêtes du Conseil d'État; political scientist, author of *Éléments de la science des finances et de la législation financière française* (Paris, 1896); and editor with Gaston Jèze of the "Bibliothèque Internationale de Droit Public."
² Boucard did oversee the publication of a French edition of *Congressional Government* in 1900. For bibliographical information, see M. Boucard to WW, July 28, 1900, n. 1.

From John Emerich Edward Dalberg Acton,
Lord Acton

My dear Sir,   Cambridge June 4, 1899

I write at once to thank you for your very kind reply,¹ hoping that this may reach you before you leave home.

I am fortunate in having secured, for that complicated period, the assistance of such a specialist as you are; and I am happy to say that we shall be in time if I receive the MS. in the course of November.

But I greatly regret to be obliged to say that I shall be abroad when you come to England, and shall miss the opportunity of seeing you, and of discussing this, and many other matters, with you. My colleague in the editorship is Dr. Ward,² late Principal of the Victoria University in Manchester, now settled 77 Addison Road, Kensington. When you are in London, I hope you will find it possible to have an interview with him.[3]

The only thing that occurs to me to add, if I did not mention it before, is that we hope to have the entire history of the States in those ten years, centering, as it does, in the approach of the conflict. You cannot tell us too much of the philosophy of government involved in it.

I remain   Very sincerely your's   Acton

ALS (WP, DLC).
    [1] It is missing.
    [2] Adolphus William Ward, historian, editor, and translator, whose interests ranged over many fields. He became Master of Peterhouse, Cambridge, in 1900 and upon Acton's death in 1902 editor-in-chief of *The Cambridge Modern History*. He was later co-editor of *The Cambridge History of English Literature* and of *The Cambridge History of British Foreign Policy, 1783-1919*.
    [3] Wilson was in London, August 1-4, 1899, but was not able to see Ward either there or elsewhere during his trip. See A. W. Ward to WW, Aug. 12, 1899.

To Charles Andrew Talcott

My dear Charlie,   Princeton, 4 June, 1899

I can't tell you how disappointed I am,—and I know that "the crowd" will miss you and wish for you every minute of the re-union. It is *too* bad! Remember that, if at the last moment,—or at any other moment,—you find it possible to break away and come, *there is room for you and a joyous welcome*. You may be sure nobody will be put in your place: it will be kept for you. Watch for a chance of escape as you would watch for a chance to show your affection for us; and don't stop to send us word,—just *come*.

In haste, deep regret, and warmest affection,
            As ever,   Faithfully Yours,   Woodrow Wilson

ALS (WC, NjP).

To Robert Randolph Henderson

My dear Bob.,   Princeton, New Jersey, 5 June, 1899.

Excuse machine-made. I am in the midst of Commencement jobs, and must take the quickest way.

Have you had the whooping cough? My children have it; Mrs. Wilson has taken it from them; I am immune. I was in hopes that the thing would be virtually over by the end of this week; but I now see that it will not be.

It does not make any one of the patients feel in the least ill; it does not interfere with domestic operations in the least,—or even with domestic comfort and convenience; the whole thing is on the mend; and it [is] absolutely and only for your sake that I write. If you have had it, all right. The doctors tell me you cannot take it away to anybody else.

Please write me, my dear fellow, whether this makes any difference to you, and whether I must place you elsewhere. It will be a sad day for me if I do have to! You must understand that it is absolutely true that it does not affect our convenience one way or the other.

In haste, chagrin, and great affection,
Faithfully Yours,   Woodrow Wilson

WWTLS (WC, NjP).

.

An Outline of a Projected Treatise

Mem., 5 June, 1899.

STATESMANSHIP.

Studies in Politics.

I.   Statesmanship: A Study in Political Action and Leadership. Systematic action of parties (Mr. A. L. Lowell's Study of English party organization)[1]

II.   Political Stability: A Study in the Nature, Sources, and Functions of Law.

III.   Political Liberty.

IV.   Political Privilege: A Study in Social Motive and Capacity.

V.   Political Progress: A Study in Statesmanship.

VI.   Political Prejudice: A Study in Social Dynamics.

VII.   Political Expediency: A Study in Statesmanship.

VIII.   Political Morality: A Study in Statesmanship.

IX.   Practical Politics: A Study in Statesmanship. Systematic action of parties (Mr. A. L. Lowell's study of English party organization)

WWT, WWsh, and WWhw outline in the notebook described at Aug. 28, 1892, Vol. 8.

[1] Wilson was presumably referring to Abbott Lawrence Lowell's forthcoming study, "The Influence of Party upon Legislation in England and America," *Annual Report of the American Historical Association for the Year 1901* (2 vols., Washington, 1902), I, 319-542.

From a Wilson Notebook

[c. June 5-Sept. 15, 1899]

Notes on *Statesmanship*. 1899

Texts

"A people is but the attempt of many
To rise to the completer life of one;
And those who live as models for the mass
Are singly of more value than they all."
Browning—Luria.

["]Drill the raw world for the march of mind,
Till crowds at length be sane and crowns be just."
• Tennyson.[1]

"Radicalism is the last and most dangerous enemy of
    Republicanism."
Jno. C. Calhoun, Letter to S. L. Gouverneur.[2]

Aristotle conceived the real problem of Politics to be, How, out of heterogeneous elements, to make the best combinations for moral progress. (See p. 7, post).[3]

Fundamental Ideas

Private Law has been described (by Thorold Rogers) as "a practical condition of life."[4] Public Law, by contrast, is a practical condition of politics.

In it, besides, the ideals of a people disclose themselves. In it are to be discerned the dynamic as well as the static forces of a nation's life.

A study of Public Law is a study of organic and functional development, and also (so far as it is a study of constitutionalism) of the emergence within the body politic of the political and social rights of individuals—as contrasted with the rights and prerogatives of 'estates' or of classes.

The life of a State cannot be summed up or exhausted in its laws. "The laws reach but a very little way," and every government must be a government of and by *men*. Laws may define, determine, balance, guide, but they do not contain life, they only express it. Institutions are subsequent to character: they do not create it, but are created and sustained by it.

After being successfully established, however, they both confirm and modify national character, forming in no small degree both national thought and national purpose.

The State is an abiding natural relationship. It is neither a mere convenience nor a mere necessity: neither a merely voluntary association nor a mere corporation, nor any other artificial thing, created for a special purpose and from time to time arbitrarily altered in form and function. It is an eternal and natural expression and embodiment of a form of life higher than that of the individual,—that common life which gives leave an opportunity to individual life, makes it possible, makes it full and complete. This notwithstanding the fact that its object may (at any rate arguably) be said to be, not its own best life, but the development of the individual in all his higher capacities. What the State exists for the sake of is, no doubt, a question by itself.

The "constitutional" State (see notes on "Constitutional" Government)[5]

The "constitutional" state, as here analyzed, obviously belongs to an advanced stage of development; but it suggests the true theory of *every* state. It is merely a question of more or less,—of a more or less definite, elaborate, conscious understanding between governors and governed.

Illustrate with Bagehot's description of a "constitutional statesman" (Peel)[6]

Themes and Topics
Central Topic,—key to the rest:
"Constitutional" Government.
Leadership (Historical sketch as in lectures on Constitutional Government, topics 2-6)
Sovereignty
"Popular sovereignty"—Democracy.
Actual Tasks of the State
Organs of the State: its Means and Methods of Action.
Written constitutions.
(See topical analysis of lectures on "Constitutional" Government.)

Text:
"I should suspend my congratulations on the new liberty of France, until I was informed how it had been combined with government; with public force; with the discipline and obedience of armies; with the collection of an effective and well-distributed revenue; with morality and religion; with the solidity of property; with peace and order; with civil and social manners."—Burke, *Reflections*.[7]

"The end of Political Science is the supreme good; and Political

Science is concerned with nothing so much as with producing a certain character in the citizens, or, in other words, with making them good, and capable of performing noble actions." *Aristotle*: Nichomachean Ethics (Welldon's trans.),[8] 22.

He therefore considered education as a political science,—and a branch or part of the art and science of legislation. "Legislation must aim at the training of the habits to make good citizens.". (Comp. Welldon, as above, p. 35.)

Note:

For a time the press took the place of the parliament or Congress as an instrument of instruction and perhaps of conviction and the tendency was for representative assemblies to go over debate and seek to register opinion developed in discussion outside themselves.

This tendency has worked itself out and given us all there was in it. Now the press itself has changed: it is nothing more than a myriad of voices, news and rumour and scarcely offers and expresses any definite mass of opinion or educated motive of action at all. Yet the representative assembly is left with the marks of the old suppression upon it.

There never was any focus to the impulses begun by the press: that focus was founded, if founded at all, in the legislative bodies. Now there is nothing for legislative bodies to focus: nothing either within them or outside them. We have leaderless and motiveless government; and the time for the reconsideration of representative institutions has come, like an embarrassing necessity.

WWhw and WWsh in looseleaf notebook (WP, DLC).

[1] From Alfred Lord Tennyson, "Ode on the Death of the Duke of Wellington."

[2] John C. Calhoun to Samuel L. Gouverneur, May 25, 1823, printed in "Calhoun-Gouverneur Correspondence, 1823-1836," *Bulletin of the New York Public Library*, III (Aug. 1899), 325.

[3] That is, the passage from Aristotle's *Nicomachean Ethics* quoted below, beginning "The end of Political Science. . . ."

[4] The Editors have been unable to find this phrase in the works of Thorold Rogers.

[5] The notes for lectures in this course are printed at Sept. 19, 1898.

[6] Walter Bagehot, "The Character of Sir Robert Peel," in Forrest Morgan (ed.), *The Works of Walter Bagehot* (5 vols., Hartford, Conn., 1889), III, 1-41.

[7] Edmund Burke, *Reflections on the Revolution in France* (London, 1790).

[8] *The Nicomachean Ethics of Aristotle*, translated by James Edward Cowell Welldon (London, 1892).

To Walter Hines Page

My dear Mr. Page,   Princeton, New Jersey, 7 June, 1899.

If you had a chair of Politics to fill, newly founded[1] and purposely left elastic in respect of subject-matter to fit the special aptitudes of the incumbent selected, whom would you nominate?

It is hardly necessary to say that it is no part of our plan to teach politics from the politician's point of view. Our immediate object is to study the new world affairs into the midst of which we find the country thrown. We want, in the man, culture, scholarship, power without acidity, tolerance for the accomplished fact. Can you help us with a suggestion?

If you can, it will make me much your debtor.

With warm regard,

Faithfully Yours,   Woodrow Wilson

WWTLS (W. H. Page Papers, MH).
 [1] About the founding of this chair, see F. L. Patton to Nancy F. McCormick, April 4, 1899.

To Albert Shaw

My dear Shaw,   Princeton, New Jersey. 8 June, 1899.

If you had a brand-new chair of Politics to fill,—a chair purposely made elastic as to subject-matter in order to be adjusted to the special attainments of the person chosen to fill it,—whom would you nominate?

I need hardly say that we are not looking for a politician. Indeed I do not think that we could afford to take any one who had been prominent in politics, unless it happened to be a man like William L. Wilson. We want a scholar, a man of culture, a man tolerant of accomplished fact. Our chief practical purpose is to study the new problems of government with which expansion has brought us face to face.

I should greatly value a suggestion from you. You are more apt than I am to know the personal equation of available men.

With warmest regard,

As ever   Faithfully Yours,   Woodrow Wilson.

Jenks[1] is just a little to much of a philistine for us.

TCL (in possession of Virginia Shaw English).
 [1] Jeremiah Whipple Jenks, Professor of Political Economy and Civil and Social Institutions at Cornell University.

From Max Boucard

Cher Monsieur,   Paris le 8 Juin 1899

Je tiens à venir vous remercier de suite de votre très aimable lettre, et de l'autorisation que vous nous donnez de traduire votre si remarquable ouvrage.

Nous acceptons avec un grand plaisir votre proposition de mettre le livre au courant des nouvelles lois,[1] et je suis certain que le public français fera un excellent et mérité accueil à votre bel ouvrage.

Veuillez recevoir encore, cher Monsieur, tous mes remerciements et me croire votre très dévoué,   M. Boucard

ALS (WP, DLC).
[1] Wilson tried to bring *Congressional Government* up to date in the preface that he wrote for the French edition. About this preface, see M. Boucard to WW, July 28, 1900, n. 1.

From Francis Landey Patton

My dear Professor Wilson: Princeton, N. J.   June 16, 1899

I have received your letter resigning from the Discipline Committee & asking that your name be not considered in the making up of the new Committee. I can well understand how natural it is for you after years of service to seek release from the peculiarly onerous duties of this Committee: but I am exceedingly sorry that you feel constrained to do so: and I know that it will be a great disappointment to Dean Winans[1] not to have your help & coöperation in the very important work which the Discipline Committee is called upon to do.[2]

I am   Very Sincerely yours   Francis L. Patton

ALS (WP, DLC).
[1] Samuel Ross Winans, Professor of Greek and Instructor in Sanskrit, who had succeeded James Ormsbee Murray as Dean of the Faculty.
[2] In fact, Wilson resigned because he thoroughly disapproved of the appointment of Winans as dean. See WW to Jenny D. Hibben, June 26, 1899; Jenny D. Hibben to WW, July 11, 1899; and J. G. Hibben to WW, July 20, 1899.

A Pocket Notebook

[c. June 18, 1899-c. Sept. 18, 1901]

Inscribed (WWhw) on front cover: "Woodrow Wilson 1899"
Contents (WWhw unless otherwise noted) include:

(a) Memorandum on a monument to himself, printed at July 19, 1899.

(b) Various names and addresses.

(c) "Articles Bought in England."

(d) Stories and cues for jokes.

(e) Memorandum of an interview with Henry Hobart Vail, printed at Jan. 20, 1900.

(f) Expenses of family trips to and from Muskoka, Ont., 1900 and 1901.

(g) Memoranda for "Philosophy of Politics," printed at Sept. 10, 1899.

(h) Random WWhw and WWsh notes and drafts for the "Colonies and Nation" series in *Harper's Magazine*, about which see the Editorial Note, "Wilson's History of the American People."

(i) Estimate of the cost of a summer home at Muskoka, printed at Aug. 29, 1900.

(j) WWsh (dated "Sept. 'oo") of opening paragraphs of "Democracy and Efficiency." The essay is printed at Oct. 1, 1900, Vol. 12.

(WP, DLC).

Two Letters from Ellen Axson Wilson

My own darling,   Princeton June 19/99

I did not realize until Mr. Hibben came back what a comfort it would be to me to have him see you off and tell me all about it.[1] It was almost as good—in some respects better!—than being there myself. And it is certainly reassuring to *know* that neither Stockton nor his wheel were left! How good too that the weather has been, and is, so perfectly delightful! Good for *me* as well as you; it is easier to be happy. I am doing finely. Indeed it was "fine" from the very beginning for *Mrs.* [Henry B.] *Fine* joined me as I came back from the station and sat a long time with me on the upper porch! After she left I made an excuse of the whaling-book, took it over to the Ricketts[2] and made a call there. The rest of the day and evening I read novels,—got through with three of them. One of them "The Well-Beloved" seems to have been recently perpetrated by Hardy. Tell Stockton if he has not read it he should do it by all means. It is a terrible warning for such as he! By the way, while Mrs. Fine was with me came a note from "Amos Hershey"[3] asking at what hour he could see you! He had arrived in Princeton the *night before*! Was not that a blissful escape for you? My pleasure in it relieved me of the last pang of regret at your departure!

Yesterday my friends rallied round me and I had a very good day. In the morning came Mr. Hibben and "Daisy."[4] Mr. Hibben told me all about you and Stockton. (He seems, by the way, to be much impressed and charmed with the latter) He also told me about *Miss Clay*.[5] Daisy is convinced that they will arrive on the other side engaged; but I smiled superior. *I* know the young gentleman. In the afternoon I went to Miss Ricketts and met all the Hibbens, Mr. Perry, & Mr. Dunn.[6] Mrs. Brown[7] would have been scandalized at the gathering,—and would not have considered the situation bettered when Mr. Dunn left to take the train. Then Mr. Perry took Mr. Ricketts off to see his *baby* and things became more normal.

Are not these great events to send across the ocean? But now comes something *really* important viz., the result of the game. It was eleven to four in Princeton's favour!—sis! boom! ah![8] Our men batted splendidly, Hillebrand[9] and Soutar[10] behaved as usual, and a freshman,[11]—I forget the name,[—] made a home run and brought in two other men. If the newsboy's uncle had not died I could have told you more, or even sent you the printed story. Thus mysteriously are human destinies linked together!

I had a nice little note from Mr. Bridges today thanking us for "the pleasantest holiday of his life," and enclosing a *dear* little Kodax picture of Jessie smiling. The letter I enclose[12] is the only one of consequence for you. I wrote to tell her you had sailed; I also answered one or two others for you. In fact I feel very virtuous for I spent the whole morning doing what I most dislike, viz. writing letters.

This evening Miss Ricketts has been over and I have had a very pleasant time, but the result is that it is now quite bed-time, so I must stop. We are all *very* well, and in excellent spirits. I love you inexpressibly my darling, my treasure! God bless you, dear love. God keep you safe & well & happy. Best love to dear Stockton,—and bestestest for you, from

Your devoted little wife.

From "Mrs. Woodrow Wilson, Princeton, New Jersey. U.S.A.["] You see I have not forgotten my former dead letter experience and am trying to make things convenient for them!

[1] Wilson and Stockton Axson had sailed from New York on June 17 on *S.S. Furnessia* of the Anchor Line.

[2] Eliza Getty Ricketts of 80 Stockton St., her daughter, Henrietta Ricketts, and one of her surviving sons, Louis Davidson Ricketts or Palmer Chamberlaine Ricketts, Jr.

[3] Amos Shartle Hershey, Assistant Professor of Political Science at Indiana University, whose note is missing.

[4] Mrs. Hibben's sister, Daisy Davidson.

[5] Mary E. Clay of Savannah, Ga., a passenger on *Furnessia*.

[6] William Ashenhurst Dunn, Princeton 1893, soon to become Professor of English at Adelphi College.

[7] Susan Dod Brown, of 65 Stockton St.

[8] The third and deciding baseball game of the annual series between Princeton and Yale, which was played at the Polo Grounds in New York on June 17.

[9] Arthur Ralph Thomas Hillebrand '00, the pitcher, who struck out nine Yale batters and got two hits himself.

[10] Herman Milton Suter, a special student, 1895-98.

[11] William Edgar Green '02, the first baseman.

[12] The enclosure is missing.

Princeton New Jersey   U.S.A.

My own darling,   July [June] 22/99

How good it is to count the days and know that your voyage at
the worst is half over,—that is, that the *worst* part of your absence,
—for me,—is half over,—the part when communication is entirely
cut off. And I am glad to hope and believe that our glorious
weather is extending out an indefinite distance into the Atlantic.
To be sure we have had one thunder-storm, but it was very good
for us and not serious enough to be bad for you, even had it
reached you. You should have seen me scudding before it across
the Stockton fields in Guinn's[1] hack, on my way to a dinner party
at the Sloanes.[2] I got there just in time to escape. Was invited to
meet Mr. & Mrs. Beaman.[3] He is Choate's law partner and had just
made the commencement address at Lawrenceville. He is one of
the most amusing men I ever met; we had a really jolly time,—
a small party & general conversation, so that we all had the benefit of Mr. Beaman's "vein." So you see I am not wearing the willow
for you at all! In fact I have been a devotee of pleasure this week;
every morning instead of asking myself as usual what I *ought* to
do that day, I shamelessly consult with myself as to what I *want*
to do! This morning I went to the Hibbens but missed her, as
usual,—the second time this week, the fourth in ten days. She is
a dreadful gad-about! I had settled with myself that in spite of
the frightfully long walk[4] I would go there often, since she was
sad, and I was lonely. But its no use, I never find her and get home
all tired out from the double walk with no rest between. This
morning however I stopped at the library and read poetry till one.
Then I brought home Mrs. Browning's general letters, the two vols.
published in '97,[5] and read them most of the afternoon. I found
them absorbingly interesting; am glad I never read them before
for they make a perfect sequel to the story in the recent vols.
Most of the letters to Miss Browning are filled with charming
anecdotes of the little "Pen" who seems to have been a fascinating,
imaginative, original, though sadly spoiled boy. It really hurts to
think that after all he should have turned out a rather poor creature. Speaking of letters, I am happy to report that so far your
correspondence has been next to nothing. I shall enclose the only
letter that needs to be forwarded.[6] I wrote Pres. Winston a line
to say that you had sailed but I would forward the letter. Since
the paragon he wants was not to be found for Princeton I doubt
if he will appear on the Texas horizon.

There is also a letter tonight from France thanking you for
the privilege of translating your book and also for your proposition

"de mettre le livre au courant des nouvelles lois."[7] I hope that doesn't mean any elaborate revision.

The only other letter was from Dunning;[8] his father has offered him a year in Europe and he wants to resign his fellowship and go at once, but would not do it without your consent. I went after tea tonight to consult Mr. [William F.] Magie and he thought he had better take the letter to Mr. [Winthrop M.] Daniels and place the whole matter in his hands, since there was no time to communicate with you.

Your accident insurance & check came too.

We are all *very* well and doing well in every respect[.] Give my devoted love to dear Stockton. Take good care of each other. I think of you all day, my darling, and dream of you by night and I *love* you love you passionately;—I am *altogether*,

Your own Eileen.

ALS (WC, NjP).

[1] William Guinn of 10 Charlton St.

[2] Professor and Mrs. William Milligan Sloane. Sloane, Seth Low Professor of History at Columbia University, continued to maintain a residence, Stanworth, at 95 Bayard Ave.

[3] Mr. and Mrs. Charles Cotesworth Beaman. A distinguished international lawyer of New York, Beaman was best known for his work on the *Alabama* Claims cases.

[4] Between Library Place and 50 Washington St., the home of the Hibbens.

[5] Frederic G. Kenyon (ed.), *The Letters of Elizabeth Barrett Browning* (2 vols., London and New York, 1897).

[6] She forgot to enclose this letter from George Tayloe Winston, President of the University of Texas, and sent it later under separate cover. It is missing.

[7] M. Boucard to WW, June 8, 1899.

[8] John Corliss Dunning, A.M., Princeton, 1899, who had been appointed the South East Club University Fellow in Social Science for 1899-1900. His letter is missing.

To Ellen Axson Wilson

My own darling,   S.S. Furnessia   At Sea, 25 June, 1899

What an age it seems since I saw you! It seemed especially long yesterday—the fourteenth anniversary of our marriage—of my making! The voyage has been very unpleasant. Not till to-day have we had a *whole* clear day. We've had, indeed, scarcely three glimpses of the sun. It has been continuously dark and drizzling, and has affected our spirits considerably. There has been no storm at all—the sea has been quiet—but one long drawn out "Scotch mist." Stock. has been nearly reduced to despair! One night we lay still and mended machinery, drifting on a still sea for six hours, and losing that much time of course out of our "run." It has been a tedious business altogether—out at sea and *just* away from home.

Tell "Jack"[1] and Mrs. Hibben that the party of professors, instead of proving bores, have proved a perfect Godsend, of course. Our fellow passengers are for the most part a painfully commonplace lot (it was so before, *going over*)[2] and these men are jolly, informal, altogether companionable and comforting. My only objection to Professor Seth[3] is that he does not talk—he listens. He is most appreciative, likes a joke, knows a good story when he hears it, smokes, and absorbs,—but will not talk. I am sure, by every sign, that he has lots in him, but he keeps it to himself, apparently only because of the amiable qualities of modesty and sympathy which make him a good listener.

Miss Clay has proved a most agreeable and unaggressive young person and we have treated her rather badly by having almost nothing to do with her. We sit in the smoking room, talk, play cards, calculate and re-calculate, and re-re-calculate the "run," tell stories, hear other groups exchange experiences, argue, quarrel,—sometimes almost fight over questions they do not understand; walk the wet deck, wonder at the dreary commonplaceness of the lines of women who sit huddled in their steamer chairs; read when we must—in any and every way try to forget that we are bored!

We hope of [to] get to Moville (the port of Londonderry) on Tuesday, and this letter will be mailed there, at the same time that my cable goes. The weather is gloriously bright now and ought to stay so till we get in; but it's going to be hard to keep Stock. from breaking with this slow line and going back on a fast steamer. He is bored as only he can be at the tedium of it all!

Ah, my Eileen, I hardly dare think of my feelings. I am deeply, pathetically homesick for you. You are all the world for me and I am wandering bereaved. Every mile of distance seems to stretch the chords of my heart the more intolerably! But I am not going to dwell on that. I am going to love you as simply, as manfully, as directly as I can, and quit analysis, for my heart's salvation. I shall know only that I am altogether and in everything

Your own   Woodrow

I was very miserable physically the first day or two out; but since then I have been "perfectly all right."

ALS (WC, NjP).

[1] John Grier Hibben.

[2] That is, when he went to England on *S.S. Ethiopia* in the late spring of 1896.

[3] James Seth. He had resigned the Sage Professorship of Moral Philosophy at Cornell University in 1898 to become Professor of Moral Philosophy at the University of Edinburgh but had remained at Cornell during the academic year 1898-99 as "Acting" Sage Professor.

From Ellen Axson Wilson

My own darling,   Princeton June 26/99

Just think, it is nine and a half days now! Surely in thirty-six hours at the latest the message will come! I am trying hard not to expect it before Wednesday morning. Yet my heart beat to suffocation almost, for a moment, this morning when the telegraph boy suddenly appeared. Alas! it was only a bill for one of Dr. Mitchell's telegrams.[1]

We are all getting on beautifully. Jessie and Nellie are practically well; Margaret and I still whoop occasionally but as gently as any sucking dove. The wonderful weather continues, adding greatly to our contentment; the thermometer keeps generally in the neighbourhood of 80°. Twice it has tried to get hot but in each case it ended with a thunder-storm after one day. I have mainly divided my time since I last wrote between making underclothing for Margaret and reading Browning literature. I brought home a great armful of the latter from the library last week, and some of it I have enjoyed intensely,—though I still like Prof. Jones book[2] best of all.

I was ashamed to find when too late for the last steamer that I had omitted to enclose in my letter the one from the Pres. of the University of Texas to which I alluded. I send it now under a separate cover. Also the one from Dunning. Mr. Magie brought it back to say that he could not find Daniels, so he himself would write to Dunning that he need not come,—as he supposed you would not want him against his will. For the rest perhaps you can send suggestions as to a fresh appointment for the fellowship. I should think that if you would send two or three names in the order of your preference one of the other men, Magie, West or Fine, might conduct the correspondence.

There have been no other letters of the slightest consequence.

Do you know that I have not Father's address and have searched for it in vain? A letter has come for him and I am quite at a loss about it.

Have just had an interesting letter from Ed.[3] He is still hard at work, taking a four weeks course in Bacteriology at the summer school of the "Tech" and also carrying on some "special research work under one of the professors." He seems to be having as much fun working as Madge[4] has playing. He is anxious to get into "sanitary work" he says.

Did I say in my last that Cousin Hattie[5] had lost another child, —the fifth to die! Isn't it sad? It is Rebecca, the baby. She was nearly five years old, a beautiful, charming little creature, Aunt Saidie[6] writes.

There is really very little news to write, either from the papers or otherwise. The papers are full of nothing but new trusts and "gigantic railroad deals." For local news we have Guyot Cameron's marriage, which was kept a great secret 'till the deed was done; no cards. Of course as yet we can only surmise (from our knowledge of him) what manner of person she must be. She is a Miss Finley from Ohio.[7] I have been trying in vain to remember whether John and Bob were from Ohio or farther west.[8] How is it?

The only other news is that Mr. Armours[9] was broken into three nights ago and a quantity of valuable silver stolen. They have been to several other places too; at the Stocktons[10] they had the silver all on the floor, packing it, when they were heard and frightened away. I hope that, now they have finally succeeded in one case, something vigorous will be done about it. As a community we have surely been much too passive in the matter;—have taken it all rather as a joke.

Good-night, my own love. Oh—for a magic mirror that I might see for myself, *now* that you are well and happy! How I wonder what you are doing *now*! "A ship sails afar over warm ocean waters, and haply one musing doth stand at her prow." Do you have time to think much about us? You are in very truth my meditation day & night. Love to dear Stock. And for yourself the whole heart of   Your devoted little wife   Eileen.

ALS (WC, NjP).

[1] Charles Wellman Mitchell, M.D., '79, who had stayed with the Wilsons during reunion week.

[2] Henry Jones, *Browning as a Philosophical and Religious Teacher* (Glasgow and New York, 1891). There is a copy of this book in the Wilson Library, DLC.

[3] Her brother, Edward William Axson, who was a student at the Massachusetts Institute of Technology. His letter is missing.

[4] Her sister, Margaret Randolph Axson, who was a student at the Woman's College of Baltimore (now Goucher College).

[5] Harriet Hoyt (Mrs. Robert) Ewing of Nashville, Tenn., her first cousin.

[6] Sadie Cooper (Mrs. Thomas Alexander) Hoyt of Philadelphia, her aunt-in-law.

[7] Anne Wood Finley.

[8] John Huston Finley, President of Knox College, and the late Robert Johnston Finley. They were from Illinois and first cousins of Anne Wood Finley.

[9] George Allison Armour, Princeton 1877, who lived in the house at 83 Stockton Street, then known as Allison House and now called the Walter Lowrie House after a later owner. The Armour and Wilson lots adjoined at the rear.

[10] The home on Library Place of Sarah Bache Hodge Stockton, widow of Samuel Witham Stockton.

To Jenny Davidson Hibben

My dear Mrs. Hibben,   S.S. Furnessia, At Sea. 26 June, '99

I want a letter to go off to you on the first mail, which we will drop at Moville, the port of Londonderry. I've already sent you a message in the letter I have written to Ellen; but I have had you and Jack and the dear, patient mother[1] upstairs so much, so constantly in mind that I find I can't rest satisfied with that. I must send a few lines direct. It was a characteristic, but none the less unusual, act of kindness on Jack's part to go with me to the steamer; it was such a comfort to see you at the train and leave Ellen with you,—two brave, sweet women together: the one knowing so well how to control herself, and the other knowing so well how to sympathize and comfort. I feel as if I could not have left home had I not been able to leave Ellen with you; and it was no small part of the distress of leaving that *I* had to miss this summer of closer drawn friendship and intimacy. But I am sure that the more you both love her the greater will my share be in the affection which has so brightened and strengthened our lives in dear old Princeton. I verily believe that, in my present state of mind about the sinister influences at present dominant in the administration of the College,[2] it would be easy for me to leave Princeton if it were not for "the Hibbens." You don't know what an anchorage our love for them has made, and is likely to make, for us!

I've already told you, in my letter to Ellen, what I think of Professor Seth and his two followers and pupils.[3] I have thoroughly enjoyed them,—and they have talked and acted in all respects like human beings. But I know you will want me to add what they said about Jack. They speak most warmly of him, and rejoice that a man of such fine tone and breadth of culture should have taken to Philosophy. He is an ornament, exclaims Lefevre, to the department. You may be sure I assented to that. You may judge, too, of the amused satisfaction with which I saw their contempt for Baldwin[4] peep out when they found that I had no susceptibilities to wound on that subject.

I shall not describe the voyage. Suffice it to say we are devoutly hoping to see land to-morrow. The weather has been abominable! This is not a letter of travel: it is a letter of love to my dear friends, whom I carry always in my heart. I am well, lonely, and
                    Your affectionate friend,   Woodrow Wilson

ALS (photostat in WC, NjP).
    [1] Elizabeth Grier (Mrs. Samuel) Hibben.
    [2] An obvious reference to President Patton and Dean Winans.
    [3] The only one who can be identified was Dr. Albert Lefevre, Seth's student at Cornell.
    [4] James Mark Baldwin, Stuart Professor of Psychology at Princeton.

To Ellen Axson Wilson

[*S.S. Furnessia*, at sea] 27 June, 1899

This, my darling, is a postscript. We expect to see land to-day, and the mail will probably be taken off to-night. I will keep this letter open to the last—so that it may be the latest possible letter news.

We have had two bright days since the first part of this epistle was written, and are in good spirits accordingly. It is misting again to-day, but that is no great matter, land being near.

I wrote to Mrs. Hibben yesterday, but did not repeat the message about Professor Seth which I put in my letter to you.

Before I forget it again, dear—I left my box of visiting cards. Will you not forward them to me by mail? They are in one of the upper divisions inside my small desk in my den. Address them, please, to the British Linen Company Bank, like the rest of my mail, and they will forward them to me.

We are still quite well,—"perfectly all right,"—though the inaction on board ship makes us feel by this time a trifle stale and uncomfortable. Stock. has fallen sleepy at the end of the voyage instead of at the beginning, and is doing a fine lot of resting. He came on board thoroughly tired out and nervously exhausted after the final rush of the college year. He was *very* much attracted by Dunn, by the way, as we knew he would be. Levermore,[1] it seems, was at first very much daunted by Dunn's youth, and took him with many misgivings: but he took him, and the rest will take care of itself.

Isn't it a comfort, my sweetheart, that this time I can *write*, and really talk with you.[2] I don't want to leave off. The trouble is, that I hardly dare give my heart leave, and when ordinary topics run out I *must* stop. I love you inexpressibly, my incomparable little wife. Your influence upon me is wholly independent of space,—you seem too thoroughly *in* my life and *of* it to be *really* separated from me. I wonder if *we* could not manage Peter Ibbetson's transmigration in our dreams and actually join one another? Do you remember the directions? (I have just read the book).[3] Lie on your back, your hands clasped under your head, your feet crossed, the right over the left. Don't lose your sense of your actual place and identity, but at the same time fix your will upon some past time and place where you want to be. Remember that *I* can't join you until five hours after your time. What nonsense! And yet the book seems so real, and has given me such an intolerable longing to join you after that delightful fashion. No doubt Miss Lucy Smith could manage it!

Ah, my sweet love, good-bye. I will write again so soon as we get settled at our hotel in Glasgow,—i.e., practically, so soon as we land. I love you unspeakably and am with absolute devotion

Your own   Woodrow

Love to all to whom I should send it—Mrs. Brown etc.
Kisses innumerable for the chicks.

ALS (WC, NjP).
    [1] Charles Herbert Levermore, President of Adelphi College.
    [2] On his trip to Britain in 1896, Wilson could write only brief letters with his left hand because he had temporarily lost the use of his right hand from a small stroke in May 1896.
    [3] George du Maurier, *Peter Ibbetson* (London and New York, 1891).

From Ellen Axson Wilson

My own darling,   Princeton   June 29/99

The cablegram[1] came to hand soon after breakfast yesterday to my great joy. Somehow I took for granted that it was from Glasgow, for it seemed to me you had had ample time to arrive there; so all day I had the satisfaction of supposing your voyage actually over. It was only at bedtime that, looking at it again, I found to my disappointment that it was from Moville. And then this morning, soon after breakfast[,] Mr. Hibben dropped it [in] and told me he had seen in the paper the notice of the ship's arrival at Glasgow. So now my mind is entirely at rest again.

We are all doing finely still; only Margaret will persist in whooping, so that I cannot send for Madge. I am naturally anxious not to leave her too long on Mrs. Reids hands.[2] She says she is having a lovely time, "especially since Edgeworth Smith[3] went away[.]" She pronounces him very tiresome.

You would suppose from the weather that Princeton had been transported bodily to the mountains. I never saw it so persistently cool; it is really glorious. It seems very superfluous for anyone to be setting off for summer resorts, but the Ricketts start on Saturday. Fraulein[4] leaves tomorrow.

By the way, your friends in conclave assembled humbly petition that you will for the present at least give up *dieting* altogether. It was discussed at the Ricketts and that was the sense of the meeting. It is stated on the highest authority that it is bad for any system to keep up a regimen of that sort too long continuously; and we think that while pursuing your present way of life you ought to be able to digest anything,—even strawberries!

There are no letters and no news, except that in the boat races Penn was first, Wisconsin second, Cornell third and Columbia last. The Yale-Harvard races come off today.[5] I will leave this open and record the result tomorrow morning.

Do excuse this specially bad scrawl; I have been drawing most of the day and my hand is quite tired. I am making a charcoal enlargement of the head of *my* Madonna, began it yesterday and got so interested that I have worked pretty steadily. I have to hold the heavy book and use a magnifying glass, which makes it fatiguing. But the head is almost finished now and it is *sweet,*— and so like my darling mother that it almost startles me. Am very glad I attempted it. Nellie Jackson[6] who was calling this morning think[s] it looks like *me*! And Fraulein thinks it like both Madge and me. It is queer.

I have just had a long evening visit from Mrs. Magie & Mary Stockton,[7] and it is now bedtime—will finish this in the morning.

Friday morning. Miss Ricketts came in for a parting visit before we left the breakfast table so now have only time to close in haste before the 10.30 mail.

Have just had a long interesting letter from Kate Wilson.[8] Business is thriving and all happy and well except that Josie[9] is a little out of sorts—works too hard. He will probably take a holiday.

Goodbye, dear love. Now, I am counting the days till my first letter. Oh, how happy it will make me! And how glad I am that you can use your right hand, for perhaps the letters will not be so short as before.

Dear love to Stock. I love you, dear, always and altogether,

Your own   Eileen.

ALS (WC, NjP).

[1] It is missing.

[2] Edith Gittings (Mrs. Harry Fielding) Reid of Baltimore.

[3] Son of the Victor Smiths of Baltimore.

[4] Clara Böhm, former German governess of the Wilson children.

[5] The first crew-racing event mentioned by Mrs. Wilson was the Poughkeepsie Regatta held on June 27, 1899; the second, the Harvard-Yale races held at New London, Conn., on June 29. Harvard swept all three of the races in the contest with Yale.

[6] She is not listed in the Princeton directories of this time and is unknown to the Editors.

[7] Mary Blanchard Hodge (Mrs. William Francis) Magie and Mary Hunter Stockton, daughter of Sarah Bache Hodge Stockton.

[8] Wife of Wilson's brother, Joseph R. Wilson, Jr. Her letter is missing.

[9] Joseph R. Wilson, Jr.

To Ellen Axson Wilson

My own darling,   The Bath Hotel, Glasgow. 30 June, 1899

We did not reach our hotel here until bed-time on Wednesday, too late to write letters for the Thursday mail, and as tired as we could be. The voyage, though "good" in one sense, was thoroughly bad in another. It was technically "good" because not rough or beset by any dangers; but it was most disagreeable and tedious in other respects. The same rain storm (the captain[1] said) followed us all the way across and we came in, most appropriately, in a mist-laden gale, which made every bit of shore we saw seem shadowy and unreal—and romantic. We lost the tide at the mouth of the river, landed and "passed the Customs" (for whiskey and tobacco and perfumery) at Greenock, and were sent up to Glasgow by train. We came up to the hotel with trunk, valise *and* bicycle—Stock in a hansum, I in a "four-wheeler"—for this primitive land knows no such Yankee inventions as delivery wagons or express companies.

We found ourselves so much fatigued by the enforced rest of the voyage that we spent yesterday in bed (an unspeakable luxury after the narrow berths of our stateroom) and loafing about the city. To-day we mean to devote to putting our wheels together and making all necessary first preparations for our ride. To-morrow we set out for Edinburgh by rail (to be there on Sunday) and thence we shall take the usual turn (via Sterling) through the lochs and Trossachs, and be here in Glasgow again, probably, by Wednesday, to take the road to Ayr. But you shall know of that as we go along. Professor Seth is to be our guide in Edinburgh, and a very kind and interesting one I am sure he will be.

We are both perfectly well—i.e. perfectly well for Stock. in *his* case,—and nothing interesting has happened to us since the voyage. The only incident I did not chronicle in my letter from the ship was the accident in mid-ocean to one of our cylinders. The high pressure cylinder was somehow (it was not explained to us how) rendered useless, and we had to make the rest of the voyage at a speed reduced by some thirty miles a day. That and the foggy mist were what made us so long in crossing. No danger whatever attended the accident, but it was very annoying—and made me fear that my darling would be anxious at not hearing of our arrival at the time she expected. We found that the Furnessia had got in the bad way of late of making slow time and so we determined not to go back on her, as we had planned. Her date of sailing is the seventh of September—and even nine days (her *best* time) would put us in New York on the sixteenth, leaving Stock only four days to get his things out of Brooklyn and himself set up in Princeton.[2] No doubt he *ought* to be in Princeton by the eighteenth, for the entrance examinations, and he could not be with the Furnessia's *usual* time. It would quite certainly make a bad impression (on Perry and the other examiners—Dr. Patton would not notice a little thing like that!) for Stock. to be late,—and the long and short of the whole matter is, that we are "booked" to sail on the City of Rome (the fastest of the Anchor Line boats,—though that is not saying much!) on the 26th of August. The Anchoria, the only boat whose time of sailing is intermediate between that and the seventh of September, is so *very* slow that it w'd not get in much ahead of the Furnessia, and Stock, who proves a bad sailor—getting frantic at the confinement—might jump overboard if the voyage lengthened to twelve days! So Stock. will be in time, and I shall see my darling (God willing) that much sooner! My heart jumps at the thought.

My heart is very light this morning anyhow, for I have your first letter and my heart sings at every line of its sweet story of daily happenings. Nothing that happens in your day can be too trivial to put into your letters to me, my sweet one. It is that I am hungry for—just the morning to night movements and thoughts and occupations of my love and her little ones. You can't make your letters too full of that or of *any*thing that has concerned you, if only for a moment. This letter I have just read is more intrinsically *interesting* than anything I have read since '96. Do it again and again and again, my Eileen, and keep me in heart through the long weeks. The news of the game did not cheer me half so much as these details of what you did. You are *so* brave and cheery and sweet,—such a splendid, bonnie girl! I could give my life for you, and you *are* giving yours for me. I love you, I adore you, I long for you with every drop of blood and every thought that is in me, and am with an unspeakable, solemn delight

Your own Woodrow

Love to *all* the dear friends—more than love to our little darlings. How is the fraülein now? I trust there has been no more fainting. Tell the telegraph office that a cable message addressed "Wilson, Princeton, N. J." will mean *you*.

ALS (WC, NjP).

1 James Harris.

2 President Patton, in his report to the Board of Trustees on June 12, 1899, had recommended that Stockton Axson be appointed as Assistant Professor of English. The trustees elected Axson by a unanimous vote at that meeting.

From Francesco Cosentini[1]

Hon. Monsieur   [Genoa, c. July 1, 1899]

J'ai l'honneur de vous communiquer que vous avez été élu "Membre correspondant étranger" de notre "Circolo di studi sociali" dont je vous envoie le programme ci-joint.

Par initiative de notre Circle il y aura à Gênes l'octobre prochain (23-29) le premier congrès sociologique italien, dont je vous enverrai bientôt le programme.

J'ai l'honneur de vous inviter, à nom du conseil de direction, à notre Congrès, et je vous prie de me communiquer votre intervention, qui contribuera certainement à accroître l'importance et le succès du Congrès.

Agréez les sentiments de la plus haute considération.

                    votre   Prof. F. Cosentini, secrétaire

ALS (WP, DLC). Enc.: printed copy of a prospectus of the Circolo di Studi Sociali of the University of Genoa.
  [1] Jurist, political scientist, and sociologist at the University of Genoa.

To Ellen Axson Wilson

My own darling,   The Imperial Hotel. Edinburgh. 2 July, 1899

Here we are in Edinburgh. I have just now returned from the "military" service at St. Giles,—the service to which the highlanders go. Stock. had a touch of his periodical pain last night and did not get up to go with me (the service is at 9:30); but I find him all right now,—no pain at all, and in excellent spirits. Besides, after two days rain, it is clearing and we are to have a bright afternoon.

Professor Seth lives here with his mother,—a dear old lady, almost as sweet but of course not so interesting as Mrs. McCosh. We reached Edinburgh just before luncheon and, as the rain forbade sight seeing, we after lunching immediately looked him up, as he had begged us to do. At his urgent invitation, we spent the whole afternoon with him, stayed to dinner, and were taken to one of Gilbert and Sullivan's operas afterwards. It was all very delightful. Albert Lefevre (son of Dr. Lefevre of Baltimore[1]), a pupil of Professor Seth's at Cornell, is here to spend the summer with his master. He was of our party on the steamer,—a thoughtful, fun-loving boy, almost, who contributed not a little to our pleasure in our smoking-room chats and amusements. We four then—with the delightful addition of Mrs. Seth at the afternoon tea table and at dinner—were the party, in that quiet, delightful, somehow strangely familiar home,—sitting most of the time beside an open grate fire in the study, by windows looking out on the tiny green garden, trim and secluded, at the rear of the solid little stone house, No. 3 Queens Crescent. Stock was beyond measure captivated—his first glimpse of the sweet privacy of the old-country life—and declares he will retire, if he ever does retire, to such a place *in Edinburgh*. For, though he saw it in the rain, Edinburgh seemed to him the most beautiful place in the world. And certainly it is not hard to agree with him—except that he has not seen Wells!

We feel that we must be off soon on our wheels, by Wednesday next, the 5th, at latest, for there are quite thirty places we want to see, and we do not wish to hurry. It would be fine to have time to linger here, if we only could. Our hotel is *very* well situated, in the *old* town, but on its open edge. The window at which I write looks out across the Princes Street Gardens to "new" Edinburgh, the Scott monument standing in the midst of the long green slopes. St. Giles is just a block away, but the level on which it stands is that of the chimney pots of this hotel, for we are at the foot of the steep rock, almost, of the castle itself. I climbed to church this morning by an endless flight of stone steps which begin to rise just by the inn door. It's impressive, I can tell you, to sit at service beside a highland regiment (the Gordon Highlanders, no less); and I can vouch for it, if this morning's sermon be a typical example, that the Gospel is preached to them with simplicity and honest force. The sermon seemed to me to strike home. Certainly I felt the force of it myself. I could not sing, though I knew the hymns. It moved me so to hear the old hymns sung to the old tunes under such surroundings that I had no voice to sing with. Assuredly my mother's blood is strong in me, and is strangely stirred in this land which gave her her breeding!

4 July

I continue my narrative in Glasgow, my sweet one: for I think you will feel that a sort of diary gives you best hold upon me.

We have been very busy since I wrote on Sunday. On Monday (yesterday) we did the historical parts of Edinburgh—the castle, St. Giles, the Parliament House, Knox's house, the Canongate churchyard, Holyrood palace, and all the rest (we had been to Greyfriar's Sunday afternoon); and to-day we went through the Trossachs and the lochs. The unusual things we did were, to lunch with Prof. Seth at the 'Union[,]' the students' club, and to dine and meet 'Company' at Prof. Seth's in the evening. Nobody could be kinder, more hospitable, more generous, or more attentive than Prof. Seth has been. The 'Union' was a most interesting democratic place, full of students, lunching, loafing, swarming in the lobbies. The Company invited to meet us in the evening was a most interesting collection of people—among the rest Mr. Hugh Brown, the principal living historian of Scotland, and Miss Amelia Hutchinson-Stirling, a most vivacious and interesting young authoress with opinions, and the words in which to express them. I was most entertained.

I have just feasted on your second letter. Ah, my darling—I wish I could tell you what these letters mean to me: they keep me alive! And to read of your systematically having a good time, —going out to dinner, browsing in the library, visting your friends, and the like, makes me love and admire you more than ever,—my precious, sane, complete little woman. Stock and I wish for you every day to tell us about everything we see! He knows almost as well as I do what an incomparable treasure you are; but nobody can love you or know how you deserve love as does

Your own   Woodrow

Love to the Hibbens and Mrs. Brown—love unspeakable to the chicks (tell them to write to me!)—Kind regards to Fraülein Clara. Both of us perfectly well and every way all right.

ALS (WC, NjP).
  [1] Rev. Dr. Jacob Amos Lefevre (1830-1905), formerly pastor of the Franklin Square Presbyterian Church of Baltimore and an old friend of Joseph Ruggles Wilson.

From Ellen Axson Wilson

My own darling,   Princeton July 3, 1899.

Before I forget it, a word as to Mr. Dunning, a letter from whom I enclose in another envelope.[1] He also wrote to Mr. Magie and was answered by him before this letter came. Mr. Magie told him he could study abroad if the faculty consented and that the consent of the faculty could be taken for granted if the "department" recommended it. But the department being in this case chiefly *you*, there was nothing that he (Dunning) could do but await your decision in the matter, though the delay of course involves a degree of hardship for him. But then as Mr. Magie says it is wholly opposed to the policy of the College to grant such a privilege except to extraordinary men, and your consent can't be *presumed* upon as a mere matter of course.

There has been absolutely *no* letter for you since I last wrote except this;—delightful, isn't it? I went today to see if I could by chance find a card or two of yours,—and lo! the whole box! You have evidently forgotten them. I enclose a few in the envelope with the letter. I see you[r] little silver travelling cup was forgotten too;—a pity!—it would have been quite convenient I should think; so compact in shape.

And what do you suppose I wanted with your cards? To take with me to the Guyot Cameron's[.] Everyone is rushing to see them, and exhorting everyone else to rush, for a singular though good natured reason. It is because the old parents[2] are behaving scandalously about it; they actually refuse to speak to either their son or his wife; and for no reason whatever except that they were madly determined that he should make a *"brilliant* marriage"!—which, I am informed[,] means that he should marry a rich *any* rich New York society girl. It seems he was engaged to this girl for years,—ever since he was a professor at Miami College (she is from Ohio) [—] and has been trying in vain all this time to get their consent, and postponing his marriage solely on that account. He is supposed to feel this sort of thing more keenly than the average American because of his Parisian training; for in France, it seems, it is actually against the law for even mature men to marry without their parents consent. So it seems we have a "stage father" among us too. I believe it is the only thing Mr. and Mrs. Cameron ever agreed upon—a fine one on which to begin!

The girl was a Miss Finley, a first cousin of John and Bob. She is a handsome, attractive girl,—has a splendid figure, is very tall and large, about the size of Mrs. Cleveland, fine colouring—rather fair, face not strikingly pretty but very pleasant in expression; has a good manner, only a trifle too much of it, dresses perfectly and seems in all respects entirely unexceptionable. *Much* too good for him I should judge. She has come to a charming little home,[3] by the way. The house is really beautiful in its furnishings; in rich but perfect taste, delightful deep rich tones of colour everywhere. And oh! the books! You ought to see them! Such a display "of red morrocco's gilded gleam, and vellum rich as country cream"! Where does he get so much money? And he has just bought a two hundred foot lot below the Magie's on our side of the street [Library Place].

Duffield, Mr Osborn's[4] understudy, is also going to buy near us (!) probably the lot this side of the Magies. Arn't we getting a job lot of neighbours! This I believe exhausts my budget of news.

We are doing nicely in every respect. The wonderful weather lasted without a break until today. It is 89° today—very hot walking, but pleasant enough here in the house. I wrote to Madge this morning to come home,—wrote with many misgivings it is true but I don't want to impose on Mrs. Reids good nature. Margaret still whoops a little but as a rule only when she has been taking exercise; and I remembered that you were able to perform the feat in question for several years when you tried to play base-ball. She must return through Balt. and wants to stop over a few days with a friend which will perhaps postpone her coming for another week.

When, oh when, will I have a letter[?] I have spent enough time in thought and abortive calculation on that point to wrest from nature some great secret if I had been a scientist. Good-night, my own love. May God bless you and bring you safely back to

Your devoted little wife   Eileen

Dear love to Stockton.

ALS (WC, NjP).
  [1] J. C. Dunning to WW, June 28, 1899, ALS (WP, DLC).
  [2] Prof. and Mrs. Henry Clay Cameron.
  [3] At 94 Bayard Ave.
  [4] Henry Green Duffield, assistant to Edwin Curtis Osborn, Treasurer of Princeton University.

A Record of a Tour through the British Isles

[July 5-Aug. 26, 1899]

— AND —

POCKET RECORD

— OF —

Bicycle Trips, Mileage, etc.

Name, *Woodrow Wilson*

Residence, *Princeton,*

New Jersey,

U. S. A.

In case of accident, notify

Address, *Mrs. Woodrow Wilson,*

address as above, — or

Club, *Cyclists' Touring Club (1899)*

Bicycle No. ~~37854~~ = 1899, 5578
59, 1899
Name, *Columbia Model* ~~40, 1896~~

Maker, *Pope Manufacturing Co.*

Cost, ~~$100.00~~   *$75.00*

Date of purchase, *1 May, 1899.*

Monthly Record,

January,		Miles.
February,		"
March,		"
April,		"
May,		"
June,		"
July,		"
August,		"
September,		"
October,		"
November,		"
December,		"

DATE	1899 ROUTE	Cyclometer Register	Arrival Hrs. Min.	Departure Hrs. Min.	House or Hotel	Expenses
5 July	Glasgow to Kilmarnock [and Alloway]	21.7			George	7 3
6 ,,	Kilmarnock to Ayr	18.8			Station	11 3
7 ,,	{ Ayr to Dumfries (rail) [and rt.]				King's Arms	9 1
	Dumfries to Ellisland	15.5				
8 ,,	{ Dumfries – Penrith (rail) Station Penrith – Patterdale (Ullswater) by wheel	14.2			White Lion	5 0
9 ,,	Patterdale to Keswick	18.2			George	
10 ,,	Keswick to Cockermouth (Return by rail)	15.5				

Actual No. of Miles, 103.9   Actual Time,

Remarks: The 15.5 (Keswick to Cockermouth) included a good deal of riding to and fro in Cockermouth, and from the station to the hotel in Keswick, on returning. The distance from Keswick to Cockermouth is 13 miles.

DATE 1899	ROUTE	Cyclo-meter Register	Arrival Hrs.	Min.	Departure Hrs.	Min.	House or Hotel	Expenses
11 July	Keswick (detained by rain)						George	
12 "	"							£ 1 8/4
13 "	Keswick to Ambleside [via Grasmere] [Stock's illness]	18					White Lion	
14 "	Ambleside, detained by						" "	£ 1.0/5½
15 "	Ambleside to Windermere (chair) Windermere to Durham (rail)	5					Three Tuns	rail 9/
16 "	Durham (Sunday)						" "	
17 "	" (Cathedral and Assizes.)						" "	£ 1 11/8 (" /5)

Actual No. of Miles, 126.9   Actual Time,

Remarks:

DATE 1899	ROUTE	Cyclo-meter Register	Arrival Hrs.	Min.	Departure Hrs.	Min.	House or Hotel	Expenses
18 July	Durham – York – Lincoln (rail)						White Hart	rail 14/2
19 "	Lincoln to Peterboro (rail)						House's	rail 5/11 4/9½
20 "	Peterboro to Ely (rail)						The Bell	rail 3/10½
21 "	Ely (waiting for luggage) Stock to Bury St. Edm.						" "	£ 1 1/
22 "	Ely to Cambridge	16.8					The Bull	
23 "	Cambridge (Sunday)						" "	

Actual No. of Miles, 143.7   Actual Time,

Remarks:

DATE 1899	ROUTE	Cyclo-meter Register	Arrival Hrs.	Min.	Departure Hrs.	Min.	House or Hotel	Expenses
24 July	Cambridge						The Bull	£ 1 11/5
25 "	Cambridge to Coventry (rail)		8	5			King's Head	9/
26 "	Coventry to Nuneaton	9.0					Newdegate Arms	19.9
	Nuneaton to Lichfield (rail)		1	7			The George	7/6
27 "	Lichfield to Nuneaton (rail)		1	7			lunch, Kenilworth,	2/7
	Nuneaton to Warwick	20.6					The Woolpack	7/11
28 "	Warwick to Stratford on Avon (via Charlecote)	10.7					The Golden Lion	8/9

Actual No. of Miles, *183.3*   *Actual Time,*

Remarks:

DATE 1899	ROUTE	Cyclo-meter Register	Arrival Hrs.	Min.	Departure Hrs.	Min.	House or Hotel	Expenses
29 July to 1 Aug.	Stratford to Oxford	40.1	(in train 6/)				King's Arms	
1 Aug.	Oxford						"	£ 1 6/6
1 Aug.	Oxford to London (rail)		(Ry 5/3½)				Covent Garden	£ 1 13/3
4 "	London to Oxford (rail)		"		"		King's Arms	£ 1 9/5
7 "	Oxford to Hungerford	32.2	(lunch 3/)				Three Swans	6/11½
8 "	Hungerford to Bath	42.8	"		2/8½		Castle Hotel	9/5
9 "	Bath to Wells,	20.2					The Star	19/9

Actual No. of Miles, *318.6*   *Actual Time,*

Remarks:

DATE 1899	ROUTE	Cyclo-meter Register	Arrival Hrs.	Min.	Departure Hrs.	Min.	House or Hotel	Expenses
11 Aug.	Wells—Langport—Taunton	33.0	Langport Lunch	2/9			The Castle	11/1½
12 "	Taunton to Exeter	33.1	Cullompton "	2/3			Half Moon	18/5
14 "	Exeter to Barnstaple	41.1	Eggesford "	2/3			Royal Fortescue	8/1
15 "	Barnstaple to Clovelly	21.0	Clovelly by lunch				New Inn	11/
16 "	Clovelly (via Hobby Drive) to Launceston	34.2	Red Post Inn Lunch	1/3			White Hart	9/
17 "	Launceston to Plymouth	25.2	Plymouth for lunch				Duke of Cornwall	18/5
18 "	Plymouth to Dublin (boat)	—	Fare 32/6				— —	

Actual No: of Miles, 506.2   Actual Time,

Remarks:

DATE 1899	ROUTE	Cyclo-meter Register	Arrival Hrs.	Min.	Departure Hrs.	Min.	House or Hotel	Expenses
20 Aug.	Dublin to Drogheda (rail)	—	Fare 2/9				White Horse	8/-
21 "	Drogheda to Dundalk	22	Dundalk Lunch 2/7				— —	
	Dundalk to Belfast (rail)		Fare 8/7				Imperial and Windsor	22/2
23 "	Belfast to Glasgow (boat)		" 13/6				Bath Hotel	21/8
26 "	Glasgow to New York (boat)	—						

Actual No. of Miles, 528.2 En route Actual Time,

Remarks: 582.6, total, including neighbourhood rides, errands about Cities, from hotels to railway stations, etc.

Pocket Notebook (WP, DLC).

To Ellen Axson Wilson

My own darling,   Station Hotel, Ayr, 6 July, 1899

We have faithfully followed our programme. We left Glasgow yesterday afternoon and spent last night at Kilmarnock. There is a very pretentious and ugly monument to Burns at Kilmarnock which would not be worth visiting were it not for the museum which it contains, with many of Burns's manuscripts and all the editions of his poems (it is said) that have ever been published,— from the Kilmarnock edition down. There is quite a little room full of the volumes, and Stock. was quite fascinated. We spent an hour in the monument this morning very delightfully,—and then rode on here and 'did' the Burns birth-place and the other interesting spots at Alloway. I am seeing things this time which I did not see in '96, because of Stock's very enjoyable enthusiasm for Burns. Stock's strong point is not enthusiasm, and it is great fun seeing him diligent to find every thing and place associated with the much loved poet. I did not see the Kilmarnock museum last time, or the inside of the poet's monument at Alloway until to-day. The Alloway monument is very absurd in point of taste—a sort of circular Greek temple standing high on a little knoll by the "auld brig" and the quiet Doon, where everything else in sight is nature's own—as sweet a rural valley, as modest and quiet a village as are to be seen in Scotland. Right beside the monument, though hidden away in the shrubbery, is a very amusing thing. In a little house evidently built for the purpose, behind a railing built to keep visitors at a respectful distance, sit Tam O'Shanter and Souter Johnie in counterfeit presentment, on a platform, drinking. Each statue is strikingly lifelike and good in itself. Each holds a drinking cup and is the very picture of the man Burns represents him to have been; but there is no table between them, no furniture or other setting as of a room is about them—they simply sit on exhibition in a bare show-room,—and outside, beyond a gate, in the open, as if cast out and rejected, sits the landlady! Why all three figures were not placed in the show room of the monument, where many other things are shown (such as the Bible Burns gave Highland Mary), I cannot imagine. No doubt the whole thing is managed by a committee! We somehow managed to escape the rush of tourists to-day and have had a most delightful time of it. We have made only forty miles on our wheels so far,—and mean to go by rail now to the Lake District, stopping for a day at Dumfries; but my last experience taught me wisdom in several matters. We are not riding for the sake of riding, but for the sake of seeing, and will try to save our time and strength for the most beautiful and memorable regions. Our plan is, to see *more* of the Lake country than I saw, going beyond the immediate Wordsworth neighbourhood to Coniston Water and through Hawkshead. Occasional use of the railway will enable us to do that kind of thing and add greatly to our enjoyment.

There is somehow an earlier demand for letters for this mail than for the mid-week, and I must get this off. We are both well and jolly. I *can't* have a *perfectly* good time without you; but, except for the ache at my heart, and the continual longing for you, which sometimes seems more than I can bear, I am happy. There is everything to make me so,—for do I not *know* your incomparable love and do I not live on the privilege of loving you,—am I not your accepted lover,   Your own   Woodrow

Love to the Hibbens and Mrs. Brown. Love beyond measure to the chicks.

ALS (WC, NjP).

From Ellen Axson Wilson

My own darling,   Princeton, Thursday July 6 1899

The letter is actually here!—came this morning, almost before I dared hope for it. I cannot tell you how happy I am over it, in spite of its news of the dismal voyage. I am *so* sorry about that, and so surprised,—was sure it was fine with you because it was so glorious here. Then Mrs. Brown heard from the Devries,[1] and their voyage was a dream of lovliness from first to last. Such weather as you describe must be frightful at sea, for it is bad merely at the *sea-shore*. I am thankful you are both well in spite of it. You did not tell me one thing which I very much wanted to know, viz., to what extent Stock suffered with sea-sickness. I was rather hoping *you* would escape better than you did.

Mr. Hibben came over this morning apparently just to compare notes as to our letters. They were evidently much pleased that you wrote them so promptly. Mrs. Hibben has been quite sick; on Monday night she had a dreadful attack of cholera-morbus. There has been no more trouble since the one night, but she is still in bed most of the day from weakness and headache. Mrs. Hibben senior is just as usual.

These things remind me of the Sloane boy's[2] case. According to Mr. Sloane there has been a wonderful advance made in surgery of which—Jamie (is that his name?) has, thanks to Dr. McCosh,[3] reaped the benefit. They are able to operate for appendicitis, and I believe for other things, without cutting *across* a single muscle; in fact they cut nothing but the skin. The muscles are separated without being severed—the knife inserted *between* them. The whole operation took less than half an hour and the wound is practically nothing. Remembering your haunting dread of appendicitis I was sure this would interest you.

We are all well and enjoying life. The children had a happy time on the fourth. They had lovely fireworks up at Mr. Wests to which I took them, upon invitation,—keeping apart from the rest of the children. After the display everyone was gorged with ice-cream and cake.

I had a letter from Ed last night saying that he would come home next week unless he was bidden not to. I have already written for Madge to come, but I am not a little uneasy about it, for Margaret has been whooping again more or less with no excuse whatever,—I mean in the way of violent exercise. I wrote Ed exactly how the case stood and he will have to decide for himself. If he takes it I don't want it on my conscience, much as I want him. Margaret's nerves are a little the worse for wear, poor child! She is beginning to twitch a little in the old way. But she is so well in every other respect and looks so splendidly that I hope it won't amount to much.

She, and all of us, had rather a shock last evening from a most terrific thunder-bolt,—the worst I ever heard. I was sure the house had been struck. Mrs. Brown says it was the worst she remembers in her long life. It came with strange suddenness; there had been no thunder before, only a beautiful sun-lit rain and we were all in the upper piazza enjoying the beautiful effects of light. And then in an instant everything seemed to go to pieces, and the children all flung themselves screaming into my arms. Jessie and Nellie recovered in a few moments but Margaret was quite hysterical for some time. The bolt, I learn today[,] struck Mr. Guyot Cameron's house and knocked down a chimney. His parents will probably consider it a "judgment" on him for his disobedience. It was rather a trying experience for one's honeymoon,—but doubtless it only afforded him a golden opportunity to show her how brave and "noble" he is.

It has been raining more or less all day; I was to go to see Mrs Hibben this afternoon, but the constant mutterings of thunder made me afraid to leave the children after they had been so unstrung.

You really tempt me to try the Peter Ibbetson experiment. But alas! I fear that faith is necessary for this miracle, as for all others, and I am of an unbelieving generation. But how delightful it would be if it were possible! beyond comparison better than the magic mirror I so often long for. Never mind! I shall at least have my letters now,—and not left-handed ones either. Now *they* have begun the worst is over,—please God. Oh my darling, *how I love you*! I love you till it hurts, but it is a blessed pain. Love to dear Stock and condolences on the voyage.

With all devotion   Your own   Eileen.

ALS (WC, NjP).
    [1] The Rev. and Mrs. John Hendrik de Vries. He was pastor of the Second Presbyterian Church.
    [2] James Renwick Sloane, Princeton 1900.
    [3] Dr. Andrew James McCosh '77, son of President McCosh, a surgeon in New York.

To Ellen Axson Wilson

My own darling,   Dumfries, 7 July, 1899

Here we are in another part of the "Burns country," still hero-worshiping, and still seeing things I never saw before. We went to the depths of a narrow court to the Globe Inn, the quaint little tavern which Burns most frequented here, and in a delightful little low ceiling'd room, just such as one's imagination would have promised with the original wainscoting and fireplace, saw the table about which the poet and his cronies used to gather, and the chair in which he used to sit and hold forth for their delectation. One Axson could at first hardly be induced to sit in the chair, but sat gazing at it with eyes big with deepest reverence,—such delectable things am I seeing! But at last he was persuaded, and sat there for a moment or two with a face full as a child's of wondering emotion. The room has several other chairs left of its "original" furniture. In another room is a window on whose panes Burns scratched some verses; but it is a bed-room and we were told, apologetically, that we could not see it: it was let to a guest. We have seen nothing yet so genuinely *like* an original as that delicious inn. We saw the outside of the house Burns lived in during most of his residence here, and both the outside and inside of the house he spent the last years in and died in; and we saw his tomb in St Michaels churchyard, hard by the latter. Here his customary ill luck has followed him and his grave is covered with a Greek mausoleum—this least Greek of our poets! Taste seemed to leave this island with the going out of the Tudors.

This afternoon we did something else out of the usual. We mounted our wheels and after not a little casting about over this beautiful country-side found, six miles away, the farm, "Ellisland," where Burns lived on first coming to this neighbourhood, and where he wrote Highland Mary and Tam O'Shanter. The house and barns and sheds are almost exactly as he built and left them; the farm-yard enclosure is the same: and all lie away from the main road, out of sight, embowered in their own grove of trees, upon the very bank of the broad and quiet Nith, running with a pleasant noise at the door, sweet walks open on its sloping banks. As ideal a little group of humble, homelike buildings as one's fancy could wish. Stock. fortunately remembered how Burns fell silent and abstracted one winter's evening (the anniversary of Mary's death), and left the house to fling himself on the hay-rick and fashion his verses to the highland lass, and how Jean followed him to warn him against the cold. He remembered, too, how she followed him by the river's bank, saw him gesticulate and heard him laugh aloud as the verses of Tam O'Shanter sprang into his thought. It was all intensely real, as we stood there in that secluded place and looked upon the unchanged scene where these things happened, and genius worked at its craft and mystery. It was a fifteen mile ride in all, the way we went, but it paid; the fine air exhilerated us and the thoughts that crowded in upon us as we looked were their own reward. There is a pang in it all for me. All these things bring *you* into my thought with painful vivid-ness, and I know to the full what it is to be separated from you. You know so much more than either of us about these things that we remember little scraps about; you could enjoy them so much more keenly, and as if in their own spirit; above all, I am myself a man who labours at thinking and conceiving and such scenes of another man's living and striving and loving make me know the part you play in my life,—how much I depend on you for sympathy and inspiration, and how nobly and in how abun-dant measure you give me all the riches of your wonderful nature. Ah me, how these thoughts *cut* me now, with my darling across the sea,—and I lonely enough to *think* of myself separately and know how unworthy I am of the little woman who has made me. My precious Eileen, my queen, how can I ever love you or praise you enough! I know that I do not praise you enough when I am with you. It hurts me yet to think that you had to *ask* for apprecia-tion of your exquisite house-keeping during our class re-union! I devoutly hope you shall not have to ask again.

"The White Lion," Patterdale, at the
head of Ulleswater, 8 July, 1899

This morning we took the train from Dumfries to Penrith,
getting luncheon by the way at Carlisle, and at Penrith railway
station we mounted our wheels and rode at once to this place,
coming the whole length of Ulleswater, along what must surely
be the most beautiful road in the world. We have had perfect
weather ever since we left Edinburgh on Tuesday morning; but
to-day seemed the most perfect day of all, with its keen fresh
air out of the West, its intense sunlight and quick-moving
shadows, showing every peak and line of the mountains, every
sloping shore, every home, or group of trees or herd of cattle in a
light chosen for the picture. No light here seems ever to be too
keen or bright. There is always a soft suffusion and touch of
mystery. The northern end of the lake lies between hills that rise
with a soft slope to no great height; but the scenery grows bolder
and grander at every turn of the way as you approach this, its
southern, end until it becomes magnificent; and all the while as
you come the road runs close to the water, in full command of
every view, and yet busy, not with that, but with taking you by
the easiest slopes first through one park and then through another, past quiet fields and neat barnyards, quite like any other
neighbourhood road, whose business it is to find a man the way
home, and regarding very much as if they were accidents the cool
avenues of ancient trees it must go through and the shining
water just beyond one of its hedges. It is all the more perfect
a road because its perfect beauty seems, not deliberate, but inevitable. We seem infinitely far away from *all* the world here in
this tiny sequestered village this evening,—from the world of England as well as from the world across the sea that holds our
treasures. An unspeakable peace rests upon this place, and our
spirits cannot escape the spell it casts. My uneasiness—the uneasiness which is never off me when I am away from you, seems
robbed of its *hurt*, though not a whit the less poignant. We passed
this afternoon through the estate which contained Wordsworth's
daffodils, and I feel when near a place identified with him that I
am near something of *yours*. So in this sweet place I feel as if it
somehow belonged to a spirit like yours, and the sense of your not
being here seems for the time harder than ever to bear. I have
the feeling I had so constantly in '96, that I am enjoying what
is more yours than mine, and an inevitable sense of guilt and
selfishness goes with the feeling. You are too absolutely unselfish
to know what I mean. It takes a certain amount of actual selfish-

ness to bring that sense of guilt: you ought really to have come with Stock., instead of me; but you can no doubt understand this: how, selfish or unselfish, this feeling brings with it a joy that almost overwhelms the pain—the joy of loving with a sort of worship,—of seeing the person I most love in all the world as it were present and glorified in these objects of exquisite beauty; which seem made for a spirit like hers to see and appreciate. This country is *yours*, my Eileen! God grant I may bring you to it *very* soon!

The George Hotel, Keswick,
9 July, 1899

If I keep up this diary form many days, my sweet one, you can do little else the day one of these epistles comes besides reading it. But I do not mean to make all of them cover so many days, and happily I am not likely to commit the usual traveller's mistake, of describing the places and scenes I visit. I want only, if I can, to give you as vividly as possible an *impression* of how I am moving about and with what emotions.

This morning at a quarter before eleven the two pilgrims set out from Patterdale, and until a quarter past four this afternoon were busy—save the time they were resting and the time they were lunching (and that leaves about three hours and a half, I believe, of actual going) in crossing the hills (?) that lie between Ulleswater and Derwentwater. In that sentence is really contained the history of the day. Since they came within the doors of the "George" they have done nothing but rest and take tea. One of them—the one who lives for you—has taken an hour's nap as his rest. The other one read Wordsworth and Baedeker instead, being somewhat moved in his mind by having reached 'these parts.' There is nothing to tell you of the day except that a boisterous wind out of the East kept Nature in a wild mood as we rode, blowing misty showers about us, and then sweeping them away to veil the tops of the mountains about us. The sun was all the while let through at intervals,—was always to be seen somewhere on the slopes or summits. It was 'clearing' all day, as we were told, but it did not clear,—and "the glass" shows a tendency to shift around to "Change" and give us some weather. The wind was *with* us, fortunately, while we were climbing the pass, it was only while we were running *down* to Keswick (the second nine of the eighteen miles) that we had to face and fight it. It was a most interesting day, and showed us every shadow and changing light the beautiful region we passed through had to show. Our eyes had their fill, and our capes were quite enough to make us indifferent to the sort of raining it occasionally chose to do. We are rather tired this evening, and rather glad to get out of the beating wind, but none the worse for wear—only a little more deliciously sleepy than usual. Stock. has found a new "Guide" to the Lakes here on the table—all about everything, and is blissfully buried in its perusal. And so the day ends in peace.

The Same, 10 July.

This morning we saw what Keswick had to show us: Greta Hall, standing on its hill beside the Greta's stream, in a sheltering group of trees; Southey's grave in Crosthwaite Churchyard, and the noble tomb within the church, with Wordsworth's lines on it,— generous and yet true too,—lines such as one might live well to deserve, if one but had a friend who could conceive and write them. Upon the tomb lies a marble effigy of Southey, almost startlingly like a sleeping man, and with features like all the portraits we had seen of the noble gentleman. It gave us a very solemn sense of reality to stand beside it. A generous portion of the old church is set apart to contain it, in a sort of separate enclosure. We finished the morning by climbing a height nearby ("Castle Hill") from which all the exquisite length and bredth and setting of Derwentwater could be seen. The greater heights were all veiled in clouds, the distances were filled with mists; but light moved here and there, the mists shifted their mystery from one valley to another, to let the lights in, and we sat enchanted. This afternoon the rain withdrew, Skiddaw unveiled, and all the land was glorious with the last level rays of the sun. We saw it as we came back from Cockermouth by the train. We rode *to* C. on our wheels, amidst the last movements of the morning's mists,—a ride to remember, beside Basenthwaite water. There was nothing in Cockermouth to see except the front of the very respectable house in which Wordsworth was born; but we wanted to see that, and to-night we are satisfied—to start to-morrow for Ambleside, where I shall mail this letter.

We are both quite well, and we both love you,—talking of you with equal enthusiasm. But Stock. does not know what it is to love as I love you: and, to tell the truth, I don't see how anybody but you *could* be loved as I love you. With overflowing heart,

Your own   Woodrow

A great deal of love to the dear Hibbens and to Mrs. Brown: love immeasurable and kisses without number to the dear chicks.

ALS (WC, NjP).

From Ellen Axson Wilson

My own darling,   Princeton, July 10, 1899

Your second letter has arrived, and oh, how my heart leaped for joy, in spite of myself, at the news that I was to expect you twelve days sooner! Of course on second thoughts I am *very* sorry for you!—and still more for Stockton, because it is his first trip,—to lose nearly two weeks of travel. I daresay he is right however; he would begin his work at a disadvantage if he were out of breath, so to say, from hasty preparation. Too bad, however, to give up *two* weeks instead of one!

I found your letter Saturday night on my return from Bryn Mawr;—for I have finally achieved my long-planned day with Florence.[1] I found her much improved, though she is still in bed and still wears the apparatus,—says she "loves it," it gives so much relief from pain. She is to continue this treatment all the rest of the summer. In spite of everything—bad nights among the rest,—she looks well. The greatest wonder to me is the expression of her face, how it can keep so sweet and serene. She certainly is one of the finest women in the world.

I reached home in a thunderstorm with rain so heavy that I was quite wet simply running from the street to the house,—having no umbrella. But of course it did me no harm. You know the street is so cut down[2] that our carriage road is temporarily useless. I suppose that when the stone is in the street it will be all right again; but if it is still below the level of our road shall I have the road sloped down to it, or wait until you come? If it involves any serious change I hardly like the responsibility.

The storm brought our cool, bright weather back; yesterday was an ideal day. The Hibbens came over for afternoon tea with me (as they also did the Sunday before). I dispense ice tea—to save the trouble of making it hot!—and lettuce sandwiches. Then I cut our regular tea,—having no further use for food of course,—and go walking with Mrs. Hibben, while Mr. Hibben goes back to his mother. She is just as usual. Mrs. Hibben is quite well again.

We have all been perfectly well until Saturday night when Margaret was taken with a little turn of indigestion; she was quite sick in the night but finally seemed entirely relieved and settled down to sleep;—and then the next thing I knew she appeared down stairs walking in her sleep! I was frightened of course and kept her in my bed the rest of the night. The attack wore off rapidly and she seemed quite well this morning, but had too much company today, I think, and too much play, so has gone to bed with a headache.

The children seem to be having a very happy summer. Margaret said the other day that she did not want to go anywhere, they were having such nice times here,—quite an admission for her to make, for she loves change and I think at first was much disappointed that we were not "going off." We have settled into a regular program now;—after breakfast stroll about the "place[,]" gather sweet peas, &c.; then we repair to the upper porch and our literary studies (!) in which we sometimes get so interested,— the children begging for more and more—that we go on 'till twelve o'clock. We are going straight through the "English Lands, Letters & Kings,"[3] with frequent extracts from Green and other things, and quantities of poetry, including Shakspere's historical plays. We are also studying the map of England very faithfully, and I am about to send for some outline maps of England and Scotland that they may record for themselves the places they read about. During the heat of the day they all read Scott devoutly. Jessie has read sixteen of the novels now. Then in the afternoon they exchange visits with Beth[4] or Margaret Sloane.[5] After tea they either stroll with me or persuade me to play croquet with them. They fell in love with croquet all over again at Beth's and began playing it with one mallet[,] three broken balls and no wickets, the sad remains of their last set,—the careless wretches! So I took pity on them and gave them a new set, "for Jessie's birthday present!"

Madge is now in Baltimore and reaches here tomorrow evening; havn't heard again from Ed yet. I had a letter from Mary Smith today[6] and a charming picture of her,—the most artistic looking thing. Mary says "it pays me such gentle flattery, and does it so quietly and firmly that I begin to believe that it is a perfect likeness." To tell the truth, though I wouldn't breathe it to her, I didn't know it! Yet in another sense it does her great injustice. It tempts me to adapt Mrs. Dowden's[7] famous remark about me. It is very *ornamental* but I wouldn't have supposed there was so much in her.

There was a nice little letter for you (which I answered) in Saturday's mail from your friend Patterson of Richmond[8] begging you to come, with us, to the [Virginia] Bar Ass. at Hot Springs, and then on to "Old Sweet,"[9] which he describes as a paradise inhabited exclusively by angels—or I *should* say by *exclusive* angels, in other words by F. F. V's.—(terms moderate!) We may consider it for next summer. I am happy to say there is no other mail for you,—was disgusted at having to put three stamps on that last long envelope,—and by the same token the others that I sent had not enough stamps;—this was the first I had weighed. I hope the others reached you. And think of 40 cts for those cards! 'Tis an imposition! If I had not sent them by Margaret they would not have gone at all—that way.

Good-night my own darling. I love you *inexpressibly*, too much to *talk* long about it under some circumstances! Love to Stock.

Your devoted little Eileen.

Margaret had a good night and says she feels all right this morning. Ed comes this week.

ALS (WC, NjP).

¹ Florence Stevens Hoyt, Ellen's first cousin, who had been graduated from Bryn Mawr College in 1898 and was suffering from tuberculosis of the bone in one of her legs.

² Library Place was being widened and paved.

³ Donald Grant Mitchell, *English Lands, Letters and Kings* (4 vols., New York, 1889-97). Two volumes of this set remain in the Wilson Library, DLC.

⁴ The Hibbens' daughter, Elizabeth Grier Hibben.

⁵ Daughter of Professor and Mrs. Sloane.

⁶ This letter from Mary Randolph Smith is missing.

⁷ Elizabeth Dickinson (Mrs. Edward) Dowden.

⁸ This letter from Archibald Williams Patterson is missing.

⁹ Sweet Springs, Va.

From Jenny Davidson Hibben

My dear Mr. Wilson,   Princeton, N.J. July 11. 1899.

Your letter delighted us. We were rather hoping we should hear from you from the steamer & were not disappointed. I am so glad that you found Prof. Seth was "human" & also delightful. I know it will give him the greatest pleasure to show you Edinburgh. It pleased me very much that he should think so highly of Jack, & you were good to tell me.

Mrs. Wilson we see very often, & it would delight your heart to see how well & pretty she looks—better than for some weeks—& your little girls are well & a great pleasure to Beth. We took tea Sunday afternoon with Mrs. Wilson. The place is so attractive now, with many of her flowers in bloom, & the recent rains have made your turf almost like the English grass you are probably seeing now.

A letter from Miss Ricketts this morning tells us that Gloucester [Mass.] is with them a success, & Mrs. Ricketts is charmed with it!

Mr. West we see constantly & his never varying kindness is making us all very fond of him. He *nightly* mutters, on our side porch as he smokes over Dr. Patton & "Dean Winans"—but never for very long—although it is constantly in his mind.

Mother continues the same, no daily change but a slight weakening week by week. I have been slightly ill, & I am afraid I am to be sent away for a week or two, but I dread so leaving Jack—with the possibility of mother's illness becoming suddenly acute. We have had delightful weather, with the exception of one week, when we had almost daily thunder storms!

I hope that you are very well & happy. See everything with our eyes too; you will have much that is delightful to tell us in the fall. We miss you constantly & never cease to wish for you—Jack is lost without you. He had one painful interview with Mr. Winans, who has finally accepted his resignation from the [Discipline] Committee, & it was so hard for him not to have your sympathy & council, at that time. When you come back we will tell you about it. With love from us both, believe me,

Ever yours,   Jenny Davidson Hibben.

ALS (WP, DLC).

To Ellen Axson Wilson

My own darling,   Keswick, 12 July, 1899

We did not get off to Ambleside yesterday, after all: it looks as if we might not get off to-day. In short, we are having a touch of English weather,—very nasty, don't you know,—and from present appearances may decide to take up our residence in Keswick. The weather report in the papers this morning calls what we are having "mists, with some rain"; but it is quite impracticable, for *us*, at any rate, to distinguish very nicely between the rain and the mist,—and the combination, or alternation, is exceeding wet, I can tell you. We sit, and think, with as little impatience as may be, of Grasmere and Rydal and Ambleside, all so near at hand and so dear to our imaginations, and yet so very far away and so inaccessible through this liquid air. Stock., I must say, endures the sitting still a little better than I do. He has no real home of his own, poor chap; but I have and to sit still under leaden skies and look at the ceaseless rain makes me unspeakably homesick and desolate for you and all that is so delicious where you are. My heart demands movement and change of scene and renewal of interest, away from you. And I don't know that it eases the pain at all to think that *next* time[1] you will be with me, and home go where we go and stop where we stop, as contentingly in one comfortable place as in another. That thought seems only to make me the more desperately eager for you now. When that time comes I know I shall be blissfully happy,—my darling with me in these scenes she will love so: but how my heart aches *now* that that bliss is so far away. I know how my darling's wonderful eyes will shine with interest and thought's content the day through, and it makes me happy only to think of it; but then that sets me thinking about the other light that comes into those sweet eyes and makes life seem to me worth living, if only to have the perfect love of so unspeakably sweet a woman. And so the bewildering alternations of pain and hope and memory go on till I deliberately stop thinking, get on a lounge or on my bed and simply ignore the passage of time and attend only to my meals. Fortunately, they have to be thought about and ordered, dish by dish. They are a welcome diversion under the circumstances.

This little inn is very humble and unpretentious, but very comfortable indeed. Landlady and servants alike are friendly and anxious to make us endure the time without annoyance or discomfort,—indeed, that's the way at every homelike, unfashionable inn we go to. These are surely the most friendly people in the world. The roughest of them knows how to be kind, and the busiest will stop to be courteous. It's always the same story: stiff and ungracious in manner when first approached, but kindly, helpful, interested, communicative when once your need or question is stated,—even the railway porters, and the stage drivers! The only persons we avoid are the *too* communicative and companionable tipsy men, who slap us demonstratively on the knee and tell us incoherent details about their own affairs, with an air of comaraderie about them that it were more wholesome not to *smell*. We had to run away from one of these comical gentry last night. He invaded the "Smoke Room" and drove us to the wet street for safety. He had some tale to the effect that he had just won £150 on a bet and had proved himself "a bloomin' prophet," —about what did not appear.

Stock. is stoically content in the perusal of an odd volume of "Leisure Hour,"[2] having exhausted Prof. Knight's "In the Wordsworth Country,"[3]—his principal find in the way of a guide book such as his soul craves. I, as usual, can't think of anything I should like to read:—you will recognize *that* mood in your difficult mate! But I am about making up my mind to read "The Lady of the Lake," which is lying here invitingly, waiting to be read. I've just been through its county, and can count upon getting vivid impressions from it, Sir Walter is so lovingly topographical in his poetry. I'd rather have my poetry a little more poetical; but one can love Sir Walter for what he gives, and forgive him what he leaves out.

"White Lion," Ambleside, 13 July, 1899

Here we are in Ambleside, after being two days imprisoned in Keswick by the rain! It paid, after all, to wait for such a day as this: glorious sunshine and yet fine, majestic clouds too, and shadows to order,—everything to show this sweet country at its best. Be the sun never so bright here, and the sky never so blue, nothing robs the atmosphere of its softness. There is no hard glitter on anything. If it is bright, it is a bright *suffusion*, that makes the green hillsides look like velvet, and the distances clear yet mysterious; and, if shadow be added, the eye does not know where longest to linger. It was familiar ground for me to-day: the sixteen miles from Keswick to Ambleside, Grasmere by the way,— Wordsworth's grave in the quiet churchyard; Dove cottage at Grasmere "town-end"; and, when almost at Ambleside, the sharp climb up a steep lane to stand at a gate and see *some* of the house at Rydal Mount, but I enjoyed it all with a new zest, and saw it all more thoroughly, with a more complete comprehension of details than last time,—and a zest too in Stock's deep, quiet enjoyment. It pays to do it again,—will pay best when done with *you*, the best enjoyer of all! And then there was the ride, along Thirlmere, Grasmere, and Rydal Water. Ullswater is the most beautiful; Derwentwater is more perfect and more perfectly set than these little lakes which we most intimately associate with Wordsworth; but, after all, theirs is the charm,—small, as if they could be claimed for one's own; set about, along the quiet roads, with homes; the air as of a sweet neighbourhood about them. To *love*, give me, before all, Grasmere and Rydal Water. But you shall see for yourself! The day would have been perfect if you had been along.

Letters awaited us here, and that has made the day brighter still—your letter announcing the arrival of my cablegram. I am so glad to *know* at last that the news has reached you. How every word of your letters interests and thrills me, my darling, with its air of home. My whole heart seems to be alive with their quiet senten[ces.] Ah, how I long for that home and for all that it means to me! I am so much interested, my love, to hear of the madonna head. It was an admirable idea to do it in charcoal, and I know what a gem it will be, and what a source of pure joy to you.

I had my laugh at the conclave of friends (much as I love them) and their sage advice about giving up the diet. Alas, I tried it for a day or two, and brought back the old familiar *misery* in my midst. Perhaps I tried too soon,—perhaps I will try again, later; but I shall make haste slowly.

Harvard's sweep of victories at New London was truly extraordinary, but miracles will happen,—and this will probably spoil her for several seasons to come. What's the matter with Yale recently? Has she forgotten how? We saw the *general* results of the races in the papers here; but it was most interesting to read the details in the cutting you sent.

But its bed-time now, my love, and this letter must go before another writing hour comes. I wish I knew how to think of you, and how to end my letters without cutting myself to the quick. It brings tears into my eyes to come too near you in my thought and try to turn my yearnings into words. Dove cottage was almost too much for me to-day. It is such a little *home*, has so much of the old home furniture in it, was actually so sweet a covert of love in all its deepest and most sacred kinds, so works upon the imagination of every man who knows what it stands for, that it quite overcame me,—overcame me with thoughts of you,—very sacred thoughts, that hurt but did me good, being holy and elevating, and giving proof that I am indeed, in a way I wish I could make you know,   Your own   Woodrow

Warmest love to the dear Hibbens and to Mrs. Brown, and as much as they could imagine to my little darlings, Margaret, Jessie, and Nen.

P.S. Your fifth letter (July 3) has just reached me, with its reference to Dunning. It may be that the terms of the Fellowship exclude foreign study. If not, (Magie can find out from the Treasurer's Office) I am for consenting—not because Dunning is an "extraordinary" man, but because he deserves all we can give him without sacrifice of better arrangements. It is out of the question to make another appointment now, and I don't want the Fellowship to be vacant. So Dunning ought to go, I think. I write to him immediately; but please show this to Magie.[4]

                              Yours in all things   Woodrow

ALS (WC, NjP).

    [1] This is the first clear evidence that Wilson had already begun to plan to ask for a sabbatical leave in the near future in order to go abroad with his family for a year or fifteen months of study. As the documents in Vol. 12 will disclose, Wilson requested and was granted leave for the academic year 1901-1902 but had to give up the opportunity on account of his father's illness.

    [2] *The Leisure Hour* was an English literary magazine published in London from 1852 to 1900.

    [3] William Angus Knight, *Through the Wordsworth Country* (London, 1887).

    [4] As J. C. Dunning to WW, July 24, 1899, ALS (WP, DLC), reveals, Wilson did write at once to Dunning giving him permission to go to the University of Heidelberg while holding the South East Club University Fellowship for 1899-1900.

From Ellen Axson Wilson

My own darling,   Princeton July 13 1899

Did you find in your 'ship library' the much talked of "David Harum"[1] and do you know all about the famous horse trade? I went over after tea to enquire after Mrs. Garland,[2] who is suffering from a fall, and to take her some sweet peas. Miss Garland is there and she lent me the afore-said "David." While waiting for the children to get "settled" for the night I read the first ever memorable chapter,—with the result that I am still scarcely sober enough to write a letter. Certainly a perfect specimen of "American humour," destined I suppose to be of the stock in trade of the travelling elocutionist for the next thirty years. I shall have lots of fun if the rest of the book is as good,—but I have every reason to suppose it is not.

Speaking of Mrs. Garland reminds me of Mr. [Moses Taylor] Pyne's accident. When I opened the paper this morning[3] I was startled to see on the first page in large type an account of his being kicked by a horse in his own stable and seriously injured. The paper said he was kicked in the side and narrowly escaped losing his life. Mr. Hibben however came in today and said that he happened to be at the house when Mr. Pyne was brought in, that he certainly had a narrow escape, but that he is not seriously hurt because the blows all came on his legs. He was kicked eight times before he could get out of the stall.

Margaret Sloane took tea with the children last night and reports her brother home again from the hospital and *well*! He was away only two weeks.

I believe this exhausts my small budget of Princeton news; there have been literally no letters for you since I last wrote. I havn't forgotten that I was to write the main *public* news, but actually there is none. I never saw the papers so dull. Every other day or so they say Mr. Alger[4] is going to resign, he denies it on the alternate days; and that is the chief excitement. Mr. Roseveldt got up some excitement for himself—and perhaps for Mr. McKinley,—by going on a royal progress through the West, being received everywhere with immense enthusiasm. He telegraphed back to New York that he was having "great fun."

One curious item of news (that will please *Stockton* more than you!) was that at an illustrated lecture on the Phillipines given in *Chicago* at the most aristocratic church there, the picture of Auguinaldo was loudly applauded, while Dewey's was received in silence! Once only they applauded Dewey's name, to wit when the speaker affirmed that he (Dewey) was leaving the Phillipines out of disgust with the policy of our government.

Margaret is quite well again now and it is Jessie's turn instead to be a little upset; only today her digestion is a little out of order. But she seems better tonight and I trust tomorrow will be "perfectly all right." The rest are quite well. We still have our fine cool weather, with frequent rains, keeping everything fresh and green and beautiful. The only penalty exacted is the unusual frequency and severity of the thunder-storms. Last night we had one that lasted from seven until after eleven. Margaret and Nellie had quite a panic,—crying &c. Jessie was as quiet as usual. By the way, by a strange fatality the thunderbolt I wrote of before struck *both* Hagaman houses,[5] injuring the roof of the one on Mercer St., tearing down the chimney of the other. It also struck a tree at the Armours.

Madge came home on Tuesday looking very well and pretty;— and in a state of adoration as regards Mrs. Reid. By the way, you know I said she was the sort of girl who would be dangerous to Edgeworth Smith? It was even so. He made a goose of himself about her,—with the reward that she thinks him "a very weak character indeed," and "*so* tiresome"! What will Mrs. Bird and Mrs. Smith[6] think if they discover that she has been cruel to their darling. Madge will have no more Sunday dinners; perhaps they will cut us all. In the meantime our young person thinks she "will never marry," she "doesn't like men well enough"! She is at the "silly age," you know, but that is a very satisfactory and unusual form for the silliness to take.

I have had no letter since Saturday. I think one should be due tomorrow. In fact I had high hopes both yesterday and today. But I try not to be unreasonable. Ah my darling, I simply live on thoughts of you, and dreams of you; and how glad I shall be of a letter recording the fact that the "fun" of the tour has really begun,—the fatigues of that unfortunate voyage all over. Love from all to both. May God bless & keep you is the constant prayer of

Your own   Eileen

ALS (WC, NjP).

1 Edward Noyes Westcott, *David Harum, A Story of American Life* (New York, 1898).

2 Mary Stebbins (Mrs. M. J. G.) Garland of 86 Stockton St.

3 *New York Times*, July 13, 1899.

4 President McKinley's Secretary of War, Russell Alexander Alger.

5 Probably the homes of Mary D. Hageman (widow of John Frelinghuysen Hageman) at 83 Mercer St. and of the late John Frelinghuysen Hageman, Jr., at 94 Bayard Ave.

6 Sarah Baxter (Mrs. William Edgeworth) Bird and her daughter, Saida Bird (Mrs. Victor) Smith.

To Ellen Axson Wilson

My own darling,   Durham, The Three Tuns, 16 July, 1899

We "played in rather bad luck," as Stockton the other day very justly remarked, in our efforts to explore the Lake District. Two days, as you know, we were shut up by rain; and the last day, Friday, Stock. himself stopped proceedings. Thursday afternoon he went down with one of his attacks of pain,[1] and of course we spent the next day quietly in the hotel, and in little strolls about Ambleside. We had intended to make Friday one of our most interesting days, by riding over to Coniston, and, by a little detour on our way back, visiting Hawkshead and identifying the scenes of Wordsworth's school days. I think poor Stock. had quite set his heart on that. But he bore the disappointment like a Stoic. Only his eyes told how deeply bored and disconcerted he was. The pain was not very severe, and passed off without much ado; but of course he had to be very careful afterward.

After all, I saw so much more this time than I saw last time in my hurried run thro. the lake country that I feel I have nothing to regret. I saw more even at Grasmere, for I did not in '96 go *into* the fine old church (St. Oswald's) in whose yard Wordsworth is buried, and I found out this time how much I had missed. This is the church, it seems, which Wordsworth describes in the fifth book of the Excursion:

> "Not raised in nice proportion was the pile,
> But large and massy; for duration built;
> With pillars crowded, and the roof upheld
> By naked rafters intricately crossed,
> Like leafless underboughs, in some thick wood,
> All withered by the depth of shade above."

That is still a description of the venerable place, which is very old indeed; singularly spacious for a village church. There are still on the walls even the "admonitory texts," "each in its ornamental scroll enclosed" just as Wordsworth describes them. There is added now, of course, the very dignified, simple, artistic memorial marble to the poet himself,—an effigy of the poet's head, in profile, in low relief, and a really beautiful inscription by Keble, the hymn writer—beautiful both in feeling and in expression, and, more than that, adequate. It was good to see it all,—and Wordsworth himself supplies me with the words in which to express my dominant thought there as at Dove Cottage and in all that exquisite county.

Ay, think on that, my heart, and cease to stir;
Pause upon that, and let the breathing frame
No longer breathe, but all be satisfied.
Oh, if such silence be not thanks to God
For what hath been bestowed, then where, where then
Shall gratitude find rest? Mine eyes did ne'er
Fix on a lovely object, nor my mind
Take pleasure in the midst of happy thoughts,
But either she, whom now I have, who now
Divides with me my loved abode, was there,
Or in my thoughts. Where'er my footsteps turned,
Her voice was like a hidden bird that sang;
The thought of her was like a flash of light,
Or an unseen companionship, a breath
Or fragrance independent of the wind.

You seem to me to own all England,—except such parts of it as are marred and spoiled!

Yesterday we came over from Ambleside (or rather from Windermere, five miles away) by train. And I can tell you it's an undertaking to *cross* England from side to side, whether you do it by bicycle or by rail! Nothing runs that way. We had to change cars four times (looking out for the transfer of our wheels each several times in the midst of crowds and hurry—for it was a Saturday), but at last our fifth train brought us to Durham, after we had spent nearly five hours going one hundred miles or less; and here we are safely ensconsed at the Three Tuns, Mrs. Brown's famous hostelry. It's good to be in a cathedral town on Sunday, if you like your worship richly done. It takes nearly two hours, but it is an exceeding handsome work of art. And this morning we had a little extra picturesqueness thrown in, not on the usual programme. Her Majesty's judges (two of them) are holding Assize here (thus is the criminal court for the trial of the more heinous offences called) and they attended service in wig and gown, coming in a[nd] going out again with the procession of the clergy and the choir (always an imposing company on any day in a cathedral) and attended (or, at any rate, accompanied) by an officer of the royal army in full regimentals. What is more, they came to the cathedral and left it in a state coach, attended by tip-staves and constables and footmen in stunning costume. They were preceded as they came and as they went by the tuneful blare of trumpets. And after all they had but to cross an open square and drive within the courtyard of their official place of entertainment! Truly, I never before saw such going to church!

One of these gentlemen (Lord (?) Grantham)² is a terror to the unrighteous,—and he looked it, with his keen, spare visage and air of acid majesty.

This is Stock's first cathedral and he is enjoying its impressive beauty after his own chastened style. It being Sunday, we cannot explore the great pile within; but we have walked around it and marvelled at its noble pose on its rocky height,—a height embowe[re]d in trees, which stand upon its steep sides and at the river's brink as if in a park, but its strength and majesty not a whit concealed by the rich shield of green boughs, which seem to reach as it were only to the knees of the crowning cathedral.

Your letters are infinitely interesting, my love. I have just read the one about Guyot Cameron's marriage, the woman he married, and their home. It is better to read your description than to see with one's own eyes. As for the attitude and iniquitous action of the old people, it is unspeakable,—the crowning wickedness of their foolish lives, whose very folly has been essentially wicked. It has been some time since I could trust myself to speak of Dr. Cameron himself,—but this is more grossly and unintelligently wrong than I supposed even he could do! It almost makes me resolve to like his son, whom he has so brutally mistreated. Let us hope that his young wife will cure him in some degree of the things we find distasteful in him, and will make him more like other men in *walk* and conversation. It is hard to think of such a mimic man (and a poor, extravagant mimic at that!) having a tragedy of his own, and choosing the way of love rather than the way of filial submission. But that fact alone invests him with a little dignity, and we must give him the benefit of it,—at any rate in our thought.

By the time this letter reaches you, my Eileen, this separation will be *half over*, think of that. From that time on we shall be approaching one another. It will be as if I turned about, and with extended arms began to walk towards you, instead of away from you. Ah, how it comforts me to think of that,—how I must guard my movements to keep from quickening the walk into a run! But I shall *feel* that my face is turned *home*wards, and that will act like a tonic upon me,—will increase every wholesome, healing influence of my vacation. I shall have to take care those days not to ride too far and too fast, as if I could make the time go faster by increasing my own speed. My heart is so *tethered*! I feel the tug of the thong every minute. You dont know, my sweet one, (or *do* you know?) how you profit by the assessment my heart makes of you these long days. I have so much time to think;—every avenue of thought leads to you;—every scene seems to remind me how much sweeter you are, and more interesting than any other thing or person I see or know or see *into*. Other men marry "such things":—I, no better than they, was permitted to marry you, and crown my life with the sweetest love, the most satisfying communion the world affords,—and so the song goes on! It has this unselfish characteristic: it is not in a single thought *egotistical*. I did not *win* this lady,—she was *given* to me, a wonderful gratuity. I can think of her in all her real beauty of mind and person and never for a moment incur the self-suspicion of admiring myself. It is the purest pleasure I shall ever know,—and probably the only blameless self-indulgence! You make me better by a great, unspeakable, abiding charm of life and character!

17 July, 1899, Monday.

Here we are still in Durham this evening, my love. We had intended to be in York to-night, ready to see the great minster to-morrow; but we found so much to interest us here that we lingered. This morning we went through the cathedral (of course we could not explore it yesterday) in all its public parts and thought we were through. But, since the Assizes were being held, we happened to wish to have a glimpse of them;—one glimpse was not enough: we became absorbed in a murder trial, held before Judge Grantham, one of the most honourably noted of the English Assize justices,—and we stayed to see it go through all its processes, to an acquittal. Stock. was as deeply interested as I was. We were both struck by the dignity, and yet efficient speediness of the trial; by the power of the judge to be a veritable trier of the case,—his privilege to tell the jury frankly what he thought the just inferences from the several items of evidence, direct and circumstantial,—and what he thought *they* ought to conclude from it all. Of course the judges came to court with the same impressive show of state as that which accompanied them yesterday to church—the Lord High Sheriff coming with them in full and splendid uniform; trumpeters and stave bearers going before them; their carriage like a thing taken out of an old picture, swung on its long springs,—and footmen in medieval grand costume; and the judges looked stern and formidable indeed as they walked solemnly in to their seats, sober and impassive under their wigs and gowns. But all the acid went out of Lord Grantham's face when he began his summing up to the jury. He is reputed the severest criminal judge in the Kingdom; but to-day he believed the accused innocent, and his face grew infinitely sweet as he spoke. It was an intellectual treat to hear him put the case—with shrewd insight, briefly, incisively, always find the word he wanted, always wanting the right word; firm, transparently fair, courteous with the perfect courtesy that is inbred and instinctive. We were charmed—I think we were a little awed. At any rate, the afternoon wore away, and we do not go to York till to-morrow. Stock. seems *"perfectly* all right" now, and full of quiet enjoyment,—as great as his temperament will allow. He provokes me sometimes, as I provoked dear Father, when my travels first began, with him in New York, and my sight-seeing, at the Centennial Exposition.[3] I am fairly put out with him for having no exclamation points in his disposition. He is as "impossible" as a New England audience. *I* am the effusive one (if you can imagine that); *I* find the adjectives and utter the praise,—in sheer reaction against the silence of our procession of two! I think I am getting more effusive as I get older,—more demonstrative,—more apt to speak my feelings and sentiments. It is the effect, I judge, of sixteen years of making love to you. I fear, therefore, that Stock. cannot be counted on to cultivate the desirable habit,—he is getting no practice,—and mere getting older will not reform him. I have lived a life of enjoyment since I have lived with you, and it would be singular indeed had I not learned to *express* pleasure. Good night, my sweet one, my matchless Eileen. You are my own constant, unquestionable, supreme joy. My heart relies on you, centres in you, lives by you, and I am altogether,   Your own   Woodrow

I believe I have not *said* that I am well; but I am, perfectly—and always must be understood to be when I do not say that I am *not*.

Give my best love to the dear Hibbens and to Mrs. Brown. Tell the children that I love them with all my heart,—and let nobody but yourself know how much I love *you*.

ALS (WC, NjP).

[1] Stockton Axson was probably suffering from chronic appendicitis. He had an operation early in the following year after an acute attack.

[2] Sir William Grantham, Judge of the High Court of Justice, Queen's Bench Division. He was never ennobled.

[3] See Wilson's diary entries for Sept. 6-8, 1876, Vol. 1.

From Ellen Axson Wilson

My own darling,   Princeton July 17/99.

Do you observe the date?—a month today since you left! Time does manage to slip away *even* when one's sweet-heart is absent. I have had *two* delightful letters since I wrote last, the Edinburgh one on Friday and today the one from Ayr. You can't imagine how happy they have made me. *Such* charming letters they are! Mr. & Mrs. Hibben enjoyed the Edinburgh one immensely when they were here Sunday,—were much pleased that you and Prof. Seth had hit it off so well. Pray sir, make a note of the fact,—you and Stockton both—that you are neither of you so unsocial as you would have yourselves believe. You *do* enjoy meeting interesting people, and it does you good; I hope you won't forget that fact when you reach Oxford, Cambridge, & London. *Can't* you manage to see Dowden?[1] I think your plan for wheeling a little less and so saving time and strength an excellent one. Have you finished with Scotland now?—or will Abbot[s]ford & the Yarrow, &c, come in on the way back?

I have just directed letters for you from Jessie and Nellie which I think you will find quite interesting. They spoke of Jessie's not being well. She has had a touch of tonsilitis for the last three days, but is much better today. Her fever has gone down from $102°$ to $100°$ and the one little ulcer on her throat has gone. There is still something of a lump on the outside of her throat. It was a *very* light attack, the doctor not putting her to bed at all. The rest of us are perfectly well, except that Margaret still whoops once in a while, so that I am afraid to "turn her loose." The rest of us I think could now present a perfectly clean health bill as regards the whooping-cough. Nellie and I went to church yesterday.

We looked for Ed both Friday and Saturday nights, but in vain! which caused both his sisters to lose their temper and declare him "as bad as Stockton." A letter today explains that the head of the Sanitary Dept. wants him "to write up the results of his experimental work and, if they seem worth it, hand them into the Quarterly for publication,"[2] which means that in order to look up references he must remain a few days longer. He hopes to be down the middle of this week.

I see the children mention Puffin's kittens! When I arose one morning recently imagine my dismay at finding five of them in *my closet*, in one of the pigeon-holes for shoes! Of course they had to be moved, which so discomposed her mind that the usual result followed: she hid them away, and that was the end of them. Yet we used the most strenuous efforts to reconcile her to her new quarters.

Well, after trying for a year to make up my mind to it I have finally, (with Mrs. Hibben's help) succeeded. I have been to New York and had my picture taken by Davis and Sanford! I really thought I *ought* to get *one* good one for the children to have when I am gone. What would *I* not give for one of Mama taken in the years when I was old enough to remember. The only ones of her, you know, were taken before I was born & when I was a baby. The proofs came today and they are a great success. It is really an embarrassment of riches, six out of eight are good. Indeed Mrs. Tilton,[3] with her usual perversity, prefers still a seventh one that everyone else thinks dreadful. How I wish you were here to settle the matter! But fortunately I can have three finished for the same price as one, so between them we surely won't miss the one that *would* have been your choice. I shall depend partly on Mrs. Hibben's judgment. She is delighted with them,—with one especially. And the Aikens[4] declare another,—which Mrs. Hibben doesn't care for,—"the most beautiful thing they ever saw in their lives." The latter is my favourite, by the way. I have had great fun over them today, the way in which people disagree about them is so comical. It happened that when I took them to the Aikens for their judgment, several people were there, and they managed to get up a great excitement over them, one and another declaring vehemently that they *"would not give up theirs"* &c. &c. You would have thought it a personal matter with them. It is certainly cause for thankfulness that they are good, for what *do* you suppose they are to cost? *Fifteen* dollars a dozen! Mrs. Hibben said the cabinets were fifteen, but we supposed of course the little ones would be less. But no, they are all the same. When they told me that I almost fainted; but I should have felt like such a fool to turn round and come back to Princeton without them, after all the trouble, that I brazened it out.

Everyone sends love and good wishes to you, dear; Mr. Hibben seems quite love-sick for you. We still have charming weather and are enjoying life thoroughly. I am *so* happy over the good reports that come from you both now. My own dearest love! I love you inexpressibly, devotedly, passionately,—I am in every heart beat, Your own   Eileen.

Love to dearest Stock from each and all by name.

July 18. Jessie says she feels "well" this morning. Such a perfectly glorious morning it is.

ALS (WP, DLC).

[1] Edward Dowden, Professor of Rhetoric and English Literature at Trinity College, Dublin. The Wilsons had met the Dowdens during the Princeton Sesquicentennial celebration in 1896.

[2] Edward W. Axson, "On Nitrites as a Product of Combustion," *Technology Quarterly*, XII (Sept. 1899), 219-25. The *Technology Quarterly* was published by the Massachusetts Institute of Technology.

[3] Caroline Stebbins (Mrs. J. R.) Tilton of 86 Stockton St.

[4] Sarah Noyes Aiken, widow of Charles Augustus Aiken, and her family of 108 Mercer St.

To Ellen Axson Wilson

My own darling,   White Hart Hotel   Lincoln 18 July, 1899

We left Durham for York this morning; reached there (by train) about half-past eleven; found, after a few hours, that we had sufficiently "done" the quaint walls and streets and the splendid minster; and took the train for Lincoln (this is the part of the country where it least pays to ride—we are saving our strength for the mid-counties and the South); and here we are. Dinner is over; we have taken a stroll in the twilight, to get a first impression of the cathedral: and out through the gate that has stood since the Romans were here; and are now ready for our evening meditations and—bed.

I was the more anxious to get on to this place because it was the next point to which my mail was to be sent,—and here is what I was longing for—the next letter from *you*. The other letters—from Mrs. Abbe[1] and the rest,—make no impression of any kind on me, because your letter makes so much. It is the letter written just after my first one had arrived,—the letter telling of the terrible thunderbolt. That was indeed a dreadful experience, and shocked me not a little. Poor little Margaret! If she gets no better of her nervousness you must certainly take her away for a change, my love. And, by the way,—though I asked you to leave me a credit of four hundred dollars, you need not leave that much by a hundred. Unless some unforeseen expense comes upon me, I am quite confident of getting through with three hundred,—and I hope to get through with less. Will not an extra hundred added to *your* side of the credit in our cheque-book make it quite feasible for you to take a trip away with the children? You know how earnestly I hope you will go, and how absolutely I must depend on you to act in the matter,—being too far away for an exchange of opinions

I am by no means so tired to-night as you might suppose from my intimation of how full a day it has been,—of sight-seeing and travel,—for, among other things, we have been about four hours on the train. But I am very well indeed, and, as always when I am well, I rest quickly, particularly with the help of a square meal,—and the English meals are eminently "square": there is no French cooking or nonsense of any kind, but plain, honest *food*; and I am pleased. I admit that, were I not taking a great deal of exercise, it might grow monotonous, and pall on my appetite; but, under the circumstances, it does not: my appetite is of the robust and honest sort that does not have to be tempted.

It was pleasant to see what deep and genuine, and unusual, pleasure Stock. got from the superb York minster. He was evidently very sensibly *impressed* by the cathedral at Durham,—one of my favourites; but it is very severe indeed, and one needs, perhaps, to be a bit experienced in cathedrals,—his cathedral sense (there actually seems a special sense for this particular enjoyment) a good deal developed,—to see how really great and admirable Durham is,—and it was Stock's first. But York is unmistakably beautiful. Its wealth of splendid old glass alone is enough to capture the eye and make it *know* that it is satisfied,—and Stock. woke up and *felt* the great pile's majesty and charm and power to awe, —and said he could see how one might develop a sort of "cathedral habit," by constant or undue indulgence. I foresee that a few more cathedrals will give him a new knowledge of what is beautiful!

The Bell Hotel, Ely, 20 July, 1899

We have added Lincoln, Peterboro', and Ely to our list of cathedrals, and Stock. is inclined to think the last the most delightful. He, by the way, sits out in the nave, a hearer, not a doer, while I attend service within the choir. The choir is generally, as you doubtless know, separated from the nave and transepts by an (often-times quite solid) screen, and the morning and afternoon daily services are conducted within the choir. Those who sit outside, in the nave can be little more than distant listeners to the music, hardly catching the words of the service at all. I go inside; sit in a stall; intone the responses with the other insiders; play the thorough-going churchman,—can you imagine it?—while Stock stays without. He says that he does not "know what to do," and that it makes him feel foolish. I, on the contrary, entirely enjoy the service. It seems, in one of these ancient cathedrals, neither artificial nor pretentious, but altogether solemn and beautiful; and the music is by no means all that I go for or take pleasure in. It is for me a real religious exercise and I feel benefitted and uplifted by it. So does Stock., for that matter, but he does not feel quite equal to actually taking part in the services.

There is, of course, nothing that I can describe about this cathedral life of ours: I can describe neither the cathedrals themselves nor the sensations they create in us. Ely is our last cathedral for the present; for, from here, our itinerary is probably, Cambridge, Bury St. Edmunds, Rugby, Warwick, Oxford:—the Universities with Shakespeare and a little monastic architecture added.

I did not write last night because at Peterboro' we went to what turned out a wretched hostelry: dirty, crowded, hardly respectable,—if we may judge by the too free manners and conversation of the young women who waited on us. There was no corner in the horrid, ill-kept place where I could write comfortably,—and I had, moreover, the feeling that it was no place from which to write to *you*. I have an almost Quixottic sense of propriety in every matter that touches you. I have a tough enough stomach in respect of what I can put up with for myself; but I cannot even write to you from a place to which I could not take you. The place is in our Cyclists' Touring Club guide book, which has never in any other instance sent us to any but first-class places,—and we are astounded and indignant that it should have made such a mistake and taken us in. The air of this island breeds "kicking" and we mean to kick. We shall write to the Secretary of the Club and protest,—urging that the house be stricken from the list. Then, at any rate, our consciences will be clear. Members of the Club might take ladies there! There is a lady I know who could not eat a mouthful of the food, if there were no other objection to the place,—not because it is bad food (it is not), but because it is served in so slovenly and uninviting a fashion, with doubtful cleanliness. But enough of that! It's over now and seems only a bad dream. Only I shall have to go to bed earlier to-night because of its noise and heat and the general discomfort which kept me awake there.

We got here to-day in time for luncheon; enjoyed the quiet town and the cathedral grounds for a little, when lunch was over; went to four o'clock service (in the manner I have already described); after service, were shown over the building by a verger in the usual manner; sat without again for a little while to look at the great structure and enjoy its proportions; had tea; and arrived at this moment of writing. Not that Stock. writes. He seems to have no correspondents,—or, else, neglects them systematically. I do all the writing,—and do all of it to you. I find that I long for these hours with you. I do not write about anything in particular, as you observe, and I dare not write much, directly, about the love that masters me and makes me so restless these wandering days, and draws me in the evening to pen and paper,—even when I am tired and have nothing to say. But there is a sense of communion in the mere multiplication of words and sheets that are to go to you,—in the mere sense of speaking directly to and for you, and there is no little solace in it all! And, faith, I need solace! This is no real living, this putting myself across the world from you, my Eileen, my queen! You must never make or let me do it again, as you love me. I am going to try to stay still for (say) a week at Oxford, but I don't know how it will go. I am infinitely restless when I am away from you. I do not want to have too much time to sit still. I may think: thinking makes me long: longing makes me

unhappy. I am quite well (and so is Stock.) but, ah me, my sweet
one, I am   Your own   Woodrow

Love to the dear Hibbens, to Mrs. Brown, and without limit to our
precious chicks.

                              Same, Friday morning, 21 July, 1899
    I am indeed rich this morning, and must add a few lines to ex-
press my happiness: a letter from you, a letter from Margaret,[2]
and a letter from Mrs. Hibben,[3]—your letter reading like a sweet
idyll, with its account of your daily life and studies with the children; Margaret's letter as sweet and interesting as possible (thank
her for it with a full heart); and Mrs. Hibben's as natural, warm-
hearted, engaging as she is. "Mrs Wilson we see very often," writes
Mrs. H., "and it would delight your heart to see how well and pretty she looks." Indeed it would! My heart can hardly endure fore-
going that delight. Your letter, my Eileen, is inexpressibly refreshing, with its direct breath and picture of the sweetest home in the
world. I declare I see very few so externally beautiful even in this
land of exquisite homes; and, as for the inside, there is not another so ideal in the world,—for there is no other presided over by
a spirit at once so sweet and so thoughtful, with the sort of
thoughtfulness which delights!
    Stock. has taken the train to Bury St. Edmunds this morning,
to spend the day there, and I am waiting here to see about our
belated boxes (otherwise trunks). For the first time, they have
failed to turn up, and we must, I suppose, wait here till we learn
what has become of them. We shall then ride over to Cambridge,
—only fifteen miles away. I thought I should enjoy a day of quiet,
and I particularly wanted Stock. to see Bury. I shall spend a good
deal of the time writing letters, which have accumulated a little
on my hands. Bless you for your letters, and for being what you
are to   Your own   Woodrow

ALS (WC, NjP).
    [1] Catherine Amory Palmer (Mrs. Robert) Abbe, wife of the distinguished New
York surgeon. Her letter is missing but may have been an invitation to Wilson
to speak to the Nineteenth Century Club of New York. See the news item printed
at Nov. 16, 1899.
    [2] Margaret Wilson's letter is missing.
    [3] Jenny D. Hibben to WW, July 11, 1899.

A Memorandum

Mem.   [c. July 19, 1899]
     I wish a monument like that to Archbishop Magee in the yard
of Peterboro Cathedral. It is an Irish (?) cross, behind the cathedral.

WWhw memorandum in the pocket notebook described at June 18, 1899.

From John Grier Hibben

My dear Wilson   Princeton July 20/99
     Your letter gave us great pleasure and Jenny has already writ-
ten you telling you how glad we were to hear from you. I wish
however to add a line or two, not of news for Princeton is moving
on in the same sleepy way, but to express to you that which you
already know of course how much I miss you. It seems that every
day something occurs which I naturally wish to talk over with you.
We have had several informal gatherings of the Faculty malcontents on Wests porch. The excitement of the early days of the
summer has subsided, and a sullen resentment seems to have
taken its place in reference to the powers that be. In a conversation which I had with the new Dean, he informed me that you
were his first choice for Dean & that he thought you better qualified for the office than any man in the Faculty. My resignation
he has finally accepted. The others, excepting [Charles Augustus]
Young, yourself & me, remain on the Committee.
     We see Mrs. Wilson very often & she is looking remarkably
well. She is good enough to read us occasional snatches from your
letters & we are in this manner kept in touch with you, much to
our pleasure. Your account of the Edinburgh visit & Seth's hospitality interested me greatly. I received a letter from him a few
days ago in which he speaks of you in terms of very warm appreciation. Last Monday the Faculty left-overs had a picnic—going out on wheels & a carriage for the fat members, to Hanging
Rock.[1] There were twelve of us altogether, & we had a very fine
time. I wished for you, but the delights of a Faculty picnic can
hardly rival the rare pleasures you are now enjoying, and it did
not seem right for me even in my thoughts to wish for you in
Princeton. I hope the summer will make you strong and vigorous
again. I would even go so far as to hope you may return quite
corpulent and aldermanic in your appearance, with a large fund
of reserve energy which additional pounds naturally indicate.
[Joseph H.] Dulles, West and I play golf every afternoon, and it

has proved a fine thing for us all. West is growing thin with his vigorous exercise. My Mother has seemed much stronger the last week—her tone seems to have been regained somewhat. It is difficult to interpret this change for the better & we hardly dare to hope that it will prove a permanent gain. We have been wonderfully favored with cool weather this summer. With the exception of a very few days, we have had a remarkable July, with a bracing air suggestive of a sea breeze. All this has been a great boon to Mother & no doubt her improvement is owing to this cause.

Jenny joins me in a great deal of love to you & my kind regards to Mr. Axson.   Faithfully your friend,   Jack

ALS (WP, DLC).
¹ A landmark near Princeton, now usually called Cradle Rock.

From Ellen Axson Wilson

Princeton, July 20 1899

My darling what a perfectly adorable letter is the one which reached me this morning!—the one from Dumfries and the Lakes. I hope you realized when you sent it some part of the happiness it would give me. I even said to myself in my haste when I first read it that it was as good as if you yourself had suddenly come back. Of course that would be far from true,—other things being equal. But then "other things["] are *not* equal, for it would be a great disappointment to have you suddenly come back before your time. So the letter wins after all! Ah, my darling, I love you *infinitely*, and it is indescribably sweet to be so loved in return,—even though I *know* that I do not deserve it,—know how out of measure your thoughts of me are. Surely, surely, you are in a land of magic and the glamour of it all has covered even me in far-away Princeton. But I am perfectly sure that whether or no I deserve such love I am the happiest woman in the world in possessing it. It seems a very miracle that such a man as *you* should so love *me*. How, I ask myself a hundred times, can he help seeing and feeling all that he is and all that I am *not*; how can he help being simply bored with me? This is a great mystery,—and I am more than willing for it to remain one, if only the facts too will remain unchanged!

But the *love* in this dear letter is only the chiefest among the many good things it has brought me. I hope you are not like Browning who strongly objected to having it said that he had, in a letter, expressed himself well, lest it should make him self-conscious,—because I really must say that it seems to me you have never written more exquisite *style* than in this epistle. I can fairly see those changing lights and shadows over mountain and valley in all their mystery and their glory. And then it is *so* good to know that all goes well with you both,—that you are so happy. Isn't it *delicious* to think of dear Stock, who has had so much to bear, having now such a truly "good time"?

All goes well with us too; Jessie is quite herself again except for a very little lump still on the outside of her throat, the rest of us perfectly well. We hopefully waited for Ed tonight but he did not turn up. I hope he will be here by Saturday at least.

The wonderful weather still continues; did you ever know of anything to equal it?—out of England! I feel especially thankful for it on the Hibbens' account. It is making the summer much easier for them than it could otherwise have been. The mother continues about the same. Beth is going soon with the house-maid to the Clevelands for two weeks.[1]

My Madonna came home in its frame tonight, and I have just unpacked it. I got for it a flat frame, rather wide, of dark grey wood, dull finish which suits the picture *exactly*. It is really a beautiful thing and is giving me no little pleasure because it has "*the* expression."

There actually is a piece of news in the paper this morning,—Alger has resigned! He could not stand the pressure any longer. It seems he went off and consulted the Vice-President who strongly advised the step telling him that by so doing he could prove to the country that "the trouble was with the *system* and not with the man," and so in the end he, Alger, would be completely justified; rather a clever line for Hobart to take, eh? All sorts of people are being talked of for the place, everyone saying however that it must be a New York man. There surely *is* something wrong with the "system" which considers state lines in making such an appointment at such a time. But all this will be an old story, even to you in England by the time this letter reaches you.

There has not been a letter for you since I last wrote; your friends—I mean your enemies—are certainly very considerate this summer! There is no town news except that they have a fog-horn to supplement the fire-bells, which latter they say did not awake the firemen. A barn caught fire last night and the sounds were simply unearthly. Poor timid Nell was of course frightened and cried bitterly.

Here in the house all goes peacefully & happily; Madge & I are absorbed in "Pan Michael."[2] After I finish with the children in the morning, she reads the greater part of the day while I sew or paint. With dear love from all to both, believe me, my own darling, in every heart-throb   Your own,   Eileen.

ALS (WC, NjP).
  1 The Grover Clevelands were at their summer home, Gray Gables, in Buzzards Bay, Mass.
  2 Henryk Sienkiewicz, *Pan Michael. An Historical Novel of Poland, the Ukraine, and Turkey*, translated by Jeremiah Curtin (London and Boston, 1893).

To Ellen Axson Wilson

My own darling,   Cambridge, 23 July, 1899

Your last letter, which came this morning to bless and delight me, disturbs me with its news that you had had no letter between Saturday and Thursday. I have been religiously careful to inquire at each place the time at which the American mail would close, and have invariably posted my letter several hours before the time stated. I am *so* sorry there should have been any irregularity. Your letters have found me with delightful regularity. The Linen Company Bank has been extremely prompt and accurate in forwarding. This morning's letter reached London yesterday afternoon at a quarter to five, and was here by breakfast time to-day. At best, the interval between mailing and receiving is nine days and that, where the heart is involved, is a dreadfully long time; but it is a vast comfort it is no longer.

Before I forget it, let me answer an important question in the letter I received at Ely,—the question about the road to the street. I hope, my love, that you will have anything done that may be necessary, and that you will have it done when and how you please. Your judgment is as good as mine in such matters, and your taste is much better. I am afraid that the street-making may be proving a great niusance to you. By the way, if it is not too late when this reaches you, will you not have sewer connections (i.e. a first section of sewer pipes) run from the manhole in which the sewer now ends to our curb line (only a few feet, you see) towards our cess-pool, so that it will not later be necessary to dig the street up to make our connections? Consult Mr. Margerum,[1] or some other responsible person about it and, if necessary, get him to superintend the work for you. No doubt the street commissioner will suggest the proper person to *do* the work. Ask Magie: he will tell you the best person to go to, or, rather, send for, and help you in every way he can.

We actually rode from Ely to Cambridge yesterday on our wheels (we had not *journeyed* on them for a week). It was only

sixteen miles (eighteen is the most I have yet felt like making
Stock take, though I should be equal, I am quite sure, to thirty)
and the easiest sixteen we are ever likely to ride,—perfectly level,
except where slightly down hill, perfectly smooth, and a smart
breeze *behind* us, modestly helping us at every stroke though we
needed no help. We had only to lift our feet and put them down
again: the wheels seemed to need no actual propulsion. And
Cambridge at the end of the ride! Oxford is more beautiful and
impressive, but surely Cambridge is beautiful and impressive
enough. We arrived about half-past twelve, and so had all the
afternoon in which to enjoy a first and general impression. The
most beautiful buildings and quads. are not five minutes walk
from our hotel (King's College, for example, and Trinity, and St.
John's) and we saw them at once, when we had had lunch, and
made straight through them to the incomparable "Backs." The
Cam you know, runs close at the rear of these colleges, with here
a broad lawn stretching between the buildings and its banks, as
at King's, and there the very walls of some shapely hall or dormitory standing with their feet in its stream (as if the road to the
station at Princeton were a river—the Cam is no wider—and
washed the very walls of Blair)[2] so that men may sit and fish
from their bedroom windows. At short intervals beautiful arched
bridges cross the little river, sometimes from lawn to lawn, sometimes from building to building,—sometimes with a single arch,
sometimes with three arches. St. Johns crowds close to the water,
stands *in* the water, indeed, on either bank and throws across the
stream an exquisite enclosed bridge of a single arch wh. is the
Bridge of Sighs in small. On the farther side of the river stretch
great lawns and splendid quiet avenues of trees, shaded walks,
and beds of flowers almost wild; and nothing breaks the fine park
except where, near its end, a building of St. John's stands, itself
an ornament. And these are The Backs, flanked in the background
by a park like public road, into which you make exit through
stately iron gates of elaborate tracery crowned with the arms of
a college. The river is full of boats for hire, and Stock. and I took
one and paddled slowly from end to end of the beautiful place,
with unspeakable, quiet pleasure. Then we sat indefinitely at the
side of one of the great lawns on the farther bank and just let
the beauty and peace and sweet air of the place soak into us.
There were pleasure seekers all about us,—enough to people without crowding the scene, and tennis courts full of young fellows
in white flannels, most of whom knew how to play the game well
enough to be worth watching. The charm is working on Stock.

and he is rapidly improving emotionally. Cambridge has quite fascinated him, and he finds words to say so! It will be some fun to be his cicerone yet, if his improvement continues at the present rate. The trouble is, we are nearly at the top of the scale in places to see. Oxford is more beautiful and more fascinating than Cambridge, but I know of no place in the Kingdom more to be desired than Oxford, and after that there will be nothing for Stock's. emotions to rise to, unless the vastness and the fulness of London should affect them, after another fashion. To-day (Sunday) it is raining, and we have stayed indoors, rather willing, on the whole, to rest and see nothing. We did not get down to breakfast until eleven o'clock. I should have got up and attended service at King's College chapel had our trunks been here, but they are not, and one would hardly dare face an English Sunday congregation in shorts! We were very much interested and amused by a notice Stock. found in yesterday morning's (London) paper. The athletic contests between Cambridge and Harvard (Yale and Oxford did not count in them, as it turned out, at all) took place in London yesterday, and London has been suffering from an uncommonly hot spell of weather. It was formally announced in the morning papers, therefore, that, in view of the extremely warm weather, gentlemen would not be obliged to wear high hats to the games! Many extraordinary and truly revolutionary things have been happening here in consequence of the heat. One of the judges in London (or was it only a magistrate?) actually took off his wig in court and invited the baristers present to follow his example! The Speaker of the House of Commons, the room being already quite too close to breathe in, broke an immemorial tradition by proceeding to a division without first closing the doors: the first instance of the kind, I suppose, in several hundred years! One wonders what would happen if they had heat such as ours. I suppose it would break down the English Constitution, wh. would seem in very fact to be a part of the established order of nature! And really it *has* been hot. Even we felt and suffered from it, *with our winter flannels on.* To-day the long desired change seems to have set in. With the rain has come back the chill the Britisher evidently dearly loves and affectionately counts on. *I* long most of the time for a cosey warm corner and a fire to sit down by. That is what you will not like. But then the winters are not so severe as ours, and we shall keep house, and an unusual supply of "coals," and shall keep warm even in summer. At Professor Seth's we found a fire in his study on a day like this, and a great comfort it was to sit by it, too, I can tell you.

The news of Pyne's accident distresses me very much. Do go to see them, love, if they are still in Princeton, and express my warm sympathy and deep concern. I hope it has turned out as they thought at the time,—that is, that the injury is indeed slight and unattended by any real danger of serious consequences. Eight kicks are a serious matter even for the legs.

Even the papers here contain such news of America as that Mr. Alger has resigned, and I am heartily glad, though it came much too late and I judge that the President's choice of Root does not improve matters very much.

24 July—Monday.

We are still in Cambridge, and shall be till to-morrow about noon. Then we shall take the train across country to Coventry, and ride our wheels thence through Kenilworth to Warwick. From Warwick we shall of course ride to Stratford, and, when we have seen that, shall go from Warwick to Oxford. Beyond Oxford our plans do not go in any definite shape,—except that there London is to be interpolated.

To-day we "did" Cambridge in true tourist fashion,—Baedeker in ha[n]d. The colleges here have a certain family resemblance: there is much more architectural consistency here than at Oxford,—with the result that there are no monstrosities here such as there are at Oxford, but a sameness of satisfying style,—except where Sir Christopher Wren has touched the original design to spoil it. We have been seeking, not so much to study the colleges individually, as to get the topography of the place clearly in mind and be able to take away a clear conception of it as a whole. And the undeniable consequence is, that we are *very* tired, and must presently go to bed. Ah, my sweet Eileen, sometimes it seems to me that the chief pleasure I have at the end of one of these interesting days is in the consciousness that I am one day nearer you! I am so continually and so intensely your lover, and, as before, all the beauty of this beautiful country seems to me to stand for you and provokes me to love you just so much the more. I know I have told you this before; but I fear I shall have to repeat it many times more—it is so constantly uppermost in my mind, this feeling that *you* are somehow *in* all that is beautiful after this exquisite, rich, refined English fashion, in scenery and ecclesiastical and academic and domestic architecture. No wonder a great literature sprang out of this life, thus environed: and if any authentic piece of literature should ever come out of my home, it will be a thing explained, provoked, shaped in some undeliberate and unconscious way by you. If there were enough wives like you in America, we should soon enough have a literature of our own. Ah, my Eileen, my queen, how passionately, and how with heart and mind alike *I love you* and know myself to be

Your own   Woodrow

Best love to the dear Hibbens and to Mrs. Brown, and to the dear chicks all that they know how to take or care for.

ALS (WC, NjP).
1 John H. Margerum, plumber, of 29 Alexander St.
2 Blair Hall, a Princeton dormitory constructed in 1896-97.

From Ellen Axson Wilson

My own darling,   Princeton July 24/99.

Your second charming letter from the lakes reached me Saturday,—the third letter last week, which made it a red letter week; perhaps I shall have to pay for it by short rations this week, some letter may have made better time than usual. I am sorry for the two rainy days, but "things like that we know must be" in England. I only hope it was not the beginning of a streak of ill luck, for I hear rumours of very bad weather in England, rain and heat both. Here we have just now rain and *cold*. Yes! it is positively cold today, like the very late fall. It will doubtless be superb when the sun comes out, just as it was before. The moon is at the full (as I presume it also is in Eng!!) and the nights are wonderful.

Ed & Madge went bicycling Saturday night, and a mile beyond Lawrenceville her front wheel jammed. So they walked to Lawrenceville where, after some adventures, they secured a wheel for her. But it turned out to be so low she could not ride it, so Ed rode it instead, pedaling with his knees almost, and she rode his. They were sights to behold; they turned up at half past eleven, Madge, according to Ed, having laughed "sans intermission" *two* "hours by the dial."

Ed came Friday morning, having taken the Fall River boat. It is a *great* comfort to have him. I havn't been exactly *afraid* of the burglars, still I was quite willing to turn over that pistol to Ed; I have slept with it at my bed-head for some time now. The burglars have been on a perfect rampage for a month, breaking in somewhere almost every night; and lately they have taken to going upstairs into bed-rooms, getting one man's purse and watch out of his pocket without his waking. They are growing perfect from practice. But one of them was caught the night before Ed came, and we think it is all over now,—else I would not have disturbed you by writing about it. Moreover we on this street have engaged a watchman and are to pay him, for the present, each $2.00 a month. He has been watching for a week past. So we are perfectly safe,—and before that it was pleasant to have "something going on."

That reminds me of an entertaining article I have just been reading in the new "Atlantic" about John Holmes of Cambridge the brother of Oliver.[1] He seems to have been as distinguished for humour as his brother was for wit. One of the most amusing extracts from his letters describes the college town in summer, and the joy of the inhabitants over an occasional burglary, that being "the only amusement." He says he misses the mosquitoes because they made things lively. I really must give you a bit of "the diary of a Cambridge citizen." "Aug. 1. Repairs of meeting-house going on,—a dorbug flew in at a window—caused alarm of bu[r]glars—great excitement in the town. Aug. 2 Repairs still going on. A tipsy man fell down but escaped without injury—great excitement in the town. Aug. 3. Repairs continued. Aug. 4. Repairs on the meeting-house going on. Aug 5 Workmen busy on the meeting-house. Aug. 6. Repairs continued. Aug 7. The meeting-house still under repair."

If you put the Cuyler studio for the "meeting-house" that would be my budget of news for the week. But now it really *is* exciting that the Cuylers[2] are building *another* house on that lot! This makes the *fourth*, for they have a little outhouse too, you know. After sacrificing the house entirely to the studio he now decides that they must live in that studio, and he must have another where he can produce his masterpieces uninterrupted. The new one is a wooden building behind the other, and just as crooked, but at a different angle. The effect is truly unique. Our crying need is evidently for someone to commit, not burglary, but arson.

As for public news of course you will see before this reaches you that Elihu Root is appointed Secretary of War. The serious strikes of streetcar men is the only other important matter at present. The militia is ordered out in some places. Yesterday they blew up a car at Cleveland full of passengers, injuring all and killing one lady. The papers are also full,—or half full,—of talk about Bob Ingersoll who is just dead.[3]

By the way, I did not tell you that Mr. Vandewater[4] is dead. He had been troubled for several days with neuralgia, and Saturday he was startled by a violent thunder-clap and simply fell back dead; the neuralgia had suddenly gone to the heart, it is said.

We are all quite well except Jessie. There is nothing much the matter with her but she looks wan and "peaked"; has not got over the effects of her last attack. All send dear love to you both. I love you unspeakibly, my own darling, and am, ah, *how happy* in your love in spite of everything. Always and altogether

Your own   Eileen.

ALS (WC, NjP).
1 Thomas Wentworth Higginson, "His Brother's Brother," *Atlantic Monthly,* LXXXIV (Aug. 1899), 175-82.
2 Mr. and Mrs. John P. Cuyler of 53 Library Place. Cuyler was a local artist.
3 Robert Green Ingersoll, the famous agnostic, who died at Dobbs Ferry, N.Y., on July 21, 1899.
4 William C. Vandewater, a hardware dealer, who lived at 45 Vandeventer Ave.

To Ellen Axson Wilson

My own darling,   "The George," Lichfield, 26 July, 1899

We are in Dr. Johnson's town to-night, as you will see by the date of this letter. We did not exactly come on his account: we came to see the cathedral; but that it was the great doctor's birthplace was an additional reason for coming. We left Cambridge yesterday, Tuesday, afternoon, having seen, I believe, all of the colleges except Girton and Newnham—that is, some fifteen in all; and it was thoroughly worth while to take time to see them. Every one has *some*thing to give it individuality, and in the aggregate they are more impressive by far than the two or three great and beautiful ones, like Trinity and St. Johns, could be if seen by themselves. Them we saw several times in the course of our three days' stay: but the others add a note of completeness and variety which was needed to make us comprehend the place in its entirety,—a place *full* of quiet chambers, secluded ancient courts, and gardens shut away from intrusion,—a town full of coverts for those who would learn and be with their own thoughts. I bring away from it a very keen sense of what we lack in our democratic colleges, where no one has privacy or claims to have his own thoughts.

I was delighted to learn that Professor Maitland[1] is back from the Canaries. I did not call upon him. He cannot be strong yet, and I dreaded the risk of his exerting himself to show me the place, or to entertain me. Such arguments, at any rate, admirably reenforced my natural shyness in such matters.

The town was full of students, reading in the long vacation,—in residence as if it were term time: going to their commons in cap and gown, observing study hours in the forenoon and enjoying all sorts of sports, on the river and in all the innumerable delicious green spaces of the college enclosures in the afternoons.

An ideal way to spend the summer, I should say. Their tutors seem (some of them, at any rate) to be at their disposal, vacation though it be; great libraries are there; and no man need wish for more delightful surroundings. There is, besides, no real heat.

We crossed country, by rail, from Cambridge to Coventry, and there we spent the night at The King's Head Hotel where is to be seen an effigy of "Peeping Tom," the conscienceless chap who dared to look at the Lady Godiva. This morning (resolved not to be so near this beautiful cathedral and not see it) we rode on our wheels to Nuneaton, and there took the train for Lichfield. We had gone to Coventry as the best place from which to ride into the Shakespeare country; but, on second thought, we determined to come here,—and Nuneaton (where we left our wheels) will serve as well to start from as Coventry. The country over which we rode this morning is the George Eliot district. Very little of it is, I am sure, as it was in her day. The road from Coventry to Nuneaton (nine miles) is like an almost continuous street, so built up is it with homes and shops and manufactories. The villages by the way,—in one George Eliot lived with her father; another is the place identified with he[r] "Scenes from Clerical Life,"—are swallowed up and merged. The passer-by on the road cannot tell where one leaves off and another begins. This is the neighbourhood, you know, of Birmingham and all that Bir'ham stands for: it teems and smokes and rings with hideous industry. And so town is confused with town, like a crowded and smudged drawing. But Lichfield, by some singular kindness of fortune, escapes. It is as near Birmingham as is either Coventry or Nuneaton: it is on the main line of the London and North Western Railway from London to Liverpool; but it has been left to enjoy its cathedral and keep its own old houses in peace and quietness. The house in which the great doctor was born still stands, as sound and well kept as if time had not been passing,— and the Three Crowns Inn, almost beside it, where the Dr. discoursed to Mr. Boswell on the virtue and sobriety of the people of Lichfield. Close by, on the same block, stands a house in which Ashmole, of Charles II's time, the founder of the Ashmolean Museum, was born:—the whole neighbourhood seems untouched and sound from of old. The house of Erasmus Darwin still stands, too, in its fine gardens, and helps the place to lay a sort of claim to his more famous grandson. And all this (there is, among other things, a hospital founded and built in 1509) in addition to the truly beautiful cathedral, which I am the happier for having added to my pleasures. Having, like almost every other cathedral in England, lost its own stained glass at the hands of the barbarous puritans, it has imported some from an old nunnery (I believe) at Liege, wherewith to make its Lady Chapel glorious,—and glorious it has made it,—like an exquisite gem. And the gem is almost perfectly set. For there is a grace and harmony and completeness about this noble church which send one away satisfied, and supplied for many a long day with images of beauty.

I can think upon my pleasures with complacency this evening because this is the *twenty-sixth* and on the next twenty-sixth that comes around I shall start for home! Ah, how that thought makes my heart sing! It is more than a month,—more by almost ten days—since I sailed *from* home; but it is *less* than that, it is *only* a month, before I sail *for* home. Nothing but the *time* moves towards you now; but then I shall move towards you (God willing) in space. It is sweet enough, Eileen, to love you,—it is enough to satisfy any really reasonable man to *be* loved *by* you—even at a distance and in days of separation! But, ah, who that *could* be with you and hold you in his arms, the best chum and companion and the most delightful lover in the world, would be satisfied with anything less than that full possession for which my heart is fairly breaking to-night? I love you and long for you with a yearning that almost passes endurance. I would give every other pleasure for the one supreme delight of having you in my arms!

"The Woolpack," Warwick, 27 July, 1899

Writing the name of the hotel reminds me that I forgot to tell you last night of an interesting association connected with "The George," at which we stayed in Lichfield. It is the same "George" at which Farquhar laid the scene of his "Beau's Strategem." I have never read the Beau's Strategem, and Stock., who has read it, cannot recall the plot of it; but it pleased our fancy to think that we were lodging at an inn made famous by the most acted and enjoyed play of its time. It made no difference at all that we did not know what it was all about! To-night we are near Shakespeare's land, and that is much better. It suggests things more real than were dreamed of in Farquhar's philosophy. We have ridden twenty miles to-day, and our road afforded us a delicious contrast. The first nine miles of it were the same nine we rode yesterday,—the dismal, grimy road between Nuneaton and Coventry. But on this side Coventry does not extend its smudgy streets into the country. You emerge almost of a sudden into the perfect country-side of exquisite Warwickshire, surely the most beautiful county in England,—a country not unlike that to the right of the

road as you ride from Princeton to Trenton, but *richer* in every
detail: more wooded; its wood distributed as if to give every
field a setting of splendid trees, and at once soften and accen-
tuate the fine line of every curving hollow and sweeping modulation of level. Our road was all the way a great avenue, shaded,
dominated, made noble, but not shut in, by trees it made one
glad to look at and be near. And the air was as sweet, almost,
as it was the morning we rode from Henderson[ville] to Arden
Park.[2] It would have been quite as sweet had *you* been here to
help me breathe it! We have had our tea and have strolled for an
hour and a half over Warwick,—seen its great castle from the
bridge and looked into all its quaintest corners,—and Stock. is
satisfied. He has been talking most of the day in superlatives,—
and I am more than satisfied.

Ah, my queen, how shall I bid you good night when my heart
is so aching for you. I love you so! I am so much in love with you.
There are no words for any of it. I can only cry out and declare
myself for the thousandth time, always and altogether

Your own   Woodrow

A great deal of love for the dear Hibbens and for Mrs. Brown,
and an overflowing measure for my precious little ones. We are
both quite well.   Your W.

ALS (WC, NjP).
  [1] Frederic William Maitland, Downing Professor of the Laws of England, Cambridge University.
  [2] On Saturday, September 15, 1883. They drove in a buggy from Asheville to
Hendersonville and returned to Arden Park so that Ellen could meet Woodrow's
mother, Joseph R. Wilson, Jr., and Annie Wilson Howe. See the Editorial Note,
"The Engagement," Vol. 2.

From Ellen Axson Wilson

My own darling,   Princeton Jan [July] 27/99

No letter for me this week so far which of course makes the
time go a little more heavily. Still we are all happy and well,—at
least Jessie, if not well, is better, I think, than when I last wrote.

I am afraid though that I had better take them away for two
weeks in Aug. after all. The cool summer here had almost convinced me that it would not be necessary. But they have had a
good deal to go through with and a little sea-change may put them
in better shape for the winter. I suppose that if I didn't go and
the cold weather found them "weakly" my conscience would reproach me for not having done the best for them in my power.
But oh! how I *hate* to go! I am about writing to see if Mrs. Top-

ping[1] can take us in. I find the places on the Jersey coast either very dear or very vulgar,—often both. I shall plan to be gone from the 19th of Aug. to the 2nd of Sept. Madge will not go with us but will pay a visit instead to Dr. Van Valzeh's[2] niece, Bertha Hayes. Ed, I hope, will go with us unless he gets something to do in the meantime. He is trying to get a place either on the Board of Health, in New York, or in Govt. research work at Washington. He is wild to get some such place, the work being so much more interesting than the routine work of ordinary analytical chemistry. His Boston professor in a letter of introduction to the Washington chief says he is peculiarly fitted for such work, being "a clear thinker, an indefatigable worker and having great skill in devising apparatus." He is certainly a worker—is busy now most of the day copying his article (which is to be published,) and a fat note-book of somebody's which will be of use to him. You should see the calculations embodying the results of the "research work,"—a paper now more than two yards long & ¼ yd. wide, covered with decimals! He has done enough to serve as a thesis for his degree, if, failing to get a place, he should decide to go back for it next year. He has also interesting photographs of the apparatus used, of his own devising.

I shall have, to my regret, to enclose you certain letters[3] from one B. F. Johnson of Richmond. I answered the first one telling him it was impossible and that I had full authority from you to decline all publisher's propositions. But you see he won't take my word for [it]. He seems to be a good sort of a goose, and being a Southerner to boot, perhaps you might write him an amiable little letter and refrain from telling him what an ass he is.

These are the only letters for you since I last wrote.

I have one from Miss Ricketts who says they are delighted with Gloucester,—that her mother seems to be enjoying it more than they dared hope. I was glad to know that they were still alive for their preparations for leaving Princeton were of such a nature that I expected nothing less than complete collapse when it was all over! They simply slaved for a week before, the house being all that time practically uninhabitable, rugs, &c. up, and as Mr. Ricketts said, moth balls a foot deep everywhere. Are you not glad I am not such a "notable house-wife"?

There is no Princeton news except that there is a fourth boy[4] at the Armour's—arrived yesterday. We have had bad weather this week and I have been nowhere and seen no one. Yesterday the three children & Beth took tea at the Sloanes and were brought back in the carriage, much to their satisfaction. It seems to have been a great frolic. This afternoon M. & N. went back for Nell's wheel, and scudded home before a thunder-storm fortunately getting in just before it burst, poor Nell, of course, sadly frightened. She held in until she reached me and then sobbed loud and long. It was a good old-fashioned storm, not too severe for enjoyment but most beautiful. I don't believe you had even in the Lakes more wonderful lights than those which transformed our little "view" when it was all over.

How I wonder where my darling is tonight and how he is! I constantly think of you in the last place from which I heard and then suddenly remember with a start that you have not been there for ten days. I should like to know in a general way your route beforehand, so that my wandering spirit which stubbornly refuses to keep at home this summer may find its quest less hopeless when it would "flee as a bird to its mountain." All send love to both. With devoted love   Your own   Eileen.

ALS (WC, NjP).
    [1] Mrs. Sidney S. Topping, who ran a boardinghouse or small hotel at Saga-ponack near Bridgehampton, Long Island, where the Wilsons had spent their vacations in 1890 and 1893.
    [2] William Ward Van Valzah, M.D., of 10 East 43rd St., New York, whom Mrs. Wilson had frequently consulted.
    [3] These enclosures are missing.
    [4] Edmund Armour.

To Ellen Axson Wilson

                                    "The King's Arms," Oxford
My own darling,   30 July, 1899

We called on the Huttons[1] this afternoon and had tea with them on the cosiest of little private lawns, such as we could have, and must have, if not in front of, then behind our own dear little home. The Huttons are in Max Müller's house,[2] you know, and most homelike and charming it is, inside and out. They are delighted with it; and well they may be. I expect to dine with them to-morrow evening. Stock. pretends he is going to London, and declines the invitation. For once, Mrs. Hutton is enthusiastic *soon*. Oxford has overcome her too critical faculty, and 'she loves it.'

We came to Oxford yesterday, I on my wheel and Stock. by train, as I've just told the children in my letters to Jess. and Nen. Stock. was not really ill, or any thing of that sort, but his digestion had become a little deranged and we both thought it would be imprudent for him to exert himself in the heat. I felt all right, and enjoyed the ride immensely, barring the mishap of the punc-

ture—and even that was fortunate in its way. It gave me a good
rest at Woodstock, a place at which it was worth while to stop.
I dont particularly admire either Blenheim castle or Blenheim
park; but Woodstock village is very pretty and attractive. I enjoyed the ride afterwards, in the cool of the evening, and over a
perfectly level road—with a following wind—and it made me so
happy to think that a letter from you was certainly at the end
of the journey. I was starved with waiting for a letter. I had not
had one for almost an entire week,—because I could not quite
calculate our movements from place to place for this week and
named Oxford as my next mail point simply to make sure,—and
so a letter had been waiting for me here for a couple of days.
By the same token, there ought to be another one to-morrow morning,—and then I shall feel the nearer home for getting two in
such quick succession[.] Ah, how *necessary* these sweet letters are
to me, and how delicious when they come! It seems to me as if I
subsisted on them.

I am so delighted, my sweet love, that you have at last got a
good photograph of yourself, by real artists,—and I judge from
what you say that you really have found photographers who
could make a success this time. If they have really got a likeness
of you, I don't doubt it is 'the most beautiful thing' the Aikens
'ever saw in their lives,' and Davis and Sanford must indeed be
artists. Your beauty is so much of the spirit,—so essentially a
beauty of character subtly married to form; the expression and
contour are so necessary to each other to make your real face that
it requires art of no mean quality to show my darling as she is.
The form by itself is infinitely sweet and touchingly beautiful, but
when your spirit is caught in the face it is radiant,—surpassingly
beautiful. If these photographers have really caught not only the
Mrs. Wilson who is in mere form so "ornamental," but also my
Eileen in all her winning reality of mixed charm of spirit and
person, I shall indeed be happy. I only wish I could have one of
the photographs before I leave this side,—to worship on the way
back on the steamer! The one I have of you is merely the *form* of
my darling, as one Mr. Perkins of Baltimore saw it. But then
perhaps a real portrait of my queen would only make me the
more intolerably anxious and impatient to see her and have her
in my arms again,—and that would not do. I could not stand it.

As usual, I saw both Warwick and Stratford more thoroughly
this time than last. Last time it was the exterior of everything
which most struck me,—the novelty and the charm of old England: castles, ruins, ancient houses,—the place where English

history had been played and English letters written,—and I did not care to look into the details and interiors of anything. It was the general impression which struck me most to the quick and the detail did not count. But this time the interiors interest me. The outside of objects and places, tho. not less attractive than before, is familiar,—no longer excites my curiosity. And so I see things I did not see before, and enjoy a new novelty. When you come with me I shall enjoy *you*,—and shall have a better, more deeply satisfying time than ever I had before in all my life,—except when I first knew that you loved me. At Warwick I went all through the Leicester Hospital, while Stockton went through the castle, which I did not care to see again. The Hospital, an infinitely picturesque half-timber building, low, irregular, rambling, curious in almost every detail of window, court, garden, and chambers, was built (most of it) in 1382, and yet its timbers are as sound as when they were put in,—have hardened indeed as they have stood. Those who hewed them out, and smoothed their surfaces rudely with the adze, followed the heart of the oak, whether that gave them a straight beam or not,—and that heart has hardened to adamant. Its surface is less damaged by the weather than the surface of old stone buildings near by. And so all interior curiosities and niceties of structure stand unaltered and oftentimes beautiful in the unchanged building. And pieces of furniture, too, which have been there almost from the first. The great Leicester endowed the "hospital" for old soldiers (it is properly a retreat); but the house was already old when he gave and adapted it for its new uses.

There was less in Stratford that I had not seen,—in fact there was nothing of consequence except Edwards School ("Edward VI's School") where Shakespeare's got his schooling. There is the great "Memorial," indeed,—half theatre, half museum, where, every April, one of the plays is given in the most elaborate and unrevised fashion, and where, for the rest of the year, all sorts of mementoes of the poet, rare editions of his works, Mr. Halliwell-Phillips'[3] Shakespearean library, paintings (most of them bad) of characters or scenes of the plays, portraits of actors, from Mrs. Siddons and Garrick down (away down) to Ada Rehan,[4] of whom there is an heroic full length, are exhibited. But all that, though interesting, is not vital; and the building is so ugly that an uglier could certainly not be conceived or executed. I did not feel that I was any richer for having seen this grotesque, interesting and valuable though some, indeed many, things in it certainly are.

31 July—Oxford.

I am not as happy as I expected to be to-day. No other letter from you has turned up,—the American mail is later than usual getting in, and I feel cheated of my feast.

I have not begun really to see Oxford yet. One reason is, that the weather is genuinely hot, and it is not pleasant to go about much; another reason is, that I have been engaged about other things. The Summer School of University Extension opened here on Saturday, and this morning I went to hear Professor Dicey[5] compare, and contrast, the English and American constitutions. I had, very much against my will, to wait for Professor Dicey at the door of the lecture room in order to get admitted: that led to all sorts of introductions, and I had to tell all sorts of small lies to get out of receiving various attentions from every body. After that—and the lecture—were over, I went with Professor Dicey to his rooms at All Souls; then I mentioned my desire to find a professor of Politics—and that led to his recommending me to consult this, that, and the other eminent person. I looked one or two of these up and could not find them: and so the day has gone. How I *hate* business, particularly the business of appointments, now that I *know* that Dr. P[atton]. cannot be depended on for anything at all. I shall have to put myself out about it, all the same, whether I like it or not. It, unhappily, does not lessen my duty that other persons neglect theirs.

It cheers me more than you know that so many messages of good will and affection are sent to me; and it really touches me that Mr. Hibben misses me so much. I could wish that *Mrs.* Hibben, too, were "love-sick" for me; but, if she is not, I may well be content with Jack's manly affection,—knowing how genuine and unselfish it is. My heart seems so filled with the unspeakable joy of your love, that I sometimes wonder why I care for anybody else's; but after all no love is comparable with the love that we have for one another, and so no love is either like it or in contrast with it, and I long for my friends' love at the very same time that I am satisfied by yours,—satisfied by you, and always and altogether, and, oh, with what pride and joy,

Your own   Woodrow

Love in full measure to the dear chicks, to the dear Hibbens, to Mrs. Brown, and to dear Madge.

ALS (WC, NjP).
[1] Eleanor Varnum Mitchell Hutton and Laurence Hutton of New York. Hutton was a literary and dramatic critic; author of many books on literature and the theater; literary editor of *Harper's Magazine*, 1886-98; and Lecturer on English Literature at Princeton, 1901-1904.

² On Norham Gardens, Oxford. Friedrich Max Müller (1823-1900) was Professor of Comparative Philology at Oxford and a prolific scholar and pioneer in the fields of Sanskrit, comparative philology, comparative mythology, and the historical and comparative study of religions.
³ James Orchard Halliwell-Phillips (1820-89), noted Shakespearean scholar and collector.
⁴ Sarah Kemble Siddons (1755-1831); David Garrick (1717-79); and the Irish-American actress, Ada Rehan (1860-1916).
⁵ Albert Venn Dicey, Vinerian Professor of English Law at Oxford.

From Ellen Axson Wilson

My own darling,   Princeton July 31/99.

I am very late beginning my letter tonight because we have a visitor and I could not manage to get away sooner. It is one of Madge's friends, Ethelyn Phipps of Balt., who is stopping for two or three days on her way to the shore. She is a nice, attractive girl and quite pretty in an irregular way,—has a rather Japanese face except as to her eyes, which are as far as possible from the Japanese type, being very large, and brown and wide-open,— superb eyes in fact. Tomorrow night we are to have almost a dinner party of young people, Ed Elliot[1] and another '97 man being invited.

Your dear letter from Ely came today and has made me very happy. The *most* interesting one from Durham reached me Saturday afternoon. There had been none all the week and when it failed to come that morning I am afraid I was rather blue for a while; but happily for me the afternoon made all right again. I am very glad you had that interesting experience at the Assize court. I was intensely interested in all you said,—so excellently well,—about it. What a noble picture you give of the essential majesty of the law, a majesty that would have seemed, I fancy, scarcely less imposing stripped of its medieval trappings,—though I like them too! At least I like them on *Monday*; on *Sunday* I prefer more humility! Your account served as an entertaining comment to me on a poem I had just been reading, Clough's "Dipsychus," in which choosing the profession of the law (and eventually becoming Lord Chief Justice of England,) is represented as literally synonymous with selling your soul to the devil! I thought with amusement, and sympathy, as I read of how justly indignant you would be at such views.

Today's letter is the one in which you beg me to go away with the children; I have already answered that, but I have not heard from Mrs. Topping yet so don't know *where* I am going. I shall have plenty of money, dear, *without* any part of the four hundred. Margaret seems very well now. I have not noticed any twitching for a long time, but alas she still whoops more or less. If she doesn't stop in the next three weeks I don't know what I shall do. I have no idea it is contagious any longer, but, all the same, imagine the indignation of summer resorters at my daring to come among them! I am afraid Margaret is going to follow your example and whoop for four years! Jessie is much better than when I last wrote, though of course still pale and thin. The rest perfectly well.

Tell Stock I had a letter from Mr. John Finley asking first for your address, and then if Stock would like a professorship in "a good western college, not Knox." I had great satisfaction in explaining the difficulty in the way of such an arrangement.

I was amused at your vivacity of language in condemning the Camerons, yet I feel more than ever today that they deserve it; Mrs. Cameron is going about talking in the most outrageous way. "The sympathy of the community is with her son and his wife now, but some day it will be with *her* when her reasons are know[n]. Oh, she could tell *such things*, if she chose, about the woman, but she will be silent," &c &c. Just think how completely such hints might ruin that poor young woman's reputation. Most fortunately, though she *is* a stranger, there is some one here who knows all about her; she is an intimate friend of Ethelbert Warfield's wife,[2] they taught in the same school and lived in the closest relations. Needless to add they declare her above reproach or suspicion in character, social standing, &c. Mrs. C. also wrote such insulting letters to her that she attempted to break her engagement, but Guyot prevail[e]d with her. And their love affair began *ten years* ago!

There are still literally no letters for you. And we still have our cool, fine weather. I never saw Princeton looking so well at this season, tis as fresh and green as in May. We still have the most beautiful sweet peas I ever saw,—such a variety of exquisite, soft tints. Mrs. Hibben, Sen. is *very* fond of them and it has been a pleasure to keep her constantly supplied,—as also Mrs. Garland, who has a crippled arm. I have gotten very chummy with Miss Tilton & Miss Garland, who is spending the summer there;—two extremely interesting women.

But I must break off here. Small space in which to tell my darling how I love him! But I despaired long ago of finding the words for that so it is no matter. How I wish I were not such a dumb creature but could find the right words like *you*, you most adorable of lovers. But you *know*, darling, that you have all the love that you want,—if not more!—from

Your devoted little wife, Eileen.

ALS (WC, NjP).

¹ Edward Graham Elliott, born Murfreesboro, Tenn., Aug. 3, 1874. A.B., Princeton, 1897; A.M., 1900. Studied at the Universities of Berlin and Heidelberg, 1900-1902; Ph.D., Heidelberg, 1902. After serving as an instructor at Bolton College in Tennessee, 1897-98, he returned to Princeton where he was Instructor in Latin, 1898-1900; Instructor in Jurisprudence and Politics, 1902-1905; Robert Stockton Pyne Preceptor in History, Politics, and Economics, 1905-1909; and Professor of Politics and Dean of the College, 1909-12. He then moved to San Francisco, where he was admitted to the bar in 1913 and soon established an extensive law practice. Lecturer on International Law, University of California, Berkeley, 1912-16; Professor of Politics and International Law, 1916-20. Vice President, Security-First National Bank of Los Angeles, 1921-47. Author of several books and many articles. He married Margaret Randolph Axson on Sept. 8, 1910. Died Dec. 12, 1947.
² Eleanor Tilton Warfield, wife of Ethelbert Dudley Warfield, President of Lafayette College.

From Jenny Davidson Hibben

My dear Mr. Wilson,   Princeton, N.J. August 1, 1899.

Your letter was a perfect delight to us, & Jack & I read & re-read it with such pleasure & felt as if we were seeing you & the cathedrals too! I hope when you reach Wells you will write us a note, & tell us about it again.

Mrs. Wilson is *still* pretty, & serene looking in spite of her liege lord's absence. You know perfectly well, that I meant that she was better after the ordeal of having you go was [a] thing of the past, instead of staring her in the face, as it had been weeks before—so you must not tease about it. We had our delicious tea with her on Sunday & a delightful letter from you she kindly read us. I do not think I can tell you, in the monotonous life we have had this summer, the pleasure your letters have been. Jack & I are so glad that Mrs. Wilson shares them with us & we appreciate her sweetness in doing it. Selfishly we rejoice that in less than a month you sail & we will have you with us again.

Mother is much the same, sometimes a little better, we dare to believe. *I* ride a *bicycle*. After much suffering & frantic struggles I can ride, & delight in it, even if I am a little wobbly. Jack plays golf, *persistently*, with Mr. Dulles & Mr. Westcott & also with Mr. Magie. Our dear Beth has gone to Gray Gables for a visit escorted by Mr. West & our faithful house-maid—so we are a lonely household.

I am so delighted that Mrs. Wilson is to take the children & go away, for a little change. We really are having a cool summer, & Princeton is very lovely now. Mother is kept constantly supplied with the most fragrant & lovely sweet peas, given by Mrs. Wilson. Your home is a very picture now & Miss Axson & Mr. Axson add not a little, as you well know to Mrs. Wilson's happiness.

This is a hastily written letter. It is done at the end of a hurried

day. Jack joins with me in warmest love for you, & appreciation
of your delightful letters.

Ever yours,   Jenny Davidson Hibben.

ALS (WP, DLC).

From Ellen Axson Wilson, with Enclosure

My own darling,   Princeton, Aug. 3/99

Your delightful letter from Cambridge came today as also the
one for Margaret, to her great joy. A charming letter it was too.
The others go about after her, while she triumphantly exhibits
it to everyone,—explaining carefully that "we too are going to
have some soon." Margaret thinks this a very "happy day," a
letter from you in the morning, and a party in the afternoon.
The party was at the Stocktons[1] and was a great success; they all
three went looking extremely sweet and pretty.

After getting them off *I* went on one of my futile trips to Mrs.
Hibbens; I havn't found her at home once this summer! When
I come staggering back tired out with the long walk and no rest
between I always vow it is the last time. But that seems unfriendly
and I go again, though I know before I start it will be no use.
This time however I loafed about the campus, resting on the steps
of one building or another and having a very peaceful, pleasant
time, enjoying the delicious freshness the long shadows and the
golden-green lights, and trying to imagine that I was at the Cambridge "backs" with you! I suppose that this time, by the way,
you found them of the true emerald tint,—not parched as they
were three years ago. I wonder if they *can* be much greener than
Princeton today. I saw Little Hall[2] for the first time lately and
found it finished as to the exterior all save a round or two of the
tower. It is very effective. I was astonished to see what an enormous amount of filling in must be done on the campus side;
why they will need to dump in a whole county.

Princeton is especially fresh today, and cool, because of the
usual thing—a thunderstorm yesterday afternoon. But though
only "the usual thing" here, it was very *unusual* elsewhere for it
almost wrecked the town of Elisabeth. We had only the edge of
it, rain and distant thunder with *extraordinary* darkness[.] There
two clouds met, and the result was a veritable tornado like those
in the west. The steeples of two churches were blown down, one
the Presbyterian, both theatres were unroofed & ruined by rain,
as were also scores of other buildings; great trees were uprooted
&c. &c. The paper says the business part of the town is in ruins.

I never heard before of such a thing in the east. But strange to relate no one was killed or even seriously hurt.

Your letter came *just* in time to have the work done as you suggest; the stones have been placed to within twenty feet of the man-hole. But I have already signed the necessary petition to the Council, and Mr. Margerum is going to have it done tomorrow.

Mrs. Topping can give us the necessary rooms,—and cheap too,—eight dollars a week, half price for children. So we go on the 19th, Ed with us I hope. It will be *such* a comfort to have him take us and bring us back and take the children in bathing while there. Jessie is *much* better, quite like herself. The *feverishness* which worried me a good deal is quite gone; there has been no touch of it for five nights. It was only *one* degree every night, but it lasted two or more weeks, and I did not like it. We are *all* quite well now. Certainly my health couldnt be better.

Miss Phipps is still with us,—don't know how long she is to stay; the girls havn't taken me into their confidence on that point! Perhaps that sounds too sarcastic,—I hasten to add that she is an unusually sweet girl and I have no objection to her staying. The young people have all gone to the observatory tonight. The other 97 man who has been hanging around is Andrus,[3] whom of course you know. What a *stunning* looking fellow he is! It is really an aesthetic pleasure to see such a man.

I should have mentioned long ago that Mr. Pyne's injuries amounted to nothing. He was out the very next day.

Was interrupted here by the return of the young folks[.] They have just gone up, & it is so late that I will finish this in the morning. Miss P. leaves, it seems, on the 9.09 tomorrow.

Friday. The young people have just gone and I sit down to finish my letter. Before I forget it I want to say that Dr. Wykoff[4] came in Wed. to see how Jessie was getting on, and I asked him about Margarets whooping. He says there is *no* danger of contagion any longer; so I shan't worry about taking her to Sagg,— though of course the women there who hear her will resent my presence, so I sincerely hope she will stop it.

I judge from the paper this morning that yesterday's account of the Elizabeth storm was greatly exaggerated; the total loss is only $100,000. The churches & theartres [theatres] are unroofed though; the trees in the church-yard were all uprooted and in the process the bones of the dead were dragged to light and scattered broad-cast.

Only think, dear, you *may* be at home a month from tomorrow! *Delightful* thought!—though I still regret your curtailed holiday.

I conclude the French trip is given up altogether. Apparently I can only write three times more with any hope of the letter reaching you. The third *may* miss you, leaving New York on the 16th. I wish I could send it direct to Glasgow.

I love you, *love* you, dear one, tenderly, devotedly, passionately. You are the very life of my life, all the world—and more—much more to,   Your little wife,   Eileen.

Of course you won't do what Mr. Finley asks! will you? He lost my letter with your address so sends this for me to mail—and incidentally gives me the chance to put a spoke in his wheel, I *hope!*

ALS (WC, NjP).
¹ It is impossible to determine which of the several Stockton families gave this party.
² A new dormitory.
³ Walter Haskell Andrus, at this time "General Athletic Treasurer" of Princeton University.
⁴ James Holmes Wikoff, M.D., of 22 Nassau St.

ENCLOSURE

From John Huston Finley

My dear Dr. Woodrow-Wilson: New York City August 1, 1899.

I suppose you have gone abroad to escape for one thing the torment of thinking to order, and to force upon your contemplation such a suggestion as this letter carries, may be a capital offense: but at the risk of losing my head and what is, in a sense, as precious, I venture to make the suggestion.

But, first, by way of preface I must let you know that we (the Harper-McClure Alliance) are about to establish a new Review,¹ which is to be not only a record of the works of the world, but also a source of political, social, industrial wisdom, inspiration and aspiration (the last to be realized through the association of such men as yourself with the enterprise). There will be between its covers from month [to month] with this record and comment, fiction for forgetfulness and facts for hope. The Review will have to do with everything that touches human life. It will be designed to reach the many. Like the soap, which an inventor was showing me the other day, it is to have within it a light material to float it—but we expect to manufacture (and at a price within the reach of working men) as good a quality of soap for political washing as the market affords.

Now, having the chronicles, the comment (in which I hope you will occasionally have a voice) and having the "floater," we want special articles on subjects of general concern and interest. A series I have thought of as timely next year, is one setting forth the world conditions at the beginning of this century and at the end—in 1800 and 1900. The series would have to do with social, economic, political, religious, industrial, educational conditions or might be less comprehensive in scope. I should like to have such a series begin in January or perhaps later and close with the year 1900—just on the eve of the new century. Would you be willing (compensation being liberal) to undertake the preparation of such a series,—of from three to twelve papers?

Possibly you have some other subjects in mind either for single articles or for a series.

I am glad to hear of Stockton's great good fortune. I recommended him recently for a college professorship in English in a Western College—but this must be the ideal position for him.

Have you found a man for the chair of politics in Princeton?[2]

With apologies for the intrusion and wishes that the remainder of your journey may be all the happier for these few minutes given to a literary beggar at your wayside, I am

Sincerely yours   John H. Finley

ALS (WP, DLC).

[1] This was either a new magazine projected by Samuel Sidney McClure to be entitled *McClure's Review*, which never materialized, or *World's Work*, first published in November 1900, which was already being planned by Finley and Walter Hines Page. Both Finley and Page had just come to New York to join McClure in the short-lived alliance between the S. S. McClure Company, Doubleday & McClure Company, and Harper and Brothers—Finley to be the editor of *Harper's Weekly*, Page to manage the book-publishing activities of Harper's. The McClure-Harper combination dissolved before the end of the year because of financial difficulties. Page and Frank Nelson Doubleday withdrew to form the new firm of Doubleday, Page and Company and to publish *World's Work*, and Finley became the editor of *McClure's Magazine* for a short time. See Peter Lyon, *Success Story: The Life and Times of S. S. McClure* (New York, 1963), pp. 160-75; and Harry J. Carman, "John Huston Finley," *Dictionary of American Biography* (22 vols., New York, 1928-58), XXII, 185.

[2] Finley himself became the first Professor of Politics at Princeton in September 1900.

Two Letters to Ellen Axson Wilson

The Covent Garden Hotel,
My own darling,   London, W.C.   4 August, 1899

According to my calculation, it will not be worth while for you to mail letters to me after the 16th. My ship sails the very day your next letter after that would be landed at Queenstown. But will you not *cable* "Woodrow Wilson Anchor Line, Glasgow," the single word "Happy" on the morning of the 25th? I shall take that to mean that you are all well and in every way all right; and I will telegraph you the same word just before we sail. We will use that word if things are on the whole all right. If they should not be, it will be best to pay for a sufficient number of words to indicate the real situation, whatever it may be.

I am later than usual in beginning my letter for this mail because I have been running about so seeing the town and getting my "business" attended to since I reached London on Tuesday evening. The "business" was, you know, to hear, if possible, of some young, or youngish, English university man who would be worth considering for the Politics chair. I wanted to see Mr. Bryce, but he is out of town. I spent the day, practically, with Professor Ashley, who lives out in Hampstead, and talked the matter over pretty thoroughly with him. I broached it, too, to one or two men in Oxford; but no name at all turns up, or seems likely to, except that of a single youngster, to whom there are, I think, one or two serious objections. I have done what I could, however, and am rather glad, so far as I am myself, selfishly, concerned, that the business does not seem likely to engage much more of my time. Yesterday afternoon I spent an hour and a half in the gallery of the House of Commons; but it is the tail-end of the session and there was little of interest to hear.

This afternoon I go back to Oxford; and on Monday I shall take to the wheel again. But this time alone. Stockton is to stay a while with his friend, Snyder,[1] you remember, and it looks as if Snyder would not (could not, kindly) be put off with a visit of only a few days. For my part I am glad of it. Stock. needs a loafing rest more than anything else, and it ought to be as long as possible. It turns out that the physical exertion of riding is bad for him. He thoroughly enjoyed our little tour, I am sure, and I think it undoubtedly did him good, mentally and physically too; but he ought not to omit a period of sheer *rest*. It would have been better if he could have had it before sailing from home; but it will do him almost as much good now,—especially amidst the beautiful and refreshing surroundings of Snyder's cottage in Surrey,—and I am heartily glad he has found both so suitable a place and the inclination. For he has found the inclination. He has *seen*, he says, all that his mind can hold, and don't *want* to see anything more this time. Knowing that I was to lose Stock. at London, either to Snyder or to the Howells,[2] my own plans have all along been vague beyond this point. My taste and instinct are just the opposite of Stock's under the present circumstances. My longing is not for the rest of inaction, but for the delicious rest of gentle change, of drifting, without too deliberate intention of sight-seeing, from scene to scene (preferably *rural* scene to scene) in this delightful country. My general idea is to go from Oxford southward and southwestward, not along the same roads as last time, but into the same country, and on into Devon if possible. But I am not going to form a fixed plan. It may be that I will swing eastward along the southern coast: or it may be that I will fetch a long turn around London and go up, from the southeast, into the central counties. It will be part of the pleasure and rest and amusement of the ride to change my direction and my object of interest when I will. And, much as I hate to break away from Stock., I shall not be lonely. Movement will cure all that. I was alone half the summer last time, you remember. I dreaded it then, but I do not dread it now. I, too, am surfeited with sightseeing; but I am in love with touring and life in the open countryside and lodging over night at villages. I shall fare famously, and not feel that I am *dragging* Stock.

I wish that I could hope that the thoughts that will come to me when alone would interpret my love to me and give me words in which to express it. It is when I am alone that I most keenly realize the part, the supreme part, that love plays and must ever play in my life,—my capacity for loving, my need for being loved,—the almost feminine sensibility I have with regard to the feeling others may have for me,—an insatiable desire to be loved,—an infinite passion of love in me, longing to be spent: and spending itself, oh, with what unspeakable delight, upon you, my incomparable sweetheart and queen! It is a source of keenest suffering to me, when I am with you and when I am away from you, that I cannot find *words* for the deepest and most beautiful thing in me. What's the use of cultivating *style* and seeking literary power if your *life* be inexpressible, and the very effort to express it a sort of exquisite torture? No doubt that is the delight of *other* means of expressing our love, when we are together,—tone, gesture, embrace, and all the sweet passionate secrets of married love. *They*, at any rate, are perfect of their kind, and do not stop short of complete and exquisite satisfaction. It amazes me when I am away from you, my Eileen, to think that *any* humour could ever make me seem, for so much as a moment, either irritated with you (Heaven forgive me!) or indifferent towards you. You are simply all the world to me: you elevate, you stimulate, you satisfy, you delight me: every part of me enjoys you with an infinite ardour. God forgive me that I should not always show my knowledge of the blessed facts as steadily and continuously when I am at home as when I am away; and do you, my pet, continue to show

your unspeakable sweetness and superiority by making his short-
comings but a further cause of indulgent devotion to

Your own   Woodrow.

Give as much love as you care to spare to the precious chicks, to
Madge and Ed., to the dear Hibbens, and to Mrs. B.

[1] He is unknown to the Editors.
[2] Probably Mr. and Mrs. Albert Howell. Howell, son of Evan Park Howell,
was a member of the Atlanta law firm of Dorsey, Brewster, and Howell.

My own darling,   The King's Arms, Oxford, 6 August, 1899
    I am glad to be out of London and back in this satisfying place
once more. I shall be more glad still when I get on the road once
again and have the air of towns out of my lungs. Beautiful and
free from most of the disadvantages of a city as Oxford is, it is
yet a city, with more than fifty-five thousand inhabitants, and
inevitably has some of the city's pent and crowded features.
    I have, of course, gone about Oxford this time looking about
me with the keenest and most constant interest, turning into
quads.; penetrating beyond quads. to delightful secluded gardens;
peeping now into one and again into another quaint corner, and
seeing a great deal; but I have not been able to bring myself to
the point of "doing" Oxford systematically, as we did Cambridge.
My sight-seeing impetus has run out, as Stock's has. What is left
is the power to *enjoy* places,—with a sort of quiet joy that forms
and penetrates the thoughts, as if one were enjoying each place
as for the time his home, and yielding himself to its influences as
if he temporarily possessed it and looked on it as if on a familiar
face. This is the sort of enjoyment that *rests* and refreshes. The
sight-seeing enjoyment fatigues at its best.
    I got here from London on Friday night last, the 4th. Yesterday
(Saturday) I lunched with one of the Balliol dons[1] and had an experience which you must remind me to recount, if I should forget
it, which is not likely. It was both irritating and amusing; but it
belongs to the sort of experiences which have to be narrated
orally. It is their detail and incidental colouring that give them
significance, and those are just what it would be tedious to put
into a letter. I mention this instance merely as a *mem*: Tell Ellen
about my lunch with the Balliol tutor.[2] In the evening I went to see
the Huttons. We must certainly show them some attentions,—
have them to dinner, etc.—next winter. They have been very
cordial to me, and I am learning to like them very much indeed,—

even to enjoy them. And it is delightful to find home people here. I found them just finishing dinner when I got to the house (a little after half-past eight). They had two very interesting women dining with them, one elderly, the other young. The older was Miss Weld, a niece of Tennyson's by marriage.[3] Her mother was Mrs. Tennyson's sister,—and she told us that when she (Miss Weld) was a girl Tennyson was *very* anxious to adopt her, having no daughter of his own and being very anxious to have one. She was a great deal with Tennyson and he "spoiled her dreadfully," she says. Like everybody who knows, she represents him as most open, approachable, affectionate, lovable at home; and says that his apparent boorishness upon occasion, in the presence of strangers, was due wholly to shyness. He did not like to be approached with flattery or praise of what he had written. He liked everyone, rather, to give him what was *in them*, —particularly good accounts of new scientific knowledge or achievement or some authentic experience. I am to take tea with Miss Weld this afternoon at half-past four,—and I understand that interesting people are generally to be met at her house.

The younger woman was Miss Townshend, her niece;—a Lincolnshire girl (?), as lively and full of fun and imitative anecdote as (I imagine) most English women are *not*. I hope I may be able to remember *some* of the good stories she told last night,—but I don't know that I shall venture to tell them if I do,—so much of their delightful quality depends on her manner of telling them.

I find it next to impossible to say what route and plan I am going to follow when I set out from here to-morrow; but I have pretty well decided that I will go southwestward, through Salisbury and Taunton to Exeter; from Exeter to Barnstaple (say) by rail, and then on my wheel from Barnstaple to Clovelly. I can turn aside, northward, if I wish, to see Wells again. My main route will take me through Bagehot's home, Langport. If I get to the northern coast (the south coast, i.e., of Bristol Channel) pretty promptly, I can there take boat northward to the Lake country once more, and thence make my way back to Glasgow, to meet Stock. a day before the steamer sails. Or, I can take a look at some part of Ireland on the way to the other Gaelic land in the north. But I mean to ride slowly, and for the sheer outing, and so shall not think of anything besides Clovelly till I get there. The *feeling* of not having to hurry is essential to my enjoyment, and I don't mean to give myself any task at all.

(*Later,* as the papers say)

I have been to the tea; met several well-known persons whose names I either did not catch or have forgotten; and one person of celebrity, Prof. [Archibald Henry] Sayce, the distinguished Oriental scholar, who called (it *was* he, wasn't it) who called Herodotus a liar.[4] He is one of the Oxford monks,—a Fellow under the old arrangement that preceded the legislation of 1872,—the old plan under which a man had to take orders to get a fellowship, and remain unmarried to keep it, but could keep it all his life if he remained a celibate. Prof. Sayce keeps his fellowship, and faith he looks it,—tall, thin, high-vested, a narrow face, like some crane-like bird's, thrust forward beyond the line of his slender, bending body. And his timid manner and rapid, thin utterance suit with his appearance, and make him a perfect type of the studious recluse. He is perfect with his shovel hat on. Fortunately (for he was *not* interesting) he came late, and I could devote most of my time to the vivacious and charming Miss Townshend, to whom, you may be sure, I stuck very close indeed until the Orientalist came in. English girls, when they are interesting, are unmistakably very attractive creatures. American girls (as surely all the world must see,—for *this* part of the world, at any rate, is full of them) have a great and obvious superiority in beauty, figure, style, grace, and a sort of *effectiveness*; but English girls are, I should judge, as a rule sweeter and easier to love in an intimate, domestic fashion. When they get beauty, too, they are very dangerous. Miss Townshend has not beauty, but she almost has it, and is pleasant to watch, as well as to hear.

The Huttons were at the tea, and bade me come around to them at seven. We are getting very thick, are we not? I have been writing the last page or two in between events; but I must break off here to dress, and come back to talk to my darling again to-morrow night, when I have started on my way towards Somerset and Devon. What a comfort it is to write to you and think about you at every turn in my wanderings, my queen. How I love you!

"The Three Swans," Hungerford, Berks 7 August, 1899
To-day I made the first stage of my journey *sole*. I am thirty miles from Oxford, and ought to get to Wells by Thursday at the latest,—even if the roads should be as bad as the last ten miles of my ride to-day. The *tilt* of the road was all right, but it was covered with loose sharp-edged flints, and I rode in constant expectation of a puncture, with my eyes glued to the path before me, painfully, anxiously picking my way. Often—where picking one's

way was out of the question—I got off and walked, the tires being safe enough without my weight. It made it very tiresome.

I lunched at Wantage, at "The Bear" (opened 1682). As I rode into the market square of the pretty little town the first thing to catch my eye was a striking monument: a boulder-like mass of stone sustaining a Saxon figure, and a tablet beneath informed me that I had ridden into the birthplace of Alfred the Great,—and a quaint, interesting little town it is. Indeed *most* of the *small* towns in England are interesting and have marked points of beauty or, at any rate, individuality. The little town I am spending the night in, for example. I know nothing about Hungerford; but its streets are arranged after a manner of its own, its inn is old-fashioned and interesting, and it is in many ways good to look at. There seem to be no towns of note or consequence that lie in my way for the next day or two: but that gives me what I want,—*plain* England,—plenty of "local colour" but no sights. I am not lonely. I can give myself up so much the more entirely to thinking about you now that I am by my lee lane. Nothing puts me so much in heart as thinking about you. You are the one part of my life and achievements (!) that it gives me unalloyed pleasure to dwell upon,—and there are so many things about you to think about and get gladness out of. Love is a positive luxury in my case. I can always please myself with you according to my mood. You are sweet, you are interesting, you are charming, you are stimulating, you are exquisite at loving:— you are sweetheart, chum, wife, counsellor, intellectual companion, playmate, as I wish. There is only one mood you do not suit, and that is sadness,—and you suit that by chasing it away. Bless you, my Eileen! You have brought blessings without number into my life: would that I knew how to fill yours with the same largess. I mean to dream of you to-night, if eager willing and loving can accomplish it, and gladden my dreams with a sight, a touch of you. Good-night, my queen, my little wife, my exquisite darling!   Your own   Woodrow

Love to the chicks, to Ed. and Madge, to the dear Hibbens, and to Mrs. Brown.

ALS (WC, NjP).

[1] Wilson was probably referring to Louis Dyer, A.B., Harvard, 1874; B.A., Oxford, 1878; M.A., Oxford, 1893; Assistant Professor of Greek at Harvard, 1881-87; Lecturer, Balliol College, 1893-96. At this time, he was a "Member," perhaps an honorary fellow, of Balliol, not a tutor there. He lectured widely in the United States and England and was also a prolific writer in classical studies, modern literature, and political economy.

[2] If the Balliol "don" was indeed Dyer, then Wilson might well have been both irritated and amused by his British affectations, to say nothing of his

pomposity, clearly revealed in his vitas in American and British *Who's Whos.*

3 Agnes Grace Weld, daughter of Nanny (Anne) Sellwood Weld, younger sister of Tennyson's wife, Emily, and Charles Weld, Secretary and Historian of the Royal Society. Miss Weld was author of *Sacred Palmlands; or, the Journal of a Spring Tour* (London, 1881), and *Glimpses of Tennyson and of Some of His Relations and Friends* (London, 1903).

4 His *Reminiscences* (London, 1923), pp. 224-25, recounts the furor in the intellectual world caused by his "impugning the veracity" of Herodotus.

From Abbott Lawrence Lowell[1]

Dear Prof. Wilson: [London] Aug. 6, 1899.

From Prof. Dicey I learn that you are still looking for the occupant of the new chair of Political Science or Colonial Government at Princeton. As I said I would keep my eyes open while here, I spoke of the matter the other day to Mr Lucas of the Colonial Office, the author of the historical geography of the British colonies,[2] & strangely enough he suggested Mr. Egerton (the author of the Short History of British Colonial Policy),[3] whose name I suggested to you last spring. I know nothing about Mr Egerton except from his book, but I thought you might be interested to know that Mr Lucas recommended him, & believed he might come.

I hope you are having a pleasant summer here & that I shall meet you somewhere before you go back.

I am staying at the Sackville Hotel[,] Sackville St. W. for a few days more, but my permanent address is Brown Shipley & Co.

Yours sincerely,   A Lawrence Lowell

ALS (WP, DLC).

1 At this time Lecturer on Government at Harvard.

2 Charles Prestwood Lucas, *A Historical Geography of the British Colonies* (5 vols., Oxford, 1888-1901).

3 Hugh Edward Egerton, *A Short History of British Colonial Policy* (London, 1897).

From Ellen Axson Wilson

My own darling,   Princeton, Aug. 7, 1899.

The dear letter from Lichfield and Warwick came duly to hand today,—and I am happy. It gives a delightful record of your doings since the last letter. I am glad to know more of your Cambridge sight-seeing; and what a lot of it you did! fifteen colleges in three days. Alas, I should never be strong enough for such wild orgies of pleasure as that! I am sorry though that you denied yourself the pleasure of seeing Mr. Maitland. It would have been just as great a pleasure to him as to you for you & he were intended by nature for friends. But I am *deeply* delighted to hear of his improved health.

With us all goes well and pleasantly,—as usual. We have had two hot days—actually!—since I last wrote, but yesterday and to-day it is cool again,—absolutely perfect weather,—"the air as sweet almost as the morning we rode from Henderson to Arden Park. It would have been quite as sweet had *you* been here to help me breathe it!" Really, my one regret about your trip is that it is so cool here! I have the unreasonable feeling that you would have gained more by going, if the summer here had turned out rather unendurable, like the last! Tomorrow morning Mrs. Hibben is coming with her brother[1] to take me to see the Pyne gardens, and especially the lotus flowers—hundreds of them. She has been raving about their beauty all summer, and urging me to go, but I wouldn't because of the dog. The Pynes are away now. Mrs. Hibben goes to Grey Gables on Thursday for a week and will bring Beth back with her; her brother in the meantime keeping Mr. Hibben company. They were all here yesterday afternoon—taking me to walk with them after. Mrs. H. was highly delighted with her letter from you.

My photographs came the day before, and they insisted that I should send one to you at once. It seems rather silly when it will reach you just a week before you start for home; but perhaps you *will* be glad to see it away off there. I send this one because it is the smallest; one,—perhaps two,—others are better likenesses, *I* think: This is Mrs. Hibben's favourite, and it is undoubtedly the most artistic of the lot in general effect. And, by the way, I was anxious to try painting from life this summer, and knowing it would make me almost helpless with nervousness and the feeling of haste to try to get my hand in on anyone but a paid model—or myself,—I rummaged out that old failure and began on it again! Whatever the result, it has afforded me lots of practice. I think I have spent *days* trying to get "some speculation in the eyes that it did stare withal!"—Ed & Madge in the meantime making all manner of fun of it, and at the end damning with faint praise. Imagine my surprise then to find that the Hibbens think it a *fine* likeness though "not a flattered one by any means," and that Mr. Wilson will be "so pleased"!—a proposition I deeply doubt. But I have also done one of Nell now, that the Hibbens think *"lovely"* and that I like a *little* myself. It is rather a spirituelle little face. I began one of Madge before her friend came that I have some little hope of. Of course I was interrupted by the guest; and now by the fact that she is having a siege with the dentist; she comes back so tired that I havn't the heart to make her pose. With the exception of one plug last summer this is the first time a dentist has ever touched her. She is in for a big bill I fear,—six or eight plugs,—all gold.

A letter from Florence Hoyt the other day brought the most surprising piece of news,—Uncle Will is going to be *married!*—at sixty-seven![2] Those poor girls! But as Florence justly remarks if any of them could have stayed with him it would not have happened. I am not even told the lady's name;[3] only that she is about Minnie's[4] age and that Minnie says she is "commonplace." If she is commonplace enough to be a good housewife and "manager" I shall find it in my heart to be glad,—when I recover from the absurdity of it! That poor man has not had a day's comfort, as you know, for forty years.

Florence says the surgeon has been out for another examination & finds her knee doing beautifully,—better than he hoped.[5] He now thinks perhaps it may not be very stiff, and she will probably be rid of the machine in two more months.

Good-night, my own darling. I love you dear,—ah, how unspeakibly I love you, tenderly passionately, absorbingly,—"with the smiles, tears breath of all my life"—I am always and altogether

Your own,   Eileen

ALS (WC, NjP).
    [1] William Newcomb Davidson of Elizabeth, N.J.
    [2] Dr. William Dearing Hoyt's wife, Florence Stevens Hoyt, had died on October 2, 1896.
    [3] She was Annie Perkins, who owned a cotton plantation near Cedar Bluffs, Ala.
    [4] Mary Eloise Hoyt.
    [5] Florence Hoyt was suffering from tuberculosis of the bone. She had to have a leg amputated in 1901. See EAW to WW, April 12, 1901, Vol. 12.

To Ellen Axson Wilson

My own darling,   "The Star," Wells, 9 Aug., 1899

Just think,—two weeks from to-morrow, only two weeks, I must be in Glasgow, to get my wheel crated and everything in readiness to sail two days later, two weeks from Saturday. Time *does* move satisfactorily, after all, even a woe-begone lover can see that it moves. I should be delighted, thankful to take the steamer *next* Saturday,—not because I am not having a good time or am not amused and happy, but because I am *so* homesick for you! You will say that it is because I am alone and that loneliness is working its natural effects upon me. But no: that's not what is the matter. I am *not feeling* very lonely, and I had exactly the same feeling while I was with Stock.—the same unutterable longing to turn back to you. The difference is, that not till these closing days of my exile have I dared indulge myself with such an examination of my heart as goes along with this avowal. I've had to be very careful indeed how I made love in my letters. I once thought of writing Mrs. Hibben a letter *about* you. I should in mere good taste have been restrained and kept myself in check in speaking of you to *any*body else,—even to her; and yet I should have had the satisfaction of dwelling on thoughts of you, and writing your praises,—with less passion, and therefore less pain, than if I had been making love directly to you, but still enough freedom to give me infinite pleasure and sure relief. But of course such a letter would have itself been in bad taste. I should have found it impossible to invent a plausible excuse for writing it. Now, by degrees at any rate, I can bring my confessions to *you*, who will demand no excuses for them.

I am sincerely glad, for one reason, that I am not coming home by next Saturday's steamer. *I* have had plenty of vacation, but you have had none at all, and, if I were coming back at once, you would not take even the niggardly two weeks you are planning for for [sic] Jessie's sake. I trust they will do you and the sweet chicks some good, short as they will be, and I *do hope* you have succeeded in getting in at Mrs. Toppings. How I wish that I were there to manage the actual trip for you and take that much trouble at least off your hands! But everything turns into a reason for wishing myself with you,—especially the thought that, if I had been less selfish and not taken this expensive outing, you and the children could have had, not two weeks' merely, but a two months' pleasuring! You and Mrs. Hibben conspired to make me think I *needed* this elaborate self-indulgence; I weakly allowed myself to be deceived; and now I am heartily and frankly ashamed of myself. There was nothing in the world the matter with me that could not have been rested out of me *any*where except, perhaps, at Princeton itself. Princeton, no doubt, would have been too full of college thoughts and regrets to afford me either rest of a good kind or recreation that would have reached my mind. But any other place would have answered, *especially with you.* Here I am simply spending money, and pining for you! Even in Wells, where take it all in all, I should rather be than anywhere else in England! I changed my route. I did not go to Salisbury at all, or anywhere near it, but came to Wells the straightest way, through Bath; and, as a consequence, arrived here a day earlier than I expected. The army is manoevering most elaborately and laboriously around Salisbury; and the roads thereabouts (never very good) are very badly cut up with the movements. Cavalry, ordnance trains, on-looking excursionists, —everything has gone over them and made them (the papers say) "quite unrideable." So I struck into the great "Bath road" from London to Bath; rode forty-three miles yesterday, and twenty to-day; and arrived at my favourite cathedral town at ten minutes before two this afternoon. There is somehow a deep content for me in this place, even *now*, if I do not allow my home-eagerness (I wont call it home-sickness—it is mere eagerness for you) to get the better of me. It is a homelike little town: one fancies that the people are steady, home-loving, self-respecting, and content, with a sort of unconscious infection of simplicity and right thinking taken from their dignified and elevating surroundings. The cathedral does not dominate the place. Even with its extensive and striking setting of ecclesiastical residences and courts and gardens, it does not belittle the town or make its simple streets seem mean. It seems too kindly and neighbourly for that. It seems to stand in the midst with a certain modesty, an air of liking to belong to the place and grace, not spoil, it. It is not as if the church or its attendent buildings were new or were set in an ostentacious way to make a show. They are old, soft-hued, grave in tone and outline, *mellow* in every tint,—in no way thrust themselves upon the eye. They seem almost, in their mellow greyness, like parts of nature (surely the Gothic is the style in which Nature *would* have piled her stones if she had herself had need of buildings!) and in their informal placing, where it was convenient and natural to have them, considering their uses and the lay of the land, they graciously stand like themselves part of the town, letting her streets and footways through, along their greens and by their doorways, opening their turfed spaces and wooded walks to serve as a park for the people,—obviously serving human uses. There is *something* of this in every cathedral town which is not a great city,—something of this sympathy and accommodation; as if in the long generations the two had grown together, had given each other character, and, like man and wife, had come almost to look alike. But in Wells it seems to me much more obvious than anywhere else, and much more delightful. And then it is not without its effect upon me, as you will readily believe, that I have seen more pretty girls in Wells than anywhere else in England; and that one of the prettiest serves my meals for me!

The ride *to* Wells was through a countryside almost as beautiful as Warwickshire,—after the bare heaths of Berks and Wilt-shire were passed and I had won my way into Somerset; but, aside from the beauty of the countryside, which one gets, ungratefully, to *expect* in riding here, there was little that was noteworthy on the way. Even in the open I sadly missed the shadows (especially one day, when it was all *one* shadow and I got caught by the rain!). It has, for the most part, been a ride in the full blaze of the sun, hardly so much as a white shred of cloud to be seen in all the sky. Shadows would have brought a coolness devoutly to be prayed for, not only, but would have brought magic into the view. But, after all, it did not *need* magic. The plain fact of it was quite fine enough. Nothing ever *stares* here in the brightest flood of burning light, if seen in the open. There is always a touch, if never so slight a touch, of mist in the air, to give to grove and hillside a softened outline that makes them seem at once far away and near at hand,—within reach to touch, as in a picture.

I spent a night in Bath and had daylight enough there to look about and find that there was nothing in particular I wanted to stay and see. It did not seem the place of pleasure and fashion I had imagined it. Perhaps I did not know where to look for the evidences of that; or perhaps the swellest fashion has turned away from Bath as it has turned away from Saratoga. Once more perhaps, it is not in the summer but in the winter that its baths and waters are taken. At any rate, it was a different kind of place altogether from what I had expected to find. I left it with no more reluctance; and find my preference for Wells sufficiently pro-nounced in any case.

You may imagine with what purturbation of mind I read of the summer's lawlessness in Princeton—burglary, arson, and everything else that the town government ought to be ashamed of. At Oxford Mrs. Hutton gave me a copy of the *Princeton Press*, which was full of it all, and which contained a very vigourous editorial about it. And my darling has had to stand the strain, the constant strain, of anxiety, sleep with a pistol by her bedside, and say nothing at all about it to her care-free lover over sea! Dear me, can I ever do it again! I am indeed thankful that Ed. has come, to stand guard, and take at least that cause of care away!

I was really deeply grieved to learn of Mr. Vandewater's death. He was an excellent, intelligent, public-spirited man, and I should say quite indispensable to the town as a merchant. It will will be hard to replace him in that capacity, unless young Farr, who was with him, can take the store and continue the business.[1]

Ah, my darling, how my heart goes back to the thought with

which it set out in this letter. It is only two weeks *to-day* before I must be back in Glasgow to get ready for *sailing*–sailing *to you.* For this page and the last four pages should be dated, not Wednesday, the 9th, but Thursday, the 10th. I have been modifying my plans, now this way, now that, to engage my fancy and kill, a little bit, my impatience. I must fill these two weeks very full to endure them. At present this is my projected route: Wells to Exeter, through Glastonbury, Langport, and Taunton; Exeter north to Barnstaple; Barnstaple to Clovelly; then southward again, by rail, to Plymouth; from Plymouth by steamer to Dublin; Dublin to Belfast on my wheel; steamer from Belfast to Glasgow. Doesn't that sound varied and interesting enough? And, while I travel, four more letters to my darling ("my Eileen" will be most appropriate when writing from Ireland, will it not?–that sweetest of all your names, because most intimate, and *mine!*), and then I shall in person carry her the love my heart almost breaks with,–go back to the infinite and only satisfaction of *living* with her and having her for my comfort and delight every hour of the day and night! Ah, my sweetheart, my delightful Eileen, I could not have pleasure or even a moment's peace *any*where were you not at least *in store* for me,–*waiting* for me somewhere, sending me love messages, touching my dreams with your sweet presence, making yourself part of past, present, and future in all my thoughts. Thoughts of you are so inextricably mixed with all my pleasures, that I am somehow conscious that they are pleasures because you are present in them,–that I am capable of pleasure, susceptible to joy *because* I am   Your own   Woodrow

Love unmeasured to the chicks; dearest love to Madge, Ed., and the dear Hibbens; and as much as she wants to Mrs. Brown.   W.

ALS (WC, NjP).
  ¹ The *Princeton Press*, Aug. 5, 1899, had already announced that Mrs. Vandewater would continue her late husband's hardware business under the management of Harry H. Farr, who had been with Vandewater for twelve years. Farr soon took over the business entirely, and it survived to 1971 as the Farr Hardware Company.

To James Bryce

My dear Mr. Bryce,   Wells, Somerset, 10 August, 1899

   I was very much disappointed, when I was in London, a week or so since, to find that you had left the city. I was very anxious to consult you about a matter of great interest to Princeton University, and which, I hoped, would prove of interest to you also.

   A friend of the University has recently given it one hundred thousand dollars (which may reasonably be expected to yield 4%) as an endowment for a chair of Politics. The term is meant to be used in the broad, Aristotelian sense; and the incumbent of the chair would be expected to be a master of his subject, of course, on the scholarly side. But the founders of the chair are two young brothers (who withhold their names as yet from publication), who are not at all sorry to see the United States make her new venture in foreign war and the government of dependencies, and their *practical* objection [objective] in making the gift was, to provide lectures of a thorough sort on Administration as a science and on the government of dependencies in particular as an experience,—on the actual methods, i.e., of success (England's success, for example) in that manner of half rule, half coaching in slow development and gradual self-help. We have thought it not unlikely that we should find the man we wanted in England. I went to Sir William Markby[1] and one or two others for advice; and I wanted to come to you.

Do you know of any man you would suggest? Mr. Egerton has been mentioned to me (the author of a short history of England's colonial ventures). Could you put me in the way of finding out all about him? I should greatly appreciate, and I am sure the Princeton authorities would be very grateful to you for any help or hints you might give us. The appointment when made would be permanent and probably at a salary of $4,000; but I think we shall during our search for the right man (naturally a rather delicate matter under all the circumstances) try the experiment of inviting a few men to deliver short courses of lectures on colonial administration, or, rather, on the government of dependencies,—of course without any form, and in some instances without any thought even on our part, of candidacy.

I cannot sufficiently regret having failed to see you. It was one of the pleasures to which I had looked forward.

Until I sail (from Glasgow) on the 26th of this month, my address will be, The British Linen Co. Bank, 41 Lombard St. London.

With much regard, and the sincere hope that you will think the importance of the matter sufficient excuse for troubling you,   Most sincerely Yours,   Woodrow Wilson

ALS (Bryce Papers, Bodleian Library).
[1] Reader in Indian Law and Fellow of Balliol and All Souls Colleges, Oxford.

To Francesco Cosentini

Wells, Somersetshire, England,
My dear Sir,   10 August, 1899

Your kind letter, informing me of my election to be a corresponding member of the "Circolo di Studi Sociale" of the Università di Genova, has been forwarded to me here, where it finds me on a vacation tour of England.

Allow me to acknowledge its receipt, and to express my very great pleasure and my deep sense of the honour you have conferred upon me. I accept with sincerest appreciation, and with the best wishes for the success of the work of the Circolo, inaugurated with so much promise of usefulness.

I wish it were possible for me to add that I would attend the Sociological Congress which you have planned to convene in October. Unhappily that is not within my choice. I must sail for America within a couple of weeks, and the Autumn there will, for me, be so full of important engagements, from which I cannot break away that it will not be possible for me to cross the water again. I am very sorry, and thank you most sincerely for the invitation.

With assurances of the highest consideration,
Most sincerely Yours,   Woodrow Wilson

ALS (facsimile tipped in Francesco Cosentini, *Woodrow Wilson e la sua opera scientifica e politica* [Turin, 1919]).

From Ellen Axson Wilson

My own darling,   Princeton, Aug. 11 1899

This is the first time since you left that I have not written at the regular time. But I was pretty sick last night with a sort of cramp colic; bowels had been troubling me all day and towards tea time the pain began; but the medicine given me long ago by Dr. V. V. for the purpose relieved me entirely by half past nine so that I thought I would then get up and write. However as soon as I stood on my feet I was seized with violent nausea & shivering so that I had to tumble into bed instead of writing letters. But this morning every symptom has gone, and except for a little weakness, I am *"perfectly* all right."

And now I can't wait another minute but must plunge at once into the surprising piece of news brought me yesterday by Mr. Hibben! Mr. Perry has been appointed editor of the "Atlantic Monthly," and has *already* entered on the duties of his office! Now

I know I will fairly take away the breath of two worthy gentlemen! He wrote it to Mr. Hibben himself, said he had considered it two weeks, was very happy in the work, but was coming back in the fall to do his work in Princeton too for this year. That was all. It is a complete mystery to us how it all happened,—what has become of Page,[1] &c. &c; there has been no whisper of any change in the papers we have seen.

It seems to me an extremely poor choice, even apart from his total want of experience; he is too light weight. Did you ever detect in him any real understanding, or even any deep interest, in public questions or indeed any serious subject of thought? However he will doubtless edit it with taste on the strictly literary side. Perhaps he is no more of a dillitante than [Thomas Bailey] Aldrich was, besides being probably more sound and wholesome in his own personal theory and practice of life.

Ah well, I am a selfish creature! I shall be thoroughly philosophical both about the fate of the *Atlantic* and the loss to Princeton if it will only result in Stocktons getting his deserts, viz. a chair of pure literature! Only I could have wished on that account that it had happened some two years later; still he has one year in which to show his paces. They may think they must have some one of large reputation as a writer, &c,—a new Lowell say,—but he won't materealize very rapidly,—look at Yales experience,—and in the meantime Stock will have made such a success that all will be well. Besides there is Dr. Van Dyke elected for no other purpose but to "make us glorious by his pen[.]"[2] I find myself for the first time truly glad that he is coming. With one such star of the first magnitude (!) in the department they may well be content for the rest to consider the true interests of the college.

Having a little shopping to do for the children before going to the shore[,] I went in Wednesday, did it first, took an early lunch; and then had a long afternoon with Florence at Bryn Mawr. It is a *great* pleasure to go to her because she is so extremely glad to see me,—poor dear girl! I saw her fathers letter in which he told her about his approaching marriage,—a very sweet, tender letter, exceedingly anxious that she should not be unhappy about it, and yet dignified too. She is a Miss Annie Perkins whom he met on a visit to a married sister in Rome. She and her mother own and live on a farm in Ala.,—so that poor Uncle Will is *again* to have a mother-in-law on his hands! Isn't that the hardest luck? He says she is "a dear old lady and will of course live with them." He says that the daughter "is considered a perfect blessing in all the neighbourhood where she lives." Minnie has met her but has nothing to say except that she "doesn't attract her"—naturally! But she, Miss Ida, and all report that she is said to be a fine house-keeper. Indeed that seems her strong point,—which is very well, as far as it goes,—and to my mind it goes quite far in this particular case. Minnie is going to keep house with one of the other teachers in Balt. next year. When Will finishes college[3] he is to join them there and study medicine; and of course they hope that by and by Florence too will be there, and Margaret[4] near them at the hospital. Florence is improving so fast now that she hopes before long to be able to tutor some; there is a great deal of it to be had at Bryn Mawr.

We are all perfectly well. Yesterday was a happy day for us for it brought your *three* charming letters from Oxford. The children were perfectly delighted. They had a happy time day before yesterday. The Morgans[5] invited them to "tea," but it turned out to be a picnic. The four of them with their nurse were driven down to Stony Brook where they had a delicious spread. Which reminds me of my (Tuesday) morning at the Pynes with Mrs. Hibben[,] her brother & Madge. It is *all* beautiful there now, Italian gardens &c. &c.—but oh! the lotus flowers! I never saw anything so glorious! Just think how we used to rave over *one* at the [Allan] Marquands and then imagine hundreds, perhaps thousands, in bloom at once, each one larger than a magnolia flower; all shades from purest white to the most exquisite deep rose. And the motions and sound of the wind in the great beautiful leaves—every one as large as a small cradle! Two thirds at least of their large (skating) pond is covered with them. But 'tis after ten o'clock. I must run no risk but close this and get it off. All send dear love to both. As for me, my darling, my *darling*, I love you so intensely that it really frightens me. God bless you and keep you safe for your little wife   Eileen.

ALS (WP, DLC).
    [1] For what had become of Walter Hines Page, see n. 1 to J. H. Finley to WW, Aug. 1, 1899, printed as an Enclosure with EAW to WW, Aug. 3, 1899. The sudden change in the editorship of the *Atlantic Monthly* had come about during several hectic weeks in July 1899, during which Page had yielded to the importunate telegrams of Samuel Sidney McClure demanding that he join the Harper-McClure alliance in New York, and the management of Houghton Mifflin in turn had summoned Perry from a fishing trip in Vermont to Boston to offer him the post on the *Atlantic*. Peter Lyon, *Success Story: The Life and Times of S. S. McClure* (New York, 1963), pp. 166-67; Burton J. Hendrick, *The Training of an American: The Earlier Life and Letters of Walter H. Page, 1855-1913* (Boston and New York, 1928), pp. 344-49; and Bliss Perry, *And Gladly Teach: Reminiscences* (Boston and New York, 1935), pp. 160-67.
    [2] Henry van Dyke had been elected in June 1899 to be the first Murray Professor of English Literature at Princeton.
    [3] Her first cousin, William Dana Hoyt, was at this time a student at the University of Georgia (A.B., 1901).
    [4] Florence's younger sister, Margaret Bliss Hoyt.

[5] Josephine Perry Morgan and Junius Spencer Morgan, who lived at the corner of Stockton Street and Elm Road. He was Associate Librarian of Princeton University.

From Adolphus William Ward

Boat of Garten Hotel, Ins.

Dear Sir,   August 12th 1899

I very much regret to have missed you in London, where I remained till the 27th of last month, and looked forward to the pleasure of meeting you as Lord Acton had told me I might do. I fear that since I shall not be back in town before the end of September there is now no chance of my seeing you this year, and I will therefore put on paper what occurs to me, begging you to let me know whether there is anything further that you would like me to add. The above address will find me during the present month.

The enclosed paper (which pray keep) will show you Lord Acton's general ideas as to the character and scope of the *Cambridge History*. You will see that he makes a special point of the bibliography. The idea is to publish two volumes in each year, one of the History of Modern Times from the Renascence in progressive order, up to the Revolutionary Epoch in the 18th century, and another of the latter half of the period beginning from that date. The first volume of the second series (in which your chapter is included) will therefore if all is well be published in 1900, and we are already receiving chapters of it. It is devoted to the *United States* and the earlier history of North America under French and English colonisation; beginning with chapters on the English and French colonies and on the conquest of Canada. Then follow the six chapters (which Messrs Hart & Bigelow[1] are to contribute) on the history of the War of Independence from its commencement to its close; and hereupon a series of which your chapter is to form part delineating the developement of American public institutions and life up to the outbreak of the conflict between North and South. Mr. Bigelow takes a chapter on the Federal Constitution, Mr. Avery[2] three chapters on Federalists, Republicans & Democrats; and then comes your chapter on State Rights. It is followed by a chapter on the Southern Confederation by Mr. Rhodes,[3] and the volume concludes with three chapters on the War, and three more bringing the history of the United States up to a recent date, and reassessing the intellectual development of the country.

The large majority of the chapters which I have hitherto read form part of the first volume of the other series referred to (the Renascence), and such observations as I might make on them with regard to overlapping and the like would hardly apply in the case of the American volume. The only chapters as to which you might feel any difficulty in the way of their touching part of the same ground as yours would be I suppose the chapters on the Federal Constitution and on the growth of the great party distinctions, for I apprehend that the chapter on the Southern Confederation would be essentially one of historical narrative. If you have any special points on which it might be well to communicate with Mr. Avery or Mr. Bigelow, kindly let me know; but I do not myself see that there is any ground for expecting overlapping. As soon as I receive either their chapters (which I have not yet had) or yours, I will of course take care to find out any portion or passage where a danger might seem likely to arise.

The length of each chapter is calculated at 30 pp., but a page or two more or less of course is of no consequence. Each page is reckoned by the printers at about 500 words; I will tell the printers to send you a specimen page to your London address to make certain.

I will ask you to be good enough to regard the information as to chapters and contributors in this letter as confidential, as nothing has yet been made public and the distribution of chapters in some of the later volumes of the work is not yet complete.[4] Pray favour me with a line to say whether I can supplement this letter, and I will let Lord Acton know in due course what has passed between us.   Yours ever sincerely   A. W. Ward

ALS (WP, DLC). Enc.: Acton's guide for contributors to the *Cambridge Modern History*, printed memorandum dated March 12, 1898.

[1] Albert Bushnell Hart and Melville Madison Bigelow, legal and constitutional historian, associated for fifty years with the Boston University Law School.

[2] Perhaps Elroy McKendree Avery, popular author who later wrote a twelve-volume history of the United States.

[3] James Ford Rhodes.

[4] As it later turned out, among the persons mentioned by Ward, only Wilson and Bigelow contributed to *The Cambridge Modern History*.

To Ellen Axson Wilson

                                        Exeter, Devon, "The Half Moon"
My own darling,   Sunday, 13 Aug., '99

It is Sunday, and I am in a cathedral town, but I can't go to church. This is *not* one of the places to which I forwarded my trunk,—it was sent forward from Wells to Plymouth, and will get there to-morrow or next day to await my sailing for Dublin,—and

I cannot make up my mind, in this most conventional of countries, to go to a cathedral service in shorts and a coloured shirt. And I stay at home and do what I must in frankness say is to me infinitely more delightful,—to talk to you!

I came away from Wells with a very heavy heart: I had spent all of Thursday there, not only because I loved the place, but also to wait for my mid-week letter from you. But it did not come; I had to leave without it,—with two letterless days of riding ahead of me. The pleasure Wells had given me, the interest of passing again through Langport and visiting Bagehot's grave once more; the keen expectation of passing from Somersetshire into Devon, which I had for so long desired to see, the delight of fine roads and satisfying scenery only partially cheered and diverted me: I wanted my Eileen's letter! And it was not here when I arrived! But I got it this morning. I can't imagine what kept it; but I don't care now: my heart is at ease again! And there ought to be another letter for me to-morrow,—for I saw that one of the mail steamers had got in at Queenstown on Friday.

Every turn of my ride brings me to things that interest me,—to some outlook upon a beautiful countryside, to some village all character and age, a beautiful church standing in its quiet yard in the midst, more noble in its proportions than most of our city churches, more lovingly finished in detail, though less ornate, an ancient monument of labour and of faith, conceived with a touch of majesty, and yet not too great for its secluded and rural seat, —only the village church; or some bright, busy town I never knew anything about, but now find worth seeing, with monuments and noble or curious buildings of its own, old and new. Taunton is such a place, where I spent Friday night. I never knew anything about Taunton. I now know that it is the place (at any rate one of the chief places) where the execrable Jefferies held his bloody assizes. I saw the great room, now bare and barn-like, in which he sat and condemned,—condemned *himself* for ever. It is in an old castle, part of which is now a museum, part (including the ancient a[r]ched gate house) an inn; and close to which crowd the pens of a sheep market, in what was no doubt once the castle yard, but is now a sort of open square. There are fine churches in the town and a noble park; its streets are wide; it is clean, alive, —a cheery place which strikes you as well-to-do, self-respecting,— a place of fine averages and some "eminent citizens." That was my last stopping place in Somerset. I left it yesterday morning at ten o'clock and by lunch time was well within Devonshire, at Cullompton, another place that surprised me with its stately

church, its air of being at once old and young, with here and there
a beautiful half-timbered house as old and as beautiful with its
simple carvings as those, more famous, in Chester,—or a stone
front with elaborately carved arms over its door and stone-mul-
lioned windows with that perfection of proportion which marks
almost no building, it seems to me, later than the workmanlike
days of the great Eliza,—not a house of consequence any longer,
apparently; given over now to some humble or common use; cut
up, it might be, into shops or offices or cottages, but dignified and
beautiful still, though with something of a decayed and chastened
air. And Exeter turns out most interesting and engaging. I reached
it about half-past four yesterday afternoon and went at once to see
the cathedral. It was, of course, to see it that I had come. It is perfectly wonderful how distinctive a character of its own each of
these English cathedrals has! One would suppose beforehand that,
going in rapid succession from one to the other through a long
series, one would get an impression of sameness. They were all
built at about the same period, for in tastes and ideals and methods of workmanship the thirteenth, fourteenth, and fifteenth centuries seem somehow essentially homogeneous and as if of the
same age. In respect of the cathedrals, moreover there was a fixed
and practically uniform plan and relation of parts. But there is no
sameness. Everywhere there is individuality and originality, and
some special character or grace or adaptation to a separate use
or unusual situation. I must say that Exeter, though apparently
less talked about than the other cathedrals and regarded as of
minor importance, is as well worth seeing as any of them, except
the very greatest, like York and Durham and the most fascinating,
like Wells. I cannot describe it, of course, but I can enjoy it; and
not only it but its surroundings: its irregular yard, or "close," set
about with houses full of a distinctive character of their own; its
"palace" gardens; the quaint quarter of the town, which it seems
to have kept to its more ancient air and character. Away from
the immediate neighbourhood of the cathedral, indeed, and its
network of narrow and twisting streets, Exeter is worth seeing.
It, too, has odd corners, old houses, some merely singular, others
beautiful, and all the layers of old and new that make these towns
so interesting, and like regions of discovery, to an American.

This dear letter of yours, just received (oh, how your letters *fill
me up*, heart and mind!) is the one which tells of Mrs. Cameron,
Sr.'s abominable conduct about her daughter-in-law. I cannot
trust myself to speak of it! Even if all that she intimates about
the poor girl were true, she ought to be tarred and feathered for

speaking of it. But it goes without saying that what such a she-devil says is necessarily false, and conceived in mere malevolence! It is indeed most fortunate that there is some one in Princeton who knows Mrs. Guyot's character and antecedents familiarly and can of knowledge offset the slanders of the false mother.

I am glad, my sweet one, that your acquaintance with Mrs. Tilton and Miss Garland is growing into such a pleasant intimacy. I know a little of how interesting and worth knowing they both are, and I know what pleasure, and it may be stimulation, too, the association will bring you. You see how frankly selfish I am,—*for you*. But I *know*, if anybody in the world does, what deep enjoyment the association with you will bring to them! They are on any reckoning the gainers. It is well worth having lived to have known you. I know of no one to whom the too hackneyed quotation, "To know her was a liberal education," applies more perfectly than it does to you (the more perfectly because you do not know or understand it); except that it is not broad enough. "Education" is not a blithe word, is not a word of enjoyment, and for you a word of enjoyment also must be found. There is assuredly pleasure in education; but it is a sober pleasure,—and you are so *bonny* and so educate one into love and deep delight.

Of course I have written Stockton of my completed plans for the next two weeks, and especially of my definite expectation of being in Dublin next Sunday; and I have invited him, in case he feels by that time thoroughly rested and entirely inclined, to join me there on the chance of finding Mr. Dowden at home. I have not liked to write to Mr. Dowden to say that we would come, and to ask him if he would be at home, for fear he would put himself out in some extraordinary way to meet us. These good people will put themselves out to any extent to be kind and hospitable. Mrs. Dowden will hardly be glad to see me, if I find them, *without you*. She, like most persons of taste and discernment, went straight to the source of all the charm and interest there is in "the Wilsons," finding it in you, and she knows that I am secondary, and distinctly inferior in flavour. I don't know why the word *flavour* has not oftener come to me when speaking of you. It is eminently descriptive of something about you which is infinitely elusive so far as words are concerned. One of my chief pleasures, you know, is to go over again and again the delightful recollections of our first acquaintance and drawing together; and I think one of the chief elements of pleasure to me in all those sweet memories is the recollection of the delicious surprise and satisfaction that came to my taste when first I perceived the exquisite flavour of all that you thought and said. It was like a distilation of all the sweet flavours of some old garden of the mind borne about by one herself fresh and of the sunshine,—no gardener there, but one for whom the garden had been made, and in whose enjoying moods it became new, a place for pleasures original and of the present,—so that one loved and wondered at the maiden for her own sake, and yet associated her with the aroma of the place in which he had found her. Of course the crowning joy of that time was the discovery that she could *love me*, who had deemed myself unlovable: and it is that love that has transformed my life, transfusing me with some touch of the sweet savour that was hers. I am like something common and stale that had been lain away in a sweet place and has come out brightened in texture and scented like a garment of state. I have grown so accustomed now to all that is exquisite in you that the surprise of those first days is now a recollection, though the delight in what caused the surprise is ever renewed; and yet sometimes I find the sense of your personality come upon me once again as if with a rush of rediscovery, and the sweet surprise is born again. Ah, but my riches are inestimable!

Dear me! Here I am at the end of my letter on the *first* day of its composition. It's no matter: there will be nothing to add tomorrow. I always keep these epistles open till the last moment, so that they shall be as recent as their day of posting. I am well, and beyond measure happy in thinking of you, my Eileen. I am, with oh such passionate love and longing,

Your own   Woodrow

You will of course be at the seaside when this arrives. Tell the chicks how much I love them. Love to Ed.

ALS (WC, NjP).

From Ellen Axson Wilson

My own darling,   Princeton, Aug. 14, 1899.

Your letter from London came today; I am surprised of course at the changes in your plans and Stockton's, but have no doubt it is all wisely done. The rest will certainly be good for him, and I think the freedom to follow your own devices will be pleasant for you. You won't have to go to the same places you did before whether you want to or not because they are the show places and Stock *must* see them. I do hope you will go to Devon! Is Stock to see absolutely nothing more,—not even Salisbury, Winchester &

Canterbury,—when they are all so near? But how stupid in me to ask questions that can't be answered!

I enclose the notice from the *Atlantic* of the change of editorship; am glad to know that Mr. Page has not come to grief in any way.[1] As Praed says, "Dame Fortune is a fickle gypsy, always blind and sometimes tipsy."[2] It strikes me that she has been playing one of her "tipsy" pranks on Mr. Perry. Think of the years he struggled on under a mountain of drudgery and other troubles! —and now when he is just relieved of all the drudgery, salary raised, his work ideal for him and everything smooth sailing, she makes him an offer so brilliant that he simply can't refuse it. He may live to regret it of course, but he would be *sure* to regret it if he didn't go. On the one side Princeton, which he always declared the ideal home for a literary worker, on the other Boston, the Paradise of all good New Englanders. Poor fellow, I am sorry for him on the whole!

We are all *perfectly* well now. We have been having a spell of bad weather but have been busily enjoying ourselves in spite of it. I reading, painting and overhauling the children's wardrobes in preparation for the sea-shore! Madge too has been sewing,—has just triumphantly finished the first waist she ever made for herself. Ed is very busy over a model of an invention of his, an automatic distilling apparatus for chemical purposes. The children spend their time embroidering, playing games, and reading Scott's novels. Jessie has read twenty and Margaret sixteen. Nellie found all of them after "Ivanhoe" and the "Talisman" too hard for her and has betaken herself to "Lorna Doone" instead. I am impressed anew almost everyday with the *value* of those novels as "educational works," with the innumerable pictures of English life, impressions of English history,—true enough for all practical purposes—with which they furnish the children's minds. In our reading together it seems to me very few things ever come up that they don't already know *something* about from reading some novel of Scotts.

Our literary researches go on famously; we have gone all the way from Caedmon to Burns now, and the children seem to enjoy it all immensely. Mr. Ike Marvel has given us some extremely readable and on the whole satisfactory books for the purpose though with some few singular errors in perspective,—or perhaps simple oversights. For instance he has seven pages about *Hannah More* and five about Lady Blessington, and not a word of Miss Austin or Miss Edgeworth![3] But it is unjust to him to pick out a fact like that for comment just because it amuses me; it is lowering myself to the level of a professional critic!

We have actually had news of Father again. He wrote me some time ago[4] and I answered at once. Then the children all wrote and he has just answered their letters. To my surprise he is still at Wilmington, not on the shore now; he says he is so well and so comfortable there that he doesn't care to go elsewhere, is enthusiastic about his boarding-house. He says Sister Annie is at Mars Hill.[5] I have not had a word from her all summer; she has been utterly lost to us. I was delighted to learn her whereabouts again and wrote to her last night.

I have an idea that this letter is an even more illegible scrawl than usual, if that is possible;—do excuse it; I have a thorn broken off in the end of my index finger and can scarcely hold a pen.

I will send the cablegram as you request if it can be sent from Sagg; I do not doubt that it *can* go from Bridgehampton, but if it *does* fail to reach you, please understand that the cause was the [that] we were away from home and could not manage it. It seems almost too good to be true, my darling, that the time grows so short;—only a day or two more than three weeks before you will be actually *at home*. My heart leaps up almost to suffocation at the thought. My last letter! and it does not seem so long after all since *your* first letter came. Indeed the time has gone quite rapidly since then; the first month when I was waiting for that letter seemed indeed interminable. Ah, my dearest, can you imagine how I love you,—how constantly my thoughts are occupied with you? "Would that my tongue could utter the thoughts that arise in me!"

But if *you* even find a difficulty and a trouble in trying to express your love imagine my dumb agony in the attempt and my dispairing abandonment of it. But oh! how every part of me echoes some of your words, dear love! *You* are all the world to *me*; you elevate, you stimulate, you satisfy, you delight me: every part of me enjoys you with an infinite ardour. You know, I am sure that these words—though they *are* scrawled,—look much better on *this* page than on yours! Everyone would declare them a lover's exaggeration in the one case, while if they read them here they would say "of course; a series of self-evident truths." It is so perfectly *reasonable* that you should satisfy and delight me,— that my thoughts should constantly hover about you in happy contemplation first of one aspect, then of another, and another. You surely cant deny the advantage I have in that you satisfy and delight my *pride* as well as my love,—that I can and do so *glory* in you.

> "Standing a man now, stately, strong and wise,
> Marching to fortune; not surprised by her.
> One great aim, like a guiding-star above—
> Which tasks strength, wisdom, stateliness to lift
> His manhood to the height that takes the prize;
> A prize not near—lest overlooking earth
> He rashly spring to seize it,—nor remote,
> So that he rest upon his path content:
> But day by day, while shimmering grows to shine,
> And the faint circlet prophesies the orb,
> He sees so much as, just evolving these,
> The stateliness, the wisdom and the strength,
> To due completion, will suffice this life,
> And lead him at his grandest to the grave."[6]

There is Browning's hero—and mine.

And now goodnight and God be with you, my own dear one. How I shall pray that in His infinite loving kindness He will bring you in safety to the desired haven,—home—to all who love you and to her who loves you more than all the rest together,

Your little wife   Eileen.

My letter is so heavy that I won't send the Perry circular. It simply said that Page had resigned to take a prominent post in directing the literary work of the allied Houses of McClure & Harper, and then gave a short notice of Mr. Perry.

By the way, I meant to tell you—for smoking-room service—say,—a good story Mrs. Brown told me last night on her eight year old grand niece. In reading the Bible they came upon the verse, "And Enoch walked with God & was not for God took him." Asked if she knew what it meant she said, "Of course, it just means that he went to heaven without dying,—like Elijah, only there wasn't so much *display* about it!" Once more goodbye, and may all be well with my darling.

ALS (WC, NjP).
1 She decided not to enclose it and gives a summary of it later in this letter.
2 A slightly edited version of lines from Winthrop Mackworth Praed's "The Haunted Tree."
3 Another reference to Donald Grant Mitchell's *English Lands, Letters and Kings*. Mitchell often wrote under the pseudonym of "Ik Marvel." Mrs. Wilson's comment about the contents of the volumes is rather puzzling. There are eight pages on Hannah More and five on Marguerite Gardiner, Countess of Blessington; but there are also six pages on Jane Austen and five on Maria Edgeworth, both of whom appear in the same volume with Hannah More and are listed in the index.

4 Dr. Wilson's letter is missing.
5 In western North Carolina.
6 Robert Browning, *Colombe's Birthday: A Play*, Act IV, lines 209-22.

To Ellen Axson Wilson

My own darling,

"Duke of Cornwall Hotel,"
Plymouth, 17 Aug., 1899

Here I am at the end of my English riding; but in the depths of confusion and chagrin! I actually *forgot* to mail my last letter to you,—kept it in my pocket until it was too late to catch the midweek steamer,—*forgot* it, when I think of you every hour of the day,—forgot it *while* thinking intensely of you, for I forgot it at Clovelly where I longed for you more constantly and more nearly intolerably than I have anywhere else;—and so you will not get it as soon even as you get this, for this will go direct to Sagaponack and that will go first to Princeton. When I got here about one o'clock to-day I thought I was properly punished: there was quite an unusual number of letters waiting for me: one from Stock., one from Mrs. Hibben,[1] two forwarded by you, etc., *but none from you,*—and I was blue with a vengeance. I went to the hotel office again and asked if they were sure they had given me all my letters; they looked again and said Yes, all; and I went out on an errand a dejected fellow, I can tell you. When I came in again your letter was handed to me! One of the women in the office had handled the letters with her parasol in her hand and your letter had dropped into *it!* Fortunately, she remembered that she had had the parasol in her hand and went at once, after I turned away from making my second inquiry, and looked within it. It would have served me poetically right if I had been cheated of the sweet letter altogether. I can only suppose that Clovelly bewitched me! I reached the wonderful little place about midday on Tuesday,— just about the time I ought to have posted the letter,—and it fairly took my breath away with surprise and delight to find it in fact what I had been told it was, as extraordinary and as interesting as the heart could desire. And yet that very fact gave me the strongest feeling of unreality. I felt as if I were walking in a picture, through a piece of stage scenery, thro. a sort of devised street built at a cunningly constructed World's Fair. And, to cap the climax, at my Inn, which was at the very heart of that incomparable precipitous street in the cloven cliff, they put me in a little house all by itself, above the roof of the hotel,—a room to which I had to climb through a little wonderfully tilted garden at the rear, all stair cases and narrow terraces. The little house was

on the topmost terrace of all, and contained nothing but my room
and a half cellar, opening from the next terrace below. The whole
of one end of the room was taken up with its door and a bay-win-
dow as wide as our hall-way oriel. The dressing table stood in the
bay, and before me as I sat at it stretched all the sea, between
the cliff-shoulders of the narrow place,—below the steep town and
the boats dancing in the tiny roadstead. I was so excited and
moved by the pleasure and novelty of it all that I caught myself
laughing aloud as I stood in my strange little room. I wandered
about with the restless curiosity and delight of a child, peeping
into every nook and corner of the place (it did not take long)
and looking into door-ways, with a child's indifference to good
manners, getting run into by other sight-seers, and almost run
into by the little donkeys whose panniers are the only possible
vehicles of the village. At last, at the bottom of the street, on the
jetty which helps make a shelter for the fishing boats, I sat down
in supreme contentment just to dream,—of the place, of the sea,
of you,—of the happiness it would be to bring you there, of the
unspeakable pity of it all that you were *not* there,—and in thinking
of you I forgot your letter written at Exeter! While I looked out to
sea and dreamed, two excursion steamers came in from Bristol,
and I went down to the pebbly beach (the pebbles are as big as
those we brought home from Gloucester) to amuse myself
watching the people at closer range; and as my eye ran with
languid curiosity through the crowds it lighted on Dr. Hazen of
Middletown! There were Mrs. Hazen and Miss Hazen,[2] too, the
Dr.'s sister, and Maynard.[3] You may imagine how I rushed at
them, escorted them all over the village, like a new guide, and
spent the evening with them. They did not go back with their boat,
but stayed all night, to drive over to Bideford in the morning *en
route* to Exeter; and yesterday morning I accompanied them on
part of their ride,—three miles through the "Hobby Drive" which
runs around the cliffs (exquisitely forested cliffs, and the drive a
continuous avenue of splendid trees) and looks down again and
again upon the village from every picturesque angle and point of
vantage,—before I turned to my own route for Launceston and
Plymouth. Mrs. Hazen told me that she had been utterly unable
to get well till she actually left home; but now, I rejoice to say,
she looks and is well,—quite like her old self again. Miss Hazen
has been studying all year on this side of the water, most of the
time, I believe, at Oxford. You would have been touched and delighted to see and hear Mrs. Hazen wish for *you* at every turn,—
and exclaim how much she would like to see your *eyes* as you

looked at this, that, or the other bit of the exquisite scene. She seems really to love you, and talks of you with the greatest enthusiasm. Of course they all sent every message of love to you and the chicks.

My rides have all been fine and exhilerating, from Exeter on, the weather remaining wonderfully fine, and Devon and Cornwall proving everything the eye could wish for. From Exeter to Barnstaple I rode thr. the very heart of Devonshire,—and it proved another Warwickshire for varied beauty, and a look upon all its face that made a fellow wish for it as a home. Yesterday and to-day I rode down the western coast and through a strip of Cornwall, topping hills from whence I could see all the fine and striking coast line, gazing out to sea, and thinking, as always, of home. Home, home is the refrain of all my thoughts. I have been too much away from you. When I get on the ship next week I shall feel like a homing bird released. Oh, for the *speed* of a homing bird. I love my darling till I *need* and cannot do without her. Life stands still till I am with her again. I am altogether

Her own   Woodrow

Love immeasurable to the chicks and to dear Ed. I was very much touched by what you said of dear little Margaret's pride and pleasure in my letter to her.

ALS (WC, NjP).
    [1] Jenny D. Hibben to WW, Aug. 1, 1899.
    [2] Frances Mary Hazen, Instructor and Professor of Latin, Mount Holyoke Seminary and College, 1865-1907. Miss Hazen had just spent a year studying at Oxford University.
    [3] The Hazens' son.

From James Bryce

Dear Profr. Wilson   [Ceppomorelli, Italy] Aug. 17/99

Your letter has just reached me. I greatly regret having missed you in London. We left on the 3rd & don't expect to be back in England till near the middle of Sept.

This endowment of a chair for τὰ πολιτικά is excellent, but I hope it won't be too specifically directed by the foundation deed to colonial matters, which may after all prove to be a comparatively small department of work for men who are to serve their country in public work. No person occurs to me off-hand in England as specially well suited for the post, & you will certainly do well to be in no hurry over making the appointment. To have a succession of lectures in the first instance will be a very good plan. I have just heard Mr. Egerton's name, but know nothing at all about it, nor how any information could be obtained. As soon as I get back to England I will endeavor to ascertain from Oxford & Cambridge friends whether they know of any men competent for such a post. There would certainly be some advantages in getting an Englishman if he were plainly of the right sort[.] It is just possible that some man who had been in India & retired early because that climate did not suit him might be available—of course assuming that he was otherwise qualified by general scholarship & ability. So it might be worth your while to write to Sir Arthur Godley, Under Secretary of State for India, asking if he knows of such a one. If you like to do this, you may use my name in writing to Sir Arthur. Anything else I can do I shall do very willingly but the article you want is rather a special one, and will want some looking for. Before you leave England, you may perhaps get some light; but August is not a good month for finding people, especially at the Universities.

With renewed regrets at not having had a talk with you, believe me   Very sincerely yours   James Bryce.

ALS (WP, DLC).

Two Letters to Ellen Axson Wilson

Drogheda, Co. Louth, 20 Aug., '99
My own darling,   "The White Horse."

I am not sure whether I am pleased with my Irish venture or not. Certainly the Dublin part of it proved a great fiasco. In the first place, the steamer from Plymouth was late, crowded, and most uncomfortable. It should have left Plymouth at noon on Friday and have reached Dublin at about six Saturday afternoon, but as a matter of fact it left at six in the afternoon and arrived at about two this (Sunday) morning. Its accommodations were like those of an ill-kept sleeping car. The crowds on board were going to the Dublin Horse Show, "the greatest horse show in the world," I am told, and an annual event of the first magnitude for all the United Kingdom. By the same token Dublin was packed; hotel rooms not to be had,—had been engaged, all of them, weeks ago. There was no place to shave or get at the contents of my trunk, and the only thing I could do was to take the first stage of my journey northward at once and by rail,—asking chance acquaintances on the boat where I should go to; and therefore I am in Drogheda. I don't clearly know yet exactly where Drogheda is! I have not been able to find a map to look it up on. I know only that it is north of Dublin some thirty or forty miles and somehow on the way to Belfast.

I did not come out of Dublin without looking at it. After I had had my breakfast, I rode about the city on my wheel and saw a great deal of it,—the Castle, the old Parliament houses, and all that I could think of as worth seeing, but most particularly, of course, Trinity College. Its gates were open, Sunday tho. it was; and I wandered through its quads. for quite half an hour with my thoughts full of Burke. The buildings are not beautiful, but they are dignified and spacious, constructed in the formal style I associate with Sir Christopher Wren,—Greek, Pseudo-Greek, or whatever it is. The magnitude of the college struck me, quad. within quad, and round about two sides spacious gardens. I should say the circumference of the whole was nearly a mile,—and that in the very heart of the city. At the front of the buildings, on the street, or, rather on sward which intervenes between the buildings and the street, stand striking statues of Burke and Goldsmith; and in the open space which the college faces (one might call it a square were it not almost triangular) there is an uncommonly fine statue, of Grattan, facing the college, but also in front of the old Parliament buildings, which also face the same space or square. Aside from these special objects of interest, the city struck me as singularly unattractive, plebeian, without distinction,—except that it must surely, from what I saw, be one of the dirtiest cities in the world. I was very much disappointed, of course, not to get a chance even to try to see Mr. and Mrs. Dowden; but they live eight miles away from Dublin, very likely are not at home at this season of the year, and—it was quite impossible to manage. I could not even get presentable linen from my trunk. At any rate Stock. did not miss it, for he decided not to join me in my Irish venture. He and Snyder have gone to Antwerp, to be back on Tuesday; and at Antwerp there is (I believe it's now "on") a most magnificent exhibition, a great many loans from private and other collections included, of Van Dyke's paintings, to celebrate some anniversary (is it the 250th?) of his birth. I envy them, I must say. That is more interesting and worth while, I am sure, than either Drogheda or the road from Drogheda to Belfast! But it's not in me to repine just now. This is the last letter before I come myself—this sails Wednesday, I sail Saturday! Ah, how my heart leaps at the thoughts that crowd about that fact! The joy of the expectation of coming to you, my *darling*, is almost too acute to give leave to, to assert itself fully. It puts me into an almost distressing agitation of mind. When I realize how much it means to me simply to come to you, my queen, I wonder how I ever endure separation at all. My delight in you is so complete, my loneliness without you so irremediable, all satisfying comradeship so impossible! I literally never know what it is to have either heart or mind satisfied, or even at rest, away from you. The explanation is plain, to me. You are the only person I ever *lived with completely*, giving my whole nature up and *using* every faculty and power of it. My love for you released my real personality, and I never can express it perfectly either in act or word away from you or your immediate inspiration. And so, without you, I feel *pent*, unnatural, *cheated* of full life,—like a flowering plant that could not bloom. The tide of my blood seems full only when I am with you. Love unlocks everything within me that it is a pleasure to me to use. I never used my mind, even, with satisfaction till I had you, —and it seems to me I never used my heart at all. My reserve was a veritable jailer before that,—and it can play, does play, the jailer yet when I am long away from you. I seem shut away from the sun and morbid. And so I feel *now* like a man about to be freed: I am going to you! No more letters this time, but after this speech face to face, my darling in my arms! I am *so* grateful to you for the exquisite photograph, sweetheart. It is, indeed, a work of art and as beautiful as any picture I ever saw,—incomparably full of sweetness and of grace. But it has not *all* your charm yet. They have done *some*thing to your perfect mouth that I don't like. I know, as I look at it,—and yet cannot say just why,—that, though this is your beauty; and *enough* beauty to satisfy anybody, it is not you. You are more winning: your *life* is not in this lovely image. I love it, but oh, how much more I love you,—even as a bit of flesh and blood, as a beautiful woman! No doubt it is impossible for the camera to see you as you are,—and no doubt you look differently when you are with me, look into my eyes with a light in your face which is not there in front of the camera! I see you, God be praised, as no one else has ever been, or can ever be, privileged to see you. Your letters have been such a blessing and delight to me this summer, my Eileen: so full of exactly what I wanted, so bright, so spirited, as if you were happy, so alight, for me, with your own quality. God keep and bless you, my precious one, till I can kiss and thank you held close to my heart. My pulses tremble at the thought of the bliss that is in store for me, when you once more look into the eyes and cling close to

Your own   Woodrow

Love unbounded to the chicks and warm love to Ed.

Imperial and Windsor Hotel, Belfast.

My own darling,   22 August, 1899

I find that there is still a wee bit of time before the American mail goes, and I cannot refrain from a few words of comment on the extraordinary news of Perry's appointment to be editor of *The Atlantic*. It is little less than amazing! He *may* succeed (I do not see how he can, unless they mean to rest content with a somewhat dillitante magazine that does not pay expenses), but I feel quite sure that the appointment would never have been made, had shrewd old Mr. [Henry Oscar] Houghton been still living, the real creator of the prosperity of the House. And what *has* happened to Page? Has he made himself obnoxious, as I feared he would, or has he gone over to the publishing side of the business, as he seemed to be doing when he so urgently solicited from me a History of the Civil War, and begged that Houghton, Mifflin, & Co might have the history he understood I was engaged on, when it was finished?[1] The latter is the supposition I incline to. It is all immensely interesting!

Don't, don't, my darling, be too sanguine about the effect on Stock's career. Stock. does not yet know the news, for your letter containing it did not reach me till I got here, and I shall not see him till he joins me in Glasgow day after to-morrow (Thursday); but I am not afraid that *he* will base confident hopes upon it; I am only afraid that *you* will, and at Princeton at present hopes, especially reasonable hopes, are deeply foolish. They will certainly want a man of wide distinction, and they will certainly not ask our advice or act upon work done in the class-room in making their selection. I shall be distressed all year (as distressed as I was pending Stock's recent appointment—and that was a wretched period indeed for me!) if I know what you are letting your hopes feed on,—if you allow yourself to imagine that Stock. is in the running for the chair Dr. Murray so recently held. We will run him if we can, and that will be strain enough, without the added expectation of your unhappiness.

But, dear me, here I am at the last moment reading you a lecture! It is because my heart is so full of you, my Eileen. Even the distant expectation of a great disappointment for you makes me unhappy. My own happiness is absolutely dependent on yours. Ah, how blessed a thought it is that my coming will make you happy! My queen! my lovely little wife! Every day my heart's excitement rises as I near the longed for sailing day. I've had holiday enough,—too much by far! The price is too great. More would do me harm, by sheer strain on my heart. I am nothing (except by force of will) away from you, for I am altogether

Your own   Woodrow

I am well and every way all right

ALS (WC, NjP).
  1 W. H. Page to WW, July 25, 1897, Vol. 10.

To John Huston Finley

My dear Finley,   Belfast. 22 August, 1899

It is mighty hard to have to say No to an editor who is also a friend, and a warmly esteemed friend at that, for whom I would gladly do anything I could.[1] But I really have no choice in this case. I've already promised more, I fear, for next winter than I can do as I like to do my work,—and the bulk of it I have promised to the Harpers. I *must* finish the History of the United States for there [their] Educational Department which I worked at all last winter, but which it will take another winter of diligent writing to finish; and I must write an elaborate chapter,—a small treatise in itself,—for the Cambridge University Press on States Rights: otherwise the history of the United States from 1850 to 1860,—to form part of their "Cambridge Modern History." I could not do more to save my life.

I need not say how much your plans interest me; how heartily I wish you success, and confidently expect that you will achieve it; or how much pleased I am that you wish me to contribute to your new Review. I thought you were the right man in the right vocation in Knox. No doubt you will prove that you are an even better man in a better place now.

With warmest regard and heartiest good wishes,

Sincerely and Cordially Yours,   Woodrow Wilson

ALS (J. H. Finley Papers, NN).
  1 Wilson was answering J. H. Finley to WW, Aug. 1, 1899, printed as an Enclosure with EAW to WW, Aug. 3, 1899.

A News Item

[Sept. 9, 1899]

Professors Woodrow Wilson and Axson and about thirty ministers, delegates to the Pan Presbyterian council at Washington,[1] were on the City of Rome which came into collision with an iceberg.[2]

Printed in the *Princeton Press*, Sept. 9, 1899.
  1 The Pan-Presbyterian Alliance, consisting of delegates from Presbyterian churches in all parts of the world, met at the New York Avenue Presbyterian Church in Washington on September 27, 1899, for a conference scheduled to last for ten days.
  2 The Anchor Line steamship *City of Rome* sailed from Glasgow on August 26, 1899, with 993 passengers and a crew of 297. In the evening of August 30, the ship struck a small iceberg in heavy fog near the Banks of Newfoundland. Since *City of Rome* was traveling at a reduced speed because of the fog and hit the iceberg a glancing blow, she suffered only slight damage. The ship arrived in New York merely a few hours behind schedule on September 4.

Memoranda

[c. Sept. 10, 1899]

P[hilosophy]. o[f] P[olitics].

No "people" has the right to rule as it pleases, independently of the rule of law,—constitutional law, if such there be, included,—or independently of moral obligations. See the decisions of the Supreme Court of the U. S. of the binding force of our constitutions upon the people, their (theoretical) makers. This points to a corporate action as not "democratic," in the ordinary misconception of that word, but under law and masters—to democracy as simply a special form of elective government under veritable *rulers.* (See Tocqueville on the character foundations of American democracy)

Institutions are subsequent to character. They do not create character, but are created and sustained by it. After being successfully established, however, they both confirm and modify national character, forming in no small degree both national thought and national purpose—certainly national ideals.

The real problem of Politics (Aristotle said) is, How, out of heterogeneous elements, to make the best combinations for moral progress.

Introduction for P. o. P.

The world is full of hope. The dreams of socialism, the visions, even the distempered visions, of democracy, the uneasy movement of labor for its betterment, the compulsions of ideals of every kind, mark a world alive with hope and with the energy of great resolutions. But hope is without moderation, without practical programs, without leaders. The most helpful service to the world thus awaiting the fulfillment of its visions would be an elucidation, a real elucidation, of the laws of leadership.

WWhw and WWsh memoranda in the pocket notebook described at June 18, 1899.

To John Grier Hibben

My dear Jack,   Princeton, 15 September, '99

We've had a housefull of company all week,—the Smith's[1] and two lunch parties of new friends whom Ellen made at Sagaponack this summer, (and one of the friends I must admit made a great impression on me;—her brow and eyes would make an impression on any man who had eyes himself; and she proved to have a remarkable and most attractive mind besides); but we have been lonely for lack of Mrs. Hibben and you, all the same, the week through, and feel that it is genuinely unselfish on our part to hope that you will stay away as long as possible. Our love for you both has put you beyond the reach of competition; and I *could* mention points of beauty (I know you'll be too modest to appropriate too much of this part of the sentence) and points of intellectual endowment in the case of the Hibbens (you and Mrs. Hibben may share this part in any proportion upon which you can agree!) which might enable them to face comparisons without embarrassment or misgiving!

Nothing is going on here. The Murrays[2] have taken possession of their new house and are now actually our neighbours, and the Winanses are moving into the dean's house,—driving wagons on to the lawn to facilitate the process. Mr. Henry M. Alexander[3] was buried here on Wednesday; and the same day Dr. Patton reached New York on the new giant liner, *The Oceanic*,—but not in time to take part in the ceremony. Dr. Purves[4] conducted the services, and made an address which he no doubt believed to be true, but which, true or not, was one of the most beautiful I ever heard, a veritable literary treat. Dr. Patton is looking uncommonly well; has shaved off his side whiskers; looks more interesting, more sure of himself, more a shrewd man of metaphysics and subtile policy than ever; and George[5] moves with him like satellite and watchful understudy. We met on the road below our house a little way—where they wandered to view again the boundaries of their principality—I jumped from my wheel to greet them with an air an actor might have studied to his advantage, and an agreeable winter has been (so far as we are concerned) smilingly inaugurated.

We rejoice to think how much cheered and strengthened you will both be by your little outing and vacation. We shall be so happy to see both your faces cleared, and we shall hope to be such companions to you as will enable you to feel that the winter before us all demands, not courage, but only the steady hand of friendship and affection to make it not only endurable but even a time of deep pleasure and profit. We all join in warmest love to you three and I am, as ever,

Your affectionate friend   Woodrow Wilson

ALS (photostat in WC, NjP).
¹ Lucy Marshall Smith and Mary Randolph Smith of New Orleans.
² Julia Richards Haughton Murray, widow of Dean Murray, and her two sons, Haughton and George Richards Murray, who had just built a new house on Library Place.
³ Henry Martyn Alexander, trustee of the College of New Jersey and Princeton University, 1863-99, died on September 9, 1899.
⁴ The Rev. Dr. George Tybout Purves, pastor of the First Presbyterian Church of Princeton.
⁵ Dr. Patton's son, George Stevenson Patton, Assistant Professor of Biblical Instruction and Secretary to the President.

To May Wright Sewall[1]

My dear Madam,   Princeton, New Jersey, 19 September, 1899.

Your letter of the fifteenth instant, received yesterday, inviting me to be one of the winter's speakers before the Contemporary Club of Indianapolis has given me very great gratification; and I sincerely wish that it were possible for me to accept.

On account of my university duties, which are crowded into the early part of each week, it is impracticable for me to accept invitations to places at a considerable distance for any evening earlier than Thursday. Moreover, there is another difficulty, which I shall take the liberty of stating to you very frankly. I have of late found my time so taken up with speaking engagements away from home, to the great detriment of my literary work, that for a year or two I have felt obliged to insist upon a "protective tariff," which shall in most cases be prohibitory. I have put it at one hundred dollars and expenses; and the embarrassment is this, that, while I should like often to make exceptions, I cannot do so without getting into very delicate situations, from which I cannot escape without giving offence to persons whom I greatly esteem and should like to serve. I do not know what to do except to maintain the rule and depend upon those who invite me to come to their own conclusions, "without prejudice," as to whether the tariff is prohibitive or not. I feel confident that you will both understand and sympathize.[2]

With much regard, and sincere thanks and regrets,
Very sincerely Yours,   Woodrow Wilson

WWTLS (May Wright Sewall Papers, InI).
¹ May Eliza Wright Thompson (Mrs. Theodore Lovett) Sewall, founder in 1890 and first president of the Contemporary Club of Indianapolis, "open to men and women on equal terms" (to quote from its constitution); first president

of the Federation of Women's Clubs; leader in the movement for woman suffrage; and author, among other works, of *Neither Dead Nor Sleeping* (Indianapolis, 1920), a book about her experiences with spiritualism.

[2] Wilson did not speak to the Contemporary Club during the year 1899-1900.

From Frederic Flagler Helmer[1]

Dear Sir,   Holyoke Massachusetts September 19 1899

Your letter reached me to-day through Lockport N.Y. It is very kind of you to give me the opportunity and I shall send you sketches of book plate designs as soon as present work allows and seemingly fit ideas come to mind. So far as work is concerned I would say in a week or so. Trusting this will be satisfactory,

Very truly   Frederic Flagler Helmer

ALS (WP, DLC).

[1] A bookplate designer and printer, about whom nothing else seems to be known.

From Thomas Shanks McPheeters[1]

My dear Mr. Wilson: St. Louis, Sept. 27/99

On account of the great intimacy of our fathers[2] and on account of the great admiration that I have for you personally, I take the liberty of calling to your attention the fact that my son, Thos. S. McPheeters, Jr., has entered this year Princeton University as a freshman. His address is 15 Dickinson St., and to say that I am very anxious to have him make your personal acquaintance and should be very much pleased if you would send for him, as I believe men more than books influence the lives of youths. I shall not expect that you will inconvenience yourself in this matter and hope that you will feel no further responsibility in it than to allow the boy to feel that he has a personal acquaintance with you rather than simply knowing you as one of the teachers.

His present plan is to study law when he finishes the University, and therefore, in the latter part of his College course will be in your classes.[3]

I am sure that you will excuse the solicitude of a parent for an only child.   Sincerely yours,   T. S. McPheeters

TLS (WP, DLC).

[1] A businessman of St. Louis.

[2] Dr. Wilson and McPheeters' father, the Rev. Samuel Brown McPheeters, had been associated in the work of the southern Presbyterian Church.

[3] He was graduated from Princeton in 1903 and received the LL.B. degree from Washington University in 1905.

From Frederic Flagler Helmer

Dear Sir: Holyoke Mass   October 2, 1899

These sketches are submitted to see if any of the ideas meet your favor. They do not pretend to give detail. If you can, from these, give me a more definite direction I will work again, at that, and submit something more carefully done. I trust you will feel very free to say what you think of these.

Very truly yours   Frederic F Helmer

ALS (WP, DLC) with WWhw notation on env.: "Book plate—Ans." Encs.: four sketches of bookplates, with WWhw comments on three of them.

To Walter Hines Page

My dear Mr. Page,   Princeton, New Jersey, 4 October, 1899.

I sit down to write you on a little piece of business; but I want first to congratulate you on your return to New York,—not because it is New York but because I know from the very fact of your leaving the *Atlantic* and breaking your interest in the literary plans of Houghton, Mifflin, & Co. that you must have found something even more to your mind and liking. I am sincerely glad; and perhaps I shall now have more chance of seeing you.

I feel some compunction in broaching the matter of business, because it involves the asking of a favour from a very busy man. But I do not know to whom else to go. We are planning some lectures here for this winter on the administration of tropical dependencies, and kindred topics, and we have naturally thought of Mr. Alleyne Ireland,[1] amongst others. But we know absolutely nothing about him personally. Can you put me on the track of learning something of his character, training, antecedents, and personality? Can you tell me *where* he is, and *what* he is at present? Is it likely that he could lecture?[2]

If you could either answer these questions or tell me who could answer them, I should be deeply indebted. At the same time let me apologize for giving you the trouble of doing so.

With warm regard,

Sincerely Yours,   Woodrow Wilson

WWTLS (W. H. Page Papers, MH).

1 English-born seaman, world traveler, journalist, and lecturer. Having spent a dozen years in British colonies in the Far East, the West Indies, and South America, he came to the United States just before the beginning of the Spanish-American War. In late September 1899, he published *Tropical Colonization: An Introduction to the Study of the Subject* (New York and London, 1899), the first of several such books by him. Wilson had asked Page about Ireland because he had published articles in the *Atlantic Monthly* in December 1898 and April 1899.

2 Page's reply is missing. Whatever plans Wilson and others at Princeton were making for a lecture series on the administration of tropical dependencies fell through.

An Address[1]

[[Oct. 13, 1899]]

SPURIOUS VERSUS REAL PATRIOTISM IN EDUCATION.

LADIES AND GENTLEMEN: The subject which has been assigned to me is Spurious as contrasted with Real Patriotism in Education. Why should a man speak this evening on patriotism by way of exhortation? Is not this immediate part of the land, at any rate, full of the voices of patriotic feeling? Are we not now worshiping at the feet of a man whom we conceive to represent the power and the dignity of the nation, a man of moderation and self-possession in peace, as well as of mastery and bravery in war?[2] And is it not true that our hearts, no matter what our opinions may be with regard to questions of policy, are at unison in rejoicing that we can produce such men? It would seem a work of impertinence to speak to a country, or to any persons connected with a country, thus stirred to tell them how they ought to feel with respect to matters of patriotism.

And yet I think you will agree with me, after very little reflection, that patriotism is, after all, not essentially a sentiment. Patriotism expresses itself in sentiment, but it does not consist of sentiment. Patriotism is a principle, not a sentiment. It is a principle of devotion, and I cannot conceive of any principle of devotion which is not suitable to the object to which we are devoted. Shall I say that I am devoted to my friend and then shall I do my friend a dis-service? Shall I praise in him what I do not honestly admire? Shall I leave unpraised what I think for his good? Shall I agree with him out of mere complaisance, and shall I show my friendship by such agreement? Surely that is not the principle of devotion. Devotion suits itself to its object and is

1 Delivered at the fourteenth annual meeting of the New England Association of Colleges and Preparatory Schools in the Fogg Art Museum of Harvard University on October 13, 1899. There is a WWT outline of Wilson's address, dated Oct. 13, 1899, in WP, DLC.
2 George Dewey, hero of the Battle of Manila Bay, who had recently been elevated to the new rank of Admiral of the Navy. Leaving Manila aboard his flagship, U.S.S. Olympia, on May 20, 1899, Dewey sailed home by way of the Suez Canal, joining the Atlantic Squadron in New York Harbor on September 26. He and his men were greeted with wild enthusiasm and feted in a series of social affairs. From New York, Dewey went to Washington to receive the plaudits of a grateful Congress. He next made a triumphal tour of New England, climaxed by a welcome by 25,000 persons in Boston on October 13, the very day on which Wilson gave this address.

careful to serve the thing served according to its character. And so I say that, although this principle of devotion breeds sentiment, it is a schooled and chastened sentiment. It is a sentiment which expresses itself in the wise and moderate counsels of real and thoughtful friendship.

If I were to undertake to describe what patriotism is, I should say that it is not a thing singular and apart, it is not a thing which we can separate from other like sentiments. When we speak of the character of a man as being unselfish, we have begun to describe him by the same terms that we would use in describing him as a patriot, for I take it that patriotism is grounded in what unselfishness is grounded in, namely, a certain energy of character expressing itself outside of the narrow circle of self-interest. We are not so small as to live only for ourselves. That is what we say to the world when we prove ourselves true friends; and when we prove ourselves true patriots we are but extending the circle of this principle of friendly interest and of energy expressed beyond the circle of self-interest. You know that when you describe a man's character as noble you are not thinking, I think I should be justified in saying that you are never thinking, of the things that he does for himself. Is it "noble" that a man should serve his own interests? It is necessary, it is desirable, it is in many forms praiseworthy; but do we describe it as noble that a man should serve himself? How does he differ from other men, and where is one man to be preferred to another in nobility, if it consists in serving one's self, for does not every man within the limits of his intelligence serve himself? No, when we say that a man is noble we mean that he serves something besides himself; that he has, if I may express it, a margin, a surplus, a free capital of character, which he can expend in undertakings which are for the general welfare as well as in undertakings for himself. He is not consumed and used up in serving himself; there is a generous remainder which he is ready to share with his neighbors and with his fellow-citizens and with his friends. And so nobility is this fine exercise of one's quality outside of the narrow circle of self-interest.

It seems to me that it is but an extension of these terms when we speak of patriotism. Patriotism is this fine, unselfish exercise of energy, and it is not, as I began by saying, a mere expression of sentiment. You know that one of the drawbacks in speaking about patriotism is that a man has a certain self-consciousness of what he himself does and does not do, and he feels that the expression of noble purpose is in itself a cheap thing. How shall a man consent to have his own patriotism examined? He shrinks from that. He fears to be suspected of cheap sentiment, and to be challenged to show where he has realized it in action. His fear is an illustration of the principle that I am insisting upon, namely, that character does not show itself in the mere utterance of the sentiments of the lip. I have heard some excellent sentiments of patriotism associated with very base conduct. I have heard some very selfish purposes served by the expression of the sentiment of patriotism. We know that the sentiment itself is cheap, but that the duty is dear, and that when men express themselves in action we then for the first time uncover ourselves and know that we stand in the presence of men who serve their country as well as themselves. I take that to be one of the things which makes us stand with no word of criticism in the presence of the great admiral whom we have so recently been honoring, because we know that he did not undertake what he undertook for glory, but in the way of service.

I was very much interested in what one of our naval officers said to me the other day.[3] He was expressing, I think with a little pique, his surprise at the astonishment of the country at the readiness of the navy for the war. "Why," he said, "I have been in the navy sixteen years, and all those sixteen years we have been ready to give a ball or go into battle in fifteen minutes." These men, therefore, have lived not to glorify themselves in this service, but as always ready for service, and when they have contained themselves after winning victories we have known in how deep a sense they were serviceable men.

The moral obviously is, that we cannot serve our country, and no man can serve his country, unless we know what the country is and what it stands for. How shall I be patriotic, how shall any man be patriotic, who does not understand the object of his devotion? It is a more serious thing, it seems to me, to be a citizen of this country than to be a citizen of any other country, unless it be the country to which we are nearest akin; because I always remember when I think of this government of ours that interesting sentence in DeTocqueville in which he says: "One is startled to perceive the variety of information and the excellence of discretion which its Constitution presupposes in the people whom it is meant to govern." The variety of information; the excellence of discretion. You are trusting a great body of men to govern themselves, and you are thereby trusting them to understand

---

3 Wilson obviously attended one of the numerous affairs given in Dewey's honor in New York, but it is impossible to determine which it was.

their polity and to adopt a policy which is suitable to that polity. This excellence of discretion will not come without knowledge, without that variety of information which DeTocqueville associates with it; and it seems to me that the first and most noble characteristic of our polity is that it is a debating and an intellectual polity. I do not know of any other polity that depends upon nicer questions of law, upon nicer balances of arrangement, and therefore it is an intellectual polity, because it requires nicety of discrimination to be understood, and it also requires that a man should know the objects for which all this nice machinery is adjusted in order that he may not put it to the wrong uses and damage it in the using. It is a debating polity. Why? If you would know why it is a debating polity, you must remember how it originated.

We have seen a good many singular things happen recently. We have been told that it is unpatriotic to criticise public action. Well, if it is, then there is a deep disgrace resting upon the origins of this nation. This nation originated in the sharpest sort of criticism of public policy. We originated, to put it in the vernacular, in a kick, and if it be unpatriotic to kick, why, then, the grown man is unlike the child. We have forgotten the very principle of our origin if we have forgotten how to object, how to resist, how to agitate, how to pull down and build up, even to the extent of revolutionary practices if it be necessary, to readjust matters. I have forgotten my history if that be not true history. When I see schoolrooms full of children, going through genuflections to the flag of the United States, I am willing to bend the knee if I be permitted to understand what history has written upon the folds of that flag. If you will teach the children what the flag stands for, I am willing that they should go on both knees to it. But they will get up with opinions of their own; they will not get up with the opinions which happen to be the opinions of those who are instructing them. They will get up critical. They will get up determined to have opinions of their own. They will know that this is a flag of liberty of opinion, as well as of political liberty in questions of organization.

I am not saying this because I am as much disposed as some are to criticise recent events, but because I love, more deeply than I love anything else, the right of other men to hold opinions different from my own. If I had to live among men who always agreed with me I know what the consequences would be on my character and development, and I do not wish to live in any so placid and complaisant a community. I wish the rigorous airs of differences of opinion, and, if I am not able to fight it out for myself, I want some better champion on my side. A man's muscles are made, as I understand it, for use, for contention, for triumph, and I take it that his opinions are made for the same thing. We belong, therefore, to a contesting, a debating, an intellectual polity, where difference of opinion is, as it were, a sort of mandate of conscience, and where things prosper and are purified, because there are differences of opinion, and not because there is unity in opinion. That is the rigorous condition upon which we live. I believe that the weakness of the American character is that there are so few growlers and kickers amongst us. We would be better served, from the street cars up, if we were all of us accustomed to make things very disagreeable (laughter). You know that Mr. Bagehot very wittily said, that the freedom of the English Constitution consisted in this, that all sorts of conveniences were afforded for making it disagreeable for the men who were governing the country; and it is because of the instinctive desire of persons to get agreeable conditions to live under that governors are conformable to the general opinion of those whom they are governing. We have heard that the government of France, under the old régime, was limited by epigram, because a laugh at its expense made the court feel uneasy, and so the court was guided in such a way as to avoid a too disagreeable laugh. Such are the conditions of conformity to the opinions of a people, and this is the sort of polity that we live under, and I rejoice in that fact.

But it lays a burden upon the teacher, such as can be laid under no other polity in respect to the matter that we have to discuss, namely, education in patriotism. I suppose that on the face of it it sounds absurd to say that you are educating people in patriotism, but it sounds absurd only if you regard patriotism merely as a sentiment. I do not know how to educate persons in generous sentiment; I know how to educate people in fear. You can make people afraid of you, if you have power enough and are disagreeable enough, but I do not know any means of making people love you—I mean deliberately; for every man remembers the days of his youth when he tried the experiment (laughter). There is no known prescription by which you can compel anybody to love you. The generous, sympathetic sentiments are not subject to compulsion. The fearful sentiments, the timorous sentiments, and the base sentiments are subject to compulsion, but you would not class patriotism with them. Patriotism is a bold and aggressive and initiative sentiment, and it is a sentiment of sympathy, above all things, and you cannot compel a sentiment of sympathy unless you display the lovable qualities which inhere in the object which you would have loved; and then you know that, if they be properly displayed, it shall be a poor spirit that does not feel its love called forth, and that it is a matter of despair to lead a nation which will not love lovely things. So that the object of the teacher, it seems to me, in matters of patriotism, should be to show what is inherent and essential in the character of American institutions, and so call out those generous sentiments which must rise at the sight of lovely objects.

And yet you will see at once that the essential objects, the essential characteristics of our government, are very abstract things. They are things which are not only abstract, but, which is worse, are abstract *and familiar*. After you have rubbed an abstraction over by constant handling it becomes almost impossible to retain it in your hand. It has become so slippery, so worn with use, so handled by the inexpert fingers of men, that it is covered over with all sorts of accretions and mistakes and it is the more difficult to recognize because it has been so much dealt with. I conceive the three central abstractions which lie in the character of our government to be these: Self-government, liberty, and equality. What man, what child, does not have to be dispossessed of prepossessions with regard to these three things? How much mistaken talk there has been about all of them. Most of the mistakes have been committed in this country, because we have supposed that self-government—we have not supposed it really, because we, after all, are not insane, but we have talked as if we supposed—that self-government and liberty and equality originated, were born and nursed in this country. No man who knows any history, or, rather, who chooses to recollect his history when he is talking about these things, can imagine that that is true. We did not originate these desirable things. We did not originate liberty or self-government. Some people think we never have invented equality yet. And we talk about these things as if, should they not be found here, it were impossible to find them anywhere. That is the first thing we have to dispossess our thought of. Any teacher who teaches a child that the flag of the United States is the only flag that stands for self-government and liberty and equality is teaching a radical error. We believe, I certainly believe, that the most serviceable forms of self-government and liberty and equality have been found under the institutions of this country; but that is all that I can say. It is a matter of comparative excellence; it is not a matter of originality or of absolute excellence. And so you have to teach your children where self-government came from and what it is, where liberty came from and what it is, where equality came from and what it is, and I take it that that is a very difficult matter.

I was led to this conclusion in preparing to make this address to you. I have never realized before so clearly as I think I realize now what the task involves; and I was naturally led to think, therefore, upon the possibility of this sort of instruction. Shall you teach young children these abstract matters of self-government and liberty and equality? And it came into my mind as I thought that it would be possible to write a book. I am not going to write it; I should have to start over again and be a bigger man; but it would be possible for a man of the right caliber to write a book which would be an incomparable suggestor of patriotism. If he were to write it so that self-government would shine in attractive instances, as concrete as the life in the midst of which we live; if he would embody liberty in the story of great passages of liberty; if he would embody equality in the fortunes of men who had lived and whose biographies we familiarly knew, he would bring these things into very life before the eyes of those who looked, because the advantage that we have in teaching these things is that we have instances at hand. I take it that French teachers could have no instances at hand of these things. I am not willing to disparage the French character, for it has many traits which we may envy, but I have noticed, in the books which I am condemned because of my profession to read, that those writers who live in countries that have not had real self-government find the question of self-government very easy to treat. I find that politics is simplicity itself with the men who have never lived any part of politics, and that it is difficult for us to speak of these things because we are "sicklied o'er with the pale cast of thought." We remember a few things, we have tried a few things, we know a few men, and we know how unlovely the mass of men are who profess these splendid principles. We have attended mass meetings of our fellow-citizens and we know of what stuff they are made and by what passions they are moved; and we know that, although you may know every man in your neighborhood, if you gather all those men in a mass meeting they will do something to surprise you. You know that the orbits of political bodies are absolutely incalculable, that the only thing you can be sure of is some sort of an eclipse (laughter), some sort of an obscuration, particularly of heavenly bodies (laughter). And, therefore, we have an advantage and a disadvantage. We can express these things in terms of life, but the difficulty is to express them in simple terms of life, such as we could imagine them expressible in if we did not know life as well as we know it. We have the disadvantage of being workmen in the stuff and knowing how unmalleable it really is, and yet the advantage of having all handled the stuff and knowing in the main what it is like. We are, therefore, safer when we think in individual instances than when we think in the abstract.

Now I think there are a few points which we can illustrate to children or to anybody else. In the first place, with regard to self-government, for I want to be very practical indeed. In regard to self-government we can illustrate the point that it is not in its essence democratic. If it were, when did it begin? You know that self-government runs back, at any rate, as far as Magna Charta. Did England have democratic institutions immediately after Magna Charta, and has she had democratic institutions during most of the period from Magna Charta down to the present time? Certainly not. And yet the history of self-government is the history of England in mediaeval and modern times, until this government was established; and ours is a very recent and modern growth. It is very easy to show children self-government, if England had it, is not necessarily democratic. You can show them if you will tell them stories about English justices of the peace—and you can get plenty of them—that English self-government in local matters consisted in the administration of those matters by appointed justices of the peace down to the year 1888; that so far as national affairs were concerned, it consisted in an imperfect system of representation down to 1832, and a not very much more perfect system since 1832; and that down to 1888 it consisted in government, administrative government all along the line, by men appointed by the Crown, the principal country gentlemen of their neighborhood. That certainly is not democratic. Why do you call it *self*-government, then? You call it self-government because it is a participation by non-official persons in the conduct of affairs; by persons who, in the case of justices of the peace, got no pay for it, made no profession of it, were appointed because of their importance in the locality, and not because of their connection with the national government; who were not officers of the central government in the sense that modern administrative officers are. And you can show that during much of the period of representation in Parliament it was merely a talking body and not a legislative body, and that its advantage was that it made the rulers feel uncomfortable rather than that they told them what they had to do. You can illustrate these things by concrete instances taken out of Parliament. Can you not describe situations in the history of England, and can you not describe how certain fearless men stood up in Parliament, under dramatic circumstances which any child's imagination will take fire at, and told the situation and made the government intolerably uncomfortable? Can you not describe that struggle, that critical struggle, between self-government and autocratic government, which came when Cromwell turned out the Parliament? Can you not find instances dramatic enough for any use all up and down English history to show how the English layman, as contrasted with the official, pressed himself into affairs and spoke his mind, and can you not make even children understand that the opportunity of laymen to speak their mind about affairs and get heard upon a public forum is self-government? That is the chief and essential feature of it. Just so long as European governments choke off discussion and put men in prison because of their opinions about personages in high places, they may have never so perfect a system of representation, and never so modern a constitution, and be without self-government. Self-gover[n]ment is the free expression of lay, non-official opinion, and I know of no other essential characteristic about it; and that is the dramatic characteristic, that is the characteristic which is concrete and illustrative.

Now, you will say, if this is true of self-government—and I ask you to excuse me from a further examination of that point and simply leave it with you in order to show you what grows out of that, which you can also illustrate—if this is the essence of self-government, this non-official participation in saying what ought to be done, and saying it in a voice and from a place where men are sure of a hearing, why, then, it presupposes, and has back of it individual capacity, has it not? It has back of it some leisure for affairs, has it not? It has back of it a spirit of honor and of devotion. These are qualities which can be illustrated out of biography in a way which will quicken any pulse—devotion to affairs, the devoting of high capacity to affairs, the pledging of unimpeachable honor in affairs, the devotion of leisure to affairs; and I believe that one reason that self-government has gone some crooked courses in this country is because we have had so few men of leisure, and so few men of leisure that we did have have devoted themselves to the free expression of opinion in public affairs. Who is the man whom the politician fears? The man whom it is no use to turn out of office. If in order to have a voice in affairs you must occupy office, the politician can silence you, because he can intrigue you out of office; but if you are going to have leisure and determination enough to keep on talking, and are going to have invitations to talk in public places, whether you are in office or out of office, what good does it do to turn you out of office? These are the men who make the scheming politician infinitely uncomfortable. If you can snap your finger in his face and say, "Give me the office, or give it to some one else and I will be a thorn in your side nevertheless," why, he will give you a berth, and if you will not prick too much he will give you a good deal of your way in affairs. We all know that when Mr. Roosevelt—for concrete instances are the most interesting—consorted with Mr. Platt, we grew uncomfortable; but Mr. Platt was a great deal more uncomfortable than we were (laughter and applause). They were bedfellows, but a thorn is an uncomfortable bedfellow. Although they were going the same course together, it was necessary that Mr. Platt should give himself less latitude of movement than he had given himself before. Why? Because this popular, this gifted man, this man whom all the nation was willing to hear speak, whether they agreed with him or not, was too big a man to have it make any difference to him whether he was in office or out of office. If he had not been governor of New York, the governor of New York would have been eminently uncomfortable because he was not, and so he would have had an important part in that governorship whether he possessed the office or did not possess the office. We may agree with Mr. Roosevelt and admire him, or not agree with him and not admire him; that is a matter of indifference to my argument. My argument is that, being a man of leisure, who can find leisure enough and energy enough to talk about affairs whether he has office or not, he is the sort of man who can carry the burdens of self-government without the assistance of machinery; and, in proportion as such men are multiplied, will pure self-government, thoroughly discussed and honestly conducted, be assured us.

Which leads to another useful observation. Not only is self-government not necessarily democratic, though I believe that democracy is the soundest basis for it, but self-government, and democratic self-government, is like every other polity in the world, though it be monarchical and despotic, in this, that the burdens of it rest upon a minority. There never has been and there never will be a government that is conducted by the majority. The majority may make all the noise they please, and a very small number of persons govern in affairs. That must always be

the case. And no man, no minority, can be successful in affairs—
I do not mean a minority in the ordinary sense, the minority who
cannot get the rest of a community to vote with them, but the
minority who are actually active in affairs and influential in affairs—no minority that carries the burden of government under
any polity can afford to give over attention to affairs and attend
to them only at intervals. We are too much inclined to govern by
committees of 100, who generally are doing nothing. If you go
into the game of politics, you must go in to be there year in and
year out, campaign or no campaign, having a passion for attending to the details as well as to the greater issues, and it is only
upon this condition that you shall have a sound and working
polity. This means that men of leisure must devote themselves to
affairs. You have, therefore, personal capacity, personal honor,
leisure, and these things are susceptible of illustration in concrete
instances. There is no child that cannot understand those things.
When expressed in terms of conduct, of individual conduct, self-
government is no longer an abstraction, it is a personal duty, and
the man ought to stay awake at nights who does not realize it as a
personal duty. I maintain that the man who does not exercise his
notion of self-government as a personal duty ought to shut his
mouth as a critic. Who is he? What has he done? Where has he
spoken? A man may have the most unimpeachable sentiments in
the world and he is not a good citizen unless he tries to get those
sentiments adopted.

That is the rigorous condition of self-government. You shall not
have exercised your duty until you have tried to make your opinions prevalent. It is a matter of agitation, and agitation is disagreeable. It is not everybody that likes to speak to a hostile audience. I think the best spirits sometimes like hostility a little
better than sympathy, because it gets the fighting blood up in
them and they do their thinking as if for life or for death. But
that is insisting upon the impact of your thought upon other
minds that do not like that impact; it is making yourself disagreeable in the long run to the vast majority of the people with whom
you associate.

Now as to liberty. Liberty does not seem to me an abstraction.
It goes without saying—it is a commonplace to say—that liberty
is not the withdrawing of all restraints. Liberty is having just
restraint enough. Do we say that a boat sails free when she is not
restrained by the wind? Is it not her obedience to the wind that
makes her free? Is it not her obedience to the great forces moving
about her that puts her own faculties, for she seems fairly to pos-

sess faculties, at her disposal? When Emerson poetically bids us hitch our wagons to a star, he means that we must go in the direction in which the solar system is going or else we will get run over. My physical freedom depends upon my obedience to the laws of nature. Am I free to move? It is because I have been trained since a toddling child to obey the laws of equilibrium, the laws of attraction, the laws of gravitation. I am a living embodiment and illustration of the laws of gravitation, and that makes me free. If I disobeyed the laws of nature, ate what I ought not to eat, how immediate my slavery would be. If you want to know when you are a slave, count the number of times the doctor visits you. You have committed an indiscretion by not being conformable to the laws of nature, and you have forfeited your liberty in respect of that, and nature says to you, "Thou fool."

It seems to me that liberty is illustrated more nearly than we at first think by such illustrations as this. Liberty is the best adjustment between governmental power and individual initiative. It does not consist in individual initiative, look you; it consists in not letting individual initiative go too far and, on the other hand, in not letting governmental power act with too arbitrary a choice of means. And it seems to me that the despotism of the despot consists in the last analysis of this, that you cannot calculate today what he is going to do tomorrow, because he will do tomorrow what he pleases without consulting you. He may be gracious to you today and send you to the block tomorrow, and you want to know how to calculate your orbit so as not to run athwart the block. You know what lawyers say. Lawyers say that swift and consistent injustice is better than slow and inconsistent justice. It is a great deal better that you should be able to know and make your calculations beforehand, know where the government is coming and where you can come, know which is your field and which is the field of government, so that there shall not be collision; and this adjustment constitutes your liberty. In proportion as the adjustment is the best adjustment (and we have never found what the best adjustment is), you have the best and completest liberty; because it is a social question and not an individual question. Do you think that Robinson Crusoe was a particularly free man? Would you be as free as you are now if you had to get and cook all your own food, and make your clothes and hats and shoes, and build your own house? Do you think you would be as free a man then as under the coöperative system under which you live? Freedom is a social question and your faculties are set free on the condition that most things are taken care of by somebody else.

You do not run the greater part of the arrangements of the world, and you thank your stars that you do not, because it leaves you, you say, free; it leaves you free to occupy your own individual little corner and do your own individual little tasks. That is your freedom, that you are a member of the coöperative society which we call the body politic.

There is a passage of Burke's that is pertinent in this connection, and whenever Burke can be read he ought to be read. "I should suspend my congratulations on the new liberty of France," he says in his *Reflections on the French Revolution* (I never have been able to understand how people thought that that was a hysterical production; but then some people have not read it), "I should suspend my congratulations on the new liberty of France until I was informed how it had been combined with government." He has just had an eloquent passage in which he admits, more eloquently than we could admit, all the excellence of liberty; but he could not congratulate a nation upon its liberty until he knew how it was combined with other things just as excellent, "combined with government, with public force; with the discipline and obedience of armies; with the collection of an effective and well-distributed revenue; with morality and religion; with the solidity of property; with peace and order; with civil and social manners." Liberty is like the ingredients in our food; it is excellent in mixture and not by itself, and in proportion as it is happily compounded you shall have an excellent thing.

You will observe, therefore, in looking down the illustrative parts of history in this connection, this circumstance. Men have seldom been unfree taking whole societies at a time. There is in almost every society, no matter how undeveloped the idea of liberty may be, some free class. And liberty has had a history of percolation downwards; so that class after class which had formerly been depressed and subordinate was elevated and put upon an equality with others in the enjoyment of this right balance between individual privilege and public power. Most of the time what has been going on has been this: that the privileged class which was free did not sympathetically understand or care for the conditions precedent to the liberty of the classes underneath them. There have been periods in history when it was perfectly evident that the governing class wished to take beneficent action for those who were depressed below them, but wished it in ignorance of what really was for the benefit of those depressed below them. Liberty has consisted in the widening of the idea, not that some men should have their privilege adjusted to the public power, but that as many men as possible should have their individual privileges rightly adjusted to the public power. The history of liberty has been a history of the spreading of an idea which men, some men, have entertained from the first, and of a thing which some classes have enjoyed from the first.

So that liberty depends upon what we have hitherto pretty nearly had in this country; and that is the reason, it seems to me, that this has been the home of liberty more distinctively, I think we are permitted to say, than other countries. You are pretty sure to have a universal acceptance of this idea, that every man is entitled to have a right adjustment between his privileges and the public power, in a country where the conditions of life are tolerably uniform, where there is no great economic or social advantage in the position of one set of men as contrasted with another, where the conditions are uniform enough to make it easy for every man to think in terms suitable to the whole community rather than in terms suitable only to the class to which he belongs in the community. Where you have equality of condition, or something like equality of condition, you have uniformity of thinking with respect to this essential matter. It is perfectly possible to illustrate to the youngest mind, it seems to me, this conception, that in order to have liberty men must consent to think of other men as they think of themselves; and that it may be shown that, although the Golden Rule is imperative upon all men, it is easiest to follow in a society of tolerable uniform economic conditions. How can I wish to do unto others as I would have them do unto me unless I know what will be beneficial to them and unless they know what will be beneficial to me? I cannot think in the terms of their experience unless I am near enough to their experience to think so spontaneously and without too great an effort of the imagination, because the imagination is a very much dwarfed faculty in most persons, particularly the social imagination. I do not know anything that needs a nicer schooling than the ability to see the conditions under which other men live, and think for other men in the terms of their conditions. That is the reason that most charity miscarries, because we cannot think of the persons to whom we would be helpful in the terms of their lives and therefore do not know how to help them. If you have a community such as this has for the most part of its history been, where men have been constantly moving from class to class and where men of the most eminent position have been at some time in a very humble position, you have a community where it is easy for men to think in the terms of each other, and therefore you have a country in which liberty is most likely to be diffused. And you have another thing. You have a community which is able to understand the general welfare as contrasted with the individual welfare. If you have movable atoms in the mass and they have experienced the atmosphere of different parts of the mass, you can explain the general atmosphere of the mass to them and they will understand, because they have been there themselves.

It is just exactly like traveling. A man after he has traveled over this country and seen his fellow-citizens in distant parts of the continent is ashamed of himself for having been so narrow a creature before he traveled, for having thought such ignorant thoughts and such superior thoughts about his fellow-citizens. The best dose for the man who would be a thinking man is to see the people he is thinking about and see the parts of the country he is thinking about, and going to see for himself what is "the matter with Kansas,"[4] because just so soon as he does he comes back *pari passu* a Kansan himself, and he is able to tell you, if he has had eyes and is an honest man, he is almost as able to tell you as if he had lived in Kansas, what is "the matter with Kansas." It is just so in moving from class to class as well as from place to place. Men who have experienced the various conditions of the societies in which they live are men who, when they are constituent parts of a political meeting, can understand the general welfare when it is explained to them, because they know the various parts and elements that go to make up the general welfare. You can illustrate this sympathy, you can illustrate this interrelationship of class, you can illustrate this common experience, you can illustrate all the terms of the simple life of this nation, better than you can illustrate the variety that is in the life of other nations; and the task of teaching the ideal liberty, that is to say, an equal adjustment of private privilege to public power, is easier here than it is anywhere else.

And then what about equality? What is equality? We no longer entertain the opinions that we used to entertain about the Declaration of Independence. There used to be a time when we took the Declaration of Independence literally; but we don't, we take it now in a Pickwickian sense. At any rate, if we believe that all men are born free and equal, we know that the freedom and equality stops at their birth (laughter), because we see what men would be blind not to see, and what of course Mr. Jefferson saw as clearly as we see, that after you have once put men upon this

---

[4] William Allen White's famous anti-Populist editorial, "What's the Matter with Kansas?," which first appeared in the Emporia, Kan., *Gazette*, Aug. 15, 1896, and was reprinted many times, particularly by the eastern press.

starting line of birth and set them on their course they do not remain equal, the one outruns the other, the achievement of one is not matchable with the achievement of another, and at the goal there is disparity, though at the starting line there may have been equality. We are not deceiving ourselves any longer by supposing that we can ever invent a machinery of government which will keep the slow runners up with the fast runners. And, moreover, we want to see a race (great laughter). We believe that the best training is in competition. We believe that keen competition is the growth of the individual, and we would not so dwarf ourselves as to give every man a handicap that would make him equal with every other man. And so we know, when we ask ourselves what we mean by equality, that we mean exactly what the sportsman means when he says "A fair field and no favor." That is all that we mean by political equality, all that it is practicable that we should mean.

What we object to in government is that it should show favor to some contestants for the prize, that it should put some men under easier conditions for competing than other men are put under. The reason we criticise the existing economic order is not because it does not give every man the same benefit of labor, but because we see that in some particulars it creates artificial advantages in competition for some men from which other men are shut out. It is not a fair field and there is favor. That is the reason we do not want lobbyists in our legislatures. That is the reason we do not want money spent in elections. That is the reason we do not want the men who already have money to have all the advantage that money is to get. It is because there is not a fair field and there is favor that we are troubled about affairs. If we can invent means, as we shall invent means, I feel confident—because so long as my digestion holds I am an optimist (laughter)—we shall find means, I firmly believe, to equalize the field at the start, so that there shall be a fair field, no interference even by the spectators, much less by the authorities of the course, and no favor shown to any contestant. That is the essence of equality. It is the equality of chance, of opportunity, and not the equality of results, for we should have a dead uniformity and the absence of growth if there were equality in result.

I have detained you long enough, it seems to me, in the illustration of what is, after all, obvious enough, but I have done so because I wished to make you appreciate, as it seems to me it is easy to appreciate, how concrete all of these things are. What characteristic and representative American biography does not illustrate this sort of equality? You can take the biography that most of all represents America, the biography of Lincoln, and there you have a man originating in a class from which we expected to find initiative stamped out, ambition long ago dead, a man from that class coming to be a prince among men because there was a fair field and no favor, and blood and origin did not shut a man out, and merit and endeavor were the only things that told. Is not that an example of equality? The adult, and I think the child also, will rejoice in the apparent paradox: the supremacy of Lincoln, the fact that he stands higher than the rest of us, is an illustration of equality. We all have the chance, if we have but fiber for it, to get to the same pedestal, and it is only when there is a fence around the pedestal and everybody is forbidden to compete for it that there is no equality.

But there is something else besides the understanding of these fundamentals which is necessary, it seems to me, to understand and to teach patriotism, and that is the right critical temper. And let me say it, I say it with the greater freedom because I am a teacher myself, I think that teachers find it more difficult than others to preserve a right critical temper about affairs, because they do the easiest thing in the world, they read books. It is easy to be wise out of books, but it is infinitely difficult to be wise in the midst of affairs. The man who sits in the calmness and stillness of a study and cavils at a man who is in the midst of the infinitely various and difficult affairs of the actual arena of public matters should be very careful to revise his judgments before he utters them and to realize the difficulties before he condemns the man. You must teach people, you must teach yourself, every man must teach himself, to learn from looking upon the face of affairs and from understanding the characters of the actors upon the stage upon which you yourselves are moving, as well as the easy task of reading out of biographies and recording past events. How often have we seen in the biographies of men dead and gone, the sufficient explanation, the honorable explanation, for things which we condemned in them while they lived, and why is it that we, if we stand near to some men in the midst of the rush of public affairs, are lenient critics of them, and those who did not see them in their private lives are harsh critics of them? Because those who did not know them do not know their tempers and do not understand their motives. We should all of us try by imagination to be statesmen ourselves, not with regard to questions which are settled, but with regard to questions which are pendent, and then we shall know what is the hard school for the right temper, the right critical temper in affairs.

There is a great deal of point, it seems to me, in this: we are constantly dissatisfied because, when we criticise affairs people will say to us, "Well, what would you do? What do you suggest?" and we say, "We have nothing to suggest, we just do not like what is being done." I say that that is very trying; but you must really submit to that if you are going to have any place in affairs. If you have nothing to propose it is not instructive that you should say that you do not like what is being done. When teachers stand up and say to their pupils, "These men did wrong," it is their business to say what it would have been right for these men to do[.] "What would you have done under the circumstances?" That is the hardest question in the world, and yet it is the only question that is worth answering in affairs. I am not interested in your opinion; nobody is interested in your negative opinion. If you have something to suggest, suggest it. You know that Mr. Bagehot wittily said that the French, with their excellent gift of language, could say anything, but that they did not have anything to say; and it was Mr. Birrell who said: "If you would have me believe you a wit, I must really trouble you to make a joke." Now, if you would really have me believe that you are wise in affairs I must really trouble you to suggest something, because it is only by positive action, and not by criticism alone, that affairs are conducted. There is a function for mere negative criticism, that is to say, there is a function for more [mere] destruction, to bring men who are doing foolish things to a consciousness of their folly, but do not propose this criticism as statesmanship until you have something better to suggest. I am not now squinting at pending questions, that would be impertinent under these circumstances; I am simply stating plainly what I conceive to be the proper position of the teacher. You have no business teaching patriotism or touching upon affairs unless you have the temper and the frame of mind to stand in the midst of affairs, and you have no place in the midst of affairs unless you have these practical standards of judgment. Something must be done, and you must get the right critical attitude toward things that are proposed.

I realize, ladies and gentlemen, that I have simply given you a very rough outline of matters which need very much more careful elaboration and statement than I have given them, but my object has been simply to assist, if I may, in some small degree, your thinking in this matter, and not to furnish a body of doctrine. I esteem it a privilege to have addressed this audience, and I thank you most sincerely for your attention.

Printed in the Chicago *School Review*, VII (Dec. 1899), 599-620.

From Lawrason Riggs[1]

My dear Woodrow: Baltimore. 16th October 1899.

I am glad always to be of any service to you and the University. I have been able to gather some information about Mr. Henry Jones Ford[2] but have delayed writing you until this morning in order that I might hear from a Pittsburgh journalist, and so bring the investigation up to the present time. The enclosed sketch of Mr. Ford was prepared in Pittsburgh, and, I believe, is correct. I have personally seen Mr. Haines and Mr. Williams[3] of the Baltimore "Sun" who knew Ford when he has [was] here. They are both men whom I could talk freely to and they assure me that he is the kind of man that Princeton could safely hear upon the lecture platform. His present position in Pittsburgh is certified to by Mr. Albert J. Barr of the Pittsburgh "Post,"[4] who writes that he is "modest, genial and well-thought of by all newspaper men in Pittsburgh."

If there is anything further that I can do for you in the matter, please do not hesitate to let me hear from you.

Yoirs [Yours] very truly,   Lawrason Riggs.

TLS (WP, DLC) with WWhw notation on env.: "In re H.J. Ford.": Enc. typed biographical sketch of Henry Jones Ford.
   [1] Princeton 1883, a lawyer of Baltimore.
   [2] Born, Baltimore, Aug. 25, 1851. Beginning work on the *Baltimore American* in 1872, he later became an editorial writer and was made managing editor in 1878. He was subsequently editorial writer for the New York *Sun*, 1879-83; city editor of the Baltimore *Sun*, 1883-85; managing editor of the Pittsburgh *Commercial Gazette*, 1885-95; managing editor of the Pittsburgh *Chronicle-Telegraph*, 1895-1901; and editor of the Pittsburgh *Gazette*, 1901-1905. Lecturer in Political Science, The Johns Hopkins University, 1906-1907; Professor of Politics, Princeton University, 1908-23. Commissioner of Banking and Insurance of New Jersey, 1912. Member of the Interstate Commerce Commission, 1920-21. Died Aug. 29, 1925.
   Wilson's attention was probably drawn to Ford by the publication of Ford's *The Rise and Growth of American Politics: A Sketch of Constitutional Development* (New York, 1898), the first of his numerous books on political science and American history.
   [3] Oakley Philpotts Haines, managing editor, and Thomas J. C. Williams, editorial writer, of the Baltimore *Sun*.
   [4] President and General Manager of the Pittsburgh Post Publishing Company.

Two News Items

[Oct. 21, 1899]

President Patton, Professors A. F. West. W. M. Daniels, Woodrow Wilson and C. G. Rockwood represented the University at the inauguration of Professor [Arthur Twining] Hadley as president of Yale University.[1]

Printed in the *Princeton Press*, Oct. 21, 1899.
   [1] Held on October 18, 1899.

[Oct. 28, 1899]

VISITATION OF CHURCHES.

The Presbytery of New Brunswick has arranged to follow up the Conference upon Spiritual Life in the Church, held in the First Church, Trenton, last Thursday, with a systematic visitation of the churches of the Presbytery.

The following are the Committees of Visitation of the Presbytery of New Brunswick to visit the churches and assist the sessions in such services as they may desire, during the coming fall and winter:

. . . Trenton First—Revs. G. T. Purves, D.D., John DeWitt, D.D., Elder Woodrow Wilson. . . .

Printed in the *Princeton Press*, Oct. 28, 1899.

An Essay[1]

[*c. Nov. 1, 1899*]

WHEN A MAN COMES TO HIMSELF.

It is a very wholesome and regenerating change which a man undergoes when he "comes to himself." It is not only after periods of recklessness or infatuation, when he has played the spendthrift or the fool, that a man comes to himself. He comes to himself after experiences of which he alone may be aware: when he has left off being wholly preoccupied with his own powers and interests and with every petty plan that centers in himself; when he has cleared his eyes to see the world as it is, and his own true place and function in it.

It is a process of disillusionment. The scales have fallen away. He sees himself soberly, and knows under what conditions his powers must act, as well as what his powers are. He has got rid of earlier prepossessions about the world of men and affairs, both those which were too favorable and those which were too unfavorable—both those of the nursery and those of a young man's reading. He has learned his own paces, or, at any rate, is in a fair way to learn them; has found his footing and the true nature of the "going" he must look for in the world; over what sorts of roads

[1] Wilson's undated handwritten copy of this essay is in the de Coppet Collection, NjP.   R. W. Gilder to WW, Nov. 3, 1899, reveals that Wilson had completed it at least by about November 1, 1899. Moreover, Wilson adumbrated the theme of the essay in a talk to the Philadelphian Society on November 2, the notes for and a news report of which are printed in the two following documents. The reasons for Gilder's long delay in publishing "When a Man Comes to Himself" are unknown.

he must expect to make his running, and at what expenditure of effort; whither his goal lies, and what cheer he may expect by the way. It is a process of disillusionment, but it disheartens no soundly made man. It brings him into a light which guides instead of deceiving him; a light which does not make the way look cold to any man whose eyes are fit for use in the open, but which shines wholesomely, rather, upon the obvious path, like the honest rays of the frank sun, and makes traveling both safe and cheerful.

There is no fixed time in a man's life at which he comes to himself, and some men never come to themselves at all. It is a change reserved for the thoroughly sane and healthy, and for those who can detach themselves from tasks and drudgery long and often enough to get, at any rate once and again, view of the proportions of life and of the stage and plot of its action. We speak often with amusement, sometimes with distaste and uneasiness, of men who "have no sense of humor," who take themselves too seriously, who are intense, self-absorbed, over-confident in matters of opinion, or else go plumed with conceit, proud of we cannot tell what, enjoying, appreciating, thinking of nothing so much as themselves. These are men who have not suffered that wholesome change. They have not come to themselves. If they be serious men, and real forces in the world, we may conclude that they have been too much and too long absorbed; that their tasks and responsibilities long ago rose about them like a flood, and have kept them swimming with sturdy stroke the years through, their eyes level with the troubled surface—no horizon in sight, no passing fleets, no comrades but those who struggled in the flood like themselves. If they be frivolous, light-headed, men without purpose or achievement, we may conjecture, if we do not know, that they were born so, or spoiled by fortune, or befuddled by self-indulgence. It is no great matter what we think of them.

It is enough to know that there are some laws which govern a man's awakening to know himself and the right part to play. A man *is* the part he plays among his fellows. He is not isolated; he cannot be. His life is made up of the relations he bears to others—is made or marred by those relations, guided by them, judged by them, expressed in them. There is nothing else upon which he can spend his spirit—nothing else that we can see. It is by these he gets his spiritual growth; it is by these we see his character revealed, his purpose, and his gifts. Some play with a certain natural passion, an unstudied directness, without grace, without modulation, with no study of the masters or consciousness of the pervading spirit of the plot; others give all their thought to their costume and think only of the audience; a few act as those who have mastered the secrets of a serious art, with deliberate subordination of themselves to the great end and motive of the play, spending themselves like good servants, indulging no wilfulness, obtruding no eccentricity, lending heart and tone and gesture to the perfect progress of the action. These have "found themselves," and have all the ease of a perfect adjustment.

Adjustment is exactly what a man gains when he comes to himself. Some men gain it late, some early; some get it all at once, as if by one distinct act of deliberate accommodation; others get it by degrees and quite imperceptibly. No doubt to most men it comes by the slow processes of experience—at each stage of life a little. A college man feels the first shock of it at graduation, when the boy's life has been lived out and the man's life suddenly begins. He has measured himself with boys; he knows their code and feels the spur of their ideals of achievement. But what the world expects of him he has yet to find out, and it works, when he has discovered it, a veritable revolution in his ways both of thought and of action. He finds a new sort of fitness demanded of him, executive, thoroughgoing, careful of details, full of drudgery and obedience to orders. Everybody is ahead of him. Just now he was a senior, at the top of a world he knew and reigned in, a finished product and pattern of good form. Of a sudden he is a novice again, as green as in his first school year, studying a thing that seems to have no rules—at sea amid cross-winds, and a bit seasick withal. Presently, if he be made of stuff that will shake into shape and fitness, he settles to his tasks and is comfortable. He has come to himself: understands what capacity is, and what it is meant for; sees that his training was not for ornament or personal gratification, but to teach him how to use himself and develop faculties worth using. Henceforth there is a zest in action, and he loves to see his strokes tell.

The same thing happens to the lad come from the farm into the city, a big and novel field, where crowds rush and jostle, and a rustic boy must stand puzzled for a little how to use his placid and unjaded strength. It happens, too, though in a deeper and more subtle way, to the man who marries for love, if the love be true and fit for foul weather. Mr. Bagehot used to say that a bachelor was "an amateur in life," and wit and wisdom are married in the jest. A man who lives only for himself has not begun to live— has yet to learn his use, and his real pleasure too, in the world. It is not necessary he should marry to find himself out, but it is necessary he should love. Men have come to themselves serving their mothers with an unselfish devotion, or their sisters, or a cause for whose sake they forsook ease and left off thinking of themselves. It is unselfish action, growing slowly into the high habit of devotion, and at last, it may be, into a sort of consecration, that teaches a man the wide meaning of his life, and makes of him a steady professional in living, if the motive be not necessity, but love. Necessity may make a mere drudge of a man, and no mere drudge ever made a professional of himself; that demands a higher spirit and a finer incentive than his.

Surely a man has come to himself only when he has found the best that is in him, and has satisfied his heart with the highest achievement he is fit for. It is only then that he knows of what he is capable and what his heart demands. And, assuredly, no thoughtful man ever came to the end of his life, and had time and a little space of calm from which to look back upon it, who did not know and acknowledge that it was what he had done unselfishly and for others, and nothing else, that satisfied him in the retrospect, and made him feel that he had played the man. That alone seems to him the real measure of himself, the real standard of his manhood. And so men grow by having responsibility laid upon them, the burden of other people's business. Their powers are put out at interest, and they get usury in kind. They are like men multiplied. Each counts manifold [many fold[2]]. Men who live with an eye only upon what is their own are dwarfed beside them—seem fractions while they are integers. The trustworthiness of men trusted seems often to grow with the trust.

It is for this reason that men are in love with power and greatness: it affords them so pleasurable an expansion of faculty, so large a run for their minds, an exercise of spirit so various and refreshing; they have the freedom of so wide a tract of the world of affairs. But if they use power only for their own ends, if there be no unselfish service in it, if its object be only their personal aggrandizement, their love to see other men tools in their hands, they go out of the world small, disquieted, beggared, no enlargement of soul vouchsafed them, no usury of satisfaction. They have added nothing to themselves. Mental and physical powers alike grow by use, as every one knows; but labor for one's self alone is like exercise in a gymnasium. No healthy man can remain satisfied with it, or regard it as anything but a preparation for tasks in the open, amid the affairs of the world,—not sport, but business—where there is no orderly apparatus, and every man must devise the means by which he is to make the most of him-

2 As in Wilson's manuscript copy.

self. To make the most of himself means the multiplication of his activities, and he must turn away from himself for that. He looks about him, studies the face of business or of affairs, catches some intimation of their larger objects, is guided by the intimation, and presently finds himself part of the motive force of communities or of nations. It makes no difference how small a part, how insignificant, how unnoticed. When his powers begin to play outward, and he loves the task at hand not because it gains him a livelihood but because it makes him a life, he has come to himself.

Necessity is no mother to enthusiasm. Necessity carries a whip. Its method is compulsion, not love. It has no thought to make itself attractive; it is content to drive. Enthusiasm comes with the revelation of true and satisfying objects of devotion; and it is enthusiasm that sets the powers free. It is a sort of enlightenment. It shines straight upon ideals, and for those who see it the race and struggle are henceforth toward these. An instance will point the meaning. One of the most distinguished and most justly honored of our great philanthropists spent the major part of his life absolutely absorbed in the making of money—so it seemed to those who did not know him. In fact, he had very early passed the stage at which he looked upon his business as a means of support or of material comfort. Business had become for him an intellectual pursuit, a study in enterprise and increment. The field of commerce lay before him like a chess-board; the moves interested him like the manœuvers of a game. More money was more power, a greater advantage in the game, the means of shaping men and events and markets to his own ends and uses. It was his will that set fleets afloat and determined the havens they were bound for; it was his foresight that brought goods to market at the right time; it was his suggestion that made the industry of unthinking men efficacious; his sagacity saw itself justified at home not only, but at the ends of the earth. And as the money poured in, his government and mastery increased, and his mind was the more satisfied. It is so that men make little kingdoms for themselves, and an international power undarkened by diplomacy, undirected by parliaments.

It is a mistake to suppose that the great captains of industry, the great organizers and directors of manufacture and commerce and monetary exchange, are engrossed in a vulgar pursuit of wealth. Too often they suffer the vulgarity of wealth to display itself in the idleness and ostentation of their wives and children, who "devote themselves," it may be, "to expense regardless of pleasure"; but we ought not to misunderstand even that, or condemn it unjustly. The masters of industry are often too busy with their own sober and momentous calling to have time or spare thought enough to govern their own households. A king may be too faithful a statesman to be a watchful father. These men are not fascinated by the glitter of gold: the appetite for power has got hold upon them. They are in love with the exercise of their faculties upon a great scale; they are organizing and overseeing a great part of the life of the world. No wonder they are captivated. Business is more interesting than pleasure, as Mr. Bagehot said, and when once the mind has caught its zest, there's no disengaging it. The world has reason to be grateful for the fact.

It was this fascination that had got hold upon the faculties of the man whom the world was afterward to know, not as a prince among merchants,—for the world forgets merchant princes,—but as a prince among benefactors; for beneficence breeds gratitude, gratitude admiration, admiration fame, and the world remembers its benefactors. Business, and business alone, interested him, or seemed to him worth while. The first time he was asked to subscribe money for a benevolent object he declined. Why *should* he subscribe? What affair would be set forward, what increase of efficiency would the money buy, what return would it bring in? Was good money to be simply given away, like water poured on a barren soil, to be sucked up and yield nothing? It was not until men who understood benevolence on its sensible, systematic, practical, and really helpful side explained it to him as an investment that his mind took hold of it and turned to it for satisfaction. He began to see that education was a thing of infinite usury; that money devoted to it would yield a singular increase, to which there was no calculable end, an increase in perpetuity,—increase of knowledge, and therefore of intelligence and efficiency, touching generation after generation with new impulses, adding to the sum total of the world's fitness for affairs,—an invisible but intensely real spiritual usury beyond reckoning, because compounded in an unknown ratio from age to age. Henceforward beneficence was as interesting to him as business—was, indeed, a sort of sublimated business in which money moved new forces in a commerce which no man could bind or limit.

He had come to himself—to the full realization of his powers, the true and clear perception of what it was his mind demanded for its satisfaction. His faculties were consciously stretched to their right measure, were at last exercised at their best. He felt the keen zest, not of success merely, but also of honor, and was raised to a sort of majesty among his fellow-men, who attended him in death like a dead sovereign. He had died dwarfed had he not broken the bonds of mere money-getting; would never have known himself had he not learned how to spend it; and ambition itself could not have shown him a straighter road to fame.

This is the positive side of a man's discovery of the way in which his faculties are to be made to fit into the world's affairs, and released for effort in a way that will bring real satisfaction. There is a negative side also. Men come to themselves by discovering their limitations no less than by discovering their deeper endowments and the mastery that will make them happy. It is the discovery of what they can *not* do, and ought not to attempt, that transforms reformers into statesmen; and great should be the joy of the world over every reformer who comes to himself. The spectacle is not rare; the method is not hidden. The practicability of every reform is determined absolutely and always by "the circumstances of the case," and only those who put themselves into the midst of affairs, either by action or by observation, can know what those circumstances are or perceive what they signify. No statesman dreams of doing whatever he pleases; he knows that it does not follow that because a point of morals or of policy is obvious to him it will be obvious to the nation, or even to his own friends; and it is the strength of a democratic polity that there are so many minds to be consulted and brought to agreement, and that nothing can be wisely done for which the thought, and a good deal more than the thought, of the country, its sentiment and its purpose, have not been prepared. Social reform is a matter of coöperation, and, if it be of a novel kind, requires an infinite deal of converting to bring the efficient majority to believe in it and support it. Without their agreement and support it is impossible.

It is this that the more imaginative and impatient reformers find out when they come to themselves, if that calming change ever comes to them. Oftentimes the most immediate and drastic means of bringing them to themselves is to elect them to legislative or executive office. That will reduce over-sanguine persons to their simplest terms. Not because they find their fellow legislators or officials incapable of high purpose or indifferent to the betterment of the communities which they represent. Only cynics hold that to be the chief reason why we approach the millennium so slowly, and cynics are usually very ill-informed persons. Nor is it because under our modern democratic arrangements we so subdivide power and balance parts in government that no one man can tell for much or turn affairs to his will. One of the most instructive studies a politician could undertake would be a study of the infinite limitations laid upon the power of the Russian Czar, notwithstanding the despotic theory of the Russian constitution—limitations of social habit, of official prejudice, of race jealousies, of religious predilections, of administrative machinery even, and the inconvenience of being himself only one man, and that a very young one, over-sensitive and touched with melancholy. He can do only what can be done with the Russian people. He can no more make them quick, enlightened, and of the modern world of the West than he can change their tastes in eating. He is simply the leader of Russians.

An English or American statesman is better off. He leads a thinking nation, not a race of peasants topped by a class of revolutionists and a caste of nobles and officials. He can explain new things to men able to understand, persuade men willing and accustomed to make independent and intelligent choices of their own. An English statesman has an even better opportunity to lead than an American statesman, because in England executive power and legislative initiative are both intrusted to the same grand committee, the ministry of the day. The ministers both propose what shall be made law and determine how it shall be enforced when enacted. And yet English reformers, like American, have found office a veritable cold-water bath for their ardor for change. Many a man who has made his place in affairs as the spokesman of those who see abuses and demand their reformation has passed from denunciation to calm and moderate advice when he got into Parliament, and has turned veritable conservative when made a minister of the crown. Mr. Bright was a notable example. Slow and careful men had looked upon him as little better than a revolutionist so long as his voice rang free and imperious from the platforms of public meetings. They greatly feared the influence he should exercise in Parliament, and would have deemed the constitution itself unsafe could they have foreseen that he would some day be invited to take office and a hand of direction in affairs. But it turned out that there was nothing to fear. Mr. Bright lived to see almost every reform he had urged accepted and embodied in legislation; but he assisted at the process of their realization with greater and greater temperateness and wise deliberation as his part in affairs became more and more prominent and responsible, and was at the last as little like an agitator as any man that served the Queen.

It is not that such men lose courage when they find themselves charged with the actual direction of the affairs concerning which they have held and uttered such strong, unhesitating, drastic opinions. They have only learned discretion. For the first time they see in its entirety what it was that they were attempting. They are at last at close quarters with the world. Men of every interest and variety crowd about them; new impressions throng them; in the midst of affairs the former special objects of their zeal fall into new environments, a better and truer perspective; seem no longer so susceptible to separate and radical change. The real nature of the complex stuff of life they were seeking to work in is revealed to them,—its intricate and delicate fiber, and the subtle, secret interrelationship of its parts,—and they work circumspectly, lest they should mar more than they mend. Moral enthusiasm is not, uninstructed and of itself, a suitable guide to practicable and lasting reformation; and if the reform sought be the reformation of others as well as of himself the reformer should look to it that he knows the true relation of his will to the wills of those he would change and guide. When he has discovered that relation he has come to himself: has discovered his real use and planning part in the general world of men; has come to the full command and satisfying employment of his faculties. Otherwise he is doomed to live forever in a fools' paradise, and can be said to have come to himself only on the supposition that he is a fool.

Every man—if I may adopt and paraphrase a passage from Dr. South[3]—every man hath both an absolute and a relative capacity: an absolute in that he hath been endued with such a nature and such parts and faculties; and a relative in that he is part of the universal community of men, and so stands in such a relation to the whole. When we say that a man has come to himself, it is not of his absolute capacity that we are thinking, but of his relative. He has begun to realize that he is part of a whole, and to know *what* part, suitable for what service and achievement.

It was once fashionable—and that not a very long time ago—to speak of political society with a certain distaste, as a necessary evil, an irritating but inevitable restriction upon the "natural" sovereignty and entire self-government of the individual. That was the dream of the egotist. It was a theory in which men were seen to strut in the proud consciousness of their several and "absolute" capacities. It would be as instructive as it would be difficult to count the errors it has bred in political thinking. As a matter

---

[3] Robert South (1633-1716), sermon on John 9:4, "The night cometh, when no man can work," *Sermons Preached upon Several Occasions by Robert South, D.D.* (2 vols., London, 1859), II, 89-90. [Eds.' note]

of fact, men have never dreamed of wishing to do without the "trammels" of organized society, for the very good reason that those trammels are in reality no trammels at all, but indispensable aids and spurs to the attainment of the highest and most enjoyable things man is capable of. Political society, the life of men in states, is an abiding natural relationship. It is neither a mere convenience nor a mere necessity. It is not a mere voluntary association, not a mere corporation. It is nothing deliberate or artificial, devised for a special purpose. It is in real truth the eternal and natural expression and embodiment of a form of life higher than that of the individual—that common life of mutual helpfulness, stimulation, and contest which gives leave and opportunity to the individual life, makes it possible, makes it full and complete.

It is in such a scene that man looks about to discover his own place and force. In the midst of men organized, infinitely cross-related, bound by ties of interest, hope, affection, subject to authorities, to opinion, to passion, to visions and desires which no man can reckon, he casts eagerly about to find where he may enter in with the rest and be a man among his fellows. In making his place he finds, if he seek intelligently and with eyes that see, more than ease of spirit and scope for his mind. He finds himself—as if mists had cleared away about him and he knew at last his neighborhood among men and tasks.

What every man seeks is satisfaction. He deceives himself so long as he imagines it to lie in self-indulgence, so long as he deems himself the center and object of effort. His mind is spent in vain upon itself. Not in action itself, not in "pleasure," shall it find its desires satisfied, but in consciousness of right, of powers greatly and nobly spent. It comes to know itself in the motives which satisfy it, in the zest and power of rectitude. Christianity has liberated the world, not as a system of ethics, not as a philosophy of altruism, but by its revelation of the power of pure and unselfish love. Its vital principle is not its code, but its motive. Love, clear-sighted, loyal, personal, is its breath and immortality. Christ came, not to save himself, assuredly, but to save the world. His motive, his example, are every man's key to his own gifts and happiness. The ethical code he taught may no doubt be matched, here a piece and there a piece, out of other religions, other teachings and philosophies. Every thoughtful man born with a conscience must know a code of right and of pity to which he ought to conform; but without the motive of Christianity, without love, he may be the purest altruist and yet be as sad and as unsatisfied as Marcus Aurelius.

Christianity gave us, in the fullness of time, the perfect image of right living, the secret of social and of individual well-being; for the two are not separable, and the man who receives and verifies that secret in his own living has discovered not only the best and only way to serve the world, but also the one happy way to satisfy himself. Then, indeed, has he come to himself. Henceforth he knows what his powers mean, what spiritual air they breathe, what ardors of service clear them of lethargy, relieve them of all sense of effort, put them at their best. After this fretfulness passes away, experience mellows and strengthens and makes more fit, and old age brings, not senility, not satiety, not regret, but higher hope and serene maturity.

Printed in the *Century Magazine*, LXII (June 1901), 268-73.

Notes for a Religious Talk

Philadelphian Society, 2 Nov., 1899.

Love the only Motive for Conduct.

Read 1 John, IV., 7-21.

Why *should* a man *do right*?

His inclination, we know, is to do wrong; *and yet his dignity*, we are none the less sure, is in doing right; and that is accepted judgment among heathen and Christian alike. *The Romans* furnished us with types of public duty and self-sacrifice.

The secret is all *in the Motive*:

(a) *Self-aggrandizement*,—summed up in two words, *Money, Power*, synonyms in fact.

(b) *Service*, devotion to *a person* or to *a cause* (patriotism).

When a man comes to himself, he finds that it is not enough to serve himself, that that does not satisfy his faculties,—that *self love is mean*.

The true spirit of Christianity is, not love for salvation's sake, but *service for love's sake*.

How can we spend ourselves better than by living for Him who is master and ruler and guide alike of Nature and of Man? This is *the only efficient ideal and motive for endeavour*.

WWhw MS. (WP, DLC).

A Report of a Religious Talk

[Nov. 3, 1899]

PROFESSOR WILSON ADDRESSES THE PHILADELPHIAN SOCIETY.

Professor Woodrow Wilson addressed the students in Murray Hall last evening on the subject of "Vital Morality." Prof. Wilson said in part:

Why should we do right? Why not do wrong, when by so doing we can advance our own interests and also follow the bent of our natures, for is it not man's nature to do wrong? Man's dignity is in doing right, and his condemnation and degredation are in doing wrong. We know this instinctively, but we desire an adequate reason for it.

The doing of right is not the command only of Christian thinking, for the heathen have standards of right. The only advantage that we have is that our Christian thinking has given us higher standards of right and wrong. The heathen countries have furnished us many unparalleled examples of lives conformed to their standards of right.

The doing of right is a matter of motive. We analyze men's characters not by their actions but by the motives underlying the actions[.] Natures in general are of two classes; first, motives of self-aggrandizement, and second, motives of service and devotion. Sometimes it is difficult for us to know to which class our motives belong, for often in serving others we strengthen ourselves and advance our own interests, so that in moments of morbidness we may despise our own actions, thinking that because we are praised we are necessarily seeking praise and honor. All conceptions of self-aggrandizement are embodied in the conception of power; by doing right man often acquires power, but if he does right merely for the sake of power we question his actions.

It is much more natural to serve persons than to serve causes, for persons are real and lovable, while causes are abstract; so it is that the law of motive is the law of love. Love is a sentiment, but it creates more power and puts more strength in the world than any other sentiment. The culmination of all praise and devotion is when we love a perfect person; in loving God we love more than a perfect person. God is powerful and we love power. We cannot love a being whose attributes we do not know and with whom we can not consort. Because Christ was a man here, we can know and love him personally. In the love of Christ we have, therefore, a perfect rule of life.

The speaker closed by emphasizing the fact that college men

are forming their characters in college. Their lives are before them and the mutual choice is the important one.

Printed in the *Daily Princetonian*, Nov. 3, 1899.

From Richard Watson Gilder

My dear Professor Wilson,   New York November 3, 1899.

Yes, indeed, we want this little essay; and we want a group of other little essays like it; and the company wants to publish them in book form.[1]   Yours sincerely,   R W. Gilder

TLS (WP, DLC).
[1] The Century Company never published a volume of Wilson's essays; however, Harper and Brothers published "When a Man Comes to Himself" in book form in 1915.

From French Ensor Chadwick[1]

Dear Sir: New York, N.Y., November 10th, 1899.

A very slight correspondence which you may have forgotten[2] and my interest in the subject on which I write are my excuses for sending you this.

As I see more of the working of our political system and approach the subject with mature thought, I am more and more convinced that we must change our methods or come to grief.

The secret legislation by committee, the absence of public discussion, the inability to produce a well considered sober piece of legislation which shall not be subject to change at the whim of an individual, or subject to the malign influences which must ever accompany secrecy; the want of the directive forces which can not exist with the want of responsibility in our system, must work for harm the more complex our needs become through growth of population and power.

The apotheosis, so to speak, of the Constitution, has prevented any serious criticism by any but a sparse number, but has not the time come when we should take another and safer attitude, the only safe attitude, that of doubt as to the perfection of all our ways.

There is, of course, no need of my going into any more details of this subject with yourself, who knows incomparably more than I do of such imperfections and consequent dangers. The real object of my letter is to ask whether it may not be possible to form an association which shall discuss these subjects (the most

vital from a political point of view which can come before us)
and try and awaken a public interest which now seems completely
dormant. I have done what little I could by putting your book[3]
and Anson's "Law and Custom of the (British) Constitution"[4] in
every ship, but the Navy has no being in the ordinary political
sense, and whatever it thought could have little weight on opinion.

My own idea of a first step is an amendment to the Constitution
which shall require the so called Cabinet officials to be selected
from members of Congress, they to retain their seats. We shall
never have our best men in Congress until we give them a chance
for a career there; there is now none practically, the headship of
a committee is the best which one can calculate upon; there is
no natural career in the true sense. The mediocrity of Congress
simply follows low [law?] as does everything else; making a step-
ping stone to the Cabinet and Presidency which may possibly be
done without a severe dislocation of our established system is the
first need to getting our ablest men in public life.

Believe me,   Very truly yours,   F. E. Chadwick

TLS (WP, DLC).
    [1] Captain, U.S.N., and commanding officer of *U.S.S. New York.*
    [2] See F. E. Chadwick to WW, May 12, 1896, Vol. 9.
    [3] *Congressional Government.*
    [4] William Reynell Anson, *The Law and Custom of the Constitution* (2 vols.,
Oxford, 1886-92).

To Richard Heath Dabney

My dear Heath,   Princeton, 12 Nov., 1899

Hurrah, and a tiger! I am deeply delighted.[1] I've been wishing
this happiness for you in my heart, and the news of it comes like
a fulfilment of hope. Alas! I cannot hope to be present: I am tied
hand and foot to my tasks at the time set; but I shall think of
you as I know you would like to have me. Commend me to Miss
Davis as a worthy person who would like immensely to know
her; congratulate her for me; and know that I count you a happy
fellow, am glad at the thought, and am now, as ever,

Affectionately Yours,   Woodrow Wilson

ALS (Wilson-Dabney Correspondence, ViU).
    [1] By Dabney's impending marriage to Lily H. Davis of Albemarle County, Va.,
on November 28, 1899.

A News Item

[Nov. 16, 1899]

NINETEENTH CENTURY CLUB MEETING.

The Nineteenth Century Club held its first meeting for the season last night at the Waldorf-Astoria. There were about two hundred and fifty members and guests present. They were received by Mrs. Robert Abbe and Mrs. Elizabeth B. Custer.[1] John A. Taylor, president of the club, gave as the subject for discussion "The Relation of the University to Affairs." Professor Woodrow Wilson, head of the department of jurisprudence and political science at Princeton University, and Dr. Charles H. Livermore [Levermore], president of Adelphi College, were the speakers of the evening.[2]

Printed in the *New York Tribune*, Nov. 16, 1899.
  [1] Elizabeth Bacon Custer, widow of General George Armstrong Custer and author of several books about army life in the West.
  [2] For his address, Wilson used the notes printed at Dec. 29, 1897, Vol. 10.

From Theodore Roosevelt

Executive Chamber
My dear Prof. Wilson: Albany   Nov. 16th, 1899.
  Just a line to say how delighted I was with your address last night! It was admirable in every way.
        Sincerely yours,   Theodore Roosevelt

TLS (WP, DLC).

From James Woodrow

My dear Woodrow: Columbia, S. C., Nov. 16, 1899.
  . . . I have often wished to write to you, but exactly the right time never came; so I have allowed myself merely to wish. Your father wrote me that you had crossed the ocean again. I hope you received great benefit and enjoyment. How has your health been? What a terrible adventure with the ice![1] . . .
  My health has been very good, almost without interruption, ever since I left the College.[2] I am not remarkably strong; but you know I never was. During the last year or two I have preached a good deal; but I will probably decline hereafter; for it hurt my throat very much for weeks after each time.
  Aunt Felie[3] is very well and active. We have been entirely alone most of the time for two years. Marion[4] is now at home.

I shall be very glad to hear from you—all about yourself and your dear family.

With much love to dear Ellen and the darling girls,

Your affectionate Uncle,   James Woodrow.

ALS (WP, DLC).
    1 See n. 2 to the news item printed at Sept. 9, 1899.
    2 That is, when he retired as President of South Carolina College in 1897.
    3 His wife, Felixiana Shepherd Baker.
    4 His daughter, Marion.

A News Report

[Nov. 18, 1899]

INTER-HALL DEBATE.

In the inter Hall debate held last night in Murray Hall to select the men who should compete for places on the Harvard Debate,[1] the following men were chosen:

S. B. Scott '00, J. B. Kelly '00, B. K. Hunsberger '00, J. H. Hill '00, J A. Jones '00, A. S. Weston '99. It has been decided to send all of the above men to Harvard. . . .

Mr. Cleveland H. Dodge '79, took Mr. Huey's[2] place as one of the judges. The other judges were Professor H. B. Fine, Professor W. M. Daniels, Professor Woodrow Wilson, and Mr. J. Aspinwall Hodge Jr., '83. . . .

Printed in the *Daily Princetonian*, Nov. 18, 1899; one editorial heading omitted.
    1 The question for the Princeton-Harvard debate, which was scheduled to take place in Cambridge on December 15, 1899, was "Resolved, That the English claims in the controversy with the South African Republic are justified."
    2 Samuel Baird Huey '63, president of the Philadelphia Board of Education.

From Ellen Axson Wilson

My own darling,   Wellesley Hills [Mass.] Nov 19/99

Here I am safe and sound,[1] and taking the first opportunity I have had to write, though it is not as early a one as I could wish. We left for church in Boston at 9.30 this morning, got back just in time for dinner, and now are just up from the dinner table. Mr. Tedcastle is to get this off for me on the train, at four.

I am having a *very* pleasant time. They are all *so* kind and *so* glad to see me,—even Miss Bachelder[2] welcoming me like a long lost friend. She is the lady who owns the house; and a *beautiful* house it is, exquisitely and perfectly artistic in every detail, and yet—in spite of its rather large size,—so cosy and home like. It is a pleasure merely to be in such surroundings. There are rather large grounds too with beautiful trees everywhere,—pines and elms. It seems she is the adopted daughter and niece of a rich old man who died two or three years ago leaving most of his money to libraries and colleges; to her he left the place and an annuity.[3] But unfortunately he did not seem to know himself how much the place cost him, for the annuity is not enough to enable her to live and keep it up without much difficulty. So she has taken the Tedcastles not as boarders but on some equitable division of expenses. It is ideal for them, giving them all the comfort and liberty of a home without the trouble, for which Agnes is not yet strong enough. Miss B. is a beautiful house-keeper; we have the most delicious things to eat.

We went in to the Central Church & heard a fairly good sermon by a dear old gentleman,—whom I met.[4] But I enjoyed the church more than the sermon; oh but it is *beautiful*,—such tone and soft colour, like old tapestry, everywhere, such woodcarving, and above all such *windows—ah*!! I havn't time to tell more about them now. There was the sweetest of music too from a singularly fine quartette. This is the church which the Tedcastles joined last winter when they were in the city. Agnes has not been back before today since mid-winter when she went to Phila., and you would have been surprised to see how the people gathered about them, and how cordial they were. You would have thought they had grown up in that church; yet they were only in it four months,—and it is a "swell" congregation. It speaks well for Boston, does it not?

I forgot to say that I had a pleasant journey; I found the "Forest Lovers"[5] unexpectedly interesting and was absorbed in it most of the time. But much of the country is beautiful too, is it not?

But I must give Mr. Tedcastle time to mail my letter, & not having a watch, I have no idea how much of it I have used,—so I begin to grow nervous.

I shan't try to tell you, dearest love, how much I want you, and love you,—love you *all*,—for then the home-sickness, which I am fighting off would inevitably prevail. Give my dear love to everyone, and *smother* the little darlings with kisses for me. Agnes sends all sorts of messages. I love, *love, love* you beyond everything, Woodrow my love;—I am always and altogether,

Your own   Eileen.

ALS (WC, NjP).

[1] Mrs. Wilson was visiting her old friends, Agnes Vaughn Tedcastle and Arthur W. Tedcastle, formerly of Rome, Ga. The Tedcastles lived on Washington Street in Wellesley Hills.

[2] Caroline Ware Bachelder (1862-1922), who married Charles C. Henry in 1900.

[3] Miss Bachelder was the niece of Mrs. Charles Tyler Wilder of Wellesley Hills and was reared by Mr. and Mrs. Wilder. Wilder had given the money to build Wilder Hall, a dormitory at Wellesley College.

[4] Central Congregational Church, at the corner of Berkeley and Newbury Streets in Boston, the Rev. Dr. Edward Lord Clark, pastor.

[5] Maurice Henry Hewlett, *The Forest Lovers: A Romance* (London and New York, 1898).

To Ellen Axson Wilson

My own precious darling,   Princeton, 19 November, 1899

Here it is Sunday evening: I took tea with the Hibbens, stayed till nine o'clock, and then came away, as I told them, "to write to a friend in Boston." I left there the bride and groom who were on the train with us going in to New York, Mr. and Mrs. McClenahan. She seems to be very sweet and attractive,—and certainly talks in real southern tones, soft and musical.[1]

I called on Mrs. Brown in the afternoon, as you suggested; so that I have had a very busy day of it, fortunately. Stock., besides, has been very good to me. Last night he sat with me and talked before the fire till ten o'clock.

There is the sort of no news which is good news. We are all *in statu quo*. The children did not go to church this morning, because it was raining a little and we could not find a *whole* umbrella in the house. I donned a mackintosh and went by myself,—not to church (when I got to the crossing I found I was too lonely and could not stand it) but to chapel, and sat with the Hibbens, and heard an extremely interesting sermon from Paul van Dyke. The intellectual form and quality of his sermon were very much the same as those of his brother's preaching, *minus* a *little* cockiness.

Stock took tea with the Daniels. I should have liked to peep in and see Fraülein[2] at one end of the table and the *other* Woodrow at the other end! Odd understudies!

I hope my darling reached her journey's end without uncomfortable fatigue and has had a day of grateful rest in a warm place. Give my warm regards to Mr. and Mrs. T.; have a roaring good time; and know that I love you more than I dare try to say!

Your own   Woodrow.

ALS (WC, NjP).

[1] Howard McClenahan, Instructor in Physics, and Bessie Lee McClenahan. She was from Baltimore, and they had been married on November 1.

[2] Clara Böhm, former German governess of the Wilson children.

From Ellen Axson Wilson

[Wellesley Hills, Mass.]
My own darling, Nov. 23 [Nov. 20, 1899]

It is after eleven but I can't go to bed in peace without sending a little love message. Have just written to Margaret some little account of my doings today. Mr. Gamaliel Bradford[,] the son of your old friend, & seventh of the name, was at dinner tonight. His father, I am told, said that if it had been *Mr.* Woodrow Wilson who was to be met he must really have insisted on an invitation for himself!

Tomorrow morning we go to Cambridge to lunch. I shan't be able to call on the Harts[1] or even the Coopers[,] our old Rome friends,[2] because we are due at the Boston Symphony concert at half past two. In the evening there is to be a "chafing-dish party"! —to my inward grief of course; but Miss Bachelder has taken a tremendous fancy to me and (very kindly) proposes to make me have as good a time as possible.

But I am *very* well and am very little fatigued by all these carryings-on. You see we drive *everywhere*; and then the weather has been very fine for our purposes, bright and bracing, but not bitterly cold. I have had a splendid time;—but for a' that I shall be the happiest girl in the world when I reach my dear home again and am in my darling's arms.

So now goodbye, my dear, *dear* love, until I see you.

Your devoted little wife, Eileen.

Dear, will you please send me from the *middle* drawer in my desk in the parlour the Boston address in Ed's handwriting—"Miss Something["] or other.[3] He wanted me to call on her if possible, & I forgot to bring it. As she lives near the Museum I *might* do it. I *shall be* (!) in Cambridge all Friday lunching there with Isabel McKee,—now Mrs. Hidden.[4] If you send me the Harts address I *might* be able to call there.

No letter from you yet.

ALS (WC, NjP).
[1] The Albert Bushnell Harts, of 15 Appian Way, Cambridge.
[2] Mr. and Mrs. John Paul Cooper, of 400 Broadway, Cambridge, formerly of Rome, Ga. Cooper was in the cotton business at 53 State St. in Boston.
[3] Florence Choate Leach, of 27 St. Botolph St. She married Edward William Axson on April 9, 1901.
[4] Wife of William Henry Hidden, Jr., Harvard '85.

To Ellen Axson Wilson

My own darling,   Princeton, 20 Nov., 1899

Margaret developed a "tired feeling" last night and a headache to-day,—in short, has a cold,—but no fever, and no signs of sore throat, or any symptom of a heavy cold. She is lying down, is instructed not to study, and gives no one any right to be in the least degree anxious or disturbed.

Our other piece of news is that the fire *is made* in the furnace (was lighted only a few minutes ago) and the radiators already feel warm,—the seige is over, on the 20th,—one day before schedule time![1] Isn't that *good* news? It may be some days yet before the new sections for your radiator arrive; the men will go away (unless the sections *happen* to come to-morrow) and return to put them in; but with a furnace which really does its work we can afford to wait for that part of the job. The present radiation will probably suffice until Christmas.

We are getting on amazingly well, considering. I have no writing job pressing on my mind and so can attend to things, and see that the house is running, without distraction; so that my new duties go smoothly, give me no trouble, and only serve to remind me too often of the sweet lady in whose stead they are performed. I went to the butcher's this morning and got what I was told by my schedule of instructions to get, giving my order alongside Mrs. Hibben, who turned up at the same moment, and watching the scales and the preliminary trimming very carefully. It wasn't at all a bore! It remains to be seen whether I shall remember it on Wednesday, when there is no class to take me down street anyway!

I broke off here to go to my four o'clock lecture, and come back to find, to my surprise and delight, a letter from you! I forgot that perhaps letters could get away from Wellesley Hills on a Sunday. I fear my first letter to you, written last night, will not reach you before to-morrow. What a pleasure, my sweet one, to learn what a good time you have *at once* proceeded to have! It makes my heart sing to read this sweet, *very* interesting letter; and I've no doubt from what you say that the good time will keep up. Hurrah, and Hurrah! This is just what I hoped for,—and it makes me more happy than I can say. I believe I *do* love you a *little* unselfishly, my darling. I am fairly astonished to see how much difference it makes to know that the separation is for your pleasure. All send more love than a letter can carry, but none to compare with the love of   Your own   Woodrow.

ALS (WC, NjP).
¹ Johnson & Company of New York and John A. Scollay of Brooklyn were installing a new heating system in the Wilson house.

To Richard Watson Gilder

My dear Mr. Gilder,   Princeton, 21 Nov., 1899

I am sending the MSS.¹ by express. It is in numbered volumes. The least satisfactory chapter is the second, on the Virginia Company. Some of it, as I *now* know, is scarcely true; and all of it was written before I had my hand in at managing the narrative. It will bear reconsideration and revision.

The matter of *sub*division is passed over in all the chapters without so much as an attempt at solution; but it can be managed very easily.

I don't know what can have been the matter with me on Saturday.² I find I had forgotten *all* my figures. The manuscript as it stands contains not more than 97,000 words; with the addition needed to round it out, it need not, I think, exceed 125,000 words.

I said Green³ contained eight hundred thousand, did I not? Well, it actually contains about four hundred and thirty-four thousand,—somewhat more than four times my present manuscript.

With much regard,

Faithfully Yours,   Woodrow Wilson

ALS (in possession of Henry Bartholomew Cox).
¹ The typed copy in three binders of the opening chapters of Wilson's "Short History of the United States." For a description of this work, see the Editorial Note, "Wilson's 'Short History of the United States,'" Vol. 8.
² November 18, when he talked with Gilder and others at the office of the Century Company in New York. For an account of the conversation, see WW to EAW, Nov. 21, 1899.
³ John Richard Green, *A Short History of the English People* (New York, 1877). This book is in the Wilson Library, DLC.

From Ellen Axson Wilson

My own darling,   Wellesley Hills, Tuesday [Nov. 21, 1899]

It is ten o'clock and I have just come up to bed after a very full and very delightful day. We went in to Boston at nine this morning and got back at half past five,—had just time to rest half an hour and then dress for dinner. We planned to go first to the Copley prints,¹ but on the way stumbled upon "Duntons," who sells the Braun photographs² and has a store full of them artistically framed already. So there we stuck, and there we made our purchases. I looked at scores and scores of them and finally go[t] a beautiful St. Anthony,—like the Perry's, you know. It is some-what larger than my Madonna with a wide dull brown frame, and the whole thing was only $8.oo[.] Agnes too got the same thing for someone's wedding. Then, after looking at scores of smaller ones for Madge what did I do but get *another* St. Anthony for her! Apparently the good Saint had bewitched us. Hers is $3.oo,—just the one figure with the child in his arms. Then we went to another fine art store and saw a great many of the Copley prints;—had a *delightful* time at both places. Then to the library where we stayed till one, when we had a delicious lunch at a swell hotel,—whose rooms by the way are works of art themselves. The afternoon we spent at the Art Museum stopping on the way to see the interior of Trinity Church, and especially a noble Tiffany window in it designed by Burne Jones.[3] Which reminds me that one of the windows in the Central church is a wonderful copy of Dagnan-Bouveret's[4] white madonna.

Tomorrow morning we are going to "Capronis,"[5] will return home to lunch, rest in the afternoon, and at night go in to see Irving in Robespierre. They are trying hard to keep me till Monday so as to go to the Sat. matinee,—(at the Wed. matinee he also plays Robespierre.) But I don't believe they could get tickets for it now, so I probably shan't lose anything by remaining firm!

But I *must* stop, *dearest—so* tired! Oh how I *do love* you! oh how I want you!

Goodnight my dear, dear love! Kiss my darlings for me. Ah, but *don't* I want to see them!

Love, dear love, to all. Your own Eileen.

ALS (WC, NjP).

1 An extremely successful series of art reproductions by Curtis & Cameron, well-known Boston photographers, and first offered in 1896. The purpose of the series was "to reproduce, in a permanent and beautiful form of photography, the best art to be found in this country. . . ." Represented were some of the works, among others, of Edwin A. Abbey, Puvis de Chavannes, Daniel Chester French, John La Farge, John Singer Sargent, Elihu Vedder, and William Blake. Curtis & Cameron published the prints in book form in 1904, 1907, and 1911.

2 The "Braun photographs" were reproductions of paintings in European museums produced by Maison Ad. Braun & Cie. of Dornach, Alsace.

3 Edward Coley Burne-Jones (1833-98), English painter and decorative artist.

4 Pascal Adolphe Jean Dagnan-Bouveret (1852-1929), French painter.

5 P. P. Caproni & Brother, Boston art dealers specializing in reproductions of sculpture.

To Ellen Axson Wilson

My own darling, Princeton, 21 Nov., 1899

Margaret is better to-day. I kept her from school. She still feels a little tired, still has a little headache, and I fancy she is a trifle deaf; but the whole thing is so slight that I believe a very little care will keep a genuine case of cold entirely off. The rest of us are *in statu quo*. The house is *too* warm now, and as *uniformly* warm as I ever knew it to be, perhaps because there is no wind blowing. The men are still working, at odds and ends, but will go away to-day, I believe,—for the extra sections of your radiator have not come.

I forgot to tell you how I spent the rest of the day, Saturday, after seeing you through the gate and down the platform (I left the door at once and watched you as far as you could be seen through the big window alongside of it,—with what feelings I will not say!) I went immediately to the office of the *Century*, and had about three quarters of an hour of somewhat interrupted talk with Mr. Gilder and then went out to lunch, at the Everett House near by, with pretty much the whole managing body of the concern: Mr. Gilder, Mr. [Frank Hall] Scott, the President of the Century Company, Robert Underwood Johnson, and a Mr. Chidester[1] (I believe), of the business side of the concern, I think, and a man I wish you could see,—one of those ruddy men with finely cut features and *white* beard and hair,—a very striking fellow in appearance,—not *so* striking in mind,—*there* of a rather uniform *grey*. Nothing was said that was new about their proposition regarding my manuscript, and of course nothing was determined. All depends upon what they think concerning the "magazine-ability" of the chapters when they read them,—and that is not wholly a question of excellence. We just had a lot of friendly, semi-professional talk, and parted pleased with one another. When I left them I went around to see Bridges at his office; from there I went to Wanamaker's "New Book" table (No, I did not buy anything); and from there to the train, where I found the bride and groom, looking very much tired out.

Ah, my love, *they* don't know what it means to be *real* lovers, years deep in the sweet business, do they? *We* could tell them what they have never yet dreamed of—couldn't we? I am really pleased with myself to find that I am a *true* lover after all—that I am actually *happy* in the midst of my loneliness because it means your pleasure. I *do* love you more than I love myself, and I am in deed and truth   Your own   Woodrow.

All send all the kisses and messages you could wish for.

ALS (WC, NjP).
[1] Charles F. Chichester, Treasurer of the Century Company.

From Ellen Axson Wilson

My own darling,   Wellesley Hills, Nov 21 [22] [1899]

Your *two* letters and the one from dear little Margaret all came at once today, to my great joy, except that I cannot help being a little unhappy to know that Margaret is not well. But I try hard to console myself with the reflection that there cannot be much the matter if she has no fever, since she generally has it on the slightest provocation. I am however most eager for later news in tomorrow's letter. Tell the dear child how much I enjoyed her sweet, interesting letter; and how much I appreciated her writing it. Please make her understand that I have almost no time to myself or I should certainly answer it. Perhaps I can later in the week.

We spent the morning in town starting at nine again;—and before that we took a *drive*! We have breakfast every morning at half past seven.

We went to Caproni's, to see the Copley prints, and to a superb art and silver store, the "Tiffany" of Boston, where also we saw much fine antique furniture, tapestries, &c. We got back to a late lunch; I have had a good rest, and now I am afraid I ought to be dressing for the early dinner and the Irving-Terry expedition. So I must bid my darling a hurried good-bye for this time. With love, *love*, *love* unspeakable for all my dear ones, and especially for the dearest of all, I am, my darling, always & altogether,

Your own   Eileen.

I am perfectly well, no trace of sore throat.

ALS (WC, NjP).

To Ellen Axson Wilson

My own darling,   Princeton, 22 Nov., 1899

By all means stay to the Saturday matinee, if you can get seats. And, while I think of it, let me give you the two addresses you ask for:

Miss Florence C. Leach
   #27 St. Botolph St.
Mrs. A. B. Hart, #15 Appian Way.
   Cambridge.

Your second letter came this (Wednesday) morning. What a good time my darling is really having, and how happy it makes me to read about it all! I wish I knew, though, what effect it is having on her dear little person,—whether she is *over*doing it or not. Take scrupulous care of my Treasure, Miss!

Margaret seems not merely much better but practically all right to-day. I have kept her at home again, to be on the safe side; but I don't think now that it was really necessary.

I sent the manuscript of the history off this morning by express. I do not think anything will come of it: I doubt whether it is in their sense "magazineable"; but it will not *hurt* to take the *chance* of paying off our debts! There need be no regrets, or disappointment either, in the matter.

Stockton is in New York to-day. He did not say why or where he was going,—perhaps it is to Brooklyn. He generally states his errand. But this time he did not even tell us he was going till he rushed in breathless to breakfast. We will hope for the best!

We are all in excellent shape and our spirits are quite respectable. I love you more passionately than I thought it possible for even me to love *any*body. I am altogether

Your own   Woodrow

A chorus of love messages goes with this.

ALS (WC, NjP).

A News Report

[Nov. 23, 1899]

FINAL DEBATE.

In the final trial last night in Murray Hall to select the men to represent Princeton in the debate with Harvard on December 15th, two members of the team were chosen: A. S. Weston '99, and J. A. Jones '00. The choice of the third debater was deferred at the request of the judges until after a further trial. The Spencer Trask Prize of fifty dollars for the best work in the preliminary debates was awarded to J. A. Jones '00.

The question was "Resolved, That the English claims in the controversy with the South African Republic are justified." The order of the first speeches was: Affirmative—J. H. Hill '00, J. A. Jones '00, and B. K. Hunsberger '00. Negative—J. B. Kelly '00, A. S. Weston '00, and S. B. Scott '00. Under the new rules for intercollegiate debating, the negative rebuttals were given first. Professor H. B. Fine, Professor W. M. Daniels and Professor Woodrow Wilson were the judges. . . .

Printed in the *Daily Princetonian*, Nov. 23, 1899; one editorial heading omitted.

From Ellen Axson Wilson

My own darling,   Wellesley Hills, Nov. 22 [23]/99

It is half past ten and I have not had a moment to myself before today, so I am afraid I must content myself with a very hurried scrawl now.

I am very glad to know that dear little Margaret is better, though the recurring deafness always makes me intensely uneasy. I am afraid we ought to lose little more time in taking her to a specialist. How *very* glad I am that the house is warm!

I shall leave Boston, dearest, at nine o'clock on Saturday and reach Central Station N. Y. at 3.30. Ah! how good it will be to see you all again,—in spite of the good time I am having!

I really had a *glorious*—a thrilling—time last night. I liked Irving better in Robespierre than in any of the Shaksperian parts in which I saw him, and Ellen Terry was as usual almost perfect. But the chief beauty of it was that *every*body, including the mob, acted so well and it was all so exciting and moving. But I havn't time to write more about it now. This morning we drove to Wellesley College and saw it all thoroughly inside and out. What an enchanting place it must be "when woods are green!" We saw a large dormitory in course of erection with the money given by Miss Bachelor's uncle.

We got back just in time for lunch and immediately after took the train for the city where we spent the afternoon at the Museum —this time with the statues. Have had a visitor this evening—and now I am very ready for bed.

With love and kisses uncounted for all the dear ones & for you my whole heart, I am, *darling*,   Your own   Eileen.

ALS (WC, NjP).

To Ellen Axson Wilson

My own darling,   Princeton, 23 Nov., 1899

It is *so* delightful to get every day from you reports of pleasure,—of holiday sightseeing. You have had so few vacations from the steady round of home duties; your trips away from Princeton have so invariably been devoted to business, that this seems to me the very first time separation from you has brought me gratification. I think I shall be still happier when you are in New Orleans, at the heart of the winter.[1]

Margaret is "perfectly all right" to-day, but there was a rain storm at school time and I have again kept her at home. Being mother for the first time, I am like a hen with ducklings. She missed dancing class and an afternoon of "fudge" making at Mildred Purves's; but she has taken it all most sweetly, and has perfectly solaced herself with reading. She gave two days to "Pride and Prejudice" and was so delighted with it that she could not lay it down till she had finished it. I could hear her audibly chuckling and sometimes laughing aloud as she pored over it in the library. She wanted to know 'which next?'—and I was a good deal non-plussed, "Pride and Prejudice" being the best. I suggested "Mansfield Park," and then thought it a foolish choice.

I go to New York to-morrow, you know, to speak to Sloane's "Seminar,"[2] and I shall have to take the 9:09, so that I am afraid I can't write, unless I find a moment for it in New York. What's worse, I don't know how I am going to learn whether you are coming Saturday or Monday,—for I am going to spend the night at the Sloane's. If you get this in time, wont you get Mr. Tedcastle to telegraph me Friday evening (Care Prof. W. M. Sloane, 109 E. 69 St., N. Y.) the day and train? I accepted Mrs. S.'s invitation to stay over night in order that I might be in New York Saturday to meet you in case you come then. But I *want* you to stay till Monday, as you know, if the *least* pleasure will be added.

My thoughts, a lover's thoughts, are with you every moment, my queen. I love you with a strength and passion which sometimes come near to disconcerting me,—they so master and make life for   Your own   Woodrow

All join in unbounded love.

ALS (WC, NjP).
    [1] Mrs. Wilson planned to visit the Smith sisters in New Orleans in February 1900.
    [2] It was probably Sloane's History 30 at Columbia University, "Transitions in American History."

From French Ensor Chadwick

Dear Sir,   U.S.S. New York. 24.11.99

I thank you greatly for your most interesting letter and address[1] which came yesterday. I must compliment you heartily on the lucidity and force of your paper. I should be much obliged if you could send me a few copies for friends with whom I sometimes discuss the subject.[2] I should be glad to have them know that there is life in it. Any such discussion is usually met with such surprise that one is disheartened by the evident magnitude of the inert mass which must be moved. But it must be moved.

I do not think you are too optimistic. I think we can, in this country, work almost any system—in a way, owing to the excellent political sense of our people and their general good sense. Our own system would not work a year in France.

I hope you did not think I was not an expansionist. I believe it is our duty to take our share of the world's troubles and difficulties. To avoid responsibilities of any kind which fall to our share simply because they are difficult is moral cowardice. We shall never rise to the heights of political goodness to which we should rise except through trouble. So long as we are not morally wrong, I rejoice in these difficulties: it is our only road so far as I can see, to better things.

Believe me   Very sincerely yours   F. E. Chadwick

ALS (WP, DLC) with WWhw notation on env.: "Ans. 21 Dec., '99."
    1 Wilson had sent Chadwick a reprint of his "Leaderless Government," printed at August 5, 1897, Vol. 10.
    2 Wilson's reply is missing, but F. E. Chadwick to WW, Feb. 28, 1900, discloses that Wilson did send additional copies.

To Albert Shaw

My dear Shaw,   Princeton, New Jersey. 28 November, 1899.

I take great pleasure in introducing to you Mr. Joseph A. Jones, of our Senior Class, who is one of our debating team to meet Harvard on the South African question. We have taken the negative side, and our men have been so much struck by what they have read in the Review of Reviews that they naturally want direct inspiration from you. I sincerely hope that you will have time to accord them an interview.

I can commend Mr. Jones to you very heartily. He will make the best and most intelligent use of any points you can give him; and I am sure that you will find him the right sort of fellow to deal with.

Hoping that you and Mrs. Shaw enjoyed your trip to Boston, and that you are both well,

With warm regard,
          Faithfully and cordially Yours,   Woodrow Wilson

TCL (in possession of Virginia Shaw English).

To Henry D. Newson[1]

My dear Mr. Newson,   Princeton, 1 December, '99

I have just heard within the hour that Harper and Brothers are to sell their educational publications.[2] I write at once to forestall any transfer of my contract to write a school history.[3]

You will remember that I offered the book to Harper and Brothers, that is, that I chose them for publishers; my preference for them was, for me, a very essential part of the "consideration" of the contract; and I should not consider it the same contract were it put into hands not of my own choosing or at least approval. In brief, I write to say that I cannot consent to the transfer of the contract to any firm with which I did not myself wish to write a book.

No doubt all this goes without saying; but in so important a matter of business I think it better to say it explicitly. It will be best to send the contract back to me to be destroyed, so that, if I finish the book at all, I may arrange for its publication *de novo*. I hope that you will see that this is done at once.

It will be no small part of my disappointment in this matter that I am not to have the pleasure of dealing with you. It has been a real pleasure to know you; and I shall hope that in many other ways we shall be brought together.

With much regard,

Sincerely Yours,   Woodrow Wilson

ALS (NNPM).

[1] Associated with Harper and Brothers in a capacity unknown to the Editors.

[2] Harper and Brothers had first fallen into serious financial difficulties in 1896, at which time the firm was reorganized as a joint stock company and began borrowing heavily from J. P. Morgan and Company. In July 1899, Morgan brought in Samuel Sidney McClure, who attempted to form a working arrangement between his own company and Harpers (see J. H. Finley to WW, Aug. 1, 1899, n. 1, printed as an Enclosure with EAW to WW, Aug. 3, 1899). However, McClure was unable to obtain the money necessary to effectuate the arrangement and abandoned his attempt in October. At this point, the members of the Harper family active in the firm called in George Brinton McClellan Harvey, owner of the *North American Review* and former managing editor of the New York *World*, to be president of the company. Harvey immediately began a sweeping program of retrenchment and reorganization. Harper and Brothers went into receivership on December 4, 1899, with Harvey named as agent for the receiver, the State Trust Company of New York. Wilson probably never knew it, but it was Harvey himself who had arranged the sale of Harper and Brothers' educational books and reference works to the American Book Company for $125,000 shortly before Harper and Brothers went into receivership. See Eugene Exman, *The House of Harper: One Hundred and Fifty Years of Publishing* (New York, 1967), pp. 171-73, 180-87.

[3] About this work, see the Editorial Note, "Wilson's History of the United States for Schools," Vol. 10.

A News Report

[Dec. 2, 1899]

THE DEBATING TEAM.

As a result of the first practice debate, held in Murray Hall on Wednesday afternoon [Nov. 29], J. H. Hill, 1900, was chosen for the third member of the team which will represent Princeton in the Harvard-Princeton debate, on December 15.

The men spoke in the following order: Affirmative—J. B. Kelly '00, S. B. Scott '00, J. H. Hill '00, B. K. Hunsberger '00. Negative —J. A. Jones '00, A. S. Weston '99. Prof H B Fine, Prof. W. M. Daniels and Prof. Woodrow Wilson acted as judges.

The next practice debate will take place in Murray Hall on Wednesday afternoon, December 5, at 2 o'clock. The second team will consist of Hunsberger '00, Scott '00, and Kelly '00, who will defend the affirmative side of the question. The members of the first team will speak, in the following order, on the negative: Hill '00, Jones '00, and Weston '99. Prof. W. M. Daniels, Prof. H. B. Fine, Prof. Woodrow Wilson, Prof. H. F. Covington and other members of the faculty will coach the team. Reading material for the use of both teams has been placed in the Debating Room of the Chancellor Green Library.[1]

Printed in the *Daily Princetonian*, Dec. 2, 1899; one editorial heading omitted.
[1] The debate took place in Sanders Theatre in Cambridge on December 15, with Simeon E. Baldwin, Chief Justice of the Supreme Court of Errors of Connecticut and Professor of Constitutional Law in the Yale Law School; Charles H. Hull, Professor of Political Economy at Cornell; and Judge Andrew Peters Wiswell of the Supreme Court of Maine as judges. Princeton defended the negative and lost. "Harvard's superiority," the *Daily Princetonian*, Dec. 16, 1899, reported, "was due to good massing of arguments and quick sharp work in taking up their opponents and meeting them squarely on the issue. Harvard was also better in form and in the power of holding the attention of the audience, and had the advantage, due, in a large degree, to the presence of sympathizers, which Princeton lacked."

From Joseph Henry Harper[1]

My dear Sir: New York. Dec. 7. 1899.

The house to which we have transferred the contract for your School History of the United States, is the American Book Company, the largest and most important school book house in the country, and one which, we have no doubt, would most cheerfully meet your views as to the method and matter of your work. We know that they would be very pleased to publish your work, but are disposed to think that it would be only on condition of your entire accord in the matter. We have explained all the details surrounding the case, to the Company, a member of which will, with your permission, call upon you, and perhaps it might be well to confer with him before definite action in the matter.

Sincerely yours   J. Henry Harper.

ALS (WP, DLC).
[1] A member of the third generation of the Harper family active in publishing, head of the literary department of Harper and Brothers, and a vice president in the new regime under George B. M. Harvey.

A recently discovered photograph of Wilson at the rear of his
home at 48 Steadman Street, later Library Place

which caused it. I am perfectly well,
but too recently out of your arms to find
writing tolerable. = I enclose marked
schedule and ticket from Philadelphia
to Princeton. You can have your trunk
checked through. The porter will see to
it for you if you instruct him to do so.
Send your trunk down early after breakfast.
— All join me in unbounded love, — of
which Stock. is to have a generous dividend.
I am more deeply than ever,
                    Your own,

Facsimile of the last page of Wilson's letter to Ellen Axson Wilson
of March 24, 1900, showing his newly designed bookplate

Ellen Axson Wilson
in the late 1890's

Samuel Ross Winans, Dean of the Faculty,
1899-1903

John Thomas Duffield,
Emeritus Professor of Mathematics

Arnold Guyot Cameron,
Professor of French

Allan Marquand, Professor of Archaeology
and the History of Art

John Howell Westcott,
Musgrave Professor of Latin

George Tybout Purves, Sr., Pastor of the
First Presbyterian Church of Princeton

Campus scene with Blair Hall in the center

Campus scene showing Whig and Clio Halls

To the American Book Company

My dear Sirs,   Princeton, New Jersey, 11 December, 1899.

I learn, through the Messrs. Harper and Brothers of their transfer to you of their school-book publishing business; and of your desire that I should write for you the History of the United States which I had promised to write for them.

I understand from Mr. J. Henry Harper, that they have explained to you the peculiar circumstances under which I made my promise to them. They did not ask me to write the projected book; I determined to write it and then picked them out and offered it to them not because they were a school-book publishing house but because, besides publishing school books they had a great general publishing business[.] I meant my book to be primarily literary and not a text. The Harpers had already published my life of Washington and I meant the book I was to write to be in some way a companion volume to that. I am told that you would like to arrange an interview with me about the matter; and of course I need hardly say that I should be glad to see a member of the Company, should he choose to call upon me. But I deem it only fair and frank to say that I do not think such an interview worth while. The proposition to write a book for the American Book Company,—a company essentially different in every way from the house I had chosen for publication of the work, would be to my mind a new proposition altogether; and not at all an attractive one. I do not care to consider it. You will understand, of course, that I take this position not upon grounds that could in any way affect the most cordial personal relationships with the American Book Company. I beg to assure you that I shall put the whole argument for the course I shall take upon grounds to which the company could have no objection at all. I am not repudiating the American Book Company; I am simply saying today what I would say to any other house of the same kind under the circumstances. I do not wish to write a book such as I had planned for the Harpers for any house not of my own choosing; it was never my purpose to write for a house exclusively or principally engaged in the publication of school books; I cannot consent to have my plans changed by such a transference as has now taken place in the school-book publishing business of Harper and Brothers; and I most respectfully but very firmly beg that you will release me of all embarrassment in the matter by acquiescing, as I feel sure you will, in my entire withdrawal from any implied obligation arising from the transfer to your hands of

my contract with Messrs. Harper. I know that you will appreciate
and sympathize with my motive under the circumstances.

⟨Very truly Yours,⟩   Woodrow Wilson

WWT and WWshLS (WP, DLC).

From William Peterfield Trent[1]

My dear Wilson,   Sewanee, Tenn., Dec. 12th, '99.

Mr. Johnson writes me that he has written you[2] respecting the
editorship of his *History*[3] & although I am afraid this will arrive
after you have averred press of work &c as an excuse for your
courteous declination I am going to write to ask you to weigh his
proposition & also to explain my connection with the affair.

Last Spring Mr. Johnson paid me a visit & we arranged for a
series of English classics which I was anxious to have started
in order to stir into a little activity the many good English scholars in the South who do practically no writing.[4] I found that he
had also set his heart on having a large history of the U.S. prepared. I knew from various sources that he was capable of pushing it & saw that he was determined to get it out. It seemed to me
therefore that it was my duty to see that he got trained men to
write it from at least not an antiquated point of view.

I accordingly suggested most of the men he has secured &
headed him off from some he was thinking of. As a result he has
secured Bassett, Petrie, Riley, Ramage[5]—all old Hopkins men—
Wm. Beer of the Howard Memorial Library of New Orleans—a
good man—& I hope Houston of Texas.[6] I promised that I would
cooperate with Ramage but I shall have time only for revising his
work. White of Washington & Lee[7] is the only man not trained
under modern influences—& he has the war period & his *Lee*[8]
shows I think that he can do military history. It seems to me I
did right in turning the work in this direction for although many
of these men will not do brilliant work they certainly will do nothing crass.[9]

Now the general editorship is, of course, important & I am very
glad Mr. Johnson sees the necessity of securing a man like yourself. If you can possibly undertake it please do it—if not recommend strongly that he get some Hopkins man—for as I warned
him to secure an untrained man to edit the young fellows he has
secured will be fatal. And he must have a man *East* of the Alle-
ghanies in order to save time.

I don't believe that a great deal of work would be requisite &

at least you could write an introduction & have an assistant editor for the dovetailing process &c.

I think the work important because Johnson has secured a strong hold on the South & because unless the good men supply him with books the impossible men (as a San Francisco paper called me, speaking of a little panegyric of mine on Milton[10]) will certainly furnish him bad stuff in plenty.

With best wishes for Mrs. Wilson & yourself

I am   Very sincerely yours,   W. P. Trent.

ALS (WP, DLC).

[1] At this time Professor of English and History and Dean of the Department of Arts and Sciences of the University of the South.

[2] Benjamin Franklin Johnson, the Richmond publisher, whose letter is missing.

[3] A projected collaborative history of the United States.

[4] There was a low-priced "Johnson Series of English Classics," but it is not clear what part Trent actually played in it.

[5] John Spencer Bassett, Professor of History, Trinity College, Durham, N.C.; George Petrie, Professor of History and Latin, Alabama Polytechnical Institute; Franklin Lafayette Riley, Professor of History and Rhetoric, University of Mississippi; and Burr James Ramage, Professor of Common and Statute Law and Dean of the Law Department, University of the South.

[6] David Franklin Houston, at this time Associate Professor of Political Science and Dean of the Faculty, University of Texas.

[7] Henry Alexander White, Professor of History at Washington and Lee University.

[8] *Robert E. Lee and the Southern Confederacy, 1807-1870* (New York, 1897).

[9] Of the scholars just mentioned, only one—Riley—ever produced a book for the B. F. Johnson Co. It was *School History of Mississippi* (Richmond, 1900).

[10] *John Milton: A Short Study of His Life and Works* (New York and London, 1899).

From Walter Hines Page

My dear Wilson: Cambridge, Mass.—13 Dec. 1899.

I was on the point of writing to you or even (as I had an impulse at one time) of going to see you the other day, because I had a feeling that perhaps I might be able to serve you in the scrape that the Harper collapse has got you into; but I said to myself in one of those laggard and unworthy moods that prevent small men from becoming great—I said to myself: "Possibly it may not be a scrape after all: how do I know? Then, too, I am in a sense an interested party & he may think that I am following only the line of my own personal interest." So, like a little man, I hesitated. Now I've been in Boston a few days and naturally grown bigger and I repent—especially since [Bliss] Perry remarked to me yesterday that you did regard yourself as a victim of—well, what shall I say? For by what *moral* right could a publisher sell to another one a mere contract with a man, even tho' he be an author, for a book that hasn't been delivered? Hard luck, that.

But our poor friends at Franklin Square were on that very day within sight of the sheriff's auctioneer, and the devil's been to play all around. Think of Gildersleeve's Pindar[1] & Lane's Latin Grammar[2] knocked off at bargain-counter prices to the A. B. C!

Well, maybe I can serve you. I don't know, but I'd like to, if I can. I don't believe that you can be held to the contract—tho' I write without a definite knowledge of its provisions. The predicament you are in requires (1) the getting out of a hole and (2) climbing up to a hill-top with the same U. S. History—a hill-top under which you *know* there's no volcano brewing lava. I happen to know most of the facts about the late irruption, from the inside: they may interest you whether they'll help you or not. I'll go down to Princeton any day next week & tell you & help you in any way I can—at the same time make a visit to my boy who is over at Lawrenceville.[3]

And you'll owe me nothing either for information or service or warning or advice or sympathy or congratulation that the actual concrete book itself wasn't there.

But if, this done & the account squared, you *should* think yourself in my debt, I'll tell you how you may pay me.

The best result of the general publisher's agitation in New York which brought doom at Franklin Square and threatened the destruction of other houses is (as I look at it) the establishment of the book-publishing house of Doubleday, Page & Co., which with the list already built up by the Doubleday-McClure Co. will now get—is getting in fact—a larger & more important list, partly refugees from Franklin Square. (But the old list includes Kipling, whose future books come to us.) The McClure interest ceases at the end of the year; & Doubleday[4] & I—go forth, already with an established & profitable business, tho' it is yet young & not large. We know the craft—he on one side, I on the other; we have money enough tho' we are not rich; we have no secrets nor side-issues. When a writer comes into our fold, we regard him as a partner & we are wholly and always at his service with all the activity we have and all the facts we know.

We haven't any history of the U. S. Almost every other publisher has. We haven't yet any definitely differentiated Educational Department, but we have a well-organized force of trained men who have sold this year from a small list very nearly as many books in general literature as the Harpers sold from their enormous list. If I didn't believe that we could do as well with your history as any publisher can do, I shouldn't tell you so; and every fact in the world that I know, about our own business or anybody else's that will help you, I'll tell you with pleasure.

And you can get the contract away from the A. B. C. if you wish to get it away.

Further (& of course in confidence)—Some fine day—next week, or next month, or next year—your George Washington, if you haven't already got it out of the wreck, will be sold by the auctioneer. If Doubleday, Page & Co. had that, they would found on it a great series of American biographies[5] (which they are going to publish anyhow) and give it two or three new markets.

Do you care to hear more? Can I serve you—with or without reference to any possible (or impossible) future arrangement with us? for it will be as great a pleasure to help you out of a wreck if I get no salvage as if I do.

My office till the end of the year will be the Doubleday-McClure Co., 141 East 25th St., N. Y.; & my home address this winter is the Hotel Margaret, Columbia Heights, Brooklyn. I go back tomorrow.   Always Sincerely yours,   Walter H. Page

ALS (WP, DLC).
  [1] Pindar, *The Olympian and Pythian Odes*, with Introductory Essay, Notes, and Indexes by Basil L. Gildersleeve (New York, 1885).
  [2] George Martin Lane, *A Latin Grammar for Schools and Colleges* (New York and London, 1898).
  [3] Arthur Wilson Page, Lawrenceville '01.
  [4] Frank Nelson Doubleday, publisher, formerly with Charles Scribner's Sons and Doubleday & McClure Co.
  [5] Doubleday, Page & Co. inaugurated its "Biographical History of the United States" in 1902 with the publication of Gaillard Hunt's *The Life of James Madison*.

A Report of a Speech on Patriotism in Waterbury, Connecticut

[Dec. 14, 1899]

OUR OBLIGATIONS.

Prof Woodrow Wilson of Princeton university gave an address on "Patriotism," under the auspices of the Waterbury Women's club, in Leavenworth hall last evening. He was introduced by C. F. Chapin,[1] and spoke for over an hour, discussing his subject both from philosophical and practical standpoints. It is safe to say that there was not one of the large audience present who was not enriched and charmed. Rarely is the privilege given to hear a speaker whose appeal, while strong, comes with so much of grace and felicity, qualities that must elude the written report.

  [1] Charles Frederic Chapin, editor of the *Waterbury American* since 1878.

At the outset Prof Wilson differentiated patriotism in its highest and best sense from the emotional and sentimental manifestations of patriotism. As anger is the product of recognized mental processes, as in righteous indignation, so patriotism results from certain other mental processes. Patriotism is distinctly altruistic and consists in the effort of the individual member of society to employ unused resources of intelligence and power without the circle of his own individual interest. It is the exuberance, as it were, of the individual mind and life. No one is ever really satisfied with living exclusively for himself. There is always present in the individual the desire to make his influence felt in society.

Coming to the practical consideration of his subject the lecturer said that it is more difficult to be patriotic to-day than in the earlier days of the country. This is due to the fact that there is now no frontier. The census of 1890 shows that the frontier has been practically wiped away. The census makers were at a loss where to draw the frontier line. What does this mean? It means that all of the vast area of the country has been brought under the civilizing influences of the age. In the days of the frontier the duty of patriotism was simple and plain. It was largely a question of brawn and courage. The needs of the country were to push forward along the frontier line and subdue the rough untamed forces of nature beyond. It required no great intelligence or discernment to see what the country required. Prof Wilson here stopped to say that he sometimes longed for those days of the past when the duty of a citizen was so simple and plain, but he looked upon such regrets as cowardly. The conditions of patriotism are much changed at the present time. The country's needs have become multiplied and complex. Perhaps not a single citizen is now able to understand all of the country's needs. The duty which confronts the citizen of to-day is to see to it that justice and equity prevail in the land and that hope in our institutions finds confirmation.

The first requisite of nationalism to-day is for the citizen to be informed as to the present needs of the country. It does not matter what one thinks ought to have been done in the past, but what is actually the condition which confronts us to-day. There is nothing which so relaxes the muscles as vain repinings. This may apply to the Philippine problem. "It was my personal wish," said Prof Wilson, "at the time that we should not take the Philippines. I do not know but that I wish we did not have them now. But that is wholly outside the question. We have the islands, and the question now is what are we to do with them. I know there are many people who think that it would be spreading our free institutions too thin to spread them across the Pacific, even though they have a half way stopping place at the Sandwich Islands. For their benefit I will call attention to two or three points which may give encouragement. In the first place what does the conquest of the Philippines mean? It means that this country has young men who prefer dying in the ditches of the Philippines to spending their lives behind the counters of a dry goods store in our eastern cities. I think I should prefer that myself. The Philippines offer an opportunity for the impetuous, hot-blooded young men of the country to serve their country according to the measure of their power.

"Again how are institutions spread? They are not spread by manuscripts. If we sent to the Philippines our institutions in manuscript they would suffer the same fate which befell a dress suit once captured by the savages. The coat was appropriated and worn by one savage, the vest by another, and the trousers by a third. Each savage had part of the suit and all were somewhat unconventional. Institutions are only spread by the people who have them. Where they go they carry the institutions."

Returning to patriotism and its obligations here at home Prof Wilson found in Tennyson the word of insight that defined them:

> "A nation yet, the rulers and the ruled;
> Some sense of duty, something of a faith,
> Some reverence for the law ourselves have made,
> Some patient force to change them when we will,
> Some civic manhood, firm against the crowd."

"A nation yet?" The recent utterance of a public man referring to a certain section of the country as "the enemy's country" was felt the more keenly by us, not because it was half untrue, but because it was almost half true. "I am convinced," said the speaker, "not only that the North and the South do not understand each other, but that people of the two sections come close to incapacity of understanding each other. The same may be said of the feeling between the East and the West. The people of one section do not understand the point of view of the people of the other section. I was thoroughly convinced of this in a trip which I made through the West, which was a constant revelation to me of things that I did not know about the West. I returned to Princeton deeply humbled and ready to do penance by not saying anything for a month. It should be the effort of every citizen to inform himself of the needs of every section of the country, and to impart such information to others about him."

Prof Wilson warned his hearers to take certain precautions as to the sources of their information. He said that there was danger of being misled in relying too absolutely on books. The writer of books only uses matter which is necessary to fill out his story. It thus often happens that he puts in certain things or leaves out certain things, and thus gives a false view of real conditions. He also warned his listeners to beware of the systematic thinker, saying that the fault of systematic thinking lay in the fact that the thinker, in trying to complete his system, fills in the spaces, adding things which have no real existence. On the other hand he warned his hearers to beware of personal bias in taking their opinions from talking men, and to weigh carefully the words of men of great persuasiveness. He said in this connection that the folly of a good man was more to be feared than the wisdom of a bad man because of the personal quality of the former which gave what he said acceptance.

Prof Wilson urged that one must, after forming his convictions intelligently and carefully, have their courage, be a partisan, realize that progress must necessarily be slow, understand what is possible under the prevailing conditions, and, hardest of all, appreciate the practical means by which the great masses of men are moved forward, by sentiment and custom more than by argument.

Printed in the *Waterbury*, Conn., *American*, Dec. 14, 1899; some editorial headings omitted.

From Henry Hobart Vail[1]

American Book Company
Dear Sir: New York 16th December, 1899.

Your very courteous favor of the 11th inst. is at hand.

On the 28th of November we contracted with Messrs. Harper & Brothers for the purchase of all their school and college textbooks and agreed to assume and fulfill all their contracts with authors for books not yet in publication.

We had full knowledge of the books now in publication and felt confident that we could continue and increase their sales in a manner that would be acceptable to the public and therefore agreeable to the authors.

With respect to contracts not yet fulfilled by publication we relied upon the reputation of the house of Harper & Brothers and felt sure that they had no contract in existence which we would not willingly accept.

You are very kind to suggest that we may have opportunity to discuss with you the matter involved in your contract with the Harpers, now assigned to us, and we are sufficiently in sympathy with the feelings you express to take no offense at your strong expression of disinclination to prepare a book that shall not be recognized by the public as a literary work rather than a mere school text book. We should, indeed, feel that we have done a positive injury to historical literature if any act of our own should serve to hinder you from completing the task you voluntarily assumed, or if any neglect of action on our part should serve as a hindrance to your work.

We are of the opinion that the highest possible literary excellence would not be amiss in an ideal history for secondary schools, and we feel that such a book would be of the greatest use to the schools.

We are not so vain as to think that we can disabuse your mind of the impression that the book, if written for us, would be a different book or serve a less useful purpose than if issued by some other house; yet we should be glad to have the opportunity to discuss the matter and we should at least not be without hope that you will write the book.

We are now extremely busy with detail work resulting from this purchase, but we shall be happy to call on you within a few days if convenient to you.

Very respectfully,   Henry H. Vail.

TLS (WP, DLC).
1 Editor-in-Chief, American Book Company.

From Horace Elisha Scudder

Dear Mr. Wilson   Boston 18 December, 1899.

We do not wish to seem intrusive in the relations of an author with his publisher, but inasmuch as we have had more than one intimation that Messrs Harper & Bros. are disposing or likely to dispose of their plates and stock, we write to say that in case you have occasion to remove from them your George Washington, we shall be happy to confer with you regarding its continued publication.

Yours very truly   Houghton, Mifflin & Co [per] S.

ALS (WP, DLC).

From Walter Hines Page

My dear Wilson: New York 20 Dec. 1899.

I had bad luck surely. When I came in, you had been gone only a few minutes, and I cannot find out where you went.

I'm going to see you Friday—never mind what come of it or if nothing come of it. There are some things better even than making contracts, & this is one of them. Besides, I never saw the day & I think I never shall, when it seemed wise to have anybody's book except the fellow who couldn't help giving it himself & of his own motion. But I've other things to talk over with you.

I do not know the time-card of the trains that stop at Princeton Junction. But I'll turn up some time during the forenoon. Follow your usual routine & see me between lectures or engagements.

Sincerely yours,   Walter H. Page

ALS (WP, DLC).

From William Goodell Frost

My Dear Friend: Boston, Dec. 20th 1899

I write to ask for three scratches of your pen!

I send in separate envelope copy of Berea Quarterly with article called *"An Educational Program for Appalachian America."*[1] This article must be republished.

Now, No. 1.

Will you tell me the points on which, without too much study of it, you see it can be improved?

No. 2.

Will you kindly write a sentence or two commendatory of my general program, mentioning your acquaintance with the region and belief in the value of its population. This I should like to publish as a kind of introduction to the article itself.[2]

No. 3.

Mr. Matthew Luce, 61 Marlboro St., Boston, is Trustee of a large estate to be used for charitable purposes. We hope he and his associates will give a considerable sum to endow our Normal Department. Cable[3] and one or two other well known publicists are writing him in our behalf. Your letter head and signature, with a few words between, would have great weight in convincing him that this *is* a matter of national concern, commending itself to those *who know.*

We are building a "President's House" in Berea, and hope you may come and spend a Sunday with me by the fireplace, as we did a year ago at Mr. Cady's.

With more gratitude than a letter can carry,

Faithfully yours,   Wm. G. Frost.

Address me here.[4]

ALS (WP, DLC).
  [1] William Goodell Frost, "An Educational Program for Appalachian America," *Berea Quarterly*, I (May 1896), 1-22.
  [2] Frost apparently never reprinted his article.
  [3] George Washington Cable, author and publicist.
  [4] Wilson's reply is printed as an addendum.

An Historical Essay[1]

[c. Dec. 20, 1899]

STATE RIGHTS

(1850-1860)

When the historian of the United States reaches the year 1850, he finds himself at a point at which it is convenient, at which it is indeed necessary, that he should pause and "look before and after," in order that he may reckon the forces amidst which he stands and scan the whole stage of affairs. The "Compromise of 1850" settled nothing; but it was compounded of every element of the country's politics and may be made to yield upon analysis almost every ingredient of the historian's narrative. Its object was the settlement of all urgent questions. Texas had been admitted to the Union with disputed boundaries which needed to be definitely determined; territory had been acquired from Mexico, by conquest and purchase, for which it was requisite to provide a government; opinion in one section of the country was demanding that the slave-trade should be excluded from the District of Columbia, the seat of the national government, and slavery itself from the new territory; opinion in another section was demanding, with an air almost of passion, that the question of slavery in the Territories be left to those who should settle and make States of them, and that property in slaves should everywhere be adequately protected by effective laws for the apprehension and return of fugitive negroes. It was the question of the extension or restriction of slavery that made the adoption of a plan of organisation and government for the new Territory perplexing and difficult, and the determination of the boundary of Texas a matter

  [1] The manuscript remains of this essay—all in the Wilson Papers, DLC—are Wilson's shorthand draft, dated Nov. 29, 1899, and the first three pages of the WWT copy, for which Wilson substituted new and revised pages in the manuscript that he sent to Adolphus William Ward.

of critical sectional interest; and yet the rapid growth and development of the country rendered it imperative that action should be taken definitely and at once. Something must be done, and done promptly, to quiet men's minds concerning disturbing questions of policy and to keep parties from going utterly to pieces. That was the object of the "Compromise of 1850."

It consisted of a series of measures framed and introduced by a committee of which Henry Clay was chairman, and urged upon Congress with all the art, energy, and persuasiveness of which the aged Kentuckian was so great a master, even in those his last days. It was agreed (1) that Texas should be paid ten million dollars to relinquish her claim upon a portion of New Mexico; (2) that California should be admitted as a State under a constitution which prohibited slavery; (3) that New Mexico and Utah should be organised as Territories without any regulation in respect of slavery, leaving it to the choice of their own settlers whether there should be property in slaves amongst them or not; (4) that the slave-trade should be excluded from the District of Columbia, but be interfered with nowhere else by Federal law; and (5) that the whole judicial and administrative machinery of the Federal government should be put at the disposal of the Southern slave-owners for the recovery of fugitive slaves found within the Free States.

Every measure in the list touched the politics of the time at some vital point. Fourteen years earlier (1836) Texas had established herself as an independent State by secession from Mexico, which Santa Anna had transformed from a republic into a military despotism; and in 1845 she had been admitted with all her vast domain into the United States. Her admission into the Union had led almost immediately to war with Mexico (1846); for her southern boundary line was in dispute. The Federal government supported her claim to the tract of land which lies between the Nueces and the Rio Grande rivers, and by occupying it with an armed force compelled Mexico to fight for its possession. In the war which ensued, the forces of the United States took possession not only of the little region in dispute but also of all the Pacific slope from Oregon to Texas, Mexico's Territories towards the north. It was this war, and the acquisition of a new and vast domain on the Pacific, which had brought Congress once more face to face with the question, What shall be done with regard to slavery in the new Territories? Shall its introduction be forbidden there, or permitted? And it was this question which had stirred parties and sections to the renewal of an old and bitter conflict, which threatened to disturb every ancient compromise and make peace and union infinitely difficult.

It was a return to the question which politicians had hoped to have dismissed in the "Missouri Compromise" of 1820, when it had been agreed that Missouri should be admitted into the Union with a constitution which legalised slavery, but that thenceforth no other Slave State should be formed out of any territory of the United States which lay north of latitude 36° 30', the southern boundary of Missouri extended; but here was new territory to which that old compromise of a generation ago, it was said, did not apply. The question was as old, almost, as the Constitution itself. It had been touched first and most definitely by the notable Ordinance of 1787—a law as old as the Constitution—which had decreed, once for all, that slavery should not enter the North-west Territory, the vast dominion made over by Virginia and her sister States to the Confederation which had fought the war for independence. But it was a matter which statutes could not quiet or conclude. So long as there was new territory to be filled with settlers, and formed into States with institutions and laws of their own, there must continue to be strife and controversy regarding what should be done in respect of slavery; for the slave-owners insisted that they should be insured by law against the risks of change, that they should be made safe against being left in a minority in a country where everything was changing and no one could surely foresee majorities either for or against any institution whatever. Such a contest could not be closed till movements of population and opinion had themselves come to an end.

Although no man could certainly foretell, even in 1850, what would be the outcome of the contest between the advocates and the opponents of the extension of slavery into the new Territories, and thus also into the new States which should be formed from them, it was very much plainer then what this was likely to be than it had been in 1821 or in 1787. Southern statesmen did not deceive themselves. They saw as clearly as anyone could see that the great movement of population into the new lands in the West was not only a natural and inevitable economic movement of men seeking to better their fortunes in new homes, but also a game of power, and a game at which they were likely, if not sure, to lose. There was no mistaking the signs of the times or the magnitude of the forces engaged. It was a contest between sections which every year became more and more widely contrasted in life and purpose.

It was slavery, of course, which made the South unlike the rest of the country, unlike the rest of the world. The contrast was to her advantage in some respects, though to her deep disadvantage in many others. She had men of leisure because she had slaves; and nowhere else in the country was there a ruling class like hers. Where men are masters they are likely to be statesmen, to have an outlook upon affairs and an instinct and habit of leadership. Privilege and undisputed social eminence beget in them a pride, which is not wholly private, a pride which makes of them a planning and governing order. It was this advantage, of always knowing her leaders, and of keeping them always thus in a school of privilege and authority, that had given the South from the first her marked pre-eminence in affairs. Her statesmen had led the nation in the era of the Revolution. The Union seemed largely of her making. Madison's had been the planning mind in its construction; Washington's mastery had established it; Jefferson had made it democratic in practice as in theory. For thirty-two out of the first forty years of the existence of the Union Virginian statesmen had occupied the presidential office, and had guided as well as presided over affairs. The coming-in of Jackson in 1829 had marked a revolutionary change in the politics of the country. The older generation and the older methods of counsel and action were thrust aside; ruling groups of statesmen thenceforth counted for less, and popular conventions for more. Delegations of local politicians were substituted for Congressional committees; the influence of unknown men displaced the authority of responsible leaders. But, even after that notable break-up, the South kept her place of authority in party counsels, in cabinets, and even in the choice and policy of Presidents. Men drawn from her school of privilege were as prominent as ever, and ruled conventions as they had ruled groups of consulting statesmen. Their initiative was not daunted or discouraged. No one could deny that the South had all along played a part in the control of parties which was altogether out of proportion to her importance in wealth or population.

But every year relaxed her hold upon affairs and more definitely and obviously threatened her mastery with destruction. The country was growing away from her. It had grown away from her in the years which preceded the coming-in of Jackson and the rough Western democracy which despised tradition; but the fact had not been upon the surface in those days. In 1850 it was plain to see. During the twenty years which had passed, the country had grown at an infinitely quickened pace, and in ways which could escape no man's observation, while the South had almost stood still. Her order of life was fixed and unchangeable. She could not expect manufacturers to make their home with her; she could not induce immigrants to settle on her untilled lands. Diversification of industry was for her, it seemed, out of the question. She had begun to perceive this twenty years ago, and had been deeply moved by the discovery. She could not forget the controversies which had raged about the tariff legislation of 1828 and 1832, or rid herself of the painful impression of what had been done and said and threatened when South Carolina made her attempt at "nullification." Time had but made the issues of that conflict more distressingly plain and significant.

The South could not compete with the North in the establishment of manufactures because she could not command or maintain the sort of labour necessary for their successful development; nor could she compete with the North in the establishment of agricultural communities and the building of new States in the West, if her people were to be forbidden to take their slaves with them into the national Territories. Her statesmen had felt a great enthusiasm for national expansion at the first, had favoured moderate tariffs and the diversification of industry, had spoken like men of a race, not like men of a section, until they saw at last how the very organisation of the communities they loved best and most passionately seemed to shut them out from sharing in the great change and growth which were to command the future. Then, as was but natural, they began to draw back and to doubt as to the course they had taken. To put tariff-charges on imports in order that manufacturers might get higher prices for their goods in the markets of the States, was, they said, when viewed from the side of the effects it would have upon their own people, only an indirect way—and not a very indirect way either—of making the South, which could not engage in manufactures, support the people of the North, who could. It would curtail the commerce of the Southern ports and markets without furnishing any countervailing advantage to offset the loss.

That had been the ground of South Carolina's "nullification." Calhoun had not led her into that singular course: he had followed her into it. He had hitherto held his mind to a national scale of thinking; but the distress of his own people swung him about, to study the causes of their disquietude. He accepted, when it was pressed upon him, their own explanation of the decline of their commerce and the falling off in the price of their cotton. He believed, as they did, that these things were due to an inequitable distribution of the burdens of federal taxation: that the South was being made to pay for the maintenance of manufactures in the North. He accordingly supplied them with weapons of defence, with constitutional arguments which went the whole length of an absolute refusal to obey oppressive and unequal laws, with the full-wrought doctrine of nullification.

Calhoun did not invent the doctrine of nullification. It had been mentioned and urged in South Carolina again and again before he had been brought to accept it—mentioned very explicitly and urged very passionately. He had turned very reluctantly from national plans to sectional defence; and only because men who were his intimate friends and close political associates at home, as well as events happening under his own eyes at Washington, convinced him of the critical peril of the Southern States. But when he did turn it was with eyes wide open and with all the passion of his nature, and with the passion of his mind also, that singular instrument of power, which gave order, precision, and a keen and burning force to whatever it touched. The doctrine of State Rights, which other men had used for protest, for exhortation, for advantage in debate, he used as if for legal demonstration. He made of it a philosophy of right, a statesman's fundamental tenet. The very coolness and precision of his way of reasoning seemed to make the doctrine a new and wiser thing. In every sentence, too, there was added to the sharp lines of reason the unmistakeable glow of conviction. Once convinced of the necessity of this his new line of action, he followed it with the zest of a crusader. "As to the responsibility necessarily incurred," he said, "in giving publicity to doctrines which a large portion of the community will probably consider new and dangerous, I feel none. I have too deep a conviction of their truth and vital importance to the Constitution, the Union, and the liberty of these States, to have the least uneasiness on the point."

He believed "the great and leading principle" of the political life of the Union to be, "that the general government emanated from the people of the several States, forming distinct political communities and acting in their separate and sovereign capacity, and not from all of the people forming one aggregate political community; that the Constitution of the United States is, in fact, a compact, to which each State is a party, in the character already described; that the several States, or parties, have a right to judge of its infractions; and, in case of a deliberate, palpable, and dangerous exercise of power not delegated, have the right also, in the last resort (to use the language of the Virginia Resolutions), 'to interpose for arresting the progress of the evil, and for maintaining, within their respective limits, the authorities, rights, and liberties appertaining to them.'" Madison had framed the Virginia Resolutions, as Virginia's protest against the Alien and Sedition Laws of 1798, which he considered "a deliberate, palpable, and dangerous exercise of power not delegated" by the Constitution, either explicitly or by reasonable implication; but he was still living when Calhoun put forth his doctrine of nullification, in imitation, as he supposed, of the precedent, and on the firm ground of the "good old Republican doctrine of '98," and he emphatically denied having meant by his doctrine what Calhoun meant by his principle of virtual resistance.

The resolutions which Kentucky had adopted in 1798 were nearer Calhoun's tone and meaning. They had declared that in case of a deliberate, palpable, and dangerous exercise of unconstitutional powers by the Federal government, "as in all other cases of compact between parties having no common judge, each party has an equal right to judge for itself, as well of the infractions as of the mode and measure of redress." But even these might be read as the terms of agitation rather than as those of revolution. The States were the only organic bodies capable of authoritative action outside the organisation of the Federal government itself, and they had seemed to the statesmen of Virginia and Kentucky the natural and proper instruments of agitation in cases where the action of the Federal government called for organised, though peaceful and constitutional, opposition and a concerted effort for redress. Calhoun's thought went much further. He conceived the States to be the only members of the Union. The people had no citizenship, as it seemed to him, except in the States under whose authority they were grouped. They had no direct connexion with the Federal government, but dealt with it, and acted in its affairs, in communities. The Union was a Union of States, and the people acted in its affairs, not directly and as a nation, but segregately, by joint action, as sovereign but associated commonwealths. The States, therefore, as the sole constituent members of the Union, were not only the natural and proper agencies of agitation; they were the only proper, the only possible parties to a change. The initiative was theirs by constituent right: and each of them must look for itself to the keeping of the general compact, acting upon its own individual responsibility.

But what if a single State should act? What if South Carolina should act alone, how far might she go? What was it her right to do? This question the Virginia and Kentucky Resolutions had not answered; but Calhoun answered it very explicitly. It was her right, he said, when all reasonable hope of redress through any other channel had failed, to call upon her electors to choose a convention, such a convention as might amend her constitution and shape her exercise of sovereignty in other matters; and that convention might declare the Acts complained of null and void, because contrary to the federal pact, and therefore not binding upon her citizens. Such a thing should not be done as an act of revolution. It should be so planned and executed, with such deliberations, delays, and postponements, and such ample opportunities for conciliation, compromise, and adjustment, that it would operate merely as a check upon the national government and give both time and motive for a final settlement. The escape from the crisis must be, not the revolt or permanent recalcitrancy of a single State, but an appeal to the power which had made the Constitution and which had the final right to interpret its intent and meaning, to the association of sovereign States. If the general government was not willing to yield in the matter in controversy, it must call a constitutional convention, such as that "for proposing amendments," which the Constitution itself provided for. With that convention, in which the States as principals to the federal compact would be present in the persons of their delegates, it would rest to determine, by a majority representing two-thirds of the sovereign commonwealths, the merits of the controversy. If these sovereign principals, by the constitutional majority of two-thirds, should declare the powers complained of to have been rightly exercised by the Federal government, it would be as if the Constitution had been amended and those powers explicitly added; and the State, or States, whose protests had brought the convention together would be in duty bound either to submit or to quit the Union. Calhoun was too sane a thinker, too sincere a lover of the Union and of the ideals which it had set before the world, too much of a statesman and master in affairs, to be guilty of so great a solecism as to maintain what some who had not examined his argument supposed him to maintain, that a State could permanently "nullify" a law of the United States and yet remain a member of the Union. Nullification was in his doctrine but a means of bringing federal action to a standstill in respect of some single matter of critical controversy until a power higher than Congress—that power which he conceived to be the real and only sovereign power under the Constitution—had acted, and a final determination had been made of the question of right. He deemed the Supreme Court of the United States an unsuitable forum in which to determine such matters of sovereign right, because it was but an agency of the very government whose powers in the case supposed were in dispute. Arbitrament must lie with the sovereign associates whose agent he conceived the Federal government to be.

Almost every Northern man who heard such views set forth considered them "new and dangerous," as Calhoun had foreseen. They seemed a little ridiculous, too, when put into practice. On November 24, 1832, South Carolina actually did declare the Tariff Acts of 1828 and 1832 null and void within her jurisdiction and in respect of her people, acting in sovereign convention, called in due form by her legislature. But no general convention of the States was called; Congress lowered the tariff duties, but would not abandon them or lower them upon the principle on which South Carolina had insisted; General Jackson was President and showed himself ready to carry out the laws of the United States, in South Carolina as elsewhere, by force of arms if necessary, like the hard-headed, practical soldier he was; and South Carolina was obliged to yield without bringing her doctrine to a final test. She had gained enough, in the alteration of the tariff laws, she thought, to make her retreat something less than a surrender, and was fain to content herself with that. She laid her constitutional weapons aside until another time.

Calhoun was unequally compounded of logician and statesman. In outlook, in sympathy, in insight, and in power among men a statesman, he was yet in all processes of systematic thought a subtle and uncompromising logician, and projected his argument without thought of time or limiting circumstance. There is in much of his writing the touch and tone of the schoolman,—so refined is the reasoning, so abstract the processes of the thought. It was this thorough-going way of reasoning, from the careful premises straight through to the utmost bounds of the conclusion, that made him seem to practical men a radical, almost a revolutionist. He made old doctrines seem "new and dangerous," because he pushed them beyond their old limits and gave them novel and disturbing applications. His doctrine of the ultimate sovereignty of the States was not new. It had once been commonplace to say that the Union was experimental, to speak of circumstances in which the contracting States might deem it best to withdraw. Webster had been prompt to challenge the doctrine of nullification and draw it out into the open in his debate with Senator Hayne; and nobody who heard him then could doubt either his extraordinary power or the breadth and wisdom and impressiveness of his conceptions with regard to the national destiny and higher law of growth. But, though he was the better statesman, Hayne was the better historian.

Webster's greatness was never more admirably exhibited than in that famous debate. His utterances on this occasion, moreover, sent a thrill through all the East and North which was unmistakeably a thrill of triumph. Men were glad because of what he had said. He had touched the national self-consciousness, awakened it, and pleased it with a morning vision of its great tasks and certain destiny. Those who heard were not so much convinced as aroused, stimulated, exhilarated. He had spoken for the new generation. But the generation in the midst of which he stood was both new and old. It was new on the whole stage of movement, of change, of struggle, of achievement, where the nation was being re-established and transformed; but it was old where change had not penetrated, where institutions had stood untouched, where the organisation of society was in fact unalterable, and where thought and habit held steady and undiverted to the old ways. The South stood still in a fixed order. Since the making of the Constitution, Alabama and Mississippi and Louisiana and Texas had been added to the South upon the Gulf, and Tennessee and Kentucky, Arkansas and Missouri within the continent; but such growth had been assured her almost from the first, and had resulted in a uniform expansion, without essential change either in conceptions or in modes of life. Wherever slavery was established, society took and kept a single and invariable form; industry had its fixed variety and pattern; life held to unalterable standards. Change had entry and freedom only in the great westward migration which followed the parallels of latitude further to the north, and in the great industrial expansion of the East. It was a process there which obliterated old political boundaries, fused diverse elements of population, created community in enterprise, quickened throughout wide regions the sense of co-operation, and made the nation itself seem to those who took part in it a single great partnership in material and political development.

No doubt the whole country had felt a certain critical coolness towards the Constitution throughout the generation which framed and adopted it. Statesmen defended, praised, expounded, fortified it; courts diligently wove its provisions into the law of the land; success added prestige to the general government which it had set up; but the little commonwealths of the long seaboard, which had agreed to live under it, kept their old pride of separateness, thought of it at first rather as a serviceable arrangement than as an unalterable law, respected it but did not love it, and were ready enough to question it, asking once and again, as they had asked at first, whether it was really, after all, calculated to promote their interests. And this was the point of view which the South, more than any other part of the country, had kept, because she more than any other part of the country had remained unchanged. She did not feel her dependence upon the national government as those did who were building up manufactures under the protecting shadow of the federal tariff laws, or as those did who were organising settlements and making new States out of the national domain in the West. These men had always an image of enterprise, union, and co-operation when they spoke of the nation; while public men in the South thought only of the general government, the agent in certain matters of the States united. For a generation or more after the founding of the Union, the South as well as the North had felt the pulses of growth and national expansion; and Calhoun had once been at the front of a group of young statesmen who were pushing forward internal improvements, advocating the acquisition of territory, and supporting every national enterprise and policy. It was when the movement quickened beyond the pace at which the South could follow it, when States threatened to multiply without end in the West, when railways shortened the road of growth, and immigration swelled more and more the tide of new peoples that poured in to join the Northern, not the Southern, hosts of settlers and State-makers, that the South began to realize her separateness and isolation. It was significant that it was in a debate concerning the right policy to be pursued with regard to the Western lands, the unoccupied national domain, that Webster and Hayne came to their issue with regard to the doctrine of nullification. It was the West that was making a nation out of the old-time federation of seaboard States. Webster was insisting upon the new uses and significance of the Constitution, Hayne was harking back to the old. The Constitution had once been deemed almost, if not quite, susceptible of the interpretation which the Senator from South Carolina still sought to apply to it; but the national life had in these later days grown strong within it, and it had become, at any rate for the major part of those who lived under it, the instrument of nationality Webster understood it to be. No constitution can ever be treated as a mere law or document: it must always be also a vehicle of life. Its own phrases must become as it were living tissue. It must grow and strengthen and subtly change with the growth and strength and change of the political body whose life it defines, and must, in all but its explicit and mandatory provisions with regard to powers and forms of action, take its reading from the circumstances of the time. In the South circumstances had not changed; in the North and West they had changed almost beyond recognition; and the men of the two sections could no longer think alike with regard to the fundamentals of their common government.

The days when South Carolina attempted nullification were the days of the first full consciousness of these momentous changes and of this disparity of interests between the sections; and by 1850 these things could escape no thoughtful man's observation. Movements which had been slow had become rapid; issues which had seemed far away were now obviously close at hand. The decade 1840-50, particularly, had seen every process of modification quickened. The age of railways and of labour-saving invention had set in, and with it the days when movements of population were to be greater than ever. Before 1842 no year had brought so many as a hundred thousand immigrants to the United States, but by 1847 the tide had amounted to 234,968, and by 1849 to 297,024. 1846 and 1847 were the years of the terrible famine in Ireland; 1848 was the year of universal political disturbance in Europe, the year of revolution which made refugees of so many thousands and unsettled the peoples of the Continent, bringing discontent, restlessness, and even a touch of despair. And the movement did not stop with the end of revolution and famine. It was but the beginning of a new era of immigration. The stream of new comers grew rather than diminished from year to year, and steadily augmented the forces of change which inevitably crossed the sea with these swarming bands of strangers. Their distribution within the Union proved easier and more immediate every year by reason of the rapid extension of the railway system of the country. More than six thousand miles of railway were constructed between 1840 and 1850,—an increase of more than two hundred per cent. over the preceding decade; and the electric telegraph was added just in the nick of time to facilitate the safe operation of long lines of transportation. Morse's invention came into actual use in 1844, and promised that the most widely separated regions of the great continent which was thus filling up with restless hosts of settlers would presently be near neighbours to one another. It was but yesterday that steam navigation had become an assured success upon the ocean (1838). The McCormick reaper was no older than 1834. The world was but just beginning to feel the full impulse towards that diversification of industry which was to transform it.

The South of course felt these forces at work within herself as well as upon her Northern neighbours and out upon the broad new-tenanted fields of the West, where everything was new. She had railways among the first; the earliest inventions of the new age had been those which made the production and manufacture of cotton easy and exceedingly profitable, and from these she had reaped a great increase of wealth. There had been a day when she had hoped for as great a development as should come to any section or any region in the world. But she had long since been disillusioned of that hope. While population grew elsewhere by leaps and bounds, hers did not sensibly increase. While new sources of wealth and power were added every year, as it seemed, to the resources of the rest of the country, none that were new were vouchsafed to her. Even her own native white population drifted away from her into the West, into the North, into the newer portions of the South itself. The census of 1860 was to show that there were in South Carolina only 277,000 white persons born within her borders, while 193,000 born within the State were living in other parts of the country. North Carolina had kept only 634,000 out of 906,000; and Virginia only 1,000,000 out of 1,400,000. Immigrants did not come down into those fertile valleys; and the great plantations, with their crowding, docile slaves, thrust out even those of native stock whose homes had been there. The race was towards the West. If Southerners could carry their slaves thither, they might remain Southerners and spread and confirm the social standards, the economic system, and the political ideals of their native region; if they could not carry their slaves with them, they must become "Westerners," lose their identity, change the whole order of their lives, and be added to those national forces from which the South feared nothing less than extinction. No wonder the whole country felt that great issues were joined in the compromise legislation of 1850.

It was significant, as one of the notable signs of the times, that one part of that legislation had been determined beforehand, by forces which politicians could neither divert nor control. While Congress was getting ready to organise California as a Territory it became a State. Gold was discovered in California in January, 1848, and all the region of the great discovery was suddenly peopled, as if by magic. The whole world seemed all at once to send its most aggressive spirits thither, a vast company of eager, resourceful, hard-fibred men, fit to work and to shift for themselves.

In they poured by shipload and by caravan, from over the seas, around the two continents by the long way of the Cape, around the northern continent by the shorter way of the Isthmus, across the endless plain by waggon and train, out of the States, out of the frontier communities of the western Territories, out of foreign lands east and west, until California showed, before the census of 1850 could be taken, a population of more than eighty thousand souls. They could not do without government: they improvised it in some rough and suitable fashion for themselves. By the autumn of 1849 they had held a general convention, framed and adopted a State constitution prohibiting slavery (for in that quickly formed community they had no slaves and wished for none, but only asked leave to live and work for themselves under rulers of their own choosing), and demanded admission into the Union. They had been encouraged to take this course by General Taylor, the frank, straightforward soldier who was then President. General Taylor was a Southerner, but he was also a democrat, and it seemed to him both legitimate and desirable that these self-sufficing pioneers in the Californian hills should choose their own government, demand their natural rights under the Constitution, and not wait upon the politicians at Washington. And they had their own way. California was admitted at once as a State, and admitted under the constitution which its inhabitants had framed.

It was a bitter disappointment to the Southern statesmen. California, with its broad and fertile valleys, its soft and kindly airs, its long area toward the south, had seemed a more likely region than any other for the extension of slavery. But these eighty thousand settlers who had rushed thither for gold had determined that question; and the most that could be offered the South by way of compensation was, that the question of the introduction of slavery into New Mexico and Utah should not also be prejudged and settled. They also had framed State governments, but with much less show of right than in the case of California; and Congress did not hesitate to ignore their request to be admitted into the Union. It organised them as Territories, with nothing said about slavery.

The only thing of substance that the Southern leaders seemed to have gained from the bundle of bills which made up the "Compromise," as they looked back upon it, was the Fugitive Slave Law; and there must have been some among them who seriously doubted the profit that would accrue to them even from that. The surrender of fugitive slaves was a matter which could never be settled in a way to satisfy both sections of the country; and it soon became evident enough that this particular effort to settle it was likely to generate passions which must grow hotter and hotter with each application of the law, promising, not accommodation, but a more perilous conflict and separation of interests. The new law was not novel in object or principle; it was novel only in character and operation, and attracted attention because of the strong forces of opinion now set hotly against it. The Constitution itself directed that not only fugitives from justice, but also all persons "held to service or labour in one State under the laws thereof, escaping into another," should be taken and returned, to receive their punishment or fulfil their service; and so early as 1793 Congress had passed a law intended to secure the return of both classes of fugitives. But this older law had proved less and less satisfactory with regard to fugitive slaves, because anti-slavery sentiment had grown apace in the North, and the officials of the Northern States had become more and more slack in assisting at the apprehension of negroes who had run away from their masters in the South. The Southern leaders, therefore, had demanded a law more stringent and effectual; and the law of 1850 had been framed to meet their wishes. Federal, not State, officials were to execute it, under heavy penalties for any neglect on their part in the thorough fulfilment of the duties it laid upon them. The mere affidavit of a master who claimed a runaway black was made conclusive evidence of ownership. The law bound federal judges and commissioners to issue the warrant of apprehension, obliged the marshals of the United States to make the arrest and safely deliver their prisoner, and operated even against the hearing of an application for a writ of *habeas corpus*. Many Southern masters used the law to the full limit of its rigour. Negroes who had been living in the North for many years were reclaimed and carried South under circumstances which greatly stirred the pity and sympathy of those among whom they had been settled. Mobs frequently attempted the rescue of apprehended fugitives, and sometimes succeeded, to the defeat of the law and the greater exasperation of feeling on both sides. Men of influence and position, besides such men as usually make up mobs, encouraged, and upon occasion took part in, even the more violent sort of resistance to the execution of the law, and did not hesitate industriously to organise every possible means of evading it. State Courts and even State legislatures put every possible obstacle in the way of the law's enforcement; and for a while men could talk of nothing else but the hateful operation of the Fugitive Slave Law.

The disturbing effects of all this upon the composition and aims of parties, and upon the action of the general government in affairs of domestic policy, were enhanced by the disappearance of the old party leaders. Calhoun died in March, 1850, the central month of the great Compromise debates—died stricken at heart, as it must have seemed to all who observed him closely, because forced in those last days to see with his keen eye of prophecy what the years to come must inevitably bring to pass. He had told those about him that the South was stronger now than she could ever be again, and must insist now or never upon what she considered her rights under the Constitution; that she had yielded too much when she consented to the Missouri Compromise of 1820, and must utterly lose the game of power if she conceded more; that the preservation of the Union depended upon the maintenance of an equilibrium between the Slave States and the Free, and that the Union must go to pieces unless that equilibrium, already destroyed, should be restored. He knew in those last sad days that it could not be restored, and that the Union he had loved and lived for must enter on its struggle with death. His own hand, more than any other man's, had wrought to bring the struggle on, because what he deemed his duty had bidden him to the work. He had drawn out the plot of the tragedy; but must have thanked God he was not to see it played out. He had designed it to be a warning: it had turned out to be a prophecy.

Webster and Clay survived him two years. Clay died in June, 1852, and Webster followed him in October. They had employed all their remaining power in the task of maintaining peace between the parties under the Compromise of 1850. Webster had gone about the country reproving agitation, speaking of the compromise measures, in his solemn and impressive way, as a new compact, a new stay and guarantee of the Constitution itself, the pledge and covenant of domestic peace. He had, indeed, sacrificed a great deal to effect the adjustment he so earnestly defended. He had lost many a friend and had infinitely saddened his own old age by advocating accommodation between the contending forces of North and South. Many thought this accommodation an utter abandonment of the gallant position he had taken in 1832, when he had faced Senator Hayne so successfully with his confident vindication of the sovereign authority of the general government. Men who had once trusted him to the utmost now denounced him with cutting bitterness as an apostate and an enemy of the

Union. But he endured the shame, as he thought, so that the Union might be saved. Clay also cried out to the last for peace, for good faith in the acceptance and fulfillment of the Compromise, for a steady allegiance in the maintenance of the old parties and the old programmes, against discontent and uproar and disquieting agitation. Both men passed from the stage before they could know what the outcome would be, hoping for the best, but doubting and distressed, their veteran heads bowed as if before a breaking storm.

The year of their death (1852) synchronised with the election of a President; and the state of parties gave cause for the gravest solicitude, to the leaders who remained as well as to those who were taken away. The Whigs uttered their usual declaration of principles, and avowed themselves entirely satisfied with the compromise measures of 1850; but they seemed to reckon for success rather upon the popularity of their candidate, General Winfield Scott, the hero of the Mexican war, than upon the attractiveness of their programme and principles. There were scores of Whigs who had no stomach for the compromise and were alienated by their party's support of it. They could not yet quite bring themselves to act with the outspoken Free-Soil party, which met in convention at Pittsburg in August and boldly pronounced the Fugitive Slave Law repugnant both to the principles of law and to the spirit of Christianity, declaring its own programme to be "no more slave States, no more slave Territories, no nationalised slavery, and no national legislation for the extradition of slaves"; but they held off from their old allegiance and would not help their party against either the Free-Soilers or the Democrats. The Democrats, for their part, spoke with their old-time confidence and acted with unity and spirit. They declared, not only that they approved of the Compromise, but also that they would "faithfully abide by and uphold the principles laid down in the Kentucky and Virginia Resolutions of 1798 and 1799." They regarded those principles, they said, "as constituting one of the main foundations of their political creed," and meant "to carry them out in their obvious meaning and import." Their nominating convention found it impossible to choose between the three leading candidates for the party's favours, Lewis Cass of Michigan, James Buchanan of Pennsylvania, and Stephen A. Douglas of Illinois, and therefore nominated Franklin Pierce of New Hampshire, an affable and prepossessing gentleman whom no one could condemn, and whom his supporters could admire for his quiet serviceableness as a member of the legislature of his State and of the

federal House of Representatives, and for his unostentatious performance of his duty as an officer of volunteers in the Mexican
war. And Pierce was elected. He received the electoral votes of
every State except Vermont, Massachusetts, Kentucky, and Tennessee—two hundred and fifty-four votes to General Scott's forty-
two. The Democratic majority in the House of Representatives
was, moreover, increased by thirty-seven, and in the Senate by
six. No influential group of public men had accepted the Compromise with quite such earnest heartiness as the Democratic
leaders had shown. They had therefore won the confidence of the
South; besides great States like New York and Pennsylvania,
which had four years before cast their votes for the Whig candidates, they had drawn North Carolina and Florida, Louisiana and
Georgia to their support. Their vote was national. The popular
vote of the Whigs had not materially fallen off, but the popular
vote of the Democrats had risen by nearly four hundred thousand,
and the vote of the avowed and aggressive Free-Soilers had diminished nearly one-half. It looked to sanguine politicians like a
clearing of the skies.

To those who could see more than the surface of affairs, however, it was even then evident that nothing of the kind had taken
place. Parties were in fact rapidly going to pieces. The Democratic
party held together for the present only because it allowed itself
to be governed by its Southern leaders, men of settled purpose and
definite opinions, experienced in counsel and in unhesitating and
concerted action. Every man who doubted and was troubled—as
what practical man was not?—by the ominous signs of the times
turned instinctively to this party, thus led, because it was at least
confident, of good courage and united counsels, knew its own
mind, and promised to bring peace and order out of confusion.
But the presidential election of itself settled nothing. Practical
questions turned with a sort of grim fatality upon the critical
matter of the extension of slavery, and came thick and fast, and
in such pressing form that they could not be put off or avoided;
and the Democrats were presently touched as near the quick by
the disintegrating influences of the time as the Whigs had been.
The field of politics began to fill more and more with new parties,
with new groups within the old parties, with dissentient factions
and a confused war of opinions.

The fact was, though politicians were very slow to perceive it,
that parties had long ago ceased to be amenable to the discipline
of the older time, when a few men trained to affairs in Virginia
and Massachusetts had been able to dominate and direct them

by the authority of a sort of oligarchy. In the old days of "the Virginian dynasty," the days from Washington to Monroe, parties had submitted to a very simple government and discipline, effected by intimate counsel among a few experienced leaders, by quiet conferences of Senators and members of the House of Representatives, by private correspondence and tacit understandings with regard to personal precedence. A change had set in with the entrance into national politics of those influences from the West which made Andrew Jackson President of the United States. Until then Presidents had been nominated by the party leaders who were in Congress or in the executive offices of the government; and a sort of succession had been observed. The Secretaryship of State, as the chief place among those held by the President's advisers, had come to be looked upon as next to the presidency itself in the line of party preferment, and statesman after statesman had passed through it to the chief national office. It was a sort of parliamentary *régime* inherited from England, where parties had long officered the government with their real leaders in legislation and policy; and it had been readily maintained because in almost all the older States the franchise had been in some degree restricted, and because there was a virtual social hierarchy in New England no less than in the South, where society was obviously aristocratic in its ideals of authority and precedence. The lawyers and the ministers, university men for the most part, and schooled to represent the prestige of training, of established forms, of learning, and of experience, still wielded in New England a power almost as substantial as that which had marked the authority of the governing class in the old colonies during the early eighteenth century; and the lawyers were of course the active politicians, an unquestioned preference being accorded all the while to certain families, as for instance the Adams family —an order of affairs which any Englishman of that generation might have recognised as natural and familiar enough. But a day came when the older States and communities of the seaboard no longer held their former undisputed place of governance in the politics of the Union. The great westward movement had set in. By 1850 Kentucky, Tennessee, Ohio, Indiana, Illinois, Missouri, Arkansas, Michigan, Iowa, Wisconsin, and California had been added to the roster of the States from the Western lands, where frontiersmen had founded a new democracy. Limitations upon the suffrage began to be discredited and broken down: the new States did not adopt them, and the old States in the face of their example could not keep them. Men without the training or the social standards of the older parts of the country made their way into affairs and grew impatient of the unsympathetic domination of the Eastern leaders by prerogative. They pushed their own propositions and candidates, and presently thrust aside Virginians and Massachusetts men to make Andrew Jackson President.

The breaking up of the old order was accompanied by many significant innovations and changes. State legislatures began to nominate candidates for the presidency; the younger men and the local political managers grew very jealous of the private and exclusive authority of congressional committees and "caucuses"; and by 1832 a new and popular machinery of nomination had been substituted, in which the part of public leadership was minimised and the art of getting votes and organising majorities magnified. This was the nominating convention, which has ever since been one of the chief instruments of party action in the United States, not only naming the candidates for the presidential office, but also giving authoritative formulation to the legislative and administrative programmes of the parties, and so binding their leaders by a sort of a *plébiscite*. In its nominating convention each party had thereafter a governing body of its own, unrecognised by law, made up under the management of the smaller sort of local politicians in the innumerable voting districts of the several States, but dictating to Congress, pledging presidents beforehand to certain courses of action; itself irresponsible, unofficial, temporary, subject to be manipulated, swayed by sudden winds of passion. It showed a singular aptitude for affairs on the part of scores of unknown men in the widely separated communities of the country that this new, miscellaneous and occasional assembly should be so promptly devised, so easily handled, and so rapidly made into an established instrument of party government. By 1852 the nominating convention had already become the regular means by which party policy was to be determined and the *personnel* of the federal Executive chosen.

The parliamentary *régime* had broken down because there was no organised method of leadership in Congress and no responsible ministry at the head of a dominant party and of the law-making Houses. The President's "cabinet," though in the early years selected from among men who had seen service in Congress and were the known and acknowledged leaders of their party, had never had a place on the floor of Congress. Congressional committees had for many years after the foundation of the government accepted the suggestions of the President and his advisers in matters of legislation; bills had often been framed in the executive departments which the Houses showed themselves very ready to adopt; and the early Presidents had counted upon exercising a guiding influence in legislation as a natural prerogative in view of their position as accepted representatives of the nation. But Congress had by degrees broken away even from this private connexion with the executive, this connexion of advice and common counsel; and there had never been any public connexion whatever. The Houses looked more and more exclusively to their own committees or to their own private members for the bills which they were to act upon, and grew more and more jealous of "outside" suggestions or assumptions of parliamentary leadership. There was still always a nominal "Administration" party, and always a party also of the "Opposition," in the House and Senate; but the "Administration" party had grown every session more and more disposed to dictate to the President rather than submit to his leadership; and Congress was not homogeneous enough to follow distinct or consistent lines of action. It was itself a miscellaneous body, made up, as the nominating conventions were made up, by the free, non-co-operative choice of separate and differing localities. There was no responsible leadership either in Congress or out of it. And so irresponsible leadership was substituted, the leadership whose function was in the electoral districts, in local campaign committees, in newspaper offices, in the management that was private and away from the forum of debate where questions of statesmanship seemed the determining factors in affairs.

The effect upon parties was profound, and, when the slavery question forced its way to the front, revolutionary. Local movements of opinion readily made themselves felt in nominating conventions. The delegates from particular localities reflected the most recent opinion of the people from amongst whom they had come; the business of a convention was not to frame legislation, or even to say how it could be framed, but only to reconcile and express opinion; the initiative was with any one who could command the votes. If men of radical views found themselves silenced or ignored in the convention of the party with which they had been in the habit of acting, they could break away and organise a convention of their own. New parties were continually springing up in times of agitation, drawing strength from the old parties, diverting attention to new and singular issues which had found no place in the ordinary party programmes, making the task of statesmanship and consistent legislation so much the more difficult and perplexing, and weakening parties without guiding them. The whole system facilitated group movement and an insistence on separate and sectional issues. Group movement inevitably made the regular parties nervous, vacillating, uncertain of their strength, prone to compromise and artificial make-shift reconciliation.

It was by such a process that the virtual dissolution of parties was being made evident in the years which preceded and followed the year 1852; and the question of slavery was the chief dissolvent. The feeling against slavery had grown very rapidly of late: not the feeling that slavery ought to be abolished in the States in which it was already established—for everyone knew that there it was a matter which the Constitution left entirely to the choice of the several commonwealths themselves and put beyond the reach of federal legislation, and beyond the reach therefore of national parties—but the "Free-Soil" feeling, the feeling against every attempt to extend the slave-holding system to new regions of settlement and force it upon new States. America had shared with the rest of the world the great philanthropic movements of the earlier part of the century. An "American Anti-slavery Society" had been established in 1833, the year which witnessed the abolition of slavery throughout the British Empire; and the men who organised that Society desired what William Lloyd Garrison demanded in the columns of the *Liberator*, founded two years before, the immediate and total abolition of slavery throughout the country, with or without the sanction of the Constitution; or, if that were indeed impossible, then the separation of the Free States from the Slave, in order that they at any rate might be purged of the offence. But such sentiments and purposes had not spread among the mass of the people. The institutions of the country had been built from the first, deliberately and consciously built, and in the sight of all the people, upon law; and a singularly vivid legal sense everywhere pervaded the nation. No one to whom the country gave serious heed proposed any interference whatever with slavery in the South or in any Slave State. But the number steadily grew of those who demanded that the purpose of the Southern leaders to obtain new territory for slavery in the West should be checked and defeated: it grew not only in New England, where the abolitionists were most numerous, but grew also, and assumed an even more practical tone and definite way of action, in the Northern tier of States to the westward, where free communities in Ohio, Indiana, Wisconsin, and Illinois lay in close vicinity to the lands concerning which the fight for "free soil" as against slavery must be fought out. Wherever there were new communities but just springing up, there was a fresh choice to be made, it seemed, with regard to slavery, in spite of nominal compromise after compromise, notwithstanding so-called settlement after settlement of the matter, in Congress. It was a question always open or to be opened until it should break national parties asunder. It could never be closed so long as unoccupied territories were at hand for which the fateful choice remained to be made.

It was the independent groups of thinking men who had made up their minds to resist the extension of slavery that began the work of disintegration which by 1852 had gone so far. At first they deliberately avoided the formation of an independent political party. They were of both parties, Whigs and Democrats; they felt the compulsion of party allegiance still strong upon them, and rejected with unaffected distaste every proposal to break away from and oppose their old associates, whose creed and practice alike they still relished and sympathised with in most things. They realised, too, the weakness and probable instability of a party whose existence was founded, and staked, upon a single issue. For long, therefore, they contented themselves with questioning individual candidates for Congress, named by the regular parties, concerning their opinions and purposes upon the slavery question, and gave or withdrew from them their support according as their replies pleased or displeased them. It was only when they saw how ineffectual this must prove, how casual, unsystematic, haphazard, that they found themselves at length constrained to take independent action. Then at last they held their own conventions, and even ventured their own independent nominations for the presidency, assuming the *rôle* of a national organisation, a distinct Free-Soil party. Democrats and Whigs alike joined them at first; but as time went on it turned out that they were to draw their strength from the Whig rather than from the Democratic ranks. The Democratic party depended for its organisation and leadership upon the South much more than the Whig party did. It formed its purposes with regard to slavery, therefore, much more readily and confidently, and kept up its spirit much more naturally and spontaneously in the face of the accumulating difficulties of the time: so that timid and busy men, and men accustomed to follow leaders and take their cue in politics from the clearest and most confident voices, left off doubting and searching for a party and followed it, electing Pierce and leaving the Whig party to go to pieces at its leisure.

The uneasiness of the time showed itself in all sorts of abnormal whims and diversions from the regular game of politics. Utter demoralisation fell upon the Whigs after their defeat in 1852, and, seeing their place vacant, a new and novel party pressed hopefully forward to take it. This was the "American" party, whose motto was, "Americans must rule America." It had been brought into existence by fears concerning the effects which the great foreign immigration of the time might have, under the country's too liberal naturalisation and suffrage laws, upon the control of affairs both local and national. It had not escaped general attention that the political disturbances then so acute in Europe had brought exiles of a new type to the United States, exiled agitators, political malcontents, men likely to be bitter, ambitious, covert, and astute in seeking their objects in a new field; and the "American" party had been formed to keep the government of the country in the hands of natives of the old stock. The organisation of the party centred in a secret club or Order, with its private councils and governing hierarchy; but no member of the Order would admit his connexion with it. They all with one accord professed entire ignorance of any such organisation; and the country dubbed them, with a sort of piqued amusement, "Know-Nothings." Regular party men were inclined to make merry over the mysterious new body. "It would seem as devoid of the elements of persistence," laughed Mr. Horace Greeley, "as an anti-cholera or an anti-potato-rot party would be." Nevertheless the Know-Nothings showed surprising vitality. To join them seemed to many of the disconcerted Whigs a hopeful way of withdrawing attention from the troublesome slavery question. In the large towns and more populous cities, too, their objects seemed very practical and desirable indeed; for there the new immigrants naturally thronged and made themselves at home in threatening numbers, and showed an ominous indifference to American standards of life and action. For one reason or another, therefore, this singular party drew strength to itself and played for a little while the *rôle* of political successor to the Whigs.

Politics moved upon a confused stage during the next eight years, years of critical interest every one of them; but determining events followed each other in quick, unbroken succession. A storm gathered and burst, and the crisis all had waited for and dreaded came at last. For a little while it seemed as if the presidential and congressional elections of 1852 had cleared the air and restored a certain calm to affairs. If other parties had been broken and thrown into confusion, the Democrats at least were united and in full possession of power. The Free-Soilers had lost, not gained, in strength. President Pierce made William Marcy his Secretary of State, a man who exercised authority as a member of the "Albany Regency," a group of astute politicians in the State of New York who understood better than any other men in the country the new art of organising conventions, and of turning local majorities not only to local but also to national use. Jefferson Davis of Mississippi had become Secretary of War, and brought to the support of the new Administration the great southern wing of the victorious party. The new heads of the government seemed established in the confidence of both sections of the country, supported alike by perfected party machinery and by a decisive general sentiment, and served and guided by capable, masterful men familiar with the movements of opinion. Both in Congress and at the executive mansion the Democrats took heart to be very bold, and to show their mastery.

Before the year of his installation was over, President Pierce had purchased still more territory from Mexico, in the region to which it seemed most likely that slavery would ultimately be extended. He had really little choice in the matter. Mexico still claimed a considerable tract of land in the far south-west which the United States deemed included in the cessions of the treaty of Guadalupe Hidalgo, a tract of more than forty-five thousand square miles lying to the south of the Gila river; and a Mexican army, under the notorious Santa Anna, had actually entered the region, as if to renew the war if Mexico's claim were not admitted. Pierce rightly thought it a prudent act of statesmanship to purchase the disputed territory for ten million dollars. The purchase was effected through Gadsden, of South Carolina, in December, 1853; and the anti-slavery men everywhere noted the transaction with profound chagrin.

But worse was to follow. Bad as it seemed to Northern men to purchase new lands which must stand open to slavery, under the compromises of recent legislation, at any rate until the day when States should be erected upon them, it was of course infinitely worse to abandon those compromises altogether, and deliberately open every part of the country not yet formed into States to the spread of the fatal institution. And yet that was what Stephen A. Douglas actually proposed and carried through Congress before the end of May, 1854. He was one of the senators from Illinois, and was but forty-one years of age, full of the rude, straightforward strength and audacity which showed him to have been bred in the free communities of the Western country. He had been born in Vermont, but had gone West as a lad to make his way, and had there grown into the short, square, coarse-fibred, thick-limbed, aggressive, vehement, eloquent man who seemed in the Senate a sort of dwarfed giant, compact of the energy and daring of the West. He confidently deemed himself, what many accepted him to be, the spokesman and leader of his party in Congress. He more boldly and explicitly than any other man pronounced the question of the extension or exclusion of slavery where the Western lands were filling up a thing to be determined by the settlers themselves, upon a free principle of self-government with which Congress and the federal authorities ought not to interfere. And there was a particular part of the Western country to which he wished to see his principle applied at once. This was the broad "Platte country" which lay within the Louisiana purchase to the northward and westward of Missouri. Across it ran the direct overland route to the Pacific, along which frequent waggon-trains moved to and fro between California and the East. There was some danger that it might be assigned as a reservation to the Indians and closed to settlement; and ever since 1843, when he was a member of the House of Representatives, before the days of the Mexican cessions, Douglas had been urging the erection of this great stretch of prairie into a Territory, not as a road to the Pacific —for in those days no one knew of the gold in California—but as a new home for settlers and commonwealths.

Early in January, 1854, being chairman of the Senate's Committee on Territories, and seeing his own party in power, he returned to his favourite scheme and introduced a bill which provided for the creation of a Territory to be called Nebraska, in the Platte country. Every previous proposal for the erection of Territories within the region covered by this bill had assumed, as a matter settled and of course, that slavery was to be excluded from it, under the Compromise of 1820; for it lay north of the southern line of Missouri; but this bill explicitly provided that the States subsequently to be formed out of the new territory were to be left to decide the question of the introduction of slavery for themselves, in accordance with what Senator Douglas called the principle of "popular sovereignty." His opponents called it the doctrine of "squatter sovereignty." The bill was presently withdrawn and amended. When reintroduced from the Committee on January 23, it provided for the creation of two Territories instead of one—a Territory of Kansas, west of Missouri, and a Territory of Nebraska, north-west of the old compromise State. But the "Kansas-Nebraska Bill" did not differ from the measure for which it was substituted in the matter of slavery. It was declared in the new bill to be the "true intent and meaning" of the Act, "not to legislate slavery into any Territory or State, nor to exclude it therefrom, but to leave the people thereof perfectly free to regulate their domestic institutions in their own way, subject only to the Constitution of the United States." It extended all laws of the United States, including the Fugitive Slave Law, to the new Territories, but explicitly excepted "the eighth section of the Act preparatory to the admission of Missouri into the Union,"—the compromise section, which had been considered one of the foundations of national politics. That section it pronounced "inconsistent with the principles of non-intervention by Congress with slavery in the States and Territories, as recognised by the legislation of 1850," and expressly "declared inoperative and void."

It was certainly an astonishing measure, conceived in the true spirit of the school of statesmen to which Senator Douglas belonged. No doubt its very audacity was what chiefly commended it to Douglas; no doubt, too, he believed it strategically as wise as it was daring. The Southern men had never dreamed of demanding a measure which should repeal the now venerable Missouri Compromise, and open all the Territories to slavery; parties wanted nothing so much as rest and oblivion of past excitements, if that might be had; a session of ordinary routine would have been welcomed on all hands as a pleasing programme of peace. But to the party leaders who hearkened to Douglas' counsels it seemed best to use their present power to have done with compromises and make all the future plain by the adoption of the simple, obvious, and consistent principle of "squatter sovereignty." Unexpected and revolutionary as the Bill was, it of course pleased the slavery men extremely, and majorities were found for it in both Houses. In the Senate 37 to 14 was the vote; and in the House 113 to 100. Forty-four Northern Democrats voted against the measure in the House; but as many more were ready to follow Douglas. Nine Southern members looked askance at the new thing and voted "No"; but most of them received it gladly. On May 30 the President signed the Bill, and it became law. He had been consulted beforehand about it, as it seems, and had expressed his approval of it, saying that he thought it founded "upon a sound principle, which the Compromise of 1820 infringed upon," and to which he was willing to return.

Notable debates had accompanied the passage of the Bill. There were men in both Houses who were ready to speak very plainly even upon this most thorny question. The most noticeable and influential group of these was to be found in the Senate. There

William H. Seward, of New York, and Salmon P. Chase, of Ohio, had been since 1849. The elections of 1849 had turned in no small degree upon the question of the extension of slavery to the great Pacific region then newly acquired from Mexico; and the Whigs of the New York legislature had sent Seward to the Senate to represent them in their wish that the new soil might be free soil. Chase had been chosen by the Democrats of the Ohio legislature to perform a like service for the "Free-Soilers" of his party. They wanted no new party. They held still very loyally to their party connexions. But upon the subject of slavery their convictions would admit of no compromise. Four years before, in the debates on the compromise measures of 1850, Seward had declared that he deemed the common domain of the Union in the West devoted to justice and liberty not only by the Constitution but also by "a higher law than the Constitution"; and had earnestly avowed the conviction that slavery even within the Slave States must eventually give way "to the salutary instructions of economy and to the ripening influences of humanity." "All measures which fortify slavery or extend it," he declared, "tend to the consummation of violence: all that check its extension or abate its strength, tend to its peaceful extirpation." This was a new voice and counsel in affairs; but since 1850 four more aggressive men of the same way of thinking had come to recruit Seward and Chase in the Senate. Ohio had added Benjamin Wade; New York, Hamilton Fish; Massachusetts had sent Charles Sumner, and Vermont Solomon Foote; and Douglas had been obliged to take account of the rising influence of every one of these in debate and upon the opinion of the country. He ought to have been warned as much by the conservative temper as by the radical speech of such a man as Charles Sumner. Sumner spoke upon occasion words of passion, but never words of revolution. He knew the limits of the Constitution and did not wish to transcend them. He had no desire, he said, to touch the system of slavery where it was already established as part of the social order and upon foundations of valid law; but he did mean to resist its extension to the utmost, and brought talents of no mean sort to the task. He believed it demonstrable that the Constitution gave Congress complete power, over this as over every other matter, in the Territories.

Nothing, however, shook the confidence or daunted the audacity of the Democratic leaders. Every compromise was abandoned, even the Compromise of 1820, which had stood and been reckoned on for a generation. The settlers upon new lands must be permitted to admit or exclude slaves as they chose. But when? Now, while the districts they were setting up homes in were under federal law as Territories; or after a while, when all the first processes of settlement were past and finished, and the time had come to frame a State constitution? The Kansas-Nebraska statute did not answer that question; but no practical man, of the stuff that settlers are made of, could hesitate long what answer must be given. It would be too late when the time for constitution-making came: by that time facts would have effectually answered it. Either the Territory would then be full of slave-holders with their slaves, or it would not be. Whoever should possess the land would make its laws. The federal authorities, it seemed, were to stand aside, neutral, uninterested: thus, then, it must be determined by the fact of possession, by whoever should have the power. Douglas and his followers must have been startled to observe how instantaneously the country saw and acted on these very obvious and practical considerations; and must have trembled when they saw a race for possession turn into civil war.

There was no longer debate; that was ended, and argument gave place to action. Kansas became the theatre of a perilous appeal to fact, which turned out to be an appeal to force. A Slave State lay neighbour to it on the east, and slave-owners were the first to pour across its borders and occupy it against the day of final settlement; but, though the men out of the Free States came later, they came in hosts and companies when they did come; they had behind them the organised assistance of societies and large funds subscribed in the Free States of the North and East; and they came bringing arms as well as tools. The country almost held its breath as it waited to hear what news should come out of Kansas; and it had not to wait long before it knew. Within two years the demoralising game for power there had been played and lost and won—won by the settlers out of the Free States; but not before blood had been shed and federal troops sent in to prevent anarchy. The Missouri settlers, being first on the ground, had very promptly acted upon their initial advantage; had organised a territorial government; and had enacted stringent penal laws against whosoever should in any way interfere with the introduction or perpetuation of slavery. But the Free-State settlers, pouring in from the North, ignored what the Missouri men had done and attempted to set up a government of their own. When they found that course forbidden by the federal authorities, they took the other, of sending majorities to the polls where a new territorial legislature was to be chosen. Partisans on both sides went armed; there were fatal riots at the voting places; blood was shed deliberately and by plot as well as in the heat of sudden brawls; fearful days of embittered passion in the distracted Territory made men everywhere presently talk of "bleeding Kansas"; but out of the fire came a definite enough settlement at last. A Free-State majority established "squatter sovereignty" very effectually; and by midsummer of 1856 the House of Representatives had passed a bill, which the Senate rejected, for the admission of Kansas into the Union under a constitution which forbade slavery.

Here was evidence plain enough for any man to read of the beneficent operation of Douglas' pretty theory of popular right in the organisation of Territories and the formation of States. The country saw with sad forebodings what it meant; partisanship everywhere was inflamed and put in a mind to go any lengths of violence; individual passion broke through all restraints; and prudent men were sore put to it to keep their comrades in affairs to the sober ways of moderation and law. It was in May, 1856, that Preston Brooks, a young Carolinian member of the House of Representatives, strode into the Senate and assaulted Sumner where he sat, for words of personal bitterness uttered in debate, striking him to the floor insensible; and it was one of the unhappiest signs of the times that such an act of blind anger and passionate folly was condoned and even applauded, not condemned, by the constituents of the man who had done it. No wonder excitement gathered head and statesmen grew infinitely uneasy when such things could happen.

The year 1856 brought another presidential election. It was a year, therefore, when every force that was astir came into the open and added to the manifest and perplexing confusion of affairs. There had been signs beforehand of what was coming. In the autumn of the very year in which the Kansas-Nebraska Bill was carried through the House of Representatives (1854), the majority which had carried it was destroyed. All "Anti-Nebraska men" drew away from it to destroy it. They did not draw together. Though "Free-Soilers," they did not relish as yet the idea of connecting themselves with the separate and avowed Free-Soil party; but joined themselves for the nonce to any independent group which promised them the satisfaction of uttering their protest against what the Democrats were doing, without withdrawing them wholly from their old allegiance. It was then that the Know-Nothings had their opportunity. A great many of the most deeply discontented voters were Whigs. They were still sensible of the compulsion of their lifelong party feeling; and it was more palatable to them to be Know-Nothings than to join with radicals who seemed inclined still further to jeopardise the peace of the country by forcing the formation of a party of revolt, upon the single and dangerous issue of slavery. In the elections of 1854, therefore, the Know-Nothings not only secured a number of seats in Congress but also elected their candidates for the governorship in Massachusetts and Delaware; and within another year they had actually carried the States of New Hampshire, Massachusetts, Rhode Island, Connecticut, New York, Kentucky, and California, besides polling votes which fell very little short of being majorities in no less than six of the Southern States, where the proper issues of the "American" party had no natural place or significance at all.

The House of Representatives chosen in the autumn of 1854 presented a curious and hitherto unknown medley of groups and elements: Democrats, Anti-Nebraskamen, Free-Soilers, Southern pro-slavery Whigs, and Know-Nothings—no regular Whig party being left, and as yet no fixed or certain combination of parties to fill its place. It took two months to elect a Speaker and organise the House for business; and, by the time that was done, the year had arrived in which a new President must be elected, and parties were once more re-forming for a fresh contest for the control of the Executive. When once the process of recombination had been definitely and deliberately begun it was pushed forward to its consummation with extraordinary rapidity. Before the presidential campaign of 1856 had been set in order for the time of voting, a new party was in the field, strong, confident, aggressive. Almost all "Anti-Nebraska men," of whatever former allegiance in politics, had drawn together as the "Republican" party; and the first year of their new organisation did not go by before they had won popular majorities in fifteen States, elected or won over to themselves one hundred and seventeen members of the House of Representatives, and secured eleven votes in the Senate. Representatives of all the older parties came together in their ranks, in novel agreement, their purposes mastered and brought into imperative concert by the signal crisis which had been precipitated upon the country by the repeal of the Missouri Compromise. They got their programme from the Free-Soilers, whom they bodily absorbed; their radical and aggressive spirit from the Abolitionists, whom they received without liking; their liberal views upon constitutional questions from the Whigs, who constituted both in numbers and in influence the commanding element among them; and their popular impulses from the Democrats, who did not leave behind them their faith in their old party ideals.

The contest for the presidency narrowed itself at once to a struggle between the Democrats and this new union of their opponents. The Know-Nothings met in convention in February, and nominated Fillmore; but when it came to the vote in November they succeeded in choosing their electors nowhere but in the little State of Delaware. The Republicans could not hold a really national convention: no States south of Delaware, Maryland, and Kentucky sent delegates to assist them at their nomination; and they nominated no statesman of their new faith, but John C. Frémont, a popular young soldier who had aided very efficiently in the conquest of California in the war with Mexico, and who had hitherto been reckoned a Democrat. In the election, nevertheless, they secured one hundred and fourteen electoral votes for their candidate, as against one hundred and seventy-four for the Democratic nominee. They carried every State of the north and north-west except Pennsylvania, New Jersey, Indiana, and Illinois; showed themselves practically the only party of opposition in the north-west; and polled a popular vote of 1,341,264, to their opponents' 1,838,169. The political field of battle was once more ordered and in set array. The issue had been very definitely joined. The Democrats had nominated James Buchanan, of Pennsylvania, who was then the Minister of the United States in London. He had been out of the country during these last years of heat and bitterness; but the platform of principles adopted by the convention which nominated him had endorsed the Compromise legislation of 1850 and what was now known to be its natural corollary, the repeal of the Missouri Compromise, as explicitly as the Republicans had repudiated them; and Buchanan himself had joined with the American ministers in France and Spain (October 18, 1854) in advising the government of the United States to acquire the island of Cuba,—by purchase if possible, by force if necessary. That was in substance to advise, as the country then looked at it, the addition of more slave territory; and the advice had been tendered just after the Gadsden purchase in the south-west, and at a time, as it presently appeared, when lawless men were planning and organising armed expeditions for the conquest of still more slave territory in Central America. Buchanan's election to the presidency meant the ascendancy, at least for a time, of the party which, frankly enough, supported the Southern interest.

The four years of his term of office (March 4, 1857, to March 4, 1861) afforded space enough in which to fight the battle of parties to a finish. For a little while the anxiety of the country was diverted from politics to business. The year 1857 was a year of very serious commercial depression, paying the penalty for years of confident and adventurous speculation. For ten years, since 1846, the country had felt the exhilaration and excitement of a rapid business expansion, which the discovery of gold in California had greatly quickened. Capital had run confidingly to new enterprises; loans had been easy to get; railroads and steamships had opened the channels of commerce, old and new, wider than ever before, both at home and abroad, and had greatly multiplied its routes in every direction; an era of invention had accompanied and occasioned unprecedented advances in the mechanic arts, affecting both agriculture and manufactures. Under the unwonted stimulus, sound business methods had not unnaturally given place to reckless speculation. Money was quickly enough invested, but was very slow to yield an increase. Enterprise after enterprise proved a dead loss. The banks of the country afforded no currency that could command confidence. Each State chartered banks of issue, and made its own laws, good, bad, and indifferent, for giving credit to their notes. There was no national regulation or oversight; no one could know which issues were safe, which unsafe. Enterprise was paid for in promises to pay, until of a sudden there came a day of reckoning: the inevitable contraction of loans; a season of failures and disillusionment; hard fact in the place of hope; painful disclosures of wholesale dishonesty, of defalcations and systematic fraud. The entire fabric of business came down with a crash, and panic had a long and doleful reign.

The population of the country had kept to its steady rate of increase from decade to decade as if unaffected by politics,—every ten years showing an increase of from thirty-two to thirty-five per cent. The decade 1850-60 was no exception. The numbers of the census rose by more than eight millions. But it was impossible that population should follow industry as fast as it was being pushed between 1846 and 1857. Railroads were built where there were neither farms nor towns to support them; sometimes upon open reaches of the continent, which the plough had never touched. The federal government had helped trade forward as it could. In 1850, while the great migration to the gold-fields of California was in full stream, it had seemed certain that an interoceanic canal would be cut through the Isthmus of Panama, and a most enlightened and satisfactory treaty with regard to its political oversight, its neutrality and disinterested management for the use of the world, had been entered into by Great Britain and the United States,—a treaty known in the United States as the Clayton-Bulwer Treaty, because negotiated by John M. Clayton, President Taylor's Secretary of State, and Sir Henry Lytton Bulwer, the British Minister. In 1854 trade had obtained the advantage of a reciprocity treaty with Great Britain, by which important rights were given and taken in respect of commerce with the British possessions in North America and the fisheries of New England and Nova Scotia; as well as of a treaty with Japan, negotiated by Commodore Perry, which secured a beginning, at any rate, of commercial intercourse between that country and the United States. But no growth of population or facilitation of trade could keep pace with the artificial work of speculation. The bubbles of fatuous enterprise were pricked, and a crisis of wholesale loss, panic, and depression occurred in spite of every token of trade and profit to come.

Congress did what it could to relieve the distress. It was feared that the high tariff rates then prevailing were drawing too much of the money needed by the banks into the Treasury of the United States; and a modification of the tariff laws was promptly effected, in the short session of Congress which followed the elections of 1856. Party interests no longer centred in financial questions: slavery had drawn passion off, and the congressional leaders cooperated with singular temperateness and sobriety in a modification of the law. Many of the raw materials of manufacture were put on the free list, and the duty on protected articles was reduced to twenty-four per cent. That was all that the government could do. The crisis could not be prevented. Throughout the year trade and industry were at a hopeless standstill: the autumn brought no revival. There was nothing for it but to wait for a slow and painful recuperation.

Even in the presence of almost universal pecuniary distress or anxiety, politics seemed inevitably to take precedence of every private concern. President Buchanan's inauguration occurred in the very midst of the troubled times in Kansas, when the struggle there still hung in a doubtful balance; and he had been in office but a few days when the Supreme Court of the United States pronounced a decision which added a new and deeply significant element both to the importance and to the excitement of the contest in the unhappy Territory. This was its decision in the case of Dred Scott *v.* Sandford. Dred Scott was a negro slave whose master, an army surgeon, had carried him for a brief period of residence first into the State of Illinois, where slavery was illegal, and then to a military post situated in the public domain further to the westward from which slavery had been excluded by the Compromise legislation of 1820; afterwards returning with him to Missouri, his home. The negro claimed that his residence in the free State of Illinois had operated to destroy his master's right over him; and the case instituted in his behalf before the Courts had come at this critical juncture, by appeal, to the Supreme Court. That tribunal held that the lower Court had had no jurisdiction: that Dred Scott, at any rate after his return with his master to Missouri, was a slave, and not a citizen, and had no standing in the Courts. That was the only point it was necessary to decide, and might have ended the matter. But a majority of the judges persuaded themselves that they should go further and expound the whole question of the status of slavery in the Territories of the United States, though they must in doing so, in the opinion of every discriminating lawyer, be speaking *obiter*. Chief Justice Taney, speaking for a majority of his colleagues, declared it the opinion of the Court that it was not within the constitutional power of Congress to forbid citizens of any of the States to carry their property, no matter of what sort, into the public domain, or even to authorise the regularly constituted legislature of an organised Territory to forbid this, though it were property in slaves: that only States could regulate that matter. If this were law, the Missouri Compromise had been invalid from the first; even "popular sovereignty," to which Douglas looked for the settlement of the question, could do no authoritative thing until it spoke its purpose in a State constitution. The Free-Soilers were beyond their right at every point.

To the Republicans the decision could seem nothing less than a stinging blow in the face. They were made to feel the smart of being stigmatised as disloyal to the Constitution. No doubt the judges had thought to quiet opinion and sustain the legislation of 1854; but instead they infinitely exasperated it. Their judgment gave the last touch of dramatic interest to the struggle in Kansas, now nearing its turning-point and culmination. In October, 1857, the Free-Soil settlers of Kansas got control of the territorial legislature at the polls; but not before the pro-slavery men, hitherto in power, had made a last attempt to fix slavery upon the future State. They had hastened before the autumn elections came on to assemble a convention and frame a constitution (September, 1857), and to see that their application for admission to the Union was at Washington in due form before the Free-Soil men could intervene and undo their work. President Buchanan decided to sustain them, judging at least the formal right of application to be really theirs. But Congress would not go with him. It was Democratic in both houses; but Douglas remembered his principles with manly consistency. It was known before Congress acted that a majority of the voters of the Territory did not in fact desire a pro-slavery State constitution; and he would not force a constitution upon a majority. There were members enough in his immediate following to control the action of the Houses, and Kansas was refused admission to the Union—pending the further contest of parties.

President Buchanan's Administration inevitably incurred the suspicion, throughout all this trying business, of being conducted in the Southern interest; and in the excitement of the time the President was suspected of things of which he was quite incapable. It was charged and believed that the decision of the Supreme Court in the Dred Scott case had been a thing concerted between the President and the Chief Justice, though the President's character made such a calumny inexcusable. He was a man of unsullied integrity, and punctilious in the performance of what he considered to be his duty. He was past the prime of life, had never possessed great courage or any notable gifts of initiative, and of course suffered himself to be guided by the men whom he regarded, and had good reason to regard, as the real leaders of the Democratic party. Only two States in the North had voted for him, and only two in the North-west: the Democratic party, which had chosen him President, was, happily or unhappily, in fact a party chiefly manned and guided from the South. He had called Southern men of influence into his Cabinet in whose character and capacity he justly and implicitly believed. He took their advice because he believed it to be honest and authoritative. But the country grew infinitely restive and uneasy to see one section rule. It was Mr Buchanan's chief fault, if fault it was, not that he yielded to improper influences, as his opponents unjustly believed, but that he did not judge and act for himself. He was weak; and weakness was under the circumstances fatal.

The year 1858 brought abundant signs of a great reaction, and it soon became only too plain that the Democratic party was driving the bulk of the country into opposition. It was the year of a general election. As the autumn approached, those who watched affairs found the critical issues of the time more and more sharply fixed and determined in their thought, and their convictions grew more and more vivid and definite. Nothing conduced more to this result than a notable debate reported from Illinois. The Republicans of Illinois had made a determined effort to keep

Douglas from re-election to the Senate. They had announced that, should they succeed in obtaining a majority in the State legislature, they meant to send Abraham Lincoln to the Senate in Douglas' stead; and the autumn campaign in Illinois became for ever memorable because in its course Douglas and Lincoln went about the State together and argued their claims for support face to face, upon city platforms and upon country platforms, in the presence of the voters. The striking individuality of the two men gave singular piquancy to the contest as well as their power of straightforward, unmistakeable definiteness of speech. Douglas was a national character, one of the acknowledged leaders of a great party; Lincoln was a comparatively unknown man, a shrewd lawyer and local politician. His long, gaunt, ungainly figure, his slouching gait, his homely turns of phrase marked him a frontiersman. His big, bony hands had wrought at the hard tasks of the forest and the farm. But his rough exterior did not repel the plain people to whom he spoke, alongside the more adroit and finished Douglas; and no one could hear his speech and think him common. He had taken his own way of learning to the bar. The passion for letters had been strong upon him since a boy, and his self-training had with unerring instinct followed a fine plan of mastery. By reasoning upon the principles of the law, as they came to him out of a few text-books, by poring upon books of mathematics, by reading up and down through such books of history or adventure as fell in his way in search of the experience of other men, by constant intimacy of talk and play of argument with men of every kind to whom he had access, he had made himself a master of brief and careful statement, of persuasion, and of oral debate: thoughtful, observant, steering in what he said by an unfluctuating compass of logical precision, and above all lucid, full of homely wit and anecdote such as was fit to illuminate practical subjects, and uttering phrases which found the heart of what he talked of, sometimes phrases which struck his opponent like a blow, but fair, unmalicious, intellectual, not passionate.

His definition of the matter to be settled between the parties was characteristic of him. "A house divided against itself," he said, "cannot stand. I believe this government cannot endure half slave and half free. I do not expect the house to fall, but I expect it will cease to be divided. It will become all one thing or all the other." Douglas found him a very uncomfortable antagonist, who drove him to awkward admissions. Before their debate was over Douglas was no longer within reach of the presidency; and Abra-

ham Lincoln had won the ear of the whole country. The Southern
men could not vote for Douglas as the nominee and spokesman
of their party. He had been forced under Lincoln's fire to admit
that Congress could not empower a territorial legislature, its
own creature, to do what, if the Dred Scott decision spoke true
law, it was itself unable to do; that Southern settlers, therefore,
could no more legalise slavery within a Territory than Northern
settlers could exclude it: that "popular sovereignty" was no solution, after all. The Republicans did not obtain a majority in the
Illinois legislature; Douglas went back to the Senate; but he went
back weakened and with loss of authority. The elections of the
autumn, taking the country as a whole, gave the Republicans
success enough to show how near at hand a crisis was. They
increased their numbers materially in both House and Senate,
carried Buchanan's own State of Pennsylvania by a handsome
majority, and made it very evident that opinion was swinging
their way. In the House of Representatives, indeed, they were put
in a position of virtual control: for no coherent party had a working majority there. The "Douglas Democrats," who had refused
to vote for the admission of Kansas with a pro-slavery constitution, were now hardly an integral part of the Democratic party;
there was still a group of twenty-two Know-Nothings; and the
Republicans held the balance of power.

And yet the President and his advisers were by no means
daunted. It was after the elections that Buchanan sent his annual
message to Congress; and in it he insisted that the United States
ought to secure possession of Cuba, assume a protectorate over
several of the nearer States of the dissolving Mexican republic,
and establish definite rights of control over the Isthmus. He was
still, as the Republicans read his motives, bent upon the acquisition of slave territory. The entrance of the Republican party upon
the stage of politics had singularly quickened the pace of affairs.
Its clear-cut, aggressive purposes seemed to give definiteness also
to the Democratic programme. A sharp rigour pervaded the air.
It startled conservative men to feel the movement as of revolution in the stir of opinion. Such debates as now marked the whole
course of politics, such contests uncompromisingly provoked and
ordered, gave plain threat of what all men dreaded, of disunion,—
nothing less. The South explicitly threatened disunion, and yet
disliked it as intensely and almost as unanimously as it resented
the exclusion of slavery from the Territories. The North dreaded
disunion infinitely; and yet dreaded the unchecked and general
ascendancy of the slave-interest even more. Both sides pushed

forward; but both with a great fear at their hearts. A sinister fate seemed riding at the front of affairs.

The power which obviously grew was the power of the North; the power which waned and was obviously threatened with extinction was that of the South. In May, 1858, the free State of Minnesota entered the Union, under an enabling Act passed by the last Congress of President Pierce's administration; and in February, 1859, the free State of Oregon was admitted by the Congress which had refused to admit Kansas under a pro-slavery constitution. Until 1848, when the slavery question came finally to the top in politics, the sections had balanced one another in the Senate: there were as many slave-holding States as free,—thirty senators from States which legalised, thirty from States which forbade, slavery. But now the balance was destroyed, as Calhoun had foreseen it would be: there were still not more than thirty senators from slave-holding States, while there were thirty-six from free States. In the House the numbers stood at ninety to one hundred and forty-seven. For in the House population was represented; and the South, which had stood equal with the North in numbers at the making of the Constitution, had long since fallen far behind. Not only had the population of the North grown very much faster, but to the North had been added the great makeweight of the North-west, from the whole of which slavery was, in fact if not in law, excluded, and, if the Republicans triumphed, excluded for ever. The ways of compromise were abandoned, discredited: the one section or the other must now secure everything or lose everything.

As if the crisis were not already sharp enough, conspiracy was added to the open battle of politics. On the night of Sunday, October 17, 1859, one John Brown, at the head of a little band of less than twenty followers, seized the United States arsenal at Harper's Ferry in Virginia, meaning to strike there a sudden blow for the freedom of the slaves, and, having set a servile insurrection aflame, make good his retreat to the mountains. It was the mad folly of an almost crazed fanatic; the man was quickly taken and promptly hanged: his flame of war had flickered and died in the socket. But that was not all. Brown was from Kansas; he had come to Virginia, at midsummer in that anxious year 1859, with the stain still fresh upon him of some of the bloodiest of the lawless work done there in the name of freedom: a terrible outlaw, because an outlaw for conscience' sake; intense to the point of ungovernable passion; heeding nothing but his own will and sense of right; a revolutionist upon principle; lawless, incendiary, and yet seeking nothing for himself. He brought arms and means to Virginia with which he had been supplied out of New England, not for use in the South, but for use in Kansas. But Southern men were not in a temper to discriminate. If Northern men would pay for the shedding of blood in Kansas, why not for the shedding of blood in Virginia also? Slavery was the object of the attack, and the slaveholders saw little difference, great as the difference was, between Abolitionists and Free-Soilers. And this terrible warning at Harper's Ferry was of a sort to put even cool men out of temper for just and sober thinking. A slave insurrection meant what it maddened Southern men to think of: massacre, arson, an unspeakable fate for women and children. If this was what "anti-slavery" meant, it must be met and fought to the death, Union or no Union.

It was in such a season of disturbed and headstrong judgment that the presidential campaign of 1860 came on. The Democrats were the first to attempt a nomination; but their convention proved a house divided against itself and went hopelessly to pieces; and the outcome was two "Democratic" nominations. One section of the party nominated Douglas for the presidency; the other, which was the Southern section, named John C. Breckinridge of Kentucky as its candidate. A new party sprang into existence, the "Constitutional Union" party, made up of those who had been Know-Nothings until the Know-Nothing party died of inanition, and of those who had left the other parties but had found it impossible to digest the Know-Nothing creed—of all who feared alike the Democratic and the Republican extremes of policy and doctrine, and still hoped the quarrel might be composed. These nominated John Bell of Tennessee, and declared in a platform of great simplicity and dignity that they recognised "no political principle other than the Constitution of the country, the union of the States, and the enforcement of the laws." The Republicans alone were united and confident. They warmly disavowed all sympathy with attempts of any kind to disturb slavery where it was established by law; but they declared as flatly as ever against the extension of slavery to the Territories; and they nominated, not Mr Seward, the chief figure of their party,—for many felt a distrust of him as a sort of philosophical radical,— but Abraham Lincoln of Illinois, the shrewd, persuasive, courageous, capable man who had loomed so big in the memorable debates with Douglas three years before. Their convention had sat at Chicago, in Mr Lincoln's own State. The cheers of the galleries and the astute combinations and diplomacy of his friends in their work among the delegates had played as great a part as his own gifts and popularity in obtaining for him the nomination. But when once he had been named the whole country began to see how wise the choice had been. Eastern men for a little while looked askance upon this raw Western lawyer and new statesman: but not after they had heard him. And when the votes were counted it was found that he had been elected President of the United States. One hundred and eighty of the electoral votes went to him; only one hundred and three to his three opponents combined.

It was a singular result, when analysed. The electoral votes of Virginia, Tennessee, and Kentucky had gone to John Bell, the nominee of the "Constitutional Union" party; the rest of the Southern votes had gone to Breckinridge; Douglas had received only the votes of Missouri and three of the nine votes of New Jersey. And yet, although these amounted to but one hundred and three votes altogether in the electoral college, the total popular vote at the back of them was 2,823,741, as against a popular vote for Lincoln of only 1,866,452,—a popular majority of almost a million votes against the Republicans,—so large was the aggregate minority in the States whose electoral votes the Republicans had won. It was a narrow victory, no popular triumph; and Lincoln, like the other leaders of his party, was disposed to use it with the utmost good temper and moderation.

But Southern men took no comfort from the figures and did not listen to protestations of just purpose. They looked only at the result, saw only that the government was to be in the hands of the Republicans, regarded the defeat as final and irreparable. Their pride was stung to the quick by the unqualified moral censures put upon them by those who were now to be in power. "The whole course of the South had been described as one of systematic iniquity." Mrs Stowe's striking and pathetic picture of what slavery sometimes led to, in her *Uncle Tom's Cabin* (1852), had been accepted in the North and by the English-speaking world at large as a picture of what it usually led to. "Southern society had been represented as built upon a wilful sin; the Southern people had been held up to the world as those who deliberately despised the most righteous commands of religion. They knew that they did not deserve such reprobation. They knew that their lives were honourable, their relations with their slaves humane, their responsibility for the existence of slavery amongst them remote"; and that now those who had most bitterly and unjustly accused them were to become their rulers. It seemed to them, too, that the North itself had of late practised nullification in its

fight against them. More than a score of the States had passed
"personal liberty" laws which were confessedly intended to bar
and render impracticable the enforcement of the Fugitive Slave
Law. The South Carolina legislature, which itself chose the presidential electors of the State, had remained in session to learn
the result of the election. When it knew that Lincoln was to be
President, it summoned a Constitutional Convention, which severed the State's connexion with the Union; and before Lincoln
was inaugurated six other Southern States had followed South
Carolina out of the Union.

The inevitable disintegration of the Union, by reason of the
operation of the institution of slavery, had worked its perfect
work. The South, which did not change, had become a region
apart; and it now put the Union aside in accordance with the
theory with respect to its authority which it conceived to have
obtained at its constitution. There was here nothing of the contradiction which seemed to lie at the heart of nullification; the
South was not resisting the Union and yet purposing to remain
within it. It had taken the final step of withdrawal: the partnership was dissolved. If that were revolution it was at least revolution within the original theory of the law as the South had
learned it.

The issue was—slavery? Yes, upon the surface. Perhaps it need
never have come to this, had Douglas kept his hand from the law.
The movement against slavery had been weak, occasional, non-
partisan until the Missouri Compromise was repealed, ten years
before. It was that which had brought the Republican party into
existence and set the sections by the ears. But now that the breach
had come, it did not seem to men in the South merely a contest
about slavery: it seemed, rather, so far as the South was concerned, a final question and answer as to the fundamental matter
of self-government. There were many men in the South who,
while they had no love for slavery, had a great love, a deep inherited veneration even, for the Union, but with whom the passion for the ancient principles, the ancient sentiment, of self-
government was greater even than these, and covered every subject of domestic policy. It was this they deemed threatened now.
Slavery itself was not so dark a thing as it was painted. It held
the South at a standstill economically, and was her greatest burden, whether she felt it to be so or not. Bad men, too, could shame-
fully abuse the boundless powers of a master. But humane sentiment held most men steadily and effectually off from the graver
abuses. The domestic slaves, at any rate, and almost all who

were much under the master's eye, were happy and well cared for; and the poor creatures who crowded the great plantations where the air was malarial and where the master was seldom present to restrain the overseer, were little worse off than free labourers would have been in a like case, or any labourers who could live there. Those who condemned slavery as it existed in the South condemned it unjustly because they did so without discrimination; and those who attacked it with adverse laws seemed to invade the privileges of self-governing States under the Constitution. Thus it was that Lincoln's election meant secession, and that the stage was set for the tragedy of civil war.

For the whole country it was to be the bitterest of all ordeals, an agony of struggle and a decision by blood; but for one party it was to be a war of hope. Should the South win, she must also lose—must lose her place in the great Union which she had loved and fostered, and must in gaining independence destroy a nation. Should the North win, she would confirm a great hope and expectation, establish the Union, unify it in institutions, free it from interior contradictions of life and principle, set it in the way of consistent growth and unembarrassed greatness. The South fought for a principle, as the North did: it was this that was to give the war dignity, and supply the tragedy with a double motive. But the principle for which the South fought meant standstill in the midst of change; it was conservative, not creative; it was against drift and destiny; it protected an impossible institution and a belated order of society; it withstood a creative and imperial idea, the idea of a united people and a single law of freedom. Overwhelming material superiority, it turned out, was with the North; but she had also another and greater advantage: she was to fight for the Union and for the abiding peace, concord, and strength of a great nation.

I. BIBLIOGRAPHIES

Lalor, J. J. Cyclopædia of Political Science and of the Political History of the United States. Chicago, 1881-8. See under special titles: Slavery, Whig Party, Democratic Party, Republican Party, Annexations, Compromises, Wilmot Proviso, Fugitive Slave Laws, Territories, Dred Scott Case.

Sparks, E. E. Topical Reference Lists in American History. Columbus, Ohio. 1893.

II. DOCUMENTS

Benton, T. H. Abridgment of the Debates of Congress, from 1789 to 1856. Vol. XVI. 1857.

The Congressional Globe gives the debates in full. The Congresses covered by this chapter are the Thirty-first to the Thirty-sixth, inclusive.

Congressional Documents, House and Senate.

Executive Documents (official).

III. CONTEMPORARY AUTHORITIES

Benton, T. H. Thirty Years' View [1820-50]. New York. 1834-6.

Calhoun, J. C. Works. 6 vols. Charleston, N. Y. 1851-5.

Clay, H. Correspondence and Speeches. 3 vols. New York. 1855-7.

Curtis, G. W. Orations and Addresses. Edited by C. E. Norton. New York. 1894.

Davis, J. Rise and Fall of the Confederate Government. 2 vols. London. 1881.

Douglass, F. Life and Times, from 1817 to 1882. London. 1882.

Grant, U. S. Personal Memoirs. 2 vols. New York. 1895.

Johnston, A. (editor). Representative American Orations. Vol. II. New York. 1884.

Keyes, E. D. Fifty Years' Observation of Men and Events.

Lincoln, A. Complete Works. Edited by Nicolay and Hay. 2 vols. New York. 1894.

McCulloch, H. Men and Measures of half a Century. New York. 1888.

Motley, J .L. Correspondence. Edited by G. T. Curtis.

Olmstead, F. L. Journeys and Explorations in the Cotton Kingdom. 2 vols. London. 1861.

Pierce, E. L. Memoir and Letters of C. Sumner. London. 1893.

Pike, J. S. First Blows of the Civil War. New York. 1879.

Poore, B. P. Perley's Reminiscences of sixty years in the National Metropolis. 2 vols. Philadelphia. 1886.

Sargent, N. Public Men and Events, 1817-53. Philadelphia. 1875.

Seward, W. H. Works. Ed. Baker. 5 vols. New York. 1853-84.

Sumner, C. Orations and Speeches. 2 vols. Boston, Mass. 1850.

—— Works. 15 vols. Boston, Mass. 1875-83.

Taussig, F. W. (editor). State Papers and Speeches on the Tariff.

Webster, D. Works. With Memoir by E. Everett. 6 vols. Boston, Mass. 1851.

IV. SECONDARY WORKS

General Histories

Holst, H. von. Constitutional and Political History of the United States. Transl. by Lalor and Mason. Vols. IV-VII. New York. 1880.

Johnston, A. History of American Politics. New York. 1879.

Rhodes, J. F. History of the United States from the Compromise of 1850. London. 1893, etc. Vols. I, II.

Schouler, J. History of the United States of America under the Constitution, 1783-1861. 5 vols. New York. 1880-91. (Vol. v.)

Wilson, W. Division and Reunion, 1829-89.

Special Works

Blaine, J. G. Twenty Years of Congress: from Lincoln to Garfield. Norwich, Conn. 1884.

Cobb, T. R. R.   Inquiry into the Law of Negro Slavery in the United States. Savannah. 1858.

Draper, J. W.   History of the American Civil War. 3 vols. London. 1871. Vol. 1 deals with events and influences preceding the war.

Goodell, W.   Slavery and Anti-Slavery. New York. 1852.

Greeley, H.   History of the Struggle for Slavery Extension or Restriction in the United States, 1776-1856. New York. 1856.

—— The American Conflict. 2 vols. Hartford, Conn. 1864-6.

Hodgson, J.   The Cradle of the Confederacy. Mobile, Alabama. 1876.

Houston, D. F.   A Critical Study of Nullification in South Carolina. (Harvard Histor. Monographs. No. 3.) 1896.

Hurd, J. C.   Law of Freedom and Bondage in the United States. New York. 1858.

Lalor, J. J.   Cyclopaedia of Political Science and of the Political History of the United States. Chicago. 1881-8. Articles: Whig Party, Republican Party, Democratic Party, Annexations, Compromises, Wilmot Proviso, Fugitive Slave Law, Territories, Dred Scott Case.

Lunt, G.   Origin of the Late War. New York. 1866.

McDougall, M. G.   Fugitive Slaves (1619-1865). Boston. 1891.

Parker, Joel.   Habeas Corpus and Martial Law. Philadelphia. 1862.

Pollard, E. A.   The Lost Cause. New York. 1866.

Sanborn, F. B.   Memoirs of John Brown. Concord, Mass. 1878.

Sherman, J.   Recollections of Forty Years in the House, Senate, and Cabinet. 2 vols. Chicago. 1895.

Siebert, W. H.   The Underground Railway from Slavery to Freedom. New York. 1898.

Smith, T. C.   The Liberty and Free Soil Parties in the North West. (Harvard Histor. Studies.) New York. 1897.

Spring, L. W.   Kansas. (American Commonwealth Series.) Boston. 1885.

Stephens, A. H.   A constitutional view of the late War between the States (argumentative and narrative dialogues).

Taussig, F. W.   Tariff History of the United States. 4th ed. New York. 1898.

Wilson, H.   History of the Rise and Fall of the Slave Power in America. 3 vols. Boston. 1872-7.

Wise, B. H.   Life of H. A. Wise of Virginia, 1806-76. London. 1899.

—— H. A.   Seven Decades of the Union. Philadelphia. 1872.

—— J. S.   The end of an Era. Boston, Mass. 1899.

Woodbury, L.   Writings, political, judicial, and literary. 3 vols. Boston. 1852.

Biographies

Coleman, Mrs. C.   Life of J. J. Crittenden. 2 vols. Philadelphia. 1873.

Colton, C.   Life and Times of Henry Clay. 3 vols. New York. 1857.

Curtis, G. T.   Life of James Buchanan. 2 vols. New York. 1883.

Davis, Mrs. V. H.   Jefferson Davis, Ex-President of the Confederate States. 2 vols. New York. 1890.

Garrison, W. P. and F. J.   W. L. Garrison, 1805-79. 4 vols. (Gives full details of the abolitionist agitation.)

Hart, A. B.   Salmon P. Chase. (American Statesmen Series.) Boston. 1899.

Herndon, W. H.　Life of Abraham Lincoln. 2 vols. London. 1893.

Johnston, R. M. and Browne, W. H.　Life of A. H. Stephens. Philadelphia. 1883.

McLaughlin, A. C.　L. Cass. (American Statesmen Series.) Boston. 1891.

Merriam, G. S.　Life and Times of S. Bowles (an influential northern editor). 2 vols. New York. 1865.

Morse, J. T.　A. Lincoln. (American Statesmen Series.) Boston, 1893.

Nicolay, J. G. and Hay, J.　A. Lincoln: a History. 10 vols. New York. 1890.

Roosevelt, T.　T. H. Benton. (American Statesmen Series.) Boston. 1887.

Schurz, C.　A. Lincoln. An Essay. London. 1891.

Seward, F. H.　Seward at Washington (1846-1872). 2 vols. New York. 1891.

——　H. W.　Autobiography of, 1801-34; with a Memoir of his life from 1831 to 1846, by F. W. Seward. New York. 1877.

Storey, M.　C. Sumner. (American Statesmen Series.) Boston. 1900.

Stovall, P.　Life of R. Toombs (a remarkable southern agitator). New York. 1892.

Tyler, L. G.　Letters and Times of the Tylers (the latter part refers to this period). 3 vols. Williamsburg, Va. 1884-96.

Weed, T.　Autobiography of; with Memoir by T. W. Barnes. 2 vols. Boston. 1883.

Printed in A. W. Ward *et al.* (eds.), *The Cambridge Modern History* (13 vols., New York and London, 1903-12), VII, 405-42, 808-10.

To Hamilton Holt[1]

My dear Sir,　　　　　Princeton, New Jersey, 21 December, 1899.

I need not say how gratified I am at your continued wish to have me contribute something to the Independent; and I wish that I could give you a part of the address I recently delivered at Waterbury.[2] But not a word of that address was written. I had simply a single page of headings and catch words from which to speak;[3] and I could therefore send you nothing that was written *de novo*, an independent essay. Even if I had a verbatim report of what I said, I could not send it to be printed: for it gives me the cold shivers to read my extemporaneous style. I am very sorry; but the simple fact is, that the address does not, objectively, exist.

With renewed expressions of obligation and thanks,

Very truly Yours,　Woodrow Wilson

WWTLS (WC, NjR).

[1] Born Brooklyn, N.Y., Aug. 19, 1872. A.B., Yale, 1894; graduate student in sociology and economics at Columbia University, 1894-97. Managing editor, New York *Independent*, 1897-1912; editor and owner, 1912-21. President of Rollins College, 1925-49. A tireless advocate of world peace and international organization, Holt was active in the League to Enforce Peace during the First World War

and a strong supporter of the League of Nations. Author of several books and numerous articles. Died April 26, 1951.

[2] A news report of it is printed at Dec. 14, 1899.

[3] He refers, undoubtedly, to the notes printed at May 30, 1898, Vol. 10.

To Richard Watson Gilder

My dear Mr. Gilder,   Princeton, New Jersey, 21 December, 1899.

I am going to take a great liberty. I feel that it is both bad form and bad business to ask you what you have decided about that torso of history I sent you; but I do so under a compulsion which I hope you will think sufficiently covers the breach of good taste.

If you are to print those chapters in the Magazine, I am mortgaged to you for next Autumn, to bring the narrative down to 1700 and give it unity, as covering a separable period worthy of detached treatment. If you have decided that it is not worth your while to do so, I am free to do other things next Autumn. Now it so happens that an unusual number of literary plans, submitted to me by reputable gentlemen connected with magazines and publishing houses,[1] are being 'held up' in my mind because I do not know to whom next Fall belongs. None of these plans is considerable. It is a matter of an important essay here and another there, of an introduction to an extensive work, etc.; but the awkward circumstance is, that if these things are done at all, they must be done before January, 1901. You will remember that the only reason I had for feeling justified in letting you see the said torso was, that my big plans of work were laid out to be accomplished after my return from the year abroad I hope to have in 1901-2, and that that fact left me an odd season of comparative freedom, the Autumn and a portion of the winter of 1900-1.

This then is my explanation and apology. Do not understand me as hastening your counsels, but only as asking, with unaffected hesitation and diffidence, whether you are able, *without* unduly hastening them, to give me some intimation as to my future freedom.

With warmest regards,

Sincerely Yours,   Woodrow Wilson

WWTLS (Berg Coll., NN).

[1] One of whom was Walter Hines Page, as the following letter makes clear.

From Walter Hines Page

My dear Wilson: New York 23, December, 1899.

Let me thank you for a pleasant day and express my hope for a happy issue out of all your publishing troubles. I wish that the old theology were true which used to try to make us believe that only the guilty suffered; but the old chaps missed it badly in holding on to that doctrine.

It occurred to me on the way home and again this morning after a conference with Mr. Doubleday, that our wish that you should make up your own mind, without influence by us, concerning your future publishing plans ought not to forbid our putting before you a more definite proposition than I made yesterday. You ought to know what we are willing to do.

Concerning the unfinished History, then,—the one-volume book the contract for which is in the hands of the A. B. C.—I do not understand that you have promised this to the Century but only that Mr. Gilder has asked you for a History of the United States for serial use in the Century & that you have not promised him anything but feel that you have an obligation of courtesy at least to let him know of this unfinished book. How great this obligation is, you must yourself judge. But at the most I do not understand that you have ever talked with him about the book rights. Under this assumption, let us make you this definite proposition:

Let Gilder have the serial rights if you wish and let us have the book-rights, & we will bring the book out as soon as its serial publication ends and pay you the following graduated royalty—

10	per cent.	on the first	5,000 copies sold.
12½	" " "	" second	" " "
15	" " "	" third	" " "
17½	" " "	" fourth	" " "
			and up to 50,000
20	" "	on all copies after 50,000—

or—

We will, of course, be glad to publish the book, if you do not care for serial publication, as soon as you have it ready;

or—

If you want serial publication and you and Mr. Gilder do not come to an agreement, we offer you our services to dispose of the serial rights to any periodical that will be acceptable to you. We, I have no doubt, could sell it for you—saving you the trouble. Down at the bottom of my immortal soul I have a prompting to ask, 'Why publish a history as a serial at all?' 'The price received for serial use' is the obvious answer, but when you have to postpone the book-publication for a year, the serial-income isn't all clear gain.

About the Washington—I doubt if the receiver of Harpers *can* sell it now. He will have to wait, probably, till permission is given by the court. But in the meantime some arrangement may possibly be made whereby you can get the use of the plates & the right to publish. I'll tell Mr. Emery[1] within a few days that you are going to see him. Now if you can get the Washington into your hands on reasonable terms, we shall be glad to take it over. I'm going to carry out the biography plan and I'm going about it early in January, making it my business to find men. If anybody occurs to you, I pray you tell me.

Now when you think of casting your fortunes—the fortunes of these two books at least—with a young publishing house, you have a right to know anything you wish to know about it; and we have no secrets from you. In general, we have the experience of three of the best publishing houses to guide us (Doubleday coming from Scribner, MacArthur[2] from Dodd, Mead & Co., & I from Houghton, Mifflin & Co), we have every one succeeded on our own account; Doubleday has already made a notable success of this house in two years & a half; we are not rich, but we have all the money we need; and we know how to sell books (this is my deep-seated conviction, for it touches the other end of the business more directly than my own department) better than anybody else in the business. But if I don't stop, I'll be bragging of my partners and that is forbidden in the constitution of the company. What I mean is, I have no secrets from you.

My regards to Mrs. Wilson and my wish for a happy holiday for you both.   Sincerely Yours,   Walter H. Page

ALS (WP, DLC).
    [1] He is unknown to the Editors.
    [2] Page seems to have been premature in claiming James MacArthur for his new publishing firm. Reader and literary adviser for Dodd, Mead and Company and joint editor of the *Bookman*, 1894-1900, MacArthur joined the staff of Harper and Brothers and of *Harper's Weekly* in January 1901.

To William Rainey Harper[1]

My dear Sir,   Princeton, New Jersey, 23 December, 1899.

I greatly appreciate your kind letter of the twentieth,[2] asking if I would be willing to consider an invitation to lecture in Chicago during your coming summer term. But I am sorry to say it will not be possible for me to do so. My winter is so full of lectures, both at home and away from home, that I find a summer's vacation from them, and a summer's leisure for literary work, a veritable necessity.

Please accept my sincere thanks and my real regrets.
                    Very truly Yours,   Woodrow Wilson

WWTLS (ICU).

1 President of the University of Chicago.
2 It is missing.

From Theodore Roosevelt

My dear Prof. Wilson: [Albany] Dec. 23rd, 1899.

Is there any chance of your being at Albany this winter? If so, remember I want you to be my guest. There is much I should like to talk over with you.

Faithfully yours,   Theodore Roosevelt

TLS (Letterpress Books, T. Roosevelt Papers, DLC).

From Joseph R. Wilson, Jr.

My dearest Brother: Clarksville, Tenn. 12-23-'99

The lovely photograph of dear Sister Ellie reached us this morning and we are certainly delighted to receive it. Just the other day Kate & I were wishing for such a photo, as we have none that does sister Ellie justice. It is, indeed, a splendid likeness and we thank you very much for it. We have a photograph of our two daughters[1] for you and it would have been sent before now had there not been an accident at the photographers which necessitated another sitting this week. It will be forthcoming shortly, however. We hope your Christmas will be a very, very happy one and your New Year will be filled with joy, prosperity and the greatest blessings of health.

I did not know until I received your letter this morning that Woodrow Kennedy is at Princeton.[2] I am glad to know that he is doing so well.

I have failed to secure passes to Wilmington, so must forego the pleasure of a visit to dear father. I regret this very much, but do not feel that I can afford to take the trip now without passes, —as I am using every cent I can get to pay for new type, machinery &c. that I have recently purchased.

We anticipate a pleasant Christmas, but I have a great longing to be with my own people at this season, a longing that I feel, at times, must be gratified regardless of expense. It is certainly a great privation to be so far away from you all with no hope of an early reunion.

We are much distressed to hear of dear Sister Annie's bad health, but hope and pray it may only be temporary.

Kate joins me in the warmest messages of love and seasonable greetings to you all.   Your devoted brother   Joseph.

ALS (WP, DLC).
[1] Alice, born May 7, 1895, and a new daughter, Jessie Woodrow Wilson, born in March 1899.
[2] Wilson's nephew, Wilson Woodrow Kennedy of Batesville, Ark., who had entered Princeton in 1899 as a sophomore and was forced to withdraw in 1900 on account of ill health. He died on November 8, 1900.

From Richard Watson Gilder

My dear Prof Wilson,   New York [c. Dec. 24, 1899]

You would have had a definite letter from me ere this—But I was sent away for a winter vacation & am off tomorrow again. Your MS. will follow me there—& you will get letters from us, in a few days. I hardly think this history will be serial material; when I asked you for just such a history it was for *book* publication. But we will have propositions to make to you which I trust will not only keep you busy—but make you feel that the Century people want you very sincerely as a "permanent author"—whose work can be put forth by them in a way that will be honorable & profitable to all concerned. So mote it be. For my part I wish the public could be made more and more to discriminate between bookmakers, & *real* writers—people *who know how to write.*

With a Merry Xmas to you & yours—

I am sincerely yours   R. W. Gilder.

ALS (WP, DLC).

To Edith Gittings Reid

My dear Mrs. Reid,   Princeton, 26 Dec., 1899

You will not fail to recognize the enclosed photograph or to realize what its sending means. Some strength and heartening, though it be unconscious, must surely come from being loved by friends whom you seldom see or hear from. You are so much talked of and admired and (singular though the word may seem) *missed* in this household that I like to think that when you are gay and your thoughts at ease we are contributing, unknown to you, to your happiness by sheer force of affection. Your and Mr. Reid's ears must often burn, (always the right ears!) because of the faraway Wilsons. The lady whose picture I send you sends very genuine love with the "counterfeit presentment."

What strange thing is this I hear about Miss King's being engaged *to another man*?[1]

With the warmest messages of affection from us both to you both and to dear Mrs. Gittings,[2]

Faithfully Yours,   Woodrow Wilson

Mrs. Wilson insists that you have no photograph of me, and instructs me to send one in her name.   W.W.

ALS (WC, NjP).
    1 Bessie King of Baltimore, who had formerly been engaged to Herbert Baxter Adams. See E. G. Reid to WW, Aug. 24, 1897, Vol. 10.
    2 Mrs. James Gittings, Mrs. Reid's mother, who lived with her.

Two Letters to Edward Ireland Renick

My dear Renick,   Princeton, 29 Dec., 1899.

I have not said anything new about Washington in these pages, but I have, I trust, given him his true Virginian setting. You and I are Virginians, and I hope that you approve it as a Virginian as well as a critic of biography. May every sight of this volume have for you the private value,—independent of all faults of execution, —of reminding you of an old and abiding friendship.

    As ever,   Affectionately Yours,   Woodrow Wilson

My dear Renick,   Princeton 29 Dec., 1899.

It is no small matter with me that men whose judgment I value as I do yours should like this little volume. It pleases me to believe that it has won its success because, whatever its other qualities, it was honestly conceived, and written with earnest conviction. No doubt you read it with the indulgence of a friend:—read it also with a full assurance of the affection of

                                        Woodrow Wilson

ALS on flyleafs torn from *George Washington* and *Mere Literature*, respectively (de Coppet Coll., NjP).

From Edward Ireland Renick

My dear Wilson: Washington, D.C., December 29, 1899.

I need not assure you that what you have written in the books I sent you has deeply touched me. Our own Lamb has told us how rare and how lovely it is to have that hand clasp ours in cordial friendship at forty which helped us in our youth to turn the pages of the *Amicitiis*.

You and I sat nearly twenty years ago reading together the Eneid, and to-day we are as fresh and warm in our regard and affection—each for the other—as in those days of enthusiasm and romance.

This I count among my dearest possessions—your genuine and *abiding* friendship.

I shall read these books—I have already read the lines they contain when first published—over and over again, always thinking of you, and rejoicing in the success that you have achieved, and the good that you have done in politics and in literature.

Both Mrs. Renick & I wish for you and Mrs. Wilson, and indeed for all your family, a happy and prosperous New Year.

Sincerely Yours,   E. I. Renick

ALS (WP, DLC).

From Frederic Flagler Helmer

Dear Sir: Lockport N.Y. December 29 1899

As apology for my obstinacy in regard to the size of your name on the book plate, let me explain that the reduction of the whole design will be considerable and as the scroll is not really large compared to all the rest I have felt that the name should be kept prominent to fulfil the use of the book plate as a personal label.

If however you feel that I have kept the name still too large, I desire to redraw the contents of the scroll till you are exactly pleased. It is *your* plate.

Kindly return the drawing to my address, 215 Chestnut St. Holyoke, Mass., and in case it is right I will then order the plate reduced in zinc etching, as usually done, and print also if you desire.[1]

I enclose a sample of gummed paper that is often desired, but any quality can be used and if you desire to have the printing done under your own order and supervision in Princeton or elsewhere I would as soon have it so. I commonly charge 75 cents for 100 prints and scale up to 2.00 for 1000. The price of sketches, final drawing and plate amounts to 7.50. But I beg you will not give out this figure (7.50) to anyone as my future price for by recent arrangement I am compelled to make it more.

Very truly yours,   F. F. Helmer

ALS (WP, DLC).

[1] No further correspondence between Wilson and Helmer has survived. The bookplate is reproduced in the photographic section of this volume.

A Newspaper Report of an Address in Philadelphia

[Jan. 3, 1900]

PATRIOTS AND POLITICS.

Professor Woodrow Wilson's Views
of Their Intimate Relationship.

The duties and responsibilities of citizenship and the ever present call for patriotism of the highest order formed the subject of a lecture last evening by Woodrow Wilson, LL.D., of Princeton University, in the current University Extension course, at Association Hall. The lecturer was introduced by the Rev. Dr. Henry C. McCook,[1] and was listened to with marked attention by a cultured audience.

"Patriotism," said Dr. Wilson, "is not mere sentiment. It is the energy of a man's character operating outside the narrow sphere of self. I conceive my devotion to my friend to be of the same kind as my devotion to my country; the two differ in the extent of their application and not in essential character. You serve your friend by reproof as well as by praise. You must serve your nation in order to benefit and perfect its character. There is no future life for nations, and if they have not won perfection on this side of annihilation they will never get perfect at all.

"I have no respect for the man who will agree with me because my party is in the majority. I should feel ashamed to belong to a nation which always gets its cue from the reigning party in Washington. The reigning party in Washington must take its cue from us, and we must not care whether we are making our neighbors comfortable or not. We must have civic manhood, firm against the crowd. Crowds cry out for revolution. The people make more slowly for progress. You must distinguish between the crowds and the people.

"The greatest impediment to progress in this country is the squeamishness of refined men in respect to politics. Some of our notions of reform are very rarefied. You must study the conditions of practical politics not to be corrupt. You can handle dirt to remove it, and it will never stain you if that be your purpose.

"Be fearless in criticism, but fearful of radical change. Talk like a radical sometimes, but don't act like one. The laws of progress demand that you shall crawl when you have found out what you think to be true. Be partisans. Associate with men who in general don't agree with you; you will find a tonic that is wholesome. Be lovers and followers of good men; love all good men and follow some."

Printed in the Philadelphia *Public Ledger*, Jan. 3, 1900.
  1 Henry Christopher McCook, pastor of the Tabernacle Presbyterian Church of Philadelphia, distinguished entomologist and prolific author on biblical and popular subjects.

Two Letters to Adrian Hoffman Joline

My dear Mr. Joline,   Princeton, 4 Jan'y, 1900

It gives me real pleasure to comply with your request,—and I am very much complimented that you should wish what you ask.

I fear the *paper* I have written on is not of a very suitable *size*, but I had no other. If you have uniform paper for binding in, and will return my note with a sheet of it, I will cheerfully copy it.

With much regard,
                    Sincerely Yours,   Woodrow Wilson

ALS (WC, NjP).

My dear Mr. Joline,   Princeton, 4 January, 1900

I wish that I could believe that I had got into this oration[1] what was in my heart and imagination as I wrote it,—a real vision of Princeton's greatness and spiritual significance for the country. If you should read it again, try to read into it what, I trust, you know to be the ideals of scholarship and of public service cherished by   Your sincere friend,   Woodrow Wilson

ALS pasted in Joline's copy of *Memorial Book of the Sesquicentennial Celebration of the Founding of the College of New Jersey and of the Ceremonies Inaugurating Princeton University* (New York, 1898), facing p. 102 (WC, NjP).
  1 "Princeton in the Nation's Service," printed at Oct. 21, 1896, Vol. 10.

To Robert Underwood Johnson[1]

My dear Mr. Johnson,   Princeton, New Jersey, 4 January, 1900.

I am sorry to say I cannot do anything for your "convention" number, much as I should like to,—for I like the idea. I have my hands as uncomfortably full for the winter, spring, and summer as the poor wight has who, having been accustomed to drive a single nag, finds himself driving six spirited racers. I am none the less obliged to you, however, and appreciate your kind letter very much.

With much regard, and very hearty greetings for the New Year,
                    Cordially Yours,   Woodrow Wilson

WWTLS (Berg Coll., NN).
  1 Associate Editor of the *Century Magazine* since 1881.

To Henry Mills Alden[1]

My dear Mr. Alden,   [Princeton, N.J. Jan. 8, 1900]

Our conversation of Saturday morning[2] has occupied my thoughts most of the time since it occurred. I was greatly gratified by what you said, and by the very fact of the visit itself. It is no small matter with me to learn that my work is really admired and desired. I was very much interested, too, and relieved to hear you speak so confidently of the rehabilitation of the great house,[3] which any man of sensibility must desire to see re-established in its place of honor and distinguished service.

When the personal feeling excited by our morning together had partly worn off, however, I found the business side of the case reassert itself in respect of my own interests. I know the necessity which forced the sale of the educational part of the business; I know the hurry that attended the sale and its character as a sale in a block; I am sure therefore that the fact that my contract was transferred with the rest was no deliberate part of the transaction. My contract, no doubt, went, unidentified, with the rest. Deeply hurt and chagrined as I was at first, I am now convinced that no intentional disservice was done me. I can, therefore, look at the whole matter quite impersonally.

The hard fact nevertheless remains that the transfer of my contract did do me a very great disservice, apparently an irreparable disservice. It will not serve my interest in the least to publish with the American Book Company; I am bound both in law and in morals to publish with them if I publish the textbook I had planned; I must give up therefore the idea of publishing it at all; and I thereby lose the only chance I ever had or am ever likely to have, to make a considerable amount of money out of a book. This has come about through the misfortunes, not through the fault of Harper's; but it does not seem to me either unfair or ungenerous in me to ask that they give me control of my Washington in order to enable me to place it where I am likely to gain for it much more than the ordinary sales. I have a chance to make it one of a series of biographies which are reasonably sure of very large sale. By so placing it, at a popular price, I should confidently expect to obtain for it a very much larger sale than it could possibly have, however thoroughly pushed and advertised, were it to continue to stand alone, an isolated work. It could in no case have anything like the sale of a textbook; but since I cannot have a textbook, I might as well make the most of what I can have.

That is the whole argument. That is why I still feel inclined to beg very earnestly that the house will let me have my Washington on as favorable terms as possible. I feel that there is nothing in this that need wound the feelings of anyone concerned. Certain I am that my own feelings are quite unengaged. I have treated the whole matter in my thoughts as purely a matter of business; and with a feeling of unqualified goodwill towards the great firm which every one must wish to see extricated from all its embarrassments. It is because I have treated it as a matter of business that I have been led to maintain my desire to put my book where there is the best and most immediate prospect of profit. I would much rather not treat any one of my books as if it were the object of commerce; but I realize that that preference is too sentimental, and has an element of weakness in it. I am trying to overcome it and to become more of a businessman than I have hitherto permitted myself to be in dealing with literary matters.

I could not conclude this letter frankly without giving myself leave to express my warm personal esteem for yourself and my very deep appreciation of your kindness to me alike in what you have said and done.

With sincerest regard,

Most sincerely Yours,   Woodrow Wilson

Transcript of WWshLS (WP, DLC).
  1 Editor of *Harper's Magazine*, 1869-1919.
  2 In Princeton on January 6.
  3 Harper and Brothers.

From Henry Mills Alden

Dear Mr. Wilson: New York City January 9th, 1900.

Do you think you could get your material in hand for a Short History of the United States (answering the same purpose for the U. S. as Green's Short History of England) so that you could give us copy by July 1st, 1900, for the First Part of a series of Twelve Parts for our *Magazine*, publication to begin in our January Number, 1901, and to be continued through the year? Copy for the Second Part would be required August 1st, 1900, and so on consecutively to the end. It is understood that, in large lines, the twelve parts taken together will be a complete history of the United States in a scope suited to serial use. Such completeness as you wish, from the point of view taken for book-form publication, you can give it afterward.

We will pay you for the serial use of this history one thousand dollars for each part, and for the book a royalty of 15% on the retail (trade-list) price for all copies sold, subject to the usual conditions in our agreements with authors.

Since writing the above I have received your letter of yesterday. I beg of you to hold in suspense this matter of the Washington book until you have considered the proposition conveyed to you in this letter.   Yours sincerely,   H. M. Alden

TLS (WP, DLC) with WWhw and WWsh notation on env.: "Ans. (doing the one work) 10 Jan'y, 1900."

EDITORIAL NOTE

WILSON'S HISTORY OF THE AMERICAN PEOPLE

In the letter just printed, Henry Mills Alden offered Wilson an opportunity to get "out of the hole" in which he said he had been left by Harper's sale of his contract for a school history of the United States to the American Book Company.[1] (The story of this abortive textbook is recounted in the Editorial Note, "Wilson's 'History of the United States for Schools,'" Vol. 10.) Alden's proposal, Wilson wrote happily, would enable him in effect to continue the school history "with no stitches dropped."[2] Moreover, he would not, as he had earlier feared, lose his "only chance . . . to make a considerable amount of money out of a book."[3]

Only two commitments prevented Wilson from accepting Alden's proposition immediately, and he set about, as he put it, getting "a clean sheet to write on."[4] The first was Wilson's obligation under the contract for the school history. This was resolved, however, when negotiations with the American Book Company led to an agreement on January 20, 1900, which, as Wilson noted, left him free to take up on "other lines" the American history for Harper's.[5]

The second commitment was more difficult to resolve because it was moral rather than legal in nature. Wilson had discussed the publication of his "Short History of the United States" (see the Editorial Note, "Wilson's 'Short History of the United States,'" Vol. 8) in both serial and book form with Richard Watson Gilder and Robert Underwood Johnson of the Century Company, and Wilson apparently thought that he had given that firm some kind of option on the manuscript. Gilder and his associates had promised to advise Wilson as to the "magazineability" of the history,[6] and Wilson had sent the typescript of the still incomplete work to Gilder on November 22, 1899.[7] The New York editor had arrived at a tentative opinion by Christmas Eve. The "Short History," he said, was hardly serial material, but he was interested in publishing it in book form, and he would have "propositions" to make to Wilson, whom he very much wanted as a "permanent author."[8]

Understandably eager to accept the offer from Harper's, Wilson moved immediately to forestall any "propositions" from the Century

[1] WW to R. Bridges, Jan. 12, 1900.
[2] WW to R. U. Johnson, Jan. 12, 1900.
[3] WW to H. M. Alden, Jan. 9, 1900.
[4] WW to H. M. Alden, Jan. 22, 1900.
[5] See the memorandum printed at Jan. 20, 1900.
[6] WW to EAW, Nov. 21, 1899.
[7] WW to R. W. Gilder, Nov. 21, 1899; WW to EAW, Nov. 22, 1899.
[8] R. W. Gilder to WW, Dec. 24, 1899.

Company. Gilder's opinion that the "Short History" would not lend itself to serialization ended the whole discussion as far as he himself was concerned, Wilson informed the Century office on January 12; and he now felt that he should put the "Short History" aside indefinitely because the situation had changed in a "manner fairly revolutionary" since he had submitted the manuscript to Gilder. Now before him, Wilson went on, were proposals so "exceedingly advantageous" that he felt constrained to turn aside from other plans and accept them.[9] To Wilson's "real relief," Gilder adhered to his earlier opinion concerning serialization of the "Short History" and also acceded to Wilson's desire to postpone publication until the work was nearer completion.[10]

Thus by mid-January Wilson felt "free to take the next step in the business," as he expressed it to Alden.[11] This was the negotiation of a contract for the twelve articles and the book.

With Harper's recent financial crisis and the transfer of his school history contract fresh in mind, Wilson approached these negotiations cautiously. That Harper and Brothers was still in receivership was ample cause for concern. Consequently, Wilson asked that each article be paid for as soon as he had delivered copy for it and, more important, that the contract be "absolutely secured . . . against sale, assignment or transfer" without his consent.[12] Additionally, he wanted insertion of a clause giving him the option of terminating the contract and buying Harper's rights in it after seven years. Much discussion ensued, but Harper's proved accommodating, and Wilson's suggestions, considerably modified, were incorporated into the contract that he signed on April 4, 1900.[13]

Meanwhile, Wilson had already begun work on the articles for *Harper's Magazine*. With the first four chapters of the school history in hand, he commenced on February 6, 1900, by returning to the fourth chapter, which he had written during the late spring of 1899, "The Approach of Revolution." It was, Wilson wrote, "architecturally, part of the one next to be written (V. The War for Independence) . . . and as some of my recent reading has led to a considerable change of perspective in my thought about things of which it treats, I am now reconstructing it."[14]

Wilson had scarcely begun before he was forced to put the work aside for a month because of illness in his family. Not until March 7 could he announce: "I got at my history again this morning, and began again the revision where I left it off. . . . I shall not hurry. I shall try, rather, to get gradually into the swing, and so cross the line to the unwritten chapter on the War for Independence."[15] He apparently worked at this slow pace and completed the chapter on the coming of the Revolution during the next three weeks.

At about this time, Wilson urgently asked Robert Underwood Johnson of the Century Company to return the manuscript of the "Short

9 WW to R. U. Johnson, Jan. 12, 1900.
10 R. W. Gilder to WW, Jan. 13, 1900; WW to R. W. Gilder, Jan. 15, 1900.
11 WW to H. M. Alden, Jan. 22, 1900.
12 *ibid.*
13 WW to H. M. Alden, April 4, 1900.
14 WW to EAW, Feb. 6, 1900.
15 WW to EAW, March 7, 1900.

History of the United States" to him.[16] With the date for submission of the first installment—July 1, 1900—drawing near, Wilson had reviewed his school history manuscript and concluded that the opening chapter[17] was not suitable for the Harper series. In its place, he decided to use the first chapter of his "Short History." Comparison of the first installment in *Harper's Magazine* with the first chapter of the "Short History" insofar as they overlapped reveals that they are virtually the same. However, Wilson did return to the school history in composing the section in the first installment on the settlement of Virginia. Although the opening paragraph and a few other parts of this section are taken from the "Short History," most of the text of this section is a repetition of the school history.

Similar analysis of the subsequent magazine installments reveals that Wilson continued to use the school history as far as it would carry him. With the school history chapters as a kind of first draft, he struck off his new copy, borrowing paragraphs here and there directly from the "Short History" and, at times, rewriting or expanding occasional paragraphs. Thus in style and length the *Harper's* articles are much closer to the school history than to the "Short History."

Late in June 1900, Wilson sent the first installment to Alden, who pronounced it "all that could be desired."[18] By the end of the year, Alden had received "The War for Independence,"[19] and a month later he acknowledged receipt of the next part which included the chapters "Between War and Peace" and "Founding a Federal Government."[20] Meanwhile, a series title, "Colonies and Nation," had been chosen, presumably by Wilson.

Actually, Wilson was drafting chapters even more swiftly than the above record would indicate. In the Wilson Papers are shorthand drafts of most of the chapters, beginning with the one on the approach of the Revolution. The fact that Wilson dated most of these enables us to see his true progress. For example, he did not send the final version of "Founding a Federal Government" to Alden until late in January 1901, but he had completed the shorthand draft of this chapter on July 2, 1900. The shorthand draft of "A Nation in the Making" is dated December 1, 1900, that of "Critical Changes," February 8, 1901. He began "The Bank and the Finances" on the next day, and he completed the shorthand version of his chapter on the Civil War, "Armed Division," on June 3, 1901. At this point, Wilson stopped his forward progress to begin revision of the articles for the book.

There are in the Wilson Papers three typed outlines or tables of contents, one of which shows Wilson's division of topics into parts for the magazine series. Probably composed in January 1901, it reveals that Wilson then thought that it would take fourteen parts or installments to bring his history to the end of the nineteenth century. Early in February 1901, he complained to Alden that he was having difficulty surveying the complete history of the United States in the assigned twelve articles, and that the best he could probably do in the maga-

---

[16] WW to R. U. Johnson, March 26, 1900.
[17] It is printed at April 8, 1898, Vol. 10.
[18] H. M. Alden to WW, June 26 and July 12, 1900.
[19] H. M. Alden to WW, Dec. 27, 1900, Vol. 12.
[20] H. M. Alden to WW, Jan. 28, 1901, *ibid.*

zine series would be to go through Reconstruction.[21] Alden readily accepted this revision, because, as he wrote "some trespass on next year's space seems to be inevitable in order to secure completeness."[22] As things turned out, however, Alden cut the series off with the December issue of *Harper's Magazine*, and "Colonies and Nation" went only slightly beyond the American Revolution.

"Colonies and Nation" will not be printed in these volumes, and the reader may find the following list of installments convenient for purposes of reference:

"Colonies and Nation. A Short History of the People of the United States. I.–Before the English Came. II.–The Swarming of the English–The Virginia Company. III.–New Netherland and New Plymouth," *Harper's Magazine*, CII (Jan. 1901), 173-203.

"[The Massachusetts Company] The Province of Maryland. The Expansion of New England. The Civil Wars and the Commonwealth," *ibid.*, Feb. 1901, pp. 335-69.

"The Restoration. New Jersey and Carolina," *ibid.*, March 1901, pp. 529-54.

"[Pennsylvania and New York] The Revolution. Common Undertakings," *ibid.*, April 1901, pp. 709-34.

"Common Undertakings," *ibid.*, May 1901, pp. 903-18.

"Common Undertakings," *ibid.*, CIII (June 1901), 115-30.

"The Parting of the Ways," *ibid.*, July 1901, pp. 285-300.

"The Parting of the Ways," *ibid.*, Aug. 1901, pp. 465-74.

"The Approach of the Revolution," *ibid.*, Sept. 1901, pp. 639-54.

"The War for Independence," *ibid.*, Oct. 1901, pp. 791-807.

"The War for Independence," *ibid.*, Nov. 1901, pp. 933-43.

"The Coming of Peace," *ibid.*, CIV (Dec. 1901), 104-10.

Preparations for publication of "Colonies and Nation" in book form had begun long before all the articles were in print. "Will you kindly let us know," Alden asked Wilson on April 24, 1901, "the number of words you intend to have in the book-form of 'Colonies and Nation,' so that we can make a close estimate of the whole number of pages before beginning the composition of the book." Alden also wanted to know whether Wilson contemplated changes in the articles so extensive that the printers could not set the book directly from the magazine series.[23] Wilson's reply is missing, but in notes which he prepared for his answer he estimated that the book would run to about 261,000 words, and that the text of the magazine articles would be altered throughout by an "infinite number of small touches [and] by little character sketches."[24]

The complete copy that Wilson supplied to the printers has survived in the Wilson Papers. Insofar as they went, Wilson cut and pasted up the extra set of revised pages of the magazine articles that Harper's had sent to him. All the *Harper's* installments are represented by mounted pages except for the final one, "The Coming of Peace." It was omitted because it was in fact an attempt by Wilson to round off the series by summarizing briefly and extracting bits here and there from

21 H. M. Alden to WW, Feb. 6, 1901, *ibid.*
22 H. M. Alden to WW, Feb. 14, 1901, *ibid.*
23 Harper and Brothers to WW, April 24, 1901, *ibid.*
24 See the notes printed at April 25, 1901, *ibid.*

the next chapter, "Between War and Peace." There are in addition
printed, mounted pages for three full chapters beyond the last installment of the magazine series. They had obviously been printed
up by Harper's before the cut-off date had been decided upon.

The changes that Wilson made on these printed pages can hardly
be described as "small touches." Actually, there are extensive handwritten and typed additions and emendations in every chapter. In general they constitute a considerable expansion of the text, although
numerous stylistic and textual alterations appear as well.

Meanwhile, Wilson had begun to transcribe the shorthand draft of
most of the balance of the book into typescript on his Hammond type-
writer. He finished the next-to-last chapter, "Return to Normal Conditions," as he reported to his wife, "at ten o'clock, copying and all,"
on May 31, 1902.[25] In June came the call to head his *alma mater*,
and he was forced to do the final work amid many interruptions. But
the shorthand draft of the final chapter, "The End of the Century,"
was completed on July 3, 1902, and its transcription and revision
moved so steadily that Wilson could announce to a concerned friend
on July 12 that the history had been finished one week before, and
that his decks were now clear.[26]

The title of the history in book form was not chosen until December 1901, when Harper's discarded "Colonies and Nation" as not "comprehensive enough" and suggested *A History of the American People*.[27]
Wilson accepted the new title somewhat grudgingly, it would seem.[28]

A History of the American People was divided into five volumes,
with the following table of contents:

I. The Swarming of the English
   1. Before the English Came
   2. The Swarming of the English,—
      The Virginia Company
      New Netherland and New Plymouth
      The Massachusetts Company
      The Province of Maryland
      The Expansion of New England
      The Civil Wars and the Commonwealth
      The Restoration
      New Jersey and Carolina
      Pennsylvania
      The Revolution
II. Colonies and Nation
   1. Common Undertakings
   2. The Parting of the Ways
   3. The Approach of Revolution
   4. The War for Independence
   Appendix
III. The Founding of the Government
   1. Between War and Peace

[25] WW to EAW, June 1, 1902, *ibid.*
[26] WW to E. G. Reid, July 12, 1902, Vol. 14.
[27] Harper and Brothers to WW, Dec. 24, 1901, Vol. 12.
[28] As WW to T. N. Page, June 16, 1902, *ibid.*, indicates.

A History of the American People appeared in October 1902 embellished by numerous maps and facsimiles and lavishly illustrated by Howard Pyle, Howard Chandler Christy, Frederic Remington, Frederick Coffay Yohn, and many others. In addition to the subscription edition, there was a trade edition and a limited "alumni" edition for Princetonians of 350 copies handsomely bound in orange and black. A "popular" edition appeared in 1910, and Harpers published a ten-volume edition in 1918 distended by a variety of original sources and documents. There were also a number of foreign editions, including a one-volume Swedish edition in 1916 and a two-volume French edition in 1918-19.

Aside from contemporary reviewers, some of whose illuminating critiques are printed in this series, only three scholars have commented extensively on *A History of the American People* and its place in the history of American historical writing. They are Marjorie L. Daniel, "Woodrow Wilson–Historian," *Mississippi Valley Historical Review*, XXI (Dec. 1935), 361-74; Louis M. Sears, "Woodrow Wilson," in William T. Hutchinson (ed.), *The Marcus W. Jernegan Essays in American Historiography* (Chicago, 1937); and Henry W. Bragdon, *Woodrow Wilson: The Academic Years* (Cambridge, Mass., 1967).

What seem to have been all of Wilson's notes for "Colonies and Nation" and *A History of the American People* have survived in the Wilson Papers. Written usually on long cards, they consist of outlines, bibliographical citations, and research notes. Hardly systematic or comprehensive, they indicate that Wilson wrote *A History of the American People* for the most part directly from printed sources and authorities.

To Julia Gardner Gayley[1]

My dear Mrs. Gayley,   Princeton, 10 Jan'y, 1900.

I am sincerely sorry to say that it is never possible for me to accept an invitation to speak at a distance from home on a Saturday evening.[2] Most of my college duties are concentrated on Mondays and Tuesdays, and I do not feel justified in using a Sunday for travel except under the compulsion of a real necessity. I am greatly gratified that the Pittsburgh chapter of the Daughters of the American Revolution should desire to have me speak to them. I hope that you will express to their Committee my very warm thanks and most sincere regrets.

I cannot close this letter without making the very humble apology I owe you. When I was in Pittsburgh last[3] you did me the honour to ask me to read a paper of yours on the Origins of Government. I asked leave to bring it away with me. When I reached home I laid it carelessly among a pile of miscellaneous papers on my table, amidst which it got buried out of sight and therefore out of mind. I forgot it. When I found it—I am ashamed to say how long afterwards,—I simply did not know what to do or say.

This is the whole truth of a matter so discreditable to me in every particular that I have been, I think, more mortified about it than about anything I ever did! I write of it because I owe it to you to do so in all frankness,—not to ask your forgiveness, for the thing is scarcely forgivable, but to beg you to believe me most deeply grieved and repentant.

I have read the paper at last with genuine pleasure and admiration; but it is almost impudent, under the circumstances, to say anything about it, even by way of appreciation.

With much regard,
Most sincerely Yours,   Woodrow Wilson

ALS (in possession of Henry Bartholomew Cox).
    [1] Wife of James Gayley of Pittsburgh, managing director of the Carnegie Steel Co.
    [2] The letter from Mrs. Gayley, to which this was a reply, is missing.
    [3] In October 1897, when Wilson had spoken to the Department of Social Economics of the Twentieth Century Club at Mrs. Gayley's invitation. See Julia G. Gayley to WW, July 20, 1897, Vol. 10.

To Robert Underwood Johnson

My dear Mr. Johnson,   Princeton, New Jersey, 12 January, 1900.

A letter received the other day from Mr. Gilder,[1] and the reference in your own recent letter to consultations about my historical matter now in your hands, have caused me a good deal of uneasiness. Instead of waiting for Mr. Gilder to return from his vacation, I think I had better write now in anticipation of a proposition from the Company.

It appears from Mr. Gilder's letter that I misunderstood him in regard to what he wanted when we had our interview here, one Sunday, in Princeton. He says in his letter: "When I asked you for just such a history it was for *book* publication" (the Italics are his). I understood him just the other way. Mr. Scott will remember that one day when I had the good luck to meet four of you at lunch in the Everett House[2] he asked me if I would be willing to make a book of the manuscript in Mr. Gilder's hands, independently of the question of its serial publication, and that I replied that I did not care to do so. He told me then, as Mr. Gilder tells me now, in his letter, that it would "hardly be suitable for serial publication." I agreed that it probably would not be: that had been my judgment from the first. I had let Mr. Gilder see it, however, in the confidence that he would know better than I what was, and was not, such material as could be made "magazinable." I am disturbed now, lest you should be giving yourselves unnecessary trouble about the formulation of propositions about making a book, when I am decidedly of the opinion that it would not be worth my while to turn aside to do that while I am in the midst of another task, from which I ought not to turn aside except to reap a very considerable and immediate advantage not to be expected to offer itself at another time. If Mr. Gilder *doubts* the availability of the stuff he has for magazine publication, I am *certain* it will not do for me to consent to its use as a serial. That, so far as I am concerned, ends the whole matter with regard to this particular manuscript. I ought, if I am wise, to let it lie in my safe until such time as I can finish it as a complete and symmetrical work.

I am the more anxious to have this understood because I have had made to me, since my experience with the American Book Company, several propositions with regard to other work, much more manageable than this which you are considering, which are so exceedingly advantageous that one or the other of them ought to be accepted. I have not felt at liberty to act without letting you know first of all exactly how I thought that the matter in negotiation between *us* ought to be settled. I have hesitated to ask what you were doing, because it seemed discourteous. But it has come to such a situation in my affairs now that I cannot refrain from asking without manifest discourtesy to you.

The new propositions to which I refer concern, not, of course, the work, or any part of the work, now in your hands, but the history I was writing for the Harpers. It has proved a matter of no little delicacy to get myself out of the hands of the American Book Company; but I now see a way out (a possible way out) of which I really ought to avail myself,—much the easiest and most comfortable escape that has offered. I hope to avail myself of it. I can then go on at once with this smaller history, taking the thread up just where I left it, with no stitches dropped, and carry out the plans I had already formed for this winter and next Autumn without interruption or embarrassment. Under such circumstances, it would be folly to increase both the work and the complications of the situation; and I ought to decline even serial publication of the other manuscript, the fragment which Mr. Gilder has been reading, should that seem worth proposing by you. The situation has changed in a manner fairly revolutionary since I sent the poor torso to your office; and I must take a clean sheet to draw my plans out on.

With warm regard,

Sincerely Yours,   Woodrow Wilson

WWTLS (Berg Coll., NN).
  [1] R. W. Gilder to WW, Dec. 24, 1899.
  [2] See WW to EAW, Nov. 21, 1899.

To Robert Bridges

Princeton, New Jersey,

My dear Gentleman of the Jury,   12 January, 1900.

Since you are a judge of the fact, if not of the law, I think you will be interested in the following recital, which I called in at your office to make, but found you out, engaged in the service of your country.

My literary history has become of late so variegated as to be fairly bewildering; but the main lines of it I can still trace with some definiteness, and you, if anybody, are entitled to have them traced for you. The latest development is, that *Harper's Magazine* has offered me twelve thousand dollars for a history of the United States in twelve parts suitable for serial publication, Mr. Alden knowing (he came to Princeton to see me the other day in the interest of the house) that the history I have actually in hand and in course of composition can easily be adapted to that purpose. He said nothing about a contract with the *Magazine* when he was here. He came merely in the general interest of the house, to dissuade me from insisting on the purchase of my "Washington," by reassuring me as to the whole situation at Franklin Square.

I went to see C. C.[1] yesterday, and asked him whether it would be *safe* to make the arrangement proposed,—whether, that is, I was likely really to get the twelve thousand,—and he thought quite decidedly that I was. The proposal seems to offer me a way to get out of my entanglements with the American Book Company through the direct offices in the matter of the Harpers themselves; and that is an additional reason why I think I ought to accept,—securing myself absolutely, of course, against the loss or transference of my copyright, either in the serial or in the book to follow.

The immense sum offered is proportioned, as you will see at once, not to my market worth, but to the determination of Harvey[2] to keep well known and rising writers at their service and on their new lists until the period of doubt about the future of the house is securely past. He must *get* as well as *keep* considerable works or else deepen the discredit of the whole undertaking to reorganize.

I have not concluded the arrangement yet, and shall not conclude it for some days, I think. For I must make all parts safe and definite. But I ought not to let an offer like this go by. I write to tell you about it first, in its initial stages, both because I tell you everything, and because I promised you to keep you posted so that Mr. Scribner might not feel that he was being cheated of any legitimate chance to get the book as a book. You will know how much of this ought to be confidential,—how much of the affairs of one firm or magazine office I ought in strict honour to communicate to another firm or magazine. Keep what is meant for you as my most intimate friend separate from what ought to be said to Mr. Scribner by way of explanation why I did not act upon his kind suggestion, through you, that he would like to serve me in my perplexity, and that he would like to consider the publication of the history under his own imprint. I really have not at any time been free to bring the matter to him with a clean sheet to write on. The Harpers seem better able to get me *out* of the hole they got me *into* than anyone else is; and they seem inclined to make it thoroughly worth my while to let them do it. It is inconceivable the little work should be of as much value to Mr. S. as it is for the present to the Franklin Square people.

With all confidence and affection,

Faithfully Yours,   Woodrow Wilson

WWTLS (Meyer Coll., DLC).
 1 Cornelius Cuyler Cuyler, Wilson's classmate and senior partner in the New York banking firm of Cuyler, Morgan & Co.
 2 George Brinton McClellan Harvey. Born Peacham, Vt., Feb. 16, 1864. Attended Peacham Academy. He began his journalistic career with small-town Vermont newspapers in 1879; served as a reporter, 1882-85, successively with the *Springfield Republican*, the *Chicago News*, and the New York *World*. He was managing editor of the New Jersey edition of the New York *World*, 1885-88, and of the Connecticut edition of the *Sunday World*, 1889-90. Managing editor of the New York *World*, 1890-93. From 1893 to 1899, he was associated with William

C. Whitney and Thomas Fortune Ryan in the development of electric streetcar lines in the New York metropolitan area. Owner and editor of the *North American Review*, 1899-1926. President of the reorganized firm of Harper and Brothers, 1899-1915. Editor of *Harper's Weekly*, 1901-13. Editor and publisher of *Harvey's Weekly*, 1918-21. Ambassador to Great Britain, 1921-23. Editor of the *Washington Post*, 1924-25. Author of several books and numerous articles; a prolific public speaker. Harvey is best known as a "President maker." He played a significant role in the renomination and election of Grover Cleveland in 1892; he was a key figure in Wilson's rise to political eminence; finally, after his break with Wilson and the Democratic party, Harvey played a prominent part in the nomination and election of Warren G. Harding in 1920. Died Aug. 20, 1928.

A News Item

[Jan. 13, 1900]

The Presbyterial Committee appointed to visit the First Presbyterian Church of Trenton fulfill their duty the coming week. The committee consists of the Rev. Drs John De Witt and G. T. Purves, ministers, and Professor Woodrow Wilson, elder.

Printed in the *Princeton Press*, Jan. 13, 1900.

From Richard Watson Gilder

My dear Professor Wilson,   New York   January 13, 1900.

I took the remaining volumes of the history off into the country with me, and greatly enjoyed reading them. It would be a thousand pities if this work, with its clear and attractive style and its broad view of the march of events in the old and new world, should not be completed in due time. Although our first idea was simply book publication, we did have the hope that this might prove usable serially, but after careful consideration it does not seem appropriate, in which case it would be doing injustice to a really noble work.

As to the book, Mr. Scott remembers clearly the conversation, and we thoroughly understand your attitude about it, namely, that your preference would be not to publish this section until the whole work is nearer completion, which, as we understand, will postpone its issue for some years. In behalf of the publishers he wishes to repeat the assurance which he gave you in conversation that The Century Co. would esteem it a great privilege to bring out this book when it is ready, and he hopes that they may have an opportunity to negotiate with you for it at the proper time.

The decision as to the serial publication has been delayed longer than we anticipated, simply, as you know, on account of my absence from the office. I have also delayed writing to you because I was in hopes that we might have a personal interview with you here in New York, in order to ascertain if there were not some other special subject that you could take up at the time you spoke of for the magazine,—preferably a historical biography. Is there one character left in American history that particularly appeals to you—if not for a great big, swinging, twelve months serial, at least for a smaller book which would run through six numbers?   Yours sincerely,   R. W. Gilder.

P.S. What would you think of a *picturesque* treatment of Webster —in half a dozen articles.

TLS (WP, DLC).

From Henry Hobart Vail

My Dear Sir: New York   13th January, 1900.

Your favor of the 18th December came duly to hand and was held on my desk from day to day in the hope that the purchase from the Harper Brothers would be concluded by a bill of sale and the transfer to us of their contracts with authors. The bargain made November 28th was evidenced only by a memorandum agreement made in duplicate and signed by both parties. Today the details of a regular bill of sale have been agreed upon and next week we may expect to see the papers. Up to the present time we have depended upon a single hasty reading of these contracts, which consumed nearly two days, and a stenographic summary of the leading features. We have not yet had in our possession the paper signed by yourself and the Messrs. Harpers and we felt that we were corresponding at a disadvantage because of a lack of precise information on our part.

Your letter of January 12th reminds me of my neglect. You are entitled to a reply even if this is necessarily an apology.

If the transfer of your contract to this house would be the cause of your giving up the writing of a brief history of the United States I should feel that this purchase had so far as this is concerned been an injury. That you should write the book is important for you and for public interest; that we should publish it may or may not be important. I am desirous to have you come to the conclusion that the book you have fully in mind is the one that was contracted for by the Harpers and conveyed by them to us, but I am more anxious to have you go forward and write it even if this should involve our full concession of rights under the contract which we certainly have purchased in good faith and paid for with our money. No officer of our Company is authorized under our By Laws to give you a free release from an existing contract without compensation, but we are far from wishing to suggest your making a monetary compensation to us.

Rest assured that we do not desire to use the contract as a means of forcing you into unwilling connection with publishers. Give us time first to learn exactly what the contract is, and second, to talk with you face to face so that we may learn what you plan to write. If after this, we can not agree to cooperate, we can certainly part in peace.

Very respectfully,   Henry H. Vail

TLS (WP, DLC).

From Adolphus William Ward

Dear Sir,   [London] Jan. 13th 1900.

Your MS. chapter on State Rights for vol. VII of the Cambridge Modern History only arrived here last night, or would of course have been acknowledged before this. We are very glad to have it, and no time will be lost in putting it forward. A proof will be sent to you in due course, with a request that you will deal with it in accordance with the enclosed circular.

We regret that there should have been delay in replying to your enquiry as to publishing this chapter in a high-class American Magazine. Lord Acton would have been glad to meet your wishes in any way possible; but such a duplicate publication would be against the practice of the C. University Press, and with a view to precedent he could not urge it in the present instance.

I am commissioned to ask whether you could give our undertaking the great advantage of further contributions to our American volume, as to the success of which we are particularly solicitous. We are desirous of including in it three chapters (9) Federalists (10) Republicans (11) Democrats, which would follow on previous chapters contributed by Mr Bigelow and bringing the narrative up to the settlement of the Federal Constitution (1789). These chapters 9, 10, 11 would immediately precede your chapter (12) on State Rights; and from what I have already read of this, I see that it would connect itself without any difficulty. Each chapter should average 15000 words, and be accompanied by a bibliography. Would you be prepared to undertake these three chapters?

We should be very glad to have these chapters by October, if this is not asking too much; but perhaps if you do us the favor of accepting our proposal, you would let me know whether this would be possible. I hope that the one attractive feature in the proposal would be to you that it would give you an opportunity of covering the whole ground in the comprehensive way which is proper to your treatment of history. Lord Acton is I know as anxious as I am for a favorable reply to this request.[1]

I remain, dear Sir,

Yours very faithfully   A. W. Ward

ALS (WP, DLC). Enc.: printed page entitled "Cambridge History."
[1] Wilson's reply is missing, but he undoubtedly said that he felt obliged to decline the invitation.

Notes for a Lecture

Freedom, in the Light of Experience.

Union League Club, Brooklyn, 13 Jan'y, 1900.

A product of *the most enlightened order* and *best all-round adjustment* between authority and individual choice attainable *under the circumstances*

BURKE: "I should suspend my congratulations on the new liberty of France, until I was informed how it had been combined with government; with public force; with the discipline and obedience of armies; with the collection of an effective and well-distributed revenue; with morality and religion; with the solidity of property; with peace and order; with civil and social manners."—*Reflections.*

Relations of Order to individual freedom,—the *institutional character of freedom.*

Freedom *not necessarily bound up in suffrage.* A "free" people is a people not subject to the arbitrary choices of rulers—*a people whose interests,* and whose individual rights *somehow get regarded with a good deal of system and without serious friction,* being made known by some adequate method of communication between rulers and subjects. The governmental action.

Idea involves (1) *Publicity,* and *freedom of opinion;*

(2) *absence of* arbitrary *economic restraints.*

(3) *Full license of concerted public agitation.*

Conditions Precedent:

(1) *A clear experimental understanding of Rights.*

(2) *Sufficient equality of conditions* to breed community of feeling.

(3) *Education and experience.*

(4) *A polity* which will breed
    (a) a habit and spirit of *civic duty*, and
    (b) *leading characters*, rather than managing talents.

13 Jan'y[1]

WWhw, WWT, and WWsh MS. (WP, DLC).
[1] Wilson's composition date.

A Newspaper Report of a Speech in Brooklyn

[Jan. 14, 1900]

LIBERTY AND ITS USES.

Dr. Woodrow Wilson of Princeton University delivered his able lecture entitled "Liberty in the Light of Experience" to a large and appreciative audience at the Union League Club last night. Dr. Wilson started out by saying that the men of the present day in their closet think as they please and please themselves. "We must square our theories with our practices," he continued. "We have been enjoying liberty. Now we are going to give others liberty. Will we give them the theory or the practice? Shall we tell them it is a spirit, or shall we tell them that it is life? If we give these people merely the theory we shall only intoxicate them.

"We must apply liberty in the Philippines in strict accordancce with the actual conditions and attitude of the people. Until we have found the best adjustment between the order which we impose and the self development which they ought to have, if that be long we must be the more patient and steadfast.

"One of the greatest luxuries a man can indulge in is thinking, but I think few people know what that indulgence is. Every man who has succeeded in thinking for himself has first learned to think the things that have been thought, so no liberty can be absolutely new. It must all have its vantage in long experience.

["]Your freedom consists of the liberty allowed you by society. The idea of freedom suggests that the government should be absolutely public, no private cliques, all open courts, always the glare and blaze of publicity. We have hitherto had a nice little home circle. We have been a fine provincial nation. It is a long way to Puerto Rico, and still further to Hawaii and the Philippines, and we can't shut ourselves up to think and do as we please. We shall have to stand criticism. We have been very genteel toward each other. We are now dealing with the world which expresses its opinions regardless of how they affect our sensibilities, and this will do us good. Let our government be open and free and I believe it will be a success in our dependencies. Pent up forces are the only ones that always cause trouble. Free forces and free thought are not in danger of doing damage.

"If we could impart liberty to the dependencies let us not impart power to those who root. If you enable the people of our dependencies to speak of us as of ourselves, they will ultimately get the self possession of experienced critics. We must have a polity in our islands led by men who will take to them not impossible ideals, but the practical, hard headed experience of the race."

Colonel W. E. Pulsifer, president of the club; Chairman William F. Fuller and members of the entertainment committee, dined Dr. Wilson after the informal reception which was held after he had concluded his address.

Printed in the Brooklyn *Daily Eagle*, Jan. 14, 1900; one editorial heading omitted.

To Richard Watson Gilder

My dear Mr. Gilder,   Princeton, New Jersey, 15 January, 1900.

Your letter, received this morning, brought me real relief. I had felt uneasy about that fragment ever since I sent it to you. I was afraid that you might want to publish it as it stood,—or, at any rate, brought done [down] to the end of the seventeenth century,— and I was afraid that, if you did, I could not in courtesy, after putting it in your hands, decline to let you do so. And yet, all the while I knew that it ought not to be published, and that I had been guilty of a weakness in letting you have it. You are the only one I have ever shown it to. I am deeply gratified that you should think it well done as far as it goes; and I am equally pleased to have my own judgment confirmed, that it ought to lie by till I can finish it. Thank you for your opinion, and for your kindness in the whole matter. It is a great blessing to deal with friends.

As for a biography, the idea is most tempting; but the temptation must be put aside for some time to come, I am sorry to say, until I am unburdened of other tasks which I feel ought to take precedence. Thank you very much. It heartens me to know that you are of the opinion that I could if I would.

Thank Mr. Scott very cordially, if you please, for his suggestion on behalf of the publishers, concerning the ultimate publication of the larger history. I do not know when I can return to it, but when I do I feel confident that there can be no more pleasant thing to do than to take it to Mr. Scott and ask him what he thinks he could do for me and it.

　With much regard,
　　Most cordially and faithfully Yrs.,　Woodrow Wilson

WWTLS (Berg Coll., NN).

To Robert Underwood Johnson

My dear Mr. Johnson,　Princeton, New Jersey, 17 January, 1900.

　I am sorry to say that my sentence about a biography (which, by the way, did refer to a biography of Webster in particular) meant that I must put the temptation behind me for an indefinite length of time. When I get through with the execution of the plans immediately ahead of me,—if I ever do finish them to my satisfaction,—I must turn first of all to the completion of the history of which Mr. Gilder has been reading a fragment. When that is finished I shall, I suspect, have reached a very mature age indeed. If I live to see a *very* ripe old age, I might enjoy crowning it with a biography; but that is beyond the range of plans. Anything that may come from my pen during the years I may reasonably hope to have, if it be not a part of plans already made, must be brief, occasional, unsystematic,—a By-product, not a "work." Does not all this sound solemn and important. Nothing like taking oneself seriously (even with a covert smile)!

　With warmest regard,
　　Cordially and Appreciatively Yours,　Woodrow Wilson

WWTLS (Berg Coll., NN).

Notes for a Religious Address[1]

Trenton, 17 Jan'y, 1900.

Proverbs, IV., 18: "*The path of the just is as the shining light, that shineth more and more unto the perfect day.*"

"*Just*" antithetical to "*wicked*" (verses 14, 19)=*righteous*, a word full of the air of *the real*, the actual, as contrasted with the *merely sentimental. But* the particular word *Just adds* the idea of *balance, clear-eyed righteousness.*

The object of the church as an organization, the *salvation of souls*,—only indirectly the *purification of Society*. That *it must effect indirectly, by example*, not by organizing vs. particular vices but by kindling a light in which no vice can live.

All vice should be *equally abhorrent to the Christian*, and he should be as active as possible in *all* reform. But *the Church should keep the* perspective, the *ideal, clear,–generating, not heat, but light.*

In matters of standard and *example, poise,* a fine *balance* and consistency of judgment,–an unsentimental *tolerance* and a capacity to feel without being unbalanced by the feeling,–*tells for more than concentrated* and passionate *attacks on particular abuses.*

Light is *still, wholesome, cleansing,*–and "shineth more and more unto the perfect day" by slow, genial diffusion. *This* light *out of heaven,*–high enough, strong enough for universal diffusion.

17 Jan'y, 1900.[2]

WWhw MS. (WP, DLC).
[1] No Princeton or Trenton newspaper carried an announcement or report of this address. Perhaps Wilson delivered it on the occasion of the visit to the First Presbyterian Church of Trenton referred to in the news item printed at Jan. 13, 1900.
[2] Wilson's composition date.

A Memorandum

[c. Jan. 20, 1900]

Interview with Mr. Vail:

Let the contract stand. They will not press me: I may write it if I can—and they would like once in a while to remind me of it and talk with me about it—but in the meantime I may write the other history, on other lines. In brief, if I write a school history they shall have it—but they will not insist that I shall write it.

WWhw memorandum in the pocket notebook described at June 18, 1899.

To Henry Mills Alden

My dear Mr. Alden,   Princeton, 22 Jan'y. 1900

I have run over the week within which I promised to try to decide the matter of writing a serial history for you for 1901; but I have not neglected the matter for a moment. I have been diligently trying, as I then said I should, to get a clean sheet to write on, so that I could feel entirely my own master. I have succeeded almost altogether, and now feel free to take the next step in the business.

I want very much to do what you ask, both because you ask it and because you make it so thoroughly worth my while; but you know, if any man does, what nervous and sensitive fellows authors are, and you will, therefore, know how entirely natural and indeed inevitable it is that I should ask the following questions.

Is it an essential part of your scheme that the serial rights should carry with them the book rights also in this case? I ask this because I had hoped to keep the two distinct in order that I might make arrangements for publication and sale of the book through agents, or at any rate in some way which would extend its sale much beyond what could be expected from ordinary advance or the usual sale of it as simply one on a general list. There is, I believe, practically only one single volume, popular history of the United States on the market, that of Ridpath,[1] which, because carried everywhere by agents, has sold up into the hundreds of thousands, in spite of its manifest crudeness and inadequacy. There is no reason, I should suppose, why a scholarly history, written in an attractive style and really handsomely illustrated, should not be given an almost equally constant and universal sale. This history of mine will run, I think, about twice the size of *Washington*. If necessary, for the sake of the illustrations, it might be sold in a two-volume illustrated edition, and also in a one-volume unillustrated edition, like the popular edition of Green's *Short History of the English People*. Agents might prefer the former, as affording a bigger commission. The latter might be sold in the ordinary way, or alternately by agents, to those who could not afford the illustrated edition.

Now I suppose the Harpers could not arrange this (or at any rate promise it definitely) in the present state of their business. And yet I should be very loath to give the idea up. It seems to me thoroughly sound and feasible, and I know that other publishers think that it is. Therefore I ask, is the book proposal contained in your letter inseparable from the proposal for the serial in the magazine.

My other questions concern both serial and book, or each separately according to our final arrangement between us. You will see at once that they seek my protection in ways which will ease my mind without in the least embarrassing or inconveniencing the house. Everything that I hear from "the street" in New York, as well as my conversation with you, convinces me that the business of the house can and will be extricated from its present embarrassment and put again upon firm footing. The men I have heard talk about it seem thoroughly interested in seeing to it, if possible. But no such transactions can be *certain* of successful outcome and I am sure that you will indulge me in this matter.

Can our agreement be so drawn as to secure me in payment for each monthly part of the serial upon the delivery of the copy therefor, according to what I know has always heretofore been your usual custom; and can the copyright of the serial and book (each or both, as the case may be) be absolutely secured to me against sale, assignment, or transfer, so that in case of any partial windup or sale of the business it cannot be transferred without my consent, and in case of any entire windup or transfer of the business the book will, in respect of copyright, absolutely revert and return to me or to my estate?

If I arrange for the book, I should like to have a clause in the contract providing that, after the expiration of seven years from the first publication, it should be within my option to buy the copyright for a sum [equal to] a capital sum of which the royalty for the seventh year would be 10 per cent. I know that this is not unusual.

You will smile when you read this; but you know I have reasons to feel anxious about transfers, etc. And as for the agreement as to payments that is your ordinary practice, or would under ordinary circumstances go as a matter of course. You know me well enough to know that such request is founded on nothing that ought in the least degree to wound anybody's sensibilities. Fortunately this is a dealing between friends and can be upon mutual undertaking of each other's characters.

As for the *Washington*, I feel that if this new agreement goes through between us, as I most earnestly hope it may, I ought to leave the book with the house. I could wish to do not only the courteous, but even the gallant thing in that matter. I very much hope, however, that the house will some day soon be in position to make a popular edition of the *Washington* (say at $1.50 list) and give it a new lease of life. It might, under the system of sale by agents,—if that can be adopted in behalf of the history,—be joined in some informal way with the history even in its present form in the canvass for the sale of the latter.

I hope that you are very well. I wish that we might some day have you out here on a visit of pleasure that had no business in it but only friendship.

With regard and appreciation,

Very sincerely Yours,   Woodrow Wilson

Transcript of WWshLS (WP, DLC).

1 John Clark Ridpath, *A Popular History of the United States of America* (Cincinnati and Philadelphia, 1876; many later editions under the same or slightly different titles).

From Harper and Brothers

Dear Dr. Wilson: [New York] Jan. 27. 1900.

Mr. Alden has referred to us your communication of the 22nd inst.

In reply, we beg leave to assure you that we shall endeavor to meet your wishes in every particular, as set forth in your letter. We propose treating your History in a similar way to Greens "History of the English People," as published by us. This work we publish in three forms: a library edition in four volumes—$2.50 a volume, with colored maps, but otherwise not illustrated, of which we have sold about 10,000 sets; an edition in four volumes, very elaborately illustrated, sold only by subscription at $20. a set, in cloth, of which we have sold about 5,000 sets; and the "Short History of the English People" in one volume, a school edition at $1.20 and a trade edition price $1.75, of which we have sold over 154,000 copies.

The subscription publishing business changes so from year to year that it is hard to tell what form of publication will be best suited for that special channel two or three years hence. At present all the best canvassers are engaged in selling large sets, and it is only the undesirable agents who could now be induced to handle a one or two volume subscription book. But the fashion may change at any time and the one volume popular edition come to the front again.

If we publish your work in serial form in the Magazine, we should most certainly have the book publication as well, and your suggestion in case of the possible sale or assignment of the book by us, can be incorporated in an agreement. Each monthly part of the serial would be paid for on delivery of copy therefor, in accordance with our usual custom. Would it be agreeable to you for us to draw up an agreement on these lines and submit it to you for consideration?

In regard to your "George Washington," we are fully in accord with your suggestion that we should bring that work out in popular form at a retail price of say, $1.50. In fact, we already had such a proposition under consideration.[1]

Very sincerely yours,   Harper & Brothers.

ALS (WP, DLC). Enc.: printed notice of voluntary dissolution of Harper and Brothers.

[1] Harper's issued a popular edition of *George Washington* later in the year.

From James Gustavus Whiteley[1]

My dear Mr. Wilson,   Baltimore Md 29 January 1900

It may be within your recollection that about two years ago I had the pleasure of calling upon you in Baltimore, through the introduction of Mr. Babcock;[2] and that we talked about the International Congress of History which had just invited me to organize a section to represent the United States.

The first meeting of the Congress at The Hague[3] was most brilliant and successful. About 17 nations were represented and the American Section was a very worthy one. It is hoped that the second reunion, in Paris in July 1900, will be even more interesting.

I am now organizing the American Committee which is to be at head of the American Section. This committee is to consist of about 8 or 10 members who are willing to give the distinction of their names, and, if possible, their advice & collaboration in the formation & controul of the American Section of the Congress. The position is chiefly honorary & there are no responsibilities attached except, of course the usual dues as a member of the Congress—that is to say 20 francs or 4 dollars.

Those who have already accepted membership on this Committee are Hon. George F. Hoar, Hon Wm. Wirt Henry, Dr Edward Eggleston, & Hon Geo Peabody Witmore. May I have the honour of adding your name?[4]

I transmit a memorandum of the French & Italian Committees. Lord Acton is, I believe, forming the English Section & Committee.

With high regard
Very Sincerely Yours   James Gustavus Whiteley

ALS (WP, DLC). Enc.: typed memorandum of the French and Italian committees.

[1] A Baltimore gentleman of leisure who described himself in *Who's Who in America* as a "writer on international law and history."

[2] The Rev. Dr. Maltbie Davenport Babcock, former pastor of the Brown Memorial Presbyterian Church in Baltimore, at this time pastor of the Brick Presbyterian Church in New York.

[3] It met September 1-3, 1898.

[4] It is not known whether Wilson accepted the appointment. His reply is missing, and the proceedings of the second Congress, which met in Paris in July 1900, do not include the memberships of the various national committees.

From Walter Hines Page

My dear Wilson: New York   January 31st, 1900

I thank you for your very kind and specific letter, and of course the information that you give shall be kept confidential.

While I should have been glad to serve you—more for the pleasure of the thing* than for the money in it—I understand your position and your decision, and I very heartily appreciate your kind attitude in the whole matter.

I am now just beginning work on my biographical scheme. For heaven's sake send me a suggestion.

Very heartily yours,   Walter H. Page

* (For we are going to make the imprint of D. P. & Co. a thing to swear by, & I wanted you in the building thereof, but—good luck & prosperity!)

TLS (WP, DLC).

A Report of an Address in Richmond, Virginia

[Feb. 2, 1900]

PROF. WILSON ON "PATRIOTISM."

An Admirable Lecture at the Academy
Last Night.

"Patriotism" was the subject on which Professor Woodrow Wilson lectured to a large audience at the Academy of Music last night.[1] It is probable that all who heard him thought "The Philosophy of Patriotism" would have more exactly indicated the character of the address.

It was an able effort and was greatly enjoyed. The lecture dealt with government and institutions and civic duties. Patriotism Mr. Wilson regards as a principle rather than a sentiment. It is a matter of love of institutions. The man who serves his country, his city, or his state or nation, is a patriot.

A very interesting portion of his address was that devoted to freedom. Americans do not govern themselves, said Mr. Wilson. They think they do. The nation consists of the rulers and the ruled. The latter think they select the former, but they don't. They are selected by a very few, and the many vote for them. The speaker said he didn't select the men for whom he voted. Frequently he didn't know them. Sometimes he didn't want to know them. He was almost prepared to say that impatience was the danger of democracy. A great reform could never be obtained in a day. A strong civic manhood was needed to keep a nation patient. Men should not allow their minds to be clouded by books when seeking to work for the good of their country. They must not allow themselves to be duped by men. Much that was valuable out of the past was to be had from books, but of the present we must learn from men.

Mr. Wilson said that when he went to look into the heart of things he read the poets. His lecture last night was evidently prepared after much poetic reading. It was a poetized version of one of his lectures on government—logical, forceful, and ringing with truths; yet there was in it a delightful vein of sentiment—a dainty touch those who are familiar with the style of Mr. Wilson were surprised to see, and pleased withal. President [Frederick William] Boatwright, of Richmond College, in introducing him spoke of the high standard Professor Wilson had set for lecturers who were to come after him when he delivered the course on government here last year.[2] The audience felt that it had not been lowered when the lecture was concluded last night.[3]

Printed in the Richmond *Dispatch*, Feb. 2, 1900.
  [1] In the Richmond Lyceum series.
  [2] News reports of these lectures are printed at Oct. 28 and 29 and Nov. 1, 2, and 3, 1898.
  [3] The Richmond *Times*, Feb. 2, 1900, had this further report:
  ". . . Dr. Wilson held the rapt attention of his audience from start to finish. The political economist was evident in the lecturer. Dr. Wilson is an exceedingly forceful speaker; he hits straight out from the shoulder, and his humor is very fine.
  " 'Nothing is so exasperating to me,' said the lecturer, 'as this talk of sectionalism, just as though we were not all one nation. Of course, we may have different interests, but we are distinctly one nation. We talk of governing ourselves; I don't govern myself. I vote, of course, but you all know the conditions under which I vote. I don't know the men for whom I vote, I don't choose the men for whom I vote, and I don't choose to know some of the men for whom I vote.'
  "Dr. Wilson, towards the close, said: 'Here is some advice that probably seems strange from a student: "Don't let yourself be clouded by books." And here is some advice natural from a student: "Don't let yourself be duped by men." If you wan't to know how little really is in books, write one yourself. If you wish to know how fallible men are, look at your next door neighbor.'
  "Dr. Woodrow Wilson will always receive a cordial greeting from the Richmond people whenever they shall have the privilege of listening to his scholarly address."

From Walter Hines Page

My dear Wilson: New York. Feb. 2, 1900.

The notion has been haunting me since I wrote to you hastily the other day that maybe I expressed so strongly my own wish that we should get your books as to leave on your mind only a feeling of my disappointment. Gad! man, you don't know how I did want 'em; and that's a fact. But that isn't the only fact, nor even the biggest one; for the most important thing is that you are content with the arrangement that you have made. That being so, all is well; for I'm not the kind of fellow to begrudge anybody anything. But I am the kind of fellow to be loyal to you through &

through, & unselfishly loyal, & to be heartily content when you have made an arrangement that pleases you. In fact if you had come to us & come with any doubt in your mind or with any reluctance, I should not have wished you to come.

My congratulations & good wishes, then; & I am as always heartily yours   W. H. P.

ALI (WP, DLC).

To Ellen Axson Wilson

My own darling,   Princeton, Sunday 4 Feb'y, 1900.

Your telegram reached me about ten this morning,[1] and eased my mind more than I realized it would. It makes me *so* happy to think of you tucked safe away from the Princeton winds, in a beautiful corner of the continent, with friends you dearly love and thoroughly enjoy,—and upon a real holiday at last, with nothing to do but have a good time. God bless you, and give you perfect health and spirits for all your pleasure!

My own journey was perfectly comfortable and uneventful. The boat on which I spent the night was convenient and comfortable. I reached Baltimore at half past eight in the morning; took a train for Washington, got the pass there, and left for home at eleven. Fifty minutes wait at Trenton, and then home at 4:35, —only four hours before you reached New Orleans! I did not make the calls I expected to make in Baltimore, but came straight through. I found I was not in the mood to *want* to make them; and felt instinctively that I would neither enjoy nor be enjoyable. I shall plan to make them on my way down to meet you.

The pain of coming home to an empty house was broken for me by the joy of finding how much all had mended. The doctor has dismissed all the children as patients,—says they need not take any more medicine; and Jessie never was sick: the syrup of figs acted as a perfect antidote and preventive. Fraülein mends slowly, very slowly, but steadily, with no setback of any kind. In short, everything is all right, and you may think of even Fraülein as practically well.

And *I* am all right now, my pet,—"perfectly all right." Of course I was blue on my journey and on first seeing the house without you,—as what man would not be upon losing the comradeship of the sweetest and most interesting woman in the world out of his life for two months. But I got my balance almost at once,—and the happiness I knew I should have has come to me in gracious abundance. It is inexpressibly sweet to know what it is all going to bring to you,–the variety, refreshment, widened friendships, and health,–the *entertainment* of spirit and body! After all, my deepest joy is in *loving* you: and that I do with a fervour, a devotion, and a delight unspeakable!

Your own   Woodrow.

You know how much love all send–and what a big portion from us all is for "Cousin" Lucy and Mary! I believe I've not *said* that Sister[2] and I are perfectly well.

ALS (WC, NjP).

  [1] The telegram is missing. Mrs. Wilson was visiting the Smith sisters in New Orleans. Wilson had accompanied her to Richmond.

  [2] Annie Wilson Howe, who had come with her daughter, Annie, to keep house for Wilson during Mrs. Wilson's absence.

From Ellen Axson Wilson

My own darling,   [New Orleans] Feb. 5, 1900

   Things in general conspired to prevent my writing yesterday so I hasten to do it early this morning, that it may if possible get off as soon as if written last night. We went to Dr. Palmer's church,[1] of course, in the morning and there was a great deal of company afterwards,–several staying to tea and remaining until quite late.

   The weather is *perfectly glorious*–it was 77° in the shade–in the house–yesterday! not in the least debilitating either. There was a delicious, soft breeze and one felt as if one could do anything,–walk any distance. The air is indescribably sweet. Today it is ten degrees cooler but still very delightful. Of course there are flowers everywhere, and I go about constantly with a bit of tea olive stuck in my bosom. That delicate fragrance,–the most perfect in the world perhaps,–constantly floating about me, seems more than anything else to give me a realizing sense that I *am* in the far south.

   Speaking of the flowers though, New Orleans has suffered in appearance,–temporarily–more than I supposed from the awful cold of last year. It has indeed robbed it for the time of most of that tropical luxuriance of vegetation which is of course its greatest charm. So that, in that respect, I have had a disappointment. Most of the great palms usually growing about every house were killed, and most of the climbing roses, thirty, forty feet high, in which the houses are usually embowered. Nearly all of these were of the fine varieties, cloth of gold &c, none of them hardy, and they were killed, roots and all. The tea olives even, which grow to the size of trees, were killed down to the roots and are now small bushes.

Your telegram[2] came at breakfast yesterday and was a great comfort. This morning comes Sister Annie's *dear* letter, which makes me very happy. The other letter forwarded was from Fraülein Bohm.[3] I think you had better write to her giving the doctor as your authority that her sister must avoid all excitement, &c. It would come better from some one on the spot than from me, away off here.

I had a very pleasant uneventful journey, was very little fatigued, thanks to dressing comfortably; indeed I slept nearly twelve hours, going to bed at eight and getting up at eight. Did you notice the young woman in black opposite me when we left Richmond? She turned out to be very nice and amusing. She was a trained nurse going to take charge of a private hospital in Greenville, S .C. Her berth was over mine. One of her funny ways was to call me "Honey" altogether. The only other acquaintance of interest that I made was the Hon. Mr. Inglis a New Jersey statesman (or politician) retired; a very handsome, stately elderly gentleman; much travelled and rather interesting, but a great egoist. *What* was he? Anybody in parti*cular!*[4]

Lucy is rather sick with a terrible cold, Mary quite well. I am *perfectly* well, and enjoying myself. I did come near having a bad time of it with home sickness the first night, but I decided it would be wiser to go to sleep instead! I fight the symptoms valiantly whenever they appear. Consequently I must avoid certain dangerous topics just now. It won't do for instance to enlarge on how much I love you,—or the children. Kiss them all over and over for me; and with a heart brimming over with love for them & above all for my darling, I am, as ever,　　Your own　　Eileen.

Dear love to Sister Annie, Stock & all. Do excuse this scrawl,— worse than the worst. I write on my knee & am out of practice in it.

ALS (WC, NjP).

　[1] The First Presbyterian Church of New Orleans, of which the Rev. Dr. Benjamin Morgan Palmer had been pastor since 1856.

　[2] It is missing.

　[3] Marie Böhm, sister of Clara Böhm.

　[4] Thomas Dunn English (1819-1902), physician, lawyer, journalist, and poet; Democratic member of the New Jersey House of Assembly from Newark, 1863-64, and of the United States House of Representatives from New Jersey, 1891-95. "He wielded a powerful and trenchant pen and had a superb command of language, which, together with his rich and varied experience out of which he drew an unending fund of reminiscence, made him a most entertaining and instructive writer." *A History of the City of Newark*[,] *New Jersey* (2 vols., New York and Chicago, 1913), II, 796.

To Ellen Axson Wilson, with Enclosure

My precious Eileen,   Princeton, Monday. 5 Feb'y, 1900.

It's fortunate, no doubt, that this is the time of year it is! Do you ask me *Why* this condescension towards the season? Because, though I am not used to being in an empty house at this or any other time of year, I *am* used, since the old Baltimore days, to being desolate in February, and in a sort of state of arrested heart action! It is equivalent to a species of hibernation; and no doubt saves my energies for subsequent use at ecstatic pressure. At any rate, I am doing very well, having a sort of grim composure and perfectly managed poise which would certainly command the admiration of any one who understood the situation. And yet I am sure Jack and Mrs. Hibben would laugh at the top of their lungs at that sentence, could they read it. For I was not exactly equable yesterday. I went around to their house, as usual, at four o'clock, to find that I was to go to Miss Ricketts' alone. Jack had yielded to his conscience (!) and they were going to attend vespers at the chapel. I went off very much disappointed, and very abusive, to spend an hour with Miss R. and the Perrys. Mrs. Cleveland was kept at home by rain and the Gilders ("the Gilders" sounds like a disease, doesn't it?). Three such good talkers left me free to say little and miss you and the Hibbens, like a sulky boy. But nobody noticed me!

Stock. began at Mrs. Duffield's[1] this morning: argal, we've not seen him since last night. I've begged him to call.

We are all doing finely. Fraülein sat up a little while to-day, and was permitted so far to depart from liquid diet as to eat an egg prepared in some wonderful way of Dr. [James Holmes] Wikoff's own. She will need a week yet; but seems sure of her health again.

Ah, darling, how we love you; and how I have to guard my tongue to keep from talking about you to everybody I meet! You fill my heart and life to overflowing. Distance seems only to intensify your influence, if that were possible. I mean to try again to tell you how much I love you,—in a day or two, but not now. Now I will tell you what lots of love we all send to the dear Smiths, who *must* be related to us somehow. If you would only look a little mature, we would adopt them.

With overflowing heart,   Your own   Woodrow

ALS (WC, NjP).

[1] Stockton Axson, who had an apartment at 10 Nassau St. and had been taking his meals with the Wilsons since coming to Princeton in September 1899, had just begun to board with Margaret Cecil Wall (Mrs. John Fletcher) Duffield, of 45 Nassau St.

From Burton Norvell Harrison[1]

Of course I had to decline; but the letter will please you.[2]

My dear Sir: New York, February 3, 1900.

I am instructed by the New York Southern Society, to invite you, as I now do, to be the guest of the Society at the Society's Annual Dinner to be given here on the 22nd inst.—and to request you then to deliver the oration on "George Washington," which is always the chief event of that occasion and is given most honorable precedence in the order of proceedings.

His Excellency the Japanese Minister[3] has graciously informed us that he will be present with us this time, and will have something to say to us with regard to the relations of his Country to ours. For courtesy's sake, he will be asked to be the first to address us; but he will be brief. Your oration will come next; and, after you, there will be certainly one other, perhaps two, to speak—one of them (if there be more than one) will be Hon. John Barrett, who was recently U. S. Minister to Siam, and who will talk about matters in what used to be the ultimate East but is now our far away Western frontier.

We do not presume to ask you to tax yourself to speak to us for more than (say) three quarters of an hour,—though we should be charmed to hear you much longer if time allowed, and if you could consent to go farther with us on so attractive a subject.

There will be about one hundred and fifty gentlemen at table— all Southern men—and among them many personal friends of yours—who will give you a cordial welcome and will be most responsive to your eloquent and delightful discussion of the greatest of our National Heroes. If you will permit me to say so, we are all of the opinion that there is nobody who writes or speaks as charmingly as you do of the days our Hero lived in, or of him or his associates; nobody who paints pictures in an atmosphere so true to Colonial or Revolutionary times or the early days of our Constitution; nobody whose studies and whose perfect literary style for such themes so qualify him to reproduce for our enlightenment and delectation the real George Washington. On him as a topic, you, best of all men, can hang a scholarly and luminous discourse about anything and everything you think useful and timely for Americans who are sympathetic with you.

Last year, George Washington was done for us by Mr. Yeomans,[4] of Columbia, South Carolina,—and admirably well done, in an oration characterized by true eloquence of the older Southern rhetoric. It was charming; but it left much for you to say to us, from your own point of view, and in your own delightful and cultured style. And, having chanced to hear you deliver an address two years ago, before an Historical Society here,[5]—when you uttered yourself about (1) foreigners who establish themselves here, get control of newspapers and lecture us in editorials every day as to what should be American opinions and the conduct of American Government, and (2) people who assume to be statesmen but, not content to go along with public opinion, must lead the people, carrying an academic banner so far to the front that, on election day they have fewer supporters than they counted on,—and when E. L. Godkin and Seth Low came up to you, afterwards, to show in their faces that they had taken you very much to heart,—having had that experience of you as a speaker, I say, I, for one, am sure your oration to us, now, will have in it much for us all to enjoy and to remember.

Your presence will do us great honor, and we sincerely hope there will be nothing to prevent your acceptance of our invitation.

Most respectfully yours,   Burton N. Harrison
Chairman Committee

TLS (WP, DLC).

1 New York lawyer, former private secretary to Jefferson Davis.

2 Wilson's note.

3 Jutaro Komura (1855-1911), Minister to the United States since 1898. He served as the Japanese Minister of Foreign Affairs, 1901-1906 and 1908-11.

4 LeRoy F. Youmans, former Attorney General of South Carolina.

5 He was probably referring to Wilson's address to the City History Club of New York on December 10, 1897, a report of which is printed at Dec. 11, 1897, Vol. 10.

From Ellen Axson Wilson

My own darling,   New Orleans, Tuesday [Feb. 6, 1900]

Lucy & Mary have gone to a funeral and I will seize the opportunity for a chat with you. It is a Catholic funeral at the home of the dressmaker they are so fond of, & they are very much distressed about it. Her sister, a pretty young thing not long married, has died in childbirth. Lucy's parting remark however was characteristic; she hoped there would be a funeral at the cathedral while I was here so that I could see it, "because the Catholic funerals are so very trying, so heartless!"

It is pouring rain and has been all day. We have had a cosy day sitting over the blazing soft coal fire, sewing and reading "Isabel Carnaby" a most amusing book, at least as far as we have gone. Then Dr. Palmer called on me and stayed perhaps two

hours. He was *lovely*,—so tender and affectionate, and so interesting. His talk consisted chiefly of reminiscences of his own and
my grandfather's younger days. When I saw him after church
Sunday he said he would call yesterday, but he didn't come—said
it being the first Monday in the month there were a number of
society meetings to attend; had meant to call during the hour
before dinner, but a man who was invited to dinner came an hour
too soon! The consequence was that we waited in vain for him
here all day, greatly to the vexation of the girls, for it was a perfect day and of course they had had some excursion planned. I
however was sufficiently entertained by merely breathing the
delicious air and loafing about the garden. We took several short
walks in the neighborhood[1] which is new & rather uninteresting,
fine broad streets with handsome trees, but ugly houses, though
many of them are expensive. Dr. Palmer lives about four blocks
away[2] practically on this street; it makes a bend near here and
beyond the bend is called "Palmer Avenue,"—they say much to
his disgust. That part of the street is really very handsome. Here
and there among the modern house[s] one comes upon one that
is really interesting,—old and beautiful and *spreading*,—in its own
noble grove of oaks and magnolias. These of course were country
houses before the city spread about them.

Tulane University is very near here,—that is the academic part,
the law and medical schools are down town. There are three or
four fine buildings, the main one very handsome of hewn stone,
the others of light pressed brick.

Several of the intimate friends of the girls called yesterday and
were all charming; "Phoebe Raymond"—most familiar of names![3]
—took luncheon with us. She is a very bright woman with a pretty,
expressive, dark face, and much charm and humour. She is thin
and worn, but was evidently beautiful not many years ago. Then
there was Cara Patterson[4] who is still a beauty. She is the one
they want to bestow upon Stockton. She looks like Carrie Henry
but with very much more animation and variety of expression.
She is evidently not wanting in spirit though her beauty is of the
exquisite, pure, lily-like type. There came with her an extremely
amusing person, Miss Augustine Lejeune (called Tiny for short)
from Pointe Coupée Parish. She and Lucy kept us laughing for
half an hour with their nonsense over some northern company
which is to provide every woman with a *silk petticoat* for *twenty
cents*; yet the company is to get five dollars for each petticoat!
This glorious result is to be achieved by some modification of the
"endless chain" system quite beyond my poor comprehension. All

of these women have gone into it for the fun of it, and Miss Lejeune brought the thrilling information that one of the petticoats had actually materialized. Some of the older sisters in Israel it seems are much scandalized, consider it a temptation of the devil and a renascence of the lottery, notwithstanding the fact that *all* women are to be provided with silk petticoats without distinction as to race, colour or previous condition of servitude.

Well, I must close,—not however without mentioning the most charming visitor of all,—a *baby*! *Ah-h-h*! *such* a baby! The most gloriously beautiful baby I ever imagined. She had eyes like those of the little Italian head in our dining-room, solemn, unfathomable, magnificent,—in fact she resembled that head at all points but was much more beautiful. Her name was Margaret & she was only fourteen months old. I consider it an epoch in my life to have seen her (!)

Goodbye dear, *dear, dear* love; with what impatience I am waiting for my first letter you can perhaps imagine.

Dear love to each and all by name

Your *devoted* little wife   Eileen.

ALS (WC, NjP).
¹ The Smith sisters lived at 1468 Clay Ave.
² At 1718 Palmer Ave.
³ Presumably the stage name of some actress well known to the Wilsons and totally mysterious to the Editors.
⁴ Of the many persons whom Mrs. Wilson met on this visit, only those of special significance will be identified if it is possible to do so.

To Ellen Axson Wilson

My precious darling,   Princeton, Tuesday 6 Feb'y, 1900.

I am expecting to-morrow to bring me a letter. I am afraid my first to you will not reach you till then; but after to-morrow all days ought to be letter days (*red* letter days!) with us both,—tho. I'm afraid even you will have to skip Sundays: for who will go to the Post Office for you?

Stock. came back at lunch time to ask us to let him use a ward in our hospital. He has an unusually heavy attack of tonsilitis, and, very sanely, did not want to stay alone at his rooms. We put him to bed in the red room, got the doctor for him (who does not speak of more than "a day or two" of confinement for him), and he is now snug and cheerful enough. Of course we have kept the children away from him. They are perfectly well. *All* of them (I mean all of *ours*) went to school to-day. I kept Margaret at home yesterday because the wind was blowing great guns and she still coughed a little. Now she seems as solid as ever. Jessie has been the *immune* this time! Fraülein Clara sits up every day now for a little while; and is well and cheerful, though weak. Sister and I keep on our way unhurt. She has caught a little cold; but I have not condescended to do even that much by way of concession to the general weakness.

I've got to work on the history; but I've gone back for a running start. The last chapter I wrote (IV. The Approach of Revolution) is really, architecturally, part of the one next to be written (V. The War for Independence); upon its right tone and conception, and even detail, depend the ease and success of No. V.; and, as some of my recent reading has led to a considerable change of perspective in my thought about things of which it treats, I am now reconstructing it,—and taking a great deal of pleasure in the process. The knowledge that I have now time to be leisurely and thorough makes the whole process easy, unanxious. I began yesterday, and could make a good deal of progress at once if only the dinner of the Scots-Irish did not demand a speech of me for Thursday night.[1]

Tell Miss Lucy and Miss Mary that when I tell people that you are in New Orleans with them, they invariably exclaim with great heartiness, "Oh, how delightful that must be!" So say I. I cannot *envy you* anything delightful, but I can wish with all my heart that I could have what would not diminish your share. We *all* send them lots of love. As for you, my Eileen, you are loved by everybody and worshipped by   Your own   Woodrow

ALS (WC, NjP).
[1] Wilson was scheduled to speak to the Scotch-Irish Society in Philadelphia on February 8. His notes for an address entitled "The Scots-Irishman as an American," dated Feb. 8, 1900, are in WP, DLC. The illness of Stockton Axson prevented Wilson from fulfilling this engagement.

To Walter Hines Page

My dear Page,   Princeton, New Jersey, 6 February, 1900.

I was away last week for several days, and returned to my desk late on Saturday to read your two letters together. It was like you to write the second, frank and generous; but I saw nothing out of the way in the first. I should have been mightily chagrined if you had *not* expressed disappointment. But what I want you to realize is, that I too was disappointed because I could not see my way to a connection with men I so thoroughly believe in and like as the men of your new firm,—yourself, I need hardly say, in particular. If I followed what seemed to be my pecuniary interest, I turned my back on the course of my preference.

I thank you with all my heart for your cordial words of friendship. You must know how heartily they are reciprocated.

As ever,   Faithfully Yours,   Woodrow Wilson

WWTLS (W. H. Page Papers, MH).

From Ellen Axson Wilson

My own darling,   New Orleans, Wed. [Feb. 7, 1900]

We have had almost a day of sightseeing, starting early and taking our luncheon down town. I have been lying down to rest, and now I write a hurried letter before dressing for their early dinner—half past five.

We have seen the French quarter, and the French market, and the French cathedral, and the Place aux Dames where they beheaded pirates and traitors, and the old Spanish Government buildings, and the octoroon ball-room, now a negro convent, and several curio shops and other things too numerous to mention. It was all immensely interesting and picturesque—and dirty! It would perhaps have been a little wiser to have waited for sunshine and dry land to appear again. After yesterday's rain the streets—including the sidewalks—were rivers of liquid mud. Yet I enjoyed it all thoroughly; perhaps the old courtyards were the most interesting, and paintable features of all, the fine iron work of the galleries the most beautiful.

But I havn't time now for description. The sun came out on our way home; the weather is beautiful again and very warm. We rode home up Charles St. the finest residence street, and it is *very* beautiful.

With love inexpressible for my *darling*, my Woodrow, and for all the rest.   Your own   Eileen.

ALS (WC, NjP).

To Ellen Axson Wilson

My precious darling,   Princeton, Wednesday 7 Feb'y, 1900.

Your first letter gladdened my heart this afternoon. It was *so* sweet to see the dear handwriting again, and read my pet's interesting account of her journey and first impressions of New Orleans. It seems almost like thinking of you *at home* to know that you are with the dear Smiths. And what a perfect symbol of *you* it is to think of your going about all day 'with a bit of tea olive stuck in your bosom,'—the most delicate and most perfect fragrance in the world,—like the fragrance of your own sweet nature, my ideal little wife and woman! I instinctively think of you as a flower, and of your character as a sort of atmosphere and fragrance that surrounds you and enters into the very heart of all who approach you.

Poor Stock. has had to go through the whole bill again. His attack of tonsilitis passed last night into an attack of pain,—more savage and longer than usual. All day he has been prostrated; but he is of course coming around all right now. It must, I think, have originated in cold. I am *so* thankful he had the discretion to come here to be taken care of. It's a good sign for the future. The rest of us are *in statu quo*.

There is absolutely no news. That we love you and miss you infinitely is certainly no news. And yet it is that which fills my mind and heart all day, till everything seems to *sing* of you away in the sunny South in the midst of flowers and a soft, sweet air,—gone to meet Spring, and maybe bring it home with you. We all send love to overflowing to the dear friends,—and to you, who can say what messages of devotion, loyalty, and longing? To love you is the whole nature and passion of

Your own   Woodrow

ALS (WC, NjP).

From Ellen Axson Wilson

My own darling,   New Orleans Thursday [Feb. 8, 1900]

Your first letter came yesterday just after I finished writing mine, the second has just been received this morning. Oh my *darling*! how I *want* you! *Why* should people who love each other *ever* be separated when they aren't obliged to be! I was deeply touched that you had not the heart to go to see your Balt. friends,—and so sorry. It would surely have brightened you up if you had gone.

Mrs. Blake took dinner here last night and was delightful. She is handsomer than ever, there are apparently no more lines in her face and the white hair adds still greater distinction to the fine, clear-cut lines of the face. She is fit to be a duchess—a French duchess of the "ancien régime" for she associates so much with the Creoles that she is very much like them in many ways. She was telling Lucy last night with the greatest indignation how the young Creoles decline to talk French—Lucy responding with deep sympathy and equal indignation. "Why Madame ——'s grandchildren were actually addressing *her* in Eng. the other day when I was there, I asked her how she *endured* it"; then Madame's answer is given at length in French with many shrugs and gestures expressive of profound despair. "I told her *I* would help it, I'd spank them all soundly. And there's Angelique Lefleur,—she's a *perfect terror*—won't speak a word of French!" Just there she broke off abruptly because she suddenly discovered that "Mrs. Wilson and Lucy were laughing at her," laughing herself very good-naturedly though.

Our other visitors since I last wrote have been the three Palmer ladies[1] and Prof Woodward & his wife of the Sophie Newcombe,[2] all very agreeable. The night before last the girls['] two artist friends were here. I am informed that they are both "in ecstasies" over *me*, and one of them—the one that can't paint,—wants to paint me. She is "Eliza Leovy," Mrs. Hall, the whimsical, egotistical but brilliant friend of whom Lucy talks so much. Tell Sister Annie she is very enthusiastic over her. They boarded at the same house in Sewanee & Mrs. Hall has a summer home there now. The other artist friend is Miss Shirer the remarkable girl who established the pottery here which does such *beautiful* [work] in underglaze decoration. We are just starting now on a visit to her works, and I am scribbling in haste to get my letter off before we go.

I *am* so thankful for all the good news from home—and I *love* you all, ah *how* I love you! Always and altogether

Your own   Eileen.

ALS (WC, NjP).
  [1] They were Dr. Palmer's daughter, Mary Howe Palmer (Mrs. John Williamson) Caldwell, and his granddaughters, Fannie Caldwell and Augusta Colcock. John Williamson Caldwell, M.D., was Professor of Chemistry and Geology at Tulane University, and Fannie was his daughter. Augusta Colcock, daughter of the late Augusta Palmer (Mrs. D. D.) Colcock, was reared by her grandfather.
  [2] Ellsworth Woodward, Professor of Drawing and Painting at H. Sophie Newcomb College of Tulane University, and his wife, Mary Johnson Woodward.

To Ellen Axson Wilson

My own darling,   Princeton, *Thursday* 8 Feb'y, 1900

I have a great piece of good news for you, which I know will rejoice you when you are over the surprise. Stock. was successfully operated on to-day for apendicitis,[1]—*most* successfully,—so that there is absolutely *no* ground for alarm of any kind, but only ground for rejoicing. Here is the whole story. The attack I have already twice told you about stuck to him, instead of passing off as usual, and, instead of being diffused, centred more and more at the apendix, with alarming acuteness,—with most distressing acuteness. Dr. Wikoff watched and studied him with admirable care and attention; and when he found, this morning, that Stock. had had another night of unbroken suffering and distress, which three injections of morphine had failed to quiet, he said, "We must have a surgeon," and see what he thinks. We *telephoned* at once to New York and got Dr. Weir.[2] He advised an operation. Stock. had grown decidedly easier during the day; but Dr. Weir thought it unwise to trust to that indication; and Stock. consented to the operation. He was in *almost* as good a condition for it, the Dr. thought (i.e. with the *de*creasing inflamation) as if he were well; and there was no telling what trick the treacherous thing *might* play. The event justified him. He found that the thing was taken *exactly* in time: that an inflamation of neighbouring parts (peritonitis) had begun, which in twelve hours might have rendered an operation impossible. So the thing was both wise *and* successful. Not a thing went wrong. The Dr. was perfectly satisfied with every step,—and confidently expects a rapid recovery. Only two cases out of a hundred go wrong anyway, by actual statistics, under such circumstances. To-night there is a trained nurse in charge; and we are tired out, but jubillant. This is the *whole* and *precise* story of the matter, as well as a sleepy man can tell it at bed-time. Jessie and Nellie spent half the day and are spending the night at the Hibben's. Margaret and Annie went to Mrs. Magie's during the commotion—and are now snugly asleep, as I hope to be in a few minutes. If you have received no telegram before you receive this you may know that everything has continued to go perfectly as it should; and may await further letters with absolute equanimity. We are all *so* glad that you are in New Orleans; will never forgive you if in the face of this absolutely full and candid recital—nothing slurred, nothing withheld,—you try to come back. That would be *too* foolish. The muscles were separated, not cut; and the Dr. virtually promised that Stock should be out within a week or ten days,—at any rate out of bed,—say six days after you read this. I *trust* you not to distress me by doing a wholly unreasonable and Quixottic thing. And oh, *how* I love you and trust you!

We are all perfectly well—Fraülein continuously better; *all* send unspeakable love;—and *I* am in every breath

Your own   Woodrow

ALS (WC, NjP).

¹ Princeton had no hospital until 1919, and the operation took place in the Wilson home.

² Robert Fulton Weir, M.D., Professor of Surgery at the College of Physicians and Surgeons of Columbia University.

From Ellen Axson Wilson

My own darling,   New Orleans, Friday, [Feb. 9, 1900]

Breakfast is just over and I shall try to write at once today before the many interruptions begin. We have had a cold change, alas! but it is not so very bad yet—45°—tonight the paper threatens a freeze. Just now I fancy it is very pleasant out of doors. We go to a reception in the French quarter this afternoon and to dinner at the Palmers at six. Among my new acquaintances since yesterday morning are Mrs. Bruns, wife of the famous doctor,¹ who called yesterday afternoon,—a pretty, rather flighty Virginian, a great friend of Miss Boxie Scott. Her father, Gen [Thomas Muldrup] Logan, was the youngest general in the Confederate army, being only twenty-two when the war ended; and he had been a general two years.

We had a very interesting time yesterday at the potteries, saw quantities of really beautiful things,—beautiful in shape, in colour and in decoration. They do it all, from the turning of the clay up; and you know it is all a development from the art department of the Woman's College, the Sophie Newcombe. They seem to be making an enviable reputation,—have cabinets of fine pieces sent them in exchange for theirs from famous potteries all about the world. One would think the Sophie Newcombe were an art school instead of a college proper; beside the potteries, they have a large handsome stone building devoted entirely to art, and six or eight art teachers—*very* good ones,—and they are doing excellent work all along the line. The feeling and taste for art must be exceptionally strong here. The grounds of the college are *most beautiful*. I have never seen finer live oaks; a great magnificent grove of them. The college had the good fortune to secure one of the finest of the old places. The house was so large and nobly proportioned that they had only to raise the roof and its massive stone coping and put on another story, to make it entirely suitable for the main college building. It is somewhat in the style of the University of Va. buildings—noble Greek stairways, spreading balustrades &c. They have also a beautiful chapel with three lovely great Tiffany windows. I have met the president and his wife,—fine people;² Mr. Dixon is also a professor at Tulane.

But it is time for me to stop. I am sorry Fraülein is getting on so slowly. I hope all this won't injure her prospects for next year at the school.³ It is certainly *too* bad that Stock had to leave! It will add to your lonliness. Perhaps you will go to see the two VanDykes at last!

Kiss the children for me over and over and over! Ah, if I could *only* do it for myself! You don't know how I love all you dear people. As for you I love you to distraction. I love you so much that it renders me wretchedly happy and blissfully miserable. I am already counting the days until my return and finding my greatest delight in imagining that time. Yet I *am* having a thoroughly "good time" here. As ever   Your own   Eileen.

ALS (WC, NjP).
  ¹ Dr. Henry Dickson Bruns and Katharine Logan Bruns.
  ² Brandt Van Blarcom Dixon and Eliza Carson Dixon.
  ³ Mrs. Scott's school in the old Evelyn College.

To Ellen Axson Wilson

My own darling,   Princeton, Friday 9 Feb'y, 1900.

Everything is all right. "He is doing as well as *any* one *ever* does after an operation," says even his pessimistic eminence Herr Doctor Wikoff. He is suffering chiefly from *intense* nervousness due to the after effects of the ether and the strain of lying always absolutely still on his back, bound as if in a vyse by the bandages. The first twenty-four hours have passed and *nothing*, absolutely nothing, has gone amiss. Dear sister Annie and I both had *all* night furloughs from duty or responsibility, by reason of the presence of the nurse, and to-day feel "quite fit," as the English say. The children are perfectly well; went to school to-day in normal fashion; and are bearing themselves like ideal persons. Could you wish for a better record than that? You may not like it, ma'am, but we are all so glad *you* are not here,—Stockton in particular. He says that that is one of the first things he thought of. There will be a great many details to tell you when you come back; but absolutely not one that will alter so much as the shading of what I have told you. Friends have turned up by the shoals and have been as good as gold,—chief among them, of course, the Hibbens and the Ricketts;—and yet it is hard to tell who *has* been chief; and our hearts are quite full because of it all. There is nothing else to tell you about,—except that dear sister and I are *not* worn out,—on the contrary well and chipper,—and what strain there is will be less every day.

I seem, alas, to have missed one of your letters,—that of Mon-

day. Tuesday's came to-day (bless your heart for it!) came to-day
[*sic*]; but none came yesterday. Did you give it to some one of
the beaux to mail, and did he forget it? This of Tuesday consoles
me for everything *but* the loss of *another* from you,—so redolent
is it from end to end with the sweet personality that fills all my
life with an endless, unspeakable charm. You *must* have *style*, my
love! I [It] can't be *all* my imagination and my loving knowledge
of you that makes your letters seem to me so to carry and contain your charm,—and that in generous measure, and not by mere
snatches! Ah, *how* I love you, *how* I love to think of myself as
living *for* you! Stock. and all of us unite in deepest love, and wish
to include the Smiths in as much as they will accept. *I* rejoice and
rejoice in being   Your own   Woodrow

ALS (WC, NjP).

From Ellen Axson Wilson

My own darling,   New Orleans, Saturday [Feb. 10, 1900]

Your letter of Tuesday, with those from Mr. Page[1] came yesterday afternoon. Am *very* sorry that poor Stockton is ill again
but relieved that he is safe in the house so that he can be well
taken care of. Please give him my special love and sympathy.

I am delighted to know that you are well into the history again
and working with ease and pleasure. The Scotch-Irish interruption is a *great* pity.

I had a *very* pleasant time at the Palmers last night; they are
a lovely family and have a delightful home. It is a handsome
house inside with very large rooms, wide halls, and high ceilings,
—massive furniture too, yet it all looks, and is, exceedingly comfortable and home-like. Tell Sister Annie I now fully appreciate
the virtues of the "hall stove" and "drum." It is destined to be the
salvation of the South! The Palmer house felt everywhere as if
heated by a furnace.

The weather is extremely bad just now, though it did not freeze
last night; it is raining in torrents instead and has done so all
night. If the weather permits we are to go to a "buffet luncheon"
at a Creole house today, and to a meeting of the "Duarante Club"[2]
in the afternoon, but I do not think we will get out. The weather
also prevented our attending the reception yesterday afternoon;
it was in the French quarter at the house of Mrs. Davis,[3] a
literary light, (her stories in the "Harper," Atlantic &c. are well
known). She is said to be *most* fascinating, and has a sort of

"salon." We are invited for any and every Friday, so we will try again next week.

The weather was fairly good yesterday morning and we had a delightful time at Audubon Park (where there are perfectly grand live oaks,) and especially in the Horticultural Hall which is in the Park and has been preserved from the time of the exposition.[4] It is extremely large and is inside a perfect dream of tropical lovliness.

But I *must* stop because of cold fingers. I am so thankful that you are all well darling. I am *perfectly* well & have been from the first. I love you, dear, tenderly, passionately, and am al-together,   Your own   Eileen.

ALS (WC, NjP).
    [1] W. H. Page to WW, Jan. 31 and Feb. 2, 1900.
    [2] Not listed in the New Orleans city directory for 1900.
    [3] Mary Evelyn Moore (Mrs. Thomas Edward) Davis.
    [4] The World's Industrial and Cotton Centennial Exposition held in New Orleans, December 16, 1884-May 31, 1885.

To Ellen Axson Wilson

My own darling,   Princeton, Saturday 10 Feb'y, 1900.

Still everything goes well,—perfectly well. Stock. called me to his bedside this morning to say that he 'was afraid he would have to trouble me to write to some of his girls,' (whose addresses he gave me from memory). They might hear indirectly of the operation and be alarmed. I might say to Miss Margaret Repplier and Miss Amy Otis, of Philadelphia, simply that he had been operated on and was all right; but it would no doubt be best to go somewhat into detail with Miss Emily Seaman, of Brooklyn. It would be best to tell her that he was here, at the house, and not at his rooms; that a trained nurse was in charge of him; and that *every*thing was going all right,—"for she is a very nervous, exciteable girl, and there's no telling what she might do. She wanted to come and nurse me once when I was ill in Brooklyn, and—there's no telling what she might do now!" You may be sure I wrote Miss Emily a very explicit, reassuring, soothing letter indeed, with my best tact! I wrote also, of course, to Madge[1] and Ed.[2] It's *such* comfort, now that its over. And it *is* over. Mrs. Daniels says that during her four years at the hospital she had more typhoid and appendicitis cases than any other sorts; and that in the appendicitis cases the first twenty-four hours were a perfect index of all. Here we have had forty-eight with steady, unbroken, unclouded progress,—without a flaw. Stock. grows more comfortable with every hour. By the way,—as an item of the warm friendship about us,—it looked, because of delayed trains,—as if the regular nurse, summoned from Philadelphia, were not going to get here Thursday night: her train was an hour late; and Mrs. Daniels was on her way here to take charge for the night when she was met and told that the nurse had arrived. They say she looked genuinely disappointed! Stock. seemed both deeply touched and very much relieved when told about it.

Sister and I are on duty,—and very mild duty it is,—from about eleven to four, while the nurse is resting, and have the nights absolutely undisturbed. After to-night the nurse herself can sleep most of the night on the cot in Stock's room (the red room, of course) and so can stay on duty for twenty-four hours,—except for a little time for exercise.

And now for a moment of love making. I am so tickled that you are away and that I had sense enough *not* to telegraph the news to you! It enables me, now that my mind is at ease, to love you with so much *happiness*,—as well as with the whole passion of my soul. There is such *satisfaction* in being

Your own Woodrow

All perfectly well. Love from all to all.

ALS (WC, NjP).
    [1] Margaret Randolph Axson, a student at the Woman's College of Baltimore (now Goucher College).
    [2] Edward William Axson, who was now working for the Buffalo Mining Co. in Mannie, Tenn.

An Announcement

[Feb. 10, 1900]

UNIVERSITY BULLETIN.

Sunday, Feb. 10th [11th].

. . . In the Second Presbyterian Church, Christian Endeavor Day will be observed by exercises held in the lecture room at 6:40 p.m. Professor Woodrow Wilson will make the address of the evening.[1] All are invited to be present.

Printed in the *Daily Princetonian*, Feb. 10, 1900.
    [1] No newspaper carried a report of this talk; however, for it Wilson used the notes printed at April 25, 1897, Vol. 10.

From Ellen Axson Wilson

My own darling,   New Orleans, Sunday [Feb. 11, 1900]

Your Wednesday's letter bringing the sad news of poor Stockton's severe attack came yesterday; today I must, as you supposed, do without my letter, for there is no delivery.

I am as much without "news" this time as you, for it is still raining steadily as it has done for forty-eight hours. I did not get out yesterday, though Lucy managed to go to the Creole luncheon. Mary and I had a cosy time reading and embroidering by the fire; Mary has "stubbed" her toe badly,—almost knocked the tip off of it jumping up hastily and running in her bare feet to unlock a door for the maid. So she is a prisoner at present. Lucy and I went to Dr. Mallard's church[1] this morning, in spite of the rain, and heard a very good sermon. I felt obliged to go once because he is an old friend of our family and a Liberty Co. [Georgia] man. But I did begrudge missing one of Cousin Ben's[2] sermons.

We have just had dinner—a delicious one,—the girls are certainly good house-keepers,—and I have come up to write to you, (and to Miss Butts to tell her to let my great-grandmother rest in peace!) after which, being very sleepy, I shall perhaps take a little nap by way of preparation for the Kentuckians,[3] who overrun the house every Sunday night, assist in cooking supper, and rob us all of our beauty-sleep.

Speaking of Kentucky I wonder what you and the "Times" think about the situation there. How I have wished all the week for New York papers. Judging from what I read I should think Taylor as dead, politically, as Goebel,—and a happy riddance too,—when the remains can be got decently out of sight.[4] His conduct since the murder seems a succession of blunders and follies. All of our young Kentuckians here are violent anti-Goebel democrats, and take his murder in a matter of course way that is truly startling,—they say it was expected by everybody; and they don't seem to *feel* the disgrace of their State! That is to me one of the saddest things about it all, for they are themselves all honorable, sober, intelligent young men! It seems to indicate a frightful state of public opinion. They were really in a sort of glee over Goebel's death! Col. Sanford,[5] the very prominent citizen, whom Goeble shot some time ago—that circumstance being the beginning of the anti-Goebel faction,—was the uncle of one of them and a near relative of the girls. Lucy had told me that he was shot down in cold blood,—shot in the back. But on repeating that version Sunday night the nephew, young Breckenridge, corrected her like the honest man that he is. "Oh no," he said. "They were shooting at each other, Uncle John just wasn't quick enough!" Did you see that Goebel wore a coat of mail, and the shot that was powerful enough to penetrate it was from a kind of "weapon" (!) issued by the government and not to be bought?

I should like, dear, to write about something *very* far removed from political quarrels today, but I simply don't dare do it to any extent. It is hard not to be home-sick in this dreary weather. I should rather enjoy a wee bit of a cry, but that would be very selfish when the girls do so much to make me have a pleasant time. But oh, I do *want* my own darlings!—and above all my love, my Woodrow, my heart's delight. But no more of this. With all my heart and soul,   Your own   Eileen.

I am *perfectly* comfortable here all the time; the weather though raw & chill of course, is not cold now, & I have a nice soft coal fire in my room night and morning & all day when I wish. I am *quite* well.

ALS (WC, NjP).
¹ The Rev. Robert Quarterman Mallard, pastor of the Napoleon Avenue Presbyterian Church of New Orleans, of which the Smith sisters were members.
² Dr. Palmer. Mrs. Wilson's relationship to him is explained in EAW to WW, May 1, 1885, n. 1, Vol. 4.
³ Numerous relatives of the Smith sisters from Kentucky.
⁴ Kentucky Democratic State Senator William Goebel lost the gubernatorial election in November 1899 to his Republican opponent, William S. Taylor. Goebel, a silver Democrat, was defeated by a combination of Republicans, gold Democrats, and Populists. The election was disputed, with both sides charging widespread corruption.
The issue was seemingly resolved when a state election board, created in 1898 at the instance of Goebel himself, declared that Taylor had won the election by a narrow margin, and when Taylor was inaugurated on December 12, 1899. However, the Goebel partisans decided to appeal to the Democratic-controlled state legislature. Politics in the state had long been inflamed by both local and national issues, and the election dispute brought hordes of armed men to Frankfort. On January 30, 1900, Goebel was shot in the capitol yard by an unknown rifleman. The legislative committee to decide the election immediately declared Goebel elected as Governor; he took the oath of office but died on February 3. His running mate, John C. W. Beckham, succeeded him as the Democratic claimant to the governorship, the Democrats retired to Louisville, and for a time the state had two rival administrations. Ultimately, the state and federal courts decided the case in Beckham's favor.
The "Goebel affair" was, in the words of the state's most eminent historian, "the most disturbing episode in Kentucky's political history." It was to lead to many years of bitter partisan strife. See Thomas D. Clark, *A History of Kentucky* (New York, 1937), pp. 605-17, and the same author's *Kentucky: Land of Contrast* (New York, 1968), pp. 202-205.
⁵ Goebel in 1895 had killed John Sanford, a Confederate veteran, in a gun duel on the steps of the First National Bank of Covington, Ky.

To Ellen Axson Wilson

My own darling,   Princeton, Sunday 11 Feb'y, 1900

Do you remember that passage in Stevenson's *Letters*: "I vote for separations; F.'s arrival here, after our separation, was better fun for me than being married was by far. A separation completed is a most valuable property; worth piles."[1] Ah, that's it, "a separation *completed*,"—and when *this* one is completed it will be "a most valuable property" indeed! I shall have such a sense of having a little *served* my sweet one! Here we are in the fourth day of Stockton's recovery without a set-back of any sort; and that charming young person his sister just now learning that he is safe along the road to fine recovery,—saved all the dread and given only that part of the news that carries relief! After all, it's the one who stays at home and serves who has the best of it,—whether a crisis comes from which the other is shielded or not; for every day there is *some*thing, though it be never so little, which the one at home can do *instead* of the one away, and there is the constant delight of *giving* the absent loved one a vacation. And yet I fear the argument proves too much! If the one who stays at home is having the better time, why is he foisting the worse time upon his sweet heart?—for love's sake? No: this time for her precious health's sake. *That's* the clinching argument. Argument or no argument, I know I am surpassing happy, and vote *this* time with emphasis for a separation.

And you are not to suppose, madam, that I am working or worrying myself to death. I leave the hard work to the nurse, and there's nothing to worry about. Besides, there are perquisites. I got out of an after dinner speech at the banquet of the Philadelphian Scots-Irish, set for the evening of the 8th (the very day of the operation) and I mean calmly to cut lectures to-morrow and next day. The whole town is interested in us,—why should we not work the sympathy for all it is worth and gain leisure to attend to our own affairs?

The children are well and jolly. In brief, you can't imagine how singularly minimized the effect of the whole thing has been upon our lives by reason of the wonderful and blessed Providence which has brought health and safety out of danger.

And, ah, my sweet one, my Eileen, my queen, how constantly and with how high an elation have I loved you through all this. It seals my confidence so sweetly that I really do love you unselfishly,—for your own sake, not for mine; what a tender touch of joy it adds to the consciousness that I am

Your own   Woodrow

All—Stock. emphatically included—send love to you all.

ALS (WC, NjP).
   [1] Letter to Robert A. M. Stevenson, Oct. 1882, in Sidney Colvin (ed.), *The Letters of Robert Louis Stevenson to His Family and Friends* (2 vols., London and New York, 1899), I, 295. These volumes are in the Wilson Library, DLC.

To Ellen Axson Wilson

Princeton N.J. 12th [Feb. 1900]
Fourth day of steady progress everything going splendidly all well   Woodrow Wilson

Hw tel. (WP, DLC).

From Ellen Axson Wilson

New Orleans, Monday afternoon
My own darling   [Feb. 12, 1900].

Both the letters—Thursday's and Friday's came this morning together, and the telegram an hour after. Oh, my darling, my darling, to think what has been going on,—what you have all been through, and I here utterly unconscious! It is easy to understand why you and Stockton,—being what you are, were glad that I was not there on Thursday, that I was spared that awful suspense and agony. But why should you be glad now? Surely I *ought* to be there now, and you will let me come,—will you not? I won't distress you, since you put your desire so strongly, by coming at once without your consent,—but it *is* almost more than I can bear to think of Sister Annie and you having all that care and I here,— going to dinners and receptions,—and I *must* go to them if I stay! *Please* telegraph me to come,—only taking care to put in the telegram that all is still well;—as if you *needed* that caution,—my *darling*!

Surely no one ever wrote so perfect a letter of its kind as yours of Thursday, from the first word to the last so reassuring, so complete,—leaving no gnawing doubts to tear at the heart-strings unnecessarily! The telegram too was a *great* comfort, though I almost fainted with terror when it came. But then I was already rather weak and sick from it all. When I got over that we were all so restless that Lucy and I decided that we would go over to the Palmers in spite of the rain. I took your letter and read it;—they were all *lovely*, and Dr. Palmer was so sweet and tender that I shall never forget it. He made the most beautiful prayer too for Stockton and all of us. The rain increased to a thunder-storm while we were there and we had to stay to lunch, after which we managed to get home again, I feeling much more like myself. Of course I have been perfectly sure for months that he had it and when I can be sure that the crisis is really passed I shall be thankful beyond words that the operation was performed. Just now, as is natural, I can only rejoice with trembling. But it does seem as though if the peritonitis were going to spread, it would have done it by the fourth day. Oh how thankful I am that it was done in the new way, separating the muscles instead of cutting! But how much,–how very much there is to be thankful for! And oh how I *love* you all, my precious ones!

Won't you let me come back to them? With love inexpressible to dearest Stockton and to my own darling, believe me, dear,
Your devoted little wife   Eileen.

ALS (WC, NjP).

To Ellen Axson Wilson

My own darling,   Princeton, Monday 12 Feb'y, 1900

As I sit with Stock. from time to time I suck nutriment out of Stevenson's *Letters*,–with sundry excellent discoveries now and again. When he says, "as if love did not live in the faults of the beloved only, and draw its breath in an unbroken round of forgiveness,"[1] he is making a very absurd generalization, surely; but he favours me with an excellent formula for a particular case I have often discussed with you. Here a [*sic*] certainly a goodly company of people about me,–no fools, neither,–who make signs as if they loved me,–or at any rate held some favourable sentiment a good deal out of the ordinary; and the "unbroken round of forgiveness" affords a very tenable theory: forgiveness for the many score things every day wherein I fall short of the standards, ideals, aspirations I profess. Your sweet letters, with their exquisite flavour of love, coming like a whiff of perfect perfume from the closing paragraph, fill me with the sense one has when blessed in all his senses by some sweet place, full of soft airs and fragrance, where he may lie alone, *possessor*, be his deserts what they may,–a place of infinite, healing peace. Your love *rests* and soothes me so, when you are away. When you are by me, it stimulates and guides. And, ah, I *need* just this when you are absent,– just this deep sense of peace, security,–all my senses at once awake and quiet in a wholesome and holy place!

There is nothing to tell you of Stock. to-day by letter: my telegram has told it all, in brief,–except that the fourth day is now *complete*, and the news the same (including "All well"); and so I may indulge myself in a *love* letter, pure and simple. The *pang* of writing such a letter has passed, with the week; and it has become a necessary indulgence,–to give the heart *vent*. It improves my character to love you thus with full and deliberate consciousness, just as it improves the imagination to look upon a noble work of art. Your own sweet spirit seems subtly to pervade me,– as it does often now at night when I lie alone in bed and cure the loneliness (at the same time that I create a new pain) by thinking of my little mate, herself alone, and lying, it may be, with thoughts full of me. Ah, with what a glory of love my life has been filled–and what deep profit it is to me that I am

Your own   Woodrow

ALS (WC, NjP).

[1] Letter to Edmund Gosse, Jan. 2, 1886, in Sidney Colvin (ed.), *op.cit.*, ii, 16.

From Ellen Axson Wilson

My own darling,   New Orleans, Tuesday [Feb. 13, 1900].

No other letter has come since I wrote yesterday afternoon, and I hardly feel like writing until it does; however the afternoon mail is due in perhaps half an hour so I will write a little now, for fear of interruptions later.

At last it has cleared after a week of bad weather,–cleared gloriously; there is not the smallest fleck of cloud in the sky,– *such* a blue sky! That it should be a winter sky seems impossible. But there is not the least suggestion of winter anywhere today. I wanted to stay at home and wait for a telegram this morning, but I had to admit that would be foolish, so instead we took a long and interesting ride on the street car, twisting and turning through the old French city, going the whole length of old Dauphine St. to Jackson Barracks and the levée. Then we had a pleasant sunny walk on the levée and my first good view of the "Father of Waters" with the city stretching along its banks behind us, and in front the plantations fading from green to blue in the distance, here and there a clump of great trees relieving the flatness and indicating yet concealing the planters home. It was all very beautiful. We walked about the barracks too, which are beautiful as well as interesting and kept in perfect order. They are very old,– were built long, long before the Civil War. The officer's houses are in the old Spanish style with great white columns in front and surrounded with roses, magnolias and palms. They have also adjoining, as a sort of general pleasure ground, a superb grove of magnolias. It was all very lovely and the sunshine was soothing, and I enjoyed it in a pensive way, though now and again something would rise in my throat at the thought that there might be a telegram at the house.

Your letter has come and is *very* comforting,–and now I must hurry away to return the calls of several people because this is their "day"!–and tonight I must go to a little "evening at home" given in my honour by one of the Tulane professors. And all the time my own brother lies ill from a dreadful operation and Sister Annie is doing my work! It is a strange situation, and a most unhappy one.

Please, dear, excuse haste. With love beyond words for all my dear ones, and my heart of hearts for my own darling, I am, as ever,   Your devoted little wife   Eileen.

ALS (WC, NjP).

To Ellen Axson Wilson

My own darling,   Princeton, Tuesday 13 Feb'y, 1900

I was rushed, by a college engagement, this afternoon, and could not get my letter off by the six o'clock mail, as I have tried to do since the operation. I hope the longer interval between letters will have caused you no uneasiness. We are far enough from the operation now to take things more at ease, and perhaps I had better return to writing in the evening, since the afternoon arrangement interferes a good deal with my necessary exercise. Everything goes well with Stock., the rest of us are in excellent shape, and there is nothing to report. Stockton has been so much and so constantly in our minds all these days, that it will be a relief now to put less of him into my letters, and turn aside for chat with my lady at a certain remove,–to try to go and spend a few minutes with her in New Orleans.

It is very cheering to me, my sweet one, to hear of your interesting doings day by day. You are certainly seeing no end of interesting things, and meeting no end of interesting people. I envy *them*! It must be such a pleasure to see you *now* for the first time in all the *maturity* of your beauty and your charm. Time has not added a single touch of age to my wonderful darling; but it has added touches of maturity, as if every sweet promise of your youth had been fulfilled with interest, and I can fancy the delicious surprise of coming upon so exquisite a woman. It was surprise that was up[p]ermost for a little in me, when I discovered the matchless girl,–and it is because that surprise was so delicious that I envy those who first see the full blown flower, full in every depth of soft petal with an ineffable sweetness, and yet a thing to gaze upon and wonder why it carries in its soft lines so clear a suggestion of strength and greatness, the light of thought and feeling. I am glad you don't *know* when people fall in love with you! There must be a power of fatal attraction in love that is perceived; and certainly women who seek it find it, to their hurt. I thrust mine upon you, and it was too strong to resist. You wouldn't have noticed me if I had not. That is one of the fascinating things about you. You do not seek love. You are lovely without deliberation, *just* like a flower, and seem to seek nothing, but simply to be yourself. Ah, how I adore you, my Eileen, and what a satisfying glory there is in the fact that you *are* actually *mine*, and that I am *accepted* as   Your own   Woodrow

We all join in love to the dear hostesses and in love *beyond measure* to the sweet guest.

ALS (WC, NjP).

From Henry Mills Alden

My dear Mr. Wilson,   New York City Feb. 13. 1900

I wish to express my personal gratification that you have decided not to withdraw your *Washington* from the Harpers & that negotiations between you & them for your History of the United States are favorably progressing. I am confident that you will feel perfectly justified in the final result.

Yours sincerely   H. M. Alden

ALS (WP, DLC).

From Ellen Axson Wilson

My own darling,   New Orleans Wednesday [Feb. 14, 1900]

There is a luncheon party on hand for today and the girls are bustling about making the pretty for it; they would not let me help so I have been basking in the sun and reading the "Guide to New Orleans,"[1] and the "Early History of Louisiana"[2] until I almost went to sleep, for we did not get to bed until one last night. So as it is now half past ten and my room is "redd up," I will try and rouse myself enough to write to you.

We have another perfect day; the warm rains and the sunshine following are bringing out the roses finely. Not all of them by any means were killed in the great freeze; Lucy has two splendid climbers almost covering the south gallery. The roses are a deep crimson, very handsome, and this morning they are superb with the sun upon them. Yesterday too I had the pleasure of seeing, at Mrs. Blake's, a yellow jassamine in bloom!

Your letter yesterday was a great comfort. Certainly all does seem to be going well; Mrs. Daniels is *lovely*! By the way, tell me about the trained nurse! Is she young or pretty or attractive? Just suppose Miss Seaman came and Fraulein's sister! Wouldn't there be a menagerie? It is rather a pity that we are forced to help Miss Seaman by giving her the countenance of the family, as it were, in her extraordinary proceedings! Now that I am beginning to be less anxious about Stockton I am greatly concerned over the interruption to your work. I hope now the nurse is sleeping at night it may not be so *very* bad;—and I am still waiting and hoping for permission to come home.

I must tell you about the party last night which was to me unusual in kind and very pleasant. The Woodwards who have no children live in a small but picturesque house, the interior exceedingly artistic, of course,—(he is the professor of art.) and they are delightful hosts; she is a pretty, charming, clever mite of a woman. There were about fifteen guests, *all* attractive, all good talkers, bright and intelligent. There was not a servant visable from first to last; Mr. Woodward admitted us himself, and about ten o'clock Mrs. W. with the help of two of the guests, and in the presence of the rest, set the table, produced a beautiful turkey, a great bowl of delicious salad, thin bread and butter, olives, pickles &c. and bottles of *beer*. Then Mrs. W. proceeded to cook oysters on a chafing dish in fine style. In short it was a regular college "spread," and was all very informal and pleasant; and as everyone present was perfectly well-bred, no one grew boisterous or silly, as young people are so apt to do on such occasions.

Among the guests were Mrs. Davis whom I mentioned before as holding a "salon[.]" She is a "character" and a truly charming one, though in appearance an old guy;[3] her husband is a nice old Colonel and a newspaper editor.[4] Then there was the younger sister of Ruth McEnery Stuart, a clever witty widow, said to be a sad flirt. Of the college people I liked best Prof. and Mrs. Sharp;[5] he is a Virginian, professor of Eng.; one gets the impression of something *fine* and finished (but not finical) about him in mind and character,—as there certainly is in manner and appearance. His wife is a lovely woman, fair, frail, flower-like. By the way, they know the Böhm sisters. He took his degree at Leipzig and met her there. She was studying music and boarded with friends of Fraülein's. Her name was Blanch Herndon. Prof. Ficklen,[6] husband of the Georgia beauty, Bessie Alexander, was also there, but not his wife as she has recently lost her mother. She is coming to see me however. He is professor of history & a tremendous admirer of yours; in fact they *all* are. Your name seems a household word; the girls did not exaggerate that at all.

But I am called for and must close abruptly. My *dear* love to Stock and all. I love you dear—love you almost *intolerably.*

Your own   Eileen.

ALS (WC, NjP).
  [1] Probably *The Picayune's Guide to New Orleans,* 3rd edn. (New Orleans, 1897).
  [2] This may have been François Xavier Martin and John F. Condon, *The History of Louisiana, From the Earliest Period . . . To Which is Appended Annals of Louisiana . . . to the Commencement of the Civil War, 1861* (New Orleans, 1882).
  [3] A term then current for an eccentric person.
  [4] Thomas Edward Davis, editor of the New Orleans *Daily Picayune.*
  [5] Robert Sharp, Professor of English at Tulane University, and his wife, Blanche Herndon Sharp.
  [6] John Rose Ficklen, Professor of History and Political Science at Tulane.

To Ellen Axson Wilson

My own darling,   Princeton, Wednesday 14 February, 1900

I will write in the afternoon to-day, after all, since a little leisure for a chat with you falls out most opportunely. Stock. continues on his equable way toward recovery,—not that *he* is equable: he is intensely nervous from long lying still on his back; but the essential parts of him are moving equably toward complete restoration, and he is nothing like so nervous as he was. Yesterday he had a free action of the bowels, and that is the final proof that they are once more a properly constituted thoroughfare,—in brief, that he is all right in respect of the healing. This is the end of the sixth day,—so you see how far along on the road he is. I thank God with all my heart for his wonderfully merciful providence in the whole matter from first to last. He has been singularly gracious to us.

I sit here and kiss your picture as I write, my darling; and my joy at the thought of all you have been spared overflows as I gaze upon it. My love and my solicitude for you pass all expression. I could not live were you not happy; and, oh, it *helps* me so that you are sane and balanced in moments of shock and sudden trouble. It has given me many a keen pang to think of the sudden pain the news of Stock's operation would bring you at its first coming; but I know you so well,—your strength and instant restoration to judgment, your power to see a situation whole, your instinctive freedom from panic and helpless dismay,—that there has been a great deal of comfort also in the picture my imagination has conjured up of what my darling would do *second* after reading the letter. I've seen her always grow calm in the face of the facts. The news is already three days old and no telegram has come to turn it from good into bad news. He is certainly safe and all right by this time.' And then the consciousness of what *I* would want you to do under the circumstances; the quiet talk about the whole matter with the dear Smiths,—a talk growing quieter and quieter, turning from soberness and anxious questioning into relief and gladness. *That's* the picture I have lived on, and seen with incomparable comfort; and as I have gazed my love and happiness have deepened and I have grown *strong* in being   Your own   Woodrow

All well. Sister and the chicks at dancing class. Fraülein down to lunch. We all love you all.

ALS (WC, NjP).

From Ellen Axson Wilson

My own darling,   [New Orleans] Thursday night [Feb. 15, 1900]

I have been rushed beyond description all day,—it is bedtime now and I am *so* tired that a real letter seems out of the question. Spent the morning sightseeing, got home late, took a hasty lunch and rushed up stairs to dress, this being their "day at home." Before I was ready came the Ficklens, at 2.15; she being in mourning wanted to make her visit early so as not to meet people. She was the first of *twenty* who called, all except one especially to meet me. The callers were still calling when the dinner guests came, viz. Dr. Palmer and Mrs. Caldwell. Soon after dinner they began to come again, spoiling,—alas!—our pleasant evening with Dr. Palmer who soon departed. I feel as if I never wanted to speak again! But most of them were *very* nice.

Good-night dear, *dear* love! Love to dear Stock & all, and to my Woodrow the whole heart of   His own   Eileen.

ALS (WC, NjP).

To Ellen Axson Wilson

My own darling,   Princeton, Thursday 15 February, 1900

The mails have been treating me in the most scurvy manner conceivable! Not till this (Thursday) afternoon did I receive your Monday letter, written just after the receipt of the news: from Monday to Thursday I had to go without any letter at all!

But, ah, how sweet the letter is now that it *is* here. How fine it is to see the *perfect* mix[ture] of grief and courage, of suffering and sense, with which my darling takes it all! Oh, but you are fine, my splendid darling! And of course you do not want me to say Come *now*, when the seventh day is over and the storm and stress all past. The nurse needs little or no assistance. We are carrying no burden, even of anxiety. It would be absurd to cut your trip short now, when you have every reason for going on to have a good time, with a lighter heart about the dear boy than you ever had before in your life. He will be feeling ready to get up and be about before you could get here; and it would distress him beyond everything to see you return. He has been bemoaning my loss of working time enough already; it would be *too* much if you were to break up your long planned outing. And you must think of *me*, sweetheart. You could *do* nothing, were you here, to help me: I am already free to do what I please, and would not do a whit more work, or anything else, were you here. And, besides, it would distress me more than you can imagine. *Please*, darling, accept the infinite blessing God in his mercy has brought us and be *glad*, not anxious, because of it. Everything is *so* cheerful here now. Fraülein comes down to meals now, and to-day took, and was much refreshed by, a little outing; the children are all well, and as happy and good as can be; sister and I have come from under the strain none the worse for wear (I am really *wonderfully* well and strong). In brief, it would be an anti-climax for you to come home now,—and you *mustn't*, as you [love] us.

How sweet the scene is to my imagination at Dr. Palmer's, as you paint it,—when you went to him for comfort,—and how I rejoice, and praise God, that you had such a comforter to go to! Bless them all! How I love them for loving my darling. You don't know, Miss, what private glee there has been in this your own household that you were out of it. We love you for your *own* sake, we would have you understand, and when we get you where we can indulge our taste in that line to our hearts' contents, we don't mean to surrender our advantage. Ah, how delightful and satisfying it is to be   Your own   Woodrow

Love unbounded from all to all.

ALS (WC, NjP).

From Ellen Axson Wilson

My own darling,   New Orleans Friday [Feb. 16, 1900].

It is a beautiful day again and we are indulging in a peaceful morning to atone for yesterday's wild whirl, from which however I have quite recovered. This too is to be a full day though; we are to go to an early luncheon at the Pattersons. Then at three or earlier with the Kings, Miss Grace[1] & her sister, to some typical Creole gathering—a club of some kind, and after that to Mrs. Davis' reception. Mrs. Davis was one of my callers yesterday. Miss Grace King was to come but was prostrated by "one of her headaches, you know," (she is very delicate) so her sister, Nan, came alone. I met Miss Grace two days ago on the street, had five minutes conversation with her, in the course of which she found time to tell how immensely she admired you, and how much she hated "Americans"! She is altogether American herself but has written about Creoles and associated with them so much that she has come to imagine herself one. She is a little unpopular it seems, rather unjustly I think, for anyone can see she doesn't mean the waspish things she says; she was laughing all the time. By the way, the whole family were devoted to Uncle Foster (Axson)[2] who was their family physician. He seems to have been most widely known and deeply loved here;—one old lady could not speak of him without tears,—and loved by rich and poor alike for Dr. Palmer says he was called all over this city "the friend of the poor," and found time to do an extraordinary amount of work among them without thought of reward.

Yesterday's junketing was an especially interesting one. We went through the old city again, the whole length of the Esplanade, the most beautiful of the Creole residence streets, down to "Bayou St. John" well-known to Cable's readers. It is bordered by very old and aristocratic Creole homes in the old Spanish style. Then to the house and gardens of the Jockey Club once a *really* "palatial" private residence, the house furnished with superb old black carved oak, the gardens indescribably romantic. There is even a beautiful stream winding through them with several little bridges,—an ideal lover's haunt,—how I wished for *you*! The guardian of this place was a truly noble looking old negro, in manners and, I might almost say, in appearance fit to be a duke. Mrs. Blake told me yesterday afternoon that he belonged to her father and that his father was an African king. He showed us the old pictures with great pride and when we asked who painted them told us that they were all "originals." From there we went on to the "Old City Park" filled with superb live oaks.

Two of them are the finest I ever saw, they are the famous "Duelling Oaks," under or near which in the old days all the duels were fought. We rode back another way passing very extensive cemetaries which seemed simply long avenues of small marble houses; they bury you know above ground because if they dig three feet they come to water. So for once the name "City of the dead'" seems really appropriate. Of course there are fine avenues of trees everywhere through the cemetaries.

Your *sweet* letter—Monday's—came before I started out yesterday; today it seems I must wait until the afternoon again. I wish I could pay you back in kind, *dearest*,—but I can't, oh I can't! But I love you as much as you want me to, and in as many ways,—and oh, I *want* you so, my darling! Give my dear love to Stockton,—equal love with thanks beyond words to dear Sister Annie, and kisses to the children. As ever,

Your devoted little wife,   Eileen.

ALS (WC, NjP).

[1] Grace Elizabeth King, author of fiction and works of local history on Louisiana and the lower South.

[2] A. Forster Axson, M.D. Little is known about his early life except that he was born in Charleston, S.C. A prominent New Orleans physician, he served for a time as Professor of Physiology at the New Orleans School of Medicine and as President of the Louisiana State Board of Health. He died on September 12, 1881. He was the brother of the Rev. Dr. Isaac Stockton Keith Axson, Mrs. Wilson's paternal grandfather, and hence was Mrs. Wilson's great-uncle.

To Ellen Axson Wilson

My own darling,   Princeton, Friday 16 Feb'y, 1900.

The mails are making up for past despites: they brought me *two* letters this evening, by the last delivery,—two letters as sweet, as brave, as engaging as the lovely little lady who wrote them. Ah, what good it does me, and how deep the good strikes, to see my bonny girl pull herself together, and face things with that fine philosophy of good sense and sweetness that is in her. You see, darling, don't you? that it would not help my *work* (or anything else) for you to come home;—that I don't work simply because my *mind* watches the dear patient. That is, I don't *write*. I do work. Fortunately, this is the season when examination papers are to be read; and I am reading them with steady and cheerful diligence. They give me just the sort of routine I need,—keep me busy with a minimum use of my mind. And they would have to be read,—and the writing put temporarily on one side for them, —whether Stockton were here to be thought about or not.

Here we are at the end of the 8th day, and still everything

goes as it should go. The poor lad is as nervous as can be; does not sleep well; and finds the bed passing tiresome, and even *sore*some to both mind and body. But the wound steadily heals; temperature, pulse, respiration, nutrition keep at normal grade; it's a mere question of wait, and not a long wait, at that, to any one but the patient. Believe me, darling, if there were anything to fear, or anything to *do*, you should know it, and be allowed to share in doing it, *at once*. That absolutely, and once for all. I verily believe that if you will but give yourself a quiet mind and have a good time without misgivings to poison it, it will contribute materially to Stock's recovery (i.e. to the *speed* of it), as it certainly would to my peace of mind and my work, and to dear sister's happiness. We are taking care of her, you may be sure, and she loves to serve; if ever a woman did, bless her heart.

So much for your additional reassurance and strengthening. Now for the real subject of my letter,—my absolute love and admiration for you. You have here, ma'am, in Princeton a lover who worships you, not with devotion merely, but with a sort of tonic elation which other men (could he tell them his secrets) could only marvel at and envy, being unmarried or married to— other women. All the pride I might have in my (neat little esoteric) literary reputation, were I a fool, has gone to make me infinitely complaisant over having become, by your sweet grace and favour,   Your own   Woodrow

It's litterally true that we are all in love with you all.

ALS (WC, NjP).

From Harper and Brothers, with Enclosure

Dear Sir: [New York] Feb. 16. 1900.

We beg leave to enclose herewith for your consideration, a rough draft of our proposed form of agreement for your Short History of the United States. We think that you would better look it over before it is put into formal shape for signature. We have endeavored to embody the various points upon which there was a substantial understanding in our correspondence, and we shall be pleased to receive any changes or amendments which you may have to propose.

Awaiting your reply, we are, dear sir,
                    Respectfully yours,   Harper & Brothers.

ALS (WP, DLC).

AGREEMENT, made this twenty second day of January, 1900, between WOODROW WILSON, of Princeton, New Jersey, hereinafter called THE AUTHOR, party of the first part, and the corporation of HARPER & BROTHERS, of the City of New York, Publishers, parties of the second part.

1. In consideration of the premises, the AUTHOR hereby grants and assigns to HARPER & BROTHERS an unpublished work, the subject or title of which is "A Short History of the United States" and also all rights of translation, abridgment, selection, and other rights of, in, or to said work, for the United States of America. HARPER & BROTHERS shall also have the right to take out copyright for the said work in the AUTHOR's name for the United States of America and to obtain all renewals of copyright, and to publish said work during the term or terms thereof.

2. The AUTHOR further covenants and represents that said work has not heretofore been published, that it is innocent and contains no matter which if published, will be libellous or otherwise injurious, or which will infringe upon any proprietary right at common law or any statutory copyright; that he is the sole Author and Proprietor of said work, and has full power to make this agreement and grant; and that he will hold harmless and defend HARPER & BROTHERS against any suit, claim, demand, or recovery, by reason of any violation of proprietary right or copyright, or any injurious or libellous matter in said work.

3. The AUTHOR further agrees that HARPER & BROTHERS shall have the Canadian market for said work and all rights in Canada growing out of British or other foreign copyright in said work, and that they also shall have the right to take such steps as they may be advised for securing to themselves independent copyright for said work in Canada, if they shall deem it expedient so to do.

4. HARPER & BROTHERS agree to take out copyright for said work in the AUTHOR's name for the United States of America and to publish said work at their own expense, in such style as they shall deem best suited to its sale; and, in consideration of the premises, they agree to pay the AUTHOR fifteen (15) per cent. on their trade-list (retail) price for each copy thereof by them sold. The trade-list (retail) price which is to be taken as the basis for this percentage shall be that of the cloth-bound copies.

Should any copies be sold for export, at less than one-half the trade-list (retail) price, they shall pay said percentage only on the price actually received for each copy so sold. No payment shall be made by HARPER & BROTHERS for permission gratuitously given to publish extracts from said work to benefit the sale thereof; but if HARPER & BROTHERS receive any compensation for the publication of extracts therefrom, or for translations, or abridgments, such compensation shall be equally divided between the parties hereto.

5. HARPER & BROTHERS agree to render semi-annual statements of account to January 1st and July 1st of each year, upon application therefor, and to make settlement in cash four months after date of each statement.

6. If, after the publication of any edition of said work, the plates be rendered useless by fire or otherwise, HARPER & BROTHERS shall have the option of reproducing them or not, and if they shall decline to reproduce them, then, after the sale of all copies remaining on hand, they shall, upon written request, reconvey to the AUTHOR the copyright and all rights herein granted, and this contract shall terminate. No insurance whatever shall be effected by HARPER & BROTHERS for the AUTHOR.

7. If, at any time after the expiration of ten years from the date of first publication of said work, the AUTHOR elects to terminate this agreement, he may do so upon the payment to HARPER & BROTHERS for the property (including the electrotype plates) of an amount equal to the capital sum of which the average royalty earned by the said work per year during the three preceding calendar years is ten (10) per cent., in which case he shall take all copies of the work in stock at half their retail price; it being understood, however, that the amount to be paid for the resumption of ownership of the work shall not be less than one-half the original cost of the plates, i.e., of the composition, the electrotyping and the illustrations, and that provision shall be made for the satisfaction of all contracts for sales made before the receipt by HARPER & BROTHERS of the AUTHOR's notice of withdrawal. But, at the request of either party to this agreement, the amount to be paid for resumption of ownership by the AUTHOR shall be determined by the arbitration of three persons, one arbiter to be selected by each of the parties concerned and the two thus selected to choose the third.

8. If, at any time, after the expiration of ten years from the date of the first publication, the demand for the said work shall not, in the opinion of HARPER & BROTHERS, be sufficient to render its further publication profitable, then they may cancel this contract, giving the AUTHOR three months' notice thereof; and thereupon the AUTHOR shall have the option to take from HARPER & BROTHERS, at one-half the cost of production, the stereotype

plates of said work and plates of any illustrations furnished therefor by the AUTHOR, should they not in the meantime have been destroyed by fire or otherwise, and whatever copies of said work they may have on hand at one-third the trade-list (retail) price, or, upon the AUTHOR's failing so to take the same, HARPER & BROTHERS shall have the right to melt up the plates and to destroy the copies of said work then on hand. In case the AUTHOR buys the plates under this provision, said AUTHOR shall not have the right to use any illustrations furnished by HARPER & BROTHERS for such work without special agreement between the parties hereto.

9. If HARPER & BROTHERS shall deem it advisable to publish said work in Great Britain, they shall have the right to do so upon the same terms and conditions as are herein specified for the publication of the work in the United States of America.

10. The above agreement for the publication of said work contemplates its sale through the ordinary channels of the book-trade, but upon the copies of said work, whether in one or more volumes, whether illustrated fully or partially or without any illustrations, which may be sold through canvassing agents, the royalty to be paid to the AUTHOR by the said HARPER & BROTHERS shall be ten (10) per cent. on the retail price of the said subscription edition in cloth binding.

11. This contract may not be assigned or in any way disposed of by said HARPER & BROTHERS except by the consent of the AUTHOR in writing. In the event of the said HARPER & BROTHERS deciding to discontinue the publication of the said work before the expiration of ten years after the first publication in book-form the copyright and publishing rights thereof shall revert to the AUTHOR upon his purchasing the electrotype plates and the stock of the work upon terms to be settled by arbitration in the same manner as is stipulated in the closing sentence of SECTION 7 of this agreement.

12. It is, however, further understood and agreed that HARPER & BROTHERS shall not be required to pay the royalties herein provided for upon any copies of said work sold by them in any country after the copyright of the same shall have terminated in such country.

13. It is hereby understood and agreed that such part of the said work as shall be selected by the editor of HARPER'S MAGAZINE shall be first published serially in that periodical in twelve monthly parts or instalments, each of which shall contain not less than ten thousand words, and in consideration thereof

HARPER & BROTHERS shall pay the AUTHOR the sum of One Thousand Dollars ($1,000.) upon the delivery to them of the Manuscript for each monthly part or instalment of said work; the Manuscript of the first part or instalment is to be delivered by the AUTHOR to HARPER & BROTHERS by July 1, 1900, and the Manuscript for the following parts or instalments are to be delivered by the AUTHOR at regular monthly intervals thereafter.

14. It is further agreed that the stipulations and agreements herein shall apply to and bind the executors, administrators, and assigns of the AUTHOR, and the successors and assigns of the Corporation of HARPER & BROTHERS.

Harper & Brothers,
The State Trust Co.,   Receiver
F. A. Duneka.[1]

T MS. signed (WP, DLC).
[1] Frederick A. Duneka, who had been with Harvey on the New York *World*, and was now general manager and secretary of the Board of Directors of Harper and Brothers.

An Amendment to a Contract[1]

[c. Feb. 17, 1900]

At any time after the expiration of seven (7) years from the date of first publication the AUTHOR may purchase and resume the rights in respect of said work acquired and exercised under this Agreement by Harper and Bros., by paying to Harper & Bros. a sum of money equal to the capital sum of which the royalties paid for said work during the year then last past is ten (10) per cent,—⟨it being⟩

WWhw MS. (WP, DLC).
[1] An amendment to the contract just printed. Wilson's reply proposing the change is missing, but see H. M. Alden to WW, March 13, 1900, n. 2.

From Ellen Axson Wilson

My own darling,   [New Orleans] Saturday [Feb. 17, 1900]

For a very interesting reason, which I will tell you about tomorrow, it has been impossible for me to write this morning. Am going out to a luncheon and scribble this line with my hat on in desperate haste.

Am quite well, weather bright but cold,—a *freeze* last night!

With dear *dear* love to all and to my darling Woodrow above all,

Your own   Eileen.

ALS (WC, NjP).

To Ellen Axson Wilson

My own, sweet darling,   Princeton, Saturday 17 Feb'y, 1900

I daresay, after the liberality of the postman yesterday, I shall get no letter at all to-day (in which case, alas! I shall have to wait till Monday),—so I will begin my letter before mail time. It must get off this evening or hang here till Monday,—provided it *can* get off in this snow storm. It has been snowing steadily and copiously all day,—and there were perhaps two inches of snow already on the ground when I got up and raised the shades this morning, so that it is a pretty respectable depth now. There are no drifts as yet, though a good wind is blowing; but there is snow enough on the level to dissuade railway trains from attempting their usual speed. The patient does well in all essentials. His nerves—no good to begin with—are worse than no good now, and give him nervous pangs all over from the long lying still; but that is one of the interesting and inevitable penalties of the situation for a gentleman built after that kind. It may prolong the period of confinement; but it does not delay the healing, and neither his pulse beat nor the thermometer deigns to take the least notice of it. Poor chap! He has been ill often enough, but I believe this is the first time he has ever had to lie a long time *flat*, forbidden so much as to turn upon his side without assistance, and sore in every joint for very stiffness.

No, the nurse is *not* young and not pretty. She is a bit grey—maybe fifty—is *Mrs.* Hand, if you please (though I doubt if Mr. H. is living) and, though as kind, thoughtful, and efficient as we could wish, and very sweet, too, in face and manner, is not dangerous. It [I] was tickled to receive your letter saying 'suppose Miss Seaman and Fraülein Marie Bohm should turn up together': for the latter *has* been here to-day and a letter to me came from Miss S. this morning offering to come and sit with Stock. "say, next Tuesday." I shall sternly discourage Miss S. (not to say forbid her) and Fraülein Marie I did not see. She was in Fraülein Clara's room except at lunch time, and during lunch I was with Stock., sister being needed to pour, and Mrs. Hand being at rest. *That* crisis, therefore, is past.

How your letters do interest me, my darling: for what novel scenes you are in and what entertainment there is in your daily programme. Bless the dear Smiths and all the interesting friends you are making and bless you for the engaging narrative of it all! Kiss all the prettiest girls and young matrons for me, and engage their interest in me against my coming myself—and all the while smile to the centre of your heart to think how deep-dyed and absolutely I am   Your own   Woodrow.

All well, and all rivals in affectionate messages.

ALS (WC, NjP).

From Ellen Axson Wilson

My own darling,   New Orleans Sunday [Feb. 18, 1900]
The Mallards have lent me a most interesting history of Liberty Co. and Old Midway Church.[1] I became completely absorbed in it this afternoon before I realized it,—besides there have been visitors,—so the result is that I have not left myself as much time as I should for writing to my darling, and feel that I deserve a scolding from him!

The visitors were Judge and Mrs. Monroe;[2] he is a very interesting and distinguished man of whom, as you may remember, the Smiths have always talked a great deal. His wife though a Creole is a Presbyterian and a very fine woman; they have *ten* children ranging from a baby in arms to a full-fledged civil engineer.

Speaking of the Creoles reminds me of the two receptions on Friday at which I met scores of them of the oldest and most representative families; it was very entertaining. The first was at the Castellanos one of the old Spanish Creole families who still live in their old home on the narrow, quaint old Rue Orleans. The six daughters, four of them married and society leaders, are of the Spanish blonde type,—very handsome. But the dear, funny old mother is the best of all with her kind heart, her delicious accent, and her perfect manner, so French and yet so simple and cordial. You should have seen Lucy,—we had no sooner entered the door than she began to speak English with an accent; and before we left I found that even I was speaking of "my friend Lucie," shrug[g]ing my shoulders and gesturing with my open palms! Really if one does'nt indulge in some demonstration of that sort one feels like a mere inanimate clod among them!

Was interrupted here by another visitor; before he left came the Kentuckians and then supper. It is now half past ten and I am almost asleep. The last visitor was Dr. Bruns whom I think you would very much like and enjoy talking to. He is a distinguished physician here, you know; but equally distinguished as a reform leader in all political issues, and as a brilliant speaker to mass meetings, &c. He is a remarkably fine talker, and evidently absolutely disinterested and high-minded in every position that he takes.

I am perfectly well in spite of the cold which has been rather severe the last two days,—temp. about 25°,—but it is already moderating a little and it is hoped will be just right again tomorrow.

Your *very* good account of Stockton in yesterday's letter was a great comfort, dear;—as was also your mention of the dancing-school party; it showed such a normal state of affairs. My *dear* love to all, and to my own Woodrow the whole heart and life of

His little wife   Eileen.

ALS (WC, NjP).

¹ James Stacy, *History of the Midway Congregational Church, Liberty County, Georgia* (Newnan, Ga., 1899).

² Frank Adair and Alice Blanc Monroe. He was an Associate Justice of the Louisiana Supreme Court.

To Ellen Axson Wilson

My own darling,   Princeton, Sunday 18 Feb'y, 1900.

Things are steadily and even rapidly clearing with us. Fraülein helped get the chicks to bed to-night, and expects to go to school again to-morrow. Stockton had a quiet, restful night and has passed a most peaceful day, with quiescent nerves and a sort of natural enjoyment of the cosy room (he has a fire on his hearth) and our little chats. He is more altogether comfortable and like himself than he has been yet. Dr. Wikoff took out the *stitches* from the wound this morning,—a decided proof of progress not only but also a cause of decreased irritation. By the end of the week, no doubt, he will be sitting up and planning where he shall go to recuperate (To-day he has been busily planning what he means to eat,—beginning with sausage and hominy!). My plan is, for him to go first, for a couple of days, to Atlantic City, and then to go South, to meet you in Savannah or Atlanta, or—where you will. Dr. Patton called the other day to bid him take two or three months, if necessary, to get well, and he can go as far as he pleases. You need not come to see him: he can go to see you! How does *that* suit your ladyship?

By the time this reaches you we shall be within a week of the end of February, and you will be in Georgia and on your way to meet him at just about the proper stage of his convalescence. Don't that sound like progress? There's less than six weeks now, my queen, between you and the gentleman to whom you are *most* dear and most necessary. I'll not deny, mum, that that gentleman seems himself deeply interested in the reckoning. He shows a fine patience in the matter (for I would do him justice, and he has some qualities which are to be commended) but no one who knows him can fail to catch a wistful look in his eyes now and again as he talks, with genuine smiles and unaffected pleasure (I must believe), of your trip and the places and people and pleasures you are seeing. One must be touched once in a while, even, by the unconscious evidences of how much he loves you. It is plain that he misses you, and yet he is keen to have you stay away and finish your trip. It is no effort—it is evidently a pleasure—to forget himself in thinking of you; and yet he is only human, after all, and you cannot wonder that there flashes a little moisture in his eye in moments of thoughtful talk. You would not have him always unconscious, I think, that his arms are empty and that the light of his life is out of the house. We are strangely made, mum! The desire to *possess* those we love, and keep them ever by us to cheer and shorten and make bright the way, burns in us like a veritable passion, and will not long be kept down; and yet this very love which seems so self-pleasing, may be unselfish and take pleasure in unselfishness! But he wishes to add a few lines for himself.

Eileen, my love, my *darling*, it is my present *joy* that you are away, that we are well without you and prosper; but it is my sustaining solace that the time goes kindly on which will, almost before we know it, bring you back, refreshed and rendered still more dear, to   Your own   Woodrow.

ALS (WC, NjP).

From Ellen Axson Wilson

My own darling,   New Orleans, Monday [Feb. 19, 1900]

Yours of last Thursday is just at hand; I wonder what *does* happen to mine! I certainly mail them regularly every day. Have more than one been lost altogether? I have been wondering that I had no answer to mine of last Monday. Of course I *do* realize that to start home now would be, as you well express it, "an anticlimax"; so I will say no more about it,—though I should like to do it!

I wouldn't say so to the girls for the world, but I fear I am looking forward with more dread than anything else to this carnival[1] business—the struggling crowds, the fatigue, the late hours. But I dare say I shall find the spirit of it contagious and enjoy it when I am once in the thick of it.

I must go to a club and luncheon combined at twelve today,—must begin to dress at eleven,—that is in ten minutes,—would have written earlier but had to mend a torn gown. After the luncheon we must try to crowd in a call or two and then go to a reception. Tomorrow there is a reception, a luncheon, and a ball at night. Wed., I am glad to say we have no engagement; I am going to hire a cab & try to make a score or so of calls. Thursday is our day at home, and at night there is a procession and ball. And so it goes!—quite too much of a good (?) thing for your quiet little wife!

Kisses for my little darlings, dearest love for each and all by name. As for my love, my Woodrow, I have no words in which to say how much I love and long for him. Always & altogether
Your own   Eileen.

The weather is mild and *glorious*; with the exception of the rain last night it has been so since Sunday when the cold wave left us. Today is ideal.

ALS (WC, NjP).
¹ That is, the Mardi Gras.

To Ellen Axson Wilson

My own darling,   Princeton, Monday 19 Feb'y, 1900

I am rich to-day—three letters, or, at least, one letter and two dear notes. Every time you write is priceless to me, and I cannot say how these letters full of the interesting things you are doing and the attractive people you are meeting fill me with delight. *What* a good time you are having, and how deeply I enjoy it all and dote upon your narrative. Perhaps the two dear sisters who are arranging and doing it all for you will let *you* kiss them *for* me. I am more deeply their debtor and lover than ever. And how delightful it is that I can *contribute* to your good time by sending you absolutely good news for the comfort of your mind. Stockton slept steadily through nearly the whole of last night and to-day is more like himself than I had expected to see him for a week yet. His nerves have "gone down" in a way that's truly wonderful. He'll be eating solid food by to-morrow, and by the end of the week sitting up. If you started when this reaches you, you could not get home in time to see him in bed! We are absolutely and finally out of the woods. There's nothing to do now but to be jolly and go about our several 'avocations.' How I wish I could hug and kiss you by way of congratulation!—and,—ahem!—for some other reasons, too. The fact is, my bonnie lassie, I find it a good deal harder to do without you now that anxiety is passed and high spirits are come back than I did while the burden of waiting was on us. It is *easy* to wish you out of all care, but, ah, it's hard, infinitely hard, to be *glad* without you. I never long to see sadness in your dear eyes,—even though that would mean seeing you and holding you as close in my arms as if I were glad; but how *passionately* I long for you when I am happy and could hold you thrilled with gladness. Sadness seems, I know, robbed of half its burden when you share it; but then I am wretched to see you sad. You seem made for gladness, and it enchants me to see you overflow with happiness. Fill your days with pleasure *now*, my Eileen: it finds its way to me straight. I see it when it is in your letters, I miss it when they do not contain it. Their mood communicates itself to me. Tell me what the people say about *you*. If you haven't room for it in your letters, jot it down, *please* ma'am, and let me enjoy it when you come back. What a good time *they* are having, meeting the little queen who is sweeter, lovlier, more symmetrically beautiful in all her traits than any other woman in the world. Such is the unhesitating credo of   Your own   Woodrow

A chorus of love to all. I lectured to-day, of course, as usual.

ALS (WC, NjP).

An Announcement

[Feb. 20, 1900]

ADDRESSES BY PROFESSOR WILSON.

Professor Woodrow Wilson will deliver the patriotic address before the students of the Hill School, Pottstown, Pa., on Washington's Birthday. His subject will be "What it Means to be an American."[1] On Friday evening, February 23, Professor Wilson has been invited to speak before the "Civics' Club" in Harrisburg, Pa., on "Political Freedom."[2] After his speech, the Princeton graduates of Harrisburg will give a smoker in his honor.

Printed in the *Daily Princetonian*, Feb. 20, 1900.
[1] Wilson delivered this address, but no notes for or newspaper reports of it are extant.
[2] See the news report printed at Feb. 24, 1900.

From Ellen Axson Wilson

My own darling,   New Orleans Tuesday [Feb. 20, 1900]

Again my letter to you is crowded into a brief half hour between engagements, for I was obliged to go down town after breakfast to get fresh gloves and have some cleaned,—Lucy too had
errands. Then on the way back we heard Dr. Palmer had fallen
down on a car track and seriously hurt his knee, so in a fright
we went there to enquire. He opened the door for us himself, to
our great relief. He limps a little, but it does not seem at all
serious. He told me with great pleasure that the trustees of
Tulane (he is one of them) had just invited you to deliver the
Commencement address; it never seemed to occur to him that
you could refuse! He seemed quite grieved and incredulous, dear
old man, when I told him, I feared you could not come.[1]

I met yesterday at luncheon a lady whom I supposed from her
conversation was married to *all* the trustees of Tulane! She insisted strenuously and at length upon your coming as President,
and assured me upon her personal responsibility that it should
not interfere in the least with your literary career. She said
Tulane had a wonderful future, and Louisiana was a glorious
field for an historian; that she herself was a whole historical
association and could put inexhaustible material into your hands!
It seems she is a Miss Kate Winter who was at the head of the
La. historical exhibit at the world's fair; ever since which she
has not known the difference between herself & La. She does
represent also in her own proper person most of the old historical
families.

The luncheon & reception yesterday were among the "smart
set," given by very rich people. I thought I should be sadly bored,
but the luncheon was very pleasant and the reception no worse
than others. It is rather amusing how nearly everyone I meet
remarks that they "have heard of me from Mrs. Davis"! She is
an impulsive, enthusiastic person and seems to have taken a
great fancy to me. It is odd to see how she belongs equally to
every set, "smart," literary, or Creole, and is loved and admired
by everyone equally. "There is only one Mrs. Davis," they all say.

By the way, will you please send me five pictures of yourself
(if you have so many) with "yours truly, Woodrow Wilson" written on them? And at the same time the little picture of *Helen
Bones* which came last Xmas. In extreme haste and with *dear*
love to all, and *above* all to you, I am as always, my darling—

Your own,   Eileen.

ALS (WC, NjP).
1 She was right; Wilson had to decline. See WW to W. O. Rogers, Feb. 26, 1900.

To Ellen Axson Wilson

My own darling,   Princeton, Tuesday 20 Feby, 1900

It seems quite natural to come home Tuesday afternoon tired
out with lecturing, as I am now,—but never too tired to talk with
my precious Eileen. I begin my letter now (6 P.M.) because at
seven I go to dinner at Paul van Dyke's, to meet a Northampton
(Episcopalian dominie) friend of his who is here over night. If I
don't finish it now, I must add a few lines after I get back to-night,
in order to get it off by the first mail to-morrow. This is the day
when the Sunday embargo tells, and I get no letter, alas! But things
are going so well and cheerfully with us that I can't in conscience
be blue. Stock. took eggs and coffee and milk toast for breakfast
and wheatena for lunch; the wound is healing, now that the
stitches are out, by leaps and bounds (so to speak[)]; he wants
everything, and is altogether a normal man again, "kicking" because the doctor says he must not meet his classes until the first of
April, but must go off and loaf somewhere. We've had a big snow
storm and several days of intense cold, with a blizzard-like wind for
a while, but the furnace is equal to the emergency, give it but
coal enough, and we have come through undamaged. We've had
a cold or two, but none worth talking about. Our life is settling
to the old routine, and if Stock. were up we could forget that
there had been an operation in the family! It's positively alarming, my sweet bewitcher, how much I think about you, now that
the skies have cleared. I could all but wish for a patient to watch,
to keep my mind otherwise employed! It makes me restless to
have leisure,—for leisure simply means thinking about you,—
thinking about the delightful little lady who *belongs in this
house*, to whom this house belongs, whom every part of it suggests, as if it were compact of the touches of her hand, a visible
embodiment of her loving thought,—of her plans for our life and
comfort and pleasure! But, ah, it's a blessed loneliness this sweet
loneliness I suffer, full of thoughts of you. I don't know what
could be more wholesome or more satisfying than the images
that fill my mind, like a light,—images of purity, of infinite
loyalty, of sufficing companionship, of a tenderness that delights, of a wonderful beauty of nature and of thought and of
person that makes my love so like an unconscious queen. My
pet, you are all the world to me, and just to *think* of you as mine
is better than it would be to possess and constantly enjoy any

other woman I ever knew,–though I must admit I know one or two who are charming. I am happy only in this, that I am

Your own   Woodrow

ALS (WC, NjP).

From Ellen Axson Wilson

My own darling,   [New Orleans] Wednesday [Feb. 21, 1900]

I certainly am in the thick of it all now, and *enjoying* it too!– the only drawback being that it seems impossible to find a quiet time to write to my love. The ball last night was *perfectly beautiful*. Of course I havn't time to describe it; will send the newspaper account tomorrow when the paper is old. This is the most exclusive and therefore the least crowded of the series. I doubt if we are quite as comfortable at Comus and Momus.[1] It was pouring rain when we started but [F.] Prévost Breckenridge, our escort, brought a carriage, so there was no trouble. We got back at twelve and had a good night's sleep. This morning we took a trolley ride, which really refreshed us, to the old St. Louis Cemetery and the "Basin," two of the most interesting of the "sights." We have just had luncheon & I am scribbling this before dressing for our visiting tour. Tonight comes the most brilliant of the illuminated processions. Mr. Blair, Mr. Patterson's friend, (he is also a friend and kinsman (!) of the Smiths,) has sent us tickets to see it from his club.

I *must* take time to tell you about my new relation! Old Uncle Mark Antony, a perfect and delightful specimen of the old time, high class, body servant, is it seems a well-known "character" and was one of Uncle Foster's old servants. He called yesterday saying he had been told that "dere was a young lady ob de name ob Axson staying here." I was produced & when I told him I was Dr. Axson's niece he almost embraced me, crying "den we's *close related!*" He told me with much feeling how many years he had driven for Uncle Foster and "took care ob him," how he had been with him when he died, "an de Madame too." Finally he remarked, "seems lak wheneber I meets anybody raal fine an elegant deys related to we all; dats de good ob belongin to de mos high up, fust families ob de lan!"

But I *must* dress. My *dear* love to poor Stock. I am *so* sorry about the nervousness,–when do they think he can sit up?

I love you my darling, my Woodrow, with all my heart and soul and mind & am in every heart-throb

Your own   Eileen.

ALS (WC, NjP).

¹ The "Momus" parade and ball was usually held on the Thursday (February 22 in 1900) before Mardi Gras; the "Comus" parade and ball, on the evening of Mardi Gras (Shrove Tuesday, which in 1900 fell on February 27).

To Ellen Axson Wilson

My own darling,   Princeton, Wednesday 21 Feb'y, 1900.

This *is* tantalizing! In Saturday's letter you say, "For a very interesting reason, which I will tell you about to-morrow, it has been impossible for me to write to you this morning," and on Sunday (which is "to-morrow") "a most interesting history of Liberty Co. and Old Midway Church" has stolen all the time, and the interesting reason is forgotten, after I have wondered about it for two days! You evidently don't know what real things your letters are to me, and how every line sticks in my memory and is the ground for a definite emotion.

Our own days slip by without incident. Stockton grows steadily stronger and better and the rest of us need nothing said about us at all, so equable is our course. To-morrow morning early (8:23) I start for the Hill School to make the Birthday address; the next day I go on to Harrisburg, to speak to the Woman's Club, —and attend, worse luck! a "smoker" given by the Princeton men afterwards, the same evening! I shall not be at home again till Saturday afternoon or evening. These, I am thankful to say, are the last engagements away from home *this year*.

The dinner at van Dyke's last night was not a success, so far as I was concerned: I was too tired, and fell sleepier and sleepier, more and more silent, as the evening advanced. But there was everything needed to make it enjoyable in the way of good dishes and good talk. Van's friend proved sensible and attractive; and the guests were Dulles, Magie, McClure, Harper, and McCay,¹— all very jolly and at their best, only I dull and without anything to say. To-day I've been working on my address at Pottstown and clearing my desk of letters,—grinding off thirteen replies at a dash. This afternoon the children and sister Annie are again at dancing school.

The only piece of news from outside that interests me is that Miss Crow, to whom I took such a fancy, was married (at her sister's home in Washington) on February 15th to Dr. Samuel E. Simmons, of Sacramento, California. One less delightful girl available for Ed's² lingering choice! Dr. Simmons is certainly a lucky man!

It is delightful, truly delightful, my pet, to hear of the interesting people you are meeting,—and you tell me enough about them, even in a few words, to give me generally a really vivid idea of what they are like. You seem to say just enough. I would give my head to hear what they say about *you*,—to know the *form* their gifted tongues give to their satisfaction. I never tire hearing people talk about you, and I am hungry to hear my darling praised, as she deserves. Every fresh image of beauty (of pure, refined, exquisite, essential beauty) that comes to my mind seems a new symbol of her! We all love you, and rejoice in your happiness beyond words; but most of all

Your own Woodrow.

Give my love to the dear Smiths, and to all who love you.

ALS (WC, NjP).

  [1] Rev. Joseph Heatly Dulles, Librarian of Princeton Theological Seminary; William Francis Magie, Professor of Physics, Princeton University; Charles Freeman Williams McClure, Assistant Professor of Biology; George McLean Harper, Woodhull Professor of Romance Languages; and Leroy Wiley McCay, Professor of Chemistry.

  [2] Edward William Axson.

To John Franklin Jameson[1]

My dear Jameson,   Princeton, New Jersey 21 Feb'y, 1900

I know you will deem me a churl; but really the thing is impossible, honourable as I should feel a place in the *Review* to be. The fact is, that the editors of the popular monthlies offer me such prices nowadays that I am corrupted. I am to appear in a serial of twelve numbers next year,—next century;—upon what subject and where I believe I am not at liberty to say yet. But it is to be a piece of work I meant to do any way,—and I alter the quality not a bit,—nor dilute the stuff, neither,—to suit the medium. I am my own master in method. It will keep me working tooth and nail the rest of the year and much of 1901.

I wrote a long chapter (1850-1860) for the American volume of Lord Acton's "Cambridge Modern History," which I should have been proud to put into the *American Historical*; but I was told the rules of the Cambridge Press permitted it not.

Mrs. Wilson is in New Orleans, to visit friends and witness the Carnival. The rest of us are *in statu quo*; the once little girls are now (two of them, at least) almost as tall as their mother; I am working steadily and as steadily growing grey; and shall ever continue, in spite of my mercenary character,

Your sincere friend, Woodrow Wilson

My warm regards to Mrs. Jameson

ALS (J. F. Jameson Papers, DLC).
¹ Managing Editor of the *American Historical Review* and Professor of History at Brown University.

From Ellen Axson Wilson

My own darling   [New Orleans] Thursday [Feb. 22, 1900]

I am actually resting quietly at home this morning, and very pleasant it is; there are to be guests however for an early luncheon. Then it is our day at home, but two of us are going to escape at four and go to a Catholic wedding at the Cathedral. At night we go to the Momus street parade and then to the Momus ball.

The parade last night was almost indescribably gorgeous; I will send the newspaper account; a very poor one however.¹ All of Canal St. was decorated and illuminated, and the total effect, together with the crowds, was wonderful. The mens clubs were especially superb, the "Boston," where we were, being beyond comparison the finest. It was voted the finest electric display of all, not excepting the procession. It is a very old, rich, and exclusive organization, and money is apparently no object. After the parade every club has an elegant supper for its lady guests. We had a great time,—were even presented with a box at the opera, but declined and so reached home at ten o'clock and had a good nights sleep. New Orleans men are certainly the incarnation of gallantry, *all* the women are "queens,"—not merely the chosen "carnival queens,"—and the men seem to exist merely to serve them. As far as I can see they never sit down in the presence of ladies! They are distinctly forbidden to do so at the balls, or the clubs, or the parades!

I must tell you one amusing incident. As we were walking through the crowd, Lucy in advance, someone said, "how do you do, Miss Smith? I hear you have a *charming* lady staying with you!" Whereupon Lucy turns to me & there follows much laughter, and pretty confusion on the part of the lady, a Mrs. Labouisse who proved to be "charming" herself.

I *am* so glad that Stockton is coming south! It will be the very thing for him. And now as to where we shall meet. Since coming here I have learned from the Palmers that Geo. Allen, one of Aunt Ella's² nephews from St. Louis, is spending the winter in Sav. in wretched health, indeed they think he is hopelessly ill, and he is a great care upon Aunt Ella. I have been a little uneasy about going myself under these circumstances, and we all know how skittish Stockton will become at the mention of them. In Atlanta you know, I thought of going to a hotel over night because of Aunt Lou's[3] small house; but she insists on my staying there; they put a bed in the parlour for guests, but of course I shall only stay two or three days. Stockton of course could be happy in Atlanta with *his* friends but *I* couldn't be with him. Rome is out of the question; Stockton can never bear the thought of going there even when he is well. So it looks as if it would be best for me to meet him at some place where there are no complications arising from kinsfolk; then I could devote myself to taking care of him. Florida would be the best because we could be *sure* of warm weather and an altogether out of door life, but perhaps the Sand Hills at Augusta[4] would do. Mrs. Richardson[5] could give you the address of a nice boarding house there. Then there is Columbia. Sister Annie could help more than any of us in deciding where it is best to go. That place Mrs. Hibben went to is good,—as to fare & climate,—and cheap, but I fear it would bore Stock to death. The only thing to do is for "you all" to decide all these things and then let me know where to go & when; I am entirely and joyfully at Stock's disposal.

In extreme haste,—I have been interrupted!—and with dear, *dear* love to all, believe me, my own darling, in every heart-throb   Your own   Eileen.

ALS (WC, NjP).
    [1] She apparently sent it under separate cover. It is a long clipping from the New Orleans *Times-Democrat*, Feb. 22, 1900, and is in WP, DLC.
    [2] Ella Law (Mrs. Randolph) Axson of Savannah.
    [3] Louisa Cunningham Hoyt (Mrs. Warren A.) Brown.
    [4] The resort area of Augusta.
    [5] Grace Ely (Mrs. Ernest Cushing) Richardson, wife of the Librarian of Princeton University.

To Ellen Axson Wilson

Hotel Lafayette. Philadelphia
My own darling,   Thursday 22 February, 1900
    It is now just a little after five o'clock, and I've been intensely busy to-day. I got up at seven o'clock, had breakfast at a quarter past, took the 8:23 train, reached Pottstown at 11:33, spoke from twelve to one, had lunch, took the 3:27 train for Philadelphia, got here some half an hour ago, and am writing to my Eileen as rest and comfort. My visit to the school was a sad one. Mr. and Mrs. Meigs[1] lost their youngest daughter, their darling, Monday,—day before yesterday, from membranous laryngitis. I never saw such fortitude of spirit, or such absolute Christian faith as they show. They submit absolutely, cheerfully. Their lives, and the life of the school, goes on as if nothing had hap-

pened. I never saw anything more touchingly beautiful. But you can see the strain, the inevitable nervous tension they quiver with. They *cannot all* the while keep the tears from their eyes. Their minds are submissive, but their hearts would break, were it not for that submission. And of course the strain communicated itself to me. I am *such* a dull, dumb beast. I cannot put any appreciable part of what I feel into words; and yet I did so yearn to say *some*thing that would cheer, were it never so little, those brave hearts! I wish I could hope for half their fortitude and faith under like circumstances! My own Christianity seems of so mild and pale a type alongside minds of such a quality as theirs.

It seems odd to be away from home and at ease about Stockton, and I think I will indulge in a frolic to-night. I will pick out some jolly play, if there is one, and go to the theatre and play I'm a boy on a holiday. The 22nd. *is* a holiday for everybody but the poor devils who have learned how to make speeches,—the poorest profession in the world,—for the professor! It goes hard with me to know that while I am away letters—dear letters—from you are lying unread at home. I had half a mind to go straight on home this afternoon and start out fresh for Harrisburg to-morrow, until I reflected that those confounded through southern mails might play me a trick and bring no letter to-day after all. Everything goes perfectly well at home. You have no idea what helpful friendliness has cheered us all through Stock's illness—and from all sides. Of course the Hibbens have been chief among all. They were on hand all the time, before and during the operation, and were of infinite use and comfort. And after all the *work* was done, they came twice a day to see how we fared. They have won our loyal love and admiration all over again, as of the true stuff from the heart out. It's all I can do to keep from making love to Mrs. Hibben! But others have been scarcely less kind and faithful—the Magies, Harry Fine, the Daniels, Mrs. Cleveland,—even Dr. Patton. I saw people come up the walk those first few days of greatest anxiety whom I had never before seen on the premises. It's good to know how kind and attentive people can be.

I shall be a *very* happy man when I get home again—my speaking engagements away from Princeton all behind me,—ahead of me uninterrupted work and the eager expectation of my darling's coming, and the end of my heart's *suspension*. I keep wonderfully well, but, ah, my Eileen, how shall I express my longing for you, or the unspeakable fervour with which I am

Your own   Woodrow

ALS (WC, NjP).
  ¹ John and Marion Butler Meigs. He was Headmaster of the Hill School in Pottstown, Pa.

From Ellen Axson Wilson

My own darling,   [New Orleans] Friday [Feb. 23, 1900]

It is after two now and the mail is collected at three, so I shall write a hurried note now, chiefly on business, and then, if un-interrupted, begin again more at leisure.

Lucy has been "talking a blue streak" about Stockton coming down here and both of us spending another month with them! I told her Stockton wouldn't do it, but I had to promise to give the invitation, though I can't reproduce her half hour's eloquent speech on the subject! Dear girls! they are certainly hospitality itself. When I told her the month was impossible she plead for two weeks, and then, her plan is, for us to go to Pass Christian, a beautiful resort on the salt water with an ideal climate, mag-nificent oaks, and a *perfect* boarding-house, kept by the two old gentlewomen, Miss Kitty and Miss Polly, of whom you will re-member to have heard them talk. I think that *would* be good and pleasant for Stock! And of course he need not stay with the Smiths two weeks, but only long enough to see and enjoy this dear old city. The objection is that it would cost him more,—for travel,—than to go to Georgia. At any rate he needn't feel squeamish about coming because of,—you know what(!) They regard him exactly as a brother! He is no more Mary's "style" than she is his, and Lucy is practically engaged to the rich planter!¹ But that is another story,—one that I have been trying to find time to tell you for a week. He had better think seriously of the Pass Christian plan; and he would enjoy going down the Bayou Teche too. Perhaps when he is strong he would like to go to Nashville on his way home.

Give my *dear* love to him, to dear Sister and all. Arn't those children ever going to write to me?

My *darling, my* Woodrow, your letters for the last few days have been heart-breakingly sweet! Oh, I *want* you, I want *you*! I love you almost to suffocation.

With love unspeakable—   Your little wife,   Eileen.

2.40 P.M.(!)

ALS (WC, NjP).
  ¹ Mr. Barton, a sugar planter whom Mrs. Wilson describes in full detail (with-out, however, mentioning his given names) in EAW to WW, Feb. 24, 1900. There are at least five and perhaps six Bartons listed as operators of sugar plantations

in the Louisiana reference works of this period, and it is therefore impossible to identify Lucy Marshall Smith's Mr. Barton.

To Ellen Axson Wilson

My own darling,   Philadelphia Friday 23 Feb'y, 1900

I am afraid it must be a short note this morning. I slept late this morning, because I must stay up late to-night. It is now nearly eleven and I am just thro. breakfast. I have to buy some shirts and some white cravats before I start for Harrisburg, and my train leaves a little after noon. I reach Harrisburg about half past three, and from that time on shall be a "guest," with all that that implies. On the train I must study my address for the evening,—a full day! But I feel quite fit. I went to an amusing opera last night,[1] and that diverted my mind; I took a very long sleep, and that comforted my body. To-day I feel refreshed and ready for anything that may [happen. All in] all, its just as well to write short letters when I am away from home *and* from you. The situation does not add to my powers of *cheerful* speech. Not that I'm low spirited. It would be a poor creature indeed who could for long be really blue while he knew that he had your love, your *chief* love,—that you, the sweetest lover in the world, loved *him* with passionate devotion. That's what my heart is always singing to me. It is one thing to know this and quite another to *enjoy* your love, I'll admit. Nothing *can* ever compensate for your absence. But a fellow may be proud, all the same, and feel that he is authenticated to the world by the love borne him, and so face it blithely. It's a rough hour for me when I don't feel *that*. With my natural self-distrust, I should be of all men most miserable, did not happiness flood in upon me with the [knowledge] of the sweet fact that I am   [Your own   Woodrow]

ALS (WC, NjP); letter damaged.

[1] There were several musical comedies running in Philadelphia during the week of February 19-24, 1900; hence, it is not possible to identify this "amusing opera." "Aida" was presented at the Academy of Music on February 22, but it does not seem likely that Wilson was referring to it.

Two Letters from Ellen Axson Wilson

[New Orleans] Saturday morning
My own darling,   [Feb. 24, 1900]

Another hurried business note for the early mail. Will write again as usual for the three o'clock.

The Palmers send a cordial and urgent invitation to Stockton to visit them, for as long as possible. If he does come here I think it would be a good idea to go out to the "Pass" first, where it is peaceful, & then to the city when he grows stronger and craves variety.

Fanny Caldwell says that Geo. Allen though very ill certainly is not confined to bed or room. Also that she knows all the domestic arrangements there and they have *plenty* of room for Stockton too.

Suppose I just go on next week as I planned to Sav, let Stock meet me there, going to a hotel first, and then we can judge for ourselves whether to accept the invitation which will certainly be forthcoming or to go somewhere else.

With *dear* love to my darling and all—

Your own   Eileen.

I shall need say $10.00 more before leaving, thanks to getting a present for the Smiths

My own darling,   New Orleans. Saturday [Feb. 24, 1900]

Yours of Wed. with the funny, dreadful photos is just at hand. Who took them? I shall begin now,—lest it be crowded out again, —with the untold tale of Sunday. It was simply that on Saturday morning, Lucy took advantage of Mary's absence to spend the whole morning, practically, talking over her love affair, and confiding to me all her doubts and difficulties in the case. I say "all" but they really resolve themselves into one,—deserting Mary or making her unhappy. She said, I think, fifty times in the course of the morning, "Mary can't *bear* the country!" She said that once she had accepted him, but Mary looked so wretched & cried so much, in *private*, that she broke it off again. Of course I told her that if she really cared for Mr. Barton—(as she seems to,) it was not just to him or herself to go on as she was doing; they need not break up the town home at once, and many things might be left to settle themselves gradually; and above all that if she *ever* meant to marry him it would be wise & kind to all concerned, including Mary, to do it *promptly*, and be done with it! She seemed decided, when we stopped talking, to marry this spring. We even discussed wedding clothes a little! But now she is almost as dubious as ever again. *She* has been out this morning and *Mary* has been talking it over with me. She doesn't think Lucy cares for him enough; says she is certainly always happiest when he is about, but that she (Lucy) "doesn't like the country," is very dependent on her crowds of friends, and the variety and excitement of city life,—in short that she is not in the state when she would feel the world well lost for Mr. Barton. She says she thought once that Lucy loved him and told him so,—tried in every way in her power to help him. He of course proposed again and she accepted him,—only to break it off later! So that now she "will have nothing whatever to do with it"!

Mr. Barton has been here off and on since the first week of my visit and he seems to me an *extraordinarily* fine man,—a man of very unusual *force* of character and mind, yet entirely without harshness or heaviness or bluntness. His voice is *beautiful*, always quiet and low & firm yet full and musical, and you feel that he could lead an army without finding it necessary to raise it one tone, or ever showing the slightest excitement. His self-control, his power of initiative, his power over men is enormous. (I have been hearing about him from others, as well as Lucy!) He manages his hundreds of negros perfectly, never any bluster, or apparent sternness, yet they obey him as if their lives were in his hand. They adore him too, and are perfectly happy and well-cared for, have good houses, a good doctor and from .75 to $1.50 a day *cash* according to the season. His business is tremendous. His plantations are worth one or two hundred thousand, his sugar houses cost him $150,000, (You know they are really manufacturies where they produce the finest grades of sugar,) it costs him $85,000 cash each year to make a crop. And yet he can lose most of a crop as he did last year by the freeze without *showing* any more concern than if he had dropped his handkerchief! He is kindness itself to all his family, and they are *devoted* to him, especially the children. In appearance he is quite fine-looking, very tall, broad-shouldered and powerful & dresses extremely well,—like a city man. He is a college man, but not a man of books,—takes an active and intelligent interest in public affairs, has been often urged to go to the legislature, &c. but is obliged to decline because of his private business.

We were to have spent today at his plantation, & sailing on the Bayou, but his little half sister [Sallie Barton] was yesterday operated on for appendicitis here in the city. She has been here two weeks, the doctors studying the case. We hear this morning that she is doing very well.

As for myself I continue my mad career in the double role of a carnival visitor and a "social success"! My engagements are too numerous to be catalogued, much less described. Dr. Jones[1] wife gave me a reception yesterday; all the sixty women who were present asked me when I was at home as they wanted to call & I was obliged to tell them I was never at home! I could have several luncheon parties given me a day if I would; (no one gives dinners any more in this time of processions and balls,—they are lucky if they can get their cooks to stay in the kitchen at night & prepare a little nourishment for themselves.) One of the luncheons crowded out is the Kings though they were willing to take me any day during my stay. I am sorry for that as I wanted to see Miss Grace more quietly than I have done. I was to have gone to the Creole club again yesterday at their house, but was too tired,—was obliged to send my excuses and rest a little for the afternoon reception.

And now it is time to dress for a luncheon. Give my dear love to all & tell the children to kiss each other for me.

I love you, dear, more than you dream of; in spite of all distractions I think of you *constantly*. I am in every heart-throb,

Your own   Eileen.

ALS (WC, NjP).
¹ Joseph Jones, M.D., and Susan Polk Jones.

A Newspaper Report of a Public Lecture and an Alumni Meeting in Harrisburg, Pennsylvania

[Feb. 24, 1900]

PROFESSOR WILSON

The Famous Princetonian Lectures on "Freedom."[1]

Prof. Woodrow Wilson, of Princeton University, was greeted in the Board of Trade auditorium last evening, where he delivered a lecture on "Freedom." Professor Wilson began by showing that Freedom does not mean license to follow inclinations injurious to the State or to gratify desires at variance with the laws of nature. The man who takes deadly poison has violated an injunction of nature and is bound to suffer. The fundamental difference between republican government and a despotism is the uncertainty of laws and their administration in the latter. It is better to have a judge render decisions contrary to law if he consistently adheres to a fixed principle than a judge who is erratic and decides one day in one manner and the next day in another, even though he observe the letter of the law in so doing. In the absolute monarchy it is not known whether the same decision will be made in the evening as in the morning regarding a similar matter. Justice is uncertain when it depends upon the caprice of the ruler who is not in the same humor each day. We must not be so hasty, however, in denouncing the fetters that are put upon public utterance in Russia, where with the exception of making allusions to certain persons there is perfect freedom of speech. In our own country we are ridiculed if we dare utter sentiments at variance with public opinion, and are denounced as un-American, which seems to be the only definition of the term. The greatest safeguard for us is to encourage free speech. A fool will kill himself if he is only permitted to have full sway and expose his folly. The only cloud that has shown itself on our political horizon, that possibly in the future may cause trouble, is the great growth of wealth and classes in society. We should not discourage industry and accumulation, the result of thrifty habits, but if ever the time should come when an alienation occurred between labor and capital and the employed and employer did not feel their interests as one, we will have trouble. Freedom is not giving the same government to all people, but wisely discriminating and dispensing laws according to the advancement of a people. It would be wrong to try to give the same government now to the Philippine Islands as we enjoy who have been schooled for centuries to the use of our liberties. We will have to learn colonial administration, perhaps painfully, but we should do everything openly and encourage those in our new possessions to express freely their opinions and show them we have only their welfare at heart.

The Civic Club are to be congratulated on the happy selection of their orator of the winter and the delightful impression made by Professor Wilson last night should bespeak for him an enthusiastic and appreciative audience if he again favors our town.

It is to be hoped that the thinking people of our city will soon awaken to the opportunities afforded them when the great minds of the country are brought to their doors and more generously support the efforts made for their pleasure and enlightenment.

With the Princeton Alumni.

At the conclusion of Professor Wilson's lecture the Central Pennsylvania Alumni Association, of Princeton, held its annual meeting in the Harrisburg Club, followed by an informal reception and collation in Professor Wilson's honor. . . .

After the business meeting the alumni and their guests proceeded to the banquet hall, where an excellent repast was served, after which Mr. Bergner,[2] in very appropriate remarks, called upon several for a few words. Professor Wilson was the first speaker, who told of the wonderful growth of Princeton and spoke of the kindly relations existing between the alumni and the faculty and university. . . .

Printed in the *Harrisburg*, Pa., *Telegraph*, Feb. 24, 1900; two editorial headings omitted.
    [1] A new title for Wilson's old lecture, "Political Liberty."
    [2] Charles Henry Bergner '74, newly elected president of the Central Pennsylvania Alumni Association. Editor of the Harrisburg *Telegraph*, 1874-83, he afterward practiced law in Harrisburg.

To Ellen Axson Wilson

My own darling,   Princeton, Saturday 24 Feb'y, 1900
    Here I am at home again,—or, rather, in Princeton,—it's not, and cannot be, real home without you! I got back sooner than I expected,—at 2 o'clock, leaving Harrisburg at 9:10 this morning. I'm very, very tired, but none the worse for that. I did not get in from the Princeton "Smoker" till half-past one this morning (after a second speech,[1] of course), and had to get up a little after seven, in order to shave before an eight o'clock breakfast (I was staying with very swell people, for whom one felt *obliged* to shave); but I am singularly well and chipper, in spite of it all, being intensely sleepy rather than physically worn out,— quite a robust person, thank you, ma'am. There's no telling what these wiry hypochondriacs can stand, the humbugs!
    It is *such* a pleasure, such a delight, to read your sweet letters, and realize what a good time you are having! So Mrs. Davis 'took a fancy to you,' did she? And how many others, that you have heard of? What do you suppose would be my estimate of the taste and intelligence of persons who did *not* 'take a fancy to you'? Somebody took a fancy to me this time, and that's a circumstance worth recording. Mr. Boyd,[2] the old gentleman at whose house I stayed in Harrisburg,—a hearty, enjoying man of affairs, and no man of books, I judge, went to my lecture. "He didn't intend to go," his son confided to me, "but since he's heard you talk he thinks he'll go." There's a practical compliment, ma'am. I went out of my way in the lecture, I'll confess, to tell a good story or two, in order that the discourse might not go *too* heavily for the old gentleman; and he seemed quite cheerful after the experiment.
    I find that Stock. is continuing his fine, unbroken progress still. He sat up yesterday (in bed, of course) to take his meals; and to-day is propped up when he will between meals. The nurse thinks him well enough to do more; but I am very content to have

him make haste very slowly, according to Dr. Wikoff's more prudent counsels. His nervousness seems to have passed away, practically altogether. He has peaceful nights and as serene days as a chap of his temperament *can* have. Ah, my love, my Eileen, how I rejoice to tell you good news, good news,—nothing but good news! Good news seems to *belong* to you, together with love and deep enjoyment, and everything that makes life full of quiet power and happiness. I adore you with all my heart. Everybody *loves* you, but I am   Your own   Woodrow

I send $50, love.—and 4 photos. I've no more photos. All send love to all.

ALS (WC, NjP).
    ¹ "After Professor Wilson's lecture the Central Pennsylvania alumni association of Princeton, held its annual meeting and tendered an informal reception to Professor Wilson, at the Harrisburg club. . . . Professor Wilson expressed his pleasure at being able to meet the alumni and guests and spoke of the wonderful and steady growth of Princeton and the delightful relations existing between the faculty and alumni. . . ." *Harrisburg Independent*, Feb. 24, 1900.
    ² The old man was James Boyd, a long-time Harrisburg businessman. His son was John Yeomans Boyd, Princeton 1884, a prominent mining engineer and businessman of Harrisburg.

From Ellen Axson Wilson

My own darling,   New Orleans Sunday [Feb. 25, 1900]

Just to think that this is the fourth Sunday that I have spent in New Orleans! And it is just such an ideal day as the first; the second was a rainy day and the third a cold one, but today is *perfect*. With every breath I draw of this delicious air I think, "Ah if *he* were only here to breathe it with me how indescribably happy I should be!" Oh, my darling, *you* are the breath of life to me; it seems to me that I literally *could* not live without you. You are all the world to me; just imagine for a moment trying to construct a life for oneself out of such elements as have filled my days since I came here, with love left out,—or even with most sorts of love left in! There is only *one* sort however that is soul-satisfying,—and that, thank God, is mine in good measure pressed down and running over. To be *so* loved by *such* a man! Think of it! I am, beyond a doubt, the happiest, the most fortunate of women. And you too, my darling, as you well know, are loved in like measure,—if you have not equal cause for happiness it is because I am not "such a woman"—not the woman to be matched with "such a man." If *I* had had the chosing of a wife for you I should not have done you such injustice! But since you have played your cards so ill, all I can do for you now is to help you make the best of it by trying constantly to be as nice as I can. With my best endeavours I can never, alas! be all that you deserve, because,—well, among other reasons because I "havn't the mind to"!

Knowing what we do of the worth of love isn't it strange that anyone could ever weigh it in the balance with anything else whatever except duty? It seems inconceivable to me that a woman could care enough for a man to even dream of *marrying* him and yet stop to consider where he lived for instance, whether in the city or the country, and what sort of "society" the neighbourhood afforded. Certainly I took no such thought for the morrow! But indeed I never even consciously considered whether or not you could "make me happy"! I *loved* you, and was more than willing to let the happiness, like everything else, take care of itself. But perhaps the chief reason for that piece of imprudence (?) was that, as you know, my mind was very much occupied with questioning whether or not *I* could make *you* happy!

Unless I hear from you to the contrary I shall of course be leaving for Sav. this week. The best train leaves here at 8 P.M. reaching Sav. the next night. I expected to leave Thursday night, but I have an engagement to lunch with the Kings, and to go in the afternoon to a Club reception given to a prima donna with an impossible name who can,—and *will*,—sing magnificently. We did not think these things would interfere with my getting off at eight, but it seems they demand my trunk in the *morning* in order to make that train, and I should be left without a proper gown for these functions. So I may have to wait for night. The ticket is more than I thought,—$21.00, I suppose without the berth. I will feel better with $25.00 more. That ought to carry me to Atlanta on my way home. Don't forget to send the *pass* to Sav.

I see in the paper that Booth Tarkington with a party of friends,—perhaps Princeton people, is here for the Carnival and will then spend some time at Pass Christian. There is a pointer for Stock. You can't imagine how happy I am over his rapid progress now. *Our* appendicitis case little Sallie Barton is also doing finely. I am perfectly well & not at all tired. It is *most* fortunate that we always get good nights sleep. We get home from the balls even by twelve & from the processions by nine or ten. So there is no danger of our getting worn out. With dear love to all.   Your devoted little wife,   Eileen.

ALS (WC, NjP).

To Ellen Axson Wilson

My own darling,   Princeton, Sunday 25 Feb'y, 1900

A night's sleep has taken Harrisburg out of my bones, and I am ready for a chat with my dear love.

To-day Stock. is to have rice and chicken; to-morrow he is to sit up in a chair. That is our bulletin,—our good news continued. I believe I told you that Fraülein Clara had resumed her duties at school.

I have received the invitation of the Tulane trustees to speak at their Commencement, June twentieth, and I *greatly* appreciate it; but, quite apart from the exacting tasks I shall then have in hand (I shall by that time be in the toils of my agreement to supply *Harpers Magazine* with not less than ten thousand words *per* month), I feel sure that it would be very imprudent for me to go to New Orleans, for a trying piece of work such as an address always is for me, at that season of the year. It's going to be hard to decline; but decline I must, and the letter shall go to-morrow.[1] I would not have even the solace of seeing the dear Smiths there in June. I wish I knew some way in which I could show my appreciation of the too high opinion the gentlemen of the Tulane Board have of me; but I can think of nothing but words. I have declined one or two Commencement invitations already, but none except this one that it gave me any pang of regret to decline. There's not another out-of-town speaking engagement on my calendar now; and I must if possible keep it clear, in order that the History may have unimperilled right of way. Speaking of work, poor Perry hasn't got the Reconstruction essay yet. I saw when you and I talked it over, just before we started for Richmond, that it sadly needed revision,—was really written from two points of view, instead of one; but I've not been able to work on it and reduce it to harmony of tone, since poor Stock. went to bed; and I fear Perry is growing nervous about it.[2] I confidently hope that this week will see it finished, not only, but work resumed on the History as well. I ought to get into the swing of that without difficulty, and write with some ease, now that my mind is cleared of all anxiety, and feels bouyant, like an athlete running free and light after practicing under weights. The portion of my work that lies immediately ahead is in a sense the most difficult of all. The story of the Revolution, so far as it is a history of opinion and of political action, needs retelling, re-colouring, reassessing from end to end. As at present told it is false and partial,—not so much in what is told as in what is not told,—not deliberately false, but essentially sophisticated and mis-conceived. Of course *I* can reconstruct it and make it true! Ah, there's the *deep* work! Not to write a decent style and keep the narrative clear and coherent, but both to see the truth and to tell it,—to be artist enough to get the picture drawn,—to believe in myself steadily enough and thoroughly enough to apply the strokes with certainty and confidence,—to be sure what to say and what not to say! See an essay entitled *The Truth of the Matter*,[3] and add to the difficulties of which it discourses what you know of the failings and weaknesses of the particular author whose case is now under consideration, and you will know the anxieties of the present situation, and the chances that *Harpers Magazine* will next year contain a work of genius, in which American history will be for the first time adequately narrated. It shall be the best piece of writing I have done yet, at least, even if it does not contain the truth! Ah, how I should like to make you glad by making it, both in truth and execution, a *really* great work. There *ought* to be a genuinely first class narrative in me somewhere,—though out and out adequacy of conception must no doubt wait for *Statesmanship: A Study in Political Action and Leadership*,[4]—may have to wait indefinitely for the next thing to be written! At any rate, thoughts of you will animate me through every page. I shall write for you as I used to talk to you in the days of our first taste of each other,—as I still talk to you, with the conscious and passionate desire to win your approval and admiration. We must be partners in this, as in everything,—else I shall grow cold to the marrow, and write without blood or life. It makes me tremble to realize how much of my life is wrap't up in you; but I glory in the sweetness and ecstasy of loving you. It is so satisfactory. I am not a fellow to be imposed upon, mad-am, by superficial charms or a first impression. Very few people, alas! wear well with me; but your charm deepens with every year,—you become more engaging to me with every taste of your quality. You are so absolutely what I expected you to be,—so much more than I had dared to hope,—and yet more in degree, not in kind,—more in unending variety of satisfying traits and powers, not in the character of your delightful gifts. Ah, my Eileen, it would be impossible for *any* one to put into words the pleasure, the wonder, the longing which flood my heart as I sit here and think of you,—the strange mixture of infinite sadness because of your absence and exultant and satisfying joy because of your love for me, your presence now as always in my life and in everything that makes me what I am. I love you, darling, with a profound and surpassing passion. God grant you may love as much

Your own   Woodrow

All well—all devoted to you, and lovers of the Smiths.

ALS (WC, NjP).
  ¹ See WW to W. O. Rogers, Feb. 26, 1900.
  ² Wilson began a shorthand draft of this article on January 5, 1900, and completed it on January 30. The manuscript of this draft is in WP, DLC. As this letter and WW to EAW, March 2, 1900, make clear, he transcribed the shorthand draft on January 31, and he and Mrs. Wilson read it together that same evening. Wilson apparently did not save this transcribed version.
  Wilson's article (printed at March 2, 1900) was to be the lead in a series on Reconstruction which the *Atlantic Monthly* published in 1901. The other authors and articles in the series were Hilary A. Herbert, "The Conditions of the Reconstruction Problem," *Atlantic Monthly*, LXXXVII (Feb. 1901), 145-57; W.E.B. Du Bois, "The Freedmen's Bureau," *ibid.*, March 1901, pp. 354-65; Daniel H. Chamberlain, "Reconstruction in South Carolina," *ibid.*, April 1901, pp. 473-84; William Garrott Brown, "The Ku Klux Movement," *ibid.*, May 1901, pp. 634-44; Samuel W. McCall, "Washington During Reconstruction," *ibid.*, June 1901, pp. 817-26; Albert Phelps, "New Orleans and Reconstruction," *ibid.*, LXXXVIII (July 1901), 121-31; Thomas Nelson Page, "The Southern People During Reconstruction," *ibid.*, Sept. 1901, pp. 289-304; and William A. Dunning, "The Undoing of Reconstruction," *ibid.*, Oct. 1901, pp. 437-49. Perry's epilogue, printed before the Dunning article, was "Reconstruction and Disfranchisement," *ibid.*, pp. 433-37. Seven of these articles, along with Perry's epilogue, have been reprinted as Richard N. Current (ed.), *Reconstruction in Retrospect: Views from the Turn of the Century* (Baton Rouge, La., 1969).
  ³ Printed under the title, "On the Writing of History," at June 17, 1895, Vol. 9. Wilson refers here to the reprint of the essay under its original title in *Mere Literature and Other Essays* (Boston and New York, 1896), pp. 161-86.
  ⁴ An outline of and the first notes for this projected work are printed at June 5, 1899.

From Ellen Axson Wilson

[New Orleans] Monday morning

My own darling,   [Feb. 26, 1900]

No time today, alas! for anything but the briefest note. We are starting immediately to make a few calls on special friends of the girls whom we can see informally in the morning,—that to save time! Then lunch and after that the "Arrival of Rex"; tonight the "Proteus" procession viewed again from the Boston Club; then supper at the club and home to bed. We have positively declined to go to the ball tonight; must save up for the grand finale tomorrow night,—the Comus rout.

The weather continues ideal; real carnival weather, and everything and everybody is very gay.

I have also two letters from you this morning to make me *really happy*; the two from Phila. But I am so sorry for the Meigs. How wonderful they are! I could *never* bear it so! I am sorry you had the distress of being there then, but am sure you were a comfort to them.

I am sure your speech[1] was splendid. I like the analysis *especially*.[2]

Dr. Jameson's letter[3] was funny, as usual!

I wonder if I have time for a good short story too! A Catholic lady here was, the other day, instructing her small boy in theology; she told him that everyone must go to purgatory but that only one person was *positively* known to be in hell, viz. Judas Iscariot. The boy meditated for a while & then remarked thoughtfully, "Well, I shouldn't think it would pay them to keep it up for just *one* person!" Is that a naughty story? Only, I suppose, on the well-known protestant tenet that it is "a sin to speak disrespectfully of the devil." But I must run. With dear love to all, and dearest of all to my darling.   Your own   Eileen.

ALS (WC, NjP).
  [1] At the Hill School on February 22.
  [2] Wilson's analysis, or outline, is missing.
  [3] Apparently Jameson's reply, which is missing, to Wilson's letter of February 21, 1900.

To Ellen Axson Wilson

My own darling,   Princeton, Monday 26 Feb'y, 1900

A Monday with a Kneisel Quartette concert in the evening[1] is certainly the busiest of all days for me. I have been *rushed* every minute since breakfast,—and we are now just about to sit down to dinner. I must write as much as possible before the concert (I am already dressed), and, if I can't finish before, finish afterwards.

And, first, as to Stock's plans. Practically none of the schemes you suggest will be feasible. He particularly wants to keep away from such places as Atlanta and Savannah, where there would be friends and therefore excitement, because he needs and longs for quiet; and he could not, and should not,—on grounds both of money and of strength for the journey,—go so far as to New Orleans or any of the other delightful places near it which you name. Besides, my love, he cannot come *now*, or very soon. He cannot come till you are well on your progress homeward. I have not had time to read him your letter yet; but I know from talks we have already had about the matter that his idea is, to go first, perhaps, for a few days to some nearby place like Atlantic City, and then go down to (say) Asheville, (where, by the way, he would probably have the advantage of having Dr. Van Valzah at hand), and there wait for you to come to your last stage, at Mrs. Dubose's;[2] and presently come home with you. He expects to return to work by the first of April, and will not, I think, wish to be at his far away resort (say, Asheville) for more than a week or ten days. I will read your letter to him, and talk the matter over with him again; and I will write you about it once more tomorrow. But he was so definite and resolute against far-away places and places where he is well or extensively acquainted that I feel quite sure the plans you suggest are to be put out of the reckoning. The one I have indicated would have the great advantage, to my mind, of making it that much the more certain that you would go to Asheville. I have set my heart on your seeing "Rose," and doing everything else that will renew your youth.

My poor head whirls whenever I write hastily and against time, as I am writing now, with thoughts of the *"charming* lady" of whom Mrs. Labouisse had heard, the guest of the Smiths'. Her charm is *painfully* vivid for me. Her image haunts me,—and startles and waylays. I hear her voice and imagine her step. I *tremble* with passionate longing. The thought of her now woos, now saddens, and again thrills me,—is always so real, so sweet, so intense, as if it were part of my actual physical life, and yet not that but a spirit going always and everywhere with me. Ah, my love, absence *has* its sweet and wholesome uses. I wonder if I ever get *used* to having you and slacken in my sense of enjoyment that I should *need* this thrilling experience of the meaning of your absence and of being

Your own   Woodrow

ALS (WC, NjP).

[1] About this famous Boston ensemble, see EAW to WW, Feb. 4, 1895, Vol. 9, n. 1. In its concert on February 26, the Kneisel Quartette presented Carl von Dittersdorf's "Quartet in E Flat Major," Schumann's "Quartet in A Minor, Op. 41, No. 1," and Arthur Foote's "Quintet for Piano and Strings in A Minor, Op. 38," with Arthur Foote as pianist.

[2] Mrs. Wilson's old friend, Rosalie Anderson Dubose, wife of the Rev. McNeely Dubose, rector of Trinity Episcopal Church in Asheville.

To William Oscar Rogers

My dear Sir,   Princeton, 26 Feb'y, 1900.

Your kind letter,[1] conveying the very flattering invitation of the Board of Administrators of the Tulane Educational Fund to deliver the address at the next Commencement of the University, reached Princeton while I was absent for a few days from home.

I am very deeply gratified by their wish, so cordially expressed, and most unaffectedly regret that it is not possible for me to accept. Next June is, for me, absolutely mortgaged, by engagements made some months ago; and I have already been obliged to decline several other Commencement invitations as a consequence. Most of these I declined without much regret; but with Tulane it is another matter. I decline her invitation with real reluctance. I should like both to visit and to serve her, were it possible.

Pray convey to the Board my very warm thanks and my most sincere assurances of genuine regret.

With much regard,

Very truly Yours,   Woodrow Wilson

ALS (LNHT).
[1] It is missing.

From Ellen Axson Wilson

My own darling,   [New Orleans] Mardi Gras day [Feb. 27, 1900]

It is already, alas! three o'clock,—too late for my letter to go on the usual mail! Soon after breakfast we left to see the procession which was to start at eleven. Had a long wait of course, but there was quite enough to divert us in watching the passing crowds, the promiscuous maskers making fools of themselves, &c. &c.

We had invitations for the Boston Club again for both today and tonight, but we decided not to venture into the dense throng on Canal Street but to go instead to a friend's gallery on St. Charles. Am very glad we so decided; as it was we could only get a car and reach home for a late luncheon. We must be dressed and ready for dinner, the night parade, and the ball by half past five. I should like to spend much of the intervening time writing to you; but what I ought to do and *must* do is to lie down and rest. Will tell you a little about the parades another day. They were superb, gorgeous, wonderful,—in fact almost every adjective you can think of except possibly the one most usually applied, viz., "beautiful." As a whole they are too fantastic, barbaric, to quite deserve that word, though some of the individual cars have been positively and undeniably beautiful.

The pictures, check, &c. came this morning. Many thanks dearest; but why so much money? With dear love to all & dearest love,—love inexpressible to my own darling, I am as always,

Your own   Eileen.

ALS (WC, NjP).

To Ellen Axson Wilson

My own darling,   Princeton, Tuesday 27 Feb'y, 1900

Stockton and I have had another talk about his trip,—and my last letter stands confirmed as written. He wants the most cordial and affectionate messages of thanks you can frame delivered to the dear Smiths and to Dr. Palmer and Mrs. Caldwell; but the distance is too great, and the expense. His choice centres on Asheville. It is, of course, impossible to say yet exactly when he will be ready to start; but, if you will begin your 'tour' practically at once, you can stay as long as you would feel comfortable in staying, under the circumstances, at Savannah and Atlanta, and even have a few days at Rome, before it is time to join him. It will be important to *meet* him at Asheville,—so that he will feel less nervous about arriving alone (he is going for a *mind* rest as well as for a body rest). But we can let you know by telegraph when he will start, and so give you time to be beforehand. Meanwhile,—or, at latest, the minute you arrive in Savannah, write, please, dear, to "Rose" and ascertain a good and moderate-priced quiet boarding house, wont you? to which to take him. We have defrauded you of your right to nurse him at this end; but you shall have your full rights at the other; and must stay with him until either he is manifestly ready to be left or ready to come back with you. In the latter case (unless it's Monday or Tuesday), I will come down to Washington to meet you both, and escort you home! Ah, what will it *not* mean to see you, my Eileen,—to touch and kiss and hold you as my own!

Miss Lucy's love story is *deeply* interesting and puzzling. I can't see the right of it at all. When you tell me Miss Lucy's side, it seems plain one way. When you tell me Miss Mary's version of the case, it seems to me rather too plain the other way. This is evidently one of the cases we'll *have* to leave to Providence. The man certainly seems splendid and worthy as you describe him.

This is Tuesday night, and I'm as tired as usual; but your dear letters keep me in spirits. It does me *so* much good to know the gay, *interesting* time you are having. You will be converted to "society" by the time you come back, and I shall have to wear a dress suit every evening.

All join me in boundless love to you,—to the dear Smiths every message of warmest affection,—and the whole heart to my Eileen of   Her own   Woodrow

ALS (WC, NjP).

From the Minutes of the Princeton University Faculty

5 5′ P.M. Wednesday, Feb. 28, 1900.

. . . The President appointed Professors Henry van Dyke and Woodrow Wilson to fill vacancies in the Committee on Elective Studies. . . .

Professors Cornwall, Woodrow Wilson and Fine were elected by ballot a Committee to appear before and confer with the Board of Trustees if required.[1]

[1] The committee did not confer with the trustees.

From French Ensor Chadwick

Dear Sir,   [New York] 28. 2. 1900.

I ought perhaps have written you long since in regard to the reception of the copies of your address, and to thank you for the one before the New Jersey Historical Society.[1]

They went as did also yr letter to the West Indies and were returned after some time.

I have distributed the Va. Bar Association address, and if you feel inclined to let me have some more, I should be glad to continue the good work. I think indeed it is the best in which a patriotic man can engage nowadays. We have come to a point where we must have a government and the first thing necessary to a change from our present condition of gristle, is a clear recognition of the fact that we are now simply in the pull and haul of an ill organized town meeting.

Believe me   Very truly yours   F. E. Chadwick

I wish I could send you a list of the beneficiaries, but I kept none: but they were all good men of the Charles Fairchild[2] sort.

ALS (WP, DLC).

[1] A reprint of "The Course of American History," printed at May 16, 1895, Vol. 9. The first page of this reprint, inscribed by Wilson, is in the de Coppet Collection, NjP.

[2] Charles Stebbins Fairchild of New York, lawyer, political reformer, and Secretary of the Treasury, 1887-89.

Notes for a Religious Address[1]

Philad. Soc'y, 28 Feb'y, 1900

CXIX Ps., 105-112

1 Tim. IV. pts. of 8 and 10.

"Godliness is profitable unto all things, having promise of the life that now is, and of that which is to come." 8. "The living God

who is the Saviour of all men, specially of those that believe."
10.

Those who think of *personal religion* as a thing merely of *emotion* or of *sentiment* must assuredly *find an awakening and a tonic in the writings of Paul,* who speaks with the precision and rational power of the trained lawyer.

The saving and regenerating power of faith is certainly as *demonstrable* a fact as the operation of the laws of nature. We have had *nineteen hundred years of observation* and experiment and can say that we know.

Godliness is profitable both for the life that now is and for that which is to come; God *is* the Saviour of *all men.*

   But specially for those that believe,—specially for *this* life, as well as specially for the life which is to come.

Simply because only those that believe get the direct and vital power of it.

   Those who do not believe get it only by *indirection, suggestion, imitation,* instead of by direct transmission,—a sort of *quack profit.*

   It requires more subtlety, more watchfulness, more anxious and doubtful calculation to be upright without belief.

Of course the supreme reason for godliness is *Love,* the only altruistic motive force in the world.

   But Love is profitable
      By reason of illumination,
               simplification,
               rectification,
         amplification.

28 Feb'y, 1900[2]

WWhw and WWT MS. (WP, DLC).
   [1] The particular circumstances of this address are explained in n. 1 to the following document.
   [2] Wilson's composition date.

A Report of a Religious Address

[March 1, 1900]

PROFESSOR WOODROW WILSON

Addresses the Fourth Religious Meeting
of the Week in Marquand Chapel.

The fourth in the week's series of religious meetings[1] which was held last evening in Marquand Chapel was addressed by

Professor Woodrow Wilson. His subject was, "Some Reasons Why a Man Should be a Christian." He said, in part:

Those who think religion is a matter of emotion wonder when they read the clear, logical writings of Saint Paul. The regenerative power of the Spirit is not a conjecture. Christians have been observing and experimenting for nineteen hundred years and they are sure that it is right and profitable. The autobiographies of godly men set forth lives which were worthy and manly and noble; those of wicked men are held as objects of derision and scorn.

Godliness is profitable in both lives; godliness not only results in salvation of the soul, but enables a man to pursue a confident course in this worldly life, like a straight course in the direction of a visible goal. It has benefited men who do not believe in Christianity, men who imitate the ways of the righteous, because it has brought to the world through the Bible, humanity, justice, higher civilization and love. It benefits the man who believes because it fills him with a living and satisfying belief in the life beyond the grave. Godliness is profitable not only during his natural life, but in the time after him. The men who have received the belief in Christianity into their hearts make up the vital force of Christian progress and expansion.

Again, in college life religion is somewhat removed from the theatre of affairs, but this is the period in a man's life when the choice is easiest. Here, where his work is ready and prepared for him his leisure is greatest. There is less time to choose when life is crowding upon him in the struggle in the outer world.

The only way to carry salvation from this world into the next is by accepting Jesus Christ, by giving him the highest form of love; the love of allegiance. Love makes duty a pleasure, not a burden. It makes life's journey one taken in the noontide hour and not in the shadows of the night. It makes the prospect so fair before a man that he cheats himself who fails to avail himself of it.

Printed in the *Daily Princetonian*, March 1, 1900.
    1 A series of religious meetings held under the auspices of the Philadelphian Society in Marquand Chapel from February 25 through March 8, 1900, with the general theme, "Why thinking men should be Christians." Other speakers in the series were Rev. Dr. Alexander McKenzie, pastor of the First Congregational Church of Cambridge, Mass., and Harvard University Preacher; John R. Mott, Y.M.C.A. leader and General Secretary of the World's Student Christian Federation; Robert Elliott Speer, Princeton 1889, Secretary of the Board of Foreign Missions of the Presbyterian Church in the U.S.A.; Professor Alexander Thomas Ormond; Rev. Dr. George Tybout Purves; Professor Andrew Fleming West; Rev. Dr. William Stephen Rainsford, rector of St. George's Episcopal Church in New York; and Professor Henry van Dyke. Wilson comments on his address and the series in WW to EAW March 1, 1900.

From Ellen Axson Wilson

My own darling,   [New Orleans] Thursday [March 1, 1900]

The fates were against me all day yesterday, allowing me not even *one* moment to write you! I slept until a quarter of ten,—the Comus ball the night before having kept us up until two,—then at 10.15, before I was quite dressed, came my first visitor, others following close upon their heels, so that when at last I was free I had barely time to rush upstairs, answer a note of invitation and dress in the greatest haste for my luncheon engagement. It was with my cousin Maud May Parker[1] (you remember the red-headed Parker boys[2] who entered Princeton with us? Maud married their elder brother,—they are a very wealthy and prominent family here.) Maud's father was my father's first cousin, the great cotton buyer & multimillionare.[3] After the luncheon we were obliged to make some calls and then go straight to meet our dinner engagement at the Leovy's.[4] I had a *delightful* evening. Dr. & Mrs. Bruns were there, and both the doctor & the Leovys are brilliant talkers. We also had the offer of a opera box for last night,—the third time we have had to refuse. Too bad! is'nt it? when I have never seen an opera.

I write now in the *early* morning that it may catch an earlier post than the three o'clock. Have to make haste and go down to the railroad office, bank, &c. &c. Then back and make a full dress toilette, before going to luncheon at the Kings, because the reception to the prima donna is at three and Mrs. Walmsley[5] has asked me to help her receive. They have a splendid house just suited for such functions. He is a bank president, and a magnate generally, and she is a great lady in the best sense of the word,—or I might say in almost *every* sense including the physical!

The carnival ended in a blaze of glory Tuesday. The whole carnival was, they say, beyond comparison the most splendid, brilliant and successful in the history of the city. And the weather was as perfect as everything else concerned. But I must not miss that mail! With devoted love,   Your little wife,   Eileen.

Since Stock was just out of bed Sunday it is only too evident he is not able yet to come here, so I go on to Sav. tomorrow night. Have heard nothing from you as to his plans for meeting me.

ALS (WC, NjP).

1 Maud May (Mrs. Robert Buskner) Parker, of 2303 Prytania St. Her husband was president of Montgomery, Parker & Co., a paint concern.

2 James Porter Parker, B.S., 1892, and Arthur D'Evereaux Parker, who entered with the Class of 1893 and did not graduate.

3 He was A. H. May (1823-99), commission merchant and cotton factor of New Orleans from 1847 to his death, who also owned extensive cotton planta-

tions in Louisiana, Mississippi, and Arkansas. He was the son of Rosa Randolph May, a sister of Mrs. Wilson's paternal grandmother, Rebekah Randolph Axson.
  [4] Probably Henry Jefferson Leovy and Elizabeth Adair Monroe Leovy, of 543 Howard St.
  [5] Caroline Williams (Mrs. Robert Miller) Walmsley.

Two Letters to Ellen Axson Wilson

My own darling,   Princeton, Thursday A.M. 1 March, 1900

It makes my heart thrill to know that this letter is going to meet you in Savannah,—that by the time my Eileen reads this she will be several hundred miles nearer me! My heart is just now very full of the love letter you wrote last Sunday, and which came yesterday, when I least expected it. Until yesterday Wednesday had been embargo day with me,—the day on which the Sunday embargo at your end took effect, and I got no letter. To get a letter not only but a letter containing more than four pages of explicit love-making quite upset my heart with joy. It came, too, just when it was most needed. I was agonizing over an address appointed for the evening in the chapel. I had to speak at a meeting of the Philadelphian Society,—one of a ten days' series of meetings, arranged, not as a means of revival in the usual sense of that word, but as a means of rousing the men to a sense of their responsibility for making or not making a choice in respect of Christ. I felt the difficulty and weight of the task in an unusual degree, and my darling's letter brought me the sweet private tonic I needed. A *sentence* of love from you, my Eileen, is more to me than the *fact* of love from anybody else. All the romance and sweetness of my life seems to be centred in it,—the fulfilment of all that I hoped for and knew that I needed from the first moment I saw you. *Don't* say that you were not good enough for me. You know how cruelly foolish that seems to me. Why did I want you so much, instinctively and at once? Why have you *satisfied* me so, in the deepest parts of my nature as well as in all the rest? You are my natural queen; no one else in the world could have reigned over my spirit as you have.

Fraülein Clara went on Tuesday to spend a week with Mrs. Dahlgren,[1] and our domestic arrangements are eased off, as a consequence. The nurse (who will probably leave within a day or two, her job done) is in Fraülein's room, instead of the day nursery, as before.

Calculate the time your letters take to reach me, my love, and keep me informed in very business like form of your plans, —with *times* set as nearly as may be,—so that I may be able to reach you by telegraph whenever we know when Stock. can start, —*and don't be alarmed by a telegram*. I *think* Stock. will be fit by the 10th.

I love you to distraction   Your own   Woodrow

A great deal of love to all the dear ones in Savannah

[1] Emilie Elizabeth Kuprion (Mrs. Ulric) Dahlgren, German-born wife of the Assistant Professor of Histology, of 12 Maple St.

My own darling,   Princeton, Thursday evening 1 March, 1900.

You would feel rewarded, and more than rewarded, I am sure, for the trouble it gave you to write a real, out and out love letter if you could but know the effect it has upon the poor hungry chap to whom it is a feast,—a feast for days after. And this time the sweet letter of Sunday is food for thought as well. Why *should* my darling keep to her superficial theory that she is unworthy of me? For it *is* a superficial theory to suppose that a man such as you imagine and describe me to be should be satisfied,—should have delight of heart and mind, unaffected, unmistakable,—for fifteen years together, in a woman not fitted by gift or acquirement to be his companion and solace; that he should see her constantly all that while in the quietest of homes, in every mood, through every sort of occupation or amusement, and find her *altogether* to his mind and taste, and yet be mistaken as to her real quality. You must either give up your judgment that I am a man extraordinarily endowed, or else you must give up your opinion that I am mistaken in you. The two ideas are mutually exclusive. Ah, my love, don't distress me with the notion any more. Accept my love for what it is, a love of a real woman whom I know,—not a fancy for an unreal being whom I have imagined you to be. I have known a good many women first and last,—have admired a great many and loved not a few; but of all the women I have ever known *you* are the one I should *now* pick out,— quickly, eagerly,—as the sweetest, most interesting, most lovely, most satisfying, most entrancing of them all,—beyond comparison the one to *live* with and die for. That is the choice and judgment I am willing to be assessed by as a man of insight and taste, —and I don't want to hear any more nonsense about it!

Alas! I must change the subject for a word of business. It is not unlikely that Stockton may be ready to start *before* the 10th, which is Saturday of next week. Please get Randolph or Palmer[1] to look up schedules for you between Atlanta and Asheville (I assume that you will go to Atlanta next week and await my telegram there) so that I can allow you enough time to get to Asheville ahead of S. Tell me the result of the inquiry and keep a note of the result yourself. Stock. grows stronger very fast,—can already walk about by himself. Ask Miss "Rose" what she knows about Mrs. Glaser, whose house (she takes lodgers, boarders) is called Oakhurst.[2] Our love to all the dear ones. My Eileen I love you beyond words or the power of devotion to express.

Your own   Woodrow

ALS (WC, NjP).

[1] Her first cousins in Savannah, Randolph Axson, Jr., and Benjamin Palmer Axson.

[2] Ellen V. Glaser, proprietress of Oakhurst, a boardinghouse of "select patronage" at 244 Chestnut St., Asheville.

From Ellen Axson Wilson

My own darling,   [New Orleans] Friday [March 2, 1900]

It is two o'clock and I am hastening to get my last letter from New Orleans off by three. Have been busy all the morning packing, answering notes &c. &c.; my trunk is locked now waiting for the transfer man, who was to call at two. As soon as I finish this I shall go to the Palmers,—unless, as they promised[,] they come here in the meantime!—and that is my last bit of business. I had a delightful evening all to myself with Cousin Ben last night. He is so sweet and tender and affectionate towards me.

We had a charming time at the King's luncheon yesterday, and then I finished my New Orleans career in a blaze of glory at Mrs. Walmsley's reception. In fact I was so petted and praised and made love to (by *women*!) that I was almost bewildered. I wore my pink dress and was voted "an incarnation of a Duchess de Brabant rose"! Arn't you afraid my head is completely turned? Mrs. Jones —Mrs. Blake's sister—says I must tell you that she has scarcely ever known any visitor make such a deep and delightful impression on New Orleans society, that I have *"charmed everybody"*! Now you *must* burn this! How could I bear to think such apparently silly bragging remained in existence? But *you know* that I repeat it, *much* against my will, because it will please you to hear it, you dear, doting, foolish darling. I couldn't give a truer evidence of my desire to please you.

Sad to relate I am leaving dear Lucy in bed; she has a feverish cold and is besides, I am afraid, worn out racing around with me. A few days of perfect rest will doubtless make all right again. I am quite well except for a bit of a back-ache & head-ache just now from trying to get everything in the trunk! There is a good deal more than a reasonable trunk-full. It makes me so tired to think of doing it four times more that I am tempted to send an express package to Princeton from Sav.

I was lucky enough to find for the girls just what I knew before they most wanted, a most *beautiful* pair of antique candle-sticks, old Sheffield plate on copper, price, replated & put in perfect order, $14.00. I was so pleased. They certainly have devoted themselves to making me have a good time. Words fail me to do that subject justice.

With love, *love, love* to all, love unspeakable to my Woodrow, I am always & altogether   Your own   Eileen.

I can't tell you dear, how much I enjoyed your Sunday letter,— how intensely interested I was in all you say about the book.

ALS (WC, NjP).

To Ellen Axson Wilson

My own darling,   Princeton, Friday 2 March, 1900.

Dr. Wikoff, with his ultra conservatism, rather frowned to-day on the idea of Stockton's leaving next week,—and said "not for two weeks yet,"—so you may be a little more leisurely in your movements. But I was not present when he said that (only Stock. and the nurse were there), and I think that his impression was that Stock. would be alone at his destination as well as on the journey. Probably when I explain the whole plan to him he will consent to (say) the 14th or 15th. I will of course write you of the exact change. Now I can say only that he will not start as early as the 10th—probably not earlier than the middle of the next week. He is gaining strength so rapidly that he can probably take his choice of time week after next. We expect to send the nurse home on Monday next.

Yesterday and to-day I have been at my writing again,—revising the Reconstruction essay for Perry,—getting it set to *one* tune throughout, instead of to two, as your own keen ear detected that it was when we read it together. I think it is pretty well in key now; and Perry gets it at once. Next week for the history, for which I feel quite fit, I assure you,—as fit as I can feel for anything with may [my] chief comfort and inspiration out of the house. I think it will be a real comfort to get you nearer! My darling is on the train as I write (it is now ten o'clock in the evening). How my heart aches to think of her travelling alone,— aches with a *special* ache, to think of my not being there to take care of her! May God keep her! That train carries precious freight,—carries my whole treasure in the world: an ineffable treasure[.] If I could once assess you in words, my Eileen, it would be in some sweet formula which would *seem* more beautiful than any possible truth; but it would not be a universal formula in which to express the quality of a perfect woman. It would be unique, because it would have your flavour,—would be the perfect image of a personality as distinctive as it is delightful. I do so rejoice in your unlikeness to all other women—much as I worship the sex—in what belongs to me, and to no other man in all the world. My Eileen is comparable with no one; no one could make me by sheer charm of her own so utterly

Her own   Woodrow

ALS (WC, NjP).

An Historical Essay[1]

[c. March 2, 1900]

THE RECONSTRUCTION OF THE SOUTHERN STATES.

It is now full thirty years, and more, since the processes of Reconstruction were finished, and the southern states restored to their place in the Union. Those thirty years have counted for more than any other thirty in our history, so great have been the speed and range of our development, so comprehensive and irresistible has been the sweep of change amongst us. We have come out of the atmosphere of the sixties. The time seems remote, historic, not of our day. We have dropped its thinking, lost its passion, forgot its anxieties, and should be ready to speak of it, not as partisans, but as historians.

Most troublesome questions are thus handed over, sooner or later, to the historian. It is his vexation that they do not cease to be troublesome because they have been finished with by statesmen, and laid aside as practically settled. To him are left all the intellectual and moral difficulties, and the subtle, hazardous, responsible business of determining what was well done, what ill done; where motive ran clear and just, where clouded by passion, poisoned by personal ambition, or darkened by malevolence. More of the elements of every policy are visible to him than can have been visible to the actors on the scene itself; but he cannot always be certain which they saw, which they did not see. He is

1 No manuscript copy of this version of "The Reconstruction of the Southern States" is known to have survived.

deciding old questions in a new light. He is dangerously cool in dealing with questions of passion; too much informed about questions which had, in fact, to be settled upon a momentary and first impression; scrupulous in view of things which happened afterward, as well as of things which happened before the acts upon which he is sitting in judgment. It is a wonder that historians who take their business seriously can sleep at night.

Reconstruction is still revolutionary matter. Those who delve in it find it like a banked fire, still hot and fiery within, for all it has lain under the ashes a whole generation; and a thing to take fire from. It is hard to construct an argument here which shall not be heated, a source of passion no less than of light. And then the test of the stuff must be so various. The American historian must be both constitutional lawyer and statesman in the judgments he utters; and the American constitutional lawyer must always apply, not a single, but a double standard. He must insist on the plain, explicit command and letter of the law, and yet he must not be impracticable. Institutions must live and take their growth, and the laws which clothe them must be no straitjacket, but rather living tissue, themselves containing the power of normal growth and healthful expansion. The powers of government must make shift to live and adapt themselves to circumstances: it would be the very negation of wise conservatism to throttle them with definitions too precise and rigid.

Such difficulties, however, are happily more formidable in the mass than in detail; and even the period of Reconstruction can now be judged fairly enough, with but a little tolerance, breadth, and moderation added to the just modicum of knowledge. Some things about it are very plain,—among the rest, that it is a period too little studied as yet, and of capital importance in our constitutional history. Indeed, it is not too much to say that there crosses it, in full sight of every one who will look, a great rift, which breaks, and must always break, the continuity and harmony of our constitutional development. The national government which came out of Reconstruction was not the national government which went into it. The civil war had given leave to one set of revolutionary forces; Reconstruction gave leave to another still more formidable. The effects of the first were temporary, the inevitable accompaniments of civil war and armed violence; the effects of the second were permanent, and struck to the very centre of our forms of government. Any narrative of the facts, however brief, carries that conclusion upon its surface.

The war had been fought to preserve the Union, to dislodge

and drive out by force the doctrine of the right of secession. The southern states *could* not legally leave the Union,—such had been the doctrine of the victorious states whose armies won under Grant and Sherman,—and the federal government had been able to prevent their leaving, in fact. In strict theory, though their people had been in revolt, under organizations which called themselves states, and which had thrown off all allegiance to the older Union and formed a new confederation of their own, Virginia, North Carolina, South Carolina, Florida, Georgia, Mississippi, Alabama, Louisiana, Texas, Arkansas, and Tennessee, the historic states once solemnly embodied in the Union, had never gone out of it, could never go out of it and remain states. In fact, nevertheless, their representatives had withdrawn from the federal House and Senate; their several governments, without change of form or personnel, had declared themselves no longer joined with the rest of the states in purpose or allegiance, had arranged a new and separate partnership, and had for four years maintained an organized resistance to the armies of the Union which they had renounced. Now that their resistance had been overcome and their confederacy destroyed, how were they to be treated? As if they had been all the while in the Union, whether they would or no, and were now at last simply brought to their senses again, to take up their old-time rights and duties intact, resume their familiar functions within the Union as if nothing had happened? The theory of the case was tolerably clear; and the Supreme Court of the United States presently supplied lawyers, if not statesmen, with a clear enough formulation of it. The Constitution, it said (for example, in the celebrated case of Texas *vs.* White, decided in 1868), had created an indestructible Union of indestructible states. The eleven states which had attempted to secede had not been destroyed by their secession. Everything that they had done to bring about secession or maintain resistance to the Union was absolutely null and void, and without legal effect; but their laws passed for other purposes, even those passed while they were in fact maintaining their resolution of secession and defying the authority of the national government, were valid, and must be given effect to in respect of all the ordinary concerns of business, property, and personal obligation, just as if they had been passed in ordinary times and under ordinary circumstances. The states had lost no legitimate authority; their acts were invalid only in respect of what they had never had the right to do.

But it was infinitely hard to translate such principles into a practicable rule of statesmanship. It was as difficult and hazardous a matter to reinstate the states as it would have been had their legal right to secede been first admitted, and then destroyed by the revolutionary force of arms. It became, whatever the theory, in fact a process of reconstruction. Had Mr. Lincoln lived, perhaps the whole of the delicate business might have been carried through with dignity, good temper, and simplicity of method; with all necessary concessions to passion, with no pedantic insistence upon consistent and uniform rules, with sensible irregularities and compromises, and yet with a straightforward, frank, and open way of management which would have assisted to find for every influence its natural and legitimate and quieting effect. It was of the nature of Mr. Lincoln's mind to reduce complex situations to their simples, to guide men without irritating them, to go forward and be practical without being radical,—to serve as a genial force which supplied heat enough to keep action warm, and yet minimized the friction and eased the whole progress of affairs.

It was characteristic of him that he had kept his own theory clear and unconfused throughout the whole struggle to bring the southern people back to their allegiance to the Union. He had never recognized any man who spoke or acted for the southern people in the matter of secession as the representative of any government whatever. It was, in his view, not the southern states which had taken up arms against the Union, but merely the people dwelling within them. State lines defined the territory within which rebellion had spread and men had organized under arms to destroy the Union; but their organization had been effected without color of law; that could not be a state, in any legal meaning of the term, which denied what was the indispensable prerequisite of its every exercise of political functions, its membership in the Union. He was not fighting states, therefore, or a confederacy of states, but only a body of people who refused to act as states, and could not, if they would, form another Union. What he wished and strove for, without passion save for the accomplishment of his purpose, without enmity against persons, and yet with burning hostility against what the southerners meant to do, was to bring the people of the southern states once more to submission and allegiance; to assist them, when subdued, to rehabilitate the states whose territory and resources, whose very organization, they had used to effect a revolution; to do whatever the circumstances and his own powers, whether as President or merely as an influential man and earnest friend of peace, might render possible to put them back, defeated, but not conquered or degraded, into the old-time hierarchy of the Union.

There were difficulties and passions in the way which possibly even Mr. Lincoln could not have forced within any plan of good will and simple restoration; but he had made a hopeful beginning before he died. He had issued a proclamation of amnesty so early as 1863, offering pardon and restoration to civil rights to all who would abandon resistance to the authority of the Union, and take the oath of unreserved loyalty and submission which he prescribed; and as the war drew to an end, and he saw the power of the Union steadily prevail, now here, now there, throughout an ever increasing area, he earnestly begged that those who had taken the oath and returned to their allegiance would unite in positive and concerted action, organize their states upon the old footing, and make ready for a full restoration of the old conditions. Let those who had taken the oath, and were ready to bind themselves in all good faith to accept the acts and proclamations of the federal government in the matter of slavery,—let all, in short, who were willing to accept the actual results of the war, organize themselves and set up governments made conformable to the new order of things, and he would recognize them as the people of the states within which they acted, ask Congress to admit their representatives, and aid them to gain in all respects full acknowledgment and enjoyment of statehood, even though the persons who thus acted were but a tenth part of the original voters of their states. He would not insist upon even so many as a tenth, if only he could get *some* body of loyal citizens to deal and coöperate with in this all-important matter upon which he had set his heart; that the roster of the states might be complete again, and some healing process follow the bitter anguish of the war.

Andrew Johnson promptly made up his mind, when summoned to the presidency, to carry out Mr. Lincoln's plan, practically without modification; and he knew clearly what Mr. Lincoln's plan had been, for he himself had restored Tennessee upon that plan, as the President's agent and representative. As military governor of the state, he had successfully organized a new government out of abundant material, for Tennessee was full of men who had had no sympathy with secession; and the government which he had organized had gone into full and vigorous operation during that very spring which saw him become first Vice President, and then President. In Louisiana and Arkansas similar governments had been set up even before Mr. Lincoln's death.

Congress had not recognized them, indeed; and it did not, until a year had gone by, recognize even Tennessee, though her case was the simplest of all. Within her borders the southern revolt had been, not solid and of a piece, but a thing of frayed edges and a very doubtful texture of opinion. But, though Congress doubted, the plan had at least proved practicable, and Mr. Johnson thought it also safe and direct.

Mr. Johnson himself, unhappily, was not safe. He had been put on the same ticket with Mr. Lincoln upon grounds of expediency such as have too often created Vice Presidents of the United States. Like a great many other Tennesseeans, he had been stanch and unwavering in his adherence to the Union, even after his state had cast the Union off; but he was in all other respects a Democrat of the old order rather than a Republican of the new, and when he became President the rank and file of the Republicans in Congress looked upon him askance, as was natural. He himself saw to it, besides, that nobody should relish or trust him whom bad temper could alienate. He was self-willed, imperious, implacable; as headstrong and tempestuous as Jackson, without Jackson's power of attracting men, and making and holding parties. At first, knowing him a radical by nature, some of the radical leaders in Congress had been inclined to trust him; had even hailed his accession to the presidency with open satisfaction, having chafed under Lincoln's power to restrain them. "Johnson, we have faith in you!" Senator Wade had exclaimed. "By the gods, there will be no trouble now in running the government!" But Johnson was careful that there should be trouble. He was determined to lead as Lincoln had led, but without Lincoln's insight, skill, or sweetness of temper,—by power and self-assertion rather than by persuasion and the slow arts of management and patient accommodation; and the houses came to an open breach with him almost at once.

Moreover, there was one very serious and radical objection to Mr. Lincoln's plan for restoring the states, which would in all likelihood have forced even him to modify it in many essential particulars, if not to abandon it altogether. He had foreseen difficulties, himself, and had told Congress that his plan was meant to serve only as a suggestion, around which opinion might have an opportunity to form, and out of which some practicable method might be drawn. He had not meant to insist upon it, but only to try it. The main difficulty was that it did not meet the wishes of the congressional leaders with regard to the protection of the negroes in their new rights as freemen. The men whom

Mr. Lincoln had called upon to reorganize the state governments
of the South were, indeed, those who were readiest to accept the
results of the war, in respect of the abolition of slavery as well
as in all other matters. No doubt they were in the beginning men
who had never felt any strong belief in the right of secession,—
men who had even withstood the purpose of secession as long as
they could, and had wished all along to see the old Union restored. They were a minority now, and it might be pretty safely
assumed that they had been a minority from the outset in all
this fatal business. But they were white men, bred to all the
opinions which necessarily went along with the existence and
practice of slavery. They would certainly not wish to give the
negroes political rights. They might be counted on, on the contrary, to keep them still as much as possible under restraint and
tutelage. They would probably accept nothing but the form of
freedom for the one-time slaves, and their rule would be doubly
unpalatable to the men in the North who had gone all these
weary years through, either in person or in heart, with the northern armies upon their mission of emancipation.

The actual course of events speedily afforded means for justifying these apprehensions. Throughout 1865 Mr. Johnson pushed
the presidential process of reconstruction successfully and rapidly
forward. Provisional governors of his own appointment in the
South saw to it that conventions were elected by the voters who
had taken the oath prescribed in the amnesty proclamation,
which Mr. Johnson had reissued, with little change either of form
or of substance; those conventions proceeded at once to revise
the state constitutions under the supervision of the provisional
governors, who in their turn acted now and again under direct
telegraphic instructions from the President in Washington; the
several ordinances of secession were repealed, the war debts of
the states were repudiated, and the legislatures set up under the
new constitutions hastened to accept and ratify the Thirteenth
Amendment, abolishing slavery, as the President demanded. By
December of the very year of his inauguration, every southern
state except Florida and Texas had gone through the required
process, and was once more, so far as the President was concerned, in its normal relations with the federal government. The
federal courts resumed their sessions in the restored states, and
the Supreme Court called up the southern cases from its docket.
On December 18, 1865, the Secretary of State formally pro-
claimed the Thirteenth Amendment ratified by the vote of twenty-
seven states, and thereby legally embodied in the Constitution,

though eight of the twenty-seven were states which the President had thus of his own motion reconstructed. Without their votes the amendment would have lacked the constitutional three-fourths majority.

The President had required nothing of the new states with regard to the suffrage; that was a matter, as he truly said, in respect of which the several states had "rightfully exercised" their free and independent choice "from the origin of the government to the present day"; and of course they had no thought of admitting the negroes to the suffrage. Moreover, the new governments, once organized, fell more and more entirely into the hands of the very persons who had actively participated in secession. The President's proclamation of amnesty had, indeed, excepted certain classes of persons from the privilege of taking the oath which would make them voters again, under his arrangements for reconstruction: those who had taken a prominent official part in secession, or who had left the service of the United States for the service of the Confederate government. But a majority of the southerners were still at liberty to avail themselves of the privilege of accepting the new order of things; and it was to their interest to do so, in order that the new arrangements might be shaped as nearly as possible to their own liking. What was to their liking, however, proved as distasteful to Congress as had been expected. The use they made of their restored power brought absolute shipwreck upon the President's plans, and radically altered the whole process of reconstruction.

An extraordinary and very perilous state of affairs had been created in the South by the sudden and absolute emancipation of the negroes, and it was not strange that the southern legislatures should deem it necessary to take extraordinary steps to guard against the manifest and pressing dangers which it entailed. Here was a vast "laboring, landless, homeless class," once slaves, now free; unpracticed in liberty, unschooled in self-control; never sobered by the discipline of self-support, never established in any habit of prudence; excited by a freedom they did not understand, exalted by false hopes; bewildered and without leaders, and yet insolent and aggressive; sick of work, covetous of pleasure,—a host of dusky children untimely put out of school. In some of the states they outnumbered the whites,—notably in Mississippi and South Carolina. They were a danger to themselves as well as to those whom they had once served, and now feared and suspected; and the very legislatures which had accepted the Thirteenth Amendment hastened to pass laws which should put them under new restraints. Stringent regulations were adopted with regard to contracts for labor, and with regard to the prevention of vagrancy. Penalties were denounced against those who refused to work at the current rates of wages. Fines were imposed upon a great number and variety of petty offenses, such as the new freemen were most likely to commit; and it was provided that, in the (extremely probable) event of the non-payment of these fines, the culprits should be hired out to labor by judicial process. In some instances an elaborate system of compulsory apprenticeship was established for negroes under age, providing that they should be bound out to labor. In certain states the negroes were required to sign written contracts of labor, and were forbidden to do job work without first obtaining licenses from the police authorities of their places of residence. Those who failed to obtain licenses were liable to the charge of vagrancy, and upon that charge could be arrested, fined, and put to compulsory labor. There was not everywhere the same rigor; but there was everywhere the same determination to hold the negroes very watchfully, and, if need were, very sternly, within bounds in the exercise of their unaccustomed freedom; and in many cases the restraints imposed went the length of a veritable "involuntary servitude."

Congress had not waited to see these things done before attempting to help the negroes to make use of their freedom,—and self-defensive use of it, at that. By an act of March 3, 1865, it established, as a branch of the War Department, a Bureau of Refugees, Freedmen, and Abandoned Lands, which was authorized and empowered to assist the one-time slaves in finding means of subsistence, and in making good their new privileges and immunities as citizens. The officials of this bureau, with the War Department behind them, had gone the whole length of their extensive authority; putting away from the outset all ideas of accommodation, and preferring the interests of their wards to the interests of peaceable, wholesome, and healing progress. No doubt that was inevitable. What they did was but the final and direct application of the rigorous, unsentimental logic of events. The negroes, at any rate, had the full advantage of the federal power. A very active and officious branch of the War Department saw to it that the new disabilities which the southern legislatures sought to put upon them should as far as possible be rendered inoperative.

That, however, did not suffice to sweeten the temper of Congress. The fact remained that Mr. Johnson had rehabilitated the governments of the southern states without asking the leave of the houses; that the legislatures which he had authorized them to call together had sought, in the very same sessions in which they gave their assent to the emancipating amendment, virtually to undo the work of emancipation, substituting a slavery of legal restraints and disabilities for a slavery of private ownership; and that these same legislatures had sent men to Washington, to seek admission to the Senate, who were known, many of them, still openly to avow their unshaken belief in the right of secession. The southern voters, too, who had qualified by taking the oath prescribed by the President's proclamation, had in most instances sent men similarly unconvinced to ask admission to the House of Representatives. Here was indeed a surrender of all the advantages of the contest of arms, as it seemed to the radicals,— very generous, no doubt, but done by a Tennesseean and a Democrat, who was evidently a little more than generous; done, too, to exalt the Executive above Congress; in any light, perilous and not to be tolerated. Even those who were not radicals wished that the restoration of the states, which all admitted to be necessary, had been effected in some other way, and safeguarded against this manifest error, as all deemed it, of putting the negroes back into the hands of those who had been their masters, and would not now willingly consent to be their fellow citizens.

Congress, accordingly, determined to take matters into its own hands. With the southern representatives excluded, there was a Republican majority in both houses strong enough to do what it pleased, even to the overriding, if necessary, of the President's vetoes. Upon assembling for their regular session in December, 1865, therefore, the House and Senate at once set up, by concurrent resolution, a joint committee of nine Representatives and six Senators, which was instructed to inquire into all the conditions obtaining in the southern states, and, after sufficient inquiry, advise the houses upon the question whether, under the governments which Mr. Johnson had given them, those states were entitled to representation. To this committee, in other words, was intrusted the whole guidance of Congress in the all-important and delicate business of the full rehabilitation of the southern states as members of the Union. By February, 1866, it had virtually been settled that the admission of their representatives to Congress should await the action of the reconstruction committee; and that purpose was very consistently adhered to. An exception was made in the case of Tennessee, but in her case only. The houses presently agreed to be satisfied with her "reconstruction," and admitted her representatives to their seats in both House and Senate by an act of the 24th of July, 1865. But the other states were put off until the joint committee had forced them through a process of "Thorough," which began their reconstruction at the very beginning, again, and executed at every stage the methods preferred by the houses. The leader throughout the drastic business was Mr. Thaddeus Stevens, of Pennsylvania, the chairman of the committee, the leader of the House. He was foremost among the radicals, and drew a following about him, much as Stephen Douglas had attached thoroughgoing Democrats to himself, in the old days when the legislative battles were being fought over the extension of slavery into the territories,—by audacity, plain speaking, and the straightforward energy of unhesitating opinion. He gave directness and speed to all he proposed. He understood better than Douglas did the coarse work of hewing out practicable paths of action in the midst of opinions and interests at odds. He had no timidity, no scruples about keeping to constitutional lines of policy, no regard or thought for the sensibilities of the minority,—being rough-hewn and without embarrassing sensibilities himself,—an ideal radical for the service of the moment.

Careful men, trained in the older ways of statesmanship and accustomed to reading the Constitution into all that they did, tried to form some consistent theory of constitutional right with regard to the way in which Congress ought to deal with this new and unprecedented situation. The southern states were still "states" within the meaning of the Constitution as the Supreme Court had interpreted it. They were communities of free citizens; each had kept its territorial boundaries unchanged, unmistakable; in each there was an organized government, "sanctioned and limited by a written constitution, and established by the consent of the governed." Their officers of government, like their people, had for a time, indeed, repudiated the authority of the federal government; but they were now ready to acknowledge that authority again, and could resume their normal relations with the other states at a moment's notice, with all proper submission. Both Mr. Lincoln and Mr. Johnson had acted in part upon these assumptions. They had objected only that the governments actually in existence at the close of the war had been chosen by persons who were in fact insurgents, and that their officers had served to organize rebellion. Let those citizens of the South who had made submission, and who had been pardoned under the President's proclamation, reconstitute their governments, repudiating their old leaders, and the only taint upon their statehood would be removed: the Executive would recognize them as again normally constituted members of the Union.

Not many members of Congress, however, accepted this view. The Republican party, it was true, had entered upon the war emphatically disavowing either wish or purpose to interfere with the constitutional rights of the states; declaring its sole object to be the preservation of the Union,—the denial of a single particular right which it could not but view as revolutionary. But war had brought many things in its train. The heat and struggle of those four tremendous years had burned and scarred the body of affairs with many an ineffaceable fact, which could not now be overlooked. Legally or illegally, as states or as bodies of individuals merely, the southern people had been at war with the Union; the slaves had been freed by force of arms; their freedom had now been incorporated in the supreme law of the land, and must be made good to them; there was manifest danger that too liberal a theory of restoration would bring about an impossible tangle of principles, an intolerable contradiction between fact and fact. Mr. Sumner held that, by resisting the authority of the Union, of which they were members, the southern states had simply committed suicide, destroying their own institutions along with their allegiance to the federal government. They ceased to be states, he said, when they ceased to fulfill the duties imposed upon them by the fundamental law of the land. Others declined any such doctrine. They adhered, with an instinct almost of affection, to the idea of a veritable federal Union; rejected Mr. Sumner's presupposition that the states were only subordinate parts of a consolidated national government; and insisted that, whatever rights they had for a time forfeited, the southern states were at least not destroyed, but only estopped from exercising their ordinary functions within the Union, pending a readjustment.

Theories made Mr. Stevens very impatient. It made little difference with him whether the southern states had forfeited their rights by suicide, or temporary disorganization, or individual rebellion. As a matter of fact, every department of the federal government, the courts included, had declared the citizens of those states public enemies; the Constitution itself had been for four years practically laid aside, so far as they were concerned, as a document of peace; they had been overwhelmed by force, and were now held in subjection under military rule, like conquered provinces. It was just as well, he thought, to act upon the facts, and let theories alone. It was enough that all Congressmen were agreed—at any rate, all who were allowed a voice in the matter—that it was properly the part of Congress, and not of the Executive, to bring order out of the chaos: to see that federal supremacy and federal law were made good in the South; the legal changes brought about by the war forced upon its acceptance; and the negroes secured in the enjoyment of the equality and even the privileges of citizens, in accordance with the federal guarantee that there should be a republican form of government in every state,—a government founded upon the consent of a majority of its adult subjects. The essential point was that Congress, the lawmaking power, should be in control. The President had been too easy to satisfy, too prompt, and too lenient. Mr. Stevens consented once and again that the language of fine-drawn theories of constitutional right should be used in the reports of the joint Committee on Reconstruction, in which he managed to be master; but the motto of the committee in all practical matters was his motto of "Thorough," and its policy made Congress supreme.

The year 1866 passed, with all things at sixes and sevens. So far as the President was concerned, most of the southern states were already reconstructed, and had resumed their places in the Union. Their assent had made the Thirteenth Amendment a part of the Constitution. And yet Congress forbade the withdrawal of the troops, refused admittance to the southern representatives, and set aside southern laws through the action of the Freedmen's Bureau and the military authorities. By 1867 it had made up its mind what to do to bring the business to a conclusion. 1866 had at least cleared its mind and defined its purposes. Congress had still further tested and made proof of the temper of the South. In June it had adopted a Fourteenth Amendment, which secured to the blacks the status of citizens, both of the United States and of the several states of their residence, authorized a reduction in the representation in Congress of states which refused them the suffrage, excluded the more prominent servants of the Confederacy from federal office until Congress should pardon them, and invalidated all debts or obligations "incurred in aid of insurrection or rebellion against the United States"; and this amendment had been submitted to the vote of the states which Congress had refused to recognize as well as to the vote of those represented in the houses. Tennessee had promptly adopted it, and had been as promptly admitted to representation. But the other southern states, as promptly as they could, had begun, one by one, to reject it. Their action confirmed the houses in their attitude toward Reconstruction.

Congressional views and purposes were cleared the while with regard to the President, also. He had not been firm; he had been stubborn and bitter. He would yield nothing; vetoed the measures upon which Congress was most steadfastly minded to insist; alienated his very friends by attacking Congress in public with gross insult and abuse; and lost credit with everybody. It came to a direct issue, the President against Congress: they went to the country with their quarrel in the congressional elections, which fell opportunely in the autumn of 1866, and the President lost utterly. Until then some had hesitated to override his vetoes, but after that no one hesitated. 1867 saw Congress go triumphantly forward with its policy of reconstruction *ab initio*.

In July, 1866, it had overridden a veto to continue and enlarge the powers of the Freedmen's Bureau, in a bill which directed that public lands should be sold to the negroes upon easy terms, that the property of the Confederate government should be appropriated for their education, and that their new-made rights should be protected by military authority. In March, 1867, two acts, passed over the President's vetoes, instituted the new process of reconstruction, followed and completed by another act in July of the same year. The southern states, with the exception, of course, of Tennessee, were grouped in five military districts, each of which was put under the command of a general of the United States. These commanders were made practically absolute rulers, until the task of reconstruction should be ended. It was declared by the Reconstruction Acts that no other legal state governments existed in the ten states concerned. It was made the business of the district commanders to erect such governments as Congress prescribed. They were to enroll in each state, upon oath, all male citizens of one year's residence, not disqualified by reason of felony or excluded under the terms of the proposed Fourteenth Amendment, "of whatever race, color, or previous condition" they might be; the persons thus registered were to choose constitutional conventions, confining their choice of delegates to registered voters like themselves; these conventions were to be directed to frame state constitutions, which should extend the suffrage to all who had been permitted by the military authorities to enroll for the purpose of taking part in the election of delegates; and the constitutions were to be submitted to the same body of voters for ratification. When Congress had approved the constitutions thus framed and accepted, and when the legislatures constituted under them had adopted the Fourteenth Amendment, the states thus reorganized were to be readmitted to representation in Congress, and in all respects fully reinstated as members of the Union; but not before. Meanwhile, the civil governments already existing within them, though illegal, were to be permitted to stand; but as "provisional only, and in all respects subject to the paramount authority of the United States at any time to abolish, control, or supersede the same."

Such was the process which was rigorously and consistently carried through during the memorable years 1867-70; and upon the states which proved most difficult and recalcitrant Congress did not hesitate from time to time to impose new conditions of recognition and reinstatement before an end was made. By the close of July, 1868, the reconstruction and reinstatement of Arkansas, the two Carolinas, Florida, Alabama, and Louisiana had been completed. Virginia, Mississippi, and Texas were obliged to wait until the opening of 1870, because their voters would not adopt the constitutions offered them by their reconstructing conventions; and Georgia was held off a few months longer, because she persisted in attempting to exclude negroes from the right to hold office. These four states, as a consequence, were obliged to accept, as a condition precedent to their reinstatement, not only the Fourteenth Amendment, but a Fifteenth also, which Congress had passed in February, 1869, and which forbade either the United States or any state to withhold from any citizen the right to vote "on account of race, color, or previous condition of servitude." The military commanders, meanwhile, used or withheld their hand of power according to their several temperaments. They could deal with the provisional civil governments as they pleased,—could remove officials, annul laws, regulate administration, at will. Some were dictatorial and petty; some were temperate and guarded in their use of authority, with a creditable instinct of statesmanship; almost all were straightforward and executive, as might have been expected of soldiers.

Whatever their mistakes or weaknesses of temper or of judgment, what followed the reconstruction they effected was in almost every instance much worse than what had had to be endured under military rule. The first practical result of reconstruction under the acts of 1867 was the disfranchisement, for several weary years, of the better whites, and the consequent giving over of the southern governments into the hands of the negroes. And yet not into their hands, after all. They were but children still; and unscrupulous men, "carpetbaggers,"—men not come to be citizens, but come upon an expedition of profit, come to make the name of Republican forever hateful in the South,— came out of the North to use the negroes as tools for their own selfish ends; and succeeded, to the utmost fulfillment of their dreams. Negro majorities for a little while filled the southern legislatures; but they won no power or profit for themselves, beyond a pittance here and there for a bribe. Their leaders, strangers and adventurers, got the lucrative offices, the handling of the state moneys raised by loan, and of the taxes spent no one knew how. Here and there an able and upright man cleansed administration, checked corruption, served them as a real friend and an honest leader; but not for long. The negroes were exalted; the states were misgoverned and looted in their name; and a few men, not of their number, not really of their interest, went away with the gains. They were left to carry the discredit and reap the consequences of ruin, when at last the whites who were real citizens got control again.

But that dark chapter of history is no part of our present story. We are here concerned, rather, with the far-reaching constitutional and political influences and results of Reconstruction. That it was a revolutionary process is written upon its face throughout; but how deep did the revolution go? What permanent marks has it left upon the great structure of government, federal, republican; a partnership of equal states, and yet a solidly coherent national power, which the fathers erected?

First of all, it is clear to every one who looks straight upon the facts, every veil of theory withdrawn, and the naked body of affairs uncovered to meet the direct question of the eye, that civil war discovered the foundations of our government to be in fact unwritten; set deep in a sentiment which constitutions can neither originate nor limit. The law of the Constitution reigned until war came. Then the stage was cleared, and the forces of a mighty sentiment, hitherto unorganized, deployed upon it. A thing had happened for which the Constitution had made no provision. In the Constitution were written the rules by which the associated states should live in concert and union, with no word added touching days of discord or disruption; nothing about the use of force to keep or to break the authority ordained in its quiet sentences, written, it would seem, for lawyers, not for soldiers. When the war came, therefore, and questions were broached to which it gave no answer, the ultimate foundation of the structure was laid bare: physical force, sustained by the stern loves and rooted predilections of masses of men, the strong ingrained prejudices which are the fibre of every system of government. What gave the war its passion, its hot energy as of a tragedy from end to end, was that in it sentiment met sentiment, conviction conviction. It was the sentiment, not of all, but of the efficient majority, the conviction of the major part, that won. A minority, eager and absolute in another conviction, devoted to the utmost pitch of self-sacrifice to an opposite and incompatible ideal, was crushed and overwhelmed. It was that which gave an epic breadth and majesty to the awful clash between bodies of men in all things else of one strain and breeding; it was that which brought the bitterness of death upon the side which lost, and the dangerous intoxication of an absolute triumph upon the side which won. But it unmistakably uncovered the foundations of force upon which the Union rested.

It did more. The sentiment of union and nationality, never before aroused to full consciousness or knowledge of its own thought and aspirations, was henceforth a new thing, aggressive and aware of a sort of conquest. It had seen its legions and felt its might in the field. It saw the very Constitution, for whose maintenance and defense it had acquired the discipline of arms, itself subordinated for a time to the practical emergencies of war, in order that the triumph might be the more unimpeded and complete; and it naturally deemed nationality henceforth a thing above law. As much as possible,—so far as could be without serious embarrassment,—the forms of the fundamental law had indeed been respected and observed; but wherever the law clogged or did not suffice, it had been laid aside and ignored. It was so much the easier, therefore, to heed its restrictions lightly, when the war was over, and it became necessary to force the southern states to accept the new model. The real revolution was not so much in the form as in the spirit of affairs. The spirit and temper and method of a federal Union had given place, now that all the spaces of the air had been swept and changed by the merciless winds of war, to a spirit which was consciously national and of a new age.

It was this spirit which brushed theories and technicalities aside, and impressed its touch of revolution on the law itself. And not only upon the law, but also upon the processes of lawmaking, and upon the relative positions of the President and Congress in the general constitutional scheme of the government, seeming to change its very administrative structure. While the war lasted the President had been master; the war ended, and Mr. Lincoln gone, Congress pushed its way to the front, and began to transmute fact into law, law into fact. In some matters it treated all the states alike. The Thirteenth, Fourteenth, and Fifteenth amendments bound all the states at once, North and West as well as South. But that was, after all, a mere equality of form. The amendments were aimed, of course, at the states which had had slaves and had attempted secession, and did not materially affect any others. The votes which incorporated them in the Constitution were voluntary on the part of the states whose institutions they did not affect, involuntary on the part of the states whose institutions they revolutionized. These states were then under military rule. Congress had declared their whole political organization to be illegal; had excluded their representatives from their seats in the houses; and yet demanded that they assent, as states, to the amendment of the Constitution as a condition precedent to their reinstatement in the Union! No anomaly or contradiction of lawyers' terms was suffered to stand in the way of the supremacy of the lawmaking branch of the general government. The Constitution knew no such process as this of Reconstruction, and could furnish no rules for it. Two years and a half before the Fifteenth Amendment was adopted by Congress, three years and a half before it was put in force by its adoption by the states, Congress had by mere act forced the southern states, by the hands of military governors, to put the negroes upon the roll of their voters. It had dictated to them a radical revision of their constitutions, whose items should be framed to meet the views of the houses rather than the views of their own electors. It had pulled about and rearranged what local institutions it saw fit, and then had obliged the communities affected to accept its alterations as the price of their reinstatement as self-governing bodies politic within the Union.

It may be that much, if not all, of this would have been inevitable under any leadership, the temper of the times and the posture of affairs being what they were; and it is certain that it was inevitable under the actual circumstances of leadership then existing at Washington. But to assess that matter is to reckon with causes. For the moment we are concerned only with consequences, and are neither justifying nor condemning, but only comprehending. The courts of the United States have held that the southern states never were out of the Union; and yet they have justified the action of Congress throughout the process of Reconstruction, on the ground that it was no more than a proper performance by Congress of a legal duty, under the clause of the Constitution which guarantees to every state a republican form of government. It was making the southern governments republican by securing full standing and legislative representation as citizens for the negroes. But Congress went beyond that. It not only dictated to the states it was reconstructing what their suffrage should be; it also required that they should never afterward narrow that suffrage. It required of Virginia, Texas, and Mississippi that they should accord to the negroes not only the right to vote, but also the right to hold political office; and that they should grant to all their citizens equal school privileges, and never afterward abridge them. So far as the right to vote was concerned, the Fifteenth Amendment subsequently imposed the same disability with regard to withholding the suffrage upon all the states alike; but the southern states were also forbidden by mere federal statute to restrict it on any other ground; and in the case of Virginia, Mississippi, and Texas Congress assumed the right, which the Constitution nowhere accorded it, to regulate admission to political office and the privileges of public education.

South Carolina and Mississippi, Louisiana and North Carolina, have since changed the basis of their suffrage, notwithstanding; Virginia and Mississippi and Texas might now, no doubt, reorganize their educational system as they pleased, without endangering their status in the Union, or even meeting rebuke at the hands of the federal courts. The temper of the times has changed; the federal structure has settled to a normal balance of parts and functions again; and the states are in fact unfettered except by the terms of the Constitution itself. It is marvelous what healing and oblivion peace has wrought, how the traces of Reconstruction have worn away. But a certain deep effect abides. It is within, not upon the surface. It is of the spirit, not of the body. A revolution was carried through when war was done which may be better comprehended if likened to England's subtle making over, that memorable year 1688. Though she punctiliously kept to the forms of her law, England then dismissed a king almost as, in later years, she would have dismissed a minister; though she preserved the procedure of her constitution intact, she in fact gave a final touch of change to its spirit. She struck irresponsible power away, and made her government once for all a constitutional government. The change had been insensibly a-making for many a long age; but now it was accomplished consciously and at a stroke. Her constitution, finished, was not what it had been until this last stroke was given,—when silent forces had at last found sudden voice, and the culminating change was deliberately made.

Nearly the same can be said of the effect of the war and of the reconstruction of the southern states upon our own government. It was a revolution of consciousness,—of mind and purpose. A government which had been in its spirit federal became, almost of a sudden, national in temper and point of view. The national spirit had long been a-making. Many a silent force, which grew quite unobserved, from generation to generation, in pervasiveness and might, in quiet times of wholesome peace and mere increase of nature, had been breeding these thoughts which now sprang so vividly into consciousness. The very growth of the nation, the very lapse of time and uninterrupted habit of united action, the mere mixture and movement and distribution of populations, the mere accretions of policy, the mere consolidation of interests, had been building and strengthening new tissue of nationality the years through, and drawing links stronger than links of steel round about the invisible body of common thought and purpose which is the substance of nations. When the great crisis of secession came, men knew at once how their spirits were ruled, men of the South as well as men of the North,—in what institutions and conceptions of government their blood was fixed to run; and a great and instant readjustment took place, which was for the South, the minority, practically the readjustment of conquest and fundamental reconstruction, but which was for the North, the region which had been transformed, nothing more than an awakening.

It cannot be said that the forms of the Constitution were observed in this quick change as the forms of the English constitution had been observed when the Stuarts were finally shown the door. There were no forms for such a business. For several years, therefore, Congress was permitted to do by statute what, under the long-practiced conceptions of our federal law, could properly be done only by constitutional amendment. The necessity for that gone by, it was suffered to embody what it had already enacted and put into force as law into the Constitution, not by the free will of the country at large, but by the compulsions of mere force exercised upon a minority whose assent was necessary to the formal completion of its policy. The result restored, practically entire, the forms of the Constitution; but not before new methods and irregular, the methods of majorities, but not the methods of law, had been openly learned and practiced, and learned in a way not likely to be forgot. Changes of law in the end gave authentic body to many of the most significant changes of thought which had come, with its new consciousness, to the nation. A citizenship of the United States was created; additional private civil rights were taken within the jurisdiction of the general government; additional prohibitions were put upon the states; the suffrage was in a measure made subject to national regulation. But the real change was the change of air,—a change of conception with regard to the power of Congress, the guiding and compulsive efficacy of national legislation, the relation of the life of the land to the supremacy of the national lawmaking body. All policy thenceforth wore a different aspect.

We realize it now, in the presence of novel enterprises, at the threshold of an unlooked-for future. It is evident that empire is an affair of strong government, and not of the nice and somewhat artificial poise or of the delicate compromises of structure and authority characteristic of a mere federal partnership. Undoubtedly, the impulse of expansion is the natural and wholesome impulse which comes with a consciousness of matured strength; but it is also a direct result of that national spirit which the war between the states cried so wide awake, and to which the processes of Reconstruction gave the subtle assurance of practically unimpeded sway and a free choice of means. The revolution lies there, as natural as it was remarkable and full of prophecy. It is this which makes the whole period of Reconstruction so peculiarly worthy of our study. Every step of the policy, every feature of the time, which wrought this subtle transformation, should receive our careful scrutiny. We are now far enough removed from the time to make that scrutiny both close and dispassionate. A new age gives it a new significance.

Woodrow Wilson.

Printed in the *Atlantic Monthly*, LXXXVII (Jan. 1901), 1-15.

From Ellen Axson Wilson

[En route New Orleans to Savannah]
My own darling,   Saturday [March 3, 1900]

I was seized with a desire to write you en route, but the car jolts so atrociously I can do nothing while it is in motion, especially as I have only a two inch stump of pencil. But I shall scribble a few lines at stations. I judge that this road, the Geo. & Ala., is not one of the main trunk lines of the continent; my car is half sleeper & half parlour car: there is one man in the sleeping compartment and I have the parlour car to myself,— which is very cosy. There is a long lounge at the back and I have had myself provided with pillows and have been lying with half shut eyes watching the great pine trees glide by in endless procession till I have begun to feel as if in a dream-world, an enchanted forest. It is all very sweet and peaceful and delightful after the whirl of the last few weeks. The air too is deliciously balmy, that of a May morning. If *you* were only here I should think it quite the most charming journey I had ever taken,—but that is a great "if"! I reached Montgomery at 6.20 this morning which means that I was awake at half past five, so I naturally feel a little lazy and dozy.

This country with its swampy pine lands makes my thoughts turn back to "Old Liberty County," the history of which I finished yesterday while resting from my labours over that trunk. It is a Puritan idyl, a pathetic one on the whole, ending in the very abomination of desolation,—"which is why," I suppose, the one incident in the book which smacks of humour is the one that has fixed itself most clearly in my memory,—so clearly that I will transcribe it for your benefit before I forget it. It is an epitaph,— of course.

> "She who in Jesus sleeps within this tomb,
> Had Rachel's face and Leah's fruitful womb.
> Abigail's wisdom, Lydia's faithful heart,
> And Martha's care with Mary's better part."[1]

But after all it is no fun writing a sentence at a time. I will give it up.

I had the pleasure of leaving Lucy *much* better, her fever almost gone. She had also begun to *talk* again; it is rather alarming when *she* falls quiet. With *devoted* love

Your little wife   Eileen

ALS (WC, NjP).

[1] The epitaph, which she quoted almost verbatim, was written by the Rev. Cyrus Gildersleeve for the tombstone of his wife, Aramintha Gildersleeve, and is printed in James Stacy, *History of the Midway Congregational Church, Liberty County, Georgia* (Newnan, Ga., 1899), p. 217. The epitaph follows:
> "She, who in Jesus sleeps beneath this tomb,
> "Had Rachel's face, and Leah's fruitful womb,
> "Abigail's wisdom, Lydia's faithful heart,
> "And Martha's care, with Mary's better part."

To Ellen Axson Wilson

My own darling   Princeton, Saturday 3 March, 1900.

I have been thinking of you all day as on the train, alone, reading, thinking over the gay, various, delightful visit behind you,— dreaming, off and on, of home, of the man who loves you and depends on you for his life, for the breath of all pleasure and stimulation and comfort, and who longs for you through every day and every night with a longing too passionate for words; of the sweet children, almost worthy of you in all the qualities which win love and convey charm; of the splendid woman, our noble sister, who does the feminine duties of the home with such a quiet *grace* of perfect capacity, with such love and pleasure at being of use to those whom she loves; and of the dear brother coming bravely and safely out of peril into assured health and strength. *I* dream of your eyes, the while, and the little, unconscious movements of lip and bosom which go along with such thoughts when the dear traveller is silent; of her lovely beauty as she sits there,—so eloquent of pure thoughts and glad devotion, so sweetened by lines of long refinement and elevated feeling, so fresh, as if of girlhood, and yet *so* womanly, so full of the peace of maturity and wifehood and motherhood. How I envy those who are in the train with that beautiful lady! If it were not giving away what I may enjoy with her, I would give a year of my life to be there in their place, even if I could only sit, as they do, and gaze, and never speak to and touch her. I would be willing she should not see me or know of my presence, if only I could see into her eyes when she *thought* of me. I *know* the extraordinary, alluring beauty then. I do not know whether I should have strength of will to sit still then. But if the conditions were to keep still or lose sight of her altogether, I think I should sit still till my heart cracked, rather than miss looking upon her. Ah me, that I should have *such* a wife, and *keep* her love, feel sure of it. I can wait any length of time for her coming without a moment of repining when I think of that. I've had love and success out of all porportion to my deserts,—out of proportion to everything except my capacity for loving in return!

We are all well, my sweet one. Stockton walks a little more every day,—looks a little stronger, eats a little more, shows increasing signs of enjoyment. But don't expect him before the middle of week after next. All join in love to all. My passion for you increases alarmingly; but I *can* rejoice and not repine, and I *do* rejoice every moment because I am

Your own   Woodrow

ALS (WC, NjP).

To Robert Bridges

My dear Bobby,   Princeton, New Jersey, 3 March, 1900.

My delay in answering Billy Isham's invitation[1] was due to my elaborate efforts to figure out how I could manage to go. But, alas! the figuring came to nothing but a disappointment. I cannot get to the function this time. I have written, of course, and told Billy that I cannot come, and how sorry I am; but it is no small part of my disappointment that I can't have my usual confab with you.

As ever,   Affectionately Yours,   Woodrow Wilson

WWTLS (WC, NjP).
[1] To the Isham dinner for 1900. About the Isham dinners, see WW to EAW, May 6, 1886, n. 1, Vol. 5.

From Ellen Axson Wilson

My own darling,   Savannah, Sunday [March 4, 1900]

Your two sweet letters were awaiting me, to my great joy, when I arrived last night. The "business" part of them however has filled me with no little concern and anxiety, for, considering how far *I* am from *you* and *both* of us from Rose, and how much correspondence will be necessary before making suitable arrangements, I don't see how Stockton is to be gotten to Asheville by Saturday. Only five days for me to write Rose, for her to look for proper places, and communicate with us, for you to complete the arrangement & telegraph me, and for me to get to Asheville! And she may have difficulties and delays in finding just what we want; boarding-houses alas! can't be ordered offhand like beefsteaks with the certainty of getting just the cut we want, just when and where we want it. But we will hope for the best. I have already written fully to Rose, asking her, in order to save time, to write directly to *you* instead of to me. Of course I won't go to Atlanta or Rome; there is no time.

Now for another point;—Uncle Randolph and Aunt Ella are *insisting* and yet again *insisting* that Stock must come straight here; they simply won't *hear* of anything else. And now I have seen the situation I can assure Stock that there is no reason why he should'nt. When there was no question of Stock's coming,— before I had even read your letters last night,—Aunt Ella said George [Allen] was absolutely no care upon her. And there is a vacant room, I have seen it myself. Of course the climate at this time of year is much better here than in Asheville; he could be out of doors all day. He would have daintier fare than in any boarding house and much more quiet,—for this is, as it has always been, the quietest family I know; and, as they say, he "is to do exactly as he pleases about everything talking included." Indeed I cannot exaggerate their evident eagerness to have him come. They say they *know* the journey is as easy as to Asheville—less than 24 hours from Phila, no change except at Washington. Then there is the question of expense,—an important one with surgeon and nurse to be paid,—no charges here, & if he get a pass (as he *ought*) from Mr. [Albert] Howell no car fare. And no *delay* and uncertainty about boarding-houses; he has simply to *come* when he gets ready. I can think of no objection to the plan whatever except that George Allen *looks* very badly,—is as white as a sheet,—and the sight might depress Stockton a bit. He, George, is a beautiful young fellow and a bright interesting talker,—very cheerful generally. He is suffering (*I* don't know about the 'dying') from the after effects of a terrible attack of meningitis. It is an obscure case. He is a young physician himself, and says all the others are waiting eagerly to cut him up. Not that he makes such remarks at the table! Oh, I must also mention, in case Stock is nervous about such things that there are a few cases of small-pox in the poorer parts of town & people are being vaccinated promiscuously. It was the same in New Orleans, but *I* never gave it a second thought; neither do the family here.

But tis tea time & I close in haste. I fear I have seemed to argue on the side of Sav. I did not mean to do that. The *most* important thing is for him to go where he *wants* to go. With dear love   Your own   Eileen.

George has been showing me his photographs for an hour. He is an *expert*. He is not exactly "dying" for he is able to spend *hours* daily developing and finishing them.

ALS (WC, NjP).

To Ellen Axson Wilson

My own darling,   Princeton, Sunday 4 March, 1900

The telegram[1] for which my heart was waiting lies open on the desk before me, and I *know* that my Eileen is safe in Savannah, and "perfectly well." How glad it all makes me,—and what a singular impression I have of a *spell* having been broken! You were *so* far away in New Orleans, and were so whirled along there in an absorbing and increasing rush of engagements, that

I felt a *special* sense of separation, as if you did not have even time enough to *think* of me,—as if you were absolutely taken possession of, appropriated, *monopolized* by those dear cordial people in the warm hearted city. Not that you *did* lose your wonderful sense of attachment to me,—not that you did not stop every day in the midst of the whirl and distraction of it all to write singularly full and infinitely tender letters to me; but you seemed more lost to me for the time being, because absorbed by the life of a city I had never seen, whose aspect I could not imagine,—appropriated by people I did not know, and never could expect to know; because so *constantly* engrossed and wrapt away, in the midst of scenes where not even my mind could follow you, where my heart groped to find you, in a bewildered quest. I did not begrudge your entertainers their temporary possession and enjoyment of you for a moment. They were pleasing and refreshing *you*, and that was enough,—that was my heart's desire for my darling, the very object for which I had stopped my life for a space. But, rub my eyes as I might, I could not *see* you,—it was almost as if you were lost! In Savannah it is different. There and in Rome and in Asheville I can *realize* you. I have seen you and loved you in all those places. The chief interest and only charm about them for me is their association with you,—with some of the sweetest passages in my life,—the sweetest things I had ever imagined till then! Sweeter things have followed. My darling has shown more alluring charms every year she has been mine; has added romance to romance in her ways, her countless ways, of making me happy; has crept to the very innermost recesses of my heart, and sounded every mystery of my nature, by the subtle growth of love and intimacy between us. It is infinitely sweeter to court her now than it was to woo her then. But the romance of those first days can never die out of my heart or lose its power of fascination over my imagination. No memories can be more perfect than the memories of our first discoveries and love of each other,—and Savannah and Rome and Asheville I *know* as places of my love's sojourning! Of Savannah in particular I have the most delightful and vivid and satisfying memories. It was to Savannah I went on that delightful run away from Baltimore,[2] certain for the first time of the reception I wanted; and our meeting there in the parlour thrills me yet. I remember what you wore and every gesture you made, and the unspeakable pleasure of that first embrace and kiss, and the wonder of love and shyness in your eyes. And every hour of that visit seems to me like stuff of deep poetry. The soft air of the place, the peace of the quiet streets, the children at holiday in the park, every breath of the Spring-like air so matched my own joy and peace, and my sense of the real Spring of life begun. And in that same sweet place you became my bride, and my life *did* begin. Every good thing in it was set free. If you can, my darling,—and if the parsonage[3] is unchanged in appearance,—will you not get a photograph of it taken for me, showing the two sides where the parlour windows are,—taken, that is, from about the middle of the *two* streets which meet there,—so that the entrance may be seen, looking toward the church, and the side of the house also, looking down the side street, towards the kitchen gate? I want this very much, and one of the boys can have it done for you. I have the pictures you once sent me, and they have a romantic interest for me (my heart gives a little flutter whenever I look at them, as it did at first, because they are of places associated with you); but they give scarcely a glimpse of the parsonage.

Stockton came down stairs for the first time to-day, and sat for a little while in the parlour,—got down and back without assistance; but he realizes now, as I do not think he did before, how such an experience as he has been through 'takes it out of' one. Neither does he realize, I think, how fast he is *gaining* strength.

It worries me, and it worries him, to keep your plans conjectural; but I don't think it need be so very long (By the way, a postal from Aunt Lou. to Stock. asks if you have gone South. Have you not written to her?) No doubt it would be safe to stay in Savannah through this week,—through next Sunday,—and then divide next week between Atlanta and Rome. It is not unlikely you will have the most, or all of it, to divide. How much will it cost you to get to Asheville from Savannah?

We are all well. George [Howe] is spending Sunday with us. *Everybody* sends love unbounded to you; and I am, with overwhelming ardour,   Your own   Woodrow

ALS (WC, NjP).
  [1] It is missing.
  [2] About this trip, see C. H. Shinn to WW, Jan. 21, 1884, n. 3, Vol. 2.
  [3] The manse of the Independent Presbyterian Church of Savannah, where Ellen and Woodrow were married on June 24, 1885. There is a picture of it in Volume 4.

From Ellen Axson Wilson

My own darling,   Savannah Monday [March 5, 1900]

Your letter written Friday is at hand and I hasten to write again to catch the midday through train to the north. I am going to ask you to *telegraph* me as soon as this reaches you whether the Asheville plan holds, (as knowing Stock I rather think it *will* (!)) or whether, in view of what I wrote yesterday of the situation here, Stockton will conclude to come to Sav. Since the trip is postponed to the latter part of next week in any case, I will, if he decides on Asheville, go on to Atlanta on *Friday night*, leaving here at 10.30, spend Saturday and Sunday with Aunt Lou, and *Monday* morning go over to *Rome*, and await your telegram *there*. I shall also write at once to Rose telling her the rooms will not be needed so soon. Does anybody there know anything of the *climate* of Asheville in March? I should fancy, judging from Rome, Atlanta, Balt. & all that middle region of country that it might be *vile*, all rain and slush. Mrs. Richardson might tell you about that, and also something about boarding-houses. Here the weather is delightful beyond description just now.

But I have no time for more this morning. I saw many old friends yesterday at church and am having a very happy time. Oh, my darling *how* I love you! How my heart leaps with delight at thought of the "shortening chain" between us. Time certainly does *not* fly under some circumstances, but at least it *can't* stand still. With love beyond words I am always and altogether

Your own   Eileen.

ALS (WC, NjP).

To Ellen Axson Wilson

My own darling,   Princeton, Monday 5 March, 1900

Your last New Orleans letter came this morning, and had an odd effect on my mind, coming twenty-four hours *after* the telegram had shifted my thoughts to Savannah; but it acted like a tonic on me,—especially that *blushing* page in which you told, *so* grudgingly, two of the compliments that had been paid you,— and fine compliments they were, too: they suited my taste to a nicety, as just what you deserved. But I suppose, madam, just because it cost you so much to tell *any*, you are under the impression that you told me a great many. Just two. *I am not satisfied*; and if you both neglect to repeat *all* the best ones in your letters *and or* forget them before you see me again, I assure you I shall never forgive you. Why, I'd rather hear praise of you than write a great book,—and you can't in conscience, if you really love me, cheat me of a deep and vivid pleasure just to save yourself a blush or two! I'll not believe it. No, miss: if you would have the blushes unseen, *write* me what they said of my darling,—or else store everything (*everything*, mind you!) in your memory and get so close to me when you repeat it all in my arms that I can't see, but can only *feel*, your surging colour. *Verbum sap.* Already I *know* that the New Orleans people are people of taste and sense; you owe it to them, after their kindness, to give me detailed proof. Ah, my sweet Duchesse: *that* compliment alone is worth several!

Five Sundays gone,—only three more, and then—! *That's* the way I count *now*, by Sundays,—unless, perchance, Stockton should need you longer! I shan't be selfish, and I shan't grumble a bit,—see if I do!

That's an excellent idea of yours, darling, to send home an express package of clothes, to relieve your trunk,—or, rather, to relieve your *back* of the strain of packing again and again. Do so, by all means, and at once, before another packing, and let me pay the charges at this end.

The nurse left this afternoon,—an excellent woman. We parted with genuine regret, as from a friend. She has been most efficient, and gave *us* not a moment's trouble. But I think she left just at the right time. Stock. is quite able to shift for himself and *ought* to shift for himself in little things, but would have remained passive and let her do everything so long as she remained. *She* thought it time to leave him. He laughs at himself in the matter. The rest of us are all right. I am *so* happy just to get my Eileen a little nearer. May God bless you and keep you, my precious one.   Your own   Woodrow

All send love to all

ALS (WC, NjP).

From Ellen Axson Wilson

My own darling,   Savannah Mar. 6/99 [1900]

Mrs. Cunningham (Miss Norah Lawton)[1] has written asking me to drive at eleven, so I have run upstairs to get my letter written beforehand, in time for the midday mail,—'tis a pity that I must always write in a hurry!

I have decided, if you telegraph that Stockton will go to Asheville, to go up to Atlanta on *Thursday* night and to Rome *Saturday* night. That will give me a Sunday in Rome—a chance to go to the old church, which I very much want. There are also many odds and ends of business to attend to there,—things to be disposed of,—now that Uncle Will's[2] house is to be sold, so that I must if possible squeeze in three working days there; I conclude from your letter that I can count on staying there until Wednesday night. You know you have never sent me that unfortunate *pass*, which I fear will be of no use if I go to Asheville, and I am afraid I will need some more money instead of it, as I have no idea what the various R.R. tickets will amount to. I have $26.00 now, so you can send the next check to Rome.

I went yesterday to Laurel Grove cemetary where our dead are laid,—also on the "belt line" around the city which enabled me to see in one morning many of the old land-marks. But Sav. is much more of a wreck than New Orleans having suffered not only from the freeze but from the terrible storms of the past few years, and from the most incredible vandalism on the part of the city authorities. The change is heart-rending. In the little park alone one storm blew down 150 trees, and then,—would you believe it?—they have simply taken down and carted away the beautiful high iron fence which gave it its special character,—a fence that a rich man at the north would gladly pay $50,000 for! The Catholics bought it, I believe. I really did not know when I *entered* the park! Worse still,—if anything *could* be worse,—they have taken down the old gray wall about the old city cemetary, leaving it too an open common. It is positively indecent to expose those old graves in that way. Their one desire seems to be to make Sav. in every respect like a new, commonplace northern town. But it will do no good to lash one's self into a fury about it.

Your *beautiful* letter written Saturday came yesterday afternoon, my darling. How exactly you describe my thoughts on that journey! How I wish I had your eloquent pen (and unlimited time,) to put them into words! I would give all I have to be able to make you as happy with letters as you make me! But *you* know, dear heart, that I *love* you as much however I fail to express it,— in words. Dear love to all, and for yourself, darling, the *whole* heart of   Your own   Eileen.

ALS (WC, NjP).
   1 An old friend of Mrs. Wilson's, she was the daughter of General Alexander Robert Lawton and Sarah Hillhouse Alexander Lawton and wife of Henry Cumming Cunningham, a prominent lawyer of Savannah.
   2 Her uncle, William Dearing Hoyt, M.D.

To Ellen Axson Wilson

My own darling,   Princeton, Tuesday 6 March, 1900
   I can't tell you how chagrined I am to have put you on the wrong track entirely about Stock's plans,—to have given you in-

finite trouble about it,—to have altered the dates again and again, —and then at last to have wiped everything out as if with a sponge in my telegram sent this evening.[1] But of course you understand. The doctor never says twice the same thing about the time at which Stock. can probably get away,—and his changes never seem to have anything to do with Stock's condition; for that has gone steadily on improving without variation of rate or interruption of any kind. Stock. himself has changed the plan as to destination with autocratic indifference to consequences. Of course we have urged arguments pro and con very mildly indeed with regard to each thing suggested or discussed, and have used absolutely no persuasion at all. The way he *feels* about it settles, and ought to settle, it. That's what the going away is *for*: to rest, amuse, please him. All along he utterly and instantly rejected New Orleans, Savannah, Atlanta,—*any* place where he would be in the midst of people inclined to see a good deal of him and to make much of him. Shrank from them all, except you alone. You he evidently longed for,—and he compromised on Asheville, among southern places, simply for the sake of meeting you *some*-where. But later came the reaction. He dreaded the journey alone, and the expense. He dreamed of Atlantic City, which everybody says is an ideal place for the purpose, in life, air, comfort,— *every*thing that makes a holiday a holiday, and where he himself went once before to recuperate and spent days which he remembers with delight,—with enthusiasm. So Atlantic City it is to be. You may regard that as settled. My telegram meant this: Suppose you spend the week beginning the 11th in Atlanta and Rome; the week beginning the 18th in Asheville, and the week beginning the 25th in Atlantic City (you *might* meet your husband there!). The place is said to have a climate—at once balmly [balmy] and stimulating—which is all its own. What do you say to that? And what is the state of your purse. The pass had to be sent back to be extended, but is expected here daily. Stock. trusts you to thank the dear folks in Sav. with all cordial love messages; but his mind is fixed. Pardon all the trouble and hurry I have caused you. I would give my head to save you *every*thing[.] My heart is wholly yours and I am   Your own   Woodrow

ALS (WC, NjP).
[1] It is missing.

From Henry Mills Alden

My dear Mr Wilson,   New York City   March 6. 1900
     Your cordial note of congratulation gave me very great pleasure
in which my wife had her full share.[1] Some day I trust we may
have the pleasure of meeting you together.
                              Yours faithfully   H. M. Alden

ALS (WP, DLC).
     [1] He had married Ada Foster Murray of Norfolk, Va., on February 22, 1900.

From Ellen Axson Wilson

My own darling,   Savannah   Mar. 7 [1900]
     The telegram came half an hour ago. I have thought it all
over and have decided to make no fresh change in my plans but
to go on to Aunt Lou's tomorrow night as I have already written
her that I would. (By the way, in answer to your question, I did
write her from Princeton, telling her when I would probably
reach Atlanta and received a letter from her which you forwarded
me to New Orleans.) I will go to Rome Saturday night and leave
it the next Friday for where ever you say,—Atlantic City or home.
I suppose it *ought* to be Atlantic City for I should think Stockton
would need to be taken care of as much in one place as another.
Perhaps since Atlantic City is so near I could go home and start
out again with him; at worst I can see *you* in Phila. But there
will be time next week to arrange all this by letter. They are
all still insisting that after gaining strength enough in Atlantic
City he must come on here. I think it would be a good plan. He
would not need me *here*, of course, and he could *so easily* get a
pass and save travelling expense. *Don't forget to send my pass!* I
can use it now. Did you get the date changed? Perhaps it does not
need change now that I start north on the 16th.
     None of you must think that I am "giving up" anything in
cutting short my visit. In fact I am *glad* to; and having got it
settled in my mind that they were to be shortened it would be a
real trial to change back again. To tell the truth it makes me very
sad to be here,—and Rome will be worse. Before, I had the children to occupy my mind and time, and that made an enormous
difference. Now I have too much time to think. It would do me
no good to make longer visits. I am so homesick now that I can
hardly see the paper I write on. To make full confession, darling,
I have been just breaking my heart for a sight of *you*. Oh, you *are*
such a comfort! You are *all the world* to me, the very light of my

eyes. I could not live without you, and with you I am the happiest woman in the world. Devoted love & kisses to my little darlings, and to my own Woodrow from   His little wife   Eileen.

ALS (WC, NjP).

To Ellen Axson Wilson

My own darling,   Princeton, Wednesday 7 March, 1900.

My spirits are dashed by every line of yours I read about the Asheville plan,—I feel so guilty to have caused you all that unnecessary trouble. Of course it was not my fault: it was nobody's fault; but it put my darling out unnecessarily, and that's enough to give me no end of uneasiness. Fortunately, everything is perfectly simplified now: you need worry and hurry about nothing; and I hope that, to relieve my feelings, you will be as happy and leisurely as possible, and do nothing that was not planned long ago;—you might even take time to write me a love letter. Your plea that you haven't my "eloquent pen," the court declines to entertain. What you can do, and have done, orally you can do in writing,—you might at any rate *try* to do to keep your lover from dying with persistent longing.

I got at my history again this morning, and began again the revision where I left it off at Stock's coming home ill. I shall not hurry. I shall try, rather, to get gradually into the swing, and so cross the line to the unwritten chapter on the War for Independence with the more confident step and the more clearly defined notions of what the journey ahead will require for its accomplishment.

Things go perfectly and without incident with us. This was dancing class afternoon, and sister (who always goes, to see that the children do not overheat themselves and then catch cold) came back looking bright and refreshed. It is hard to get her to go out, as hard as to get you to take the air when you are at home; but it does her so much good when she *does* go. Stockton hardly needs looking after now, except at meal times and the like. He must not *lift* things, must not stoop too much,—or, rather, too low,—must move with great deliberation, &c., &c., but in most things he can be as independent as he likes. He has a beard, of course, but I think he means to shave before he leaves for Atlantic City. It goes without saying that he sends messages of devoted love to you every day. *Every*body sends you love who asks about you or speaks of you. My love for you passes all bounds. It leads me about from mood to mood at its will. Every faculty seems in some way or degree involved. Your portrait affects me (especially when I see it away from home,—as on Mrs. Hibben's desk) like a touch of sun,—makes me quiver with a sudden ardour: every moment of the day I am reminded by one pang or another, sweet or doleful, that I am   Your own   Woodrow.

Dearest love to all.

ALS (WC, NjP).

From Ellen Axson Wilson

My own darling,   [Savannah] Thursday [March 8, 1900]

It is breakfast time, but while waiting for the bell to ring I will begin to write, as I am going to be pressed for time today, having to get my trunk ready this morning and go to prayer-meeting after dinner.

Before I forget it,—Uncle Randolph wishes me to tell Stockton that he had yesterday a letter from the Southwestern R. R. asking his whereabouts, as he had not drawn his last dividend. I should think Stock would be more than willing just now to "draw" all he could!

I have just had a sweet letter from Rose in answer to my first two letters. Oakhurst she says is a very nice place, much sought after. Mrs. Glasser can let Stockton have a nice sunny room up only one flight of stairs for $10.00 a week. She didnt ask for a room for me, as I requested, because she is "*determined*" to have me with her unless tis "absolutely necessary" for me to be in the house with Stock. Of course I wrote her yesterday that we would not go to Asheville at all, but it seemed just as well to let you know that a nice place is secured in case he would like to change his mind. Rose says we must not expect to find spring there. It does not begin until the last of April. Until then it is about as wintry as the north. I think myself Stockton is wise in deciding against Asheville. If he came south at all he should come *all the way*. I *do* wish he could be in the *real* south where he could be out of doors all day; there is something so soothing to the nerves in this soft air.

I had a long, delightful talk yesterday with Daisy King,[1]— Rose's sister—and Mrs. *Anderson* herself, who is spending the winter here. Also saw the old doctor[2] and Daisy's two lovely girls.[3]

But it is time for me to be about my packing. I will not send the express package because now I shall not have to unpack at all in Atlanta and perhaps not altogether in Rome.

I am sorry I wrote a homesick letter yesterday, darling. I am all right today; that is I am taking as I ought full comfort in the thought that you are what you are, and that you *love* me. So I am leaning and depending on your love and finding perfect happiness in it, even though I cannot just yet find it in your arms. But that after all is a *mere detail*! You see how reasonable I have become! Always and altogether   Your own   Eileen.

ALS (WC, NjP).
    [1] Mrs. Clarence King, sister of Mrs. Wilson's friend, Rosalie Anderson Dubose.
    [2] Dr. and Mrs. H. M. Anderson of Sewanee, Tenn.
    [3] One of whom was Carol King.

To Ellen Axson Wilson

My own darling,   Princeton, Thursday 8 March, 1900

Mr. Henry Savage Landor lectures here to-night on Thibet, but neither sister nor I feels like going: we are both afraid that he will describe the tortures to which he was subjected,[1] and we've had enough surgery and the like, of late, to last us a long, long while,—and Thibet will keep. It's immeasurably pleasanter to sit here and write to my Eileen. All delightful thoughts centre about her. Whether I'm tired or sad or worried—or gay or hopeful or full of confidence, it's a tonic to turn to her. Thoughts of her cure the fatigue, dissipate sadness or worry, confirm gayety and hope and confidence amidst hazards of fortune. You have been my solace and the substance of happiness for me, my darling, ever since you promised to be my wife,—my ground of hope ever since I first met you!

The incumbency of Dr. Murray's chair[2] was settled by the trustees to-day, in a perfectly characteristic way. The secret was perfectly kept to the last, and that was, of course, the most important matter of all: that we should all feel that we were outsiders hearing a piece of news. Harper was transferred from French to the English chair; it is given out that Guyot Cameron *will* get the vacated French chair,[3] being brought over from the scientific to the academic side (though I am told this was not actually done to-day); and some one, inexpensive of course, will be put in Cameron's place. How complete it all is: not a pound added to our working force; not a name added to our list, or prestige; money saved and second-rate men promoted! Of course I do not refer to Harper, whom I love and admire, and who is wholly worthy of the place, if he wants it. I refer to the whole familiar process by which *choice* and *development* are avoided. Harper was ten years ago very eager for a place in English, I know; but I supposed he was by this time drawn by French to another task and training altogether. But that's his affair, and, so far as he is personally concerned, I am delighted. A more complete surprise could hardly be imagined. A trustee was elected, I understand, but I can't find anybody who knows *who*,—probably, I should guess, Howard Duffield.[4] That would round out the day's work symmetrically!

We are all well, darling, and in excellent form every way. My work is slowly and satisfactorily gathering momentum; and as the days of our separation shorten I can see peace and happiness approach.   Your own   Woodrow

ALS (WC, NjP).

[1] An English artist, lecturer, and world traveler, Landor had recently published *In the Forbidden Land; An account of a journey into Tibet, capture by the Tibetan Lamas and soldiers, imprisonment, torture, and ultimate release* . . . (2 vols., New York and London, 1899).

[2] The Holmes Professorship of Belles Lettres and English Language and Literature, held by James Ormsbee Murray until his death in 1899 and then by Bliss Perry until his departure to become full-time editor of the *Atlantic Monthly* in 1900.

[3] George McLean Harper was given the Holmes chair, and Arnold Guyot Cameron became Woodhull Professor of French. Both were elected at the meeting on March 8, 1900.

[4] Wilson's guess was wrong. De Witt Clinton Blair was elected a trustee on March 8, as Wilson reported in his letter to his wife of March 9.

From Ellen Axson Wilson

My own darling,   Atlanta, Friday [March 9, 1900]

Here I am safely at the end of another stage in my journey; I reached here two hours ago, at 7.30, and found Uncle Warren[1] awaiting me. It has been very bad weather here, as it was in Savannah yesterday, but now the sun is coming out gloriously.

They all seem very well and cosy in their comfortable little cottage;[2] perfectly absorbed in the baby, little Philip,[3] who is a great, fine fellow. While coming up I asked Uncle Warren how he liked living in Atlanta and he replied simply, "Oh, I'm satisfied wherever your Aunt Lou is."

My time is so short that I won't write a long letter (especially as the ink seems to be *watered*!) Your letter suggesting that I spend a week in Asheville was received yesterday, but I can't think that would be right. If Stockton needs me at all he certainly needs me *most* when he *first* leaves home, and while he is still weak. I had already written Rose that I would not get to Asheville.

So just write, or telegraph if necessary, when I shall leave Rome for Atlantic City and where I shall go when I get there. I presume I must come back to Atlanta to start, on account of the *pass*. That will take me and my trunk as far as Washington, and as yet I have no idea how to get from there to Atlantic City. Perhaps you can write me. I am going to try to find out here for I know I can't in Rome. I am perfectly well & happy. With dear, *dear* love to all, and above all to *you*, believe me, my own Woodrow, always & altogether   Your own   Eileen.

I have $14.00 left now.

ALS (WC, NjP).
  ¹ Warren A. Brown, husband of Mrs. Wilson's Aunt Louisa Brown.
  ² At 333 N. Boulevard.
  ³ Philip Evans, youngest child of Mrs. Wilson's first cousin, Loula Brown (Mrs. James Philip) Evans. Loula Brown Evans had died a few weeks after Philip's birth in 1898, and he was living with his grandparents, Mr. and Mrs. Warren A. Brown. James Philip Evans and his four older children were living in Gainesville, Ga., at this time.

To Ellen Axson Wilson

My own darling,   Princeton, Friday 9 March, 1900.
    Your letters written from Savannah after the receipt of my telegram about Stockton's plans came, together, to-day. And so you calmly decline to do as you are advised, madam! You will not go to Asheville at all, but will come straight away north on the sixteenth. Well, my sweet one, I will not insist upon your going against your inclination and your judgment both, if you've "thought it over." But *have* you thought it over? Think, Eileen: I cannot often spare you thus: it would infallibly shorten my life, if I did. When again will you have a *chance* to spend a few days with "Rose"? Don't, I beg of you, act upon an impulse. You were too homesick when you were in Savannah to exercise calm judgment. Think of the pang to Rose, whom you have loved all your life, and the abiding pang for you, if you do *not* see her now, when you can. *I* am going to take Stock. to Atlantic City; and you can join him there later just as well as at the beginning of his stay. I can see you for a few hours at Philadelphia when you come,—will of course meet you and take you to Atlantic City (by the way: select a train wh. reaches Philadelphia rather early in the day, and be sure to select it in time and let me know exactly what time it arrives); but then,—*separation again*, and the tantalizing pain of having you only three hours away! I believe in my heart it will be harder to bear than having you in New Orleans or Savannah! *I* wont have you any more than I did when you

were in the South. I had set my heart on having you go to Asheville. Think of these things again, my pet, think of them all again, and,—whatever you decide then I will accept without another word.

It looks as if the pass were going to fail us again! "Coming," "coming,"—but it never comes. No matter. It shall be sent, post haste, if it comes: if it does not come, no matter. I took it for granted you would extend your stay in Savannah after receiving my telegram, and so sent you a cheque for fifty dollars there. For fear it may not follow you in time, I enclose a duplicate. If you need both (as you may if you go to Asheville) keep both. If you do not, destroy one, and let me know, please ma'am.

Ah, love, God knows how my heart aches over this whole business. I almost dread to have you near and yet as much out of reach of voice or caress as ever. I am torn by a thousand conflicting desires and judgments, just because I *am*

Your own   Woodrow

Clinton Blair, old Jno. I's son, is the new trustee. Love to uncle Will.

ALS (WC, NjP).

From Ellen Axson Wilson

My own darling,   Atlanta Saturday [March 10, 1900]

Please excuse pencil; that ink is impossible especially when one is in something of a hurry. We are going out to ride down Peach-tree St., see it and Ed's[1] new house at the farther end of it.[2] Ed is to meet us out there. It is a *beautiful* day, and almost as mild as Savannah, and yesterday afternoon was the same.

I had a most amusing adventure looking for Mr. Bones.[3] The address you remember was in the "Gould Building." Mr. Henderson took Minnie[4] and me there but he was not at the number designated. Then he asked some official if there was "a Mr. Bone" in the building, getting, it seems, the name a little wrong. He was told there was, at a certain number to which we betook ourselves. There we were met by a very pleasant gentleman[5] who regretted that Mr. Bone was out of town; so I handed him my card asking him to give it to Mr. Bones and tell him that I was *exceedingly* sorry to miss him! (Think of leaving such a message for a strange man!) But as soon as my new friend saw the card he became *violently* excited, jumped out of his chair, and almost danced. "What!" he cried, "Woodrow Wilson's wife? Tommy

Wilson!" I've known him since he was a baby, I'm from Staunton Va.[6] & my wife is *Mattie Brown*![7] And how is Annie?—and how's everybody? &c. &c. In fact he almost fell on my neck, and I was equally glad to meet him for of course I knew all about the Browns. Then he suddenly started up again saying he must go & telephone to Mr. *Bones*! "But," I said, "I thought you just told me he was out of town!"—and so the comedy of errors reached its dénoument! Mr. Bone was a young man in his employ. Mr. Bones was in his office very near; we proceeded thither and he accompanied us to see my old friends the two Mrs. Kingsbury's.[8] I was fortunate enough to find them both at home; so altogether I had a delightful afternoon. Dear Mrs. Bowie[9] is out of town with one of her daughters; it seems Mr. Bowie *died* two years ago.

Mr. Arnall and his wife, Mattie, called and spent the evening. She was very sweet & sent all sorts of love messages to Sister Annie. But I am called for. With *devoted* love I remain in every heart-throb   Your own   Eileen.

No letters for me, alas! until I get to Rome.

ALS (WC, NjP).
   [1] Her first cousin, Edward Thomas Brown, at this time practicing law in Atlanta.
   [2] A large stone house at 962 Peachtree St., between 14th and 15th Sts.
   [3] Wilson's maternal uncle-in-law, James W. Bones.
   [4] William A. Henderson and Minnie Brown Henderson, Mrs. Wilson's first cousin. Henderson was at this time local manager of Baker-Vawter Co., manufacturers of office supplies and equipment. He and his wife lived with Minnie's parents, Mr. and Mrs. Warren A. Brown.
   [5] Charles S. Arnall, general agent in Atlanta for the Phoenix Life Insurance Co. of Hartford.
   [6] Born in Augusta County, Va., June 18, 1839, Arnall had worked in a bank in Staunton, Va., before the Civil War. He had moved to Atlanta in 1883.
   [7] Martha Brown, who had married Arnall about 1880.
   [8] Rosa Bowie (Mrs. Charles Sanford) Kingsbery and Caroline F. (Mrs. Edwin) Kingsbery. The Kingsbery brothers were in business together as C. S. Kingsbery & Co., Wholesale Clothing, Shoes and Hats.
   [9] Lucy Smith (Mrs. John A.) Bowie. Bowie, a prominent fire insurance agent, had actually died on December 13, 1896. Mrs. Wilson had known the Bowies as a child in Rome, Ga.

To Ellen Axson Wilson

My own darling,   Princeton, Saturday 10 March, 1900.

A word of supplement to my letter of yesterday. In my telegram I said that Stockton would go to Atlantic City about the 19th. But it is not *necessary*, I think, for him to wait so long. If you are to start north on the 16th, he and I can, I feel quite confident, leave here the same day, and on the 17th I can meet you in Philadelphia and take *you* to Atlantic City. It would, I am sure, be painful for you to come home and then tear yourself away again immediately. But, of course, if Stockton *can't* leave before the 19th, you ought to come straight here on Saturday, and start out again with him on Monday. I can communicate with you at the last moment about that, if necessary, by telegram. But *we* think Stock. could go *now* without the least risk. He has walked out of doors both yesterday and to-day, and is quite steady enough to travel.

No letter yet to-day (I write earlier than usual on Saturdays to escape the Sunday embargo); and no letter to-day means no letter till Monday. A late mail may bring one; but it's not at all likely that you were able to write and mail a letter yesterday forenoon,—the morning of your arrival in Atlanta;—and so I will avail myself of my usual resource under such circumstances: I will make love to you, to ease my heart off in its loneliness. I can't venture *very* far. I have had all through this separation to think of you, not as in my arms (I could not bear to dream of that and not have it so!), but within my sight only,—where I could see and think of you, but could not approach or speak to you,—and so could keep my self-possession and not *kill* myself with longing. I have had to confine my dreams very rigourously to thinking of myself as your lover, but not quite as your husband. If I were to let my longing take *full* possession of my imagination, I feel it would rack me to pieces. I think of you as my sweet, sweet lady love, so beautiful, so alluring in voice and grace of mind, so full of *meaning* in all her nature, such a treat to the mind in her talk and to the heart in her sentiments, so unlike, so delightfully unlike anyone else, so wonderfully mixed and compacted of charm and sense,—the woman to *live* with and never exhaust, never run out of sweet surprises, dear discoveries of latent things,—so made by every gift as to be queen and mistress in the heart and imagination of

Her own   Woodrow

No pass yet.

ALS (WC, NjP).

To Frederick Jackson Turner

My dear Turner,   Princeton, New Jersey, 10 March, 1900.

It has been a long, long time since we exchanged letters, and I have felt the separation (for it is nothing less) more, I am afraid, than I could make you realize.

I heard only the other day that you had lost one of your children.[1] Nothing that I could say, I very well know, could bring you real comfort; but I can at least tell you what a pang of genuine grief it brought me, and how it has lingered in my mind ever since as a source of sadness. It must be a terrible thing to lose a little one (thank God, I have never had to go through that darkness!), and Mrs. Wilson and I have both thought and talked of you both again and again, wishing that we might in some way be able to make you feel how deeply we sy[m]pathized with you.

I am busier every year of my life; and to be busy is, I fear, to be selfish also, because absorbed. I am the more rejoiced, therefore, that a matter of business should turn me to you, and to a renewal of our correspondence.

We want a Professor of Politics; and I make bold to ask you this question: If you had such a chair to fill, whom would you invite to fill it?

The conditions here are such that a mere specialist would not do. We must have a man who is also a gentleman and a scholar in the broad and genial meanings of those words. Our most immediate object is to have intelligent study and lecturing on the new things with which recent events have brought us face to face: the administration of dependencies in particular, and the actual administration of government in general. I myself try to take care of the theory of Politics.

If you know of a man whom you have seen and sampled as a man, and whom you think thoroughly worth considering for our appointment, will you not tell me about him? The endowment of the chair is one hundred thousand dollars, and we could, therefore, offer a salary of four thousand.

With warmest regards to you both, and to Haskins,

Cordially and faithfully Yours,   Woodrow Wilson

Carl Becker[2] has just written to me.[3] What does he amount to?

WWTLS (F. J. Turner Papers, CSmH).
 [1] As Wilson soon discovered, the Turners had actually lost two children—Jackson Allen and Mae Sherwood—in 1899.
 [2] At this time he was Instructor in History and Political Science at Pennsylvania State College.
 [3] His letter is missing.

From Ellen Axson Wilson

My own darling,   Rome [Ga.] Sunday [March 11, 1900].

I reached Rome safely last night and found Uncle Will awaiting me at the East Rome depot with his buggy; found also your sweet letter, written Wednesday, awaiting me. And this morning we got another from the post office on our way home from church; so I am very happy.

I know too that you will be glad for my sake to hear that this Sunday in Rome is a perfect spring day,—a real May day, as lovely as any we had in New Orleans. Weather makes a great difference always in my feelings,—as I presume it does in everyones! The jassamine, the daffodils and the hyacinths are in bloom, the grass is green, and the town looks very attractive while the hills about it, veiled in a soft blue haze, are *beautiful,—* as always.

I held, of course a reception after church and met almost all the people here I most care for; several said they were coming over this afternoon—so, now that dinner is over and we have strolled about the place while Uncle Will smoked his cigar, I have come up to write to you before their arrival. The new wife[1] is a decided success, and the poor old uncle is more comfortable than he has been since he left his mother's roof. It really seemed queer to be ushered into a sweet, fresh, dainty room in *this* house. And the food is perfectly cooked and well served. She is an attractive woman too, with a very sweet manner. In appearance she is a good deal like *Minnie!*[2] type and colouring exactly the same, but her manner is more quiet and restful. The old mother[3] is very nice looking, peaceful and inoffensive. They have a family boarding with them, a Mr. Hastings from Montgomery, a very nice young man; his wife and child are absent just now.

I found a letter from Madge here asking permission—but stay— I will enclose her letter to save time.[4] I think there is no objection to the plan; it will be a fine frolic for her. Will you please send her a check for $20.00?

I had no chance to find out anything in Atlanta about the journey to Atlantic City; the wretched station being always so packed with people and in such confusion. Am afraid you will have to help me with my schedule. Since I cannot, with the pass, take the "limited" I must leave Atlanta at half past twelve at night; that will bring me to Washington at eight the next night and to Phila.—if I went straight on,—at *three* the next morning; that would be *very* bad! I would better leave that train at Washington and if possible go by some direct route to Atlantic City. The Atlanta people seemed to think that could be done. My programme is a puzzle altogether. If I leave here *Friday* night I get to Atlantic City too soon, besides travelling on Sunday; the only alternative is to leave Monday night and get there too late.

Besides I am to see *you* somewhere, you know, and you could not leave home on Monday. *You* will just have to settle it all,—its too much for me!

I am disgusted beyond expression at the work of the trustees. I never heard of a more perfect botch. Mr. Harper is a nice fine fellow but will of course add no prestige to the department and I fancy will do the work only fairly well! But you have said all that I think on the subject and it will do no good to fill my letter with grumbling. I am glad you have your own work to engage your mind and keep the best of your thoughts from dwelling on so hopeless a situation. Ah, how eagerly I read every word you write about that work! With what delight do I read between the lines that you are working with some satisfaction to yourself! How I should *love* to hear the dear voice reading the daily "stint." But that will come *soon* now! And when I have you I shall hold you fast. I shan't be sent away again except for absolute necessity. Was interrupted here by the callers,—close in haste to get this mailed. With devoted love   Your little wife   Eileen

ALS (WP, DLC).
  [1] Dr. Hoyt's new wife, Annie Perkins Hoyt, additionally described in EAW to WW, Aug. 7, 1899, n. 3.
  [2] Dr. Hoyt's daughter, Mary Eloise Hoyt.
  [3] That is, Mrs. Hoyt's mother.
  [4] It is missing.

To Ellen Axson Wilson

My own darling,   Princeton, Sunday 11 March, 1900.

It excites me beyond measure to think that I *may* spend *next* Sunday with you! I have not heard from you since you left Savannah,—I did not really expect to hear,—but I take it for granted that you are in Rome to-day, and I have a subtle consciousness of your *approach* to the last stage of your journey homeward. I cannot, I fear, put into words the tender thoughts which crowd into my mind when I think of you in Rome,—sitting in the church where I had my first glimpse of your exquisite face,—first felt the keen thrill that has ever since gone with every thought of your sweet presence![1] A blessing on the place,—and an unmeasured blessing on the little woman who has brought everything that is good into my life. May her sadness in the midst of all the memories the place excites be tempered with *some* happiness, at thought of what first came to her there,—the promise of infinite love, the sweet home in far away Princeton, and a life widening into greater usefulness and quiet power for good than any *girl* could reckon. Ah, my love, Rome would have only sweet associations for me, did I not know what memories it holds for you,—what an unutterable sadness and sense of loss.[2] For me, it is easy to think of it wholly as a place of romance, and of you, in connection with it, only as the heroine of that romance,—my romance,—the source of all that is poetic and stuff of inspiration in my life. Oh, I *hope*, my Eileen, that *those* memories will come to you, too, and be strong enough sometimes to crowd the others out. Think *what* a conquest you made there: how complete, how lasting, how blessed for the man you love. Think of what began there, and be glad that you were born to bring so much happiness into the world. I am afraid that if *I* were with you in Rome now, I should pass all bounds of feeling and *worship* you. It goes to my head, like a delicious intoxication, to think of the fulfillment of all the dreams I dreamed as I walked those streets and roads with you, or watched for glimpses of you as I passed; to think how the charm that thrilled me there thrills me yet and is never stale,—not only abides, but grows, by unending surprises of fresh discovery, so that I am always falling in love anew. The delight I first felt in Rome has grown upon me ever since. I know that when you come back it will be better than getting married was, more exciting, more delicious, more romantic even: happiness is now of such assurance with us, of such known and certain zest! I hope that you have thought of all this, my love, and that sadness has been swallowed up in the thoughts that are sweetest of all.

Give my warmest regards to Miss Anna Harris, and to all friends who ask after me to whom you *wish* to give such a message. I did not know that you had any *business* to attend to in Rome. Perhaps, by the way, you can buy from uncle Will that sofa you always admired so much. Do so by all means, if you wish,—and anything else that you think would prove handsome and useful for us. I suppose you have a great many books in the house, which you will have to have boxed and started northward by freight.

We are all getting on as usual. Stockton looks brighter and stronger to-day than he has looked any day yet. I've no doubt he can start for Atlantic City whenever he chooses. I had the bad taste to have a little stomach attack last night,—an exceedingly mild version of that feeling of *distention* around the waist that I had once or twice quite violently in Middletown. But this afternoon it is practically gone, and I feel only a little tired and worse for wear. I took the bismuth and calomel at night and sprudel salts this morning, and shall repeat the doses two more nights and mornings, as I did before you went away, and it's evident that is going to set me right. The rest are all well.

Our only piece of news is, that the Hibbens are going to Europe,—will sail May 26th, and stay until February of next year! Doesn't that make you feel a little blank? It does me, very. They are not going for pleasure, as you see by the period set, but for work. Jack has felt for some time that he needed a little time and stimulation under European masters to keep him from going stale in his subjects, and he is now determined to freshen up,— next term promising to be as easy to skip as any he is ever likely to have. But, dear me, *what shall we do without them*? And five months, or less, after they get back we ourselves go, to stay eighteen months,—so that we shall have only five months with them out of two years and four months,—shall be practically two whole years separated from them. It's hard, very hard to bear the thought! Isn't it, sweet heart? That's the worst of having friends whom one really loves,—the pain of the inevitable separations. The thing to think about is our own home,—the absolute satis-faction and all-sufficiency of our love for each other. I can bear *any*thing so long as I am accepted and cherished as

Your own   Woodrow

No pass yet!

ALS (WC, NjP).
 [1] See the Editorial Note, "Wilson's Introduction to Ellen Axson," Vol. 2.
 [2] On account of the death of her mother, Margaret Jane Hoyt Axson, in Rome on November 4, 1881, and the illness of her father, Samuel Edward Axson, in Rome in 1883.

From Ellen Axson Wilson

Rome [Ga.] Monday morning
My own darling,   [March 12, 1900]

Your letter with the second check came before breakfast this morning. I am about to go driving with Uncle Will and am writ-ing a few *very* hurried lines while waiting for him to see a near by patient. The weather is just as it was yesterday—*perfect*!

You are right in all you say about the Asheville trip; it is a matter of poignant and lasting regret to me that I did not see Beth[1] in all those years, and I would like if possible to avoid the same heart-ache in regard to Rose. It *will* be a *great* disappoint-ment to her too it seems, and as she has had so much trouble of late and is not well,—is to have another baby,—I should like to avoid that. So I *have* "thought it all over again," and I think I can crowd in two days at least with her without failing Stockton; I don't *want* to go home for one or two days and then start again. That would be *too* hard! The only objection is that if I go to Asheville that ill-fated *pass* will probably be of no service; but hurry it on, if it comes, and let me see.

I was interrupted by a visitor, then had to go driving immediately with Uncle Will; we were out until dinner time and had a *beautiful* drive. I am just up from the dinner table, and will now proceed with my subject.

In the mean time I have been to the R. R. office and enquired about ways and means of getting to Asheville. The ticket is $8.50 and if I leave here at three P. M. I get there at *five* the next morning! That doesn't suit me at all; I will inconvenience my friends and see nothing of the scenery. So I shall leave here Friday at three—

Was interrupted at this point by old Martha.[2] While still talking to her a visitor arrived and soon the parlour was filled; the last one has just left at six o'clock. As I was about to observe I shall leave here at three on Friday, reach Knoxville at eight P.M., spend the night there, leave at eight in the morning and reach Asheville about one in the afternoon. Then if there is a good train Monday night I can take it and get to Phila. at some decent hour the next day. The only trouble will be about your lectures on Tuesday; you won't want to cut them. Perhaps if Stockton is strong enough to be alone so long you would prefer on that account that I should reach Phila. Wed. morning. But I *don't* want to be selfish in making him secondary to my comfort or pleasure. Don't be concerned at my stopping over night at Knoxville. There is a nice hotel[3] there at which I spent the night alone when I was a girl,—the second night after we became engaged.

I have had a delightful afternoon seeing old friends. There certainly are many dear, delightful people here,—especially women, and they are perfectly devoted still to Papa and Mama. Of course I love the Rome people exactly in proportion to the degree in which they individually loved my parents. My affections may in some instances be misplaced, but that is my principle!

But I *must* stop for I have not yet written to Rose and it is almost tea-time. You don't know what a heavy heart I have because of my own decision to go to Rose, and so postpone seeing you for a few days! I don't like to think about it or write about it, but I know I will be glad I went when it is all over and I *am* at home again. I love you my Woodrow, my *darling*, with all my heart, soul, and mind, and I am always and altogether,

Your own   Eileen.

ALS (WC, NjP).
  [1] Elizabeth Adams (Mrs. Hamilton) Erwin.
  [2] A servant.
  [3] The Hotel Imperial, as EAW to WW, March 16, 1900, discloses.

To Ellen Axson Wilson

My own darling,   Princeton, Monday 12 March, 1900.

I stayed away from lectures, etc., to-day out of abundant caution in respect of that minor, and really very well behaved, "gastric crisis" reported in my last. I have really felt very well all day, barring a slight self-consciousness at the spot concerned; but the wind is abroad in its might, the thermometer is now down to scandalously small figures, and no doubt it was best for me to stay within. It's a pretty slow business, none the less, and would have been without cheer had not your two letters from Atlanta come to me smiling this morning, with pleasant news and the air of happiness which goes with you in all that you do in normal humour.

I can hardly count on getting more than two letters more to you,—so here's for information. You reach Atlantic City from Philadelphia (*we* reach it from Trenton); but all you have to do is to let me know, as exactly as possible, the schedule of your train (it's *number*, if may be), especially it's time of arrival at Philadelphia,—which should, if you can manage it so, be Saturday forenoon. There is, e.g., a train (No. 38) which leaves Atlanta at noon and reaches Phila. at 10:15 the next morning. If I don't send you the pass by my next letter, dismiss it from your mind, and come straight from Rome, if that is just as convenient as *via* Atlanta. The doctor says Stock. can leave "any time" now; but there's no reason why you should start before the time you have already fixed upon (Friday, the 16th). We shall pretty certainly not leave before Thursday, and I can stay with him till I go to fetch you from Phila., not only without inconvenience but with pleasure and profit. It will do me no harm, and brace me for the shock of being happy again,—and once more miserable, when I *leave* you at Atlantic City! How I can take you in my arms again and ever let you go out of my sight afterwards is more than I can just at this moment imagine or endure the thought of! But I have had strength given me for many things, and shall not yet fall coward. And yet the fact is, my Eileen, that

I love you tragically,—with a movement at the deepest parts of my heart which *might*,—should anything ever happen to you,—rise to a thrashing storm that would dash me to pieces. God keep me very far from that tempest! And one glimpse of your eyes will be unspeakable tonic and refreshment to

Your own[1]

AL (WC, NjP).

[1] In lieu of his signature, Wilson here pasted a small snapshot of himself.

From Frederick Jackson Turner

My dear Wilson,   Madison, Wisconsin 12 March 1900

Your letter was most welcome—not so welcome as a view of you in the flesh—but next to it, for you can make your letters bring you more nearly in person than can anyone else I know.

I know I have your sympathy; and I am glad you can only write from your sense of what it must be, and not from experience. I grew to married manhood without meeting death in my family, or among my closest friends, and the loss of my little girl and little boy inside of a year has made havoc with my hopes and joys. Mrs. Turner's health has sadly suffered, too, and she is now in a rest cure to build up her strength in Chicago. She, I am happy to tell you, is gaining steadily in strength and the doctor gives me reason to hope for excellent results. Her mind and spirit are as strong as ever, but her poor little body could not stand so heavy a load.

In regard to your position, I am sure it ought to command a very strong man. Looking to available men, I will say that I should carefully consider Morse Stephens[1] who is a thorough student of modern history, and especially of colonial politics. He is a force, has influence over students and is full of ideas.

We are this month to have a special course of lectures from him on Colonial Politics; but I have not heard him lecture. You should get acquainted with him, at any rate.

Our own expectations rest on Dr. P. S. Reinsch[2] who is soon to have a work on World Politics for Macmillan.[3] He is one of our own products, but has travelled and studied abroad, has successfully practiced law, and has lots of growth in him. He has developed from a German youth without particular social advantages, but he has the natural instincts of a well bred gentleman and is an inspiring teacher. At present I could not say he was up to a $4000. place; but I believe he will soon be; and that he would fit at Princeton. I say this reluctantly, for we wish him to stay and grow with us. However, you have a right to a knowledge of him. Administration has not been his particular field; but he would get it up easily in time. Reinsch is one of the men whom I take pride in claiming as in part a product of my shop.

Carl Becker would make an excellent instructor. He has a fine literary sense; is a well grounded fellow; has taken our fellowship, and one in political science at Columbia. If I have a place in American history before long, he is one of the men I should consider. As a student he was retiring, but he was developing in this direction rapidly. He is a good man for a *starting* position in a large college or university, and would hold down a professorship in a smaller college. His force is not of the obvious kind, but he has good metal to work on. If you have an instructorship he is well worth considering.

We are missing [Charles Homer] Haskins this semester, who has leave of absence to lecture in Harvard (Colonial Club). Special lectures by Morse Stephens & Jewett,[4] of Minnesota have been arranged to fill the gap in part.

We hoped for you in our Summer Session. Moses Coit Tyler, Macy, Giddings, Kuno Francke and others are to be here.[5] I am overcrowded just now, as I conduct a seminary in Chicago to help fill the breach caused by Professor von Holst's illness[.] It is more than doubtful if he will ever give University courses again.[6] What do you think of Chicago's future in graduate work in history?   Yours affectionately   Frederick J. Turner

ALS (WP, DLC) with WWhw notation on env.: "(Ans. 4 April, 1900.)"
    [1] Henry Morse Stephens, Professor of Modern European History at Cornell.
    [2] Paul Samuel Reinsch, Assistant Professor of Political Science at the University of Wisconsin.
    [3] *World Politics at the End of the Nineteenth Century, As Influenced by the Oriental Situation* (London and New York, 1900).
    [4] James Richard Jewett, Weyerhaeuser Professor of Semitic Languages and History, University of Minnesota.
    [5] Moses Coit Tyler, Professor of American History, Cornell University; Jesse Macy, Professor of Political Science, Iowa College (now Grinnell College); Franklin Henry Giddings, Professor of Sociology, Columbia University; and Kuno Francke, Professor of German Literature, Harvard University.
    [6] Hermann Eduard von Holst retired from the University of Chicago in 1899 on account of ill health and spent the rest of his life in Europe. He died in 1904.

From Ellen Axson Wilson

My own darling,   Rome [Ga.] March 13 [1900].

Your letter written Saturday is at hand and shows us again a bit at cross purposes! for acting on the supposition that Stockton would not leave 'till next week I have written to Rose and settled everything as I wrote you yesterday. It is too bad! I hope he does not *care* to change his plan but was only doing it for my and your convenience.

I spent some time after breakfast ransacking the lumber-room. Then I went driving with Annie[1] returning just in time for dinner, and I am again trying to get my letter written before visitors arrive. Am to go driving again with Anna Harris; would prefer to stay at home and meet friends who call, but she is so sensitive that I did not like to refuse. The weather is as fine—Oh dear!—a caller!

A continual stream of visitors until Anna came!—and indeed we were fortunate to have an interval in which to escape for as we drove away we saw another coming up. Poor old Anna came to take me to drive in a fine livery-stable carriage and pair! We are just back at half past six and I am expecting the tea bell every moment. Ah me! this is an unsatisfactory sort of intercourse with my darling! But the days are numbered now! Please explain to the dear girlies why I *can't* answer their dear little letters, and tell them how *very* glad I was to get them,—and how *dearly* I love them. Best love to all, and for you my own Woodrow the whole heart and life of   Your little wife   Eileen.

No tea bell yet—will scribble till it rings! We had a beautiful drive this afternoon—another new, "river road," along the banks of the Coosa, with a high rocky "bluff" on the other side covered with ferns and vines.

This morning we took *our* river road,—and also went to Fort Jackson hitching the horse at the bottom and climbing up through the beautiful fragrant pine forest with its clean, smooth, brown carpet. And oh, the view from the top is *glorious*! This is certainly a singularly beautiful country.

ALS (WC, NjP).
[1] Annie Perkins Hoyt.

To Ellen Axson Wilson

My own darling,   Princeton, Tuesday 13 March, 1900.

Stock. tells me that the *direct* route north from Rome (*via* Chattanooga, &c.) is roundabout, and that much the shortest way is to take the Southern Railway at Atlanta. Perhaps, therefore, since the pass, the unlucky pass, has not come to us, you had better write to your cousin Ed. Brown and ask him to go to Mr. Howell's office (Dorsey, Brewster, & Howell, 203-212 Law Building, Atlanta), inquire about the errant document, and, if he can get hands upon it, meet you at the (noon ?) train and deliver it. You *might*, if you cared to, go down to Atlanta the evening before starting and get Ed. to do the errand the next morning while you waited. But, in any case, my love, don't give yourself any particular trouble or concern about the wretched thing. I'd *rather* pay than take favours, anyhow, as you know; and the pass, if obtained, would save very little at best. If you *do* get it, your train will stop long enough in Washington for you to get for yourself, or send the Pullman conductor for, a ticket from Washington to Philadelphia. *All* trains make stops of from ten to twenty minutes there,—even if late, I think.

Your husband is all right to-day. He is delivering his lectures, as usual, and feels as chipper as a fellow can who took Sprudel salts before breakfast. His blood quickens as the week advances: his real cure and tonic will come when he has seen you and touched your lips. When you are really at home again everything in the world will seem to him new and beautiful and his whole life will swing along heartily as if to music. And to have you at Atlantic City will mean that on each Saturday and Sunday that you are there he will slip off to steal enough life out of your eyes and your caresses to keep him in heart and zest for the week of work. It's this *long*, slow *starvation* that tells on the system like an intimation of death. Forty-eight, or even twenty-four, hours' of delight a week ought to keep the blood going finely! And it will be so fine to *see* you *on a holiday*. There will be precious little taking care of Stock. to do; and I shall expect you simply to expand like a flower (Duchesse!) in the sweet air of that favoured place. I shall come simply to caress you and enjoy your happiness and beauty. Dream all the journey up, my Eileen, of the new courtship and happiness we shall have,—of the joy, strength, *fervour* of peace and delight you will presently see in the face of   Your own   Woodrow

ALS (WC, NjP).

From Henry Mills Alden

Dear Mr Wilson,   New York City   March 13. 1900

I enclose for your consideration a substitute for the section you wished inserted in the agreement between you & Messrs Harper & Brothers for the serial & book-publication of your "Short History of the United States."[1]

Your concession of ten in the place of seven years for the undisturbed operation of the contract[2] places the publishers in a position where they may hope, notwithstanding the great initial expense for magazine use & the subsequent expense for continued & wide-spread advertisement (to which must be added the limitation of the publishers' margin of profit by reason of unusual discounts to the trade to further the sales,) to realise a reasonable profit. We hope, of course, to be aided in this by subsequent writings of yours in this field of U. S. history which will keep you before the reading public, & which we hope to publish.

You must be aware of the fact that but for our publication of the book we could not have made you so large an offer for serial use; & it is also true that but for our publication of the book we could not afford to make one-half the outlay which we purpose to make for illustrations. Ordinarily the magazine publication is supposed to cover at least one-half the cost of text & illustrations for a work to be subsequently published in book-form. In the present case it falls short of doing this. The expense for illustration is more likely to exceed than fall below ten thousand dollars for the twelve parts.

One half this expense for illustration must be included in what is designated in the agreement as "one-half the cost of production of the plates."

Now, in the case of the publishers' wish to discontinue publication at any time after the expiration of ten years, it is evident that in the estimate of the publishers the work has no considerable market value; & when, in such circumstances, they offer to sell the plates at half cost to the author, (as an alternative to melting them,) they would naturally be willing to make accommodations. For example, if, or in so far as, the illustrations are wholly separate from the text, i.e. occupying pages by themselves, they would be willing to allow the author his choice to include or exclude these, in his resumption of ownership; & if he exclude them they still remain under the control of the publishers for whatever purpose they may serve. This is the case of an abandoned book.

Obviously the situation is quite different where the publisher is willing to continue publication & the author wishes to withdraw & resume ownership. At the time of making the original contract it is impossible to estimate what after ten years will be the market value of the work. It is equally impossible to predict the author's motive for withdrawal. He may, without any dissatisfaction with the results of the publishers' efforts, simply wish to gather all his works together in a uniform edition to be issued by the publisher having control of most of them. The method of withdrawal may vary. For instance, he may wish a sumptuous uniform edition, leaving the popular edition undisturbed in the control of the original publisher, or *vice versa*, he may wish to withdraw for a popular uniform edition, leaving the elaborately illustrated edition in the original control.

But whatever the circumstances or method of withdrawal, one point seems clear—namely that there is a market value sufficient to make the book desirable to another publisher as a commercial undertaking—in which case its purchase value could not be less than one-half the original cost of the production of the plates, including half-cost of illustrations.

But the market value of the book might well be twice or even ten times the value thus estimated, & this value would be in good part due to the enterprise & sacrifice of the original publisher. This market value will always be equal to what would be a fair price in its disposal by sale to another publisher desiring to undertake it.

Our concession is this that, while at the end of ten years we might not wish to part with your book, we leave ourselves no option against your wish to withdraw it; & it is manifestly fair, in such a case, that we should receive the equivalent of its market value.

You will see how very difficult it is to establish in set terms a standard for this valuation; & while we have done our best in the formula submitted herewith, it is quite likely that much is left open to such final negotiation—in case you ever withdraw your book—as may, in the actual circumstances, seem mutually satisfactory.[3]

The royalty upon copies in more expensive binding, as well as those in sheets, would depend on the cloth price. This is in accordance with the general usage in the trade, both for books sold in the ordinary channels & for those sold by canvassing agents.   Very truly yours   H. M. Alden

ALS (WP, DLC). Att.: WWhw estimates.
[1] The enclosure is missing.
[2] Wilson made this concession in a letter which is missing.
[3] As H. M. Alden to WW, March 26 and April 3, 1900, disclose, one part of the substitute section which Alden had sent for Wilson's consideration proposed arbitration as one possible means of determining the fair value of the history in the event that Wilson desired to recover ownership at the end of ten years.

From Ellen Axson Wilson

My own darling,   Rome [Ga.] Wednesday [March 14, 1900]

I have had two letters from you today[.] The sweet, *sweet* one written Sunday—

I was interrupted here,—have not had *one single minute* all day to write,—ten o'clock now,—this *must* go [to] the mail box at once! It was *so* good in you to send the telegram.[1] I was feeling very heavy-hearted about my change of plan,—indeed I still regret it desperately, but the telegram made me feel better   Devotedly,

Your own   Eileen.

ALS (WC, NjP).
  [1] It is missing.

Two Letters to Ellen Axson Wilson

[Princeton, N.J., c. March 14, 1900]

I took the liberty, sweetheart, of reading this.

Your W.

ALI (WP, DLC). Enc.: Lucy M. Smith to EAW, March 11, 1900, ALS (WP, DLC).

My own darling,   Princeton, Wednesday 14 Mar., 1900.

Your letter, changing your plans to work in a little visit to Asheville, has just reached me,—and meets with my delighted approval. I *know* you would have had a wretched heart-ache whenever you thought of Rose, if you had omitted this visit.

Never mind *our* change of plan. Stock. is abundantly able to stay alone at Atlantic City: if he is not, you may be sure I will stay with him, and have never a compunction about the Monday and Tuesday lectures, and on Wednesday (as my telegram suggests) I will meet you in Philadelphia and take you to him. We shall leave to-morrow at 2:15, and I shall have a good loaf with him, and no doubt be greatly refreshed.

I got a clean bill of health from the doctor[1] to-day in New York. I had treated myself so scientifically that he found practically nothing the matter with me. I hurried back on the 2:20 train so as to get my letter off in time to my darling. I brought Stock. a cheering message from the doctor. *I* had confidently predicted that this operation would radically mend Stock's general condition; but *my* view in the matter made painfully little impression upon him. Now I bring the same judgment exactly from the doctor,—and Stock's face shone upon the delivery of the message.

Hurrah! Stock's eyes look like a boy's again, anyhow,—and the rest of his face, too, so far as it is to be made out through the beard.

We are all well. I have not seen the children yet since I got back. They,—and sister A.,—are at dancing school.

I am just now seeking and getting advice from all quarters by correspondence about the chair of Politics and am elated to think that I am at last on the track of a man or two. One of the men I have drawn into the circle of advice is no less a person than the Governor of New York![2] Another is the President of Yale.[3] What a virtuous feeling it will give us to actually *add* a *man* to this emasculated Faculty!

God bless you, my Eileen, on your visit. Give my love to Mrs. Dubose; enjoy her as a *girl*, and believe me with *all* my heart

Your own   Woodrow

ALS (WP, DLC).
[1] J. Douglas Nisbet, M.D., 10 East 43rd St., New York.
[2] Theodore Roosevelt, whose letter to Wilson of March 13, 1900, is printed as an Enclosure with WW to EAW, March 15, 1900.
[3] Arthur Twining Hadley. His correspondence with Hadley is missing.

To Joseph Anderson[1]

My dear Sir,   Princeton, New Jersey, 14 March, 1900.

I am very much complimented by your kind letter of March twelfth,[2] and unaffectedly wish that I could accept the kind invitation which it conveys. But I am not a free man for the rest of this year. On the first of July next copy must begin to go in to one of the Magazines from my desk, and not stop until the first of July, 1901 (for an all-year serial for 1901), and if I am not to break my neck at the task, I must let nothing entice me away from my desk, and, at my desk, turn aside to the preparation of nothing but the aforesaid copy.

I am very sincerely obliged, and as sincerely sorry; but you see that it is a case of *must*.

With much regard,

Sincerely Yours,   Woodrow Wilson

WWTLS (in possession of John J. Meng).
[1] Pastor of the First Congregational Church of Waterbury, Conn.
[2] It is missing.

From Ellen Axson Wilson

My own darling,   Rome [Ga.], Mar. 15/1900 six P. M.

I have had another hurried day with no time so far for writing, but it is snowing so I hope I will be left in peace now. It rained all the morning and snowed all the afternoon, but I had engagements which I was obliged to keep in spite of it. Annie drove me over just after breakfast to see Anna Harris who was to remain at home especially to see me at that time. I got back just in time to dress and go out to dinner at Mrs. Goetchius;[1] from there to an afternoon tea at an old school-mate's, from which I have just returned. Yesterday Susie Bowie, Mrs. Terhune, gave me a beautiful luncheon, and every moment of the day & evening when I was not there I was either seeing visitors or calling on sick friends or elderly ones who could not see me. It is fortunate that I am not to stay here longer for I am getting rather tired. But Annie has a little pony of her own and drives me everywhere,— a *very* pleasant arrangement! They are *so* good to me! Indeed all the dear kinsfolk in Savannah, Atlanta, and here, have treated me like a little princess for whom nothing was quite good enough. They really make me feel ashamed,—so many special dainties to eat, and of course always my favourite luxury[,] the bed room fire!—made before I rise in the morning and kept up all day. Ed "shut up shop" so to speak and devoted himself to me in Atlanta. By the way, he is just finishing a *beautiful* $25,000 house on Peachtree St. I went all over it with much interest and pleasure.

I enclose a little note which came today from Rose. Ah, well! I know I shall be glad I went to her this time next week,—but *now*! If I had not once *planned* to see you on Saturday!—but it does hurt to change back; and how every allusion in your letters to seeing me this week makes my heart-ache! Certainly I have managed very badly to prepare an unnecessary disappointment for you; and I have been very heavy-hearted over it. And you were *so* sweet to send the telegram! I am sure no one was ever so kind and thoughtful as you!

My "business" here was only to collect a few odds and ends of my posessions and see about having them forwarded, and to see about the graves.[2] I don't want to *buy* anything, and even if I did, the sofa belongs to the girls and they mean to keep it.

But I must finish before tea, so that "the boarder" may mail it & I need not have Uncle Will expose himself later. Love and kisses to all. I love you darling in a way that *hurts*. The separation is almost more than I can bear these last few days. And yet your love is *just* the comfort you wished it to be. It and it alone has made my visit here a pleasure instead of a pain as I expected it would be.

Always and altogether   Your own   Eileen.

ALS (WC, NjP). Enc.: Rosalie Anderson Dubose to EAW, March 14, 1900, ALS (WP, DLC).
    [1] Antoinette Wingfield (Mrs. George Thomas) Goetchius, wife of the pastor of the Rome Presbyterian Church.
    [2] Of her parents in Myrtle Hill Cemetery.

To Ellen Axson Wilson, with Enclosure

My own darling,   Princeton, Thursday 15 March, 1900

I confidently expected to write to you to-day from Atlantic City; but we are having what, were the wind but a little stronger and the cold a little keener, would be fairly entitled to be called a blizzard. The snow is, I should guess, four inches deep,—but fine and soft, and likely to go the minute the sun gets at it. There *may* be a blockade to-morrow, but we confidently expect the sun and our own departure. Our trunks are both packed. For I am going to carry a trunk,—my little steamer trunk,—half empty,—so that your ladyship may when you reach Atlantic City, relieve the plethora of your own much suffering travelling companion by sending unnecessary extras home with me. Am I not a model of forethoughtfulness?

Bad as the day is, dear sister is out,—but not far away. She is lunching with Miss Ricketts, the other guests being but two, Mrs. Cleveland and Mrs. Morgan,[1]—a cosey, interesting party, I should say, whose pleasant confab I should dearly like to hear,—to *over*hear, did good manners permit. For the rest, there is absolutely nothing, I believe, to report; except that we are all very well (the children walked to school, the snowfall having then but just begun, and rode back in a hack), and that I am getting some interesting letters (actually containing practicable suggestions, some of them) in answer to my requests for nominations to the chair of Politics. I enclose a note from Mr. Roosevelt, because I think it will interest you as showing a side,—a very sane, *academic* side of him,—not known by everybody so much as to exist, but constituting his hope of real and lasting eminence. You need not return it.

It gives me such *deep* satisfaction, my sweet one, that you are to go to Asheville. I should myself have been so unhappy about it, if you had *not* gone,—knowing, as I do, what the disappointment would have meant to you. It is no matter that I have to spare you that much longer,—my love would be a poor thing if it could not make all sacrifices to accomplish the right and ideal thing for you. My love is of stout and lasting and weather-proof stuff. I am *for* all things and *in* all things

Your own   Woodrow

ALS (WC, NjP).
1 Josephine Perry (Mrs. Junius Spencer) Morgan.

ENCLOSURE

From Theodore Roosevelt

My dear Mr. Wilson: Albany.   March 13th, 1900.
    I need hardly say that that is peculiarly a position in which I take the greatest interest. I think I know exactly the *type* of man you want, but I am not at all sure that I know the *man*. Indeed at the moment I cannot think of one. He must be a scholar, a man of broad culture—emphatically an academic man in the sense of having received a thorough training and being in hearty sympathy with the men who know that, from the days of the Fed[e]ralists down and up, the theorist is the safe guide for the practical man; and yet he must also be thoroughly practical in the sense that he must understand that theories have to be proved in practice. Now to combine these traits with the capacity to teach would be a rather difficult problem. I shall try my best to think over some man and to let you know.

Faithfully yours,   Theodore Roosevelt

TLS (WP, DLC).

Two Letters from Ellen Axson Wilson

My own darling,   Rome [Ga.] Friday, 1 P.M. [March 16, 1900]
    I have finished my packing, been down town for ticket and money and also over to the cemetary and back, and now I will write a short note to you before dinner. I suppose I ought not to selfishly devote *too* much of this last day to writing you,—though I should like to do it! but Uncle Will seems to be letting his patients take care of themselves, while he "stays around" all day for my sake, so I ought to show my appreciation. The weather is freezing cold, but bright today,—a great improvement on yesterday. I have had no letter as yet today but hope for it on the next train. I especially want one more before I leave, so as to be sure you are *quite* well again. I was distressed to hear of your attack. Are you *sure*, darling, that you told me the whole truth about it, and that it is entirely over?

I havn't had time to speak of my 'business' at the cemetary. I found the lot and the graves dreadfully washed down; it should have been levelled and walled up on the sloping side years ago. When I was here before the plan was for the other half of the lot to be sold promptly & the proceeds used for that purpose, but it was not sold for some years, & now though sold (for $40.00) it has not yet been paid for. So I have arranged to have this very necessary work done at once. It will cost about $30.00.

Give dearest love and kisses to all. I love you, darling, so *desperately* that I hardly dare talk about it just now. I am in every heart-throb   Your own   Eileen

My own darling,
Hotel Imperial, Knoxville, Tenn.,
Friday. 10 P.M. [March 16, 1900].

Would you like a few lines from me from a *bran new* place? Here I sit most shocking lonely, (that is a forbidden subject however) but very cosy by a blazing soft coal fire, having just finished in dignified retirement my supper of tea and toast! This is an old-fashioned place in which the rooms are not heated,—only the hallways. They make you a bed room fire to order, a l'Anglaise;— an order which, as it is extremely cold, I very promptly gave, and find the result most cheering. I reached here at nine; formal supper over and nothing to eat in the house, was told that I could get something at a café in the neighbourhood, but took fright at the very idea and resigned myself, with a sinking stomach, to a Lenten fast. See how inconvenient it is to be a woman! I wonder if those who are more accustomed to the role of unprotected female would have gone to that café! However the porter came to my rescue by offering to fetch me some tea from the said café. So at the cost of 20 cts for the food—and something more for the porter—I have had quite a dainty supper and feel almost as if I were in a English Inn. I had a delightful journey this afternoon through a beautiful hill country,—I might almost call them mountains. It was a fine afternoon,—brilliant sunshine with breaking clouds, causing lovely effects of light and shade, and finally a *glorious* sunset.

But I find it hurts my eyes to write by a feeble light seven feet in the air, so I must stop. I will go to sleep and dream of you. My darling, you feel very, very near to me here, where all the other voices are still and my heart can commune with you alone. I am very busy too with memories of that other night I spent in this house, sixteen years ago last September just after I had given you my "promise true." How happy I was that night,—and how much more happy now! What a wonderful day it had been, coming down from Asheville through those glorious mountains with a heart full of "thoughts that did often lie too deep for tears." A sweet beginning to a more perfect happiness than I dared even *dream* possible! I am looking forward eagerly to tomorrow's journey; you will be with me in spirit all the way,—and I will try not to long *too* sorely to feel the dear hand actually in mine, to see with my very eyes the love-light shining in those beautiful eyes of yours.

Goodnight, and God bless you, my love, my own Woodrow. Always and altogether—   Your own   Eileen.

ALS (WC, NjP).

Two Letters to Ellen Axson Wilson

My own darling,   Princeton, Friday 16 March, 1900.

The weather has relented, and we go to-day. There is a perfect fairly [fairy] land about us this morning. The night coated the trees to the tips of every twig with ice; and now the sun makes each of them a mass of light. The papers represent the storm as having been general, in the South as well as in the North. I hope it has not banked *your* road with snow. The railways in *your* part of the country do not know how to handle the troublesome stuff. I wonder if you will telegraph me from Knoxville to-night.

I enclose your Southern R'wy schedule northward from Asheville. You will have three whole days with Rose. You leave Asheville, as you will see, at 1:37 Tuesday afternoon and reach Phila. the next morning at a quarter past ten. You know my plan is, to leave Stockton in Atlantic City while I come back and attend to my Monday and Tuesday duties here. I will go from *here* to meet you Wednesday morning. The 9:44 (as it now is) reaches Phila. 11:13, just about an hour after your train gets in. Unless I can manage, therefore, to get up and take the 8:23 (as I confidently expect to, at this writing) you may have to wait for me in the Phila. station that length of time. I write this simply that you may not be disturbed if you do not find me standing at the Exit gate when your train rolls in. I shall not write after to-morrow. A letter written on Sunday would have very little chance of reaching you before Tuesday noon. Will you not telegraph me just before you *start* on Tuesday, my love, so that I may *know* that you are off,—off on the train indicated on the enclosed schedule? There is a through sleeper Asheville-New York on that train. Ask Mr. Dubose to engage a lower berth on it for you as soon as this letter reaches you. It might be crowded. I am actually so inured to loneliness, my Eileen, that the *end* of our separation seems to me hardly real! At any rate, I hardly dare let my thoughts dwell on having you again where I can see and hear and touch you, and round out my days with a perfect satisfaction. No doubt your two weeks at Atlantic City will break the sweet shock of it all enough to keep it from killing me. I shall of course *visit* you there, madam, and so slowly appropriate you to myself again. Your taste of freedom will, perhaps, make you prefer to be taken possession of again gently and by degrees; and I will be as moderate and considerate as I can. For I am, my Duchesse, entirely and with every wish to serve you,

Your own   Woodrow

The Chalfonte   Atlantic City, N.J.

My own darling,   Saturday 17 March, 1900.

How it thrills my heart to think that my next words to you will be *spoken*! Wednesday is a long way off, and these last days of waiting are the hardest of all, but two of them at least are engrossing days, of lectures, letter-writing, chores of all kinds,—less time to muse, less time merely to endure,—and I shall do famously, thank you!

Stockton and I are very comfortably ensconced here, at one of the smaller, quieter hotels, but in the midst of all there is to be in the midst of. You will be very happy with the dear brother here, and I shall leave you with a clear conscience (I mean with *my* conscience clear). I go back home this afternoon at three, by way of Philadelphia, catching the five o'clock there. I don't think Stockton will be at all rattled at being left alone; but he is looking forward with the greatest eagerness to your coming,— as who would not who knew you never so slightly! You are the most delightful person to look forward to in the world, the most delightful to *be* with, the most delightful to *live* with. Be the association long or short, there's nobody in all the world half so enjoyable as my darling; but to be with her a *little* while is dangerous: it makes the long while without her so intolerable. And to be a long while *with* her makes the little while without her seem an age! Surely there never was a longer period than these seven weeks have been! And yet I have been happy. I have so deeply and thoroughly enjoyed your vacation—marred though it has been by the anxious news from home. Another time, better fortune, my love! And let us pray that *next* time at least we may take the vacation together. It will not seem long before we begin our preparations to go abroad. But meantime, *meantime*, my Eileen, you are coming to me! Happier, almost, than my own exulting sense of being about to have you in my arms again, and all day at my side, is the knowledge that *you* delight in the thought of coming to me. How fervently I thank God for that,—and what a zest of *achievement* it gives to my love of you. Ah, my pet, may God keep you and bless you and bring you safe and well and laughing to the arms of   Your own   Woodrow

Love from Stock. Warmest regards from us both to the Duboses

ALS (WC, NjP).

From Theodore Roosevelt

My dear Prof. Wilson: [Albany] March 17th, 1900.

I am perfectly ashamed to say that I have been unable to think of a single man to give you. If I was not in such a whirl with Ramapo,[1] taxation of franchises, forestry, fish & game commission appointees, and the machine and everything else, with the legislature in its death throes, I might be able to think of someone, but as it is I simply cannot. You see that for the last five years I have been in such very active political life that I have not had a chance of associating with scholars and students, save for the must [most] hurried glimpses, and I simply do not know who the new men are. I am awfully sorry.

                    Faithfully yours,   Theodore Roosevelt

TLS (Letterpress Books, T. Roosevelt Papers, DLC).
    [1] A bitter and protracted struggle over a contract between the Ramapo Water Company and New York City. The company was to furnish part of the city's water supply at a rate that reformers and businessmen thought was exorbitant. In 1901, Roosevelt won his fight to have the company's charter repealed and other provisions made to assure New York City of an adequate water supply. G. Wallace Chessman, *Governor Theodore Roosevelt: The Albany Apprenticeship, 1898-1900* (Cambridge, Mass., 1965), pp. 244-49.

From Louis Dyer

                              [Oxford] St. Patrick's Day
Dear Professor Wilson   [March 17] 1900
    I take advantage of the leisure I enjoy on this newly instituted national and international festival to commend to your perusal the enclosed circular from my undergraduate friends of the

American Club of Oxford.[1] They are an able trio and their corresponding circular addressed to the heads of all Oxford Colleges is a document in which Seward has shewn something like his great-uncle's diplomatic ability. People here are pleased with the young men's purposes and plans.

Yours sincerely   Louis Dyer.

ALS (WP, DLC).
[1] Harry Allen Overstreet, Samuel Swayze Seward, Jr., and Reginald Shippen Huidekoper to "Dear Sir," printed letter, March 1, 1900 (WP, DLC), announcing the formation of the American Club of Oxford. Dyer was an "Honorary Adviser."

From Ellen Axson Wilson

My own darling,   Asheville   Sunday [March 18, 1900]

Here I am prosperously arrived at the last stage of my journey, and, in spite of my eagerness to be gone, having a very happy time with my dear Rose and her lovely family. They are unusually sweet, handsome interesting children,[1] all of them, and you ought to see St. Pierre, the twenty-two months old baby; he is simply magnificent, with his great shining dark eyes and brown curls. He is immensely big and strong and rosy and full of life and fun. One would think he had never been ill in his life. She is fortunate in one respect at least; all the dreadful illness of last year has left no "after effects[.]"[2] They are all well and strong now; and it is really amazing to see how well she looks, and is, on the whole, in spite of all she has been through, and her present condition. She is as lovely as ever if not more so; always serene and sweet, and self-controlled, but almost always very grave; the smiles do not come quite easily. That is the chief change I see in her.

I reach Philadelphia, darling, at *10.15* on Wednesday morning, on an excellent through train which leaves here about 2 P. M. on Tuesday, and stops in Washington for breakfast about 7 A. M. Only three nights more before I see my love! The thought excites me so that I can hardly write! Ah, if you had only been with me on that journey yesterday through the snow-covered mountains. It was *wonderful!* an entirely new experience for me, and one that I shall always remember with delight. The snow was of the soft clinging sort; every twig was covered with it, every branch drooping with the weight of it;—and transfiguring it all the most *brilliant* sunshine! It was a fairy scene. I passed at *exactly* the right time. Three hours more of such a sun and the glory would have departed.

I am writing in haste (as usual) because we are just going to evening prayers at All Souls, the Vanderbilt church,[3] and we must start almost immediately on the street cars.

Dear love to all, and love beyond all words for my own Woodrow from   His little wife   Eileen.

ALS (WC, NjP).

[1] They were McNeely Dubose, Jr., Margaret Dubose, David Rainsford Fairbanks Dubose, and St. Pierre Dubose. The last child, Marion St. John Dubose, was born on June 24, 1900.

[2] That is, the illness of another Dubose child, Julia, who died on February 28, 1899, of meningitis.

[3] All Souls Episcopal Church, the church of Biltmore Village on the estate of George Washington Vanderbilt.

From Bliss Perry

                                        The Atlantic Monthly, Boston.
My dear Wilson,   March 19, 1900.

Here comes the bit of business of which I spoke on Sunday. Would three hundred dollars be a satisfactory compensation for your Reconstruction article? You know, of course how modest is the scale of Atlantic prices. That sum would be about twice our usual rate of payment for articles of the better class, but then we were about four times as glad to get it as we should have been over an ordinary article, and I realize that you are making a financial sacrifice to write for us at all. Please send me a line.

If you think the honorarium should be increased, I rely upon you to say so frankly, and I will in that case make my assault upon the powers that be.   Cordially,   Bliss Perry

TLS (WP, DLC).

To Henry Mills Alden

[Dear Mr. Alden,]   [Princeton, N.J.] March 20, 1900.

This clause will have to answer, and I hope it will be embodied in the Agreement. If I understand you aright, the illustrations will probably cost about ten thousand dollars; of this sum the Magazine will bear about half; the rest will be part of the book's "cost of production." Supposing, then, that the plates of the book, including composition, electrotyping, etc. cost an additional thousand (about this I can only guess) the "cost of production" in this case will be about six thousand. Half that would, of course, be three thousand; and that would be the minimum price at which

I could resume the rights; paying besides, a sum, at which I cannot even guess, for the copies of the book on hand. Of course whoever has the rights should assume the outstanding contracts. Lastly, under the concluding clause, I should have, very likely, under easily imaginable circumstances, to pay more still; which does not seem very cheerful.

But then I might, also, have to pay less; and I do not know anything about the business. The obvious conclusion is, that I had better depend, as I have no doubt I can in this case depend, upon the good temper and the sense of justice of the publishers; and the other clauses of the Agreement make it impossible that I should be handed over to any others. Pray have the whole thing drawn out in form and sent to me for my signature. I have no doubt I shall sign it.

I am sincerely obliged to you for all the trouble you have taken in the matter, and for your very full and satisfactory letter of the sixteenth [thirteenth]. I would have replied earlier had it been possible for me to do so.

With warm regard,

Faithfully yours,   [Woodrow Wilson]

TCL (WP, DLC).

From Theodore Roosevelt

My dear Mr. Wilson: Albany. March 20th, 1900.

I have yours of the 19th inst.[1]

I hardly know enough of Mr. Homer Folks[2] to answer you without qualification, but he seems to me to be an excellent man, and is certainly well worth carefully considering. He has through his work in the State Charities Aid Association and his experience in local politics gained the information that it seems to me advisable, where it is possible, for a man to have in such a position as that which you are seeking to fill. I wish he could have been elected to the legislature last fall, and he would have been, if there had not occurred one of those exasperating hitches due in part to the base misconduct of the machine politicians, and in part to the equally exasperating folly and vanity of the professional reformers—which combined make it so difficult for us to accomplish results, in New York City.[3] I do not know whether he has looked at national politics with the breadth of vision, and insight, that you would require. In municipal politics I think he is well qualified. If you say so I will make a point of seeing him to discuss some of our matters here, not making the slightest allusion to you or the professorship, and then I will let you know my judgement.   Sincerely yours,   Theodore Roosevelt

TLS (WP, DLC) with WWhw notation on env.: "Ans."
    [1] It is missing.
    [2] Associate Editor of *Charities Review*, Secretary of the State Charities Aid Association of New York, and an alderman of New York City, 1897-98.
    [3] The Republican and Citizens' Union parties of the 29th New York Assembly District nominated Homer Folks as a fusion, reform candidate for the state Assembly in June 1899. Folks lost the election in November to his Democratic opponent, Moses R. Ryttenberg, by about 150 votes out of some 7,000 cast. Folks failed to carry this normally Republican district primarily because the coalition of machine Republicans and reform Citizens' Unionists did not work well in practice. The reformers refused to endorse the Republican candidate for alderman, and many Republicans failed for various reasons to support Folks. See Walter I. Trattner, *Homer Folks: Pioneer in Social Welfare* (New York, 1968), pp. 73-74.

To Ellen Axson Wilson

My own darling,   Princeton, 24 Mar., 1900

I reached home last night at half past six, to find all well and just as I had left them on Wednesday,—to find myself pensive, but not sad,—full of a deep, deep gladness, rather; aglow in every part of me with the unspeakable happiness I have just been through! I find myself quick with the same feeling this morning; and I am sure it will last, like a delicious intoxication, till you come, and I can renew the draughts which caused it. I am perfectly well, but too recently out of your arms to find writing tolerable.

I enclose marked schedule *and ticket* from Philadelphia to Princeton. You can have your trunk checked through. The porter will see to it for you if you instruct him to do so. Send your trunk down early after breakfast.

All join me in unbounded love,—of which Stock. is to have a generous dividend. I am more deeply than ever,

Your own,[1]

AL (WC, NjP).
    [1] Here Wilson pasted one of his bookplates, reproduced in the photographic section of this volume.

From Ellen Axson Wilson

My own darling,   Atlantic City, Sunday [March 25, 1900]

I came up to my room yesterday afternoon intending after I had washed my hair to write to you. But when I had finished that I discovered that I had stupidly allowed Stockton to go off to see his "Adelphi girls" with my purse and trunk key in his pocket! So I had nothing to write withal, and was of course too unpresentable with my damp hair to go down and write at a desk. It was just as well perhaps; for after our happy time together one does feel, as you confess, more than usually impatient of pen and ink.

All goes well with us. Yesterday the weather was more perfect than ever—as balmy as Savannah. We sat for an hour with the [Harry Fielding] Reids on that same seat—you know,—and the air was deliciously, dreamily soft; what little wind there was being behind us, so that we were quite sheltered from it.

Stockton is *charmed* with Mrs. Reid! I wish they could have stayed longer, but they went yesterday. I was begging her yesterday to come over to our hotel and stay until I left, letting Mr. Reid go home without her, whereupon I discovered that Stockton had the night before (when they called,) been teasing her to do the same thing!

Who do you think is our latest acquaintance, sitting next me at table? Prof. Hiram Corson of Cornell![1] Isn't that luck? I only discovered this morning who he was, so of course at dinner I took advantage of such exceptional opportunities and began a conversation!

He is certainly a queer looking specimen but *very* interesting. You would be bored with him because he thinks Goldwin Smith a greater writer of English than Cardinal Newman even! Isn't that amazing? But I can forgive him even that for the sake of hearing him talk about Browning,—something that he is abundantly willing to do! I had heard that he told every new acquaintance within half an hour or so how well he knew Browning personally; so I took care not to mention the poet, waiting to see if it would happen. And sure enough it did! We heard all about it before we left the dinner table.

Your little note and the express package both came last night! Many thanks, darling. I shall be there Wednesday on the train you have marked. How my heart leaps up at the thought! I am positively so excited at the prospect that I can scarcely write. To have the long separation *entirely* over,—to be with my darling for keeps! It seems almost too good to be true. Ah me! *How* I love you!—tenderly, absorbingly, passionately,—"with the smiles, tears, breath, of all my life."

I look with sentimental interest at the door of No. 114 whenever I pass! It is a shame that they turned me out. It is *our* room! Yet a fat commonplace, stupid old couple are now presuming to

make themselves perfectly at home in it. Never mind! Soon we will have things all our own way, and will not be separated, even for a lecture tour, for months and months! With dear love to all, and for your *dear delightful* self just as much as you want from—
Your little wife,   Eileen.

ALS (WC, NjP).
    [1] Professor of English Literature at Cornell University.

To Ellen Axson Wilson

My own darling,   Princeton, Sunday 25 March, 1900

    Things are going quite as usual with us, and we are all well. It is wonderful (and pitiful, too) how placid and normal the surface of things can keep, when the *heart* of them is out! The *routine* of this dear household is exactly the same when you are away as when you are here: we do the same things and keep, apparently, the same spirit in them; but, ah me! how deep the real difference is,—how different the *colour* of life without you, its sweet, informing spirit! What I said yesterday I still abide by. The glow and delight of those two days of exquisite happiness,— which made last week a red letter week for me,—is on me yet, and will be till you are in my arms again, to stay. But, oh, the wrench of that parting,—the dreariness of coming "home" without you,— the pang of *leaving* home at Atlantic City! I wish I "carried an atmosphere," as you do! It might be a comfort. It might refract and colour all one's views; and he might manage to make life look, not like the cold fact, but like an emanation of one's own self,—full only of the things one loved. Your presence is so *individual*; mine is so naked and subject to be dominated by what surrounds it. It must be an inestimable protection to be thoroughly individual,—to influence instead of being influenced. I have often seen you, serenely and without effort or consciousness, keep your individuality when I was painfully aware that my own had gone hopelessly and ridiculously to pieces. I am defencelessly impressionable; you keep your poise and choose what to be impressed by. I record a mere breath, like a mirror; you receive only those impressions which your nature welcomes. The only complete compensation for my weakness I was denied: I ought to have been a poet, so that I might have been vocal with the sounds of all the world. As it is, I am condemned to use nothing but dumb prose.

    But I did not mean this to be a moan about myself: I meant it to be a little essay in praise of you. No doubt that is what brought me to the chagrin of not being a poet,—for you cannot be praised in an essay: you need a poem: the poem which my heart sings without words,—of which my pen knows only the refrain,   "I am her own   Woodrow."

Love from all to you both, and God bless and keep you.
I sent $30 by Express yesterday. Did you get it?

ALS (WC, NjP).

To Robert Underwood Johnson

My dear Mr. Johnson,   Princeton, New Jersey, 26 March, 1900.

Do you happen to know what Mr. Gilder did with my MSS.[1] which you were some time ago thinking about publishing? I am very anxious to get hold of it (for I am really in immediate need of part of it), and I know that he is abroad. It occurs to me as not unlikely that he brought it to the office and left it there. It was in three volumes, bound in cloth covers by clasps at the back. Will you not be kind enough to make some inquiries about it; and, in case its whereabouts is not known at your office, will you not send me Mr. Gilder's present address?
    In haste,
    With warm regard,
                    Sincerely Yours,   Woodrow Wilson

WWTLS (Berg Coll., NN).
    [1] Of his "Short History of the United States." See WW to R. W. Gilder, Nov. 21, 1899.

From Henry Mills Alden

My dear Mr Wilson,   New York City March 26. 1900

I ought to say in connection with your letter to me of March 20 that your interpretation of what is meant by "half the cost of composition, electrotyping & illustrations" is not the one intended in the agreement, i.e. there is no deduction for previous magazine use of the illustrations. There is no such deduction in the sale of the plates of a book by one publisher to another. The phrase is worded precisely as in the case of the sale of the plates of an abandoned book to the author, & it is assumed that a living book would not be estimated as of less value. But as in the event of your withdrawing the book the purchase of plates is made obligatory, & since the valuation on this basis might, in certain supposable circumstances, be too high, there is the possible reference of the matter to arbitrators, though a mutually satisfactory arrangement might be made (& probably would be) by the parties directly concerned without such reference.

The purchase of stock on hand, in like manner, might prove unduly burdensome if it could be supposed that the publishers overprint, having in view the obligation of the author to purchase, so as to purposely have on hand at the end of the specified ten years an unusual amount of stock. But, of course, after the author's notice of withdrawal, there would not be any addition to stock except to meet actual demand or to satisfy contracts already made—any attempt to unduly increase the amount of stock after such notice being readily apparent from the publishers' record of orders to print. To over-print before notice of withdrawal would be obviously at the publishers own risk.

But, in the case as between you & the Messrs Harper, no trick is supposable. Still here, as in every point connected with the possible transfer of ownership, there is open the reference to arbitrators.

It seems to me that the arbitration clause provides for the settlement of any point upon which there may be a difference of opinion not adjustible by arrangement between the parties directly concerned.   Yours sincerely   H. M. Alden

ALS (WP, DLC).

From Ellen Axson Wilson

My own darling,   Atlantic City, Monday [March 26, 1900]

We have been shut in this morning by a drizzling rain into which Stockton of course was afraid to venture. We have just finished dinner and I have come up to write to you while Stockton smokes; then since the clouds are breaking and the blue increasing overhead, we may have our walk yet.

Stockton has gone off to smoke with Prof. Corson. We three are getting extremely chummy. He apparently considers us quite a Godsend for he says he has been wretchedly lonely. He is not at all well; is being massaged &c.—and says he will *never* leave home again without Mrs. Corson. He has offered to read us his lecture on "The Ring and the Book"; isn't that delightful? You know he is a wonderful reader, and the lecture consists largely of quotations. I have the most vivid and delightful recollections of hearing him give his two lectures on Tennyson, with readings, when I was thirteen, in Sav.; few things in my childhood gave me more pleasure. He was very fond of Tennyson then, but now he (T.) has been completely crowded out by the "expulsive power of a new affection." He even makes spiteful remarks about him. You know, by the way, that he is singularly like Tennyson in personal appearance and used to be thought very proud of that fact.

I have just finished a delightful book by Principal Shairp on "Culture and Religion"[1] which I found in the library here. I am feeling quite stirred by it and can scarcely get my mind off of it. What a very extraordinary collection of books there is here for a hotel library!

Tell dear little Margaret that her sweet letter came this morning and I was *delighted* to get it. Am very glad to hear of such fine progress in Latin, &c.

I have had nothing from you as yet, but perhaps it will come tonight. Only two more nights away from my love! We are making progress indeed! Once upon a time, long, long ago, it was two *months*. Time does move after all though it doesn't "gallop withal." Only my pulse does that at the thought of where I will be two days from now. And so good-bye my darling, until then, and may God bless you! With love unspeakable

Your little wife,   Eileen.

ALS (WC, NjP).
[1] John Campbell Shairp, *Culture and Religion in Some of Their Relations* (Edinburgh, 1870; many later edns.).

To Ellen Axson Wilson

My own darling,   Princeton, Monday 26 March, 1900

I take leave to observe that you are not *quite* as generous to me in the matter of letters as I am to you. This is the third I've written to Atlantic City, and as yet (1 P.M.) I've received not a line. Ah, well! it can't last long, this dismal *living on letters* as a thing more necessary than food to keep even *life* in the blood! I ought not to *need* further evidence of your love; but it would be absurd, after all, to say that I ought not to need further food. The thing is inscrutable,—and inevitable! Everybody is asking about you, and about the time of your home coming, in the most affectionate manner. Dear old Mrs. Brown seems genuinely eager to see you,—speaks of it with a light on her whole face,—and our Sunday afternoon circle was all alive with interest about you. Come back and relieve us of the tension,—unless Stockton really needs you after Wednesday. I am forlorn, of course; but I am well, and so are the rest of us,—except for dear sister Annies incessant, distressing headaches. Love to Stock,—and for you, my Eileen, besides love from all the rest, the unbounded, eager, *painful* love of   Your own   Woodrow

ALS (WC, NjP).

Francis Landey Patton to John James McCook

My dear Colonel McCook: [Princeton, N.J.] March 30, 1900.

I received your letter of March 29th, and also its enclosures in reference to the new chair of politics at Princeton. I hope indeed that we are on the track of the right man for this place.

In reference to what you say in your closing paragraph, let me make simply this explanation. Whenever a vacancy occurs in a chair in Princeton or whenever a new chair is created, it is my habit to consult the professor or professors in the department in which the vacancy occurs, or in the department contiguous to the vacancy, respecting the choice of a suitable man to fill the position. I am as careful always to consult the professors in the department where the vacancy occurs as I am not to consult any outside of that department. In the present case, I felt that Professor Wilson would naturally be the most competent man in our faculty to judge respecting qualifications of the incumbent of the new chair, and would be most likely to know who the men are that are active in the department of Political Science. I therefore asked him to make the inquiries which have led to the letter a copy of which you sent me. There was the greater reason for my doing so in the present case, in view of the fact that the donors of the new chair I have reason to believe are in close relation of confidence and friendship with Professor Wilson. And I am particularly anxious that in the establishment of this chair of Politics, Professor Wilson should be able to find an associate with whom he could work comfortably and who would be a marked accession to our productive and teaching force. I know that you will entirely concur with me in this matter, both as to the wisdom and expediency of my course.

I am anxious to see you, and shall arrange shortly for a conference on some important matters.

Very faithfully yours,   Francis L. Patton

TLS (Patton Letterpress Books, University Archives, NjP).

From Henry Mills Alden

My dear Mr. Wilson   New York City   April 3. 1900

I am confident that you will not regret the completion of the contract (which will be duly signed & forwarded) on its present basis. The premises of the section concerning repurchase by the author are in accord with arrangements between publishers with reference to such transfer of property. When the case actually occurs various circumstances will affect the precise details of an amicable arrangement. The most important of these circumstances relate to the motions for & the method of withdrawal, as indicated in the next to the last of my letters to you.

If the Messrs. Harper had all but one of your books & wished to make their edition complete they would be glad to purchase that other at its full value; they would, if the case were reversed, expect to receive no more, & no less. In case of disagreement as to valuation arbitration furnishes a ready means for fair determination.

I trust your book will remain with us during the whole term of its natural life, & that you will also find it profitable to arrange with us for the publication of all your important historical work. We shall offer you every legitimate temptation to secure this.

For the present it is a very great satisfaction to me editorially to be able to count upon you for the important contribution you are about to make, & to this is added the gratification of my personal acquaintance with you.

Mr. Yohn[1]—whom we spoke of for the illustration of your history—is now abroad &, I regret to say, expects to remain abroad during the present year.

Yours cordially   H. M. Alden

ALS (WP, DLC).

[1] Frederick Coffay Yohn, painter and illustrator of New York. He was abroad to prepare illustrations for Theodore Roosevelt's "Oliver Cromwell," being serialized at this time in *Scribner's Magazine*.

To Frederick Jackson Turner

My dear Turner,   Princeton, New Jersey, 4 April, 1900.

Your letter has been a part of my thoughts ever since it came. Your sorrow was so much deeper than I had heard,—*both* your dear little ones gone, and Mrs. Turner's health temporarily broken,—and the whole tone and matter of the letter brought you so vividly before my eyes, that I felt stirred, as if I had talked with you face to face and had *seen* you in your work and trouble.

I assure you, my dear fellow, that my feeling for you is not of the ordinary kind: separation does not seem in the least to lessen or weaken the sense of comradeship and the genuine affection you have excited in me since I first learned to know you. It is, as you know, one of the abiding disappointments of my life that we cannot be colleagues; and, now that you are in trouble, I feel more keenly than ever the pain of not being able to take you every day by the hand and help you with sympathy at least, if with nothing more. There are not many men to whom I am led to say such things, for all I am an outspoken southerner; but with you it seems inevitable.

I need not say how much obliged I was for the suggestions you made with regard to my quest for a Professor of Politics. For any other chair I should think Morse Stephens the very man; but there is one consideration in this case that would be absent in other cases. He is an Englishman, and in this absurdly sensitive country of ours I feel confident it would create a bad impression to set an Englishman up in one of our universities to teach us Politics,—especially the colonial politics concerning which we must, whether we will or not, take our lesson from England in any case. The mere fact that the chair is called a chair of Politics makes the selection a matter of delicacy.

I have a tolerably long and important list now to choose from. It ought, I think, to be easy to make a satisfactory selection. I wish I had time to go over the list with you, and discuss pros. and cons. with regard to the several names on it.

I wish I could give you a definite opinion about the future of graduate work at the University of Chicago; but I do not feel that I have ever really seen inside the place. My impression (most superficicially formed, and from a distance) has been that it lacked academic steadiness, certainty of aim, dignity, the patience that does not pant for "results": that it was infected with the hurry, and I should suspect superficiality, of the "intensive" methods indicated by their six weeks' concentration on groups of electives, etc. But I am very old fashioned and conservative; and all "hustling" seems to me the very negation of progress in thoughtful study. I should, for myself, be afraid of the lack of reserve and the feverish progressiveness which I suppose to characterize the place. I know so little about it, however, that I would not say this to any one who did not know me. I should think Chicago a splendid place to work in a hundred years from now, when Dr. Harper was dead and the place had cooled off, and fads had been exploded.

Let me hear, wont you, how Mrs. Turner comes on in her search for strength? Give her my most affectionate regards and assurances of sympathy (in all of which Mrs. Wilson most heartily joins), and believe me, my dear Turner,

Faithfully and affectionately Yours,   Woodrow Wilson

WWTLS (F. J. Turner Papers, CSmH).

To Henry Mills Alden

My dear Mr. Alden,   Princeton, New Jersey, 4 April, 1900.

Thank you for your letter of yesterday. While I could have wished that particular clause a little more liberal, I have promptly signed the contract, and return it this morning.[1] I have no doubt at all that I shall be fairly treated in any case; and certainly your own part in the matter has been most gratifying to me.

I am deeply disappointed to hear that Mr. Yohn is not available. I suppose there is no chance of getting a picture or two from him at long range?[2] I do not know any illustrator whose dramatic quality seems to me so great as his, or so true.

With warm regard,

Faithfully Yours,   Woodrow Wilson

WWTLS (Berg Coll., NN).
    [1] There is no copy of the contract in the Wilson Papers.
    [2] Yohn in fact became available and supplied some of the illustrations for the series, "Colonies and Nation."

From Franklin Henry Giddings

Dear Professor Wilson: [New York] April 4, 1900

I have given careful consideration to the question which you put to me, and have tried to look at it exactly as I would do if I had to make the decision. Every name that seemed to have possibilities in front of it I have made the subject of an inquiry, covering history, work published, age, temperament and various other things. The list finally sifted down to these:

Jenks, Cornell
Willoughby, J. H. U.
Rowe, Penn
Loos, Iowa
Ford, Pittsburg.[1]

Each of these men is strong in one or another way. Jenks I put easily ahead of all others; but I do not know that his engagements and prospects are such that he could or would change. If he is not a possibility I should look most carefully into the qualifications of Henry Jones Ford. He is in newspaper and not in academic life but his writings[2] show a clearer grasp and a sounder knowledge of American politics than do those of anyone who has recently addressed the public. Third in order I should rank Loos.

I wish I could be of more real help to you than I can be in this very general expression of preference.

Sincerely yours,   Franklin H. Giddings.

ALS (WP, DLC).

[1] Jenks and Ford have already been identified in this volume. The others mentioned were Westel Woodbury Willoughby, Associate Professor of Political Science, The Johns Hopkins University; Leo Stanton Rowe, Assistant Professor of Political Science, University of Pennsylvania; and Isaac Althaus Loos, Professor of Political Science, State University of Iowa.

[2] At this time, Ford had published one book—*The Rise and Growth of American Politics: A Sketch of Constitutional Development* (New York, 1898)—articles in scholarly journals, and numerous articles in popular magazines and newspapers.

A Report of a Lecture

[April 20, 1900]

MONDAY NIGHT CLUB.

Professor Woodrow Wilson addressed the meeting of the Monday Night Club[1] last evening, at 2 North Dod, on "Fashion in Literature."[2] He said that the general tendency in modern literature is to centre everything about two or three characters, and thus narrow the sphere of a book; that modern authors seem to lack the ability to put themselves into all their characters with the same ease and naturalness, a quality which is essential to lasting literature. The fashion of literature he declared to be determined by no abiding qualities, but rather influenced by the changes of the times. He then discussed both the historical and the problem novel in the light of his subject and criticised some of the modern novels as being too narrow in their portrayal of character and in their application to life. He mentioned the fact that the true form of the essay, which is characterized by an impartial view of the subject, is coming into vogue again.

Printed in the *Daily Princetonian*, April 20, 1900.

[1] Established by members of the Class of 1894, this was an organization composed of seniors, which met periodically during the academic year for lectures on and discussions of philosophical, scientific, and literary subjects.

[2] For this lecture, he used the notes printed at Oct. 27, 1897, Vol. 10.

From Albion Woodbury Small[1]

My Dear Prof. Wilson: [Chicago] Apr. 20th 1900

With the understanding that I am writing entirely on my personal responsibility, without the knowledge of any of my colleagues, and with a pledge to keep entirely to myself anything that you may say, may I ask you to write what you are willing to say about the following?

Would an invitation to assume the headship of our department of History be sufficiently attractive to you to make it a matter of serious consideration?

We want this department to take a leading place in the University and in the country. It is already strong for undergraduate work, but it needs a head who has outlook and force and generalship. The present members of the department would rally around him. The cognate departments would hail his advent as reinforcement for themselves, quite as much as for his own immediate division of the work. The University as a whole would breathe more freely if the present serious gap were filled.

Pres't Harper will be in Europe until early in June. Some of us are quietly looking over possibilities so that he will have as detailed accounts of the situation as possible when he returns.

Whatever be your answer, I will use it entirely in accordance with your wishes. In case you should indicate in any way that you would consider yourself among the possibilities, I can use the fact without in any way committing you. On the contrary if you should tell me that my suggestion is out of the question, I should be able to guide the attention of our men in the direction of other possibilities.

It is needless for me to say that it would be a delight to me personally if you could join us. The opportunity for influence upon the future of the Central West, and so of the country as a whole, needs only to be observed on the spot to be recognized. It is not Chicago bluster, but it is the calm calculation of our cool heads, that in some respects we have the most important distributing centre for influence in the whole field of the social sciences, that this country offers. I should be glad to go into particulars if you say the word.[2]

Sincerely   Albion W. Small.

ALS (WP, DLC).

[1] Professor and Head of the Department of Sociology of the University of Chicago.

[2] Wilson's reply is missing, but in it he undoubtedly discouraged Small.

From the Minutes of the Committee
on the Graduate Department

Apl. 25, 1900

Examination of Robert McNutt McElroy, Princeton 1896, for the degree of Ph.D.

In the absence of the President, Prof. Magie presided.

The thesis entitled, History of the Commonwealth of Kentucky, had been read & accepted by Profs. Woodrow Wilson & Paul van Dyke.

Prof van Dyke examined in Gen'l History	2:15
	3:00
Prof. Wilson examined in American History	3:00
	3:30
Prof. Daniels examined in Political Economy	3:30
	3:45
Prof. Hibben examined in Logic	3:45
	4:10

The examinations were declared satisfactory and it was resolved to recommend Mr. McElroy for the degree of doctor of philosophy, *cum laude.*[1]

Adj.   W. F. Magie

"Minutes of the Committee on the Graduate Department [1895-1901]," bound minute book (UA, NjP).

[1] Insofar as is known, McElroy was Wilson's only doctoral student at Princeton, and this was the only doctoral examination in which he participated. The "Minutes of the Committee on the Graduate Department," p. 29, disclose that Wilson read Max Farrand's dissertation in 1896; however, he was not among the examiners when Farrand took his final examination on May 30, 1896. *Ibid.*, p. 25.

From Miles J. Renick[1]

My dear Mr. Wilson,   Washington, D.C. April 25, 1900.

I received with regret your telegram informing me that it would be impossible for you to be present at Mr. Renick's funeral. We were so anxious to have you serve as one of his pall-bearers knowing how great the affection was he bore you. I have been very anxious to let you know the circumstances of his death but I have had to attend to so many matters of business, in addition to caring as best I could for my poor mother, that I have not had time in which to write.

About the middle of February Mr. Renick sailed for France in company with my mother[2] and the Count & Countess Castellane,[3]

having been sent by the Coudérts,[4] who were acting for the Goulds, to Paris to take charge of Castellane's affairs and disburse the income of his wife and himself and reach a settlement with their creditors.[5] Prior to sailing Mr. Renick had been working quite hard in fact all the past winter and once arrived in Paris he did not spare himself and in addition to worry and hard work his ignorance of the language proved a constant source of annoyance to him. The weather too was terrible—only two days of sunshine in the first month of their stay. After having been in Paris nearly a month he was compelled to go to bed with what they at first supposed was cold and fever. At the end of a week the Doctors pronounced his malady typhoid and stated that they had no doubt he would pull through nicely, though they frankly admitted that he was in a very "run down" condition and expressed concern at this feature of the case. Two skilled nurses were secured and a man-servant engaged to lift him in and out of the cold baths and my mother says that every-thing possible was done for him, and in all, four physicians attended him—three being called in consultation. But each day he grew weaker and finally after an illness of eleven days he passed away, his death occurring the afternoon of Sunday April the first, at the Hotel Continental, where they had been stopping. I know you will be glad to learn that apparently he did not suffer at all and he died calmly, peacefully and without pain. You can imagine, my dear Mr. Wilson, what a terrible visitation this was to my poor mother, alone in a strange land—far from us all. Friends were raised up for her though, and some how I found her alive and seemingly calm when I went on board the "New York" at quarantine the night of the 14th of April. Think of what that journey home, without him, was to her. Mr. Renick's remains came home also by the same ship and on Tuesday the 17th we took leave of him forever and laid him to rest, in the evening, at Oak Hill Cemetery (here in Washington), a most beautiful place. It seems so bitter a thing, when we recall how full and happy his life was, how he gloried in his chosen work, and how fair was the promise of the future for him, that he should be taken away. For he was a man loving life and enjoying it to the full. However he is gone and we are left to bear it as we may.

I wish to quote the closing passage of his will, a noble one and one whose every word brings him clearly before us:

"In testimony of the sincere friendship I bear Woodrow Wilson, of Princeton, New Jersey, my former law partner, James

Keith Marshall Norton of Alexandria, Virginia, my classmate at the University of Virginia, Mr. Crammond Kennedy, of Washington D.C., of late years my office mate and benefactor, Paul Fuller and Frederick R. Coudert Jr., of New York, who kindly gave me profitable and congenial employment almost on the day when I was asked to resign the office of Chief Clerk of the Department of State after thirteen years of faithful service in the Departments, in posts gained without political influence, and as a result (except the last one) of examinations—to each of these, my good friends, I direct that my executor shall give books or other mementos."

With kindest regards from my mother and myself, I beg to remain, as always,

Yours very sincerely,   Miles J. Renick

ALS (WP, DLC).

[1] Foster son (his father was James S. Turpin) of Edward Ireland Renick, Wilson's law partner in Atlanta. At this time he was a clerk in the Office of the Commissioner of Internal Revenue.

[2] Isabel Evans Turpin Renick.

[3] Marie Ernest Paul Boniface de Castellane, scion of an ancient French family, and his wife, the former Anna Gould, daughter of the railroad magnate, Jay Gould.

[4] Coudert Brothers, the New York law firm.

[5] The New York newspapers of January 18-20, 1900, ran reports taken from Paris newspapers that the Comte de Castellane had lost heavily in stock speculations and gambling and even hinting that he was fleeing to the United States to escape his creditors. The Count vehemently denied the allegations upon his arrival in New York on January 22; however, the remarks in Renick's letter suggest at least that his finances were in serious disarray. The "Goulds" mentioned above were George Jay, Edwin, and Frank Gould, brothers of the Countess. The *New York Times*, February 16, 1900, reported that Count and Countess de Castellane had sailed for France on February 15 but did not mention the Renicks.

A News Item

[April 28, 1900]

Among the long list of those who have accepted Chancellor MacCracken's invitation to serve as judges for filling the very remarkable Hall of Fame at New York University[1] are Woodrow Wilson '79, and William M. Sloane, now of Columbia. It is a goodly list of Americans and the names have a familiar sound,[2] but their's must be an embarrassing job. The easiest way out of it will be simply to elect themselves unanimously.[3]

Printed in the *Princeton Alumni Weekly*, 1 (April 28, 1900), 48.

[1] Henry Mitchell MacCracken, Chancellor of New York University, in 1899 had originated the idea of a Hall of Fame as a memorial to outstanding Americans. In March 1900, Helen Gould (Mrs. Finley Johnson) Shepard donated the money for a structure to be called "The Hall of Fame for Great Americans," to be erected on the University Heights campus of New York University.

[2] The first College of Electors, chosen by the New York University Senate, consisted of 100 prominent Americans in the fields of education, science, journalism, humanistic studies, literature, and the law. To name them all would be to name the intellectual leadership of the United States in 1900.

[3] The first College of Electors in 1900 chose twenty-nine persons for the Hall of Fame. Wilson served just one term as an elector and participated only in the first election.

From William B. Pritchard[1]

My Dear Prof. Wilson: New York, April 30th 1900

Meyrowitz informs me that he has forwarded battery as directed. I write therefore to give instructions as to method of use: One electrode (you can easily tell by shape which one) should be placed back of the neck covered of course with a folded towel wet in hot water[.] The other electrode should [be] placed over the affected side of face moulded somewhat to fit contour of face. Both electrodes should be kept in steady contact without any interruptions. The current should be gradually turned on through rheostat up to 5 miliamperes. The seance should last about twenty minutes daily.

I should be glad to hear from you from time to time as to progress.   Sincerely,   W. B. Pritchard

ALS (WP, DLC).
[1] A physician of 105 West 73rd St., New York.

Notes for an After-Dinner Speech

Princeton Inn   3 May, 1900.
Dinner to Bliss Perry:

A delicate task; but I trust, my dear Perry, that you will not be overwhelmed by a eulogy spoken here to your face.

We have had close comradeship here,—and there can be no embarrassment in listening to praise from a comrade's lips.

You owe us compensation. You are about to go away taking more than you brought. You brought your fine equipment of mind, your fine qualities of nature: you take these away enhanced and perfected by use,—and our hearts besides.

We have not often enough told you how deeply we have esteemed and valued you.

We have loved you

(1) For what you did for the University, to which our first allegiance is due, by your teaching,—and reputation.

(2) For what you did [for] us, by your spirit and example.

(3) For the illustration of high academic and literary ideals
in your public lectures and addresses.

(4) For working like an artist and genuine man of letters.

We say our formal, collective good-bye tonight; but you cannot
really break with us. Our friendship goes with you, and you
leave with us all the wholesome comfort of what you have
done and been amongst us.[1]

WWhw MS. (WP, DLC).
[1] There is no account of this dinner in the Princeton newspapers. A printed
menu of the dinner in the Wilson Papers bears the date of May 5, 1900.

From Max Boucard

Monsieur: Paris   4 Mai 1900

Vous avez bien voulu me donner l'autorisation de traduire
votre ouvrage "Congressional Government."[1]

Je viens vous annoncer qu'il est actuellement à peu près com-
pletement imprimé!

Mais avant de le livrer au public, je viens vous demander si
vous n'avez pas quelques *retouches* à y apporter, et si vous ne
seriez pas assez aimable pour nous écrire un mot de *préface* pour
les lecteurs français.[2]

En vous remerciant encore, Monsieur, je vous prie d'agréer
mes meilleurs sentiments.   Boucard

ALS (WP, DLC).
[1] See M. Boucard to WW, Jan. 25, 1899, printed as an Enclosure with Houghton, Mifflin and Co. to WW, May 26, 1899, and M. Boucard to WW, June 8,
1899.
[2] About Wilson's preface to the French edition, see M. Boucard to WW, July
28, 1900, n. 1.

From George Washington Miles

My dear Doctor: Radford, Va., May 7, 1900.

Is there any change in the situation with you at Princeton so
that you could consider the proposition I made you two years
ago?[1] It can be readily revived.[2] We need somebody as chairman
of the University faculty who will make it a national University
in the best sense of the word and will serve its great good will and
assist in attracting a more extensive endowment.

I have never known the University of Virginia in such fine
attitude to the country at large and to the State of Virginia. The
last legislature gave it an annuity of $50,000, with an additional
appropriation of $10,000 for its own electric light plant. We
should like to give you the position as outlined in our former cor-

respondence. We have nearly 700 students this year, but things are not going quite yet according to our notion.

With cordial regards, I am

Very truly yours,   Geo. W. Miles.

TLS (WP, DLC).

¹ That is, when they exchanged a number of letters concerning Wilson's acceptance of the Chairmanship of the Faculty and a professorship in the Law School of the University of Virginia. In fact, Miles had brought the matter up a second time in G. W. Miles to WW, March 4, 1899.

² We may be sure that Wilson did not permit it to be revived.

To Harper and Brothers

Princeton, New Jersey,

Messrs. Harper and Brothers,   9 May, 1900.

I am sorry to have mistaken the purpose of the receipt which I returned to you. I ought to have noticed that it was meant to cov[er] sales only up to December 4. If you will have it sent to me again (it was not returned with your letter), I will sign and forward it at once.

Allow me to thank you for your kindness in sending me half a dozen copies of the popular edition of my "George Washington." I am very much pleased with it indeed.

Some passages of the book need correction; and I hope that before you go to press with it again, you will let me send you the corrections. They can be made, I believe, in the plates as they stand.   Very sincerely Yours,   Woodrow Wilson

WWTLS (Berg Coll., NN).

To Robert Bridges

My dear Bobby,   Princeton, New Jersey, 16 May, 1900.

I am delighted that you are to have a run abroad, and hope with all my heart that you will have just as much satisfaction and pleasure as can be packed into the time. I wish I could get a little glimpse of you before you go just to shake hands and say good-bye. It gives me an uneasy feeling to have the sea between me and those I tie to.

Yes, the "London"¹ is here. I send it by the same mail that carries this. I am ashamed to have kept it when I was not using it.

Mrs. Wilson joins me in warmest wishes for your pleasure and safe return, and I am, as ever,

Your affectionate friend,   Woodrow Wilson

WWTLS (WC, NjP).

¹ Undoubtedly a guide book.

An Announcement

[May 26, 1900]

UNIVERSITY BULLETIN.

Sunday, May 27.

. . . 5 p.m. Vesper Services in Marquand Chapel, conducted by Professor Woodrow Wilson.[1]

Printed in the *Daily Princetonian,* May 26, 1900.
  [1] The local press carried no report of this service, but for his talk Wilson used the notes printed at April 4, 1895, Vol. 9.

From John Franklin Genung[1]

My dear Sir: Amherst, Massachusetts, May 28, 1900

Will you pardon me for addressing a question to you in the interests of some work of my own, but through that also, as I trust, in the interests of literary study? It is this: in rewriting my text book of Rhetoric[2] I have come upon the chapter relating to the theme and flow of a composition, and have been studying your charming essay "The Truth of the Matter," in "Mere Literature," with a view to condensing its subject-matter into a single proposition. I was led to do so by reading it as a kind of supplement to Macaulay's Essay on History, which I had treated in the same way. Now I write to you to know if the following proposition would represent you, I won't say fully, but fairly as far as it goes:

The art of writing history, which ought to display facts as they are, cannot do so except through that realizing imagination which so colors and vivifies facts that they appear to us as they did to the actors in them.

My writing to you involves two questions which I hope will not appear to you too audacious. First, may I make such use of your essay? and secondly, if so, may I have your opinion of the above-given attempt at evolving a theme, and still better, if your time permits, such revision and correction of it as will make it fairly represent your essay?

I don't know whether my name will mean anything to you or not. I have seen you and heard you once at the Authors Club in New York;[3] and Professor Winchester, with whom I think you have studied, is an acquaintance of mine. And all that I have seen of you, and what I have read of your writings, make me wish to become better acquainted.

Yours very truly   John F. Genung

ALS (WP, DLC).
¹ Professor of Rhetoric at Amherst College.
² Genung's *The Practical Elements of Rhetoric* (Boston, 1866) went through several expansions and editions before appearing in its final form as *The Working Principles of Rhetoric Examined in Their Literary Relations* (Boston, 1901).
³ See Wilson's diary for 1897, entry dated Jan. 1, 1897, Vol. 10.

To John Franklin Genung

My dear Sir,   Princeton, New Jersey, 30 May, 1900.

Your letter of May twenty-eighth has gratified me very much. I am by no means entitled to call myself a professional critic; I am only a writer on history and politics who turns his hand sometimes to criticism by way of pleasing himself, and, incidentally, clarifying his ideas about the art of writing which he practices. I am the more complimented, therefore, that you, a professional critic, should wish to summarize a bit of my critical work, and I shall be most complacently pleased to have you do so.

I venture to suggest the following, as perhaps a little more comprehensive of the whole meaning of my essay than the sentence you ask my opinion upon:

History is not a record of all the facts: that were impossible. It is a record of some of the facts, selected for their significance, and set forth in such order and combination, with such a touch of realizing imagination, with such colour and life as shall cause them, if possible, to make the same impression upon us that they must have made on those who were actors in the midst of them.[1]

I am sincerely glad to have made your acquaintance, if only by letter, having known of your work and its high character a long while. I shall hope for a face to face meeting in the near future.

With much regard,

Sincerely Yours,   Woodrow Wilson

ALS (de Coppet Coll., NjP).
¹ There are WWsh and WWhw drafts of this paragraph in WP, DLC. Genung quoted this paragraph on pp. 423-24 of the book just cited.

To the Editor of the *Princeton Alumni Weekly*

Dear Sir: [Princeton, N.J.] June 4, 1900.

The football game with Yale this fall will be played in Princeton and our association must provide seats for the spectators.

It is folly to sink five or six thousand dollars in temporary stands as has been done twice in the past—for the Harvard game in '95 and the Yale game in '98—but no other course seems possible unless the Alumni will contribute the money with which to erect permanent ones. In fact it is doubtful whether the income of the Football Association this fall will be sufficient, when bills for running expenses and such fixed charges as the salary of General Athletic Treasurer, the rental of grounds, and interest have been met, to pay the cost of temporary stands. The season of '98, in which the conditions were similar, closed with a deficit of about four thousand dollars.

So far as we have been able to inform ourselves, the cost of permanent stands will not be less than fifteen thousand dollars ($15,000), but we are confident that this sum can be raised, if the alumni are made to realize the seriousness of the situation.

Princeton is the only one of the larger universities which does not already possess permanent stands, and the lack of them contributes very much to the difficulties of our position. With them we should be quite independent financially, but without them we are sometimes compelled to consent to arrangements which please neither the captain of the team nor ourselves—and even then cannot always make ends meet.

This embarrassing situation is due to a definite cause, the inauguration of the policy of "college games on college grounds"—a policy which, of course, has our most cordial support. We wish to say very explicitly that it is *not* due to extravagance in the management of our athletics. A year ago, at the request of the Graduate Advisory Committee[1] and the Athletic Association itself, we undertook the supervision of the athletic budget, and we speak with full knowledge of the facts, when we express the conviction that the athletics of no other university are managed with greater economy than our own.

A generous alumnus has already subscribed a thousand dollars "to start the ball rolling." It would be difficult to find a Princeton man who is not proud of our athletics. We believe that there are many who will be ready to respond to this call for the money needed to place them on a sound financial footing.[2]

Very truly yours,   H. B. Fine '80,
W. B. Scott '77,
Woodrow Wilson '79,
Faculty Committee on Outdoor Sports.

Printed in the *Princeton Alumni Weekly*, I (June 9, 1900), 161-62.
[1] About this body, see J. L. Williams to WW, Sept. 25, 1891, Vol. 7.

2 The *Princeton Alumni Weekly*, I (Oct. 20, 1900), 229, reported that permanent stands to seat 12,000 people and costing $12,000 were under construction. These stands were completed about November 1, but they did not prove to be very permanent. The *Princeton Alumni Weekly*, XIV (April 1, 1914), 515, commented that "in recent years, the Athletic Association, because of lack of permanent and adequate seating capacity for the big football games, has been at an expense of about $10,000 each autumn to erect and remove the temporary stands at University Field." The same issue of the *Princeton Alumni Weekly* hailed the gift of a stadium by Edgar Palmer '03 as a memorial to his father, Stephen Squires Palmer, a member of the Princeton Board of Trustees, 1908-13. Formally presented to the University on November 13, 1914, Palmer Memorial Stadium, with a capacity of 41,000 persons (later enlarged to its present capacity of 46,000), proved to be the permanent solution to the seating problem at Princeton football games.

From John Grier Hibben

My dear Woodrow,   [At sea] S. S. Anchoria, June 5/00

   This is the last day of our voyage. We expect to land tomorrow morning. We seem very far away from Princeton and our dear friends, not only by the measure of space but of time too, for the early days of our voyage were interminable owing to the severe sea sickness which laid us all low. You know what a keen east wind was blowing on the Saturday morning that we sailed. We were not well out of the harbor before the pitching & rolling of the ship began & continued for two days. Jenny & Daisy were in their stateroom for five days. These were the long days of the voyage. Beth was only ill two days, [Joseph Heatly] Dulles & I about the same time. Since the first week we have passed from the state of mere existence and holding on with teeth set & eyes shut, to a quiet and enjoyable life on deck and in the sunshine. In the latter respect we have been highly favored—clear skies after the first two days without exception. The nights have been wonderful, the twilight & the dawn coming together without any real night. Tell the children that Beth has been very much interested in the various animals she has seen from the ship,—the blowing of several whales, numerous schools of porpoises, seagulls, and although not to be classed an animal, a wonderful iceberg which floated down on the Labrador Current within a quarter of a mile of us & seemed to have a personality of its own. The Captain [Campbell] told us that he estimated the height of this iceberg to be about 150 feet—and its length about 600. The Captain, by the way, has spoken of you several times, and the pleasure which he had in knowing you.[1] We have found him most agreeable, and Jenny has plied him with innumerable questions about Scotland, and its history, people etc. He seems well informed & has given us much valuable information as to our pro-

posed tour through the Highlands. We have often spoken of Mrs.
Wilson & yourself. We appreciate your going to New York &
standing by us to the last. With all the pleasure which is before
us we are constantly reminded of that which we have left behind
us, and the little circle of friends which forms for us the heart
of Princeton. It is a satisfaction to know that strong friendship
holds through all separation. We all join in warmest love to Mrs.
Wilson & yourself   Your affectionate friend   Jack.

ALS (WP, DLC).
¹ Wilson had come to know Captain Campbell when he returned from his
first trip to Great Britain in 1896 aboard *S.S. Anchoria.*

From John Franklin Genung

Amherst, Massachusetts.

My dear Professor Wilson,   June 11, 1900

Your kind response to my somewhat impudent letter has gratified me very much. And now may I trouble you just this once
further. I have been analyzing the essay in order to get at the
steps of the plan; a plan which even the rapid reader feels to be
admirably homogeneous, but of which also the studious reader
likes to convince himself more in detail. And it has carved up so
well that I wish to use it as a further illustration of how an orderly
moving mind thinks in plan. I enclose the result of my morning's
study of the essay. May I ask you to look it over and see if it
amounts to anything?¹

I think that as you wrote you did not exactly skeletonize it as
this would indicate, but, so to say, steered your remarks successively toward certain large landmarks of thought, which land-
marks stand out generally as summarizing sentences at the ends
of paragraphs. The order is rather inductive than deductive,—as
befits the process of getting at a new view of truth. Am I not
write [right] in thinking that the modern "dispassionate" ideal
of writing history (of which, to my mind, Professor [Samuel R.]
Gardiner is very nearly a typical representative) furnished perhaps the more immediate spur and occasion for your writing the
essay? At all events, the essay meets the actual state of things
in a very masterly way. I have had the same thoughts, though I
had not systematized them, as called out by the way our friends
the Higher Critics have been approaching the old Biblical records.
Just for lack of historic imagination they have made what is at
present a grotesque of the whole Jewish history; and it will take
a new John Richard Green, endowed with what Green lacked, to

straighten it out. The art of making commentaries suffers in the same way: men interpret books in the spirit of Hebrew grammar rather than in the spirit of what the book stands for. As I have specialized a little in these departments, you can see how I may have been led by another way to the point where your remarks on history are very refreshing and vital.

If you will please return the plan after looking it over, and, without giving yourself unnecessary inconvenience, comment on it, I shall be greatly obliged and honored.[2]

Yours very truly   John F. Genung

ALS (WP, DLC).

[1] It was an outline of "The Truth of the Matter," which Genung printed in *The Working Principles of Rhetoric*, p. 439.

[2] Wilson returned the enclosure in a letter which is missing. *The Working Principles of Rhetoric*, p. 405, prints the following extract from Wilson's letter:

"My literary and critical essays are by-products of my desk, written for the most part to ease the strain of my regular and, so to say, professional writing. They are, therefore, not thought out by plan before being composed, but form themselves under my hand as I turn and return to them from time to time. I am the more pleased that this one should turn out to possess something so nearly like a systematic plan."

From John Nolen[1]

My dear Professor Wilson: [Philadelphia] June 12, 1900

We have not lost sight of your disinclination to accept invitations to lecture and yet we are going to ask you to give one of our afternoon courses in Philadelphia next winter. Your lectures represent so exactly what we want that we feel compelled to invite you again and again, in the hope that some time—we hope this— you will be in a position to consider our request favorably. The lectures would be given in a Hall—probably Witherspoon—in the central part of Philadelphia at four o'clock in the afternoon, at weekly intervals from the early part of January to the middle of February. We can promise you a large, cultivated and appreciative audience. Great Leaders of Political Thought,[2] for which you have a prepared syllabus,[3] would be a most acceptable subject, but we could, I have no doubt, adopt your preference. The fee that we have usually paid is $300, but we should like in this, too, to meet your wishes.

Will you be so good as to turn this matter over in your mind, and, if possible, send me a favorable reply. The course would be one of the two afternoon courses given annually under the direct auspices of the Society.[4]   Faithfully yours,   John Nolen

TCL (in possession of Henry W. Bragdon).

[1] Associated with the American Society for the Extension of University Teaching, 1893-1903; later a prominent city planner and landscape architect.

2 Six lectures on Aristotle, Machiavelli, Montesquieu, Burke, De Tocqueville, and Bagehot, which Wilson first delivered in 1895-96. About this series, see the Editorial Note, "Wilson's Lectures on Great Leaders of Political Thought," Vol. 9.

3 Woodrow Wilson, *Syllabus of a Course of Six Lectures on Great Leaders of Political Thought* (Philadelphia, 1895).

4 Wilson's reply is missing. However, he did repeat this series in Witherspoon Hall in Philadelphia in January and February 1901. See the news item printed at Jan. 12, 1901, Vol. 12.

From Charles Francis Adams, with Enclosure

My dear Prof. Wilson: Boston. June 13, 1900

I have undertaken to deliver an address at Madison, Wisconsin, during the first week in October, at the formal opening of the new State Historical Society building which has there been constructed.[1] In preparing this address, there are certain subjects in regard to which I am desirous of getting information, and I fancy you would be able to assist me.

I propose, therefore, to solicit your aid.

Enclosed, I send you a printed list of queries. I want to get answers from you to such of these queries as you can give answers to without imposing any undue amount of labor upon yourself.

My purpose is to find out, if I can, what is the present tendency as respects historical reading of the young men in our advanced educational institutions. There is an impression abroad that, since my time,—that is , within the last forty years,—a great change has taken place in what might be called the reading capacity and inclination of the coming generation. The impression is that those composing it have no longer the patience to apply themselves to any considerable task, and that, accordingly, what might be called the continuous reading of authors has passed out of vogue.

For instance: I would like to be advised whether you know of a single young man in recent years who, for his own pleasure and information, has undertaken to read through Gibbon's "Decline and Fall," or even Macaulay's "England," or Bancroft's "United States"; or, indeed, any other historical work running into more, we will say, than two volumes.

Have you any means of informing yourself on this subject? Also, I want to ascertain who are the favorite historical writers of the present day. In my time,—that is, between 1850 and 1860,—there were certain historical writers who were in great vogue. They were regarded somewhat as prophetic voices, or instructors. Mommsen, Thomas Carlyle, Macaulay and Grote were among the number. Are there any such now?

I should be under exceeding obligation to you if you would kindly consent to throw such light on these problems as may be in your power. You are in touch with the coming generation; I am mot [not]. So far as information of this sort is concerned, I am distinctly a "back number."

I am sorry to trouble much occupied men like you in such a matter, but I know no other way of getting what I need.

Believe me, etc.,   Charles Francis Adams

TLS (WP, DLC).
[1] *The Sifted Grain and the Grain Sifters: An Address at the Dedication of the Building of the State Historical Society of Wisconsin at Madison, October 19, 1900* (Cambridge, Mass., 1900).

E N C L O S U R E

A Questionnaire

I

What is your impression in regard to what may be described as the habit of steady, or "course," historical reading, and sustained thought, among the Undergraduates of the present day, as compared with those of your own time? *Their studies apt to run more to topical reading than to "course" reading; their pleasure they find in poetry and fiction rather than in such historical reading as I remember to have been the delight of my own undergraduate days.*

2

For instance, among the young men of your present, or recent, classes, how many have read through Gibbon's "Decline and Fall?" *Yes* Are Carlyle's "French Revolution" and "Frederick the Great" much read? *No.*

3

Who, among American historical writers, are read consecutively, and as books?

Is Bancroft? *Much more than Motley.*

Is Motley?

Are the historical writings of John Fiske read? *More than others.*

To what extent are Parkman and Prescott read; especially the former? *Parkman less than Prescott.*

Are Captain Mahan's books read? *Do not know.*

4

Who are now, by our American college students, regarded as models of historical method and composition? Is the tendency towards Macaulay, Carlyle, or Green?—or is it towards other, and more recent methods? *Other and more recent methods, so far as it is not towards historical fiction.*

5

What, if any, historical works of any considerable length are now read through from beginning to end, as was formerly the not unusual practice among college students with Gibbon, Hume[,] Macaulay, etc.? *Fiske, Parkman, Macaulay*

Printed questionnaire with transcripts of WWsh replies and WWhw replies italicized (WP, DLC).

From Jenny Davidson Hibben

My dear Mr. Wilson—   Edinburgh, Scotland 13 June 1900.

Your letter welcomed us to Edinburgh, where we came with confused heads from our sea-voyage last Thursday. We were so very glad to hear from you. In the midst of all our new pleasures we find our thoughts very constantly in Princeton, & with our dear friends there. You & Mrs. Wilson were so kind in coming to the steamer. I enclose the photograph that I took of you all just before you left us.

We are in love with Edinburgh always barring the climate which as you know is more fickle than the proverbial woman. To-day we went to Queensferry & Forth Bridge, on top of a coach, & were rained upon for fully ten miles & only one umbrella for five people! Perhaps you remember that lovely road going past Lord Roseberry's beautiful place. Jack is daily at the University hearing lectures & working in the library. Part of the day he gives to us & then we are veritable sightseers, & go from Holyrood to the Castle & up & down the streets of Edinburgh. We went to St. Giles Cathedral on Sunday, & thought of the service you wrote us about last year. It is so beautiful there, I think—& the service quite perfect. We sat in great craved [carved] stalls & it was pretty to see Beth almost lost in one. To-morrow we go to North Berwick to spend the day with Prof. James Seth & his mother, who remembers you & Mr. Axson with such pleasure

We are in most comfortable lodgings, in a very attractive part of Edinburgh, & with our books & picture & writing materials! & open fire & flowers in our drawing room we have almost a little

home. We shall be here, at least one week longer, possibly more &
then go to St. Andrews probably for ten days. My sister was
greatly interested in your news of the Harvard game.[1] We shall
hope for letters often from you & Mrs. Wilson. They are more
than welcome. Our warmest love take over to the dear Ricketts,
& tell them to write to us—& will you tell us about our house & garden for we think of it so much. Our love for Mrs Wilson, the little
girls & for you from Jack & myself.

Ever your friend,   J. D. Hibben

ALS (WP, DLC).
   [1] Harvard defeated Princeton 4 to 0 in the baseball game played at Cambridge
on May 26, 1900.

To Robert Underwood Johnson

My dear Mr. Johnson,   Princeton, New Jersey, 15 June, 1900.

I write to ask a question which I trust you will not deem impertinent.

I am very anxious to get out another volume of essays in the
autumn, and I cannot make up a full table of contents without
the two which are in your safe awaiting publication in the
Magazine. Will you kindly tell me whether it is your plan to
publish them soon or not? They are the essays on Burke and on
"When A Man Comes To Himself."[1] I would greatly appreciate
your indulgence of this inquiry. If it is possible for you to get
them in in season for my plan for a volume it would gratify me
more perhaps than I could readily explain. Suffice it to say that
the book hangs fire till those essays appear.[2]

With warm regard,

Very sincerely Yours,   Woodrow Wilson

WWTLS (Berg Coll., NN).
   [1] "Edmund Burke and the French Revolution," printed at Feb. 23, 1898,
Vol. 10, and "When a Man Comes to Himself," printed at Nov. 1, 1899.
   [2] For reasons unknown to the Editors, the new volume of essays was never
published.

Francis Landey Patton to John Work Garrett and Robert Garrett

My dear Sirs: [Princeton, N.J.] June 15, 1900

I have great pleasure in saying to you that at the last meeting
of the Board of Trustees I reported to them the receipt of your
very handsome gift of $100,000 for the erection of a chair of

Politics in Princeton University. I understand that this money has been invested in Baltimore & Ohio 4% bonds.

After giving the subject the most careful consideration and taking every pains to inquire in reference to the character and standing of several gentlemen who might be regarded as available for the position, Professor Woodrow Wilson and I agreed that the best man to be the first incumbent of your professorship is Dr. John H. Finley, formerly President of Knox College, Galesburg, Ill. I have had a long and very satisfactory conversation with Mr. Finley. I have made inquiries through several channels in reference to Mr. Finley's antecedents, character, attainments, and qualifications generally, and I had the most unhesitating confidence in recommending him to the Board of Trustees. He was unanimously elected, and I have no doubt that he will accept the position and enter upon his duties if all goes well, in the autumn.

The Trustees, I assure you, are profoundly impressed with the loyalty and devotion that you have shown to your Alma Mater, and are deeply grateful for this very handsome expression of your discriminating sense of the most pressing needs of the University.

I am,   Very faithfully yours,   Francis L. Patton

TLS (Patton Letterpress Books, University Archives, NjP).

Two Letters from Henry Mills Alden

My dear Mr Wilson,   New York City June 26. 1900

I was delighted to receive to-day the first part of your history, which I shall give myself the pleasure of reading as soon as we have given full attention to the work of illustrating it. As you have heard from Mr Harper,[1] Mr Yohn is now in New York, & it seems likely that he will be inclined to undertake the illustrations. We will promptly find out if Mr Pyle is in a situation to do in time such pictures as you want from him.[2] The suggestion of Appleton Clark for the Slave-ship picture is a good one.[3]

Thanking you for your promptness in forwarding the text, I remain, with affectionate regard

Yours sincerely   H. M. Alden

ALS (WP, DLC).
  [1] Joseph Henry Harper, in a conference in Princeton.
  [2] Pyle assisted very significantly in the illustration of the series.
  [3] Walter Appleton Clark of New York, illustrator for *Scribner's Magazine*. As it turned out, Howard Pyle painted the picture of the slave ship.

My dear Mr. Wilson: New York, June 27th, 1900.

As I wrote to you yesterday, your letter referring to the illustrations was taken up immediately, and in view of the fact that arrangements have already been made with Mr. Yohn, I think it highly advisable to have him go ahead instead of calling upon Mr. Pyle. One of the principle reasons why I arranged with Mr. Yohn was because Mr. J. Henry Harper told me that when he was in Princeton you expressed a very strong desire to have Mr. Yohn illustrate your History. Furthermore, I am confident that Mr. Yohn will do the illustrating entirely to your satisfaction; and I think it would be a very good thing if you and Mr. Yohn would keep in close touch during the progress of the work.

Upon hearing favorably from you I will request Mr. Yohn to go to Princeton at stated intervals in order to consult with you, and in order to do everything possible to carry out your wishes in this matter.   Yours very truly.   H. M. Alden

TLS (WP, DLC).

From William B. Pritchard

My dear Prof. Wilson: New York June 29, '00.

I should like very much to hear from you with reference to the present status of that "tic" of yours. I am much interested personally & impersonally in the result. You should by this time be in a position to determine with more positiveness the value of the plan of treatment suggested. I have no doubt you have been faithful in the matter of detail
                    Sincerely   W. B. Pritchard

ALS (WP, DLC).

To William B. Pritchard

My dear Dr. Pritchard,   Princeton, New Jersey, 5 July, 1900

I think you have just cause to complain that I have not let you know how your treatment prospered. The distractions of Commencement have been upon us, and the engrossment of final examinations, with hundreds of papers to be read, in addition to routine tasks which never stop, and I have thought of nothing but getting through each day with reasonable equanimity.

By the same token, I have to confess that the treatment has not been kept up with absolutely unbroken regularity. There have been days when it seemed practically impossible to find twenty minutes in which to sit by the battery. But, on the whole, I have observed your instructions with steady faithfulness in the matter of the electricity, and it has unquestionably done me good. I have the most sensitive of stomachs, and I have not taken the arsenic as you directed, fancying that it upset my digestion. No doubt I have erred in that. Now that a little more quiet order of life is possible for me, I will take it regularly.

The "tic" varies noticeably with my general nervous condition. When I am over tired, when I am embarrassed by the expectation that it *will* show itself, when I am for any cause not at my best, it manifests itself with provoking vigour. But its frequence and its violence are greatly diminished. The whole effect of the electricity is stimulating, and gives to my face a feeling of greater firmness. The muscles seem less flabby.

I remembered after leaving you that I had answered one of your questions incorrectly. I *had* often noticed a sound in my ear, a burring sound, like the flutter of something. I had for the moment forgotten, because the sound had of late been infrequent. It has returned now, occurring almost every time the twitching comes.

I shall get away for a vacation about the first of August and I fear that I shall not be able to make the battery part of my luggage.

Thanking you most sincerely for your note,

With much regard,

Very truly Yours,   Woodrow Wilson

TLS (in possession of Frederick F. Herzberg).

From John Lambert Cadwalader

My dear Professor Wilson: New York. July 9th 1900

I enclose you a check of $1500 in the matter of providing the maintenance of a part of the trip to Europe of your coming assistant,[1] as agreed upon. You may possibly require the money or a part of it, and I therefore send it to you. Will you inform Dr. Patton on his return.

Yours faithfully,   John L. Cadwalader

ALS (WP, DLC).

[1] A two-year fellowship to enable Edward Graham Elliott, Instructor in Latin, to go to Germany and obtain a Ph.D. in political science and jurisprudence. Wilson had agreed to advise Elliott about his course program, and there was an understanding between the two and President Patton that Elliott would return to Princeton to assist Wilson in his courses.

Two Letters to Edward Graham Elliott

My dear Mr. Elliott,   Princeton, New Jersey, 10 July, 1900.

You will be pleased to hear that the money is in hand, and will be ready for your use just as soon as you need it, for example, to make the payment for your passage. We can arrange all the details as soon as you are here again.

George Howe's address is, Care Dr. J. W. Flinn,[1] Woodburn Farm, Pendleton, South Carolina.

I sincerely hope that you continue to get the best reports from your brother.[2] Give him my regards and congratulations[3] when you write.

With warmest regard,

In haste,   Faithfully Yours,   Woodrow Wilson

WWTLS (WC, NjP).

[1] The Rev. Dr. John William Flinn, Chaplain and Professor of Philosophy at South Carolina College, an old friend of the Wilson and Howe families.

[2] James Johnson Elliott, Princeton 1896.

[3] Upon beginning the successful practice of law.

My dear Mr. Elliott,   Princeton, New Jersey, 10 July, 1900.

I have followed the simplest course and deposited the seven hundred and fifty dollars sent by Mr. Cadwalader to your credit at the Bank here.[1] You can get your letter of credit from Ed. Howe,[2] if you choose, and the whole matter will be without red tape or bother or delay. I enclose the memorandum handed me by Howe.

In haste, as always, apparently,

Faithfully Yours,   Woodrow Wilson

WWTLS (WC, NjP). Enc. missing.

[1] As future documents will reveal, Wilson turned the balance of $750 over to the University Treasurer for Elliott's use in 1901-1902.

[2] Edward Howe, President of the Princeton Bank (now the Princeton Bank and Trust Company) of 12 Nassau Street.

Three Letters from Henry Mills Alden

My dear Mr Wilson,   New York City July 10. 1900

We had some interviews with Mr Yohn after his arrival in New York, & felt confident that he would undertake the illustration of your U. S. History. We are, therefore, somewhat disappointed to hear from him that his engagements with the Scribners will not leave him time enough to do justice to the work we had in view for him.

We see now no other way than to engage the best work we can secure from several artists eminent in work of this kind. We shall see at once what we can expect from Mr Pyle, Mr Appleton Clark & Mr Keller;[1] & we are not without hope of having some illustrations from Mr Yohn. We believe, moreover, that this plan of procedure is best for your History.

With warm regard   Yours faithfully   H. M. Alden

[1] Arthur Ignatius Keller, painter and illustrator of New York.

Dear Mr Wilson   New York City   July 11. 1900

I am at fault for the delay in sending you the payment for the 1st Part of your History. This was owing to the distraction of my mind by concern as to illustrations. A cheque will be forwarded at once, & regularly hereafter on the receipt of your copy

Yours faithfully   H. M. Alden

My dear Mr Wilson,   New York City   July 12, 1900

I want to congratulate you upon the first instalment of your History, which I have just read. It is all that could be desired & fully meets my expectation. I only hope that we may do our part as well as you have done yours

Yours sincerely   H. M. Alden

ALS (WP, DLC).

To Edward Graham Elliott

My dear Mr. Elliott,   Princeton, New Jersey, 17 July, 1900.

We expect to get away (to Canada) by the first of August,— not sooner, but not much later, either. If you cannot manage to be here by that time, I will make out, from the Universitäts-kalendar,[1] a provisional programme for you, to be modified later by your own experience and information on the other side.

I am still chained to my desk, working to forget the heat. I am delighted to hear the good news of your brother.

With warmest regard,

Cordially Yours,   Woodrow Wilson

WWTLS (WC, NjP).
[1] F. Ascherson, *Deutscher Universitäts-Kalender. Achtundfunfzigste Ausgabe. Winter-Semester 1900/1901* (Berlin, 1900). This was a handbook listing university course programs in Germany, Austria, Switzerland, and the Baltic provinces of Russia.

To Azel Washburn Hazen

My dear Dr. Hazen,   Princeton, 18 July, 1900

I am afraid I am suffering from atrophy of will—or conscience—for I have taken thirty-six hours to make up my mind to do my duty!

It really takes a great deal of moral courage to say No to a letter and a request like yours.[1] I have an affection for Middletown and its people out of all proportion to the length of my residence there—in proportion to the extraordinary kindliness and attractiveness of the community. I could wish that I might seem really to belong to it, as I might were I to speak on such an occasion. And, then, you convey the invitation, and my affection for you I have not tried to disguise.

But it is my duty to decline. I really have no other wise choice in the matter. I am to publish a twelve number serial in *Harper's Magazine* next year, which is only in part written (a history of the U. S.); I must keep six months ahead of the press; every moment I can devote to it after my vacation (like every moment at the present writing) really belongs to it by contract,—as a mere question of obligation; there's an article promised to the *Atlantic*[2] besides—which I sadly fear will not be written—; and I dare not venture upon anything else that would involve preparation. I doubt the prudence of going away from home for the two or three lectures I have promised which do *not* require preparation.

That is the whole story. I *owed* you the whole story in reply to such an invitation. You may be sure I would accept it if I could accept *any* invitation of the kind.

And now accept, both for yourself and the Committee, my heartfelt thanks. My regrets this whole epistle is intended to express.

Mrs. Wilson joins me in the most affectionate messages to you all; and I am, as ever

    Cordially and faithfully Yours,   Woodrow Wilson

How delightful about the Clovelly ivy![3]

ALS (photostat in RSB Coll., DLC).

[1] Dr. Hazen's letter is missing.

[2] The essay that became "Democracy and Efficiency," printed at Oct. 1, 1900, Vol. 12.

[3] Wilson had run into the Hazens at Clovelly in Devonshire in August 1899. (See WW to EAW, Aug. 17, 1899.) The Hazens had brought back a cutting of ivy from Clovelly, and it was doing well. See WW to EAW, April 11, 1901, Vol. 12.

From Max Boucard

[Paris] 28 juillet 1900

"Merci, mille fois,"[1] cher Monsieur; veuillez recevoir de suite et *nos compliments* et *nos meilleurs souvenirs.*

Votre bien dévoué   M Boucard

Je suis heureux de vous annoncer que c'est Mr Wallon[2] "le père de notre Constitution" qui présentera votre ouvrage au public français.

ALS (WP, DLC).

[1] For Wilson's preface to the French edition of *Congressional Government.* Wilson completed a shorthand draft of this preface (MS. in WP, DLC) on July 14, 1900, and transcribed it and sent the copy to Boucard very soon afterward. Dated July 14, 1900, the preface (translated into French) appears in Woodrow Wilson, *Le Gouvernement Congressionnel: Étude sur la Politique Américaine,* in "Bibliothèque Internationale de Droit Public," published under the direction of Max Boucard of the Conseil d'État and Gaston Jèze of the University of Aix-Marseilles (Paris, 1900), pp. xxiii-xxxi.

Except for its opening paragraph, which was addressed to French readers, the preface to the French edition is the same as the one to the fifteenth American edition printed at August 15, 1900. The preface to the French edition is therefore not printed herein.

[2] Henri Alexandre Wallon (1812-1904), French historian and statesman, was Professor of History at the École Normale Supérieure for many years and the author of many historical works. A member of the French Legislative Assembly, 1849-50, he withdrew from public life during the Second Empire. Member of the National Assembly, 1871-76. His most notable achievement was his constitutional provision, adopted in January 1875, which stipulated that a President should be elected for a seven-year term and be eligible for re-election. Adoption of this provision determined that France would be a republic, not a constitutional monarchy. Wallon was a member of the Académie des Inscriptions (one of the sections of the Institut de France) from 1873 to his death and was elected a senator for life in 1875.

Henri Alexandre Wallon's Preface to the French Edition of *Congressional Government*

[c. July 28, 1900]

Dans sa préface au 1er volume de la *Bibliothèque internationale du Droit public* publiée sous la direction de MM. Max Boucard et Gaston Jèze (le *Gouvernement parlementaire en Angleterre,* par A. Todd), M. Casimir Perier a signalé, avec juste raison, l'importance politique de cette entreprise. Si l'on veut rechercher la meilleure forme de gouvernement, non pas seulement en théorie, mais en pratique, il est bon de s'éclairer des expériences déjà faites, dans les diverses nations qui offrent un champ convenable aux études de législation comparée. Au point de vue parlementaire, l'Angleterre devait tenir le premier rang: car c'est chez elle que cette forme de gouvernement a pris naissance et qu'elle s'est développée, transformée depuis la grande Charte, ou du moins depuis la *Déclaration des Droits.* C'est de ses exemples que se sont inspirés les États qui ont aujourd'hui adopté ce régime, avec les différences résultant de leurs origines, de leur histoire, de leur position et de leurs mœurs. Après l'Angleterre, on devait attendre les États-Unis d'Amérique, issus de l'Angleterre et affranchis de sa domination avec le concours de la France; et les éditeurs de cette collection avaient une raison toute spéciale pour l'offrir, en second lieu, au public français; c'est que les États-Unis ont avec le France cette affinité de plus: tandis, en effet, que l'Angleterre, à travers ses révolutions, est restée monarchique, la France, à l'exemple des États-Unis, est devenue République. Elle a, comme les États-Unis, son président élu pour un temps limité, elle a deux Chambres, une Chambre de représentants et un Sénat; mais là s'arrêtent les ressemblances, et les différences sont profondes. Elles ne tiennent pas seulement à la diversité des races, elles tiennent au mode de formation des deux nationalités. En France, c'est la royauté qui a fait l'unité de la nation: royauté procédant de la loi des Francs, sous Clovis, et de l'Empire romain comme de la royauté franque, sous Charlemagne; effacée pendant un temps par la féodalité, mais prévalant à la fin, grâce à la suprématie qu'elle tenait de son titre et ramenant sans défaillance toutes les parties de la Gaule à l'unité nationale, œuvre capitale, maintenue et fortifiée par la Révolution. En Amérique, ce sont des colonies, formées indépendamment les unes des autres, qui, s'affranchissant du joug de la métropole et associées dans la lutte après la victoire, se sont constituées en nation.

C'est de là que part le livre de M. W. Wilson.

L'objet de ces essais, dit-il, n'est pas de présenter d'une manière complète la critique du gouvernement des États-Unis; il est simplement de mettre en relief les traits les plus caractéristiques de la pratique du système fédéral. Prenant le Congrès comme le pouvoir central et prédominant du système, l'objet de ces essais est d'illustrer tout ce qui touche au Congrès.

Il faut pourtant que le lecteur se rappelle ce que l'auteur suppose trop bien connu, je veux dire quelles sont les différentes pièces de la machine dont il se propose d'apprécier le jeu dans son livre:

Pouvoir législatif attribué à un congrès qui se compose d'un Sénat et d'une Chambre des représentants: la Chambre des représentants nommée pour deux ans, en nombre déterminé pour chaque État; le Sénat comptant deux sénateurs par chaque État et renouvelable par tiers tous les deux ans;

Pouvoir exécutif confié à un Président, nommé pour quatre ans en même temps qu'un Vice-Président, son remplaçant de droit en cas de destitution, de démission ou de mort.

On aimerait à suivre, d'étape en étape, les évolutions qu'a subies en réalité la constitution américaine depuis qu'elle a été signée le 17 septembre 1787. M. Wilson, je l'ai dit, ne le fait pas : il s'attache surtout à la juger telle qu'elle est pratiquée aujourd'hui. Disons qu'il n'en pense pas tout le bien possible ; et je ne sais si le lecteur français trouvera dans ce tableau des traits applicables à la réforme de notre Constitution. Une Chambre des représentants, divisée en grands comités qui sont comme autant de petites législatures menées par leurs *leaders* (p. 113), une Chambre où la discussion est étranglée par un règlement draconien (p. 122), où les bills n'ont chance de passer que par des suspensions du règlement obtenues presque subrepticement à la dernière heure (p. 123) ! et qui est-ce qui crée ces comités presque souverains ? Est-ce le vote de la Chambre tout entière ? Est-ce au moins le sort ? non : c'est le *Speaker* ou président de la Chambre, homme de parti, et il les compose absolument comme il le veut (p. 158) ! Nos réformateurs qui songent aux comités de la Convention ne prendront assurément pas modèle sur ces comités d'Amérique, ils ne prendront pas non plus modèle sur le Sénat des États-Unis, pour réformer notre Sénat qu'ils attaquent dans les projets de revision, comme empiétant sur les droits de la Chambre. Qu'ils lisent cette page du présent livre.

La conduite du Sénat, quand il s'agit de bills financiers, rend inutiles les efforts laborieux de la Chambre.

Le Sénat possède, par précédent, le droit d'amendement le plus complet pour ces lois aussi bien que pour toutes les autres.

La Constitution ne dit pas dans quelle Chambre les projets de loi pour l'affectation des crédits devront être proposés d'abord. Elle dit simplement que tous les projets de loi pour la fixation des recettes doivent venir de la Chambre des représentants, et que, dans l'examen de ces projets, le Sénat peut proposer ou accepter des amendements comme pour les autres lois (art. 1, sect. VII) ; mais "par une pratique aussi ancienne que le gouvernement lui-même, la prérogative constitutionnelle de la Chambre a été considérée comme s'appliquant à tous les "*general appropriation bills*" et on a accordé au Sénat les droits d'amendements les plus étendus.

Dans quel esprit se feront ces amendements ?

La Chambre Haute peut y ajouter ce qu'elle veut ; elle peut s'écarter complètement des stipulations de la Chambre, et y ajouter des dispositions législatives d'un caractère tout à fait nouveau, qui changent non seulement le montant mais l'objet des dépenses, et qui font avec les matériaux que leur a envoyés la Chambre populaire des choses d'un caractère tout différent. Les *appropriation bills*, tels qu'ils sortent de la Chambre des représentants, pourvoient à des dépenses très inférieures aux crédits demandés dans les *estimates*; quand ils reviennent du Sénat, ils proposent des crédits de plusieurs millions de plus, car cette Assemblée moins sensible a porté les dépenses presque, sinon complètement, au niveau du chiffre des *estimates*.

Comment s'en tire-t-on?

Après avoir subi l'épreuve d'un examen rigoureux au Sénat, les *appropriation bills* reviennent à la Chambre avec de nouveaux chiffres. Mais quand ils reviennent, il est trop tard pour que la Chambre les remette au creuset du Comité de la Chambre entière. Le Comité des appropriations de la Chambre n'a guère présenté ses bills avant le milieu de la session, on peut en être certain; une fois arrivés au Sénat, ils ont été soumis au Comité correspondant; le rapport de cette Commission a été discuté avec la lenteur qui caractérise la façon de procéder de la Chambre Haute; de sorte que les derniers jours de la session ne sont pas éloignés, quand les bills sont renvoyés à la Chambre avec toutes les modifications que leur a fait subir le Sénat. La Chambre n'est guère disposée à accepter les changements importants introduits par le Sénat, mais on n'a plus le temps d'engager une querelle avec la Chambre Haute, à moins de prendre le parti de prolonger la session jusqu'au milieu des chaleurs de l'été, ou de rejeter le bill en acceptant tous les ennuis d'une session extraordinaire. Si c'est la courte session, qui se termine, d'après la Constitution, le 4 mars, on n'a que l'alternative encore plus désagréable de laisser régler les appropriations par la nouvelle Chambre.

Il y a donc là aussi des conflits.

Voilà pourquoi il est d'usage de régler ces conflits au moyen d'une conférence entre les deux Chambres. La Chambre rejette les amendements du Sénat sans les lire: le Sénat refuse énergiquement de céder; il s'ensuit une conférence dirigée par une Commission de trois membres de chaque Chambre; on arrive à un compromis en amalgamant des propositions contraires, de façon à ne donner la victoire à aucun des deux partis. . . (p. 171-174).

Quant au Pouvoir exécutif, nous offre-t-il plus d'exemples à suivre, soit dans l'élection du président, soit dans l'exercice de ses droits.

Pour l'élection du Président rappelons encore ce que M. Wilson n'avait pas à apprendre à ses concitoyens, mais ce qu'un lecteur français doit savoir.

Chaque État nomme un nombre d'électeurs égal à la totalité des sénateurs et des députés qu'il a le droit d'envoyer au Congrès. Ce corps électoral nomme tout à la fois et le Président et le Vice-Président qui n'est, comme on vient de le voir, que sa doublure, un *en cas*, mais qui, du vivant du Président, a pourtant un rôle: il préside le Sénat. Le vote se fait distinctement pour chacun d'eux dans chaque État, et les deux listes contenant tous les noms, avec indication des suffrages obtenus, sont envoyées au siège du gouvernement. Si l'un des candidats obtient pour la présidence la majorité absolue, il est proclamé Président; sinon, la Chambre des députés choisit immédiatement au scrutin parmi les trois qui ont obtenu le plus grand nombre de suffrages; mais dans ce choix du Président fait à la Chambre, les votes sont pris par État, la représentation de chaque État n'ayant qu'un seul vote. Les deux tiers des États représentés constituent le *quorum* nécessaire pour la validité du vote; et, le *quorum* atteint, l'élection se fait à la majorité des États.

Les rouages, convenons en, sont un peu compliqués; mais on y voit cet avantage; c'est que le Collège électoral est dissous une fois la besogne faite et on estime que le Président se trouve ainsi dégagé de tous liens envers ses électeurs. Est-ce bien sûr? car en dernier lieu l'élection peut dépendre du vote de la Chambre; et le Président a-t-il aussi pleinement le pouvoir exécutif qu'on le prétend? Que dire de l'intrusion du Sénat dans le Pouvoir exécutif, de ses réunions en "sessions exécutives," de la part qu'il prend non seulement à la conclusion des traités (cela en effet est bien aussi du domaine législatif) mais dans la nomination des ambassadeurs et même des fonctionnaires civils.

Le Président, dit l'auteur, n'a point de voix dans les décisions du Sénat au sujet de ses transactions diplomatiques ou au sujet des matières pour lesquelles il le consulte; et cependant si l'on n'a point de voix dans la décision, il n'y a pas consultation. Quand il ferme ses portes et qu'il se rend à la "session exécutive," le Sénat ferme ses portes au Président aussi bien qu'au reste du monde. Il ne peut répondre aux objections que fait le Sénat à ses déterminations que par le moyen encombrant et insuffisant d'un message, ou par les bons offices d'un sénateur qui veut bien lui offrir son concours, mais qui n'a point d'autorité. Bien souvent même le Président ne peut pas savoir quelles ont été les objections du Sénat. Il est obligé d'aborder cette Assemblée comme un domestique qui confère avec son maître et qui est naturellement plein de respect pour ce maître.

Pour les nominations l'intervention du Sénat est sans doute plus contestée.

Ce sont les nominations, dit l'auteur, qui amènent le plus de désaccord entre le Président et son Seigneur le Sénat (page 254).

Et il ajoute:

Quand on examine les rapports du Sénat avec les fonctions civiles et les abus qui accompagnent ces rapports, on discute une phase du gouvernement par le Congrès qui promet d'être bientôt un simple souvenir historique (p. 256).

Il faut dire d'ailleurs que cette pratique ne résulte pas de la Constitution, c'est une des évolutions abusives qu'elle a subies et sur laquelle on peut revenir.

Mais le Sénat, à qui l'auteur reproche d'être "le seigneur du Président, n'a-t-il pas pour Président le Vice-Président des États-Unis," que fait ce membre du Pouvoir exécutif à la tête du plus haut organe du corps législatif?

Il ne serait pas convenable, sans doute, dit l'auteur, de ne pas dire un mot du Président du Sénat dans une étude sur le Sénat; et cependant il y a très peu de chose à dire du Vice-Président des États-Unis. Sa position est extraordinairement insignifiante et très incertaine. En apparence et strictement parlant, il ne fait point partie de la législature—il n'en est évidemment pas membre—et cependant ce n'est pas non plus un fonctionnaire de l'Exécutif. . . C'est simplement un fonctionnaire judiciaire chargé de régler les actes d'une Assemblée dont les règlements ont été faits sans son avis et ne sont point changés d'après son avis.

Et il conclut:

Ce qu'il y a de plus embarrassant dans l'examen de ses fonctions, c'est qu'en montrant qu'il y a peu de chose à dire sur son compte, on a évidemment dit tout ce qu'il y a à dire (p. 259, 260).

Dans cet examen critique des pouvoirs publics aux État-Unis comme ils sont aujourd'hui, ce que l'auteur a surtout devant les yeux, c'est la Constitution de l'Angleterre, non pas dans sa totalité: La Constitution de l'Angleterre, défalcation faite de la royauté et des lords! Son idéal, c'est la Chambre des communes avec un ministère formé selon l'esprit qui y domine; la Chambre des communes c'est le Congrès comme il le veut, et le ministère un vrai comité de gouvernement; les deux réunis réalisent pour lui le Gouvernement congressionnel. Le *Gouvernement congressionnel* c'est le titre de son ouvrage et l'objet de ses vœux. Mais ce Gouvernement congressionnel, c'est dans nos souvenirs le Gouvernement Conventionnel: la Convention, en Amérique, tempérée il est vrai par le fédéralisme, chez nous la Convention avec son comité de salut public; nous sommes payés pour n'y plus revenir. Quant au présent, ni le Pouvoir législatif en France, partagé, à titre égal, entre deux Chambres issues, quoique par deux modes différents, d'un même suffrage, ni le pouvoir exécutif qui a toutes les prérogatives d'une monarchie constitutionnelle n'ont rien à envier au système américain, à une condition pourtant, c'est que les deux Chambres sachent se maintenir dans les limites respectives de leurs droits et le Président de la République user du sien; quoiqu'il en soit des projets de décentralisation que l'on agite aujourd'hui, il est certain qu'on n'ira pas en France jusqu'à reconstituer nos anciennes provinces en donnant à chacune d'elle une législature qui lui soit propre; et quant à l'élection du Président, il me paraît douteux qu'un système qui, en Amérique, met tout le pays en agitation pendant toute une année, un an sur quatre, soit jugé préférable au procédé qui, chez nous, peut réduire la crise à une seule journée tous les sept ans.

En somme, tout n'est pas à imiter dans le tableau que nous présente l'auteur, ni à recommander dans les tendances qu'il manifeste; mais indépendamment des renseignements précieux qu'il nous fournit, il nous donne un bon exemple à suivre: c'est de faire, comme il le fait pour l'Amérique, l'examen impartial de notre propre état. Voyons d'où vient le mal dont nous souffrons, s'il résulte de notre Constitution même ou de la façon dont on la pratique; notre Constitution, par les facilités qu'elle offre à la révision, comporte toutes les réformes; l'examen que M. Wilson nous suggère nous montrera si c'est elle que nous devons réformer.

HENRI WALLON
Sénateur, Membre de l'Institut.

Printed in Woodrow Wilson, *Le Gouvernement Congressionnel: Étude sur la Politique Américaine* (Paris, 1900), pp. ix-xxii.

To Edward Graham Elliott

My dear Mr. Elliott,   Princeton, New Jersey, 3 August, 1900.

Now that I have really studied the matter, I am less confident than I was that I can give you safe advice *in detail* about the course you are to pursue in Germany. I can know here only what the several men are as writers (except in one or two instances, presently to be mentioned), whereas for you the important question is, who are good and stimulating teachers.

After thinking the matter over, therefore, I have concluded that the best advice would be as follows:

Go first to Heidelberg, and spend the winter under Jellinek.[1] Though not, I learn, an agreeable person, he is a most competent teacher. He covers, moreover, just the fields of Politics and of International Law which it is your special object to cover.

After you have thoroughly got hold of Jellinek's method and point of view and principles of study, go next to the University where you shall by that time have learned that the best *group* of masters are to be had in general Rechtswissenschaft, in Roman Law, and in International Law. By the "best," I mean those out of whom you are likely to get the most by way of example and stimulation, as well as direct instruction. I should expect that you would find that Berlin is that place. But try, if only for a few weeks, to hear the great Rudolf Sohm at Leipzig.[2] He is great, I understand, as a lecturer as well as as [sic] a scholar.

That, then, is your steering principle: the best masters in General Jurisprudence, International Law, Roman Law, and Politics,—Politik (if, for lack of time, you have to make the choice) rather than Allgemeine Staatslehre or Allgemeines Staatsrecht, though the Allgemeines Staatsrecht ought to be taken if time serves.

Write to me at any time for such advice as I can give. With these general sailing orders, I feel quite sure that you can fill the two years with the men and the subjects you wish without my assistance, keeping your ears open and finding out by the free masonry of university students which are the men and the places to seek out.

During the rest of the summer, until about the fifteenth of September, my address will be, Care T. J. Snow, Judd Haven, Ontario, Canada.[3] I am delighted to hear that you have arranged to go with George [Howe].[4] My best wishes and warmest regards go with you. Let me know of your arrival and safety.

Give your brother my best congratulations and best wishes, and believe me in all things

Faithfully and Cordially Yours,   Woodrow Wilson

WWTLS (WC, NjP).
    [1] Georg Jellinek, Professor of Political Science at the University of Heidelberg and author of works frequently cited by Wilson.
    [2] Author of *The Institutes of Roman Law*, which Wilson had used and cited frequently.
    [3] Where the Wilsons would spend their vacation.
    [4] Who was about to go to the University of Halle for graduate work in the classics.

From Henry Mills Alden

Dear Mr. Wilson: New York City August 7, 1900.

I have received Part III of the "History of the United States" and will send you payment therefor at the end of August.

I have taken note of your Canadian address. Cordially wishing you a pleasant holiday, I am

Sincerely yours,   H. M. Alden

TLS (WP, DLC).

From John Grier Hibben

My dear Woodrow,   London Aug 13/1900

We have just received your letter from which we have gained much pleasure, and the assurances which it contained of friendship and affection were especially grateful. You must not judge of our devotion to you by the number of letters you receive from us. Travelling and sightseeing have seemingly destroyed any habits of regular performance which I may have possessed in times past. We often refer to you, quote you & oftener think of you. We are delighted to know that you and all of your family are now in Canada where I hope you will find rest and strength. As Bridges said of you in the last conversation I had with him just before leaving, "If Tommy Wilson would only loaf for a while and drink Scotch whisky, he would be all right." That programme need not be followed literally, but in the spirit of it, there is wise counsel. Jenny wrote to you I think from Grasmere.[1] Since that time we have been through Ambleside, Windermere, and on the other side of the lake district as far as Coniston. Ruskin's grave impressed us by reason of its dreary loneliness. It is the only grave in the village cemetery that seems to be absolutely alone, not even within the railing of one of the usual plots which enclose the graves of those bound by the ties of kin and love. We drove along the border of the lake to the beautiful forests of Brantwood, which are unique in their native wildness. They were evidently left without cultivation that nature might not be spoiled by the interference of man. We were greatly interested in the Ruskin museum which had been opened to the public for the first time that week. From Coniston we turned our faces towards London, stopping a few hours at Haworth; and at Rowsley also, where we spent two days, visiting Haddon Hall, and Chatsworth. We have succeeded in finding most comfortable lodgings here in London on Jermyn St., just off of Piccadilly. Last week I went to Cambridge for a day, to hear the opening address before the Summer School, delivered by Mr. Balfour. He was most interesting, a fine figure and attractive presence. His address was original and suggestive.[2] I heard him again at one of the sessions of the House of Commons, when he and Mr. Labouchere had a passage at arms. I was very much interested also in Mr. [Joseph] Chamberlain, especially at one time during the session, when the whole of the opposition half rose, leaning far forward with derisive shouting & hissing, while he stood facing them very white but defiant, until the storm had passed, then, he spoke quietly but with a keen cutting sarcasm which made every word hurt and wound.[3] He is a man of undoubted power, but with an indirect shrewdness that is not conducive to a perfect trust in him.

Since I have been in London, I have been writing an article on "The Scottish University," which I have finished I am glad to say & as soon as it is typewritten, I shall send it to Scribners.[4] I have a number of pictures which Jenny took while in Scotland, which I will send with it to serve as illustrations. The pictures at least are very interesting. We are planning to leave here on Friday, going to Oxford; thence to Cambridge, and about the first of September we go to the Continent, taking in Holland on our way to Germany. I hope that we shall hear from you often. Give our warmest love to Mrs. Wilson & the children.

Ever affectionately yours   John Grier Hibben

ALS (WP, DLC).

[1] Jenny D. Hibben to WW, July 22, 1900, ALS (WP, DLC).

[2] Arthur James Balfour, *The Nineteenth Century. Inaugural Address Delivered in the Senate House, Cambridge . . . August 2, 1900* (Cambridge, 1900).

[3] On August 3, 1900, Arthur Balfour and Henry du Pre Labouchere clashed briefly over the schedule of business for the House for Monday, August 6. *Parliamentary Debates*, Fourth Series (London, 1900), LXXXVII, 657-58. Joseph Chamberlain made a spirited defense of the government's colonial policy on August 3. *Ibid.*, pp. 661-93.

[4] John Grier Hibben, "The Scottish University," *Scribner's Magazine*, XXIX (June 1901), 741-55.

The Preface to the Fifteenth "Edition" of *Congressional Government*

[Aug. 15, 1900]

I have been led by the publication of a French translation of this little volume to read it through very carefully, for the first time since its first appearance. The re-reading has convinced me that it ought not to go to another impression without a word or two by way of preface with regard to the changes which our singular system of Congressional government has undergone since these pages were written.

I must ask those who read them now to remember that they were written during the years 1883 and 1884, and that, inasmuch as they describe a living system, like all other living things subject to constant subtle modifications, alike of form and of function, their description of the government of the United States is not as accurate now as I believe it to have been at the time I wrote it.

This is, as might have been expected, more noticeable in matters of detail than in matters of substance. There are now, for example, not three hundred and twenty-five, but three hundred and fifty-seven members in the House of Representatives; and that number will, no doubt, be still further increased by the reapportionment which will follow the census of the present year. The number of committees in both Senate and House is constantly on the increase. It is now usually quite sixty in the House, and in the Senate more than forty. There has been a still further addition in the number of the "spending" committees in the House of Representatives, by the subdivision of the powerful Committee on Appropriations. Though the number of committees in nominal control of the finances of the country is still as large as ever, the tendency is now towards a concentration of all that is vital in the business into the hands of a few of the more prominent, which are most often mentioned in the text. The auditing committees on the several departments, for example, have now for some time exercised little more than a merely nominal oversight over executive expenditures.

Since the text was written, the Tenure of Office Act, which sought to restrict the President's removal from office, has been repealed; and even before its repeal it was, in fact, inoperative. After the time of President Johnson, against whom it was aimed, the party in power in Congress found little occasion to insist upon its enforcement; its constitutionality was doubtful, and it fell into the background. I did not make sufficient allowance for these facts in writing the one or two sentences of the book which refer to the Act.

Neither did I give sufficient weight, I now believe, to the powers of the Secretary of the Treasury. However minutely bound, guided, restricted by statute, his power has proved at many a critical juncture in our financial history—notably in our recent financial history—of the utmost consequence. Several times since this book was written, the country has been witness to his decisive influence upon the money markets, in the use of his authority with regard to the bond issues of the government and his right to control the disposition of the funds of the Treasury. In these matters, however, he has exercised, not political, but business power. He has helped the markets as a banker would help them. He has altered no policy. He has merely made arrangements which would release money for use and facilitate loan and investment. The country feels safer when an experienced banker, like Mr. Gage, is at the head of the Treasury, than when an experienced politician is in charge of it.

All these, however, are matters of detail. There are matters of substance to speak of also.

It is to be doubted whether I could say quite so confidently now as I said in 1884 that the Senate of the United States faithfully represents the several elements of the nation's make-up, and furnishes us with a prudent and normally constituted moderating and revising chamber. Certainly vested interests have now got a much more formidable hold upon the Senate than they seemed to have sixteen years ago. Its political character also has undergone a noticeable change. The tendency seems to be to make of the Senate, instead of merely a smaller and more deliberate House of Representatives, a body of successful party managers. Still, these features of its life may be temporary, and may easily be exaggerated. We do not yet know either whether they will persist, or, should they persist, whither they will lead us.

A more important matter—at any rate, a thing more concrete and visible—is the gradual integration of the organization of the House of Representatives. The power of the Speaker has of late years taken on new phases. He is now, more than ever, expected to guide and control the whole course of business in the House,— if not alone, at any rate through the instrumentality of the small Committee on Rules, of which he is chairman. That committee is expected not only to reformulate and revise from time to time the permanent Rules of the House, but also to look closely to the course of its business from day to day, make its programme, and virtually control its use of its time. The committee consists of five members; but the Speaker and the two other members of the committee who represent the majority in the House determine its action; and its action is allowed to govern the House. It in effect regulates the precedence of measures. Whenever occasion requires, it determines what shall, and what shall not, be undertaken. It is like a steering ministry,—without a ministry's public responsibility, and without a ministry's right to speak for both houses. It is a private piece of party machinery within the single chamber for which it acts. The Speaker himself—not as a member of the Committee on Rules, but by the exercise of his right to "recognize" on the floor—undertakes to determine very absolutely what bills individual members shall be allowed to bring to a vote, out of the regular order fixed by the rules or arranged by the Committee on Rules.

This obviously creates, in germ at least, a recognized and sufficiently concentrated leadership within the House. The country is beginning to know that the Speaker and the Committee on Rules must be held responsible in all ordinary seasons for the success or failure of the session, so far as the House is concerned. The congressional caucus has fallen a little into the background. It is not often necessary to call it together, except when the majority is impatient or recalcitrant under the guidance of the Committee on Rules. To this new leadership, however, as to everything else connected with committee government, the taint of privacy attaches. It is not leadership upon the open floor, avowed, defended in public debate, set before the view and criticism of the country. It integrates the House alone, not the Senate; does not unite the two houses in policy; affects only the chamber in which there is the least opportunity for debate, the least chance that responsibility may be properly and effectively lodged and avowed. It has only a very remote and partial resemblance to genuine party leadership.

Much the most important change to be noticed is the result of the war with Spain upon the lodgment and exercise of power within our federal system: the greatly increased power and opportunity for constructive statesmanship given the President, by the plunge into international politics and into the administration of distant dependencies, which has been that war's most striking and momentous consequence. When foreign affairs play a prominent part in the politics and policy of a nation, its Executive must of necessity be its guide: must utter every initial judgment, take every first step of action, supply the information upon which it is to act, suggest and in large measure control its conduct. The President of the United States is now, as of course, at the front of affairs, as no president, except Lincoln, has been since the first quarter of the nineteenth century, when the foreign relations of the new nation had first to be adjusted. There is no trouble now about getting the President's speeches printed and read, every word. Upon his choice, his character, his experience hang some of the most weighty issues of the future. The government of dependencies must be largely in his hands. Interesting things may come out of the singular change.

For one thing, new prizes in public service may attract a new order of talent. The nation may get a better civil service, because of the sheer necessity we shall be under of organizing a service capable of carrying the novel burdens we have shouldered.

It may be, too, that the new leadership of the Executive, inasmuch as it is likely to last, will have a very far-reaching effect upon our whole method of government. It may give the heads of the executive departments a new influence upon the action of Congress. It may bring about, as a consequence, an integration which will substitute statesmanship for government by mass meeting. It may put this whole volume hopelessly out of date.   WOODROW WILSON.

Princeton University, 15 *August*, 1900.[1]

Printed in *Congressional Government* (Boston and New York, 1900), pp. v-xiii.
[1] Wilson's handwritten copy of this preface is in WP, DLC.

Two Letters to Winthrop More Daniels

                                    Judd Haven, Ontario, Canada
My dear Daniels,   16 Aug., 1900
   Your letter of the thirteenth brings us our first news from Princeton. We are rejoiced to hear of the arrival of your little son,[1] and wish you lasting joy in him with all our hearts; but we are gravely disturbed by what you say,—or rather imply,—about Mrs. Daniels. Please drop us a line to say how she is faring. I don't think she knows what admiration and deep friendship she has won in Princeton, or what grief it would bring to us all, should her health be impaired. Give her our warmest regards, accept our deepest sympathy in your anxiety; and let us know, if you possibly can, her progress towards recovery. She seemed so well before the baby's coming that I cannot believe there can be any very serious or lasting difficulty now.
   Evidently we are not rid of Mr. Edgar[2] yet,—alas! The plea about the proportion of conditions of course does not hold; but the record of removal of first term conditions is good, and the excuse of illness is awkward to dismiss,—is, indeed, never dismissed unless it lack substantiation,—is it? I doubt whether we can refuse him the chance to try for a removal of all of the six hours of condition at the opening of the year. Is not this your judgment in the matter?
   With warmest regard and sympathy,
      Cordially and faithfully Yours,   Woodrow Wilson

ALS (in possession of R. Balfour Daniels).
[1] Robertson Balfour Daniels, born Aug. 6, 1900.
[2] Andrew James Edgar, a special student who was not graduated.

Judd Haven, Ontario, Canada,
My dear Daniels,   24 August, 1900.

The people at the Post Office are very slow to learn who the "Professor of Political Economy" at Princeton is, and the enclosed belongs to you.

We are *very* anxious to hear how Mrs. Daniels is. We get absolutely no news from Princeton, and must beg you again to drop us a line. Not a word since your note about Edgar.

With warm regard and sympathy from us both,

Faithfully Yours,   Woodrow Wilson

ALS (in possession of R. Balfour Daniels).

An Inscription

24 August, 1900.

No man can serve a living government unless he comprehend it. Blindness to its faults will not make it sound simply by leaving it unscrutinized. Criticism sets it in the way of realizing its best qualities by removing its adventitious clogs and blemishes,— setting its qualities free from its mere temporary machinery.

Woodrow Wilson

WWhw inscription in *Congressional Government,* "fourteenth impression" (Boston and New York, 1900) (WC, NjP).

A Memorandum

29 Aug., 1900

Estimate—Muskoka establishment:

Residence,	$2500
Boat-house,	400
Ice-house,	100
Bath-houses,	100
Wharf,	400
Boats,	205
	3,705

WWhw memorandum in the pocket notebook described at June 18, 1899.

To Allen Wickham Corwin[1]

Judd Haven, Ontario, Canada

My dear Mr. Corwin,   10 September, 1900

Your letter of the fourth has had to seek me out in this obscure corner of the continent, and has had, consequently, to await an answer longer than I should have kept it had I been at home.

I wish I *were* at home to look up some references for you. As it is, at this distance from my books and notes, I feel quite helpless in regard to a topic which, so far as I now recollect, has never been extensively or systematically developed.

"The Consent of the Governed" is a part of constitutional theory which has, so far, been developed only or chiefly with regard to the adjustment or amendment of established systems of government. Its treatment with regard to the affairs of politically undeveloped races, which have not yet learned the rudiments of order and self-control, has, I believe, received next to no attention. The "consent" of the Filipinos and the "consent" of the American colonists to government, for example, are two radically different things,—not in theory, perhaps, but in practice,—and practice is the "whole duty of man" in politics,—i.e. what is practicable, workable. But this difference has, unfortunately for some thinkers (or would-be thinkers) never been fully or adequately explained. You will have to work on your own muscle,—and I shall be very much interested to know where your thinking lands you. I shall have to tackle the problem myself more formally than I have yet tackled it. I have spoken a good deal on it, but, as yet, have published nothing at all.

I hadnt the slightest difficulty in recalling you. I only wish I could send you a more satisfactory answer to your letter.

With much regard,

Faithfully Yours,   Woodrow Wilson

ALS (WC, NjP).

[1] Princeton 1895; LL.B., Harvard 1898; at this time practicing law in Hudson, N.Y.

ADDENDA

To Andrew Jackson George[1]

My dear Sir,   Princeton, 9 April, 1897

Allow me to thank you most warmly for your kind letter of April sixth and for the excellent little edition of Burke's "Conciliation with America"[2] which reached me to-day. I think I could answer satisfactorily Mr. Birrell's question for parliamentary candidates, "Have you read your Burke?" and every time I see him given proper setting it appeals to my sense of piety.

My "Mere Literature" contains very earnest matter,—if it reads as it was meant to read; and I heartily agree with all that you say about the teaching of English literature. No method "made in Germany" can ever get at the heart of our great literature, and by using such methods we are cheating ourselves out of a great heritage, stupidly if not deliberately.

With renewed thanks,

Most sincerely Yours,   Woodrow Wilson

ALS (photostat in WC, NjP).
   [1] Head of the English Department of the Newton, Mass., High School, 1888-1907, prolific author and editor in the field of English literature.
   [2] Andrew Jackson George (ed.), *Burke's Speech on Conciliation with America,* 1775 (Boston, 1895).

To George Sidney Webster[1]

My dear Mr. Webster,   Princeton, 17 January, 1899

I was glad to be able to telegraph this afternoon my acceptance of the invitation to speak for Berea which you so kindly urged upon me.[2] I write only to add that I shall claim the hundred dollars you mentioned only so far as to ask that it be given to Dr. Frost[3] as my contribution to the expenses of the college.

With much regard,

Very Sincerely Yours,   Woodrow Wilson

ALS (W. G. Frost Papers, KyBB).
   [1] Pastor of the Presbyterian Church of the Covenant in New York, who was making arrangements for a meeting on behalf of Berea College, to be held in the Brick Presbyterian Church in New York on January 29. This and the following letters from the Papers of William Goodell Frost, in the Berea College Library, were received after this volume had been set in pages. The Editors are indebted to Miss Elizabeth G. Gilbert, Librarian of Berea College, for photographic copies of these letters.
   [2] Wilson's speech is printed at Jan. 29, 1899, a news report of the meeting at Jan. 30, 1899.
   [3] William Goodell Frost, President of Berea College.

To William Goodell Frost

My dear Dr. Frost,   Princeton, New Jersey, 13 February, 1899.

What I enclose is the nearest approach to a speech that I could make in the quiet of my study to a stenographer.[1] It seems to me singularly vague and rhetorical, containing the main ideas of my speech at the Brick Church only in their most general statement, with a reminiscence here and there of a phrase I actually did use.[2] But it is at your disposal,—absolutely. If you think it too little like what I said to answer your purpose, please do not print it. I shall be all the better pleased. But, if you think it good enough as a summary and suggestion of what my speech contained, use it in any way you choose. I do not think I should have done this for anybody else. You have somehow engaged my feelings in respect of yourself and your work more deeply than I should have supposed possible.

With warmest regard, and sincerest hopes that your health is res[t]ored,   Very cordially Yours,   Woodrow Wilson

WWTLS (W. G. Frost Papers, KyBB).
[1] This is the first evidence known to the Editors that Wilson had dictated a speech or literary piece to a stenographer.
[2] This letter makes it clear that the item, "Our Last Frontier," printed as an address at Jan. 29, 1899, was in fact Wilson's reconstruction of the speech and should have been dated c. Feb. 13, 1899.

To William Goodell Frost

My dear Friend,   Princeton, 17 February, 1899

I did not know that you were to be so long in the North[1] (though I might have guessed it), and so I sent the speech,—or, rather, its poor ghost,—to Berea, some days ago. Perhaps it was buried in the blizzard!

What you say of the speech delights me as much as it surprises me. I think that our talks together beforehand had probably put you in a way to know *me*, and so what I meant much better than I said it, and that much of the merit of the little address consisted in the interpretation your thought illuminated it with. I wonder if there can be a similar explanation of the keen pleasure *your* address gave *me*![2] It was so unlike most such things,—had such substance and dignity and was so warm with a broad generous humanity! It seemed, consequently, impersonal,—not like an appeal, but like something told out of the general story of humanity. I shall long carry the impression.

Mrs. Wilson is expecting the "bed kiver" with grateful pleasure. It was like you to be so generous and so thoughtful.

With warmest regard,

Faithfully Yours,   Woodrow Wilson

Regards to the household

ALS (W. G. Frost Papers, KyBB).
   1 Wilson was replying to W. G. Frost to WW, Feb. 15, 1899.
   2 That is, Frost's appeal on behalf of Berea College at the Brick Church on January 29.

To William Goodell Frost, with Enclosure

My dear Friend,   Princeton, New Jersey, 27 December, 1899.

I do what you ask with the greatest pleasure. I had to wait a little to find time to read the Educational Program before replying to your letter.[1] I find I had read it before. Now, as then, I wholly approve it. I feel that in any case I could hardly make any suggestions about it. You know the region from this side so much better than I do that I should deem it presumption to correct your ideas, even if I thought that they needed correction, as I do not. Moreover, I think you wise and conservative; and no man at a distance, whatever his general acquaintance with the problem, can give helpful advice to wise men in the midst of the work. God speed you in all you have undertaken, and in all you hope for!

I write the commendatory lines with zest and pleasure. You will find them enclosed on another sheet.

A letter to Mr. Luce[2] shall follow this this afternoon.

Thank you for your invitation to us to visit the "President's House" at Berea. We shall keep that invitation in store among our hopes for future pleasure. Thank you for thinking of us.

I trust that you have had a most profitable and successful time in New England; and that you are strong and well.

With warmest regards, and every good wish for the new Year, and for many, very many, to follow,

Cordially and Faithfully Yours,   Woodrow Wilson

   1 W. G. Frost to WW, Dec. 20, 1899.
   2 He is identified in the letter just cited.

ENCLOSURE

To William Goodell Frost

My dear Friend,   Princeton, New Jersey, 27 December, 1899.

Your "Educational Program for Appalachian America" has my heartiest endorsement. I know the Cumberland region myself a little; but I can see that you know it very thoroughly; and the educational plans you are following seem to me in every respect sound and wise. With the proper money resources, you ought to be able, with God's blessing, to begin not only, but also to carry no small way towards consummation a veritable transformation of the great region you have set yourself to serve, to bring from darkness to light. May God lead and prosper you!

Sincerely Yours,   Woodrow Wilson

WWTLS (W. G. Frost Papers, KyBB).

NOTE ON THE INDEX

The alphabetically arranged analytical table of contents at the front of the volume eliminates duplication, in both contents and index, of references to certain documents, such as letters. Letters are listed in the contents alphabetically by name, and chronologically within each name by page. The subject matter of all letters is, of course, indexed. The Editorial Notes and Wilson's writings are listed in the contents chronologically by page. In addition, the subject matter of both categories is indexed. The index covers all references to books and articles mentioned in text or notes. Footnotes are indexed. Page references to footnotes which place a comma between the page number and "n" cite both text and footnote, thus: "624,n3." On the other hand, absence of the comma indicates reference to the footnote only, thus: "55n2"—the page number denoting where the footnote appears. The letter "n" without a following digit signifies an unnumbered descriptive-location note.

An asterisk before an index reference designates identification or other particular information. Re-identification and repetitive annotation have been minimized to encourage use of these starred references. Where the identification appears in an earlier volume, it is indicated thus: "*1:212,n3." Therefore a page reference standing without a preceding volume number is invariably a reference to the present volume. The index supplies the fullest known forms of names, and, for the Wilson and Axson families, relationships as far down as cousins. Persons referred to in the text by nicknames or shortened forms of names can be identified by reference to entries for these forms of the names.

A sampling of the opinions and comments of Wilson and Ellen Axson Wilson covers their more personal views, while broad, general headings in the main body of the index cover impersonal subjects. Occasionally opinions expressed by a correspondent are indexed where these appear to supplement or to reflect views expressed by Wilson or by Ellen Axson Wilson in documents which are missing.

Skiddaw (mountain), 159

Slavery and Anti-Slavery: A History of the Great Struggle in Both Hemispheres; with a View to the Slavery Question in the United States (Goodell), 347

Sloane, James Renwick, 153,n2, 167

Sloane, Margaret, 161,n5, 167

Sloane, William Milligan, *2:91,n2; *5:418,n1; 131,n2, 162n5, 193, 289, 538; Mrs. (Mary Espy Johnston), 131,n2, 165n5, 193, 289

Small, Albion Woodbury, *6:135,n1; *7:578,n1; 535,n1

Small, Maynard & Company, 115n1

Smith, Edgeworth, 138,n3, 168

Smith, Edward, 115,n1

Smith, Goldwin, 525

Smith, James Passmore, 42n1; Mrs. (Mary Adams), 42n1

Smith, Lucy Marshall, *10:310,n1; 87, 88,n2, 137, 241,n1, 288n1, 385, 385,n1, 386, 387, 389, 390, 392, 393, 394, 395, 399, 402, 403,n1,3, 405, 409, 412, 421, 422, 424, 425, 427, 429, 432, 435, 437, 438, 444, 446, 448, 450, 457, 458, 480, 512n

Smith, Mary Randolph, *10:310,n1; 88,n2, 161,n6, 240n1, 288n1, 385, 385n1, 386, 387, 389, 390, 392, 393, 399, 402, 403n1,3, 405, 409, 412, 421, 422, 424, 425, 429, 435, 437, 438, 444, 446, 448, 450, 458

Smith, Theodore Clarke, 347

Smith, Thomas Ralston, *42,n1, 55,n3

Smith, Victor, 138,n3; Mrs. (Saida Bird), 138,n3, 168

Snow, Thomas L., 565

Snyder (friend of S. Axson), 205, 235

Sohm, Rudolph, 565,n2

Somersetshire, England, WW in, 216, 224

South, Robert, 271,n2

South Carolina College, 277,n2

Southern History Association, 40

"Southern People During Reconstruction" (Page), 446n2

Southern Railway, 508, 518

Southey, Robert, 159

Southwestern Railroad, 492

Speer, Robert Elliott, 453n1

Spring, Leverett Wilson, 347

Sparks, Edwin Erle, 345

"Speech on Moving His Resolutions for Conciliation with the Colonies" (Burke), 28n5

Spirit of the Laws (Montesquieu), 63, 65

Stacy, James, 422n1, 480n1

Star, The (hotel), Wells, Somerset, 150, 213

State Papers and Speeches on the Tariff (Taussig, comp.), 346

state rights, 303-45

State Trust Company, New York City, 420

statesmanship, notes on, 124-26

Station Hotel, Ayr, 148, 152

Staunton, Va., 497

Stephens, Alexander Hamilton, 347, 348

Stephens, Henry Morse, 506,n1, 507, 532

Stevens, Thaddeus, 469, 470, 471

Stevenson, Robert Alan Mowbray, 404n1

Stevenson, Robert Louis, 403-4,n1, 406; Mrs. (Fanny Van de Grift Osbourne), 403

Stirling, Scotland, 140

Stirling, Amelia Hutchison, 144

Stockton, Mary Hunter, 139,n7

Stockton, Samuel Witham, 135n10; Mrs. (Sarah Bache Hodge), 135,n10, 139n7

Stocktons, 201

Storey, Moorfield, 348

Stovall, Pleasant A., 348

Stowe, Harriet Beecher, 343

Stratford-on-Avon, Warwickshire, 186; WW in, 150, 195, 196

Stryker, William Scudder, 90

Stuart, Ruth McEnery, 410

Stubbs, William, 116

Studies in Constitutional Law: France—England—United States (Boutmy), 97,n1

Success Story: The Life and Times of S. S. McClure (Lyon), 204n1, 221n1

Sumner, Charles, 330, 346, 348, 470

Suter, Herman Milton, 130,n10

Sweet Springs, Va., 161,n9

Talcott, Charles Andrew, *1:240,n3; 118n2, 122

Talcott, James, 96

Talisman (Scott), 228

"Tam o' Shanter" (Burns), 156

Taney, Roger Brooke, 337, 338

Tariff History of the United States (Taussig), 347

Tarkington, Booth, 443

Taunton, Somerset, 208, 217; WW in, 151, 224

Taussig, Frank William, 346, 347

Taylor, Hannis, 109

Taylor, John A., 277

Taylor, William S., 402,n4

Taylor, Zachary, 316

Teachers College, Columbia University, 104-5

Technology Quarterly, 174,n2

Tedcastle, Arthur W., *2:461n1; 278,n1, 279, 280, 289; Mrs. (Agnes Vaughn), *2:334n; 278,n1, 279, 280, 283-84

telephone, 396, 497

AND WOODROW WILSON

Ah, my darling, I love you *infinitely*, and it is indescribably sweet to be so loved in return,—even though I *know* that I do not deserve it,—know how out of measure your thoughts of me are, 181; How I wish I were not such a dumb creature but could find the right words like *you*, most adorable of lovers, 199; As for me, my darling, my *darling*, I love you so intensely that it really frightens me, 221; *You* are all the world to *me*; you elevate, you stimulate, you satisfy, you delight me: every part of me enjoys you with an infinite ardour, 229; My *darling*, *my* Woodrow, your letters for the last few days have been heart-breakingly sweet! Oh, I *want* you, I want *you*! I love you almost to suffocation, 435

HEALTH

I was pretty sick last night with a sort of cramp colic, 219

OPINIONS AND COMMENTS

I am of an unbelieving generation, 155

[Bliss] Perry has been appointed editor of the *Atlantic Monthly*. . . . It seems to me an extremely poor choice. . . . 220

Princeton, which [Bliss Perry] always declared the ideal home for a literary worker . . . 228

I am disgusted beyond expression at the work of the trustees [professorial appointments of 1900], 501

WOODROW WILSON

AND ELLEN AXSON WILSON

Every time I am separated from you I realize that the chief part of my strength and the chief part of my delight in living are cut off, 66; [At sea] I am deeply, pathetically homesick for you. You are all the world for me and I am wandering bereaved, 133; Your influence upon me is wholly independent of space, —you seem too thoroughly *in* my life and *of* it to be really separated from me, 137; I wish I knew how to think of you, and how to end my letters without cutting myself to the quick, 166; I would give every other pleasure for the one supreme delight of having you in my arms! 191; It is when I am alone that I most keenly realize the part, the supreme part, that love plays and must ever play in my life, 206; The tide of my blood seems full only when I am with you. Love unlocks everything within me that it is a pleasure to me to use, 236; Your love *rests* and soothes me so, when you are away, 406; Time has not added a single touch of age to my wonderful darling; but it has added touches of maturity, 408; You have here, ma'am, in Princeton a lover who worships you, not with devotion merely, but with a sort of tonic elation which other men (could he tell them his secrets) could only marvel at and envy. . . . 416; I love you tragically,—with a movement at the deepest parts of my heart which *might*,—should anything ever happen to you,—rise to a thrashing storm that would dash me to pieces, 506

APPEARANCE

I am working steadily and as steadily growing grey, 431

[EAW to WW] Yours of Wed. with the funny, dreadful photos is just at hand. Who took them? 437